CIRCULATING

FILM

LIBRARY

CATALOG

THE

MUSEUM

OF

DERN

ART

Copyright © 1984 by The Museum of Modern Art
All rights reserved
Library of Congress Catalog Card Number 83-62353
ISBN 0-87070-327-7

Designed Jill Korostoff
Assisted by Dayna Burnett
Typeset, printed and bound by
Edwards Brothers, Ann Arbor, Michigan
Cover printed by
Rae Publishing Co., Inc., Cedar Grove, N.J.

The Museum of Modern Art
11 West 53 Street
New York, New York 10019

Printed in the United States of America

Cover: Segments from films by John Whitney

Contents

PREFACE

The Museum of Modern Art established a Film Library in 1935 in order to accord to the motion picture its proper place as a major art form. Its purpose, as stated by John Hay Whitney, first President of the Library, and A. Conger Goodyear, President of the Museum, was to assemble "a collection of motion picture films suitable for illustrating the important steps historically and artistically in the development of motion pictures from their inception, and making the said collection available at reasonable rates to colleges, schools, museums and other educational institutions."

Since then the Library has expanded to become a Department of Film with an archive of over 8,000 titles of international film and video art, an extensive exhibition program covering contemporary trends as well as pioneering developments, and study centers with films, videotapes, stills, posters, scripts, and related materials. The Circulating Film Library has grown to over a thousand films that span the history of cinema from the 1890s to the present. It continues to be the goal of the Library to make a wide range of films available to viewers who otherwise would not have the opportunity to see them. To this end the Library has drawn upon the archive's rich holdings of silent films, particularly the Biograph collection from the early part of this century. In addition, the Library draws upon the exhibition program; for example, its recently assembled collection of historical documentaries and animation films from the National Film Board of Canada that was based on the Film Board retrospective presented at the Museum in 1982.

Over the past several years the Library has reexamined its holdings, replaced worn prints, and updated the selection of historical and contemporary, independently produced films. We most gratefully acknowledge funding for these purposes from the D. H. and R. H. Gottesman Foundation, the National Endowment for the Arts, Washington, D.C., and the New York State Council on the Arts. We also appreciate the ongoing support from the Hans Richter estate for the acquisition of works by independent filmmakers.

The catalog of the Circulating Film Library has been prepared by Department of Film staff members, together with a team of scholars who researched and verified background information about each film and contributed annotations and essays that enlarge our understanding of film history. The catalog also owes a great debt to the pioneering efforts of Margareta Akermark, who for many years was in charge of the Circulating Film Library, and whose advancement of the work of young artists contributed importantly to the field of independent filmmaking.

For her generous support of the research, writing, and publication of this catalog, we wish to express our very warm appreciation to Celeste Bartos. Her enthusiastic encouragement of this project reflects, as always, her sensitive and thorough understanding of the collection and exhibition activities of the Museum and its Department of Film.

Finally, we offer our thanks to William Sloan, who joined the Department of Film staff as Librarian in 1980, having been Film Librarian of The New York Public Library since 1958. While continuing to broaden the holdings of new independent work, and to strengthen the collection of documentaries and classic narratives, he has taken on the enormous task of organizing this, the most comprehensive, scholarly catalog of the Circulating Film Library. He deserves our admiration as well as our gratitude.

Buster Keaton in
THE GENERAL (1927)

Richard E. Oldenburg
Director
The Museum of Modern Art

Mary Lea Bandy
Director
Department of Film

A COLOUR BOX (1935) by Len Lye

INTRODUCTION AND ACKNOWLEDGMENTS

The Department of Film began circulating films almost half a century ago, when the motion picture itself was less than half a century old. The Circulating Film Library in those early years stood almost alone in making the film classics available to the educational field. Gradually, as commercial sources developed for the feature-length fiction film of the sound period, the Circulating Film Library began to extend its efforts to other periods and genres to better serve the needs of the scholarly community. Today the circulating collection has unique and special strengths in the areas of the European and American cinema of the silent period, the avant-garde, and the documentary, as well as the British independent and Canadian film. In order to make these parts of the collection more accessible and useful to teachers and students, we have supplemented the annotations with interpretive essays by specialists, several on the staff of the Department of Film—"Silent Fiction: Reframing Early Cinema" by Eileen Bowser, Curator; "International Avant-Garde Film: Scattered Pieces" by Larry Kardish, Associate Curator; "The Documentary Film: Trends in the Nonfiction Tradition" by William Sloan; and "American Experimental Film: Breaking Away" by Lucy Fischer, Coordinator, Film Studies Program, University of Pittsburgh; "Contemporary British Independent Film: Voyage of Discovery" by John Ellis, film critic and lecturer and former member of the British Film Institute Production Board; "National Film Board of Canada: Four Decades of Documentaries and Animation" by Sally Bochner, Public Relations Officer, National Film Board of Canada.

The Circulating Film Library was conceived and developed to encourage and facilitate the study of film history. With the passage of time, however, many of the films have come to be recognized as valuable artifacts of their period and as such hold a fascination for historians, anthropologists, sociologists, and psychologists. For instance, many of the early silent films reveal enormous amounts of information about turn-of-the-century America, including aspects of family life, relations between men and women, work, racism, crime, wealth and poverty, costume and manners. In order to achieve the maximum usefulness of the collection for the widest number of users, especially in academic disciplines other than film, we expanded the film descriptions from previous editions of the catalog, and added a subject index.

Concurrent with the preparation of the catalog, the prints in the collection have been examined for quality, and worn prints withdrawn and replaced so that our users could be assured of the best attainable print quality. Many of the programs that the Circulating Film Library has offered for several years have been restructured to reflect our contemporary knowledge of film history and better serve the needs of our users.

The successful completion of this catalog is the result of the devoted work of a large number of people. We are grateful indeed for the dedication they brought to the project and for their scholarship, which makes this catalog a valuable reference tool. Ron Rollet deserves special thanks for his work as editor of this book, as author of many of the experimental annotations, and as contributor to the development of a computerized data base for the collection.

We are especially grateful to the team of catalogers-researchers who have worked in the Department of Film for several years to bring this project to completion. Herbert Reynolds served as historian for the catalog; edited texts; supervised research and indexing; and contributed annotations for the Sound Fiction, Documentary Film, Experimental Film, and Film Study sections. Marita Sturken wrote annotations for Sound Fiction, Documentary

Film, Experimental Film, Contemporary British Independent Film, and Films on the Arts; assisted in editing texts; and coordinated research and indexing. Jytte Jensen did additional research and translations from German, Swedish, and Danish; and Alison Dineen did substantial research. Indexing and research were performed by Barbara Salvage and Vivian Wick.

Eileen Bowser authored the Silent Film sections, Lucy Fischer wrote American Experimental and Sound Fiction annotations, and Larry Kardish wrote European Experimental and Contemporary British Independent annotations. We would like to thank John Whitney for the use of his photograph—created from his film frames—for the cover.

We are profoundly grateful to Rob Wilke who entered the entire catalog into the computer with great skill and accuracy, and who organized the data base in structure and content. A vast amount of work was undertaken by the Museum's Publications Department: Jill Korostoff, the designer; Susan Weiley, the copy editor; Dayna Burnett, design assistant; and in particular Susan Schoenfeld, in charge of production. We also received advice and support throughout the project from Chris Holme.

Michael Miller and David Van Bibber of the Circulating Film Library staff were of crucial assistance in performing a variety of duties, always with good will. Mary Corliss, Curatorial Assistant, Film Stills Archive, ably assisted in the selection of the stills. Nancy Legge edited the first stage of the catalog and helped establish its organization. Martha Deline provided valuable assistance to the editor. Finally, Mary Lea Bandy, Director of the Department of Film, deserves special thanks for her invaluable help and guidance that extended from practical advice on production to philosophical issues involving the goals of the circulating film collection.

William Sloan
Librarian
Circulating Film Library

ORGANIZATION OF THIS CATALOG

The films in this catalog are divided into eight categories: Silent Fiction (including early actualities) from 1894 to 1930; Sound Fiction (1927 to the present); Documentary Film (from early commercial newsreels to the present); Experimental Film (the international avant-garde and American independent cinema from the 1920s onward); Contemporary British Independent Film (from the 1950s); the National Film Board of Canada (documentaries and animation); Films on the Arts (nonfiction work on the arts, exclusive of filmmaking); and Film Study (examinations of film history and film production intended specifically for the teaching of film as art). These groupings will be familiar ones for most readers, though the assignment of any given film to one or another category is obviously discretionary: refer to the Title Index for a full listing of films and their locations within the catalog.

Within each section, films are arranged *chronologically by year and alphabetically within each year*. As a rule, the actual release dates have been listed in preference to dates of production. (For independent works where no formal release or specific public showing took place, the date of completion is preferred.) This system produces some abnormalities (for example, in the alphabetical listings for 1925, Eisenstein's *Potemkin* preceeds *Strike*, even though *Strike* is the earlier work), but the chronological organization provides a general historical perspective within each category.

In the case of programs comprising films from more than one year, the entire program is listed under the year of the earliest film in the group. Thus in the Silent Fiction section *Early Films of Interest* (1895–1918) will be found under 1895. On rare occasions, films within a single program represent more than a particular category, and the entire program is included in the section that is more representative: *Animation Program* (1908–33) spans both silent and sound eras, but appears in the Silent Fiction section under 1908 because most of the films in this program are silent. Cross-references in each section will help locate additional films, and the indexes can assist further.

For simplicity and accessibility, films are listed under their most familiar titles (usually the English title for foreign films). In the annotations film titles appear in bold italics; bold roman face is used to distinguish series titles (like WHY WE FIGHT and THE MARCH OF TIME) and the titles of programs comprised of a number of shorter works (such as THE COMING OF SOUND). Alternate titles follow main titles in parentheses; these include original titles for foreign works, transliterated if necessary. (Whenever possible, all titles by which a film is known are given in the Title Index, with reference to the title under which the film is listed here.) Each film is followed by its country of production, production company (if applicable), and major credits, which are generally listed in order of importance.

In addition to the Title Index, titles are listed in the Country Index, Filmmaker Index, and Subject Index. In the Country Index, titles are listed under the producing country, which is not necessarily the country in which the film was shot (refer to the Subject Index for locations actually depicted in films). In the Filmmaker Index, all of the filmmakers represented in this catalog, including several important producers, are listed along with their films. The Subject Index provides an overview of the collection, with films listed under headings of historical and social issues, location, technique, and various other topics.

Films are offered in their full, original versions, with English subtitles or intertitles where necessary, except as noted otherwise. In the case of films that are silent, a projection speed is recommended—either at 18 or 24 frames per second (abbreviated "fps"). These rates correspond to the approximate "silent" and "sound" speeds available on most 16mm projection equipment. In the absence of uniform standards during the silent period, running speeds varied from around 16 fps to well above 24 fps, even within a single film. Our recommendations, which often are based on the rates suggested by musical cue sheets and other contemporary sources, necessarily represent a compromise between the two speeds available to most users, with the proper speed generally the one that looks most natural.

The information given in this catalog reflects current scholarship as much as possible, and supersedes dates or other references that may appear on the prints themselves. (Significant discrepancies between the information in the catalog and that on the actual prints is noted in the text.) In order to maintain accuracy in future editions of the catalog we welcome suggestions from our users.

See the Price List for information on ordering films.

Dorothy and Lillian Gish in AN UNSEEN ENEMY (1912)

Silent Fiction: Reframing Early Cinema

by Eileen Bowser

With this new edition of the Circulating Film Library Catalog, we hope to encourage some revisions of early film history. When The Museum of Modern Art began to make films accessible for study in 1935, it had an inescapable influence on film history because the films selected were the ones that could be seen and reseen. As a result, the films obtained from the Museum were those that were written about as forming our cinema heritage. Since that time many other organizations have entered nontheatrical distribution, making a much larger number of films available for classroom use. Television has brought hundreds of films of the past into our living rooms. Although the body of films available from the silent period has not increased greatly, the Museum's film archive has continued to collect, preserve, and restore significant films from this period. Forgotten films have come to light, some of which may change the way we see our past.

Among the Museum's greatest film treasures are the large collections of original negatives from Biograph and Edison, two leading production companies during the first two decades of cinema. Our prints from these negatives are usually of extraordinarily high photographic quality. Many of them are now available for rental and sale for the first time through the Circulating Film Library. Many more may be restored if we find there is sufficient demand and enough curiosity on the part of our users to seek out films that are not yet discussed in standard film histories. In addition to newly-restored Biograph and Edison films, this catalog includes silent films recently discovered in foreign archives and private collections. Teachers of film history may easily find ways to vary basic courses by selecting some of these lesser-known, but not necessarily less significant, films to illustrate the development of cinema as art and social document. For those able to explore particular aspects of silent cinema in more depth, this catalog offers greatly increased resources.

Film history did not begin with D. W. Griffith, or even Edwin S. Porter. *The Life of an American Fireman* (1903) and *The Great Train Robbery* (1903) will probably always be regarded as important films, but we do not see them clearly unless we look at them in the context of what Noël Burch has described as the "profound *otherness*" of films before Griffith.[1] It is that context that we hope to provide through the films now available. Early cinema was once considered to consist of clumsy attempts to find the way to a kind of film narrative style that was "intrinsic" to the medium, the style we now call classic cinema. In fact, the films of the early period are the results of other, equally valid ways of seeing. Classic cinema draws the eye and the mind of the spectator *in* and exerts a control over what is seen and felt, whereas early cinema was a phenomenon to be looked at, a show to be enjoyed and examined in detail. Changes came about through the varying conditions of production, distribution, exhibition, technology, popular culture, and the audience, as well as through the ideas of the individual film-maker. Looking back at early cinema can freshen our vision. A film of 1905 may be as significant within its terms of reference as one from 1925.

Before the rise of the nickelodeon in 1905–07, the major film exhibition places were the vaudeville stage, the music hall and burlesque show, the dime museum, the circus, and the itinerant show, and the leading creator was often the narrator-showman. He was responsible for the order in which the films (many of them consisting of a single shot) were shown, and might make changes according to audience reaction. He could run a film faster or slower, or even backward. His monologue explained the action and directed the spectator's attention. Audiences were primarily from the urban working class, including the new immigrants. The films they saw reflected an anarchic, comic, and often amoral view of urban life, in which social institutions were frequently burlesqued. Films in this period were full of comic stereotypes—racial, religious, national, and professional. The country bumpkin, policemen, cooks, tramps, nursemaids, and grocery store proprietors were all the victims of practical jokes. Many erotic films were made, primarily for peep shows, burlesque houses, and smokers, but the spirit they conveyed is shared by many other films of the period (see THE CLASSIC AMERICAN MUTOSCOPE [1897–1907]).

During the first decade of cinema, the actuality film far outweighed the staged film. Such films show scenes of both everyday life and far-off, exotic lands (see FILMS OF THE 1890S [1894–99] and LUMIÈRE PROGRAMS I AND II [1895–98]). They were shown as a novelty within the vaudeville program, where the free mixture of artifice and reality apparently did not disturb the audience. As Erik Barnouw has pointed out, it may be that all films, including actualities, were considered in the first place as illusionism, or magic tricks.[2] In any case, the most popular actualities were based on sensational news events: war, riots, fires, bank and train robberies, kidnapping, and murder. When cameramen could not be present at the event or were unable to satisfy the demand for pictures of it, they recreated events in staged scenes. The look of news films had some influence on the style of staged films in such matters as camera placement and movement of action in front of the camera. When a real event was filmed, the action was apt to move diagonally to the picture plane, to approach or recede, or to be seen at a high or low angle—in contrast to staged acts performed, as in the theater, parallel to a fixed camera position. When the filmmaker wanted to imitate a news event, he copied the look of the real thing[3] (see EARLY FILMS OF INTEREST [1895–1918]).

Staged films were also made from the very beginning. They gradually overcame the actuality film in numbers produced during the second decade. These films found their sources not only in recreated news events, but in vaudeville acts—its songs and dances, its slapstick comedy, its "living pictures," and its magic acts. Many early filmmakers were first magicians, and the camera, with its possibilities for trick effects such as stop-motion, was for them another kind of illusionism (see *The Execution of Mary Queen of Scots* [1895], MAGIC FILMS [1898–1905], GEORGES MÉLIÈS PROGRAM [1899–1912], *Tit for Tat* [1905], *Whence Does He Come?* [1905], and many others). The comic strip provided yet another source for picture ideas.

In the beginning the form of the narrative film may have been most strongly influenced by the popular lantern slide show with lecture. Many were travel lectures; some were narratives. Early catalogs advertised films and slides together, and a showman could combine them in various ways in one optical show. The first films contained only one shot, or in the case of stop-motion trick films, two or more shots designed to appear as one. By its nature, the lantern slide show consisted of self-contained images. The lecturer would fill in gaps and interpret, just as the narrator in early film exhibition would point out to the audience what the images meant. Even after the filmmaker began to combine two or more shots, he continued to think of them as self-contained, and would try to complete an action with a given shot, often splitting the frame into spatial areas or panning extensively to keep the action within the frame. The showman was still given several options and could order a film in different lengths, according to his needs. The combined shots did not necessarily follow a temporal progression. A part of the action, as in slide shows, would often be repeated from another point of view in the succeeding image. This tradition is particularly evident in the films made by Edwin S. Porter, himself a showman first and filmmaker second.[4] The temporal overlap inherited by early cinema from preexisting modes of representation forms one characteristic of what Tom Gunning calls the "noncontinuous" style,[5] which is most clearly demonstrated in the fire-rescue scenes of the restored *The Life of an American Fireman* (1903).

Pans, traveling shots, and close-ups exist in these early films, but they are not used as part of the classic film grammar we know today. Close-ups were first employed in the one-shot films as a novelty known as "facial expressions," in which actors sneeze, laugh, leer, perform impersonations, or, as in *The Irwin-Rice Kiss* (1896), embrace. They were often photographed with the performer looking directly at his audience. Later, such shots serve as introductions or closures to simple narratives (*The Great Train Robbery* [1903], or *Rescued by Rover* [1905])—setting up a theme or introducing the leading characters, but not participating in the narrative. When close views are edited into a narrative, as the semi-close-up is in *The Strenuous Life* (1904), they often repeat the action of the long shot in which they are inserted and interrupt the narrative flow. Pans and traveling shots, as mentioned above, were methods of keeping the action self-contained in one shot.[6]

If we accept the trick film as essentially an expanded magic act from vaudeville and tent shows, then the first original film genre to be codified was the comic chase film. The chase has remained a basic element of cinema from its beginnings to the present day. In 1903–04 it took narrative filmmaking away from the stage set and the painted backdrop into outdoor space. In *Maniac Chase* (1904), *Boarding School Girls* (1905), *The Runaway Horse* (1907), and *Jack the Kisser* (1907), one may see the conventions of the genre, conventions that would remain little changed until the advent of parallel editing after 1907. The early comic-chase film has no cuts between the pursued and the pursuers. They are shown running, falling, and tumbling over obstacles, the ladies in their long skirts providing glimpses of their ankles. The chase crosses the field of vision from background to foreground in diagonal and curving lines, until the last straggler has disappeared, before the scene changes to a new location, where the action is repeated. The camera sometimes pans to keep the chase in sight interminably. Only the capture brings an end to these early narratives. Diagonal exits to the left or the right of frame near the camera may have suggested a way to link shots by movement from one shot to the next, one step in the development of an integrated narrative style. But the desirability of linking shots to make a coherent narrative emerged only when changing modes of production and exhibition began to eliminate the showman-narrator.

By 1907 the popularity of the nickelodeons had created a demand for films that could be satisfied only by assemblyline factory production. Creative control over what the audience would see and understand, and in what order, shifted from the showman to the producer, cameraman, or director, and this had a profound effect on film narrative style. In 1907 there were still numerous comedies in which the shots are linked together only by a device that would be common to all episodes, named by John Fell "the motivated link"[7] (see *Laughing Gas*, *Jack the Kisser*, and *The Rivals*, all from that year). What was lacking, for the most part, was a way to express more complex narrative—ways to explain temporal and spatial relationships as well as character relationships. Probably because such devices as close-ups in early cinema practice were considered to be outside the temporal progression and disruptive to a smooth narrative flow, they were used less frequently until they reemerged in 1912–13 as a new and expressive element. And while filmmakers concentrated on ways to link shots in an edited continuity, they also used fewer camera movements to extend the single shot, until these too reemerged as another expressive element. Early cinema's modes did not disappear altogether and the shift in emphasis was gradual, even sporadic. Among the earliest steps toward the new narrative mode were the centering of significant action within the frame, making both shorter and an increased number of shots, relating shots by movement and composition, eliminating temporal overlap and repeated action, and cutting directly on action. As early as 1906, in *The 100 to 1 Shot*, for example, the first stages of cutting that would lead to parallel editing are evident.

Some stages of that development took place in early British cinema (see THE BEGINNINGS OF BRITISH FILM [1901–11]), which played a leading role in the first years of the century, and in French cinema (see FERDINAND ZECCA PROGRAM [1905–10] and COHL, FEUILLADE, AND DURAND PROGRAM [1907–12]), which dominated the world market during 1905–10, while American producers wasted time in legal wrangles over the control of the new industry and failed to understand the need for a steady flow of product. In 1908 the American film industry achieved a temporary measure of stability in the establishment of a consortium of the major producers, known as "The Trust," and began to grow steadily. Even before World War I, the event usually attributed as the causal force, the American film industry had begun to assume its long domination of world film production. At the same time, the nickelodeon parlors began to give way to more permanent movie houses, and in a few years some were magnificent picture palaces, lavishly furnished and designed.

Just as the vaudeville houses had made a conscious effort to attract a more respectable middle-class and family audience at the turn of the century, the increasingly organized film business sought to discard its disreputable associations and draw a similar audience. Nickelodeons came under attack by the press, politicians, and guardians of moral conduct. They were labeled unsafe and unhealthy, and the films were accused of corrupting the morals of their audiences. In answer to this attack, the antisocial spirit of many early films was eliminated. After 1907 the melodrama, endowed with a moral base and protective of established social order, became the major film genre. Even the popular comic film dropped in numbers for a few years, although it was to return with vigor as the slapstick comedy, embracing the anarchic spirit of early cinema, as soon as the melodrama was firmly established. In France a similar urge for greater prestige led to the establishment of the Film d'Art, ambitious productions starring great stage actors in film versions of their most celebrated performances (see THE

FILM D'ART [1908–12] and GREAT ACTRESSES OF THE PAST [1911–16]).

In 1908 the stage was clearly set for the coming of a D. W. Griffith. Although he was by no means the only filmmaker to help establish the film style that we now call classic cinema, he was a major figure. The films now available from the original Biograph negatives make it possible to study his work in depth and progression from year to year and to see the many methods he explored to enrich the expressive qualities of the narrative film. The pre-Griffith films make it possible to understand what constituted his cinema heritage, while the Biograph films demonstrate what it is he did with it. Perhaps what chiefly lifts Griffith above his contemporaries is his ability to convey feelings and emotions, which he is able to do within early, as well as later, cinema styles. The new emphasis he gave to certain preexisiting techniques grew out of his desire for a greater degree of expressivity that was surely shared by many of his contemporaries. His previous acting experience in touring melodramas prepared him to be a leading exponent of the major film genre, and his lack of experience in the earlier modes of exhibition practice made it easier for him to abandon some of the early film conventions, although they are still found in his first films.

Probably first in order and importance was his development of parallel editing from its sketchy beginnings in pre-Griffith cinema to a basic component of classic cinema structure. Parallel editing is the interweaving of two or more streams of action into a narrative continuity and often includes the compression or expansion of time and space. One important function of parallel editing is its ability to thrill audiences with suspense and excitement, as can be seen in *The Lonely Villa* (1909), *Rose O' Salem-Town* (1910), *The Lonedale Operator* (1911), *The Girl and Her Trust* (1912), *An Outcast among Outcasts* (1912), *An Unseen Enemy* (1912), and *Death's Marathon* (1913). Parallel editing is also used for contrast in films of social and moral purpose, as in *A Corner in Wheat* (1909), *The Usurer* (1910), *The Broken Cross* (1911), *Conscience* (1911), *The Two Sides* (1911), and *What Shall We Do with Our Old* (1911). In several of these, the contrast is ironic, comparing through cross-cutting the sufferings of the poor with the luxuries of the rich who may be responsible for their poverty.

Griffith increased the pictorial beauty and the emotional power of his films through the use of nature, as well as through the use of movement and rhythm, and a variety of camera positions, as may be seen in *The Mended Lute* (1909), *The Broken Doll* (1910), *His Mother's Scarf* (1911), *Black Sheep* (1912), and *An Outcast among Outcasts*. Through the various techniques of repetition he gave intensity as well as psychological and emotional meaning to specific settings, or created metaphors, in *The Country Doctor* (1909), *The Unchanging Sea* (1910), *The Way of the World* (1910), *The Spanish Gypsy* (1911), *The Eternal Mother* (1912), and *The Painted Lady* (1912). The isolation of significant details through disjunctive editing and the development of a natural and intimate acting style made possible the creation of individual characterization in *Bobby, The Coward* (1911), *The New York Hat* (1912), and *The Mothering Heart* (1913). Griffith used close-ups sparingly until late in the Biograph years, but he began to explore their expressive and dramatic function in some of the 1911 Biographs by bringing the actors forward during a long shot to close-up position, and by 1912–13, when close-ups cut into longer shots were an accepted part of his repertoire, in such films as *Death's Marathon*, *The Lady and the Mouse* (1913), and *The Mothering Heart*. By the end of his Biograph period in late 1913, the strategies that provide the basic framework for classic cinema were common to filmmaking everywhere and the shift to a self-sufficient linear narrative structure had been essentially completed.

While the majority of films during this period were standardized as a product one or two reels long, especially in the production of the major American companies within "The Trust," the longer film came into acceptance in European countries and also in America with the independent producers who now challenged the Trust. By 1913 five-and six-reel films were not uncommon, and by 1915 the feature film was established as the norm. Early Danish cinema (unfortunately not yet represented in the Circulating Film Library) gave emphasis to the longer film. Italian historical spectacle films (*The Fall of Troy* [1910], *Quo Vadis?* [1912], *Cabiria* [1914]) added their weight to the growing interest in longer and more ambitious films. *The Birth of a Nation* arrived at the very beginning of 1915 and was so remarkable that historians ever since have marked it as a watershed. Remarkable it is, not as a new kind of film after which everything would be different, but rather as a culmination of everything that had gone on before. There were still other changes to occur before the classic cinema style that dominated American films for many years would be complete. For example, in Griffith's films, the editing process is not only clearly visible, but is brought to the viewer's attention. The tendency in classic cinema was to cut on action in such a way that the viewer would not be conscious of the separate pieces of which a film is made.

The growth of the entertainment industry into big business led to a conservatism, especially in America. Films were produced on a regular basis to fill a program: romances, melodramas, fantasies, westerns, and comedies. The kinds of films produced and the classic cinema style might be altered and refined, but radical change became more rare. Among the films intended only as profit-making products, designed to amuse and enthrall a public, some nevertheless emerged as works of art. Within the established conventions, American filmmakers produced some great films admired the world over, as did filmmakers from within the industry in other countries.

The concept of film as a major new art form had been discussed as early as 1908 and had taken root in the thinking of some artists by 1913. By the twenties, for many filmmakers if not the general public, the question was no longer whether films might be art, but rather of what elements that art is composed. The last decade of the silent film was a ferment of aesthetic debate. The Museum of Modern Art was born out of the modern art movement of the twenties, and from its founding in 1929 it was envisioned that film would take its place among the other art forms to be collected and enjoyed. Most of the deliberate attempts to create works of art in the medium during the twenties came from outside the established film industry. Such a film was Griffith's *Broken Blossoms* in 1919, made independently, and widely influential in this country and abroad.

However, much of the experimentation and theoretical discussions took place in European countries. Eventually, European trends were absorbed into the body of American film technique. In France, an active group of independent filmmakers, working outside the industry and coming from literature, theater, poetry, music, and the fine arts, explored aspects of film art in theory and in practice. Their impressionist and avant-garde films modified or challenged classic cinema, lessening the importance of narrative in favor of formal concerns about the nature of the medium. In Germany, experimentation was actually encouraged within certain branches of the film industry. Since the country was suffering severe economic difficulties following its defeat in World War I, in order to build up its film industry it provided subsidies and constructed large studios in which craftsmanship was perfected. The Expressionist movement in theater and art, notably Max Reinhardt's Deutsches Theater and the Kammerspiele, provided stimuli for trying out new kinds of films and new styles. In the newborn Soviet Union, resolved to establish a film industry that would forward the goals of the socialist revolution, experiment was everywhere in all the arts but particularly in cinema, where formal aspects of the medium were taken apart and examined and tested.

In their different ways, French, German, and Soviet filmmakers challenged the tradition of cinema as based on narrative logic, symmetry, objectivity, and continuous space. They questioned the all-pervasive melodrama and its traditional heroes. Toward the end of the decade, these new trends flowed together in the European International Style. Ideas and filmmakers freely crossed national borders. The moving camera, rapid montage, rhythmic cutting, subjective camera, oblique camera angles, new lighting effects, and the self-sufficient (titleless) narrative gave increased expressiveness to the silent film medium. These experiments greatly enriched classic cinema style. At the same time, however, there was another movement toward greater objectivity, frequently in films of social purpose, toward a greater degree of illusionism, stressing a seamless continuity in which the formal means are subordinate to the narrative. With the coming of sound, itself another addition to an illusory reality, the latter movement would come to dominate over the twenties' preoccupation with film aesthetics and formalism.

Through the films described in the following pages it is possible to study rather closely the history of the silent film and its impact on western culture. In one sense the silent film era came to an end with *The Jazz Singer* (1927); in another sense it still lives in every film that is made.

Notes

[1] Noël Burch, "To the Distant Observer: Towards a Theory of Japanese Film," *October*, no. 1 (Spring 1976), p. 32, n. 1.

[2] Erik Barnouw, *The Magician and the Cinema* (New York: Oxford University Press, 1981).

[3] David Levy, "The 'fake' train robbery: les reportages simulés, les reconstitutions et le film narratif americain," *Les Cahiers de la cinémathèque*, no. 29 (Winter 1979), pp. 42–56.

[4] Charles Musser, "Edwin Porter at the Eden Musée: Exhibitor as Creator: 1891–1900," a paper presented at the Society for Cinema Studies Conference, April 1981, City University of New York, New York.

[5] Tom Gunning, "Le style non-continu du cinéma des premiers temps (1900–1906)," *Les Cahiers de la cinémathèque*, no. 29 (Winter 1979), pp. 24–34.

[6] Jon Gartenberg, "Camera Movement in Biograph and Edison films, 1900–1906," *Cinema Journal*, vol. 19, no. 2 (Spring 1980), pp. 1–16.

[7] John Fell, "Motive, Mischief and Melodrama: The State of Film Narrative in 1907," *Film Quarterly*, vol. 33, no. 3 (Spring 1980), pp. 30–37.

ANNOTATIONS
Eileen Bowser

FILMS OF THE 1890S

1894–99. U.S.A.
Total program: 18 min. B&W. Silent.
18 fps.

CHINESE LAUNDRY

1894.
Edison Kinetoscope film. With Robetta and Doretto.

THE EXECUTION OF MARY QUEEN OF SCOTS

1895.
Edison Kinetoscope film. Directed by Alfred Clark. With Mr. R. L. Thomae as Mary.

DICKSON EXPERIMENTAL SOUND FILM

ca. 1895.
Edison Company. Directed by, and with, William K. L. Dickson.

THE IRWIN-RICE KISS

1896.
Edison Company. From the play *The Widow Jones*. With May Irwin and John C. Rice.

FEEDING THE DOVES

1896.
Edison Company.

MORNING BATH

1896.
Edison Company.

BURNING STABLE

1896.
Edison Company.

THE BLACK DIAMOND EXPRESS

1896.
Edison Company.

NEW YORK STREET SCENES

ca. 1897.
Identification uncertain.

FATIMA

1897.
The International Film Company.
Identification uncertain.

A WRINGING GOOD JOKE

1899.
Edison Company.

DEWAR'S SCOTCH WHISKY

1897.
The International Film Company.

The short films on this compilation program are typical of production in most countries before the turn of the century. The first pictures in the program were made for the Edison Kinetoscope, a peephole device developed by William K. L. Dickson. Later, events were filmed and projected as we know them today. The fiction film began with shorts like this one about the execution of Mary, Queen of Scots, and the documentary has its roots in these small scenes of babies being bathed and stables burning. Stop-motion filming, the basis for later trick films, is seen in *The Execution of Mary Queen of Scots*, made before Georges Méliès had seen his first film. The first uses of the close-up appeared in the "facial expression" genre, exemplified by *The Irwin-Rice Kiss*, a sensational and much imitated film in its day. Experiments with synchronizing sound and picture began as early as the Dickson film (which now lacks the sound recording). *Dewar's Scotch Whisky* is considered to be one of the first advertising films, projected by Edwin S. Porter on an outdoor billboard in New York's Herald Square before he became a producer for the Edison Company.

—

EARLY FILMS OF INTEREST

1895–1918.
Total program: 22 min. B&W. Silent.
18 fps.

EXCURSION OF THE FRENCH PHOTOGRAPHIC SOCIETY TO NEUVILLE (DÉBARQUEMENT, OU, ARRIVÉE DES CONGRESSISTES À NEUVILLE-SUR-SAÔNE)

1895. France.
Lumière. Directed by Louis Lumière.

GOLD RUSH SCENES IN THE KLONDIKE

1898. U.S.A.
Edison Company.

THE FUNERAL OF QUEEN VICTORIA

1901. Great Britain.
Produced and directed by R. W. Paul.

REPRODUCTION OF MCGOVERN-CORBETT FIGHT

1903. U.S.A.
American Mutoscope and Biograph Company. Photographed by G. W. (Billy) Bitzer.

SAN FRANCISCO EARTHQUAKE

1906. U.S.A.
Edison Company.

MEETING OF THE MOTION PICTURE PATENTS COMPANY

1909. U.S.A.
American Mutoscope and Biograph Company.

MISS DAVISON'S FUNERAL

1913. Great Britain (?).
Pathé.

FIRST WRIGHT FLIGHT IN FRANCE

1908. France.
Gaumont. Photographed by Félix Mesguich.

SINKING OF THE AUSTRIAN BATTLESHIP "ST. STEPHEN"

1918.
Identification uncertain.

Most films made in the first decade of cinema were actualities or news events. Even before the creation of the formal newsreel in 1910, the camera was recording the scenes and incidents that were to become newsreel staples. These typical clips range from the Lumière Neuville excursion, which may be the first instance of camera reporting, to the prize fight (mistakenly identified on the print as the Jeffries-Corbett fight) staged at the Biograph studio against a painted canvas of enraptured spectators. Some of the early fiction films were attempts to recreate news events, and the events themselves often influenced the staging of early narrative cinema. *San Francisco Earthquake* is another typical example of this, as is, in a certain sense, *The Great Train Robbery* (1903). *Miss Davison's Funeral*, a true news film, covers the demonstrations that accompanied the rites for Emily Wilding Davison, the great English suffragette.

—

EARLY GERMAN FILMS

1895–1911. Germany.
Total program: 33 min. B&W. Silent.
18 fps.

PIONEER FILMS BY MAX SKLADANOWSKY

1895–96.
8 min.

DON JUAN'S WEDDING (DON JUAN HEIRATET)

1909.
Duskes Kinematographen-und-Film Fabriken. Directed by Heinrich Bolten-Baeckers. With Joseph Giampietro. English intertitles.
14 min.

MISUNDERSTOOD (VERKANNT)

1911.
Messters Projektion. With Henny Porten, Friedrich Zelnik. Identification uncertain. English intertitles.
11 min.

Max Skladanowsky was a producer of optical shows using animated slides and drawings in the pre-cinema period. He exhibited films for the first time on November 1, 1895 at the Wintergarten in Berlin. This group of his early presentations contains examples of his early lantern slides as well as live-action subjects: acrobatic acts, Berlin street scenes, and some slapstick comedy scenes filmed on a trip he made to Stockholm in 1896. At the end Skladanowsky appears in person to bow, and is seen in a close-up. ***Don Juan's Wedding*** is a farce about the troubles of a Don Juan on his wedding day when three of his former loves kidnap him from the arms of his bride. He escapes by pretending to hang himself, which we see in a point-of-view shot through a keyhole-shaped matte. Employing the conventions of pre-Griffith cinema, the film uses camera pans to follow action and several semi-close-ups inserted in long shots. This film was formerly attributed to Oskar Messter. ***Misunderstood*** is among the earliest films starring Henny Porten, Germany's most popular silent film star. The title is in question (see *Deutsche Stummfilme* by Gerhard Lamprecht) and the film is incomplete. However, enough survives to show that this is a melodrama with a strong role for an actress. Anna robs her father's safe to get money for her secret lover and lets her brother, a gambler, go to prison for the deed. Overcome by her guilty conscience, she confesses. Domestic scenes are intentionally intercut with scenes of the brother ruining himself at gambling. Figures filmed at full-length are sometimes brought forward to dramatic semi-close-ups at the close of a shot.

— —

LUMIÈRE PROGRAM I: FIRST PROGRAMS

1895–96. France.

The Auguste Lumières in FEEDING THE BABY (1895)

Lumière. English titles.
Total program: 21 min. B&W. Silent. 18 fps.

WORKERS LEAVING THE LUMIÈRE FACTORY (SORTIE D'USINE)

1895.

ARRIVAL OF EXPRESS AT LYONS (ARRIVÉE D'UN TRAIN)

1895.

FRIENDLY PARTY IN THE GARDEN OF LUMIÈRE (PARTIE D'ÉCARTÉ)

1895.

FEEDING THE BABY (REPAS DE BÉBÉ)

1895.

BOYS SAILING BOATS, TUILERIES GARDEN, PARIS (BASSIN DES TUILERIES)

1896.

THE FALLING WALL (DÉMOLITION D'UN MUR)

1896.

BATHS AT MILAN, ITALY (BAINS DE DIANE, MILAN)

1896.

FRENCH DRAGOONS (DRAGONS)

1896.

Identification uncertain.

GONDOLA PARTY (ARRIVÉE EN GONDOLE)

1896.

SACK RACE (COURSE EN SAC)

1895.

MILITARY REVIEW, HUNGARY

Identification uncertain.

GERMAN HUSSARS JUMPING FENCES (DRAGONS ALLEMANS, STUTTGART)

Identification uncertain.

FEEDING THE SWANS (CYGNES, LYON)

1896.

BOILER LOADING

Identification uncertain.

The first motion pictures reached the screen almost simultaneously in France, England, and the United States. In all three countries, the first programs consisted largely of the films of the Lumière brothers, Louis and Auguste. This collection contains some of the Lumière films that were exhibited on opening nights in Paris, London, and New York, as well as some Lumière films that were not in those programs. During cinema's first decade, the largest number of films were actualities—featuring soldiers, workers, trains, and babies (**Feeding the Baby** shows Auguste Lumière with his wife and daughter). In other words, the fabric of everyday life was shown in images as magical to the first audience as any trick effects. Even these simple subjects were staged for the camera, however, and their composition, their use of space and movement contributed to what was to become the art of cinema.

—

LUMIÈRE PROGRAM II: EARLY LUMIÈRE FILMS

1895–98. France.
Lumière. French titles.
Total program: 20 min. B&W. Silent. 18 fps.

I. Miscellaneous Views (Vues Diverses)

BOAT LEAVING THE HARBOR (BARQUE SORTANT DU PORT)

1896–97.

TEASING THE LION (LION)

1896–97.

FEEDING THE BABY (REPAS DE BÉBÉ)

1895.

WOOD CUTTERS (SCIEURS DE BOIS)

1896–97.

CHILDREN'S PLAYMATES (SCÈNE D'ENFANTS)

1896–97.

GAME OF BACKGAMMON (PARTIE DE TRIC-TRAC)

1896–97.

WORKERS LEAVING THE LUMIÈRE FACTORY (SORTIE D'USINE)

1895.

NEGROES BATHING (BAIGNADE DE NÉGRILLONS)

1898.

II. Comic Views (Vues Comiques)

TEASING THE GARDENER (L'ARROSEUR EST ARROSÉ)

1895.

RUSSIAN DANCE (DANSE RUSSE)

1896–97.

PAINTING CONTEST (JURY DE PEINTURE)

1896–97.

III. France

COKE OVENS AT CARMAUX (DÉFOURNAGE DU COKE)

1896–97.

FISH MARKET AT MARSEILLES (MARCHÉ AUX POISSONS)

1896–97.

FLOOD AT LYONS (INONDATIONS 1896: QUAI DE LYON)

1896.

IV. Military Scenes (Vues Militaires)

HORSES' WATERING TROUGH (ABREUVOIR)

1896–97.

CHARGE OF THE CUIRASSIER (CUIRASSIERS: MÊLÉE)

1896–97.

DRAGOONS SWIMMING THE SAÔNE (DRAGONS TRAVERSANT LA SAÔNE À LA NAGE)

1896–97.

SOLDIERS' FUN IN CAMP (DANSE AU BIVOUAC)

1896.

LEAPING OVER A HORSE (SAUTS AU CHEVAL EN LONGUEUR)

1896–97.

PLACING AND FIRING GUN (MISE EN BATTERIE ET FEU)

1896–97.

The Lumière brothers brought out their Cinématographe in 1895. Light and compact, it was used by photographers all over the world to send back a steady stream of brief actualities to Paris. The exotic and the everyday subjects were of great curiosity to early cinema viewers. Although the Lumières became known for their actuality films and topical subjects, this program also includes some examples of their slapstick comedies: the famous **Teasing the Gardener**, in which a mischievous boy steps on the gardener's hose and then releases the water in his victim's face (subsequently imitated by many film companies), and the delightful **Painting Contest** in which a disgruntled artist breaks his canvas over a juror's head. Two of the films, **Feeding the Baby** and **Workers Leaving**

the **Lumière Factory**, appear also on **Lumière Program I** (1895–96), as they were among the earliest Lumière films made. The twenty films in this collection are grouped as they were in the Lumière catalogs, under various types.

—

THE CLASSIC AMERICAN MUTOSCOPE

1897–1907. U.S.A.
American Mutoscope and Biograph Company (known as American Mutoscope Company until 1899). Compiled in 1966 by Douglass Crockwell.
Total program: 10 min. B&W. Silent. 24 fps.

THE TRAMP AND THE MUSCULAR COOK

1899.

REGINALD'S FIRST HIGH HAT (incorrectly identified as *A [W]RINGING GOOD JOKE*)

1899.

THE HORSE THIEF (one shot from an eleven-shot narrative film)

1905.

AN AFFAIR OF HONOR

1897.

HOW THE OLD MAID GOT A HUSBAND (incorrectly identified as *OLD MAID AND THE BURGLAR*)

1900.

A FIGHT FOR A BRIDE

1905.

THE CONVICT'S BRIDE (incorrectly identified as *JAIL BREAK*)

1906.

WALTZING WALKER

1907.

SHE BANKED IN HER STOCKING, OR, ROBBED OF HER ALL

1905.

W. K. L. Dickson, after designing Edison's Kinetoscope, left the company and made another peepshow device, the Mutoscope, for what was to become the American Mutoscope and Biograph Company. It carefully avoided Edison's patents. Individual film frames are printed on cards and mounted on a wheel that, when revolved inside a box, gives the illusion of movement. Douglass Crockwell, the experimental filmmaker well known for **Glens Falls Sequence** (1946) and **The Long Bodies** (1947), collected old Mutoscopes and rephotographed these onto film; however, the movement is a little slow even at sound speed, and Crockwell's dating (1902–05) is imprecise. The films are each a single shot filmed from a fixed camera position, using stage sets or painted backdrops. They are staged vaudeville or burlesque acts, with an emphasis on slapstick comedy and the erotic. The single exception is a shot from **The Horse Thief** which, like the other shots in that film, is made outdoors with a panning camera. The practical jokes and teasing display of female limbs are characteristic of most early film production. Biograph, however, due to the success of the Mutoscope, kept the little erotic films in production later than the other companies, even after going on to longer and more serious films. Many of Biograph's short productions served equally for Mutoscopes and projected films.

———

MAGIC FILMS

1898–1905.
Compiled by Lucy Fischer.
Total program: 22 min. B&W. Silent. 18 fps.

VANISHING LADY

1898. U.S.A.
Edison Company.

THE MYSTIC SWING

1900. U.S.A.
Edison Company.

A MYSTIC REINCARNATION

1901. U.S.A.
American Mutoscope and Biograph Company.

TEN LADIES IN ONE UMBRELLA (LA PARAPLUIE FANTASTIQUE, OU, DIX FEMMES SOUS UNE OMBRELLE)

1903. France.
Produced and directed by Georges Méliès.

THE FUGITIVE APPARITIONS (LES APPARITIONS FUGITIVES)

1904. France.
Produced and directed by Georges Méliès.

JUPITER'S THUNDERBOLTS (LE TONNERRE DE JUPITER)

1903. France.
Produced and directed by Georges Méliès.

ALCOFRISBAS, THE MASTER MAGICIAN (L'ENCHANTEUR ALCOFRISBAS)

1903. France.
Produced and directed by Georges Méliès.

THE BALLET MASTER'S DREAM (LE RÊVE DU MAÎTRE DE BALLET)

1903. France.
Produced and directed by Georges Méliès.

PIERROT'S PROBLEM

1900. U.S.A.
American Mutoscope and Biograph Company.

THE ARTIST'S DILEMMA

1901. U.S.A.
Edison Company (?).

A DELUSION

1902. U.S.A.
American Mutoscope and Biograph Company.

A PIPE DREAM

1905. U.S.A.
American Mutoscope and Biograph Company.

The first films to exploit camera tricks—stop motion, dissolves, and double exposures—were frequently based on magicians' stage acts. In this program camera magic is added to the magician's stock of illusions with **Vanishing Lady, The Mystic Swing, A Mystic Reincarnation,** and **Pierrot's Problem** set against drop curtains or scenic painted backdrops, just as they would have appeared on the vaudeville stage. Male magicians make scantily-dressed women appear and disappear. They are dismembered, reassembled, levitated, and not infrequently changed into men or skeletons. The Frenchman Georges Méliès operated a theater devoted to magic and spectacle and his films are characteristically more ambitious (see also **Georges Méliès Program** [1899–1912]). He constructed elaborate imaginative sets, and his films in this program tend to have scene changes and are not restricted to the single shot. (The stop-motion films contain more than one shot, but give the illusion of only one.) **The Fugitive Apparitions** uses slow dissolves for the magic appearances and disappearances instead of the abrupt and "invisible" cut of most stop-motion filming. Because **The Artist's Dilemma** has an ornately-designed set and appears as early as 1901, we suspect that it may actually be one of the Méliès films that the Edison Company commonly duped and distributed as their own. Lucy Fisher has noted the unconscious symbols implied by these films' images of women. **A Pipe Dream** is a reversal of these exploitative images: a young woman in three-quarter shot blows cigarette smoke in the palm of her hand and calls forth a tiny miniature man. However, when she tries to call him back again, she is powerless to do so. One might also note the erotic

THE CONQUEST OF THE POLE (1912) (p. 22)

22

tendencies of these films: in **A Mystic Reincarnation** the magician handles the young lady's stockings and leers knowingly at the camera. All of the prints in this program are reconstructions from the paper prints deposited for copyright purposes in the Library of Congress and lack the brilliant photographic quality of the originals, which were often hand-tinted in bright colors as well.

—

GEORGES MÉLIÈS PROGRAM

1899–1912. France.
Produced and directed by Georges Méliès.
Total program: 47 min. B&W. Silent. 18 fps.
A Trip to the Moon is also available individually.

THE CONJURER (ILLUSIONNISTE FIN DE SIÈCLE; L'IMPRESSIONNISTE FIN DE SIÈCLE)

1899.
1 min.

A TRIP TO THE MOON (LE VOYAGE DANS LA LUNE)

1902.
11 min.

THE PALACE OF THE ARABIAN NIGHTS (LE PALAIS DES MILLE ET UNE NUITS)

1905.
19 min.

THE DOCTOR'S SECRET (HYDROTHÉRAPIE FANTASTIQUE)

1910.
9 min.

THE CONQUEST OF THE POLE (À LA CONQUÊTE DU PÔLE)

1912.
7 min. French intertitles.

All early filmmakers were fascinated at first with the camera's possibilities for tricks and illusionism. In fact, many were magicians before becoming filmmakers. But it was Georges Méliès, the French magician, producer of spectacles, actor, artist, and poet, who had the imagination and enthusiasm to fully exploit its marvels. His films are spectacles that amaze and delight. He created fantastic visions—all of them curious, some of them comic. Although he made many kinds of films, even actualities, the titles in this program are typical of his pro-

ductions. **The Conjurer** is a transformation film in which a magician brings a doll to life, makes her disappear, and then disappears himself, all through the magic of stop-motion filming. **The Doctor's Secret** is a comedy in which a fat man is subjected to drastic and cruel weight-loss treatment. The other three films illustrate Méliès's more elaborate super-productions, with richly decorated sets he designed himself, beautiful women, and fantastical scenes. They were longer and more costly than most films of their time. **A Trip to the Moon** is undoubtedly the most well-known, especially since its imaginative science fiction has become fact. In thirty scenes, members of the Astronomic Club prepare for their moon-launching, take off, land on the moon, and finally splash down in the sea as they return to earth. In **The Palace of the Arabian Nights**, Prince Charming goes through fantastic adventures armed with his magic sword from the sorcerer Khalafar, in search of the great treasure in the Palace of the Arabian Nights. **The Conquest of the Pole** is a late Méliès film, and another science fiction adventure in which teams of scientists race each other to the Pole in a helicopter and a balloon. En route they meet the terrible Giant of the Snows who eats scientists for lunch. On their return to Paris, they are greeted by the giddy chorus line that saw them off.

—

THE BEGINNINGS OF BRITISH FILM

1901–11. Great Britain.
Total program: 29 min. B&W. Silent. 18 fps.

THE FUNERAL OF QUEEN VICTORIA

1901.
Produced and directed by R. W. Paul.
3 min.

RESCUED BY ROVER

1905.
Produced and directed by Cecil Hepworth.
6 min.

THE AIRSHIP DESTROYER

1909.
Warwick Trading Company. Produced by Charles Urban.
8 min.

TATTERS: A TALE OF THE SLUMS

1911.

Cricks and Martin. Directed by A. E. Coleby.
12 min.

The imaginative innovations in the earliest British cinema made it a rich source for filmmakers in other countries. This reel includes a dramatic news event, the funeral procession of a famous queen; a cleverly-made trick film that shows the contemporary fascination with flying machines; and two melodramas. The classic **Rescued by Rover**, about the rescue of a kidnapped baby by the family dog, shows a careful observance of screen direction and action from one shot to the next. It begins with an introductory close-up of the baby with the dog and ends with a change of camera position to reveal a closer view of the homecoming scene. (Child-kidnapping was a popular film subject and served as the topic of the first film directed by D. W. Griffith.) **Tatters** is a Dickensian melodrama in which a boy of the slums rescues a rich boy from his kidnappers. Painted backdrops are alternated with natural settings, in accordance with the early cinema style, which demonstrates that British cinema by this time was becoming out of step with trends in world cinema and was losing its position as a leader. The highly stylized acting, formal and expressive, also comes from the earlier style.

—

EDISON PROGRAM

1903–04. U.S.A.
Edison Company.
Total program: 8 min. B&W. Silent. 18 fps.

EGYPTIAN FAKIR WITH DANCING MONKEY

June 8, 1903.
Directed by A. C. Abadie.
2 min.

WEARY WILLIE KIDNAPS A CHILD

June 7, 1904.
Directed by Edwin S. Porter.
3 min.

NERVY NAT KISSES THE BRIDE

September 30, 1904.
Directed by Edwin S. Porter.
2 min.

SCARECROW PUMP

December 9, 1904.
Directed by Edwin S. Porter.
1 min.

The vaudeville houses were the major exhibitors of this period, and filmed vaudeville acts, in addition to the popular actuality films, were staple fare. The films in this program are typical of the kinds of films shown there. *Egyptian Fakir*, while it could be taken for a vaudeville act, was actually filmed by A. C. Abadie in Cairo during an Edison Company trip to the Near East. It consists of two shots from the same camera position showing a monkey act. *Nervy Nat Kisses the Bride* is a little comedy extended into three scenes about a pickpocket who steals a train ticket in the station and once on the train steals a kiss from a lady, for which he is thrown off the train in a scene using trick effects. *Scarecrow Pump*, in the tradition of Lumière's *Teasing the Gardener* (see **Lumière Program II** [1895–98]) and others of the "mischievous boy" genre of early film comedy, shows a boy camouflaging a water pump to look like a scarecrow in order to soak the farmer. In this film, the act is staged in front of a painted backdrop as it might have been presented live on the vaudeville stage. *Weary Willie Kidnaps a Child* was filmed outdoors in a park. The result is that the action approaches close to the camera in one of the shots, expanding the normal stage presentation. Weary Willie, the stereotypical vaudeville figure of a comic tramp, finds an unattended baby in the park and steals it to try to sell it to another couple, but is caught by the careless nursemaid and her boyfriend the cop.

───

EDWIN S. PORTER PROGRAM I

1903–08. U.S.A.
Edison Company.
Total program: 33 min. B&W and color.
Silent. 18 fps.
The final three films in this program are also available individually, *The Great Train Robbery* in both black-and-white and color versions; the first is also included in *The Life of an American Fireman* (*Two versions*) (1903).

THE LIFE OF AN AMERICAN FIREMAN

January 21, 1903.
Directed by Edwin S. Porter.
6 min. B&W.

THE GAY SHOE CLERK

August 12, 1903.
Directed by Edwin S. Porter.
1 min. B&W.

THE GREAT TRAIN ROBBERY

December 1, 1903.
Directed by Edwin S. Porter.
11 min. Color version.

THE DREAM OF A RAREBIT FIEND

February 24, 1906.
Directed by Edwin S. Porter.
7 min. B&W.

RESCUED FROM AN EAGLE'S NEST

January 16, 1908.
Directed by J. Searle Dawley. Supervised by Porter.
8 min. B&W.

This program includes the most well-known films by the inventive Edwin S. Porter. As projectionist-exhibitor during 1896–1900, he assumed the editorial function that would later belong to the filmmaker, combining single-shot films and slides in a variety of ways. This experience shaped his approach to filmmaking when he later became head of production at the Edison studio. *The Life of an American Fireman* is restored from an original print recently discovered by the American Film Institute Archives Program and should finally resolve the perplexing problem of its editing. If Porter had intercut the fire rescue scenes, as previous versions had it and as film histories have given him

claim, he would have been quite out of step with his contemporaries. Instead, we find him a leading exponent of the noncontinuous narrative style of much of early cinema. The other Porter films will bear this out. Unusual among films of 1903 or earlier, *The Gay Shoe Clerk* has an extreme close-up inserted in mid-scene. In it, the shoe clerk's hands move nervously over the young lady's shoe as she reveals a tempting ankle. One of the little erotic comedies in early cinema, the film implicates the spectator as voyeur. *The Great Train Robbery* (now available in an original color version) was undoubtedly the most popular film of early cinema, in release long after 1903. Contemporary advertisements describe it as "a faithful duplication of the genuine 'Hold Ups' made famous by various outlaw bands in the far West," showing that Porter may have intended it as a reconstruction of actual events rather than a fiction film. Its editing, too, might be carefully studied in the context of Porter's other films for a better understanding of film style before Griffith. Its temporal strategies are sufficiently ambiguous, making it possible to see *The Great Train Robbery* mistakenly as an example of classic editing style rather than the early cinema style that it actually represents. *The Dream of a Rarebit Fiend* demonstrates Porter's technical virtuosity with the trick film. The

THE GREAT TRAIN ROBBERY (1903)

surreal dream of this rarebit fiend takes him on a flight over New York's skyscrapers by means of a horizontally-split screen and an actuality film of the type known as panorama. Winsor McCay's comic strip of the same name was running at the same time and may have helped to exploit this very popular film. *Rescued from an Eagle's Nest*, although representative of popular theater at the time, may also have been inspired by what was said to be a real event that took place in the Adirondack Mountains, commemorated in a waxwork at the Eden Musée (Porter's former employer) in 1906. A baby is stolen by an eagle and rescued by his intrepid woodsman father, played by D. W. Griffith in what was not his first film role but his first starring one. The mixture of artificial sets and backdrops with the real woods of the Palisades on the Hudson River is typical of early cinema, but such discrepancies were already beginning to be criticized in 1907–08, when film melodrama was beginning to take on its own style and greater verisimilitude was considered desirable.

—

EDWIN S. PORTER PROGRAM II: SOCIAL ISSUES

1903–07. U.S.A.
Edison Company.
Total program: 46 min. B&W. Silent. 18 fps.
The final three films on this program are also available individually; the first two are also available as a pair.

A SCRAP IN BLACK AND WHITE

July 8, 1903.
2 min.

THE WATERMELON PATCH

October 20, 1905.
11 min.

THE WHITE CAPS

September 14, 1905.
12 min.

COHEN'S FIRE SALE

June 14, 1907.
13 min.

LAUGHING GAS

December 5, 1907.
8 min.

These films were all directed by Edwin S. Porter for the Edison Company and show the ethnic stereotyping and racial attitudes prevalent during this period. With the exception of *The White Caps*, they are all comedies exploiting racial stereotypes, a trend also common in popular entertainment. The program may refute the notion that real blacks did not appear in early cinema, even though some black roles were taken by whites wearing blackface. It should be remembered that the indigenous American entertainment the minstrel show was a forerunner of vaudeville, as vaudeville was a forerunner of cinema. *A Scrap in Black and White* is a one-shot film showing a boxing match between two little boys, one black and one white. *The Watermelon Patch* is a longer film, including a comic chase and an inserted semi-close-up, showing a group of poor black men stealing watermelons for their families. They are pursued by a gang of white men who smoke them out of their cabin. *The White Caps*, a more serious film, also takes a pro-vigilante stance. It shows a clan of hooded men, like the Ku Klux Klan, tarring and feathering a white man for beating his wife. *The Watermelon Patch* and *The White Caps* both illustrate the general acceptance at the time of people taking the law into their own hands, a frontier ideal that provides the background for understanding *The Birth of a Nation* (1915). *Cohen's Fire Sale* has a very funny comic chase through New York City streets, with painted sets and reality boldly mixed in it. It concerns a Jewish hat-shop owner who sets fire to the store in order to collect the insurance. *Laughing Gas* uses the device of close-ups to open and close the film, the better to enjoy the engaging personality of its black star who, after taking nitrous oxide for a toothache, infects everyone with uncontrollable laughter.

—

THE LIFE OF AN AMERICAN FIREMAN (Two versions).

January 21, 1903. U.S.A.
Edison Company. Directed by Edwin S. Porter.
12 min. B&W. Silent. 18 fps.

Porter's original version is here followed by a later reedited version employing intercutting in the culminating rescue scene. This reel serves as an example of the common practice of reediting films from the early cinema to conform to editing principles in the post-Griffith period and the problems it presents for historians of the medium. Films may have been reedited consciously by their distributors a few years later in the case of a film as popular as this, or it may have been done innocently many years later by those unfamiliar with early cinema style, who could have considered the print to be in error. The careful analysis of these two prints will help in understanding the nature of early cinema and how it changed in the course of a few years.

RUBE AND MANDY AT CONEY ISLAND

August 13, 1903. U.S.A.
Edison Company. Directed by Edwin S. Porter.
13 min. B&W. Silent. 18 fps.

This is a comedy in which two leading vaudeville performers play country bumpkins taking in the wonders of Coney Island in 1903. It is a series of comic episodes connected by a common motif rather than an integrated narrative. It demonstrates how early cinema employed close views as a coda to the main structure of a film, with its final shot of Rube and Mandy enjoying hot dogs.

THE EX-CONVICT

November 19, 1904. U.S.A.
Edison Company. Directed by Edwin S. Porter.
10 min. B&W. Silent. 18 fps.

Porter explores a social issue in this early story film about a former criminal forced to return to a life of crime because his prison record makes him unemployable. His heroic act, however, of saving a child from a street accident, finally leads to his redemption. The eight loosely-connected episodes were filmed in outdoor locations, combining real exteriors with interior painted sets. It contains a dialogue title, rare in early cinema, but characteristic of the period, that occurs long before the scene in which it is spoken.

FIGHTING THE FLAMES, DREAMLAND and *HIPPODROME RACES, DREAMLAND, CONEY ISLAND*

1904–05. U.S.A.

Total program: 11 min. B&W. Silent, 18 fps.

FIGHTING THE FLAMES, DREAMLAND. AN ATTRACTION AT CONEY ISLAND

September 11, 1904.
American Mutoscope and Biograph Company. Photographed by G. W. (Billy) Bitzer.
6 min.

HIPPODROME RACES, DREAMLAND, CONEY ISLAND

June 29, 1905.
Edison Company. Directed by Edwin S. Porter.
4 min.

Both films record the kind of open-air spectacle that provided entertainment for the crowds at Coney Island around the turn of the century. *Fighting the Flames* is action-packed, showing street crowds, the firemen's ceremonial parade, and the staged action of the show itself. Firefighting intrigued American audiences at the time, as is evident from the many films on the subject and the great success of Porter's *The Life of an American Fireman*, made in 1903. *Hippodrome Races* shows horse races taking place on a dirt track lined with spectators, as well as a show composed of Roman chariots, a parade of costumed figures, and teams of horses with women standing on their backs. The show may be similar to the one used in Kalem's *Ben Hur* (1907).

MANIAC CHASE

October 7, 1904. U.S.A.
Edison Company. Directed by Edwin S. Porter.
10 min. B&W. Silent. 18 fps.

A close copy of the Biograph title, *The Escaped Lunatic*, made in January 1904, this is a typical comic chase film. To the annoyance of Biograph, Porter freely plagiarized several of their films, not only using the same story but even similar locations, shots, and editing strategies. It has a circular structure beginning and ending in the maniac's cell (we know he is crazy because he dresses and poses as Napoleon) and between those shots there is a chase through woods, field, and stream. The camera pans freely to follow action, even swinging back to pick up the thread of the chase; reverse motion shows the maniac leaping up into a tree. This film, with its Biograph predecessor, marks the real beginnings of the comic chase film in America.

THE STRENUOUS LIFE, OR, ANTI-RACE SUICIDE and WAITING AT THE CHURCH

1904–06. U.S.A.
Edison Company. Directed by Edwin S. Porter

Total program: 12 min. B&W. Silent. 18 fps.

THE STRENUOUS LIFE, OR, ANTI-RACE SUICIDE

December 19, 1904.
5 min.

WAITING AT THE CHURCH

July, 1906.
7 min.

Two amusing comedies by Porter are combined in this program. *The Strenuous Life* is about a new father who is presented with more babies than he expected. It is a good demonstration of the rare use in early cinema of close views cut into mid-scene. The semi-close-up of the baby being weighed is a repetition of what is shown in the long shot and is not integral to the narrative structure. *Waiting at the Church*, showing what happens when a miscreant married man is tempted to propose to a young lady, is a typical chase comedy. It contains a "daydream" inserted in the same shot with the woman who imagines it, the kind of trick effect that was a Porter specialty. The film was probably suggested by the popular song of the same title, newly introduced to the American public by the British vaudeville star Vesta Victoria.

BOARDING SCHOOL GIRLS

September 1, 1905. U.S.A.
Edison Company. Directed by Edwin S. Porter.
15 min. B&W. Silent. 18 fps.

This variation on the popular chase film formula follows a group of school girls on a class trip to Coney Island. Much to the consternation of their pursuing chaperone, they enjoy a fun-filled day. The camera pans freely, following their movement, and the action is nearly continuous as the young ladies try out all the amusements with delightful abandon and a careless unconcern about showing their ankles.

A DETECTIVE'S TOUR OF THE WORLD (TOUR DU MONDE D'UN POLICIER)

1905. France.
Pathé Frères.
17 min. B&W and color. Silent. 18 fps.

A detective is assigned to trail a bank embezzler and the journey takes him all over the world. This fascinating film combines Pathé's documentary stock footage from exotic places with some cleverly matched stage sets. It has point-of-view shots seen through mattes designed to resemble telescopic views. There is also a cut-in to closer view on a set, and an opium dream in double exposure. The trip through the Suez Canal to Calcutta, Bombay, and Yokohama culminates in New York before the detective returns to Paris with his captive in hand. The print is partly tinted and the final tableau has been hand-colored.

THE DREAM OF THE RACE-TRACK FIEND

October 14, 1905. U.S.A.
American Mutoscope and Biograph Company. Photographed by G. W. (Billy) Bitzer.
8 min. B&W. Silent. 18 fps.

A drunken gambler dreams about winning a fortune at the track and entertaining his friends aboard his yacht with wine, women, and song. He falls overboard and wakes up trying to swim in his bathtub. With the typical inventiveness of early cinema, the film was built around actuality shots of New York's busy harbor filmed from aboard the yacht Tevo. One of its more erotic shots became another film called *How Millionaires Sometimes Entertain Aboard Their Yachts* (1905). The dream was a very common motif of early cinema. For another example, see *The Dream of a Rarebit Fiend* (1906) on the **Edwin S. Porter Program** I (1903–08).

FERDINAND ZECCA PROGRAM

1905–10. France.
Pathé Frères.
Total program: 45 min. B&W. Silent. 18 fps.
Fun After the Wedding is also available individually.

WHENCE DOES HE COME? (D'OÙ VIENT-IL?)

1905.
3 min.

SCENES OF CONVICT LIFE (AU BAGNE)

1905.
10 min.

SLIPPERY JIM

1910?
9 min.

A FATHER'S HONOR (L'HONNEUR D'UN PÈRE)

1905.
5 min.

FUN AFTER THE WEDDING (NOCE EN GOGUETTE)

1906.
10 min.

THE RUNAWAY HORSE (CHEVAL EMBALLÉ)

December 21, 1907.
4 min.

REBELLION, MUTINY IN ODESSA (RÉVOLUTION EN RUSSIE)

1905.
4 min.

The director chiefly responsible for the very popular Pathé films that dominated the world market for more than five years was Ferdinand Zecca. The seven films in this program demonstrate his great versatility and skill. **Whence Does He Come?** and *Slippery Jim* are examples of his charming trick films. The first shows a bather who leaps out of the water and assumes his clothing by reverse film, a trick that contemporary audiences found very amusing. Slippery Jim is an elusive crook who escapes justice by changing his form and defying the laws of space, time, and gravity. Zecca's famous **Scenes of Convict Life** is a grim social drama showing the harshness of prison conditions and a revolt, using a mixture of artificial sets and location shooting, and lengthy panning shots to follow action. **A Father's Honor**, equally grim but more literary, concerns a father's murderous revenge against the killer of his daughter. Although filmed in the outdoors with extensive panning shots, it retains the flavor of the nineteenth century melodrama. **Fun After the Wedding** is a knockabout slapstick comedy set amidst the revelry of a wedding celebration. It ends with the whole company falling in the river in their finery. **The Runaway Horse**, otherwise a conventional chase comedy, is of importance for the effective crosscutting of the action in the beginning sequences. A horse eats stolen grain while it waits at the sidewalk for its master, while the latter makes deliveries inside the house. The editing shifts between interior and exterior scenes, revealing the amount of grain being reduced as the skinny horse becomes a sleek, plump one. The last film on the program utilizes documentary footage of the Odessa port and its ships as an introduction to the staged presentation on painted sets of the events that would be immortalized twenty years later by Eisenstein in **Potemkin** (1925). Zecca's film is instructive as a contemporary account of the 1905 rebellion when compared to the later film.

THE LITTLE TRAIN ROBBERY

September 1, 1905. U.S.A.
Edison Company. Directed by Edwin S. Porter.
8 min. B&W. Silent. 18 fps.

The great popularity of **The Great Train Robbery** (1903) inspired many similar subjects, even outright imitation. Porter made his own amusing burlesque version with little children playing the roles, and even a miniature train. This chase film contains some remarkably lengthy panning shots going first in one direction and then the other in order to keep the action in frame, a frequent alternative in pre-Griffith cinema to breaking the action into separate shots.

SPOOK MINSTRELS

January 9, 1905. U.S.A.
Edison Company.
17 min. B&W. Silent. 18 fps.

This film is a real curiosity, a unique record of a minstrel show by Havez and Youngson. Several acts can be seen in it, shot from a variety of camera set-ups, all at stage distance. It is, in fact, only the visual part of the show, which toured the country's major cities with members of the company standing behind the screen to provide the jokes and the songs. In 1907–09, there was a revival of the concept in the troupes of actors who could be hired to travel with a film to provide the dialogue and songs from behind the screen, one of the solutions to the problem of making the first attempts at a more complex narrative understandable to their audiences. Such performances were limited to vaudeville houses, as the little nickelodeons could not have afforded such expense. This film would have been available only with the traveling company, and it was not copyrighted.

TIT FOR TAT

1905. France.
Pathé Frères.
4 min. Color. Silent. 18 fps.

Although the director and original title of this film are unknown, it is typical of the kind of films Pathé produced in great numbers and used to dominate the market at a time when American companies were still too involved with legal squabbles to develop a steady production. **Tit for Tat** is a charming little trick film, essentially a music hall turn, featuring young ladies becoming butterflies and their consequent misadventures. In it, the ladies take their revenge on a butterfly collector by pinning him

in a startling trick shot that simulates an overhead camera angle. The vivid hand-coloring of the original nitrate is reproduced in our prints. Compare the subjects included in **Magic Films** (1898–1905).

THE TRAIN WRECKERS

November 25, 1905. U.S.A.
Edison Company. Directed by Edwin S. Porter.
12 min. B&W. Silent. 18 fps.

This popular thriller features a brave and resourceful heroine who foils the efforts of outlaws to wreck a train. It represents an intermediate stage between films such as **The Great Train Robbery** (1903) and **Rescued by Rover** (1905), and Griffith's 1909 thriller, **The Lonely Villa**. By separating the actions of its characters into different scenes it contains the suggestion of parallel editing yet to come, although not in the work of Edwin S. Porter. Filmed on real locations, the film is visually exciting, fast-moving, and full of action, with a care for screen direction as it moves from one shot to the next. It set an Edison Company record for number of prints sold of any one title up to that time.

GETTING EVIDENCE

October 8, 1906. U.S.A.
Edison Company. Directed by Edwin S. Porter.
12 min. B&W. Silent. 18 fps.

This is a minor Porter comedy about the misadventures of a private detective assigned to get a photograph of an illicit couple. It has what John Fell has called the "motivated link" of much film construction in this period and is not a truly integrated narrative. It includes an extreme close-up in order to show the photograph, inserted into the middle of a scene. The chase sequence was filmed at Asbury Park, New Jersey, and includes bathing beauties who chase the detective. The voyeuristic theme is not exploited by point-of-view shots as in the much-imitated 1903 Biograph film **A Search for the Evidence**; this film is important as a forerunner of the Mack Sennett slapstick comedies.

THE 100 TO 1 SHOT, OR, A RUN OF LUCK!

1906. U.S.A.
Vitagraph Company.
10 min. B&W. Silent. 18 fps.

This important, recent discovery is a melodrama in which the winnings from a lucky bet at the racetrack stave off the eviction of the old folks from their home, in a last-minute ride to the rescue in an automobile. The parallel editing in the final scenes is an early indication of the kind of cutting that Griffith would make his own in 1908, and marks a significant shift away from the conventions of early cinema. It should be seen by anyone studying the development of parallel editing in Griffith's films. The director of this film is not yet known.

MAX LINDER PROGRAM

1906–12. France.
Pathé Frères.
Total program: 23 min. B&W. Silent. 18 fps.

MAX LEARNS TO SKATE (LES DÉBUTS D'UN PATINEUR)

1906.
6 min.

TROUBLES OF A GRASS WIDOWER

1908.
8 min.

MAX AND HIS DOG (MAX ET SON CHIEN DICK) (title on print, MAX UND SEIN HUND)

1912.
9 min. German titles.

Every gag of the slapstick comedy to come was exploited in the filmed vaudeville acts of early cinema. The rise of skilled and inventive comic personalities such as Max Linder turned slapstick into a major film genre. Mack Sennett and Charlie Chaplin both acknowledged their debt to the dapper little French comic. In **Max Learns to Skate**, Max endures all the humiliation of a beginner at ice skating. In **Troubles of a Grass Widower**, Max's wife goes home to mother after a quarrel and he has to learn to keep house for himself. There are several cut-ins to close views in the middle of long shots, to show Max trying to wash dishes or cook a chicken, each effort ending in disaster. In **Max and His Dog**, Max instructs his dog to notify him should his rival call on Max's new bride in his absence: the dog does so by placing a telephone call to him across the streets of Paris. It is shown in a triple-screen image, Max and his dog on opposite sides of the screen and the cityscape in the middle panel, reminiscent of the scene in Porter's **College Chums** (1907). Linder's films, like those of Porter, often exploit his interest in special effects.

THE PUMPKIN RACE (1907)

BEN HUR

1907. U.S.A.
Kalem Company. Directed by Sidney Olcott and Frank Oakes Rose. Screenplay by Gene Gauntier, from the novel by General Lew Wallace.
14 min. B&W. Silent. 18 fps.

It is hard to imagine that this crudely-made spectacle film was popular, but it was, perhaps as an early example of the power of advertising. "Positively the Most Superb Moving Picture Spectacle Ever Produced in America," Kalem's advertisement claimed. Kalem rented the scenery left over from a summer exhibition staged by Pain's Fireworks Company on the racetrack at Sheepshead Bay, New York, and the Brooklyn Fire Department staged the chariot race. **Ben Hur**'s place in film history was guaranteed thanks to the first copyright infringement suit over a film script. Filmmakers had not bothered to ask any permission for the material they used, but when Kalem lost the suit in 1911, that practice changed completely.

COHL, FEUILLADE, AND DURAND PROGRAM

1907–12. France.
Gaumont.
Total program: 30 min. B&W. Silent. 18 fps.
The Pumpkin Race is also available individually.

THE PUMPKIN RACE (LA COURSE AUX POTIRONS)

December 21, 1907.
Directed by Louis Feuillade and Romeo Bosetti (formerly attributed to Emile Cohl).
6 min.

A TRULY FINE LADY (UNE DAME VRAIMENT BIEN)

1908.
Directed by Louis Feuillade.
4 min.

LES JOYEUX MICROBES

1909.
Directed by Emile Cohl. French intertitles.
5 min.

LE PEINTRE NÉO-IMPRESSIONNISTE

1910.
Directed by Emile Cohl. French intertitles.
7 min.

ONÉSIME HORLOGER

1912.
Directed by Jean Durand. With Ernest Bourbon. French intertitles.
8 min.

The Gaumont studio was a rival to Pathé Frères. Both companies were founded in 1895 in Paris and are the only film companies of that period to survive today. Gaumont produced melodramas, newsreels, and many wonderful comedies like those represented in this program. Louis Feuillade was one of the originators of what we now recognize as the Parisian style, one filled with charm, wit, and gentle understatement. *The Pumpkin Race*, formerly attributed to Emile Cohl, is a delirious chase film carried to surrealist levels. Two mischievous boys upset a barrow of pumpkins which then take on a life of their own, rolling up and down hills, into houses, chimneys, and sewers, while energetically pursued by a group of people. *A Truly Fine Lady* shows what happens when an unusually attractive young lady walks through the streets of Paris serenely oblivious to the havoc she creates among the Parisian males, until the police find it necessary to hustle her away under wraps. Emile Cohl, the pioneer French animator, is represented here by **Les Joyeux microbes**, a film of transformations in which a microbe is changed into and out of various human forms, and *Le Peintre néo-impressionniste*, a delicious satire on modern art, in which a customer visiting an artist's studio is bewildered by being shown a white sheet representing a polar bear at the North Pole and similar works. In *Onésime Horloger*, the director of many of the best French comedies, Jean Durand, gave a psychological substance and an insane logicality to the trick film. Onésime, the character played by Ernest Bourbon in a long series of comedies, takes liberties with time, through the technique of fast-motion photography, in order to speed up receipt of his inheritance. Films such as these greatly intrigued the French Surrealists, and *Onésime Horloger* had an influence as well on René Clair's *The Crazy Ray (Paris qui dort)* (1923).

———

COLLEGE CHUMS

November 27, 1907. U.S.A.
Edison Company. Directed by Edwin S. Porter.
11 min. B&W. Silent. 18 fps.

In this light comedy a young lover, after lying to his fiancée about the identity of the "other woman," enlists his roommate to impersonate a nonexistent sister to prove his innocence. It was shot in five days largely on a single set and in apparent long takes (actually made up of several shots), but its staged quality in no way inhibits the fun and action. There is an unusual animation segment, to show the participants in a phone conversation within one time frame but separated by space, with the words of their exchange floating across the screen from one caller to the other (see also *Max and His Dog* in the **Max Linder Program** [1906–12]). In the

search for ways to make more complex narratives comprehensible to audiences of 1907, Porter employed actors behind the screen to supply the voices.

DANIEL BOONE, OR, PIONEER DAYS IN AMERICA

January 3, 1907. U.S.A.
Edison Company. Directed by Edwin S. Porter. With Florence Lawrence.
13 min. B&W. Silent. 18 fps.

This was one of Porter's more ambitious story films. It is a historical drama, filmed out-of-doors. Florence Lawrence, later to be known as the Biograph Girl, plays Daniel Boone's daughter. She befriends an Indian girl who later comes to her aid when she is kidnapped by the Indians. The incomplete print has been partially restored by Charles Musser with the help of production stills and descriptive titles to supplement the existing footage.

JACK THE KISSER

October 4, 1907. U.S.A.
Edison Company. Directed by Edwin S. Porter.
11 min. B&W. Silent. 18 fps.

Jack the Kisser is among the more entertaining examples of the chase comedy. The plot involves a lecherous fellow who insists on kissing every pretty woman he can find in the parks and streets. The film observes the genre's well-established conventions at the same time that it elaborates on the motive for the chase. Porter adds visual excitement by using some unusual locations for the chase, including a factory yard stacked high with sewer pipes.

LOST IN THE ALPS

April 1907. U.S.A.
Edison Company. Directed by Edwin S. Porter.
13 min. B&W. Silent. 18 fps.

Seemingly improvised to take advantage of a fresh snowfall, this film was shot in Central Park and Gloversville, New York. Neither location has much resemblance to the Alps. It is the lost-child-dog-rescue genre made popular by such films as *Rescued by Rover* (1905) but without that film's careful use of screen direction. It ends like its predecessor, with a close-up of the dog hero. The clock hands, although pointed out by the child's mother to indicate the lateness of the hour, are painted on and do not move during the course of the film—a common phenomenon of these early films, but soon to disappear.

THE RIVALS

August 27, 1907. U.S.A.
Edison Company. Directed by Edwin S. Porter.
10 min. B&W. Silent. 18 fps.

This comedy is a series of episodes linked by a common motif. Two fellows, rivals for a girl's love, play all kinds of tricks on each other, including the blowing up of an automobile. The camera pans to follow action in a variety of outdoor locations, from parks to a graveyard, the seashore, and a church. Charles Musser, who restored this film, reports that there is one missing scene, but in this kind of loose narrative construction it makes little difference to the story. Scenes could easily be added or deleted according to the ambition of the filmmaker toward his material.

SCULLIONS' DREAMS (UN RÊVE DE MARMITON)

ca. 1907. France.
Pathé Frères. Directed by Ferdinand Zecca.
8 min. B&W. Silent. 18 fps.

The dream, popular in early cinema, was an appropriate frame of reference for the surrealistic happenings of a trick film. In this one, the kitchen servants fall into a drunken stupor. A dwarf with magic powers cruelly cuts off their hands which, disembodied, perform all the work of preparing dinner, chopping the vegetables, and polishing the silver. Into the dominant setting of a big crowded kitchen, the filmmaker inserts extreme close-ups. Some show the hands at work with a knife, others show a sleeping scullion, and one shows a bald head with the Pathé Frères trademark written across it. It is a delightful dream for anyone who has to do housework.

STAGE STRUCK

August 8, 1907. U.S.A.
Edison Company. Directed by Edwin S. Porter. With Herbert Prior.
12 min. B&W. Silent. 18 fps.

Another popular erotic comedy from early cinema, *Stage Struck* is a chase comedy about a traveling actor (played by Herbert Prior) who persuades three young women from the country to run off with him to the city. There they appear on the stage at Coney Island, where they are pursued by the family and the police through various amusements until they are finally caught, and thoroughly spanked.

THE "TEDDY" BEARS

February 23, 1907. U.S.A.
Edison Company. Directed by Edwin S. Porter.
15 min. B&W. Silent. 18 fps.

The familiar fairy tale of "Goldilocks and the Three Bears" is given a topical twist by its references to Theodore Roosevelt's much publicized passion for hunting that resulted in the contemporary craze for "Teddy" bears. The bears in the story are costumed actors, cruelly shot by a hunter representing Roosevelt, who, as he claimed to do in the public press, spares the baby bear. However, the real novelty of this film, and one that Porter is said to have been particularly proud of, is a sequence of puppet animation. The little girl peeks through a knot-hole and sees a scene (matted in) of toy bears moving about by stop-motion effects.

THE TRAINER'S DAUGHTER, OR, A RACE FOR LOVE

November 15, 1907. U.S.A.
Edison Company. Directed by Edwin S. Porter.
10 min. B&W. Silent. 18 fps.

This suspense thriller tells the story of a villain's attempt to rig a horse race in order to marry the trainer's daughter, who is to be awarded to the winner. The print has been restored from an incomplete original by Charles Musser, using stills and the original catalog description. It has a moving camera point-of-view shot characteristic of early cinema, representing what a man sees as he watches the race through binoculars. The film is of interest for an early stage of parallel editing: the shot in which the man blows the horn to start the race, enclosed in a round matte, is cut into the shot in the stables where the characters react to hearing the horn. It is one of several instances in this period of a parallel cut to indicate that someone hears a sound.

ANIMATION PROGRAM

1908–33.
Total program: 58 min. B&W. Silent and sound: the first five subjects are silent, 18 fps; the final three are sound, 24 fps.

Felix Gets the Can is also available individually.

A LOVE AFFAIR IN TOYLAND (DRAME CHEZ LES FANTOCHES)

1908. France.

Gaumont. By Emile Cohl.
4 min.

GERTIE THE DINOSAUR

1914. U.S.A.
By Winsor McCay.
9 min.

MUTT AND JEFF IN THE BIG SWIM

ca. 1918. U.S.A.
Produced by Raoul Barre, based on the Bud Fisher comic strip. Animation by Dick Huemer(?) and others.
8 min.

NEWMAN'S LAUGH-O-GRAMS

1920. U.S.A.
By Walt Disney.
3 min.

FELIX GETS THE CAN

1924. U.S.A.
Produced by Pat Sullivan. Animation by Otto Messmer.
9 min.

STEAMBOAT WILLIE

1928. U.S.A.
Produced by Walt Disney. Animation by Ub Iwerks.
8 min. Sound.

THE MAD DOG

1932. U.S.A.
Produced by Walt Disney.
7 min. Sound.

CARMEN

1933. Germany.
By Lotte Reiniger.
10 min. Sound.

This collection of early animation contains some of the pioneer efforts, including examples of the commercial animated cartoon series, and other work by animation artists. In France, Emile Cohl was among the earliest animators. His *A Love Affair in Toyland* uses pencil drawings on white paper reversed into negative image. Winsor McCay, the leading American cartoon-strip artist, performed drawing acts on the vaudeville stage, where he created the material for his amusing *Gertie the Dinosaur* (see also **Winsor McCay Program** [1911–21]). McCay "talks" to his creation by way of titles, as he did in person in his stage act. *Mutt and Jeff in the Big Swim* represents the early animated cartoon series, and this example has Jeff trying to swim the English Channel. In *Felix Gets the Can* from the **Felix the Cat** series, Felix, hungry for salmon, ends up in

Felix the Cat, featured in
FELIX GETS THE CAN (1924)

Alaska. Otto Messmer was one of the first animators to use inner thoughts and physical movement to develop a character's personality, and his Felix was among the most original and well-loved cartoon characters until Mickey Mouse came along. The program includes three Disney films, the first showing his earliest work, which was produced for Newman's Theatre in Kansas City. Disney himself appears in the film, but there is not much true animation. The second Disney animation, *Steamboat Willie*, is the first public appearance of Mickey Mouse and also the first sound cartoon. Mickey uses the animals aboard a steamboat as musical instruments. This film revolutionized the animated cartoon. *The Mad Dog* shows a later evolution of Mickey and includes a new character, Pluto, who swallows a cake of soap and is taken for a mad dog. The program concludes with an example of the delicate silhouette animation of Lotte Reiniger, in a film suggested by the Bizet opera.

═══

AT THE CROSSROADS OF LIFE

July 3, 1908. U.S.A.
American Mutoscope and Biograph Company. Directed by Wallace McCutcheon. Photographed by G. W. (Billy) Bitzer and Arthur Marvin. With D. W. Griffith, Marion Leonard, Robert Harron.
12 min. B&W. Silent. 18 fps.

A typical melodrama of 1908, this is a story of the theatrical world and the dangers it holds for young women. D. W. Griffith wrote the script and plays a leading role as the would-be seducer, in the days just before he took over as a director at the Biograph studio. Although there were signs of a shift to a new style of narrative in 1907 and 1908, this film reflects the earlier approach. The figures are shot from single camera positions at stage distance, the gestures of the stage melodrama characterize the acting, and there is a kind of split-screen effect with a partition dividing the space in order to show action in adjoining spaces within a single shot. One shot of a street scene contrasts vividly with the staginess of the rest of the film.

THE FILM D'ART

1908–12. France.
Total program: 56 min. B&W. Silent. 18 fps.

THE ASSASSINATION OF THE DUC DE GUISE (L'ASSASSINAT DU DUC DE GUISE)

1908.
Film d'Art. Directed by Charles Le Bargy and André Calmettes. With Le Bargy and Albert Lambert. French titles. 13 min.

QUEEN ELIZABETH (LES AMOURS DE LA REINE ÉLISABETH)

1912.
Produced by Henri Desfontaines. Directed by Louis Mercanton. With Sarah Bernhardt, Lou Tellegen. English titles. 43 min.

When American producers turned to the popular melodrama in an effort to attract a more respectable middle-class audience, the French were drawing on the Comédie Française and its great actors and actresses for their classic performances. *The Assassination of the Duc de Guise* was among the first productions of Film d'Art, and its opening performances were accompanied by a score composed for it by Camille Saint-Saëns. The story is a historical reconstruction of the events that occur when the Duke, ignoring the warnings of his friends, insists on accepting Francis II's treacherous invitation to the palace, where death awaits him. Seen in the context of other historical films of its time, the acting is of high quality and the staging carefully planned—showing the professionalism of those involved in the production. *Queen Elizabeth* stars the most

celebrated stage actress of the day: Sarah Bernhardt. The "divine Sarah's" grand style, one not suited to the intimacies of the motion picture, was already beginning to evolve into a more naturalistic one. Her fame guaranteed that this film would receive great attention, especially in America, where her repeated tours had made her known across the land. The film covers the events in the Queen's life in which Nottingham and Bacon conspire against Essex, whom the Queen believes to be unfaithful and has beheaded. Adolph Zukor's distribution of the film in the United States launched his career and that of Famous Players, and contributed toward the acceptance of the feature-length film. (See also **Great Actresses of the Past** [1911–16].)

—

FIRESIDE REMINISCENCES

January 16, 1908. U.S.A.
Edison Company. Directed by Edwin S. Porter.
10 min. B&W. Silent. 18 fps.

In this melodrama a man who believes his wife to be unfaithful casts her out of his home. Three years later, sitting by his fireside, he thinks about his past, and in the fire he sees the first meeting with the girl who became his wife, their wedding, their children, and their happy home. Characteristically for Porter, he chooses to show these "flashbacks" successively within the same shot, matted in to the fireplace image. The scene also employs a cut-in to a closer view to make these flashbacks more visible to the audience. The print has been restored from a deteriorating original and many images are blemished by chemical damage.

THE POLICEMAN'S VISION (LE RÊVE D'AGENT)

ca. 1908. France.
Pathé Frères. Directed by Ferdinand Zecca.
10 min. B&W. Silent. 18 fps.

The magic of cinema frequently suggested to early filmmakers the dream image. In Zecca's imaginative and amusing trick film, two policemen fall asleep and dream about an ingenious and maddening thief with unusual powers. He can change his shape at will, assuming a two-dimensional shape in order to slide under doors; he can also become invisible and pass through walls, easily evading the pursuing comic cops. Although we do not know the precise date of this film, its use of close views

to begin and end the film, enclosing the dream, and another cut-in to show the thief removing coins from the safe, suggest the approximate year of its production.

THE COUNTRY DOCTOR

July 8, 1909. U.S.A.
Biograph Company. Directed by D. W. Griffith. Photographed by G. W. (Billy) Bitzer. With Frank Powell, Gladys Egan, Florence Lawrence, Mary Pickford.
14 min. B&W. Silent. 18 fps.

Made about a year after Griffith began directing, this is a melodrama about a dedicated doctor compelled to choose between saving the life of a neighbor's child and that of his own beloved daughter. Griffith builds the suspense of this situation by cutting between the two households with ever shorter shots. The most extraordinary element in this film, however, is the building of genuine feeling, not through the acting, which is still characterized by the gestures of the stage melodrama, but with camera movement and composition. An opening slow pan across a wide valley creates a pastoral mood, ending at the door of the doctor's house from which the happy family emerges. The reverse pan across the same landscape that ends the film after the child's death is elegiac. It was photographed in Greenwich, Connecticut.

GRIFFITH BIOGRAPH PROGRAM

1909–12. U.S.A.
Biograph Company. Directed by D. W. Griffith.
Total program: 69 min. B&W. Silent. 18 fps.

These films are also available individually (except **The Lonedale Operator**, which rents with **The Girl and Her Trust**; see separate annotation [1911]).

THE LONELY VILLA

June 10, 1909.
Script by Mack Sennett. Photographed by G. W. (Billy) Bitzer and Arthur Marvin. With Marion Leonard, Mary Pickford.
11 min.

A CORNER IN WHEAT

December 12, 1909.
Script by D. W. Griffith. Photographed by G. W. (Billy) Bitzer and Arthur Marvin. With Frank Powell, Henry Walthall.
14 min.

THE LONEDALE OPERATOR

March 23, 1911.
Script by Mack Sennett. Photographed by G. W. (Billy) Bitzer. With Blanche Sweet, Wilfred Lucas.
14 min.

THE MUSKETEERS OF PIG ALLEY

October 31, 1912.
Photographed by G. W. (Billy) Bitzer. With Lillian and Dorothy Gish, Walter Miller, Elmer Booth.
15 min.

THE NEW YORK HAT

December 5, 1912.
Script by Anita Loos. Photographed by G. W. (Billy) Bitzer. With Mary Pickford, Lionel Barrymore.
15 min.

This program contains five of D. W. Griffith's outstanding and most well-known films made for the Biograph Company. A year after Griffith began directing, he made *The Lonely Villa*, a classic example of the suspense thriller with last-minute rescue. He improved the suspense of earlier versions of the genre by crosscutting freely among three strands of the narrative at once—the burglars trying to break into the house, the frightened mother and children inside, and the father rushing home to protect them—while at the same time creating an accelerating tempo by shortening the shots near the end. The original negative of *A Corner in Wheat*, the famous film of social comment, has recently been found, resolving the vexing problem of the proper placement of the shots. This powerful film contrasts the harsh life of the farmers and the poor who depend on the price of bread with the exotic luxury indulged in by the wheat speculator. The contrast is made explicit by parallel editing, although the various characters never meet on the screen. Griffith anticipates the modern freeze frame in a posed shot of the poor waiting in the bread line, and adds a high degree of lyricism with the repeated image of the farmer sowing wheat—slow and lovely shots with a gradual fade to dark at the end. *The Lonedale Operator* shows Griffith at the height of his suspense-building powers in a thriller about the heroic girl telegrapher at an isolated railroad station fending off thieves while waiting for her engineer sweetheart to come to the rescue in his train. A carefully orchestrated combination of a parallel editing pattern, a larger than usual number of shots, and a closer camera to show expressive faces help to build the excitement to a fever pitch. *The*

Musketeers of Pig Alley, celebrated as an early gangster film for its social theme of poverty and crime in the big city and for the documentary quality of its New York street photography, is remarkable most of all for its extraordinary composition and the cinematic ballet created by the movements of the gangsters as they track each other through the city streets. Finally, *The New York Hat* is a charming comedy that demonstrates the subtle natural charm of Mary Pickford's acting—built of small and sensitive details and telling gestures. She plays the role of an innocent orphan who becomes the subject of a scandal because her minister-guardian anonymously gives her an expensive hat. Pickford undoubtedly had an influence on Griffith's discovery of a natural acting style eminently suited to the intimacy of the motion-picture camera.

—

THE MENDED LUTE

August 5, 1909. U.S.A.
Biograph Company. Directed by D. W. Griffith. Photographed by G. W. (Billy) Bitzer. With Owen Moore, Florence Lawrence, James Kirkwood.
16 min. B&W. Silent. 18 fps.

In Cuddebackville, a small town where New York businessmen spent summer holidays, the Biograph Company found beautiful scenic locations for their popular Indian pictures. *The Mended Lute* was the first film made there. Set in 1854 among the Dakota or Sioux Indians, the film is a love story that illustrates the legendary stoicism of the first Americans, and it features a chase on the river in canoes. The outdoor locations give a variety to camera setups, and the actors frequently come closer to the camera than usual in Biograph's interiors made in the studio. The lovely scenery and fluid action give a poetic quality to this idealized Indian story.

MEXICAN SWEETHEARTS

June 24, 1909. U.S.A.
Biograph Company. Directed by D. W. Griffith. Photographed by G. W. (Billy) Bitzer.
5 min. B&W. Silent. 18 fps.

The Biograph Bulletin claims "high class acting" for this tale of Latin lovers and their passions. A flirtatious senorita makes her sweetheart jealous by her attentions to an American soldier and must resort to tricks to save the soldier's life. Not every Griffith film ventured into the new narrative style, and especially not in this year, when he reached his high-

Blanche Sweet in
THE LONEDALE OPERATOR (1911)

est rate of production, turning out films with the regularity of a production line in a factory. This film is shot in one set from a single camera position and the actors are compelled to carry the narrative by their exaggerated gestures.

MRS. JONES' LOVER, OR, "I WANT MY HAT"

August 19, 1909. U.S.A.
Biograph Company. Directed by D. W. Griffith. Photographed by G. W. (Billy) Bitzer. With Florence Lawrence, John Cumpson.
7 min. B&W. Silent. 18 fps.

There were twelve in the Mr. and Mrs. Jones comedy series that Griffith began in 1908. In this, the next to last of them, Jones is unreasonably jealous because he finds a strange hat in the hallway and doesn't wait to find out that it belongs to the repairman. The performances are in well-timed high comedy style, played to the camera as in early cinema. In the Jones series, the setting is the urban social scene and the couple is wealthy and childless, while the stage conventions of the domestic farce are explored. The Muggsy comedy series that followed was set mostly in a rural village and featured a pair of young innocents (Mary Pickford and Billy Quirk) in a vanishing world that Griffith returned to in later feature films.

THE REDMAN'S VIEW

December 9, 1909. U.S.A.

Biograph Company. Directed by D. W. Griffith. Photographed by G. W. (Billy) Bitzer. With James Kirkwood, Arthur Johnson.
15 min. B&W. Silent. 18 fps.

Griffith's earliest Indian films tend to be remarkably sympathetic to native Americans and their plight. This example shows how the white man forced the Indians from their land and pursued them ever westward. An Indian brave declares his love for the maiden on the very day that the white men arrive and order the tribe to move on. They detain the girl as their slavey and the brave, torn between love and duty, leaves her there to accompany his old and ailing father. When the old chief dies, we are shown a traditional Indian funeral. Later reunited beside the bier, the couple stands with heads bowed. This poetic evocation of the noble redman myth is one of Griffith's loveliest films. The acting is restrained, and the images are filled with mountain vistas and sunlight. The Indian tribe on the move travels across the horizon, or diagonally in curving lines toward the camera. Without the complex editing structures and use of close-ups that would characterize his late Biographs, Griffith is nonetheless able to fill this film with deep feeling.

"1776," OR, THE HESSIAN RENEGADES

September 6, 1909. U.S.A.
Biograph Company. Directed by D. W. Griffith. Photographed by G. W. (Billy) Bitzer and Arthur Marvin. With Mary Pickford, Linda Arvidson.
16 min. B&W. Silent. 18 fps.

In this early film Griffith first sketched the subject to which he would return in the later *America* (1924). The Revolutionary War fascinated him as much as did the Civil War, and he had already written an unproduced play on it. *1776* was filmed in the scenic locations of Cuddebackville and used an old stone building still standing there as part of the set. The Hessians, portrayed as cruel mercenaries, come searching for a young American dispatch-bearer in his father's house and kill him. Seeking revenge, the father and his daughter overcome a sentry and replace him with the girl dressed in his uniform. She holds the post while the father calls forth a motley army of his neighbors, composed of old people and women with tools for weapons, who overcome the Hessians. Young Mary Pickford plays the role of the brave girl who pretends to be the sentry.

THOSE AWFUL HATS

January 25, 1909. U.S.A.
Biograph Company. Directed by D. W. Griffith. Photographed by G. W. (Billy) Bitzer.
3 min. B&W. Silent. 18 fps.

A comic novelty to be used in place of the customary slide, "Ladies, please remove your hats," this film shows in slapstick fashion the forced removal with a giant pair of tongs of the large picture hats worn by ladies at the time. This reconstruction of the film is not historically accurate: probably the original was made by double printing the movie image onto the blank screen. Here it has been accomplished with a modern traveling matte, and because the film to be printed in had partly deteriorated, it has been completed with a sequence from *At the Crossroads of Life* (1908), showing Griffith as actor. The tone of the film is comically surreal, and it seems significant that Mack Sennett appears as one of the most animated members of the audience.

THE BROKEN DOLL

October 17, 1910. U.S.A.
Biograph Company. Directed by D. W. Griffith. Script by Belle Taylor. Photographed by G. W. (Billy) Bitzer. With Gladys Egan.
15 min. B&W. Silent. 18 fps.

This film combines the popular Indian subject with another of Griffith's favorites, the child-centered melodrama. A little Indian girl, treated kindly by the settler family and given a doll, warns them of the impending Indian attack and dies in the ensuing battle. Unlike many of his other Indian stories, this one represents the red man as savage and cruel. Filmed outdoors in breathtaking landscapes, the film is full of action—fast-moving and fluid in its direction. There was a rumor that David Belasco had a hand in the direction of this picture. The rumor was denied by "Spectator" of the *New York Dramatic Mirror*, but it was acknowledged that Griffith had been called the Belasco of motion pictures.

THE FALL OF TROY (LA CADUTA DI TROIA)

1910. Italy.
Itala Film. Directed by Giovanni Pastrone.
27 min. B&W. Silent. 18 fps.

This early Italian historical epic covers the events of the Greek-Trojan war: the love affair of Helen and Paris, the revenge of the betrayed King Menelaus of Sparta, the battle outside the fortress, the giant wooden horse that brings the Greek soldiers secretly inside the gates, and the burning of Troy. The Italian silent cinema was noted for its spectacle films, which contributed toward the rise of the feature film in America. This film was originally about three minutes longer than the surviving copies and twice the length of the ordinary film of 1910. It is notable for its lavish production, its interesting use of spaces in which the action is played, and the use of alternating camera pans to follow the action. Pastrone was to use camera movement in even more complex ways in his most famous film, *Cabiria* (1914).

OVER SILENT PATHS

May 16, 1910. U.S.A.
Biograph Company. Directed by D. W. Griffith. Photographed by G. W. (Billy) Bitzer. With Marion Leonard.
15 min. B&W. Silent. 18 fps.

Filmed in the California desert, this western tragedy tells of a girl who without knowing his identity falls in love with the man who murdered her father. When she discovers it, she turns him over to justice. The barren desert landscape inspired Griffith to very somber dramas. This one is set at the time of the gold mining days. It bears evidence of the growing fluidity of his style. The shots are becoming shorter, some of the entrances and exits are dropped off, and some scenes begin in mid-action. The actors move in diagonal directions, approaching very near the camera in some shots.

THE ROCKY ROAD

January 3, 1910. U.S.A.
Biograph Company. Directed by D. W. Griffith. Photographed by G. W. (Billy) Bitzer and Arthur Marvin. With James Kirkwood, Stephanie Longfellow, Blanche Sweet.
15 min. B&W. Silent. 18 fps.

This grim story is replete with melodramatic coincidences, in the style of the nineteenth-century stage melodrama. A deserted wife and mother loses her mind, abandons her baby, and years later, just before falling dead, manages to stop the wedding of her grown daughter to her own father. The film is made with care and skill, and its location filming (in Hackensack and Edgewater, New Jersey) gives it a vivid reality.

ROSE O' SALEM-TOWN

September 26, 1910. U.S.A.
Biograph Company. Directed by D. W. Griffith. Script by Emmett Campbell Hall. Photographed by G. W. (Billy) Bitzer. With Dorothy West, Henry Walthall.
16 min. B&W. Silent. 18 fps.

Filmed in Marblehead, Massachusetts and the Delaware Water Gap, this historical thriller takes place in 1692. A hypocritical Puritan deacon, whose advances are rejected by a young maiden, accuses her and her mother of witchcraft. A trapper leads his Mohawk Indian friends to the rescue, just before the girl is to be burned at the stake. Griffith's theme of the evil done by fanatic reformers is made very exciting by the staging of the last-minute rescue. The locations in the sunlit forest and on the rocky New England coast make this an exceptionally beautiful film as well. Very short shots, 43 of them in this film, increase the excitement.

THAT CHINK AT GOLDEN GULCH

October 10, 1910. U.S.A.
Biograph Company. Directed by D. W. Griffith. Photographed by G. W. (Billy) Bitzer. With Dell Henderson, Charles West, Gertrude Robinson.
16 min. B&W. Silent. 18 fps.

This western, made in the scenic location of the Delaware Water Gap, has a Chinese laundryman for its hero. The butt of the cowboy's jokes, he sacrifices his sacred pigtail in order to capture the outlaw who has been holding up the pony express. Though he reunites the film's lovers, he sadly leaves town, for he can never return to his homeland once he has cut off the pigtail. The "Chink" is rather a comic figure but in many ways is an interesting forerunner to the idealistic Chinaman played by Richard Barthelmess in Griffith's **Broken Blossoms** (1919). The film is action-filled, with more and shorter shots, 46 of them, than other films of 1910, when the average was about 30.

TONTOLINI AND POLIDOR COMEDIES

1910–12. Italy.
With Ferdinando Guillaume. English titles.
Total program: 27 min. B&W. Silent. 18 fps.

TONTOLINI PAYS A VISIT (TONTOLINI IN VISITA)

1910.

Cines Company.
5 min.

TONTOLINI AND THE AMERICAN COUSIN (TONTOLINI FINTO AMERICANO)

1911.
Cines Company.
9 min.

POLIDOR HAS STOLEN THE GOOSE (POLIDOR HA RUBATO L'OCA)

1912.
Pasquali Film.
7 min.

POLIDOR STATUESQUE (POLIDOR STATUA)

1912.
Pasquali Film.
6 min.

The popular Italian comic Ferdinando Guillaume was the son of a circus family of French origin who were naturalized in Italy. He played an eccentric acrobat until he left the circus for the cinema in 1909. As Tontolini, he made 100 slapstick comedies for Cines during 1910–12. In the latter year he did a brief comedy series for Milano under the name of Cocciutelli, and that same year he metamorphosed as Polidor for the Pasquali Film Company in another long-lasting series. **Tontolini Pays a Visit** is a delightful surreal comedy built on camera magic. Tontolini is so clumsy that he is thrown out of a fashionable soiree and down the stairs, rolling up in the stair carpet as he goes. The traditional comic chase follows, as Tontolini defies the laws of gravity while inside his magic carpet, knocking people down, traveling up walls and over rooftops. Made in the second year of the Tontolini series, **Tontolini and the American Cousin** presents the character as a tramp who wanders into a magnificent house where he is mistaken for a cousin who has spent many years in America. His bad manners and peculiar behavior are attributed to his foreign experiences. When the real cousin arrives, his costume and behavior are even more eccentric. The film has elements of both the chase film and slapstick. In **Polidor Has Stolen the Goose**, an example from the first year of the Polidor series, our hero steals a goose and hides it under his coat, leading to considerable awkwardness as well as sexual innuendos when he is invited to join a wedding party at an inn. The slapstick comedy ends in a chase and a magic trick scene: the goose takes wing, Polidor flies through the air and ends up clinging to a wrecking ball in mid-air. In **Polidor Statuesque**, Polidor is asked to dust the works of art in a sculptor's studio. When he breaks the statue of a classical gladiator, he puts on a costume and stands in its place. Carried off to the home of a customer, he attempts to keep up the pretense, guaranteeing hilarious results. There are frequent cut-ins to a closer point of view, and a modified chase sequence. Polidor escapes capture by the police in the end by posing against a public monument. (See also **Polidor Comedies** [1912–13].)

———

THE UNCHANGING SEA

May 5, 1910. U.S.A.
Biograph Company. Directed by D. W.

Arthur Johnson and Linda Arvidson in THE UNCHANGING SEA (1910)

Griffith. Suggested by Charles Kingsley's poem "The Three Fishers." Photographed by G. W. (Billy) Bitzer. With Linda Arvidson, Arthur Johnson, Mary Pickford.
15 min. B&W. Silent. 18 fps.

Made during the first trip of the Biograph Company to California, this is one of the series of films by Griffith showing women waiting for their men to return from the sea. Linda Arvidson (Griffith's first wife) grows old as she searches the waves in vain for a sign of her fisherman husband's return. He has been shipwrecked and lost his memory, and only after their little daughter grows to womanhood does chance bring him home. The repetition of the image of woman and sea becomes a metaphor on human mortality and the eternity of nature, making this one of Griffith's most moving and poetic films.

THE USURER

August 15, 1910. U.S.A.
Biograph Company. Directed by D. W. Griffith. Photographed by G. W. (Billy) Bitzer. With George Nicholls, Alfred Paget, Kate Bruce.
15 min. B&W. Silent. 18 fps.

With mounting power, Griffith stages one of his grim social dramas in the tradition of **A Corner in Wheat** (1909). Through editing he contrasts the sufferings of the poor, who cannot meet their debts, with the rich life of the money lender. While his collectors visit the delinquent debtors to carry out deeds such as removing the bed on which a sick child rests, the usurer enjoys a rich banquet. He meets a just and ironic fate when, accidentally locked in his bank vault overnight, he suffocates to death in the midst of his useless wealth.

THE WAY OF THE WORLD

April 25, 1910. U.S.A.
Biograph Company. Directed by D. W. Griffith. Photographed by G. W. (Billy) Bitzer. With Henry Walthall.
15 min. B&W. Silent. 18 fps.

The San Gabriel Mission in California, where this film was made, inspired Griffith to poetic allegories. The ringing of the mission bells, ignored by the world's workers and pleasure seekers, serves as a repeated motif throughout this tale of an idealistic young priest who enters the world as a laboring man in the hope of saving souls. His efforts only meet with scorn, except for the salvation of a fallen woman. The acting is somewhat stylized to suit this allegory, and special lighting effects add to its symbolism. The intertitles are original in their text but without the Biograph type style of 1910.

BOBBY, THE COWARD

July 13, 1911. U.S.A.
Biograph Company. Directed by D. W. Griffith. Script by Dell Henderson. Photographed by G. W. (Billy) Bitzer. With Robert Harron.
15 min. B&W. Silent. 18 fps.

A drama of New York City slums, this is a character study of a young boy trying to get a job to support his invalid father and younger sister. Intimidated by the street hoodlums, he nevertheless finds the courage to fight off thieves who threaten the safety of home and family. This film records the spontaneous energy of the tenement streets of 1911: the passersby in some street scenes appear so unaware of the film being made that one might assume the camera was hidden. As his skill in narrative construction increases, Griffith infuses his films with enriching details that do not necessarily advance the story but contribute to characterization and atmosphere.

THE BROKEN CROSS

April 6, 1911. U.S.A.
Biograph Company. Directed by D. W. Griffith. Script by Harriet Quimby. Photographed by G. W. (Billy) Bitzer and Percy Higginson. With Florence La Badie, Charles West.
15 min. B&W. Silent. 18 fps.

This romance develops one of Griffith's favorite themes: the conflict between city and country values. His cross-cutting between the faithful woman waiting for her fiancé to return and the young man's flirtation with a devious vamp at a city boarding house heightens the contrast between the two worlds. A broken cross symbolizes the engaged couple's love, while the repeated close-ups emphasize its importance as the narrative progresses. Many American films of the period, not only those by Griffith, celebrate the old-fashioned virtues implicit in a rural and vanishing past, as against the breakdown in moral values represented by the city. It was, of course, a conservative attitude.

CONSCIENCE

March 9, 1911. U.S.A.
Biograph Company. Directed by D. W. Griffith. Photographed by G. W. (Billy) Bitzer. With Alfred Paget, Dell Henderson, Stephanie Longfellow.
15 min. B&W. Silent. 18 fps.

A psychological drama about the power of man's conscience, this film is also intended to point out, in the words of the Biograph Bulletin, "the fallibility of circumstantial evidence and the injustice often induced by the third degree." At his hunting lodge, a man is overheard threatening his wife with a gun, although he is only teasing her for providing bad coffee. When another hunter, drunk, mistakes the wife for a deer in the woods and kills her, the husband is forced by police grilling to confess to a murder he did not commit. The real culprit's conscience finally drives him to admit his guilt. Griffith intercuts vivid images of the murderer's struggle and the scenes of the husband's arrest and questioning.

ENOCH ARDEN

Part I: June 12, 1911; Part II: June 15, 1911. U.S.A.
Biograph Company. Directed by D. W. Griffith. Adapted from Alfred Lord Tennyson's poem "After Many Years." Photographed by G. W. (Billy) Bitzer. With Wilfred Lucas, Linda Arvidson, Frank Grandon.
30 min. B&W. Silent. 18 fps.

Griffith's second two-reel film is a remake of his 1908 adaptation of a Tennyson poem, "After Many Years." This later treatment develops the subject more fully and reveals Griffith's growing ability as a director. A wife, thinking her husband has been lost at sea, remarries. As in **The Unchanging Sea** (1910), a woman looking out to sea becomes a metaphor, but this time of faithful love. Griffith's skillful editing links distant locations and establishes psychological and emotional bonds between characters. The wife and husband seem to "see" each other across time and space by the placement of their figures within the composition from one shot to the next.

GREAT ACTRESSES OF THE PAST

1911–16.
Total program: 76 min. B&W. Silent. 18 fps.

MADAME SANS-GÊNE (excerpt)

1911. France.
Film d'Art. Directed by André Calmettes. With Gabrielle Réjane.
13 min.

LA DAME AUX CAMÉLIAS (excerpt)

1912. France.

Film d'Art. Directed by André Calmettes. With Sarah Bernhardt, Lou Tellegen.
16 min.

VANITY FAIR (excerpt)

1913. U.S.A.
Edison Company. Directed by Eugene Nowland. With Minnie Maddern Fiske.
16 min.

CENERE (excerpt)

1916. Italy.
Ambrosio-Caesar-Film. Directed by Febo Mari, Arturo Ambrosio. With Eleanora Duse, Febo Mari. English titles.
31 min.

To attract a higher class audience, film producers lured to the cinema the world's greatest theatrical stars in their most successful stage vehicles. Although the merciless camera sometimes made the grandiose stage gestures of celebrated actors and actresses appear ridiculous to the general public, the effort was successful in terms of prestige, bringing a new audience and a new critical attention to the movies. The costly production values and the feature length of these films gave weight to the trend toward longer, more elaborate films. The films in this program constitute an invaluable record of theatrical acting styles of their time. Réjane and Bernhardt belonged to a style of acting that was fading out, while Fiske in America and Duse in Italy were proponents of the newer naturalistic style. For Duse, in particular, this meant a moving and honest performance well suited to the intimacy of the motion picture camera. Gabrielle Réjane's **Madame Sans-Gêne** is about the rise of a washerwoman to be Duchess of Danzig through the favors of Napoleon. Sarah Bernhardt plays Marguerite in *La Dame aux camélias*, the familiar Dumas story about the woman of low origins loved by the noble Armand Duvall, who is kept from her by his family until she is dying of consumption. *Vanity Fair*, from the stage version of Thackeray's novel, stars Mrs. Fiske as the Victorian adventuress Becky Sharp making her way in society. *Cenere* is the moving story of a poor woman who commits suicide because, through a misunderstanding, she thinks she has ruined her son's marriage into good society. A familiar strain of the sufferings inflicted by respectable society on the lower-class woman and her noble behavior runs through these roles in which celebrated actresses achieved glory on the stage. For another Bernhardt performance, see **Queen Elizabeth** (1912) on **The Film d'Art** (1908–12). *Cenere* is also

available in a complete version (see separate annotation [1916]).

—

GRIFFITH'S WESTERNS

1911. U.S.A.
Biograph Company. Directed by D. W. Griffith. Photographed by G. W. (Billy) Bitzer.
Total program: 61 min. B&W. Silent. 18 fps.

These films are also available individually.

WAS HE A COWARD?

March 16, 1911.
With Blanche Sweet, Wilfred Lucas.
15 min.

THE CHIEF'S DAUGHTER

April 10, 1911.
With Stephanie Longfellow, Jack Dillon.
15 min.

HIS MOTHER'S SCARF

April 24, 1911.
With Charles West, Dorothy West, Wilfred Lucas.
16 min.

IN THE DAYS OF '49

May 8, 1911.
With Claire McDowell, Charles West.
15 min.

The four films in this reel group together westerns made by Griffith for the Biograph Company while on location in California in 1911. The conventions of the western and the myth of the western hero are by now well enough established that Griffith can play against them on occasion. *Was He a Coward?* introduces a new brand of western heroism. An easterner staying at a ranch for his health refuses to engage in fisticuffs with his rival for the ranch owner's daughter, but redeems himself in her eyes by caring for an Indian and her own father when they come down with the dread smallpox. *The Chief's Daughter* introduces a story that trade journals at the time called ticklish subject matter: interracial romance. A prospector wins the love of the Indian chief's daughter only to cast her aside when his eastern sweetheart unexpectedly arrives on the scene. The Indian maiden wins revenge in the film's humorous ending. With *His Mother's Scarf*, Griffith begins to reach toward the epic western. It is a dramatic tale of two brothers who fall in love with

the same woman, the sole survivor of an Indian attack. One is prevented from killing the other only by the fortunate sighting of the scarf given to them by their dead mother. The spectacular western landscape is seen in deep, dramatic long shots, and the wagon train massacre is staged in extreme long shots, seen from a hill in the viewpoint of those watching. The grandeur of the scenery and the openness of the space leads Griffith to a freer style, closer views intercut with extraordinarily deep long shots, and a greater number of short shots. The actors move in a greater variety of directions than conceivable in the studio. *In the Days of '49* benefits from these formal developments as well. It is set in the time of the gold fever and based on a Bret Harte story. The miner sends for his wife, but on the stagecoach she meets an itinerant gambler. She is torn between her honest, hardworking husband and the romantic stranger until the latter helps her come to her senses.

—

HER AWAKENING

September 28, 1911. U.S.A.
Biograph Company. Directed by D. W. Griffith. Photographed by G. W. (Billy) Bitzer. With Mabel Normand, Harry Hyde.
15 min. B&W. Silent. 18 fps.

The moralizing tone of the melodrama was in strong contrast to the pre-Griffith cinema which had been heavily attacked by ministers, politicians, and the public press. Subtitled "The Punishment of Pride" in the Biograph Bulletin, this film takes up the themes of vanity, guilt, and forgiveness. An otherwise dutiful daughter is ashamed of her old, decrepit, and lame mother. Out walking with her well-heeled sweetheart whom she met while working in a laundry, the girl pretends not to know her own mother. Moments later, the mother is run over and killed by a passing car, filling the daughter with belated, intense remorse for her cruel behavior. Action cutting accelerates the pace of this drama.

A KNIGHT OF THE ROAD

April 20, 1911. U.S.A.
Biograph Company. Directed by D. W. Griffith. Script by Dell Henderson. Photographed by G. W. (Billy) Bitzer. With Dorothy West.
15 min. B&W. Silent. 18 fps.

Set at harvest time on an orange ranch in Southern California, this comedy explores the myth that a hobo's life is more desirable than conventional employment. A tramp, attracted by the ranch owner's daughter, protects her from burglars. Offered a job and a place to live in reward, he quietly steals back to his friends of the campfire. The ending anticipates Jean Renoir's **Boudu Saved From Drowning** (1932). A critic for the *New York Dramatic Mirror* complained that the extraordinary number of shots in this film made it difficult to follow.

THE LONEDALE OPERATOR and THE GIRL AND HER TRUST

1911–12. U.S.A.
Biograph Company. Directed by D. W. Griffith. Photographed by G. W. (Billy) Bitzer.
Total program: 28 min. B&W. Silent. 18 fps.

THE LONEDALE OPERATOR

March 23, 1911.
Script by Mack Sennett. With Blanche Sweet, Wilfred Lucas.
14 min.

THE GIRL AND HER TRUST

March 28, 1912.
Story by George Hennessy. With Dorothy Bernard, Wilfred Lucas.
14 min.

The Lonedale Operator is Griffith's classic suspense thriller. The daughter of the telegraph operator at an isolated railroad station takes her father's place when he becomes ill and bravely defends the station against thieves until her engineer sweetheart can come to the rescue in his engine. With 97 shots, more than he had ever used before, Griffith builds the suspense through powerful parallel editing. He brings his camera closer to the heroine to show her expressive face and in an extreme close-up exposes her ruse in pretending that a monkey wrench is a gun. In original prints, the scenes following the extinguishing of the lamp would have been tinted blue to convey the semi-darkness that enables her to fool the crooks. *The Girl and Her Trust* is virtually a remake, appearing just one year later. Griffith's development is revealed by comparing the two films. The basic parallel editing pattern is the same, as is the setting. But the camera is brought even closer, and a new dynamic element is added to the ride to the rescue with tracking shots of the train. The resourceful heroine this time throws herself bravely in front of the handcar and is carried off by the thieves. A new lyric ending shows the girl and her hero riding away into the distance seated on the cowcatcher of the train.

MACK SENNETT PROGRAM I

1911–16. U.S.A.
Total program: 49 min. B&W. Silent. 18 fps.

Comrades and *The Surf Girl* are also available individually.

COMRADES

March 13, 1911.
Biograph Company. Directed by Mack Sennett. With Sennett, Jack Dillon, Frank Grandon.
15 min.

MABEL'S DRAMATIC CAREER

September 8, 1913.
Keystone Company. Produced and directed by Mack Sennett. With Sennett, Mabel Normand, Ford Sterling.
13 min.

THE SURF GIRL

July 30, 1916.
Triangle-Keystone. Produced by Mack Sennett. Directed by Glen Cavender. With Raymond Griffith and the Keystone Cops.
21 min.

Sennett was the master of the uniquely cinematic genre, the American slapstick comedy. The films of the French comics Max Linder and André Deed were a particular inspiration, but it was Sennett who perfected the form. The slapstick comedy exists in a surreal universe where ordinary logic is suspended: it takes advantage of all the magic of camera tricks and editing devices to create fantasy and illusion. It turns upside down the conventions of society and challenges us to see them differently. *Comrades* is believed to be the first film directed by Sennett. An actor at Biograph for several years previously, he took over the direction of comedies at that studio from this film until he left to form his own company in the fall of 1912. *Comrades*, not a true slapstick comedy, is about two tramps and their adventures when one decides to impersonate Marmaduke Bracegirdle, a British Member of Parliament scheduled to pay a visit to an American family. *Mabel's Dramatic Career* lacks photographic tricks, chases, and Keystone Cops, but it has the violence of slapstick, the charm of Mabel Normand, and

a glimpse of movie production and exhibition in 1913. When Mabel's hick boyfriend goes to the city in search of her, he finds her on the screen, playing a role in a Keystone production. The film plays on the tension between film and reality in a comic way by showing the boyfriend shooting at the screen villain who threatens Mabel. *The Surf Girl* is typical of hundreds of Sennett films. In a seaside amusement park, the lifeguards are after the daughters, the philandering husband is after the bathing girls, the jealous wife is after the husband, and the Keystone Cops are after them all. In this surreal world, time stops, reverses itself, and speeds up. The whole cast lands in the ocean, and the cops are there to pull them out, but their paddy wagon is too high to go under the first low doorway. So the cab and the body separate, and half of it grows legs and walks off.

THE NEW DRESS

May 15, 1911. U.S.A.
Biograph Company. Directed by D. W. Griffith. Photographed by G. W. (Billy) Bitzer. With Dorothy West, Wilfred Lucas.
15 min. B&W. Silent. 18 fps.

The Biograph location trips to California gave rise to dramas based on Mexican or Spanish stereotypes and the Latin temperament. In this romance of modern Mexico, a young bride loses her mind at the thought of her husband's betrayal when he gives the new dress she longs for to a strange woman. She recovers her sanity when she gives birth to her first child. The idea of emotional shock driving a young woman insane, which is given a tryout here, is more successfully realized in *The Painted Lady* (1912), and it is useful to compare the two films.

THE PRIMAL CALL

June 22, 1911. U.S.A.
Biograph Company. Directed by D. W. Griffith. Photographed by G. W. (Billy) Bitzer. With Claire McDowell, Wilfred Lucas, Frank Grandon.
15 min. B&W. Silent. 18 fps.

In a comedy reminiscent of D. H. Lawrence—but with a lighter touch—Griffith embroiders his tale with details that delightfully build comic characterization. The daughter of a society woman with high ambitions and a need for money is prepared to do her duty to her family by marrying a rich count. But on a pre-wedding trip to the seashore, she meets a more primitive type, a sailing man who treats her roughly, and she loves it. The heroine's delicate picnic fare is contrasted with the contents of the workingman's lunch pail. A minister who is beachcombing samples the contents of the picnic basket after looking around to see if anyone is watching. When the girl gives in to the primal call and agrees to run off in the sailor's boat, he scoops up the providential minister and takes him along to perform the marriage ceremony. A most unexpected film to come from Griffith.

PRISCILLA'S APRIL FOOL JOKE

March 27, 1911. U.S.A.
Biograph Company. Directed by Mack Sennett (?). With Florence Barker, Edward Dillon.
10 min. B&W. Silent. 18 fps.

In 1911, Mack Sennett took over the direction of Biograph's farce comedies. With the **Priscilla** series, he tried his hand at creating a comedy team based on the characters of two young lovers who have all kinds of difficulties over misplaced jealousy. It was not very promising material and the series was soon dropped. In this one, two friends play a joke, setting up a situation in which Priscilla thinks her sweetheart has betrayed her. The lovers turn the tables by pretending they have each drowned themselves in the sea. The California coastline provides scenic background.

THE ROSE OF KENTUCKY. A ROMANCE OF THE FIELDS OF TOBACCO

August 24, 1911. U.S.A.
Biograph Company. Directed by D. W. Griffith. Photographed by G. W. (Billy) Bitzer. With Wilfred Lucas, Marion Sunshine.
15 min. B&W. Silent. 18 fps.

Several years before **The Birth of a Nation** (1915), Griffith portrayed the Ku Klux Klan in an unfavorable light in this romance of the Kentucky tobacco fields. The tobacco-grower refuses to join and in revenge the Klan rides out to set fire to his barn. The tobacco farmer has brought up an orphan girl and fallen in love with her, but is prepared to step aside for his younger partner. While defending the barn, the younger man proves himself a coward and the young girl takes his gun to stand side-by-side with her benefactor. The Klan is presented here primarily as a *modus vivendi*; the story is about an old man's love for a young girl, presented with moving

tenderness. Nonetheless, this film is of great interest for providing a contrasting view of the Klan from the heroic version in **The Birth of a Nation**.

THE SPANISH GYPSY

March 30, 1911. U.S.A.
Biograph Company. Directed by D. W. Griffith. Photographed by G. W. (Billy) Bitzer. With Wilfred Lucas.
15 min. B&W. Silent. 18 fps.

This "romance of sunny Andalusia" was shot on the California coast. The story is built on literary stereotypes of the supposed passionate nature of Latin lovers. When the fickle troubadour José deserts the gypsy dancer Pepita for another, Pepita becomes crazed with the desire for revenge. Fate intervenes in the form of an accident that permanently blinds José and his new girl deserts him. When Pepita discovers his pitiful state, she has a change of heart. The film demonstrates Griffith's dramatic use of repetition to build tension, returning more than a dozen times to the same view of the gypsy camp by the sea where Pepita first meets José, where he leaves her, and where she obsessively sharpens her dagger on a grindstone.

TEACHING DAD TO LIKE HER

March 20, 1911. U.S.A.
Biograph Company. Directed by D. W. Griffith. Photographed by G. W. (Billy) Bitzer. With Vivian Prescott, Dell Henderson.
15 min. B&W. Silent. 18 fps.

Although Griffith had begun to confine comedies to the split-reel length and to delegate them to other directors, occasionally he took one over as a full reel "feature." In this amusing example, the son of a wealthy widower wants to persuade his father to let him marry a chorus girl. Realizing that the father couldn't help but like the girl if he only knew her, the lovers arrange a chance meeting with him. The problem is that the father likes her too well and wants her for himself. In comedy, the style is more apt to revert to the conventions of early cinema, as here when the son mimes directly to the camera, intending to involve the audience in his troubles. In other ways, however, the film is very much in the Griffith style of 1911. He expands a telephone call to thirteen shots, divided between the two participants, and much of the film is in three-quarter-shot, approaching semi-close-up at the exit from a scene.

THE TWO SIDES. A VIVID CONTRAST OF THE WORLD'S PROSPEROUS AND POOR

May 1, 1911. U.S.A.
Biograph Company. Directed by D. W. Griffith. Photographed by G. W. (Billy) Bitzer. With Dell Henderson, Gladys Egan.
16 min. B&W. Silent. 18 fps.

In this film the Mexican ranch hand is the brave hero, breaking with the Mexican "greaser" stereotype common to Griffith's and others' westerns of the period. Additionally titled "a vivid contrast of the world's prosperous and poor," the film uses parallel editing to compare the life of the ranch owner and his spoiled child with that of the Mexican laborer and his sick baby. Discharged only because the ranch owner wants to increase his profits, the Mexican is tempted to ignore the fire in the barn until he learns the owner's child may be trapped inside. Parallel editing again adds to the suspense of the rescue of the child from the flames. The camera is placed consistently closer to the actors, most of the scenes in three-quarter-shot, although the film does not use close-ups.

WHAT SHALL WE DO WITH OUR OLD

February 13, 1911. U.S.A.
Biograph Company. Directed by D. W. Griffith. Photographed by G. W. (Billy) Bitzer. With Claire McDowell, W. Christy Miller.
14 min. B&W. Silent. 18 fps.

Unfortunately, this stirring social drama, based on "an actual occurrence in New York City" according to the Biograph Bulletin, is not complete. The shots that would demonstrate most clearly the contrast that Griffith set up between the sufferings of those too old to work and the idle rich are missing: the old carpenter who has lost his job because of age sees a wealthy lady get out of her automobile with great solicitude for her pet dog, carried in her arms. However, scenes of the man's sick wife are intercut with sequences in which he robs a grocery store and goes to court and then jail for the crime, adding a bitter note of irony when help comes too late.

WINSOR MCCAY PROGRAM

1911–21. U.S.A.
Animation by Winsor McCay.
Total program: 49 min. B&W and color. Silent. 18 fps.

LITTLE NEMO

1911.
Live-action sequences by J. S. Blackton.
With John Bunny.
12 min. B&W and tinted.

DREAMS OF A RAREBIT FIEND: BUG VAUDEVILLE

1921.
28 min. B&W.

GERTIE THE DINOSAUR

1914.
9 min. B&W.

This program presents three works by Winsor McCay, one of the earliest creators of animated film. McCay's background was in the graphic arts. As a young man he worked as a billboard and poster designer, and later achieved prominence as a newspaper illustrator and comic-strip artist. Most famous were his "Little Nemo in Slumberland" strip, created in 1905 for the *New York Herald*, and "Dreams of a Rarebit Fiend," which ran in the *New York Telegram*. Both were dream fantasies, but the former was particularly distinguished by its metamorphic imagery and its intricate architectural drawings, influenced by art nouveau design. At some point McCay fashioned a vaudeville act around his drawings and shortly thereafter began experimenting with translating his comic strips into films. **Little Nemo** presents animated versions of the characters Flip,

Impy, and Nemo from the comic strip and frames them within a live-action sequence reenacting the production of the film. *Bug Vaudeville* is an episode from the **Dreams of a Rarebit Fiend** series and involves a hobo's indigestive fantasies of insect life. Finally, **Gertie the Dinosaur** is based on McCay's theatrical act, in which he would talk to a film image of Gertie, which responded to his commands. Here the intertitles perform McCay's role and order Gertie to come out of the cave or bow to the audience. This print contains excerpts of the live-action sequence that framed the McCay animation. Because of the evolution of McCay's work from newspaper graphics through vaudeville performance to animated film, this set of films affords a unique opportunity to observe the interrelated histories of these various popular arts. *Gertie the Dinosaur* is also available on the **Animation Program** (1908–33).

———

THE BABY AND THE STORK

January 1, 1912. U.S.A.
Biograph Company. Directed by D. W. Griffith. Script by George Hennessy. Photographed by G. W. (Billy) Bitzer. With Edna Foster.
15 min. B&W. Silent. 18 fps.

The idealized innocent child of Victorian times is to be found at the center of many of Griffith's Biograph films,

influencing the moral attitudes of the adults. In this gentle comedy, however, a touch of reality is permitted to the little boy who becomes jealous over the arrival of a new baby in the family. Believing the old tale about the stork, he takes the baby to the park and tries to give it back. The alarmed parents think there has been a kidnapping, until the children are found. Edna Foster frequently played the part of boys. Location shooting gives pictorial interest to this simple, well-crafted film.

BLACK SHEEP

July 29, 1912. U.S.A.
Biograph Company. Directed by D. W. Griffith. Script by George Hennessy. Photographed by G. W. (Billy) Bitzer. With Charles West, Dorothy Bernard, William Carroll.
16 min. B&W. Silent. 18 fps.

This western drama is set on a ranch in the great Southwest. The ranch foreman's son is a secret drinker and gambler but he is nonetheless loved by the ranch owner's daughter. She saves him at the last moment from being strung up for a crime he did not commit. The real villain is the racially stereotyped brutal Mexican. Made in California, the action, which takes place in wide vistas of the rugged western landscape, is shot either in great depth or near the camera with many layers of depth behind. It demonstrates Griffith's growing tendency to use short, fast shots, rapidly intercut to increase the excitement.

Winsor McCay (at easel) in GERTIE THE DINOSAUR (1914)

A BLOT IN THE 'SCUTCHEON

January 29, 1912. U.S.A.
Biograph Company. Directed by D. W. Griffith. Script by Linda Arvidson, from Robert Browning's poem. Photographed by G. W. (Billy) Bitzer. With Dorothy Bernard, Edwin August.
23 min. B&W. Silent. 18 fps.

The first of Griffith's two-reelers to be released as a single subject was a costume melodrama based on Browning's poem and set in the 17th century. The cruel family pride of Earl Tresham leads him to kill the seducer of his motherless younger sister even though he had agreed to their marriage before he knew of their love affair. The girl dies of the shock when he shows her his bloody sword. Literary adaptations grew more rare in Griffith's late Biographs and this one, scripted by his wife Linda Arvidson, seems not to have inspired him to the poetic imagery found in other of his films taken from literary sources. However, its extra length, lavish costumes, and sets seem to show that the company considered it a prestigious undertaking. The titles, quoting lines from the poem, are longer than usual.

BRUTALITY

December 2, 1912. U.S.A.
Biograph Company. Directed and written by D. W. Griffith. Photographed by G. W. (Billy) Bitzer. With Mae Marsh, Walter Miller, Elmer Booth, Lionel Barrymore.
15 min. B&W. Silent. 18 fps.

Brutality is a reworking of the theme of Griffith's earlier *A Drunkard's Reformation* (1909). A young man (played by Walter Miller) with a brutal temper, inflamed by drinking, is reformed while he watches the murder of Nancy in a performance of *Oliver Twist*. The acting of this later version is considerably more subtle and sophisticated. The camera placements are more varied: when the action on the stage becomes more violent, the camera is placed closer to the actors, reflecting the increased attention and emotion of the spectators. The exterior scenes at the beginning, in which Mae Marsh falls in love with the man she comes to fear, were filmed in Fort Lee, New Jersey. During the performance of the play, one may spot well-known Biograph actors in the audience.

A DASH THROUGH THE CLOUDS

June 24, 1912. U.S.A.
Biograph Company. Directed by Mack Sennett. Script by Dell Henderson. Photographed by Percy Higginson. With Mabel Normand, Fred Mace.
12 min. B&W. Silent. 18 fps.

This farce comedy was directed by Sennett during his final year at Biograph, before leaving to form his own company dedicated to the slapstick comedy. It exploits the current fascination with flying machines, still a very recent invention in 1912. Mabel Normand's boyfriend is a tutti-frutti gum salesman. When he goes to a Mexican border town to sell his product, his attraction for women gets him into a difficult situation with the Mexican men. Meanwhile, Mabel's interest has turned to a glamorous aviator and she has taken up flying. When her boyfriend calls for help, she stages a thrilling rescue in the aviator's biplane. Mabel does her own flying, giving evidence of the risks expected of early actors and actresses.

THE ETERNAL MOTHER

January 11, 1912. U.S.A.
Biograph Company. Directed by D. W. Griffith. Photographed by G. W. (Billy) Bitzer. With Blanche Sweet, Edwin August, Mabel Normand.
16 min. B&W. Silent. 18 fps.

The Biograph Bulletin calls this one a "symbolism." A young farmer is lured from his happy marriage by the fascinations of the woman next door. His wife generously gives him a divorce to marry her. When the second wife dies in childbirth, the first one agrees to bring up his child. After long years of atonement, the unfaithful husband is reconciled with his first love in their old age. The film is a testament to Griffith's belief in the strength of women. His use of repetition, contrasting light and shade, and slow fades brings lyricism to the film, and the increasing acting skills of his cast contribute to an extraordinary psychological tension. Without the use of extreme close-ups to isolate details, a sultry gaze from Mabel Normand is sufficient to indicate the sexual power she exerts, and Blanche Sweet's smallest hand gestures betray her every thought and feeling.

HER CHOICE

September 30, 1912. U.S.A.
Vitagraph Company. Directed by Ralph Ince. Script by Mrs. Brevil. With Julia Swayne Gordon, Zeena Keefe, Anita Stewart.
9 min. B&W. Silent. 18 fps.

Vitagraph films are still rare enough to justify the inclusion of this incomplete and rather poor quality print, even though half of the film is missing. The film's story is there in all its essentials: a wealthy schoolmistress anonymously gives scholarships to her two nieces to attend her exclusive girls' school. One of them is a vain girl (in the missing portion she demands new clothes to attend the school) who snubs her more humble cousin. The generous girl wins her reward when her aunt names her as heir to the school. The film does not represent the best work of Vitagraph or Ralph Ince, but it may be of interest to compare with Biograph's style in this year. A different kind of camera placement is consistently used, closer to the actors and at a slightly lower angle; the principals are generally brought up to something closer than three-quarter shot; and the director cuts freely to semi-close-ups within a scene.

ITALIAN MELODRAMA

1912–14. Italy.
Total program: 46 min. B&W. Silent. 18 fps.

LYDIA (I DUE AMORE)

1912.
Milano Films. With Pino Fabbri.
English titles.
39 min.

THE NAKED TRUTH (LA DONNA NUDA) (excerpt)

1914.
Cines Company. Directed by Carmine Gallone(?). Adapted from the play "La Femme nue" (1908) by Henri Bataille. With Lyda Borelli. Italian titles.
7 min.

Concurrent with the historical spectacle films, Italy produced melodramas of high life in which statuesque women reacted, or over-reacted, to grand passions. In *Lydia*, a poor girl employed in a dressmaker's establishment is led astray by her desire for wealth. After extravagant adventures, gambling, a duel between her lovers, she ends up dying of consumption and abandoned, except for the arms of her loyal artist lover. The dating of this film as 1912 is tentative, but the date of 1910 on the film seems too early for its style, which includes a variety of camera positions, cuts into semi-close-up, and many short shots. Made from a worn copy, it has inadvertent jump cuts and too much contrast. Like *The Naked Truth*, however, it features picturesque shots and unusual compositions. It makes use of deep space and plays its action both in foreground and background: Lydia's longing for rich jewels is shown through the window of a shop, the traffic moving in the street behind her; a matted keyhole shot of the rich Count Guy de Lys reveals that Lydia is secretly watching her amorous acquaintance. The scene from *The Naked Truth* is that in which Borelli learns of her betrayal by the man she loves. It, too, makes use of playing areas in foreground and background, divided this time by glass doors, through which Borelli sees her man make love to another woman. Above all, these two films feature the flamboyant Italian diva, suffering nobly and with graceful gestures. *Love Everlasting* (1913) also belongs to this school.

———

THE LESSER EVIL

April 29, 1912. U.S.A.
Biograph Company. Directed by D. W.

Griffith. Script by George Hennessy. Photographed by G. W. (Billy) Bitzer. With Blanche Sweet, Alfred Paget, Edwin August.
15 min. B&W. Silent. 18 fps.

This typical Griffith suspense thriller takes place at sea, after a girl who stumbles on a gang of smugglers is kidnapped to keep her quiet. Her sweetheart leads the harbor police in a wild chase at sea, while the captain of the smugglers defends the girl from the attack of his drunken and mutinous crew. There is a lot of rapid cross-cutting (114 shots, the highest number in any Biograph up to this time), and spectacular sea scenes. This rendition of the genre has some curious overtones. The smuggler captain is brutal to his men and lusts after the heroine, but then protects her and is about to shoot her with the last bullet in his gun to save her honor. After the rescue, she lets him escape overboard and watches through binoculars until he is safe on shore, then she sighs happily and sits down next to her sweetheart while the film comes to an end in a slow fade. The character of the smuggler captain has certain resemblances to the uncouth strong-man hero of an earlier Griffith comedy, *The Primal Call* (1911).

AN OUTCAST AMONG OUTCASTS

May 30, 1912. U.S.A.
Biograph Company. Directed by D. W. Griffith. Photographed by G. W. (Billy) Bitzer. With Blanche Sweet, Frank Opperman.
15 min. B&W. Silent. 18 fps.

The kindness of the postmaster's daughter to a "blanket tramp" (one who is outcast by his fellow tramps) is returned to her when some thieves waylay her for the mail she is carrying from the railroad station. The tramp brings help to rescue her in a thrilling sequence reminiscent of *The Lonedale Operator* (1911) and other films of this genre. The special interest of this film lies in the striking imagery composed of bright sun and dark shadow (it was shot in California) and the unusual compositions in almost every shot. The circular structure explored by Griffith in earlier Biographs is revived here in the beginning and ending shots of the disappearing railroad track along which the tramp enters the story and at the end walks away to fadeout. The final image, charged with pathos, suggests Chaplin's *The Tramp* (1915) (see **Chaplin's Essanay Films** [1915–16]). It also had personal meaning to Griffith who, when he was a struggling actor, sometimes hopped freights.

THE PAINTED LADY

October 24, 1912. U.S.A.
Biograph Company. Written and directed by D. W. Griffith. Photographed by G. W. (Billy) Bitzer. With Blanche Sweet, Joseph Graybill, Charles H. Mailes.
15 min. B&W. Silent. 18 fps.

Following her father's teachings, the eldest daughter refuses to powder and paint, or to flirt, and is ignored at the church picnic. She is all the more vulnerable to the advances of the stranger who courts her only to gain knowledge of her father's house for purposes of robbery. Her discovery of the betrayal of her love drives her mad. The atmosphere of this unusual film changes from comedy to tragedy in its course, with minimal action. Long takes enable Blanche Sweet to develop the character to an unusual degree for a 1912 film. Griffith returns again and again to the wooden bridge where the lovers first meet, endowing its physical space with emotional significance.

POLIDOR COMEDIES

1912–13. Italy.
Pasquali Film. With Ferdinando Guillaume. English titles.
Total program: 52 min. B&W. Silent. 18 fps.

POLIDOR LOVE SICK! (POLIDOR FACCHINO PER AMORE)

1912.
8 min.

POLIDOR DANCING MASTER (POLIDOR MAESTRO DI BALLO)

1912.
7 min.

POLIDOR'S WONDERFUL FRIEND (POLIDOR E L'AMICO INTIMO)

1913.
6 min.

POLIDOR'S DEBT (POLIDOR E IL SUO DEBITO)

1913.
7 min.

POLIDOR AND THE ELEPHANT (POLIDOR E L'ELEFANTE)

1913.
7 min.

POLIDOR AND THE LIONS (POLIDOR E I GATTI)

1913.
10 min.

POLIDOR'S FIRST DUEL (IL PRIMO DUELLO DI POLIDOR)

1913.
7 min.

Ferdinando Guillaume stars in this group of comedies from the Polidor series made for the Pasquali Film Company during 1912–13. The former circus acrobat began his career as a screen comic in 1910 for Cines in the Tontolini series—see **Tontolini and Polidor Comedies** (1910–12). In *Polidor Love Sick!*, Polidor is favored as a suitor by the girl's father but her mother prefers the great musician Potetoff. She throws Polidor out of the house, but he sneaks back in and hides in the piano during Potetoff's performance, ruining his rival's reputation as a musician. In *Polidor Dancing Master*, it is the father who throws Polidor out of the house of the girl he loves, but the persistent suitor returns in disguise as applicant for the position of the girl's dancing instructor. He might have succeeded if his beard hadn't fallen off. Guillaume turned out over 100 comedies in the Polidor series and *Polidor's Wonderful Friend* is one of the stranger ones. His "wonderful friend" is a giant, and most of this film's humor comes from the contrast in size with little Polidor (as in *Polidor and the Elephant*, see below). This print is probably not complete. Polidor is a poor artist who cannot pay his rent in *Polidor's Debt*. His solution to the problem is ingenious: he disguises himself in turn as a policeman, a chemist, and a dentist, collecting from the landlord himself all the money that he owes him. Polidor is on his way to a wedding in *Polidor and the Elephant*, but stops to remove a thorn from the foot of a large pachyderm and wins his heart. Enraptured, the elephant insists on following Polidor into the most inappropriate places, breaking up the wedding party and causing a chase. In *Polidor and the Lions*, Polidor loses his master's pet cats while he is away, and decides to steal some replacements from a caravan. Unfortunately, it is a circus caravan and his cute little kitties are lion cubs. The film survives today only in a poor copy. Even though elements of classic narrative style in 1912–13 are used in these films—for example, closer views are cut into mid-scene—Polidor still mugs to the camera, calling the attention of the audience to his performance as in the days of early cinema. Such mannerisms survive much later in comedy than in melodrama and are used occasionally for comic effect even today. In *Polidor's First Duel*, the style belongs more to pre-Griffith cinema and seems old-fashioned for 1913. Polidor is a tailor who has a terrible time getting a customer to pay his bills. The customer is a fencing master and insists on challenging the persistent Polidor to a duel. In the surreal world of slapstick comedy Polidor wins the contest, with Guillaume showing off the acrobatic skills acquired in his early circus career.

———

QUO VADIS?

1912. Italy.
Cines Company. Directed by Enrico Guazzoni. From the novel by Henryk Sienkiewicz. With Amleto Novelli, Gustavo Serena, Lea Giunchi. French and German titles only.
116 min. B&W. Silent. 18 fps.

This early version of the much-filmed Sienkiewicz novel ran a full eight reels and helped establish the feature film in America. In the same year U.S. filmmakers produced two seven-reel films and six six-reel films, but the policy of the Motion Picture Trust companies kept the majority of film production to one or two reels. *Quo Vadis?* opened in New York on April 21, 1913, where it played for 22 weeks at a top admission price of $1.00. The burning of Rome, the chariot race, the lions set loose upon the Christians, the solid three-dimensional sets, and the use of masses of extras made a great impression. Although the grandiloquent Italian acting style may appear overdone today, it was very well received at the time. No close-ups are used, and distance demands broader and more stylized gestures. There are cuts in mid-scene, changes of camera position, and some miniatures, special lighting effects, and double exposure. The long titles, in the style of early cinema, explain the action to follow. The Italian spectacle film was considered the pinnacle of film art for a few years, until the first World War brought a hiatus to European film production.

REVENGE OF A KINEMATOGRAPH CAMERAMAN (MIEST KINEMATOGRAFITSCHESKOGO)

October 17, 1912. Russia.
Khanzhonkov. Directed by Ladislas Starewicz. English intertitles.
12 min. B&W. Silent. 18 fps.

Ladislas Starewicz, a Pole born in Moscow in 1890, was director of a natural history museum before he began making films. His early puppet animation films, made with modelled or jointed figures animated by stop-motion pho-

tography, featured insects with human characteristics. The insects, who are involved in slapstick comedy adventures, are scientifically correct and are not rendered lovable and "cute," as in later puppet films. This film is about the philanderings of Mr. and Mrs. Beetle, he with a dragonfly, she with a grasshopper. After catching his wife in dalliance, Mr. Beetle takes her to the movies, where his own love affair is shown on the screen by the grasshopper cameraman-projectionist. The gag is reminiscent of several early live-action films. Here, following the ensuing fight, there is even a nitrate fire.

A STRING OF PEARLS

March 7, 1912. U.S.A.
Biograph Company. Directed by D. W. Griffith. Photographed by G. W. (Billy) Bitzer.
15 min. B&W. Silent. 18 fps.

Another of Griffith's social dramas that contrast the life of the selfish rich with the sufferings—and the joys—of the poor. The film draws a parallel between the material string of pearls worth a quarter million dollars and the spiritual string composed of the kindly and generous neighbors living in the slum tenement. The millionaire's employee is dying of consumption and must go to the country to recover. His sister goes to the employer's house to plead for help, but he, while giving the string of pearls to his wife, refuses to listen. The boy's neighbors pool their meager re-

sources to send him away and share the family's happiness when he returns, recovered. Life in a tenement is vividly depicted by a large cast of the Biograph actors.

THE TOURISTS

August 5, 1912. U.S.A.
Biograph Company. Directed by Mack Sennett. With Mabel Normand, Charles West.
6 min. B&W. Silent. 18 fps.

A farce comedy improvised by the Biograph players on their way to or from California, this bit of nonsense shows four tourists who get off the train in Albuquerque to look at the Indian wares on sale at the station and are left behind. To fill in the time before the next train, Mabel Normand begins a flirtation with the Big Chief. The Indian women are upset by this and join forces to turn the affair into a chase comedy. Real Indians, who can't help grinning at being in the midst of the frenetic activity, are used as extras. Some documentary shots of Indian crafts and a lovely young Indian girl weaving at her loom add a note of ethnographic interest.

AN UNSEEN ENEMY

September 9, 1912. U.S.A.
Biograph Company. Directed by D. W. Griffith. Photographed by G. W. (Billy) Bitzer. With Lillian and Dorothy Gish, Robert Harron.

REVENGE OF A KINEMATOGRAPH CAMERAMAN (1912)

15 min. B&W. Silent. 18 fps.

Griffith's old reliable formula, the suspense thriller, continued to serve him well in the late Biographs. It is brought to even more intense heights of excitement in this new version of the story of *The Lonely Villa* (1909). Griffith uses close-ups, an increased number of shots, skilled performances, and the interweaving of four lines of action into one complex pattern: the frightened Gish girls are threatened with a gun, the thieves in the next room blow the safe, the car bringing rescue is stuck at a drawbridge, and the boyfriend hovers anxiously outside the window. The thriller is enriched by adding a love scene at the beginning, before the action has started, with an arresting high-angle shot of shy young lovers in a field of ripening corn.

VITAGRAPH COMEDIES

1912–17. U.S.A.
Vitagraph Company.
Total program: 56 min. B&W. Silent.
18 fps.

STENOGRAPHER WANTED

February 26, 1912.
With John Bunny, Flora Finch.
13 min.

GOODNESS GRACIOUS, OR, MOVIES AS THEY SHOULDN'T BE

February 7, 1914.
Directed by James Young. Script by J. Stuart Blackton. With Clara Kimball Young, Sidney Drew.
30 min.

PROFESSIONAL PATIENT

1917.
Directed by Sidney Drew. With Drew and Lucille McVey (Mrs. Sidney Drew).
13 min.

In an era of slapstick comedy, Vitagraph made a tradition of the social comedy, based more on the humor of situation and character than the nonsense gags and surrealism of vulgar slapstick. The early success of the John Bunny/Flora Finch comedies laid the basis for a comedy based on everyday life. *Stenographer Wanted* uses a plot familiar from the earliest days of cinema: two businessmen choosing a secretary select the prettiest candidate but when their wives visit the office they replace her with the ugliest one. John Bunny, a former stage actor, was one of the most

well-loved screen personalities up to his death in 1915. His success in films derived from more than his physical appearance: his acting as well as his face was larger than life. In contrast to his monumental rotundities, the skinny Flora Finch was the perfect foil. *Goodness Gracious* is an exception to the Vitagraph social comedy. It is the broadest of burlesques, a parody of melodrama and its acting style adapted from the theatrical tradition. The film ends in a wild chase sequence, the action speeded up by slow cranking of the camera. Of historic significance, it records for us the old Vitagraph studio in Flatbush and the surrounding streets. The premiere of this film was at the opening of the new Vitagraph Theatre, among the earliest of New York's picture palaces. In *Professional Patient*, Sidney Drew gets a job in a dentist's office pretending to be a patient who can testify to the painless character of the dentistry for the benefit of waiting clients. He is soon in danger of being discovered when he falls in love with a girl in the waiting room. Drew was a member of a celebrated theatrical family and an uncle to the Barrymores, and was nearing fifty when he left the vaudeville stage to join Vitagraph. He and his wife, who wrote his scripts, believed that comedy should be based on real life and have characters with which the audience could identify. They rejected the vulgarity of slapstick and hoped to appeal to a more refined audience. Drew's relaxed and natural acting style lent itself well to the medium and his gags were fresh and inventive.

—

A VITAGRAPH ROMANCE

September 18, 1912. U.S.A.
Vitagraph Company. Directed and written by James Young. With Clara Kimball Young, James Morrison, Edward Kimball.
8 min. B&W. Silent. 18 fps.

The special delight of this drama is that it shows the Vitagraph lot in Brooklyn and the making of movies there. The plot revolves around a Senator's daughter who is disowned when she marries a penniless writer and reconciled with her father after becoming a famous motion picture actress. The Vitagraph Company executives appear in the film as themselves: Albert E. Smith, James Stuart Blackton, William T. Rock, and the director James Young. The print is only half complete, but fortunately the studio scenes, showing cameras, sets, and lights, survive intact.

BRONCHO BILLY WESTERNS

1913–18. U.S.A.
Total program: 41 min. B&W. Silent.
18 fps.

BRONCHO BILLY'S CAPTURE

1913.
Essanay Company. Written and directed by Gilbert M. ("Broncho Billy") Anderson. With Anderson, Marguerite Clayton.
13 min.

SHOOTIN' MAD

1918.
Golden West Producing Company. Directed by Jesse J. Robbins. With Gilbert M. ("Broncho Billy") Anderson, Jay Lewis.
28 min.

In 1906 Gilbert M. Anderson organized the Essanay Company in Chicago in partnership with George K. Spoor. For the next ten years he concentrated on producing, writing, directing, and starring in mostly one-reel westerns. He used real locations in the far west, and his instinct for natural surroundings was one of the factors that gave him such popularity—especially abroad, where audiences recognized a unique genre. His films were full of action, using short shots and dynamic compositions dictated by the outdoor locations. He was the first western star, a legendary one because so few Essanay films survive. In *Broncho Billy's Capture*, made at the peak of his career, he is forced to do his duty as a sheriff and arrest the woman he loves, discovering too late that she is in partnership to rob the stage with a Mexican "greaser" (as Mexicans were then stereotyped in hundreds of westerns). *Shooting' Mad* represents Broncho Billy's attempt at a comeback in 1918, after two years of retirement. In this film Billy is blamed for the murder of a settler to whom a gambler has given his farm in his absence, but Billy escapes from the sheriff's office long enough to save the settler's daughter from the gambler and expose him as the villain. It is significant that the two films on this program differ very little from one another, except that Broncho Billy looks older in the later one. While the American film had changed in style in the intervening years, Anderson had not changed with it.

—

BY MAN'S LAW

November 22, 1913. U.S.A.
Biograph Company. Directed by William Christy Cabanne. Script by William E. Wing. With Mae Marsh, Robert Harron, Alfred Paget, Donald Crisp.
30 min. B&W. Silent. 18 fps.

It would be easy to mistake this very intriguing film for one of Griffith's. The other directors who worked at Biograph absorbed his style, his themes, and inherited his well-trained group of young actors. This two-reel film has a strong social theme. An oil magnate ruthlessly buys up independent rivals, then cuts wages and closes factories, causing much suffering among the working classes. The film hints at another sensational topic of the time, the white slavery that threatened poor, unprotected females. Yet another Griffith theme enters into the depiction of the hypocrisy of the do-good reformers. Excellent photography in real locations adds to the interest of the film.

DEATH'S MARATHON

June 14, 1913. U.S.A.
Biograph Company. Directed by D. W. Griffith. Script by William E. Wing. Photographed by G. W. (Billy) Bitzer. With Blanche Sweet, Henry B. Walthall, Walter Miller.
15 min. B&W. Silent. 18 fps.

Griffith's well-known thrilling ride to the rescue did not always arrive in time. In this grim drama from Griffith's late Biograph period, an inveterate gambler embezzles funds from his firm and when he approaches ruin, determines to commit suicide. Nearly half of the film's 112 shots are dedicated to the suspenseful phone conversation in which Walthall threatens his estranged wife with his suicide, while her former suitor races by car to prevent it. Repeated close-ups of the anguished facial expressions of Blanche Sweet or the crazed Walthall fondling his gun increase the intensity of the drama and explore the psychology of the characters. Blanche Sweet's frozen expression of horror as she hears the fatal shot over the telephone reveals the outcome.

FANTÔMAS. Episode 2: JUVE VS. FANTÔMAS (JUVE CONTRE FANTÔMAS)

1913. France.
Gaumont. Directed by Louis Feuillade. With René Navarre, Bréon, Georges Melchior, Renée Carl. English titles.
64 min. B&W. Silent. 18 fps.

This is the second episode of the series of five films that comprised Feuillade's adaptation of the serial novel by Pierre Souvestre and Marcel Allain. The feature-length films are about the exploits of the mysterious master criminal Fantômas and the efforts of the detective Juve to capture him. In this episode, Fantômas baffles his pursuers by an ingenious method of staying under water. These films were a combination of melodrama, fantasy, and intrigue, set in the cityscape of Paris and its suburbs and in wonderfully-designed interiors. Their lyricism and fantastic atmosphere were much admired by the Surrealists, and the films were popular all over the world.

A HOUSE DIVIDED

1913. U.S.A.
Solax Company. Directed by Alice Guy-Blaché.
13 min. B&W. Silent. 18 fps.

A House Divided is a light domestic farce which offers a comic vision of marriage. Its plot hinges on a series of mistakes and coincidences that lead a husband and wife to unjustly suspect each other of infidelity. A further coincidence, of course, ultimately leads to the resolution of their marital difficulties. Alice Guy-Blaché was one of the first women directors in the film industry. She began her career in France with Gaumont, but eventually came to the United States and in 1910 became the president of Solax Company. Although Solax ceased production in 1914, Alice Guy-Blaché directed continuously until 1920.

THE LADY AND THE MOUSE

April 26, 1913. U.S.A.
Biograph Company. Directed and written by D. W. Griffith. Photographed by G. W. (Billy) Bitzer. With Lillian and Dorothy Gish, Lionel Barrymore, Henry Walthall, Kate Toncray, Robert Harron.
15 min. B&W. Silent. 18 fps.

The kindly storekeeper can't pay off the mortgage because he is unable to refuse the needy, but his invalid daughter must have a change of climate. A tramp, treated with kindness, turns out to be a millionaire and saves the day. Griffith devotes much of this film's 120 shots to developing characterization and allows the only comic relief to become the major sequence and to give the film its title. Lillian Gish plays the storekeeper's other daughter, who finds a mouse in a trap and feels sorry for it. Her attempts to drown it provide a captivating sequence, not only because of her charm and comic gifts, but also due to Griffith's extended editing pattern emphasizing details and reactions.

LOVE EVERLASTING (MA L'AMOR MIO NON MUORE)

1913. Italy.
Gloria Films. Directed by Mario Caserini. With Lyda Borelli, Mario Bonnard. English titles.
70 min. B&W. Silent. 18 fps.

This Italian melodrama has a characteristically flamboyant role for the diva Lyda Borelli. She plays a celebrated opera singer with a past who, when the man she loves discovers it, commits suicide by poison, dying on stage in full view of her public. The production is lavishly over-decorated; the titles and takes are long. There are some changes of camera set-up within scenes and semi-close-ups are used sparingly for dramatic emphasis, including the final oval vignette enclosing the dying woman's head hanging upside down with her lover leaning over her. The great Borelli's gestures and stances, however mannered, are executed with such devastating grace that they banish, for the time being, all other criteria of great acting.

LOVE IN AN APARTMENT HOTEL

February 27, 1913. U.S.A.
Biograph Company. Directed by D. W. Griffith. Script by William M. Marston. Photographed by G. W. (Billy) Bitzer. With Blanche Sweet, Henry Walthall, Mae Marsh.
16 min. B&W. Silent. 18 fps.

Mae Marsh is a chambermaid in a hotel who dreams about the rich guest above her station in life (played by Henry Walthall). She gets locked up in his closet by a would-be thief and thus nearly becomes the cause for breaking Walthall's engagement to the lovely Blanche Sweet. When the truth emerges, Mae Marsh learns she would be better off to accept her humble lover the bellboy. This slight little comedy is very fast-moving, containing nearly 120 shots, many so short that some were apparently used twice to increase the rapid intercutting, according to notes by the cameraman, G. W. Bitzer. The print lists the director and cast credits, something never done by Biograph up to this time, but they may have been added when this popular film was reissued in 1915.

THE MOTHERING HEART

June 21, 1913. U.S.A.
Biograph Company. Directed by D. W. Griffith. Script by Hazel H. Hubbard, George Terwilliger(?). Photographed by G. W. (Billy) Bitzer. With Lillian Gish, Walter Miller, Peggy Pearce.
30 min. B&W. Silent. 18 fps.

As much as any other of his films, this one demonstrates Griffith's supreme mastery over the emotions of his audience. Lillian Gish gives one of her most moving portrayals as the young wife betrayed by her husband. Her performance is greatly enhanced by Griffith's skillful use of suggestive details and unusual compositions. There are close-ups of faces to reveal emotion, but when Gish watches from behind a tree as her husband goes off with the other woman, all we see is her hand slipping on the tree trunk and a brief glimpse as she runs, in long shot, back into her house. When her baby dies, Gish registers her numbing first shock in a close-up, but we know her grief and anger in a beautiful iris shot as she furiously beats the rose bush in the garden. By 1913, Biograph permitted Griffith to make two-reel films, but this film is so emotionally compressed that one has the impression he could have used even more screen time to develop his characters.

SWEDISH CINEMA CLASSICS

1913–24. Sweden.
Svensk Filmindustri in cooperation with the Swedish Film Institute. Compiled in 1959 by Gardar Sahlberg. English version narrated by Alan Blair. The compilation includes excerpts from the following films, all of them produced by Svensk Filmindustri or its forerunner (through 1919), Svenska Biografteatern.

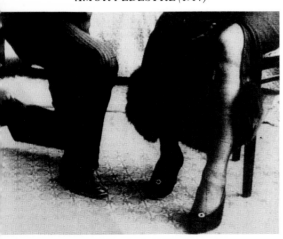

AMOR PEDESTRE (1914)

Total program: 36 min. B&W. Sound. 24 fps.

Directed by Victor Sjöström:

GIVE US THIS DAY (INGEBORG HOLM)

1913.
With Hilda Borgström.

A MAN THERE WAS (TERJE VIGEN)

1916.
With Sjöström, August Falk.

THE OUTLAW AND HIS WIFE (BERG-EJVIND OCH HANS HUSTRU)

1918.
With Sjöström, Edith Erastoff, John Ekman.

THE GIRL FROM THE MARSH CROFT (TÖSEN FRÅN STORMYRTORPET)

1917.
With Greta Almroth.

THE SONS OF INGMAR (INGMARSSÖNERNA)

1919.
With Sjöström.

KARIN, DAUGHTER OF INGEMAR (KARIN INGEMARSDOTTER)

1920.
With Sjöström, Tore Teje, Bertil Malmstedt.

LOVER IN PAWN (MÄSTERMAN)

1920.
With Sjöström, Greta Almroth.

THE PHANTOM CHARIOT (KÖRKARLEN)

January 1, 1921.
With Sjöström, Olaf Ås.

Directed by Mauritz Stiller:

EROTIKON (RIDDAREN AV IGÅR)

1920.
With Anders de Wahl, Tore Teje, Lars Hanson.

THE TREASURE OF ARNE (HERR ARNES PENGAR)

1919.
With Mary Johnson.

THE JUDGEMENT (GUNNAR HEDES SAGA)

1922.
With Einar Hanson.

THE STORY OF GÖSTA BERLING (GÖSTA BERLINGS SAGA)

1924.
With Lars Hanson, Greta Garbo.

This survey of the highlights of Sweden's golden age of silent cinema concentrates on films by the two greatest directors of the period, Sjöström and Stiller. It also contains a few early cinema scenes, not all of them Swedish, and documents of the film industry, including production footage. Because filmmaking began slightly later in Sweden than elsewhere, Sjöström and Stiller were very much under the influence of American films, in particular the work of D. W. Griffith and Thomas Ince. However, in place of the American West, their films featured Scandinavian character and landscape. Based largely on the national literature, notably on the novels of Selma Lagerlöff, their films have a heroic character, frequently portraying people at variance with society. The Swedish films stressed visual detail and composition, used natural lighting and restrained acting; the Scandinavian settings, landscapes, and weather served as carriers of emotion and drama. In turn, Swedish cinema influenced other major national cinemas in the first half of the twenties. *The Outlaw and His Wife* (1918), *The Phantom Chariot* (1921), and *The Treasure of Arne* (1919) are available in full-length versions—see individual annotations.

———

AMOR PEDESTRE

1914. Italy.
Ambrosio Company. Directed by Marcel Fabre.
15 min. B&W. Silent. 18 fps.

Marcel Fabre was a French clown of Spanish origin (his original name was Fernandez Perez) who starred in a series of some ninety comedies for Ambrosio during 1910–15 as Robinet (the series was known as Tweedledum in the U.S. releases). He came to America at the end of 1915, where he made comedies for Vim Comedies and then Jester Comedies. After losing a leg in an accident, he became a gagman at Universal under the name of Marcel Perez, and directed a series of Jimmy Aubrey comedies as well as a number of feature films during the twenties. *Amor Pedestre* was a novelty, based on an idea that had already appealed to a number of early filmmakers because it permitted an erotic suggestiveness: the entire narrative is told by showing only the feet of its characters. Similar ideas caught the fancy of some avant-garde filmmakers at a later date. This is one of the cleverest of the genre. According to their feet, we see a man pursue a woman who is married and become her lover. When he is caught by her husband, a duel follows in which the interloper is wounded.

THE AVENGING CONSCIENCE

July 16, 1914. U.S.A.
Reliance-Majestic. Directed and written by D. W. Griffith. Photographed by G. W. (Billy) Bitzer. With Spottiswoode Aiken, Ralph Lewis, Blanche Sweet, Henry Walthall.
84 min. B&W. Silent. 18 fps.

Griffith drew on Edgar Allen Poe for this strange psychological study of a man who dreams of murdering his uncle and is finally driven mad by his guilty conscience. The use of double exposures, allegorical scenes, lighting contrasts, extreme close-ups, elaborate editing structures, and framing devices that change the size and shape of the image, add up to a showy style that Griffith would never return to. Some of its devices were, however, taken up later by German Expressionism and the French avant-garde. The most impressive sequence creates an atmosphere of foreboding doom. Through the rhythmic cutting of close-ups of a clock pendulum, the guilty man's nervous fingers, and the questioning detective's tapping pencil and foot, Griffith convincingly portrays inner tension and guilt.

THE BATTLE AT ELDERBUSH GULCH

March 28, 1914. U.S.A.
Biograph Company. Directed by D. W. Griffith. Photographed by G. W. (Billy) Bitzer. With Lillian Gish, Robert Harron, Mae Marsh, Alfred Paget.
27 min. B&W. Silent. 18 fps.

Made in 1913 and not released until long after Griffith left Biograph, this two-reel western represents the director at the peak of his excitement-building power. With the western genre now set in its conventions, Griffith readily abandons the noble red man of his early Biographs for the traditional savage Indian. White settlers are attacked by Indians after one of their tribe is killed during an attempt to steal a little girl's dog. After much terror and many killings, they are rescued by the cavalry. There are spectacular dust-filled battle scenes, appealing close-ups of young children and puppies threatened by the danger, and the familiar image of Indians racing around the settlers' cabin that will reappear in the final sequences of **The Birth of a Nation** (1915).

CABIRIA (1914)

CABIRIA

1914. Italy.
Itala Film. Directed and written by Giovanni Pastrone. Photographed by Segundo de Chomon. With Marcellina Bianco, Almirante Manzini, Bartolomeo Pagano. English and Italian titles.
116 min. B&W. Silent. 18 fps.

This famous historical spectacle film takes place during the struggle for supremacy between Rome and Carthage in the Second Punic War. Cabiria, daughter of a Roman family, is sold into slavery in Carthage and destined to be sacrificed to the pagan god Moloch. She escapes with the help of a gigantic Roman slave, Maciste, played by a former docker, Bartolomeo Pagano, who enjoyed a subsequent screen career as a mythic superhero. Elaborate sets, spectacular battle sequences employing large casts of extras, and the use of the process shot contributed to the grandeur of this film. The traveling shot, used to follow action, isolate characters, and emphasize the depth perspective of sets was considered revolutionary and came to be known as the "Cabiria movement." The film added suspense and excitement to the Italian historical genre and film historians since that time have debated its possible influence on Griffith's **Intolerance** (1916). The Museum's print has reissue credits and is not as long as the original.

CHAPLIN'S KEYSTONE FILMS

1914. U.S.A.
Keystone Company. With Charles Chaplin.
Total program: 73 min. B&W. Silent. 18 fps.

These films are also available individually.

MAKING A LIVING

February 2, 1914.
Directed by Henry Lehrman. With Alice Davenport, Minta Durfee, Henry Lehrman.
12 min.

THE KNOCKOUT

June 11, 1914.
With Fatty Arbuckle, Minta Durfee, Alice Howell, Al St. John.
28 min.

THE MASQUERADER

August 27, 1914.
Directed and written by Charles Chaplin. With Fatty Arbuckle, Minta Durfee, Charles Murray, Fritz Schade.
12 min.

THE ROUNDERS

September 7, 1914.
Directed and written by Charles Chap-

lin. With Fatty Arbuckle, Minta Durfee, Al St. John.
11 min.

GETTING ACQUAINTED

December 5, 1914.
Directed and written by Charles Chaplin. Photographed by Frank D. Williams. With Phyllis Allen, Edgar Kennedy, Mabel Normand, Mack Swain.
10 min.

In 1914 Mack Sennett's Keystone comedy factory acquired an English music hall performer who was soon to become the best-known and loved figure throughout the world. Charlie Chaplin made thirty-five films that year in the fast-moving slapstick comedy style prevalent in the Sennett studio and during that time he began to develop the character that would eventually emerge as the little tramp. In the Sennett films there was seldom time to develop comic characterization or complicated gags, but many of Chaplin's little comic bits and gestures are as memorable as anything he did in later years. In a short time he became the writer and director of most of his films. In his first, *Making a Living*, he wears the costume and makeup of his stage act as an impoverished English nobleman. He tries to get a newspaper job and when rejected, snatches a camera out of a reporter's hands in an attempt to get a scoop that will get him hired, precipitating a chase. *The Knockout* is a Fatty Arbuckle film in which Chaplin plays a small but wonderful part as a referee at a boxing match getting the worst of the blows. By the time *The Masquerader* was made, Chaplin was beginning to get control over his own material—or as much control as producer Sennett would permit. In it Charlie is trying to become a movie actor but gets fired because he ruins scene after scene. To get himself rehired, he exercises his coy charms disguised as a woman. Arbuckle and Chaplin team up in *The Rounders* as a couple of husbands spending a night out on the town, pursued by their irate wives. Trying to escape their wrath, they take refuge in a sinking rowboat. *Getting Acquainted* finds Chaplin and Mabel Normand flirting in a park, each of them married to someone else. Charlie's wife is bigger and stronger than he is and Mabel's husband is a cop, resulting in the expected mayhem.

———

A FOOL THERE WAS

1914. U.S.A.
Fox Film Corporation. Directed by Frank Powell. Screenplay by Roy L. McCardell, from a play by Porter Emerson Brown based on Rudyard Kipling's "The Vampire." Photographed by Lucien Andriot. With Theda Bara, Edward Jose, Mabel Frenyear.
82 min. B&W. Silent. 18 fps.

A Fool There Was gave the word "vamp" to the English language. As the incarnation of this aggressive variety of the femme fatale, Theda Bara became famous overnight. Using wiles that may appear absurd to us today, and perhaps as well to much of the 1914 audience, the vamp lures a man from his wife and child, ruins his reputation, and drives him to drink, only one among her victims. In Victorian times, she might have been the dark side of the traditional innocent virgin, but in 1914 her aggressiveness could be considered as a symptom of the growing need of women to have a degree of power, of whatever kind, in a man's society. Of the some forty films Theda Bara made in the next five years, only this one and one other, *East Lynne* (1916), survive. It serves as an example of the average feature film of the year in which it first gained general acceptance.

HOME, SWEET HOME

May 17, 1914. U.S.A.
Reliance-Majestic. Directed and written by D. W. Griffith. Photographed by G. W. (Billy) Bitzer. With Henry Walthall, Lillian Gish, Mae Marsh, Robert Harron, Donald Crisp, Owen Moore, Blanche Sweet.
64 min. B&W. Silent. 18 fps.

Griffith's third feature after leaving Biograph is actually a group of one-reelers linked by a common theme, and in that sense is a kind of first exploration of the construction of *Intolerance* (1916), although the stories are not intercut. The structure is even more reminiscent of the little comedies of 1905–07, wherein single-shot episodes were linked by a common motif. The prologue tells about the life and death of John Howard Payne, composer of the title song, and the subsequent stories tell how the song was heard at crucial moments in the lives of their characters: a simple love story with Mae Marsh and Robert Harron as its charming lovers; a drama of fratricide in which the last minute ride-to-the-rescue along the spectacular California coastline arrives too late; and one in which a wife is tempted to run off with a lover. In an allegorical epilogue, Henry Walthall as Payne struggles (held back by Lust and Greed) to reach his sweetheart (Lillian Gish), reincarnated as an angel suspended perilously by wires.

Raoul Walsh (as John Wilkes Booth) and Joseph Henaberry (as Lincoln) in THE BIRTH OF A NATION (1915)

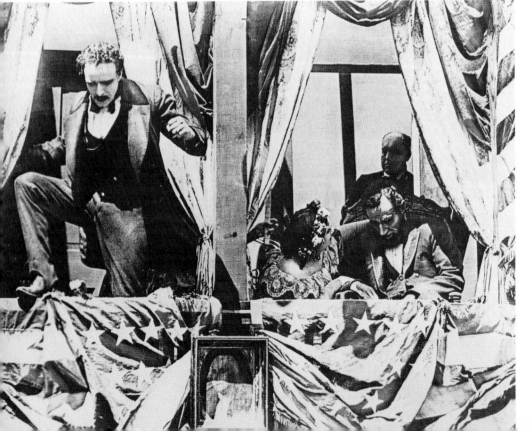

JUDITH OF BETHULIA

March 8, 1914. U.S.A.
Biograph Company. Directed by D. W. Griffith. Photographed by G. W. (Billy) Bitzer. With Blanche Sweet, Henry Walthall, Mae Marsh, Robert Harron, Lillian and Dorothy Gish.
68 min. B&W. Silent. 18 fps.

Griffith's first feature was made in the spring and summer of 1913, against the wishes of Biograph's executives, who held up its release until long after Griffith left the company. Based on the Apocrypha and the play by Thomas Bailey Aldrich, it tells the story of Judith, who sacrifices herself for the people of the fortified city of Bethulia by going to the tent of Holofernes, whose Assyrian army holds the city in siege. Although she falls in love with him, she carries out her appointed task to kill him. Filled with stirring battle scenes and strikingly composed crowd scenes, Griffith brings to the historical spectacle film all the Italians had done and more. He gives it human dimensions with intimate portrayals of individuals. Film historians who have tried to link *Cabiria* (1914) to *Intolerance*(1916) have overlooked this earlier film, made long before *Cabiria* was shown in America.

THE LAST OF THE LINE (PRIDE OF RACE)

December 24, 1914. U.S.A.
Produced by Thomas H. Ince. Directed by Jay Hunt. Script by Thomas H. Ince and C. Gardner Sullivan. With Sessue Hayakawa.
28 min. B&W. Silent. 18 fps.

Ince's films are all stamped with his personality, no matter who the director. Though he rarely directed after 1913, he supervised scripts, ordered them shot as written, and then edited the material himself. Ince made his first reputation as a director of westerns using California landscapes and authentic cowboys and Indians. The star of this film, however, is Japanese, and a popular matinee idol at the time. *The Last of the Line*, bearing the reissue title *Pride of Race*, perpetuates the myth of the noble red man. Chief Gray Otter's son turns renegade after his government schooling and leads an attack against the stagecoach. His father shoots him down to prevent his killing of the cavalry leader and arranges matters to look as though his son died a hero, for which the son receives a military burial. Ince's westerns were epic in nature, swiftly cut on action, with bare landscapes that lent grandeur to the simple sentiments.

ASSUNTA SPINA

1915. Italy.
Caesar Film. Directed and written by Gustavo Serena, from a play by Salvatore Giacomo. Photographed by Albert G. Carta. With Francesca Bertini, Gustavo Serena. English and Italian titles.
66 min. B&W. Silent. 18 fps.

This film is an outgrowth of the Italian artistic movement known as *verismo*, which attempted naturalistic portrayals of the lower classes. Related to the neorealism of post-World War II Italy as a precursor, it remains within the traditions of melodrama. It is the tragic love story of a Neapolitan laundress with a jealous lover, for whom she goes to prison when he kills his rival. It stars Francesca Bertini, Italy's foremost silent film star, who infuses the film with raw vitality despite her flamboyant histrionics. Filmed in the crowded streets of Naples and in natural light, it has a documentary quality. Its remarkable compositions in deep focus, linking the varying spatial planes by the movement of the actors, not only give a depth to its photography but also add to the psychological overtones of certain emotional scenes.

THE BIRTH OF A NATION

January 1, 1915. U.S.A.
Epoch Producing Corporation. Produced and directed by D. W. Griffith. Screenplay by Griffith and Frank Woods, based on Thomas Dixon's novel and play *The Clansman*. Photographed by G. W. (Billy) Bitzer. Assistant cameraman: Brown. With Lillian Gish, Mae Marsh, Henry Walthall, Miriam Cooper, Robert Harron.
180 min. B&W. (Also available in a color version, 167 min.) Silent. 18 fps.

Griffith's historical spectacle film of the Civil War and its aftermath is told through the intertwined stories of two families, one on each side of the conflict. As an important part of our cultural heritage, it should be seen by everyone, despite its inflammatory subject matter. Griffith poured his whole heart and all the emotional power of his style of filmmaking into his southern-based view of the war that tore a nation apart. It is difficult for anyone seeing this film not to cheer the ride of the Ku Klux Klan in the stirring climax, whatever one's feelings about that vigilante group today. The film is filled with spectacular battle scenes and intimately moving moments: a mother welcoming home her weary soldier son, a sentry's sigh over the sight of a lovely young girl, a soldier falling in the battlefield. It was made as the culmination of hundreds of popular Civil War films and of the development of what has become known as classic cinema style, and in this sense it is not the "first" of anything, regardless of what the history books say. It was probably the most successful and popular film ever made, though surrounded by controversy from the time of its first showings as **The Clansman**. A new color version made from a tinted print is now available. Excerpts of the battle sequence and the homecoming sequence are also available (see Film Study).

CHAPLIN'S ESSANAY FILMS

1915–16. U.S.A.
Essanay Company. Directed and written by Charles Chaplin. With Chaplin and Edna Purviance.
Total program: 82 min. B&W. Silent. 18 fps.

These films are also available individually.

THE TRAMP

April 11, 1915.
Photographed by Roland Totheroh, Harry Ensign. With Leo White.
24 min.

A WOMAN

July 12, 1915.
With Charles Insley.
19 min.

THE BANK

August 9, 1915.
With Carl Stockdale.
19 min.

POLICE

March 27, 1916.
With Wesley Ruggles.
20 min.

Chaplin, in leaving Sennett for the Chicago-based Essanay Company, left behind some of the roughhouse and vulgarity of slapstick comedy. He wrote and directed as well as starred in all the films in this program. He gave more time to story development, slowed his pace, and elaborated his comic character. New elements of pathos and irony and a self-confidence in his performance contributed to making these films among his most memorable. In *The Tramp*, Charlie as a hobo rescues the farmer's daughter from crooks and wins himself a job on the farm. His efforts to learn

Edna Purviance and Charles Chaplin in A WOMAN (1915) (p. 47)

farm work provide fruitful material for gags. The discovery that he is mistaken in thinking himself worthy of the girl's love adds a note of pathos to the comedy. His final walk away from the camera down a long road, shoulders dejected; and the recovery of his spirits with a shrug and a skip became a Chaplin trademark. In *A Woman*, Charlie does one of his famous female impersonations in an effort to gain entrance to the home of the girl he loves. Most of his bits of comic business arise from this play on the tensions of his male-female identity. *The Bank* returns more emphatically to the comic pathos of *The Tramp*. As a janitor in a bank, he mistakes the attentions of the lovely stenographer. In compensation, he dreams of rescuing the lady from bank robbers, but wakes to the sad reality, kicks the wilted flowers she has rejected, and walks away. In *Police*, Chaplin introduces a note of ironic social commentary. An ex-convict, Charlie is being persuaded to reform his way of life by a reformer who turns out to be a thief himself. Led into robbery by his former cell-mate, Charlie is redeemed by a beautiful girl in the house he intended to rob. By adding the elements of irony and pathos to the slapstick comedy, Chaplin produced a new form of high comedy.

THE COWARD

November 7, 1915. U.S.A.
Triangle-Ince. Produced by Thomas H. Ince. Directed by Reginald Barker. Screenplay by Thomas H. Ince. With Frank Keenan, Charles Ray.
74 min. B&W. Silent. 18 fps.

The Coward, like *The Birth of a Nation* earlier the same year, rode the crest of the wave of Civil War films that were produced in enormous numbers between 1911 and 1915. While Ince did not neglect the spectacular aspects of the conflict, he focused primarily on the personal experiences of the people of the South. This film was primarily designed as a vehicle to introduce the stage star Frank Keenan to the screen. He plays the father who forces his "cowardly" son to enlist in the Confederate Army. When the son deserts, his father takes his place, but the young man redeems himself by stealing the battle plans of the Union soldiers who take over his house. At a time when many films subordinated all other elements to movement, *The Coward* makes conspicuous dramatic use of pause, even of immobility, to draw the spectator close to the emotional core of the action. "Soul-fights" was the period's phrase to describe the performances in Ince's films, created as much by camera angle and by cutting as by the actor.

ENOCH ARDEN (Extant reels: Conclusion)

April 8, 1915. U.S.A.
Reliance-Majestic. Supervised by D. W. Griffith. Directed by William Christy Cabanne. With Lillian Gish, Wallace Reid, Alfred Paget, Mildred Harris.
30 min. B&W. Silent. 18 fps.

The third time Griffith drew on the Tennyson poem that provided the material for *After Many Years* (1908) and *Enoch Arden* (1911), he produced a five-part feature, finding at last the scope he needed to tell the pathetic story of Annie and Enoch, separated for long years by a shipwreck that stranded him on a deserted island. All that survives of the film is the last two reels, which tell of Annie's reluctant remarriage and Enoch's long-delayed return, too late for his happiness, which he sacrifices for hers. Griffith did not direct this version but his influence is felt in every shot, especially in the repeated metaphor of faithful love, the image of a woman alone looking out to sea. William Christy Cabanne had been trained by Griffith at Biograph. While still there, Cabanne directed films that are often difficult to distinguish by their style from those of Griffith. This excerpt will be found useful for comparison with the 1911 version to illustrate the changes in film style that four years had brought, particularly the expressive use of close-ups and the changes of camera position within scenes. It also demonstrates Lillian Gish's maturing acting style.

KENO BATES, LIAR (THE LAST CARD)

August 27, 1915. U.S.A.
New York Motion Picture Company. Produced by Thomas H. Ince. Directed by William S. Hart. Screenplay by J. G. Hawks and Ince. With Hart, Louise Glaum, Margaret Thompson.
30 min. B&W. Silent. 18 fps.

It is his lofty romantic idealism, characteristic of the William S. Hart screen image, that makes a liar of Keno Bates. In an act that almost causes his death, Keno falsifies the circumstances surrounding the death of a thief in order to prevent the man's sister from knowing about his dishonor. This is the last of a series of two-reelers that Hart made before beginning feature-length westerns for the newly-formed Triangle Film Corporation, still under Ince's supervision. "Here," writes Richard Griffith, "the techniques of the western can be seen in mid-development, with film devices taking on increasing dramatic significance: 'fades' are concerted with the action, close-ups show us what the characters, as distinct from the audience, see, and the flashback is used with easy confidence." This is a reissue print, bearing the title **The Last Card**.

THE MARTYRS OF THE ALAMO

November 4, 1915. U.S.A.
Triangle-Fine Arts. Directed by William Christy Cabanne. With Sam De Grasse, Walter Long, Alfred Paget.
74 min. B&W. Silent. 18 fps.

This historical spectacle film concerns the events of 1835–36 in Mexico that resulted in the battle of the Alamo and led to the formation of the state of Texas. It was probably inspired by the success of **The Birth of a Nation** earlier in the same year and was produced by Griffith's own Fine Arts Company, but it is doubtful that he was in any way involved in the production since he was then fully occupied with **Intolerance** (1916). It has all the action and spectacle of a Griffith film and the same attempt to be authentic in all the details of the history it tells. However, trying to place the motive for the conflict on Mexican insults to American womanhood is perhaps not sufficient explanation for what actually happened. There are impressive long shots and battle scenes and a particularly startling shot of the dead body of James Bowie (played by Alfred Paget) with two bayonets impaled in his chest. The film appeals to Texan patriotism in its finale with flags dissolving into flags. In the end, it lacks both the individual characterization and the emotion that gives Griffith's own films such conviction.

RUMPELSTILTSKIN

1915. U.S.A.
New York Motion Picture Company. Produced by Thomas H. Ince. Based on Grimm's fairy tale "Lumber Leg." With Clyde Tracy, Elizabeth Burbridge, J. Barney Sherry.
57 min. B&W. Silent. 18 fps.

In the first decade of cinema, fairy tales were popular as subject matter because their stories were part of the common cultural knowledge of adults and children alike, and all could enjoy seeing them visualized without the need for an integrated narrative style that was not yet known. When Thomas Ince made this fairy tale in 1915, they were no longer as fashionable. **Rumpelstiltskin** was intended for children, and its distributor announced it as the first in a series of children's films. Based on Grimm's tale of the wicked dwarf who covets the miller's daughter and convinces the king

that she is capable of spinning straw into gold, it is an imaginative, well-designed production that makes use of the camera tricks of the early cinema, adding to its old-fashioned look in 1915.

THE TAKING OF LUKE MCVANE (THE FUGITIVE)

1915. U.S.A.
New York Motion Picture Company. Produced by Thomas H. Ince. Directed by William S. Hart. With Hart, Enid Markey, Clifford Smith.
29 min. B&W. Silent. 18 fps.

After shooting a man in a saloon quarrel, Luke McVane becomes an outlaw and flees the sheriff and his posse. When the sheriff is wounded, McVane refuses to abandon him, and dies defending him from an Indian attack. Such is the behavior of a Good-Bad Man in western mythology, a man who must follow the code of the frontier. William S. Hart was not the first Good-Bad Man, but he was the best, his noble features forcing belief in his simple feelings. He shared with Thomas Ince a desire for increased authenticity in details such as costume, props, landscape, handling of horses and cattle. His firm belief in the heroic frontier aided him in giving conviction to his films, many of them classic renditions of the genre and its myths. The Museum's prints carry the reissue title of **The Fugitive**.

CENERE

1916. Italy.
Ambrosio-Caesar-Film. Directed by Febo Mari, Arturo Ambrosio. Script by Eleanora Duse, Febo Mari, from the play by Grazia Deledda. With Eleanora Duse, Febo Mari. English titles.
45 min. B&W. Silent. 18 fps.

Cenere is the moving story of a poor woman who commits suicide because, through a misunderstanding, she thinks she has ruined her son's marriage into good society. Although the great Duse was later to regret that her only screen appearance was in such an inconsequential vehicle, it is clear that the vehicle is redeemed by the appropriateness and transparent honesty of her performance. Unlike many of her contemporaries (Bernhardt is one example), Duse knew what film demands and, correspondingly, gave one of the great film performances. (For an excerpt, see **Great Actresses of the Past** [1911–16].)

CIVILIZATION

1916. U.S.A.
Thomas H. Ince. Directed by Raymond

B. West and Irvin Willat. Script by C. Gardner Sullivan. Photographed by Irvin Willat. With Herschel Mayall, Howard Hickman, Enid Markey.
95 min. B&W. Silent. 18 fps.

Like **Intolerance** (1916), this picture consisted of an already completed feature (**He Who Returned** [1916]) to which new material was added. Ince's desire to rival Griffith is evident but the film has more important sources. Just before America's entry into World War I, the country was more or less politically polarized. Ince's film is an apt rendering of the ideas and sentiments of the pacifist side. It is a superproduction on a vast scale, an allegory about the ambitions of the ruler of a mythical 20th-century country that brings about war, carnage, and the starvation of civilians, while opposed by a secret army of women pledged to end the fighting. The production includes, in addition to massive battle scenes, visions of heaven and hell and the appearance of the Christ figure. The editing is economical and functional, and the scope is impressive although, lacking the intimacy of the Griffith spectacles, the film is remarkably impersonal. This version of the film is the 1931 reedited version, but is silent. The original ran about 130 minutes.

HER DEFIANCE

January 14, 1916. U.S.A.
Universal. Directed by Cleo Madison and Joe King. Script by Harvey Gates. With Cleo Madison, Willis Marks, Edward Hearn.
23 min. B&W. Silent. 18 fps.

Cleo Madison's career began as an actress for Universal Studios. By 1916, however, she was directing and starring in her own two-reel productions. **Her Defiance** is noteworthy for its own defiance of thematic taboos and its avoidance of a stereotypical portrayal of women. It concerns a young girl (played by Madison) who becomes pregnant and believes herself abandoned by her lover. She refuses to comply with her brother's plans to have her marry a rich old man, and runs away from her wedding. Instead, she bears her illegitimate child and goes to work as a cleaning lady in order to support it. Madison's technique is, in general, conventional; but one sequence stands out for its novelty. When the girl finally encounters the father of her child and he explains to her his apparently irresponsible behavior, Madison mattes out part of the frame and superimposes a flashback scene to illustrate the man's verbal account. Thus, rather than intercut be-

INTOLERANCE (1916)

tween moments of the past and the present, Madison maintains them both within the borders of the frame. It is a survival of early cinema style; see *Fireside Reminiscences* (1908).

HIS BITTER PILL

1916. U.S.A.
Triangle-Keystone. Produced by Mack Sennett. Directed by Fred Fishback. With Mack Swain, Louella Maxam, Edgar Kennedy.
26 min. B&W. Silent. 18 fps.

Given the great popularity of the western genre and especially those William S. Hart made for the Ince studio, the temptation of Mack Sennett to satirize it could not be resisted. Ince's films were the third division of Triangle; the other two sides of the company were composed of Griffith's Fine Arts productions and Sennett's Keystone comedies. *His Bitter Pill* is apparently a genuine western, complete with heroic sheriff, the girl he loves, a villain, and hard riding; but it is seen through an ingeniously distorted lens, and the values are consistently overemphasized or misplaced. Mack Swain does a delicious bit of work satirizing the nobility of the William S. Hart hero.

INTOLERANCE

August 4, 1916. U.S.A.
Wark Producing Corporation. Produced, written, and directed by D. W. Griffith. Photographed by G. W. (Billy) Bitzer. Assistant cameraman: Karl Brown. Music arrangement by Joseph Carl Breil and D. W. Griffith. With Mae Marsh, Robert Harron, Howard Gaye, Margery Wilson, Constance Talmadge, Lillian Gish.
170 min. B&W. (Also available in a color version.) Silent. 18 fps.

Intolerance is considered among the formal masterpieces of the cinema and has exercised enormous influence, particularly in post-revolutionary Russia, where it was closely studied. Before the release of *The Birth of a Nation* (1915), Griffith had almost completed a new film, *The Mother and the Law* (1919), and when he returned from the openings of *Birth* he decided to make it a part of a larger work, interweaving it with three parallel stories of other times: modern industrial strikes and slum life contrasted with 16th-century persecution, ancient Babylon, and the Calvary. The whole was to serve as a mighty sermon against hypocrisy. The complexity of the structure baffled the audiences of its time and it was as great a failure as *Birth*

had been a great success. Time has brought a greater appreciation of it. Griffith's own words describe it well: "The stories begin like four currents looked at from a hilltop. At first the four currents flow apart, slowly and quietly. But as they flow, they grow nearer and nearer together, and faster and faster, until in the end, in the last act, they mingle in one mighty river of expressed emotion." Our printing material comes from an original nitrate tinted print.

MACK SENNETT PROGRAM II

1916–20. U.S.A.
Produced by Mack Sennett.
Total program: 76 min. B&W. Silent. 18 fps.

A Clever Dummy and *Astray from the Steerage* are also available individually.

HIS BREAD AND BUTTER

1916.
Triangle-Keystone. Directed by Edward Cline, assisted by Hank Mann. Script by Hank Mann. Photographed by K. G. Maclean. With Hank Mann, Slim Summerville, Peggy Pearce, the Keystone Cops.
25 min.

A CLEVER DUMMY

July 15, 1917.
Triangle-Keystone. Directed by Herman Raymaker in collaboraton with Ferris Hartman and Robert Kerr. Photographed by Elgin Lessley. With Ben Turpin, Chester Conklin.
23 min.

ASTRAY FROM THE STEERAGE

1920.
Paramount. Directed by Frank Powell. With Billy Bevan, Louise Fazenda.
28 min.

His Bread and Butter is a classic Sennett ballet of movement. The plot is of little importance in this dizzy whirl of happenings. Hank Mann is an incompetent waiter in a restaurant where his pretty wife gets a job as a cashier and attracts the attention of the proprietor. Somehow it all ends up in the usual Keystone Cops chase sequence. In the opening scene, Mann says goodbye to his wife in the morning and by means of reversed film and editing he flies backward through the air into a streetcar, out the other side, and lands in an open car beside an indignant matron. The rhythm and pace are precise, the laws of logic are disrupted with perfect aplomb.

There is no reason for the scene beyond its own beautifully ridiculous nature. *A Clever Dummy* stars the little cross-eyed Ben Turpin, impersonating a mechanical dummy, or robot, in order to be near the woman he loves. When he is discovered, he becomes the object of a typical Sennett chase, riding a motorcycle through brick walls and on railroad tracks. Turpin could make vulgar gestures or execute a classical dance routine with equal elegance, grace, and precision. He seemed to feel no pain or to be disturbed by any rules of propriety. In his own narrow specialties, he was the best performer to come out of the Sennett school. In *Astray from the Steerage*, the solemn experience of going through U.S. immigration procedures falls prey to Sennett's burlesque. The officials are quite mad, the process is entirely surrealistic, as it may have seemed to bewildered immigrants with little or no English at their command. When Billy Bevan is given a physical examination, they spin him upside down in a chair until he becomes only a blur. When they remember to stop him, his giddiness is expressed by an image of the entire scene revolving, followed by a superimposition with Bevan at the center while the room spins around him. Finally, returning to an objective camera view, Bevan executes a masterful little dance of imbalance.

THE MYSTERY OF THE LEAPING FISH

June 11, 1916. U.S.A.
Triangle-Keystone. Directed by John Emerson. Script by Tod Browning. With Douglas Fairbanks, Bessie Love.
28 min. B&W. Silent. 18 fps.

Though Fairbanks was originally signed on as a more restrained actor of polite stage comedy, his comic and acrobatic agility became so evident that Griffith is said to have advised him to enter the Sennett studios if he wanted to remain in films. This picture is a burlesque of detective fiction with an absurd plot, much caricature, and a dizzying pace. Fairbanks plays a dope-addicted Sherlock Holmes, uncovering a gang of smugglers who use the inflated rubber beach toys as a means of bringing in their drugs. Later Hollywood drug tragedies led to the subject being treated seriously and then banned from the screen by the Motion Picture Production Code, but here it is strictly slapstick comedy.

REACHING FOR THE MOON

November 18, 1917. U.S.A.

Douglas Fairbanks Pictures. Directed by John Emerson. Script by John Emerson and Anita Loos. Photographed by Victor Fleming and Sam Landers. With Douglas Fairbanks, Eileen Percy.
70 min. B&W. Silent. 18 fps.

Douglas Fairbanks appeared in a series of breezy satires on contemporary fads, embodying the boundless optimism of the average American and his faith in physical culture and success in business. Here he is seen as a button-counter clerk who dreams of hobnobbing with royalty. In the dream he himself becomes royal with nightmarish results until he awakens to realize that being ordinary is best. In addition to poking fun at taking on the snobbery of association with royalty, the comedy satirizes New Thought, a current fad concerning the power of mental concentration over physical events. Vigorous pace and infectious enthusiasm drive the film forward with the energy that made Fairbanks a screen star admired the world over.

TEDDY AT THE THROTTLE

1917. U.S.A.
Triangle-Keystone. Produced by Mack Sennett. Directed by Clarence Badger, assisted by Burt Lund. Photographed by J. C. Bitzer. With Bobbie Vernon, Gloria Swanson, Wallace Beery.
22 min. B&W. Silent. 18 fps.

This Sennett comedy, among the last he contributed to the Triangle association, is an amusing burlesque melodrama in the *East Lynne* tradition. There is a rascally guardian who steals orphans' fortunes, a heroine who is chained to the railroad tracks, and a rescue by a heroic dog, all carried to ridiculous extremes. A terrifying storm includes rain flowing horizontally. Teddy, the marvelous Keystone dog, performs impossible deeds. Bobby Vernon, only about seventeen years old here, had a long and varied career as a slapstick comic. Beery and Swanson had met in the Chicago studios of Essanay and were briefly married before they went their separate ways to stardom, Beery as villain and character actor, Swanson as the most glittering symbol of twenties glamour. Clarence Badger became one of the top directors of comedy in the silent era.

WILD AND WOOLLY

July 5, 1917. U.S.A.
Douglas Fairbanks Pictures. Directed by John Emerson. Script by Anita Loos based on a story by H. B. Carpenter. Photographed by Victor Fleming. With Douglas Fairbanks, Eileen Percy.
67 min. B&W. Silent. 18 fps.

At the end of 1916, Douglas Fairbanks formed his own production company and signed a distribution contract with Paramount-Artcraft. The team that had contributed so much to his success, John Emerson and screenwriter Anita Loos, went with him. This film is a satire on westerns, not a burlesque as in *His Bitter Pill* (1916), but a self-mocking view of America's belief in the western heroic myth. Fairbanks plays a restless young railroad clerk with romantic misconceptions based on reading dime novels and movies. The inhabitants of Bitter Creek play a joke on him by staging an act to match his ideas of the west. With a double twist, the pretense turns into reality when a genuine holdup and Indian attack take place, and Fairbanks turns out a hero. His cheerful ingenuousness, high spirits, and energetic athletics make this a lively and amusing film.

CARMEN (GYPSY BLOOD) (Escape from prison sequence) (1918). *See* Film Study

FATHER SERGIUS (OTETS SERGEI)

1918. Russia.
Yermoliev Company. Directed by Yakov Protazanov. Script by Protazanov and Alexander Volkov, based on a story by Leo Tolstoy. With Ivan Mozhukhin, Natalie Lissenko. English titles.
104 min. B&W. Silent. 18 fps.

Film was introduced to Russia by French production companies. Gradually native talents emerged and the country's great literary and theatrical traditions supplied material. *Father Sergius*, the last and most important film made before the October revolution, shows signs of a loosening of censorship. Based on a Tolstoy story that was considered rather scandalous when it first appeared, it is the story of an officer at the court of Nikolas I who determines to enter a monastery after a broken love affair. Along the way, he encounters many temptations, and reveals the corruption at the court and in the church. In intensity of character and emotion, *Father Sergius* equalled the best of Swedish production at the time, and in it Ivan Mozhukhin gave one of his great performances as the prince turned monk, eternally pursued by the desires of the flesh. Protazanov, chief director of the Yermoliev studio since its founding in 1914, used actual settings to give authenticity to his film and made a break with the staginess of much of the French-influenced Russian cinema.

Pola Negri in MADAME DU BARRY (1919)

HEARTS OF THE WORLD

April 4, 1918. U.S.A.
D. W. Griffith Corporation. Directed by
D. W. Griffith. Script by M. Gaston de
Tolignac (pseudonym of D. W. Griffith). Photographed by G. W. (Billy)
Bitzer. Technical supervision by Erich
von Stroheim. With Lillian and Dorothy Gish, Robert Harron, George Siegmann.
147 min. B&W. Silent. 18 fps.

This propaganda film was intended to
arouse America's fighting spirit, but
World War I was nearly over before it
was ready for release. Distributed later
in a cut-down version, its reputation did
not long survive the war, in part because its direct appeal to the emotions
was no longer wanted. Today, leaving
aside the propaganda about Hun atrocities, it can be seen as one of Griffith's
major films. The battle scenes are stirring, though Griffith wisely decided to
portray the horrors of war chiefly
through the view of a few individuals in
a small village that changes hands as the
fortunes of war sweep over it. This decision resulted in some memorable portrayals: Dorothy Gish wearing a black
wig in a comedy role that led to her long
career in a successful comedy series;
Lillian Gish trying to guide her confused grandfather to safety as the village is bombarded; and the unforgettable image of Lillian wandering in a
daze through a battlefield, wedding dress

clutched in her arms, searching for the
body of her lover.

MICKEY

December 1918. U.S.A.
Mabel Normand Feature Films. Produced by Mack Sennett. Directed by F.
Richard Jones. With Mabel Normand.
102 min. B&W. Silent. 18 fps.

Mickey is a tomboy orphan raised by an
old western prospector and finds herself a terrible misfit when sent to live
with her wealthy aunt in the east. Mabel
Normand's first feature comedy, made
independently in late 1916, found no
bookings until the end of 1918, when it
went on to become her biggest success.
Mickey starts out to be a "more genteel"
comedy, its story akin to those starring
the adored Mary Pickford, but its sentimental ideas soon go by the board to
make way for Mabel's stunts and the
maddest of chases in the customary logic-defying Sennett world. Mabel Normand was sometimes called the female
equivalent to Chaplin, and some of her
mannerisms do indeed recall his, like the
flapping hand at the end of a stiff arm
and the impulsive hugging of her knees.

A MODERN MUSKETEER (Extant reels: Opening)

January 3, 1918. U.S.A.
Douglas Fairbanks Pictures. Directed by

Allan Dwan. Script by A. Dwan, based
on *D'Artagnan of Kansas* by E. P. Lyle,
Jr. Photographed by Victor Fleming.
With Douglas Fairbanks, Marjorie Daw,
Kathleen Kirkham, ZaSu Pitts.
42 min. B&W. Silent. 18 fps.

This film survives as the first three reels
of a five-reel film, the remainder having perished through chemical deterioration. It provides a link between Fairbanks's American comedies and his
subsequent cloak-and-dagger costume
romances. It was, perhaps, a trial balloon. A Kansas boy seeks to emulate
D'Artagnan in acrobatic sequences in his
own life; the delicious "vision" sequences predict *The Three Musketeers*
of three years later. Fairbanks supplies
one of his best routines as he playfully
uses the architecture of a Kansas town
as his private gymnasium, to the general annoyance of the inhabitants.

THE OUTLAW AND HIS WIFE (BERG-EJVIND OCH HANS HUSTRU)

January 1, 1918. Sweden.
Svenska Biografteatern. Directed by
Victor Sjöström. Script by Sjöström and
Sam Ask from the play by Johan Sigurjonsson. Photographed by John Julius (pseudonym of Julius Jaenzon). With
Sjöström, Edith Erastoff. English titles.
130 min. B&W. Silent. 18 fps.

Set in Iceland, this famous film is about
a thief who attempts to escape his fate,
and the woman who abandons her home
to follow him into the wilderness.
Sjöström's use of the northern light, the
poetry he found in landscape and
weather, the skill with which he handled parallel editing and flashbacks, the
restrained acting style, and a more sophisticated handling of character than
found in other films of the period made
his work a revelation. Sjöström's innovations made Swedish films a major force
in world cinema at this time. So striking
is the outdoor photography in this film
that Louis Delluc wrote that, in addition
to the outlaw (played by Sjöström himself) and his wife, the third leading
character is the landscape.

BLIND HUSBANDS

December 7, 1919. U.S.A.
Universal Pictures. Written and directed by Erich von Stroheim. Photographed by Ben F. Reynolds. With von
Stroheim, Francellia Billington, Sam de
Grasse, Gibson Gowland.
98 min. B&W. Silent. 18 fps.

Before directing his first film, the Austrian-born Erich von Stroheim had
worked under D. W. Griffith as an ac-

tor and assistant director. **Blind Husbands** is about a triangle, composed of a preoccupied husband, neglected wife, and a predatory "love pirate" (played by von Stroheim), vacationing in the Austrian Alps. It was immediately evident that the new director had an unusual skill in handling classic cinema techniques and a particularly acid view of human relationships. He embellished the plot with such significant and often bizarre detail and displayed such visual penetration that the result is fantastic and memorable melodrama. Extravagant in his demands for perfection, unconventional in his disregard for what had become the established Hollywood production methods, von Stroheim created a number of films which were never released in the form he wanted. His first film was no exception—he did not intend the happy ending.

BROKEN BLOSSOMS

May 13, 1919. U.S.A.
D. W. Griffith Corporation. Directed by D. W. Griffith. Script by D. W. Griffith based on "The Chink and the Child" by Thomas Burke. Photographed by G. W. (Billy) Bitzer. Special effects by Hendrick Sartov. With Lillian Gish, Richard Barthelmess, Donald Crisp.

Available in three versions: B&W, silent; color, silent; or color, sound. All 92 min., 18 fps (see further explanation below).

The search for the elements of film art that took place in the twenties led filmmakers to neglect the natural world in favor of the studio-made film, where it was easier to control these ingredients, particularly settings and lighting, more precisely. Following his big spectacle films, Griffith turned in this direction. He changed from the large canvas to this allegorical story of a waif of the London slums, loved by a gentle and idealistic Chinese boy, and beaten by the brutal Battling Burrows. **Broken Blossoms** is small in scale, with few characters, filmed in the artificial settings of the studio and characterized by its poetic atmosphere and psychological intensity. It was immediately influential on a worldwide basis. Audiences were overwhelmed by this new kind of film and especially by its intimate acting style. Filmmakers took note of its rhythms: a slow cadence, harmonious images, shimmering lighting, soft-focus, contrasted with sequences of quick cutting, disordered compositions, sharp lens, stark lighting, and bare sets. Together these served to express the differences between an

idealistic world and a savage, uncivilized one. Our recently acquired color prints are taken directly from the beautifully tinted original nitrate footage. The film may be ordered silent, or with orchestral accompaniment, including Gaylord Carter at the organ, from the original score by Louis Gottschalk and D. W. Griffith. This sound version must be projected at 18 frames per second, with the sound turned on, using a projector that has the technical capability to play sound at this slower speed.

HIS MAJESTY THE AMERICAN

September 28, 1919. U.S.A.
Douglas Fairbanks Pictures. Directed and written by Joseph Henabery. Photographed by Victor Fleming and Glen MacWilliams. With Douglas Fairbanks, Marjorie Daw, Lillian Langdon.
114 min. B&W. Silent. 18 fps.

The first stage of Douglas Fairbanks's screen career consisted of a series of comedies of American life in which he played what Alistair Cooke characterized as "The Popular Philosopher," an ingenuous fellow imbued with boundless energy and optimism. A number of the comedies included the elements of action and fantasy, as in this example, which would soon dominate his work in a series of swashbuckling adventure films. Here Fairbanks plays a wealthy and adventurous New Yorker whose only unhappiness is that he never knew his parents. His escapades as the rescuer of a woman in a skyscraper and the captor of Pancho Villa are intercut with a secondary plot about political revolution in a mythical kingdom. The two story lines merge when Fairbanks is revealed to be the heir to the throne. Fairbanks's athletic prowess comes to the fore in a chase sequence in which he eludes his pursuers by sliding down

roofs, jumping across buildings, and swinging on flagpoles.

MADAME DU BARRY (PASSION)

September 18, 1919. Germany.
Union-Ufa. Directed by Ernst Lubitsch. Script by Fred Orbing, Hans Kraly. Photographed by Theodor Sparkühl. With Pola Negri, Emil Jannings, Harry Liedtke. English titles.
124 min. B&W. Silent. 18 fps.

Madame Du Barry is a historical spectacle film about the rise of Du Barry from milliner to mistress of Louis XV and her execution at the hands of the French Revolution. It led the way to what was to be known as "the foreign invasion" of Hollywood in the twenties. Lubitsch's historical spectacle films differ from the Italian examples in focusing on the human emotions of the major historical figures. It seemed to audiences that Lubitsch brought history to life. They differ from Griffith's spectacles, which portrayed the life of ordinary people affected by historical events. Lubitsch handles the people in the great mass scenes as decorative elements, moving them about in patterns according to the principles of the Max Reinhardt stage spectacles. To American audiences, Pola Negri appeared to be a new kind of actress, full of passion and fire. She was soon brought to Hollywood, where she became the personification of the glamorous and temperamental star of the twenties.

MALE AND FEMALE

November 30, 1919. U.S.A.
Paramount-Artcraft. Directed by Cecil B. De Mille. Script by Jeanie Macpherson, from J. M. Barrie's *The Admirable Crichton*. With Gloria Swanson, Thomas Meighan, Lila Lee, Bebe Daniels.

Gloria Swanson in MALE AND FEMALE (1919)

133 min. B&W. Silent. 18 fps.

Male and Female represents the American feature film as it was to develop in the twenties, forecasting with great prescience and impact the postwar revolution in tastes and manners. At the dawn of the Roaring Twenties, De Mille began to make smart, sophisticated comedy romances, set against a background of beauty and luxury, with heroines who were neither wicked vamps nor innocents, but believable women whose love affairs were slightly daring. Intimate scenes took place in bedrooms and bathrooms, gorgeous with the make-believe trappings of the very wealthy. Flashback sequences to an earlier time of history—here, to ancient Babylon—served to point a moral. This version of the Barrie play *The Admirable Crichton*, about the role reversals occurring when an aristocratic English girl and her family are shipwrecked on an uninhabited island with the competent family butler, allows De Mille to display his visual wit and points to the Chaplin and Lubitsch comedies later in the decade.

THE MOTHER AND THE LAW

1919. U.S.A.
D. W. Griffith Corporation. Produced, written, and directed by D. W. Griffith. Photographed by G. W. (Billy) Bitzer. Music by Louis F. Gottschalk. With Mae Marsh, Robert Harron, Miriam Cooper, Walter Long.
104 min. B&W. Silent. 18 fps.

Production on this film was nearly completed in 1914 and early 1915 when Griffith decided to make it part of ***Intolerance*** (1916). After the failure of the latter, he recut it, added new material, and released it as a separate feature in 1919. However, this film is primarily a product of 1914. It may well be a stronger film on its own than as it appeared when interwoven into the great canvas of ***Intolerance***. It represents Griffith at his best in evoking powerful feeling by all the compositional means he had at his command. The forces of capitalism and institutionalized morality bear down hard on the lives of the poor. After a factory strike leaves them unemployed, some poor people drift to the city, where they encounter the poverty and crime of the slums. A baby is taken away from its mother, a young man is unjustly sentenced to be hung for murder, and a last-minute ride to the rescue brings the governor's pardon.

A ROMANCE OF HAPPY VALLEY

January 26, 1919. U.S.A.
Paramount-Artcraft. Directed by D. W. Griffith. Script by Capt. Victor Marier (pseudonym of D. W. Griffith). Photographed by G. W. (Billy) Bitzer. With Lillian Gish, Robert Harron.
80 min. B&W. Silent. 18 fps.

In what he described as a "short story series" begun in 1918, and following the failure of ***Intolerance*** (1916), Griffith turned backward toward the simpler narratives of his Biograph days. *A Romance of Happy Valley* is a look at his own youth in rural Kentucky. It is a charming slight comedy about the boy who leaves home to seek his fortune in the big city with all its temptations, and returns, successful beyond dreams, to rescue his family from poverty and marry the quaint country girl who has waited faithfully for him. A similar plot was used in ***The Son's Return*** in 1909. The portrayal of backwoods life and the narrow attitudes of the southern revivalist church could have come directly from Griffith's own experience. If one takes the boy's success as a parallel to Griffith's own in the movie business, it is a most amusing symbol: employed in a toy factory, all his effort is directed toward making a toy frog that can swim.

THE TREASURE OF ARNE (HERR ARNES PENGAR)

1919. Sweden.
Svenska Biografteatern. Directed by Mauritz Stiller. Script by John Julius (pseudonym of Julius Jaenzon) from a story by Selma Lagerlöf. With Hjalmar Selander, Rickard Lund, Mary Johnson.
83 min. B&W. Silent. 18 fps.

Based on one of the Selma Lagerlöf novels, this historical film is set in the 16th century. Three mercenary soldiers escape from prison and burn down the house of Sir Arne, killing the whole family except for an adopted daughter, for a treasure chest. The ship in which they intend to escape to Scotland is delayed by the frozen sea. The daughter having fallen in love with one of them, finds out he is a murderer, and kills herself to prevent his escape from arrest. Stiller's greatest film is a rich tapestry of characters, sets, costumes, and landscape. The snow and ice are used as symbols of guilt and imprisonment. The heroine's death is followed by a memorable funeral procession of women, filing in a line across the frozen sea, as behind them, miraculously, the thaw comes and the seas open. In theme, in its foreboding atmosphere, and in its snow-covered landscape, the film exemplifies the national character of the Swedish silent cinema.

TRUE HEART SUSIE

June 1, 1919. U.S.A.
Paramount-Artcraft. Directed by D. W. Griffith. Script by Griffith based on a story by Marion Fremont. Photographed by G. W. (Billy) Bitzer. With Lillian Gish, Robert Harron.
86 min. B&W. Silent. 18 fps.

Another in the series of modest pictures Griffith made in 1918–19, this one recalls the country village as it was before the Jazz Age, where the opportunities were few, the choices limited, and the outlook narrow. In such a place, the ambitious ones left home; in doing so, most Americans felt, they left behind certain irreplaceable rural values. The film has the peculiarly luminous quality of a time remembered. The innocent and self-sacrificing Susie anonymously supports her childhood sweetheart's

Douglas Fairbanks and Herbert Grimwood in WHEN THE CLOUDS ROLL BY (1919)

going away to school and when he returns ordained a minister, loses him to a more modern woman. A heroine so innocent and selfless could exist only in the past, but as Lillian Gish portrays her, she has great depth of character: she grows through tragedy from a funny, happy adolescent to a mature and dignified woman. Her performance, and the visual poetry of landscape, light, and weather make this film one of Griffith's minor masterpieces—and for some present-day viewers their favorite Griffith film.

WHEN THE CLOUDS ROLL BY

December 29, 1919. U.S.A.
Douglas Fairbanks Pictures. Directed by Victor Fleming. Script by Tom Geraghty, Lewis Weadon, based on a story by Douglas Fairbanks. Photographed by William McGann, Harry Thorpe. With Douglas Fairbanks, Kathleen Clifford. 93 min. B&W. Silent. 18 fps.

This hilarious Fairbanks comedy satirizes what was then the popular conception of the new science of psychoanalysis. The star plays a superstitious young businessman who is the unknowing subject of a psychological experiment to discover how much the human mind can withstand. In dream sequences, we see the food Fairbanks has failed to digest bouncing around in his stomach and then pursuing him. A slow-motion dream chase articulates Fairbanks's exquisite physical coordination. A flood sequence gives the ebullient Fairbanks character a big swimming pool in which to display his diving skill and the rooftop of a floating church as an appropriate place for a wedding ceremony.

THE CABINET OF DR. CALIGARI (DAS CABINET DES DR. CALIGARI)

January 1920. Germany.
Decla-Bioscop. Produced by Erich Pommer. Directed by Robert Wiene. Script by Carl Mayer from a story by Hans Janowitz. Art Direction by Hermann Warm, Walter Röhrig, and Walter Riemann. Photographed by Willy Hameister. With Werner Krauss, Conrad Veidt, Lil Dagover. English titles. 72 min. B&W. Silent. 18 fps.

This fantastic nightmare film was the catalyst for aesthetic debates all over the world. It is the first film to realize the tenets of German Expressionism as it had developed in literature, theater, and the arts. It is the story of Dr. Caligari, head of an insane asylum, who directs his somnambulist victim to commit

Lil Dagover and Werner Krauss in THE CABINET OF DR. CALIGARI (1920)

crimes and himself ends up in a straightjacket. In a framing story, it is only a tale told by a madman. The special qualities of the film are primarily linked to the production design, the product of a group of artists associated with *Sturm.* The use of painted flats was a reversion to early cinema but the design was ultramodern in its deliberate distortions. The flatness is ameliorated by a perspective that destroys natural space and by the use of dramatic contrast lighting. The actors adapt stylized movement and gesture to suit this Expressionist style. Later films abandoned the painted backdrops but utilized light and shadow to create similar distortions and to suggest the mystery and horror that dominated Expressionist cinema. "Caligarism" entered the language.

THE CRADLE OF COURAGE

April 25, 1920. U.S.A.
Paramount-Artcraft. Directed by Lambert Hillyer. Script by Hillyer from a story by Frederick Bradbury. With William S. Hart, Gertrude Clair, Thomas Santschi. 74 min. B&W. Silent. 18 fps.

Hart's Good-Bad Man character is transferred intact to a rare nonwestern role. In this lively action film, made on location in San Francisco and filled with allusions to the postwar scene, Hart is a former crook reformed by the ennobling experience of fighting for his country in World War I. He returns home to become a policeman, torn between two sets of values, providing scope for another of the "soul-fights" familiar from the earlier Ince films. It contains an outright parody of white-haired Irish motherhood as conventionally portrayed on the silent screen: Gertrude Clair as Hart's mother throws him out of the house for becoming a cop.

EXCUSE MY DUST

1920. U.S.A.
Paramount-Artcraft. Directed by Sam Wood. Script by Will M. Ritchey based on "The Bear Trap" by Byron Morgan. With Wallace Reid, Ann Little, Theodore Roberts. 68 min. B&W. Silent. 18 fps.

Reid was another of the silent stars—like Hart and Fairbanks—who imprinted his style upon an entire series of films. He usually appeared in light comedy vehicles designed to show off his handsomeness, good humor, and off-hand acting technique. They were modest productions with a formula of romance and thrills (here he plays a racing-car driver) designed for an audience that came to see the star more than the story. This film is the sequel to **The Roaring Road** (1919), which launched Reid on a series of car-racing comedies, describing the tumultous competition of the early automobile industry and reflecting contemporary attitudes about big business and success.

THE GOLEM (DER GOLEM)

October 29, 1920. Germany.
Union-Ufa. Directed by Paul Wegener and Carl Boese. Script by Wegener. Photographed by Karl Freund. With Wegener, Albert Steinruck, Lyda Salmonova. English titles.
106 min. B&W. Silent. 18 fps.

The legend of the Golem, a creature made from clay by Rabbi Loew in 16th century Prague to defend the Jews in the ghetto against pograms, was filmed several times. Paul Wegener codirected and acted in a 1914 version as well as another in 1917. This is his most ambitious version, made with all the resources of the Ufa studio. The "monster without a soul" terrifies the multitudes, rebels against his creator, falls in love with the Rabbi's daughter, and is destroyed when a child removes the Star of David from his chest. The enormous looming sets by Hans Poelzig were inspired by the medieval architec-

Paul Wegener in THE GOLEM (1920)

ture of Prague. Special lighting and the composition of crowd scenes contribute to the haunting atmosphere of this fantasy. The hulking figure of the Golem, played by Wegener, influenced the portrayal of the monster in **Frankenstein** (1931).

HIGH AND DIZZY

July 11, 1920. U.S.A.
Produced and directed by Hal Roach. Script by Frank Terry. Photographed by Walter Lundin. With Harold Lloyd, Mildred Davis.
30 min. B&W. Silent. 18 fps.

Harold Lloyd's slapstick comedies were the most popular to come from the Hal Roach Studio. This is a transition film between slapstick and the situation comedy in which he achieved his greatest heights. He has already adopted the horn-rimmed glasses, and begun to develop his comic character of a timid and naive young man endowed with the ambition and optimism of the twenties. Here he is a new doctor beginning medical practice. He falls in love with a girl who wanders into the waiting room and gets drunk drinking up a batch of home brew that is popping its corks. In pursuit of the girl, he ends up out on the window ledge of a high building: the early manifestation of the comic thrills he would make his specialty in **Never Weaken** (1921) and **Safety Last** (1923).

THE MARK OF ZORRO

November 29, 1920. U.S.A.
Douglas Fairbanks Pictures. Directed by Fred Niblo. Based on "The Curse of Capistrano" by Johnson McCulley. Photographed by William McGann and Harry Thorpe. With Douglas Fairbanks, Marguerite de la Motte.
90 min. B&W. Silent. 24 fps.

This film created the prototype for the comic-strip superhero of the forties. Fairbanks, with his superb physical powers, was almost superhuman in real life. Like Batman, his nearest imitator, the character of Zorro has a double identity: the weary, languorous, and foolish Don Diego stands in comic contrast to the masked Zorro who conquers injustice and rights wrongs with typical Fairbanksian zest and athletic grace. Zorro's mission is to protect the California landowners, in the time when it was still part of Mexico, from the ruthless militia of the governor. For the double role here, Fairbanks divides up his screen character so that the buffoon is implicit in the hero. This was the beginning of Fairbanks's swashbuckling adventure films.

THE MOLLYCODDLE

June 14, 1920. U.S.A.
Douglas Fairbanks Pictures. Directed by Victor Fleming. Script by Tom Geraghty from a story by Harold Mac-Grath. Photographed by William McGann and Harry Thorpe. With Fairbanks, Ruth Renick, Wallace Beery.
94 min. B&W. Silent. 18 fps.

In his third film for United Artists, Fairbanks burlesques the effete European playboy, wearing a monocle, using a cigar-holder, and carrying a cane. In fact, the character is a fifth-generation American who has been brought up in Europe: all he needs to recapture the virile spirit of his ancestors is to be returned to his native land. He ends up in the scenic landscape by way of pursuing an American girl aboard a yacht and being mistaken for a government agent on the trail of a diamond smuggler. The Hopi Indians appear in this film.

THE TOLL GATE

April 18, 1920. U.S.A.
Paramount-Artcraft. Directed by Lambert Hillyer. Script by William S. Hart and Hillyer. With William S. Hart, Anna Q. Nilsson.
77 min. B&W. Silent. 18 fps.

One of William S. Hart's finest and most moving westerns, and nearly his last. In the changing ethics of the Jazz Age, Hart's depiction of moral conflicts in an authentic portrayal of the Old West were no longer wanted. The public preferred the simple fantasy and action of Tom Mix westerns. In this film, Black Deering, a typical Good-Bad Man role for Hart, is an outlaw who wants to quit his gang but is trapped during a train robbery. Escaping and on the run, Deering saves a baby from drowning at the risk of his own capture. The Sheriff clearly admires this survivor of the old frontier morality, and after Deering has proved his bravery once more, lets him ride away across the frontier alone.

WAY DOWN EAST

September 3, 1920. U.S.A.
D. W. Griffith Corporation. Directed by D. W. Griffith. Script by Anthony Paul Kelly from a play by Lottie Blair Parker. Photographed by G. W. (Billy) Bitzer and Hendrick Sartov. With Lillian Gish, Richard Barthelmess.
154 min. B&W. Silent. 18 fps, or 104 min. (reissue version with music added, 24 fps.)

The stage melodrama on which this film is based was already laughably old-fashioned when Griffith bought the rights to it. Anna Moore is seduced and abandoned, her illegitimate child dies, and she finds work on a New England farm. When the truth comes out, the squire drives her out of the house in a raging blizzard and she nearly drowns on the ice floes of the river. The sentimentality of this film, it was thought, had little to do with the new era ushered in by 1920. But fine naturalistic acting by Lillian Gish, Griffith's ability to evoke feeling, and the ultimate in exciting last-minute rescues, made the film his most popular one after *The Birth of a Nation* (1915). It should be noted that Anna is not just a helpless victim: she is a vigorous spokeswoman protesting the double standard of treatment for men and women, and she wins her point.

THE BLOT

September 4, 1921. U.S.A.
Lois Weber Productions. Directed by Lois Weber. Photographed by Philip R. DuBois, Gordon Jennings. With Claire Windsor, Louis Calhern, Philip Hubbard, Margaret McWade.
104 min. B&W. Silent. 18 fps.

Lois Weber is one of the most important woman directors of the silent era, having made some 400 films between the years of 1908 and 1934. *The Blot* was filmed in Weber's own studios by the production company she formed in 1917 after leaving a successful career at Universal. Characteristic of Weber's films, *The Blot* deals with a social issue—the plight of intellectuals (college professors, ministers) in American society whose work is underpaid and accorded minimal status. Weber contrasts their struggle with the success of the *nouveau riche* merchant class. Significantly, she focuses on women and emphasizes how their economic destinies are determined by marriage. Weber's narrative style is static, depending little on the dynamic of parallel editing. Her concern is with psychology, and she stresses the point of view of female characters.

DESTINY (DER MÜDE TOD)

1921. Germany.
Decla-Bioscop. Directed by Fritz Lang. Script by Lang and Thea von Harbou. Photographed by Erich Nietschmann, Hermann Salfrank, Fritz Arno Wagner. Art Direction by Walter Röhrig, Hermann Warm, Robert Herlth. With Lil Dagover, Walter Janssen, Bernardt Götzke. English titles.
122 min. B&W. Silent. 18 fps.

Fritz Lang's gothic fantasy film consists of three fairy tales enclosed by the story of a girl who defies death to win back her lover. The figure of Fate tells her she may have her wish if she can save but one life that is doomed. She tries her best in tales set in a Moslem city, in Renaissance Venice, and in the ancient Chinese Empire. Lang creates a stylized, macabre atmosphere, using camera magic and extraordinary, bizarre sets, creatively lighted. There is a wall so large it fills the entire frame, with tiny figures standing before it; a flight of endless stairs; a huge dark space filled with thousands of flickering candles. Fairbanks saw this film in Europe and bought a print in order to study its special effects before he made *The Thief of Bagdad* (1924).

FIÈVRE

1921. France.
Alhambra-Film. Directed and written by Louis Delluc. Photographed by Alphonse Gibory, Lucas. With Eve Francis, Gaston Modot, Edmund Van Daële, Leon Moussinac. Titles are missing.
40 min. B&W. Silent. 18 fps.

Film enthusiast and theoretician Louis Delluc was the central force of French impressionist cinema. This film, inspired by *Broken Blossoms* (1919), creates an atmosphere of psychological tension in a seamy old waterfront cafe. A Corsican and his wife manage the cafe, which is patronized by sailors and their prostitutes. The woman keeps bar and dreams of her first love, a sailor who deserted her. He reappears with a Chinese wife who, he explains, cared for him in his illness. The sailors dance and drink, and passion and jealousy lead to violence and murder. The little Chinese girl is a fixed counterpoint in a frenzy of emotion. Delluc's interest in film rhythm as a component of the art of film is clearly expressed in the varying cadences evoked by the editing of *Fièvre*.

LEAVES FROM SATAN'S BOOK (BLADE AF SATANS BOG)

1921. Denmark.
Nordisk Film. Directed by Carl Theodor Dreyer. Script by Dreyer based on Marie Corelli's *The Sorrows of Satan*. Photographed by George Schneevoigt. With Helge Nissen, Clara Pontoppidan. English titles.
116 min. B&W. Silent. 18 fps.

Danish cinema played a leading role in world cinema during 1910–14. Based on the naturalistic style of the theater of Ibsen, these films emphasized the erotic and psychological more than action and concentrated on settings and atmos-

Dorothy (below) and Lillian Gish (above) in ORPHANS OF THE STORM (1921) (p. 58)

phere. Denmark's greatest director, Carl Dreyer, participated in this period as scriptwriter and editor, but by the time he directed his first film this early wave was over, and he remained nearly alone to extend the Danish film tradition abroad. This is his second film, begun in 1918 after a viewing of *Intolerance* (1916). While he does not intercut them, he also uses parallel stories through the ages to elaborate a single theme. The story tells of Satan's temptation of Judas, and subsequent episodes set in the Spanish Inquisition, the French Revolution, and the Russo-Finnish War of 1918 amplify the theme with tales of people tempted to betray their trust. This early film is already characteristic of Dreyer's emphasis on flat architectural spaces framing people and isolating faces, intensifying feeling and defining character.

THE NUT

March 19, 1921. U.S.A.
Douglas Fairbanks Pictures. Directed by Ted Reed. Script by Kenneth Davenport, William Parker, Lotta Woods. Photographed by William McGann, Harry Thorpe, Charles Warrington. Art Direction by Edward Langley. With Douglas Fairbanks, Marguerite de la

Motte.
86 min. B&W. Silent. 18 fps.

The Nut brings to an end the first phase of Fairbanks's career in the light comedies that burlesqued American fads. Here he parodies both American ingenuity and charitable "do-gooders." Fairbanks plays an inventor engaged to a girl enamored of a scheme to bring slum children into refined homes for a dose of moral uplift. The film opens with an animated sequence of the hero's machine, which is designed to save himself effort in getting bathed and dressed. The opening titles acknowledge his debt to Chaplin, but perhaps Chaplin's feeding machine in **Modern Times** (1936) owes a credit to Fairbanks as well. A chase sequence serves as a vehicle for Fairbanks's agility and acrobatic skill.

ORPHANS OF THE STORM

December 28, 1921. U.S.A.
D. W. Griffith Corporation. Directed by D. W. Griffith. Based on the play *The Two Orphans* by Adolphe D. Ennery. Photographed by Hendrick Sartov. With Lillian and Dorothy Gish, Monte Blue, Joseph Schildkraut.
176 min. B&W. Silent. 18 fps.

For this historical spectacle, Griffith set the events of the old melodrama *The Two Orphans* in the French Revolution. Two orphans are separated by events and hurled into the frenzy of the revolutionary mobs in the streets of Paris. They are reunited only after one of them has been rescued from the guillotine in the typical Griffith last-minute race. The first half is crammed with a murder,

kidnappings, orgies, duels, last-minute escapes, and the famous scene in which Lillian Gish hears her adopted blind sister singing as a beggar in the streets but cannot reach her. The second half shows the Revolution itself, the masses surging into streets and squares, and Lillian Gish caught up by them against her will. In several shots the top and bottom of the screen are masked, anticipating the wide-screen ratio.

THE PHANTOM CHARIOT (KÖRKARLEN)

January 1, 1921. Sweden.
Svensk Filmindustri. Directed by Victor Sjöström. Script from Selma Lagerlöf's novel *Thy Soul Shall Bear Witness*. With Sjöström, Astrid Holm, Hilda Borgström. English titles.
84 min. B&W. Silent. 18 fps.

The Phantom Chariot, made at the peak of the great period of Swedish silent cinema, met with a critical enthusiasm comparable only to that which met **Broken Blossoms** (1919), and like Griffith, Sjöström chose to make his film almost entirely within studio sets. The story is based on a Swedish legend that the last person to die each year must drive the chariot that collects the dead. When a drunken brawler dies at midnight New Year's Eve, the driver decides to take him back to life and give him the chance to correct his errors. The extraordinary beauty of the ghostly superimpositions and the complex flashback structure of this poetic allegory were much admired. F. W. Murnau saw it before he made his **Nosferatu** (1922), a darker and more chilling fantasy.

THE THREE MUSKETEERS

August 28, 1921. U.S.A.
Douglas Fairbanks Pictures. Directed by Fred Niblo. Script by Edward Knoblock, based on the novel by Alexandre Dumas. Photographed by Arthur Edeson. Art Direction by Edward Langley. With Fairbanks, Adolphe Menjou, Marguerite de la Motte.
172 min. B&W. Silent. 18 fps.

With this film, Fairbanks entered the phase of his career for which he is best known, the archetypical swashbuckling romance. He plays D'Artagnan, "the best swordsman in France," given the mission to recover the Queen's jewels from Buckingham in England and return with them to Paris before the King can discover they are gone. The film is an outstanding achievement in the construction of action scenes and in dynamic editing. Enough stunts have been crammed into the fight with the Cardinal's guard, lasting less than two minutes on the screen, to serve another filmmaker for an entire production. It is only the beginning for Fairbanks in this, his most popular film.

TOL'ABLE DAVID

November 21, 1921. U.S.A.
Inspiration Pictures. Directed by Henry King. Script by King and Edmund Goulding from "The Happy Life" by Joseph Hergesheimer. With Richard Barthelmess, Ernest Torrence, Gladys Hulette.
109 min. B&W. Silent. 18 fps.

This is the classic demonstration of American film narrative style, frequently cited by Pudovkin in his *Film Technique*. Into the poor but idyllic life of a poor tenant farmer and his family comes the violence and brutality of the outlaw Hatburns. The younger son grows to maturity when forced to act as head of the family and combat the evil doers. With brilliant disjunctive editing and expressive images, Henry King expands and compresses time, creates suspense, and conveys feeling in a manner worthy to be compared only to D. W. Griffith (who actually wrote the original adaption for this film, part of which was used in the final scenario). This is one of the few major American films of the twenties to be made on location away from the studio, using King's own native Virginia hills. Even today, this film has more emotional power than most of the famous films of the early twenties.

BLOOD AND SAND

August 15, 1922. U.S.A.
Paramount Pictures. Directed by Fred

Eugene Pallette, Douglas Fairbanks, Leon Barry, and George Siegman in
THE THREE MUSKETEERS *(1921)*

Niblo. Script by June Mathis, based on a novel by Vincente Blasco Ibáñez and a play by Tom Cushing. With Rudolph Valentino, Lila Lee, Nita Naldi. 113 min. B&W. Silent. 18 fps.

By the time this film was released, Valentino had attained a fame that few film stars have ever exceeded. His sense of poise and rhythm, his graceful gestures, and his sultry lovemaking made him *the* matinee idol. This picture remains one of his sturdiest vehicles, despite the fact that Spanish novelist Ibáñez's theme—an expose of the brutality and psychology of the bullfight—was much diluted. Niblo, like others of his day, evidently thought that the way to translate literary material to the screen was to seek out and emphasize its pictorial aspects. Nevertheless, the film works as a star vehicle. During the summer of 1922, Otis Skinner was a big hit in the same role in a stage version.

DR. MABUSE, THE GAMBLER (DR. MABUSE, DER SPIELER)

May 26, 1922. Germany.
Decla-Bioscop. Directed by Fritz Lang. Script by Lang and Thea von Harbou based on a story by Norbert Jacques. Photographed by Carl Hoffman. Art Direction by Otto Hunte, Stahl-Urach. With Rudolf Klein-Rogge, Aud Egede Nissen, Alfred Abel. English titles. 100 min. B&W. Silent. 18 fps.

This, the first of three films that Lang devoted to the master criminal Mabuse, originally ran to over twenty reels. This episodic version is the American release of 1927, cut down to nine reels. Through a myriad of convoluted plots, settings, characters, and Mabuse's varied disguises, it follows his pursuit of power for its own sake, and Inspector Wenk's efforts to control him. Lang's use of off-centered composition, low angles, sharply-contrasting light and dark areas, and intense editing extends the director's power over an audience, often leading to mysterious and fearful paths. The character of Mabuse is a descendent of Louis Feuillade's *Fantômas* (1913), and traces of his intrigue may still be found in today's James Bond series.

FOOLISH WIVES

January 15, 1922. U.S.A.
Universal Pictures. Directed and written by Erich von Stroheim. Photographed by William Daniels, Ben F. Reynolds. With von Stroheim, Mae Busch, Maude George. 118 min. B&W. Silent. 18 fps.

Max Schreck in NOSFERATU (1922)

As in the earlier **Blind Husbands** (1919), von Stroheim's passion for the perverse and his inordinate attention to detail make the story—gullible Americans visiting decayed aristocracy in Europe—a naturalistic study of uncommon force. The film was severely cut from its original 210-minute length, however, both before and after its release, and this print can be considered only a part of the original. What remains is a fully developed portrait of a continental seducer enacted with brilliant depravity by von Stroheim himself.

NOSFERATU (NOSFERATU. EINE SYMPHONIE DES GRAUENS)

March 5, 1922. Germany.
Prana. Directed by F. W. Murnau. Script by Henrik Galeen based on Bram Stoker's *Dracula*. Photographed by Fritz Arno Wagner. With Max Schreck, Gustav von Wagenheim, Greta Schröder. English titles.
88 min. B&W. Silent. 18 fps.

Nosferatu is the legendary story of the vampire who plagues a village until the sacrifice of a pure young girl dispels his curse. Murnau's chilling rendition of Bram Stoker's *Dracula* was filmed on location in the Baltic, an exception to the German tradition of the studio-made film. Within this natural world, he created an overwhelming sense of desolation and terror. He used negative im-

ages to turn trees white and skies black, stop-motion filming to create unrealistic motion, and double exposure for ghostly effects; but more important, he somehow endowed with foreboding commonplace landscapes photographed in natural light. Max Schreck portrays the most terrifying of a long line of blood-sucking counts.

ROBIN HOOD

November 5, 1922. U.S.A.
Douglas Fairbanks Pictures. Directed by Allan Dwan. Script by Elton Thomas (pseudonym of Fairbanks). Photographed by Arthur Edeson. With Douglas Fairbanks, Enid Bennett, Wallace Beery.
121 min. B&W. Silent. 24 fps.

The legendary Robin Hood was a natural role for the athletic Fairbanks in his new swashbuckling career. In the time when Richard the Lion Hearted is abroad fighting in the Crusades, the Earl of Huntingdon becomes an outlaw in Sherwood Forest and gathers an army to defeat the usurping prince when the king returns from the Crusades. It was Fairbanks's most ambitious production to date and its Maxfield Parrish-style romantic atmosphere, its enormous sets, and its horde of costumed extras greatly impressed audiences of its day. The intrigue and decor have the effect of subduing the Fairbanks personality until the second half of the film, when the pro-

THE COVERED WAGON (1923)

duction comes to vivid life with his extraordinary stunts.

SKY HIGH

January 22, 1922. U.S.A.
Fox Film Corporation. Directed by Lynn Reynolds. With Tom Mix, Eva Novak, J. Farrell MacDonald.
66 min. B&W. Silent. 18 fps.

In the twenties the most popular cowboy star was Tom Mix. He had a personality closer to Fairbanks than to Hart. He was frank, friendly, cheerful, and given to comedy and acrobatic turns. The results, while entertaining, are usually devoid of that sense of reality that characterizes Hart's films. *Sky High* takes place not on the legendary frontier but in an equally unreal modern west. Mix is a U.S. immigration inspector bent on uncovering the activities of a gang of smugglers of Chinese laborers and rescuing the girl who falls into their clutches. He ropes a car of smugglers as he would a recalcitrant calf, rides his horse and climbs ropes among the cliffs of the Grand Canyon, and drops from an airplane into water, all with a lively sense of fun that tells us not to take any of it seriously.

SQUIBS WINS THE CALCUTTA SWEEP

September 1922. Great Britain.
Welsh-Pearson. Directed by George Pearson. Script by Pearson and Hugh E. Wright. With Betty Balfour, Hugh E. Wright, Fred Groves.
78 min. B&W. Silent. 18 fps.

According to Thorold Dickinson, "between Cecil Hepworth and Alfred Hitchcock, George Pearson was the out-standing personality in British silent cinema." His reputation is not one of a pioneer or innovator, but rather of a sensitive practitioner of the narrative film medium. This is the second in a series of films Pearson directed featuring Betty Balfour in the role of a cockney flower-seller. The first film in the series, *Squibs* (1921), was originally made without any sequel in mind, but distributors cut a final scene involving Squibs's marriage to her policeman boyfriend so that sequels could be produced. This one reveals a distinctly British tone of humor. The plot, which has Squibs winning a large sum of money in a lottery, provides an opportunity for Pearson to mock affectionately the British class system.

ANNA CHRISTIE

July 26, 1923. U.S.A.
Thomas H. Ince Corporation. Directed by John Griffith Wray. Script by Bradley King, based on the play by Eugene O'Neill. Photographed by Henry Sharp. With Blanche Sweet, George F. Marion, William Russell.
75 min. B&W. Silent. 24 fps.

By the twenties Ince had abandoned his westerns for a broader spectrum of topics. Here he reached for the prestige of filming Eugene O'Neill's big success of the previous Broadway season. The play, about a world-weary prostitute's first encounter with her father, a sentimental old seaman, and their disillusionment about each other, was a daring topic for Hollywood in the twenties and only O'Neill's great reputation at the time made it possible. O'Neill himself approved of this faithful rendition. The vulnerability in Blanche Sweet's performance makes her rendition of Anna a moving one and her portrayal of a prostitute acceptable to movie morals of the period. Less stagebound than the later Garbo version, which had to cope with early sound equipment, this version builds the atmosphere of the sleazy waterfront cafe and the foggy sea-mists into a convincing setting for O'Neill's melancholy imagination.

THE COVERED WAGON

March 16, 1923.
Famous Players-Lasky (Paramount). Directed by James Cruze. Script by Jack Cunningham from a novel by Emerson Hough. Photographed by Karl Brown. Edited by Dorothy Arzner. With J. Warren Kerrigan, Lois Wilson, Alan Hale.
98 min. B&W. Silent. 18 fps.

This western epic about the pioneer trek across the continent in covered wagons marked a renewal of the western genre. Its love story—the leader of one wagon train falls in love with the daughter of another wagon train leader, but has to clear himself of false charges as a cattle thief before he can win her—is secondary to the majestic sweep of the covered wagons moving westward. The wagon trains cross wide rivers, are attacked by Indians, and later divide up, some carrying gold-seekers to California, others taking land-settlers to Oregon. Much of the film was made on location, and the landscape, weather, and the dust, richly photographed by Karl Brown, engraved images on the frontier mythology. Made at a time when most Hollywood production was studio-bound and dedicated to star vehicles, this film was a revelation, and was followed by a rash of big-budget westerns made on location. Our print is the general release version, about fifteen minutes shorter than the first road-show prints.

THE CRAZY RAY (PARIS QUI DORT)

1923. France.
Films Diamant. Directed by René Clair. Photographed by Maurice Desfassiaux, Paul Guichard. With Henri Rollan, Madeline Rodrigues, Albert Préjean. English titles.
62 min. B&W. Silent. 18 fps.

René Clair's first film exploits stop-motion filming in a comedy about a night watchman on the Eiffel Tower who wakes one morning to find the city of Paris asleep below. He is joined by a small group of people who were in an airplane when everything on earth was frozen in time by a mysterious ray invented by a mad scientist. The French avant-garde looked back to early cinema in their quest for the elements of film art. Here, it is the comic trick film that intrigues René Clair (see **Onésime Horloger** [1912]). However, it is the process of moviemaking that is the subject of this film. Basic elements of cinema, time and movement, are its chief characters. Stasis and motion are constantly placed in counterpoint. Another preoccupation of the twenties evident in this film is the fascination with abstract forms of machinery, shown here as the camera glides around the steel curves and fretwork in its exploration of the Eiffel Tower from every angle.

THE SMILING MADAME BEUDET (LA SOURIANTE MADAME BEUDET)

January 20, 1923. France.
Vandal-Dulac-Aubert. Directed by Germaine Dulac. Based on a play by André Obey, Denys Amiel. Photographed by A. Morrin. With Germaine Dermoz, Alexandre Arquilliere. French titles.
40 min. B&W. Silent. 18 fps.

Germaine Dulac was a film theoretician and leading force of French impressionist cinema, of which this film is an outstanding example. In later films, Dulac moved on to other phases of the French avant-garde. **Madame Beudet** explores the relationship of a bored couple in a dreary provincial town from the woman's point of view. Basing her film on a play by André Obey and Denys Amiel, the director translates into cinema their aesthetic of the "theater of silence," a theory that the silences engulfing characters could be more articulate than their speech. Silent actions betray the conflicts in the marriage, and inanimate objects are made to carry psychological meaning. Dulac shows us Madame Beudet's view of her husband through a distorting lens, or her own romantic imagination in abstract visions. Ironic contrast provides a strong counterpoint.

THE STREET (DIE STRASSE)

November 29, 1923. Germany.
Stern-Film. Directed by Karl Grüne. Script by Grüne, Julius Urgiss, Carl Mayer. Photographed by Karl Hasselmann. With Eugen Klöpfer, Aud Egede Nissen, Lucie Höflich, Max Schreck. English titles.
86 min. B&W. Silent. 18 fps.

The Street is the beginning of a long line of films (later to be called *strasse* pictures) that injected a note of realism into the German cinema of the twenties. This film, though made almost entirely in the studio and still utilizing an Expressionist-like chiaroscuro, emerges as an engrossing naturalistic study of a middle-aged man who leaves the security of home one night for the unknown adventures awaiting him in the city. Lured by a prostitute, he is falsely accused of murder and tries to hang himself in the police station; released, he returns to his boring domestic routine. The lighting suggests the influence of the Max Reinhardt theater, as does the acting style; the unity of time is characteristic of the *kammerspiel* film. The original used no titles; this print has a few added to it.

WARNING SHADOWS (SCHATTEN)

July 26, 1923. Germany.
Dafu. Directed by Arthur Robison. Script by Rudolf Schneider, Arthur Robison. Photographed by Fritz Arno Wagner. Art Direction by Albin Grau. With Fritz Kortner, Ruth Weyher, Gustav von Wangenheim. English titles.
95 min. B&W. Silent. 18 fps.

An Expressionist film, this claustrophobic and dream-like picture concerns a group of chateau-bound aristocrats who play with life and love as if they were shadow-puppets. A shadow-maker puts under his spell the members of the household and they act out the ultimate conclusions of their emotions. The jealous husband forces his wife's admirers to kill her, after which they turn on him. Awakening, the wife returns to her husband and the others leave. Stylized sets, acting, and camera conspire to create the withdrawn, ego-ridden, slightly schizoid atmosphere of Expressionist art. In its observation of the unities of time, place, and theme, and using almost no titles, it may also be related to the *kammerspiel* film.

THE WHITE ROSE

May 21, 1923. U.S.A.
D. W. Griffith Corporation. Directed by D. W. Griffith. Script by Irene Sinclair (pseudonym of D. W. Griffith). Photographed by G. W. (Billy) Bitzer, Hendrick Sartov, Hal Sintzenich. With Mae Marsh, Carol Dempster, Ivor Novello, Neil Hamilton.
136 min. B&W. Silent. 18 fps.

The image of women is central to this film about a young girl seduced by a minister and who bears an illegitimate child. The theme shares a relationship to **Way Down East** (1920), but in place of New England landscapes and the harshness of snow and ice, Griffith puts rich and romantic images of his beloved Old South, atmospheric with live oaks and Spanish moss. The irony of the minister's sermons contrasted with his weak (not evil) behavior forms a counterpoint to the highly-expressive visions of women as moral and spiritual forces, and as mystical beings, especially in motherhood. Mae Marsh, returning to Griffith's direction after many years, gives a magical performance that alone would make this a memorable film.

AMERICA

February 21, 1924. U.S.A.
D. W. Griffith Corporation. Directed by D. W. Griffith. Script by John Pell, adapted from a story by Robert Chambers. Photographed by G. W. (Billy) Bitzer, Hendrick Sartov, Marcel Le Picard, Hal Sintzenich. With Neil Ham-

Albert Préjean in THE CRAZY RAY (1923)

ilton, Carol Dempster, Lionel Barrymore.
173 min. B&W. Silent. 18 fps.

This is a patriotic historical spectacle about the American Revolution. It combines a love story with the events and battles from Virginia to New England, while the second half of the film concentrates on the Mohawk Valley campaign. It was made with the cooperation of many official bodies who anticipated an ideal vehicle for teaching school children about their heritage. The personal story, involving conflicts between love and patriotism for the lovers on opposing sides, was not as emotionally effective as in Griffith's **The Birth of a Nation** (1915), and the result was more a textbook illustration of history. Nevertheless, the battles of Lexington and Concord are as stirring as any of those in Griffith's earlier films, superbly expressing the surge of a people fighting for freedom. This version, called **Love and Sacrifice**, was made for British release, with some slight changes in intertitles.

ENTR'ACTE (1924): *See* Experimental Film

THE EXTRAORDINARY ADVENTURES OF MR. WEST IN THE LAND OF THE BOLSHEVIKS (NEOBYCHAINIYE PRIKLUCHENIYA MISTERA VESTA V STRANYE BOLSHEVIKOV)

1924. U.S.S.R.
Goskino. Directed by Lev Kuleshov. Script by Vsevolod I. Pudovkin and Nikolai Aseyev. Photographed by Alexander Levitsky. Production design by Pudovkin. With Porfiri Podobed, Boris Barnet, Vsevolod I. Pudovkin. Available with either Russian or English titles: please specify.
90 min. B&W. Silent. 18 fps.

This is a satiric comedy about the trip of an American dignitary to the Soviet Union, accompanied by a cowboy bodyguard and with absurd misconceptions about the country. He falls into the hands of a gang of counter-revolutionaries who exploit his naiveté, until he is rescued and given a tour of the actual Soviet Russia. The film was the first success of Lev Kuleshov's famed Workshop, which was influenced by Meyerhold's theories. Kuleshov was himself a major film theorist and this film demonstrates the early use of his anti-Stanislavkian, anti-psychological acting style, emphasizing instead the actor's appearance and movements. Sergei Eisenstein studied film direction in Kuleshov's Workshop, and this amusing comedy was made with the help of two other major Soviet directors who also appear in it: Boris Barnet and V. I. Pudovkin.

THE IRON HORSE

August 28, 1924. U.S.A.
Fox Film. Directed by John Ford. Script by Charles Kenyon, John Russell. With George O'Brien, Madge Bellamy, Delbert Mann.
110 min. B&W. Silent. 24 fps.

John Ford's first big critical success, **The Iron Horse**, was Fox's answer to Paramount's **The Covered Wagon** (1923). It is an epic film about the building of the first transcontinental railroad. Against this background, the plot has a classic western motif: the hero searches for the murderer of his father to get revenge. The main theme is never forgotten because the building of the railroad and the ceaseless activities connected with it continue literally in the background of the scenes of personal drama. John Ford had already been directing films, chiefly westerns, for many years when he won this assignment. His skill in handling action sequences, and his ability to create characters firmly rooted in their time and the world of nature around them, made this a major piece of Americana and the prototype for the many railroad-building epics that followed.

ISN'T LIFE WONDERFUL

December 4, 1924. U.S.A.
D. W. Griffith Corporation. Directed by D. W. Griffith. Script by Griffith based on a story by Major Geoffrey Moss. With Carol Dempster, Neil Hamilton.
135 min. B&W. Silent. 18 fps.

Griffith's last film as an independent is a sharply realistic study of poverty, hunger, and the debasement of people in the German postwar period. It was partly filmed on location in Germany and used local people as extras. Scenes such as that in which the family of Polish refugees sits dully at their dinner of turnips are masterpieces of observation. The film stops short of slice-of-life naturalism, however, and is imbued with the lyrical affirmation of life expressed by the reiteration of the title. The final chase sequence is unlike any other Griffith chase: there are no contrived effects and the suspense is not pushed beyond belief. The two lovers with their precious store of potatoes hurry home through the tall trees, pursued by the desperate workers who at last overtake and rob them. The film originally ended here, but within a few days Griffith had tacked on a happier ending, which weakens the simple and poetic conclusion. Made the year before Pabst's **The Joyless Street**, this film had a wide influence on European and American filmmaking.

THE LAST LAUGH (DER LETZTE MANN)

December 23, 1924. Germany.
Ufa. Directed by F. W. Murnau. Script by Carl Mayer. Photographed by Karl Freund. Art Direction by Robert Herlth, Walter Röhrig. With Emil Jannings, Maly Delschaft.
107 min. B&W. Silent. 18 fps.

THE EXTRAORDINARY ADVENTURES OF MR. WEST IN THE LAND OF THE BOLSHEVIKS (1924)

This famous film is the study of a hotel doorman who loses all self-respect when demoted to the rank of washroom attendant and forced to give up the impressive uniform that is his glory. The important place of this film in cinema of the twenties is due in part to its occurrence at a kind of crossroads of movements and the richness of elements it combined from all of these styles. It was made at the end of Expressionism and contains the strong diagonals, exaggerated gestures, and distortions of that movement. It was released at the height of the *kammerspielfilme* and observes its intimacy and the unities, but it is also what Kracauer called the culmination of the "instinct film," in which lower class characters act in direct response to emotions and where subtitles are not needed because of this transparent motivation. Some historians also find elements of the growing trend in Germany to realism. The chief influence of this film, however, was in its dazzling use of the moving camera. Here, the camera becomes the leading character, frequently expressing a subjective point of view. The film's play of light—in reflections and shadows, windows, mirrors, shiny objects, gleaming wet pavements, and electric light bulbs—creates the effect of a nebulous world of emotions.

THE MARRIAGE CIRCLE

February 3, 1924. U.S.A.
Warner Brothers. Directed by Ernst Lubitsch. Script by Paul Bern based on the play *Nur ein Traum* by Lothar Goldschmidt. With Adolphe Menjou, Marie Prevost, Florence Vidor, Monte Blue. 118 min. B&W. Silent. 18 fps.

This witty and elegant comedy about the flirtations and misunderstandings of two married couples marked a turning point for Ernst Lubitsch, the German director of historical spectacles. Brought to Hollywood by Mary Pickford, Lubitsch was influenced by the Hollywood style of filmmaking and, more directly, by Chaplin's *A Woman of Paris* (1923). Chaplin's indirect method of revealing character, the use of close-ups of inanimate objects, subtle or fleeting facial expressions, and his cool ironic tone were adopted not only by Lubitsch but by a whole school of filmmaking. Lubitsch himself continued to make films in a similar vein and contributed his satiric touch to the polish for which Hollywood films are noted. The close-up was made for him. Lubitsch's clever and pointed use of the camera to make satiric comment became an important part of his style. At its sharpest, his camera

Paul Richter in SIEGFRIED (1924)

is imbued with his personality; Lubitsch invites the viewers to join him in smiling at human follies.

MONSIEUR BEAUCAIRE

August 18, 1924. U.S.A.
Famous Players-Lasky (Paramount). Directed by Sidney Olcott. Script by Forrest Halsey from the novel and play by Booth Tarkington. Photographed by Harry Fischbeck. Art Direction by Natasha Rambova. With Rudolph Valentino, Bebe Daniels, Lois Wilson. 106 min. B&W. Silent. 24 fps.

Based on the Booth Tarkington novel about a duke in the time of Louis XV who flees to England and poses as a barber until exposed, this film was staged primarily as a starring vehicle for Valentino. It was his "come-back" after a hiatus caused by Paramount's breach-of-contract suit over his marriage to Natacha Rambova (who served as art director on this film). Everything in it is subordinated to the star and everything is calculated to make him appear to best advantage. The lavish lighting, the sa-

tiny sheen of the costumes, and the dexterity with which the chief character is kept glamorously and sympathetically in the foreground deserve attention. This was the epitome of "box office," and through it all Valentino moves, radiantly poised and incomparably photogenic.

DIE NIBELUNGEN

1924. Germany.
Decla-Bioscop. Directed by Fritz Lang. Script by Thea von Harbou. Photographed by Carl Hoffmann, Günther Rittau. Art Direction by Otto Hunte, Erich Kettlhut, Karl Vollbrecht. Special effects by Walter Ruttmann. With Paul Richter, Margarete Schon.

Part I, SIEGFRIED (TEIL I: SIEGFRIEDS TOD)

February 14, 1924. German titles.
86 min. B&W. Sound (music track). 24 fps.

Part II, KRIEMHILD'S REVENGE (TEIL II: KRIEMHILDS RACHE)

April 26, 1924. English titles.
90 min. B&W. Silent. 24 fps.

Fritz Lang's gigantic two-part vision of the Nibelungen legend employs two film styles to differentiate between the part set in the Burgundian court and that set in the land of the barbarous Huns. In Part I, Siegfried slays the dragon and visits the court, falls in love with Kriemhild, and dies through the machinations of Queen Brunhild. It is told in architecturally composed compositions, light and dark are used for allegorical significance, its sets are geometrical and monumental, its actors seemingly frozen in time. In Part II, Kriemhild seeks revenge for the killing of her husband. She marries Attila, King of the Huns, and incites the Huns to massacre her enemies among the Burgundians. This part is dynamic and spectacular, with battle scenes and a great fire; its cutting rhythms express the awesome nature of the events, in contrast to the pictorial quality that was predominant in Part I. The enormous resources of the German studios were called upon for this saga of German nationalism.

THE THIEF OF BAGDAD

March 18, 1924. U.S.A.
Douglas Fairbanks Pictures. Directed by Raoul Walsh. Script by Elton Thomas (pseudonym of Fairbanks). Photographed by Arthur Edeson. Art Direction by William Cameron Menzies, assisted by Edward Langley. With Douglas Fairbanks, Julanne Johnston, Anna May Wong.
135 min. B&W. Silent. 24 fps.

Douglas Fairbanks, ever the showman, was impressed by the opulence of German superproductions, and particularly inspired by Lang's **Destiny** (1921), from which he borrowed many special effects. He launched this fairy-tale fantasy, outdoing even his **Robin Hood** (1922) in the splendor of the sets and scope of the production. Trees were painted, objects and architecture were designed out of human proportion, and a highly-polished black floor was devised to reflect buildings. Art Nouveau set the style of decoration. In keeping with the artistic goals of the production, Fairbanks adapted a stylized form of acting. There are few of his acrobatic stunts, but his grace is that of a ballet dancer. Spectacle and magic effects form the chief entertainment of this story of the thief who pretends to be a prince to win the princess's love and, when discovered, is sent on a quest which ends in his rescuing Bagdad and the princess from the Mongols.

CHESS FEVER (CHAKHMATNAIA GORIATCHKA)

1925. U.S.S.R.
Mezhrabpom-Russ. Directed by Vsevolod I. Pudovkin. Script by Pudovkin and Nikolai Shpikovsky. Photographed by Anatoli Golovnya. With Vladimir Fogel, Anna Zemtzova, Jose Capablanca. English titles.
25 min. B&W. Silent. 18 fps.

Pudovkin's first film is a comedy filmed during the International Chess Tournament in Moscow. The hero's love of chess distracts him from the girl he loves until she too succumbs to "chess fever" and joins him. This witty comedy uses the principles Pudovkin learned in the Kuleshov Workshop, ingeniously combining newsreel footage taken at the chess tournament with shots of actors' hands and objects photographed in the studio. The chess motif is an influence even in the checked patterns of the costumes and sets.

THE CHRONICLE OF THE GRAY HOUSE (ZUR CHRONIK VON GRIESHUUS)

February 11, 1925. Germany.
Union-Ufa. Directed by Arthur von Gerlach. Script by Thea von Harbou. Based on a novel by Theodor Storm. Photographed by Karl Drews, Fritz Arno Wagner, Erich Nitschman. Art Direction and sets by Walter Röhrig, Robert Herlth, Hans Pölzig. With Paul Harmann, Lil Dagover. English titles.
100 min. B&W. Silent. 18 fps.

This dreamy, slow-paced, atmospheric fantasy is set in medieval times and is about the fight of two brothers and their wives (one high-born and the other of humble origins) over their legacy of the family castle and property under feudal law. Filmed in northern Germany, as was Murnau's **Nosferatu** (1922), and employing the same designers and chief cameraman as the earlier film, this production captures the barren landscapes of the moors and its mists to add to the mysterious mood of gray tonality that characterizes the claustrophobic, low-arched, shadowy interiors. The use of the tableau and long shot at moments of dramatic intensity reflects the theatrical background of Arthur von Gerlach, who contributed only four films to the German cinema before his early death in 1925. This is the American release version, about 45 minutes shorter than the original length.

DON Q, SON OF ZORRO

September 20, 1925. U.S.A.
Elton Corporation (Douglas Fairbanks).
Directed by Donald Crisp. Script by Jack Cunningham based on "Don Q's Love Story" by K. and Hesketh Prichard. Photographed by Henry Sharp. Art Direction by Edward Langley. With Douglas Fairbanks, Mary Astor, Donald Crisp.
113 min. B&W. Silent. 24 fps.

In this sequel to **The Mark of Zorro** (1920), Fairbanks recaptures the vitality of the earlier film, which his fans had missed in his more ambitious spectacle films. Instead of having a double identity as in **The Mark of Zorro**, Fairbanks plays double roles: as Zorro, the father, thirty years later, and his young son, Don Q. Don Q returns from California to his ancestral home in Spain and there falls in love and runs afoul of intrigue. Framed on a murder charge, he defends himself against his enemies with a bullwhip, displaying a new skill Fairbanks has added to his repertory. At this time about forty-two, and playing a boy of twenty with convincing freedom and grace, Fairbanks is no longer the purely athletic film star. His movements have become as graceful and rhythmic as those of a ballet dancer and yet still lightly touched with the spirit of comedy. The flow of movement supplies the structure for this rapidly paced adventure film. The illusion that Zorro and Don Q are separate persons is maintained by skillful and clever editing.

THE JOYLESS STREET (DIE FREUDLOSE GASSE)

March 1925. Germany.
Sofar. Directed by G. W. Pabst. Script by Willy Haas based on a novel by Hugo Bettauer. With Asta Nielsen, Werner Krauss, Greta Garbo. English titles.
126 min. B&W. Silent. 18 fps.

Social realism emerged as a style in modern art in the latter half of the twenties, a movement known in Germany as the New Objectivity. **The Joyless Street**, representative of the new style, was shocking to its audiences. Few films had tried to deal with the reality of the inflation-ridden postwar society. This one dealt with the struggle for existence in Vienna and showed the brutality of the profiteering butcher, the corrupt speculator, and the brothel keeper to the victims of inflation and war. Pabst's quest for social realism did not take him outside the tradition of the German studio-made film, and his compositions are arranged, as in cinematic expressionism, for emotional and pictorial effects. However, the techniques he developed for cutting on movement was in the direction of realism. At the same time that the Soviet filmmakers were building a theory of montage that dramatized the cut between shots, Pabst's method subdued the mechanics of film-making in the interests of creating the illusion of real life. He nevertheless depended on parallel editing for contrast within sequences. An example is the sequence showing women standing in line all night at the butcher shop intercut with scenes of women relaxing in the luxurious bordello. The film was censored in most countries and no complete print exists: this one has been pieced together by Pabst's assistant on the film.

LADY WINDERMERE'S FAN

December 26, 1925. U.S.A.
Warner Bros. Directed by Ernst Lubitsch. Script by Julien Josephson based on Oscar Wilde's play. Photographed by Charles Van Enger. With Ronald Colman, May McAvoy, Irene Rich, Bert Lytell.
85 min. B&W. Silent. 24 fps.

Oscar Wilde's comedy of manners fell into the hands of the director most able to translate its precise nuances to the screen. The scandalous Mrs. Erlynne returns to London to save her daughter from disgrace and sacrifices her own reputation by claiming the fan left by Lady Windermere in the apartment of Lord Darlington. Lubitsch almost entirely replaces Wilde's epigrams with visual images as clever and polished, capturing the essence of Wilde's spirit in a model of elegant pictorial wit. His use of pointed close-ups, the subtle gestures and fleeting expressions of his actors, his assured and silken style, make of this delightful comedy a virtuoso exercise in American silent film style and in his own "Lubitsch touch." In the late twenties there were numerous Hollywood imitators of his style but none to match it.

MÉNILMONTANT

1925. France.
Produced, written, and directed by Dimitri Kirsanov. Photographed by Leonce Crovan and Kirsanov. With Nadia Sibirskaïa, Yolande Beaulieu, Guy Belmore. No titles.
36 min. B&W. Silent. 18 fps.

This independently-produced work of French Impressionism marks the passage of that style into various experimental modes included in the term avant-garde, a movement populated by modern artists and poets. Kirsanov was a musician, an Estonian émigré to Paris. The drama of two orphan girls seduced by the same man and their hopeless futures—to become prostitutes or to work

May McAvoy and Ronald Colman in LADY WINDERMERE'S FAN (1925)

in the artificial flower factory—is only a pretext for a lyric evocation of atmosphere. The emotions of the heroines are reflected in associated images: empty streets convey loneliness, streets full of speed and movement express the state of happiness. Traveling shots capture transitory impressions and feelings in a cinematic equivalent to poetry. The brilliant opening sequence, a forty-second cascade of images, rivals Soviet montage. Sibirskaïa's sensitive performance was greatly admired.

POTEMKIN (BRONENOSETS POTEMKIN)

December 21, 1925. U.S.S.R.
Goskino. Directed by Sergei Eisenstein. Script by Eisenstein from the scenario "1905" by Nina Agadzhanova-Shutko. Photographed by Éduard Tisse. With Vladimir Barsky, Grigori Alexandrov, Alexander Antonov. English titles.
72 min. B&W. Silent. 18 fps.

With *Potemkin*, the new Soviet cinema took a central place on the world scene. The effects of this radical style are still felt wherever revolutionary movements look for a cinematic means of expression. To characterize the meaning of the Soviet revolution, Eisenstein used the

events of the 1905 rebellion in the port of Odessa. There are five major sequences: the rebellion of the Potemkin's sailors over rotten food; the mutiny on the quarter deck; the display of the martyr's body on the quay; the massacre on the Odessa steps; the triumphant sailing of the battleship to meet the fleet. All of them merit prolonged study for Eisenstein's conscious manipulation of film materials. His brilliant editing, his use of details and repetition and contrast, his compression or expansion of time, the collision of images for their shock value, ran counter to the trend toward a seamless illusion of reality found elsewhere. The film was censored in many countries, but this is the complete version. The famous Odessa Steps sequence is also available as an excerpt (see Film Study).

STRIKE (STACHKA)

April 28, 1925. U.S.S.R.
Goskino. Directed by Sergei Eisenstein. Photographed by Eduard Tisse. With Alexander Antonov, Grigori Alexandrov, Mikhail Gomorov. English titles.
97 min. B&W. Silent. 18 fps.

Eisenstein's first film is about a 1912 rebellion of factory workers and their brutal repression by the Czarist bosses. Influenced by his work in the Proletkult Theater Collective and the Kuleshov Workshop, Eisenstein looked for a way to express the meaning of the revolutionary movement. He shot the film in real locations but aimed for abstractions in which the detail can stand for the whole. He substituted stereotyped figures as collective symbols where other films had individual heroes. The symbolic meaning is underlined by comparative editing, intercutting shots of animals with people, or in the massacre sequence, cutting in the slaughter of cattle in an abattoir, and by editing for contrast. Actors are selected for their facial characteristics as types. The theatrical tradition is still evident in the geometric patterns and decorative settings, but it is also clear that a new style is emerging out of the elements of classic cinema.

VARIETY (VARIETE)

November 16, 1925. Germany.
Ufa. Directed by E. A. Dupont. Produced by Erich Pommer. Script by Dupont based on *The Oath of Stephan Huller* by Friedrich Hollaender. Photographed by Karl Freund. With Emil Jannings, Maly Delschaft, Lya de Putti. English titles.
82 min. B&W. Silent. 18 fps.

Variety is told as a prolonged flashback by a convicted murderer. As a circus acrobat, he runs off with a young girl and loses her to another, leading to his crime of passion. Photographed by Karl Freund, the cameraman of *The Last Laugh* (1924), the film is a dazzling display of camera movements, subjective viewpoints, unusual angles, and continuous movement. It is a more deterministic melodrama than is readily apparent in this American release version, which had to satisfy the censors by eliminating the sequence in which the man first deserts his wife to run away with the girl. While expressionistic elements still linger through a decorative manner, lighting, and composition, in other respects this is a film of the New Objectivity in its use of a sordid, slice-of-life milieu. The circus setting lends itself to kaleidoscopic images, and extreme tension is built into the trapeze sequences, with fast cuts and a swooping camera. It was a very influential film in America.

BEAU GESTE

August 25, 1926. U.S.A.
Famous Players-Lasky (Paramount). Directed by Herbert Brenon. Script by Paul Schofield, adapted by John Russell and Brenon from a novel by Percival Christopher Wren. Photographed by J. Roy Hunt. With Ronald Colman, Neil Hamilton, Noah Beery.
109 min. B&W. Silent. 24 fps.

Much of Hollywood production in the twenties was sheer romantic escapism. This lavish superproduction combines exoticism, adventure, action, and spectacle with elements of mystery. Three brothers join the French Foreign Legion over an episode concerning a stolen jewel; they engage in a revolt against a cruel commanding officer; and there is an Arab attack on the garrison. The mystery is created by the device of withholding information at the beginning and gradually revealing it. Filmed in the desert sands of Arizona, the majestic scenery provides a setting for the grand emotions of the film's characters. Noah Beery as Sargeant Lejaune runs away with the picture in one of the great villain roles: hard, cruel, ready for murder, yet admired by the men who suffered under him when he shows courage under fire and brilliance as a military leader. This popular adventure film was remade in 1939 and again in 1966.

BED AND SOFA (TRETYA MESHCHANSKAYA)

March 17, 1926. U.S.S.R.
Sovkino. Directed by Abram Room. Script by Room and Victor Shklovsky. Photographed by Grigori Giber. With Nikolai Batalov, Ludmilla Semyonova, Vladimir Fogel. English titles.
85 min. B&W. Silent. 18 fps.

Other themes besides revolution were entering Soviet cinema, among them the changing role of the individual in the new society. The background setting for this comedy is Moscow's housing shortage. A husband, who has come to take his wife for granted, brings home a friend to sleep on the sofa; before long it is the husband who has to sleep on the sofa. Pregnant without being sure of the father, the wife goes for an abortion and then changes her mind (the policy on abortion was changing while this film was in production to a stance of opposition). She then abandons both men, revealing a high degree of women's liberation for a film of the twenties. Room's careful selection of details depicts the psychology and tensions of the characters in the crowded little flat. This satiric comedy was not widely seen outside of the Soviet Union due to its forbidden subjects of adultery and abortion.

POTEMKIN (1925) (p. 65)

BY THE LAW (PO ZAKONU)

1926. U.S.S.R.
Goskino. Directed by Lev Kuleshov.
Script by Kuleshov and Victor Shklovsky based on "The Unexpected" by Jack
London. Photographed by Konstantin
Kuznetzov. With Sergei Komarov, Vladimir Fogel, Alexandra Khokhlova.
English titles.
85 min. B&W. Silent. 18 fps.

Kuleshov, theoretician and teacher of
the first Soviet filmmakers, made this
remarkable film on a very low budget
as an experiment. It is based on a Jack
London story set in the Alaskan wilderness. Three people involved in a murder are isolated by winter storms; eventually two of them condemn the guilty
one. Although the film has American
sources, the compressed psychological
tension of the film is more akin to Dostoyevsky, from whose work an episode
has been borrowed. In the Kuleshov
Workshop actors learned that hands,
arms, and legs could be as intrinsic a part
of performance as facial expressions.
The effect of isolation and extreme tension in this film is achieved through the
emphasis on significant detail and gesture. Kuleshov's rational, mechanistic
approach might be related to that of
Alfred Hitchcock. This film has also
been mentioned as a possible influence
on Dreyer's *The Passion of Joan of Arc*
(1928).

THE CLOAK (SHINEL)

May 11, 1926. U.S.S.R.
Leningradkino. Directed by Grigori
Kozintsev and Leonid Trauberg. Script
by Yuri Tinyarov based on "The Cloak"
and "Nevsky Prospect" by Nikolai Gogol. With Andrei Kostrichkin, Anna
Zheimo, Sergei Gerasimov. English titles.
51 min. B&W. Silent. 18 fps.

The Factory of the Eccentric Actor, or
FEX, was an experimental studio and
theater organized by Kozintsev and
Trauberg, dedicated to creating new
forms and drawing on the circus,
vaudeville, American slapstick, adventure films. Where Kuleshov relied on
the manipulation of film's unique properties, FEX translated the experimental
theater forms directly to film. The grotesque characters of Gogol lent themselves to FEX's eccentric acting styles.
The complete version of this film has a
kind of prologue based on Gogol's
"Nevsky Prospect" in which the lowly
civil service clerk undergoes a painful
youthful adventure. This version contains only the second part, based on Go-

Mack Swain (at stake) and Raymond Griffith (center) in HANDS UP! (1926)

gol's "The Cloak," in which the clerk has
his all-important cloak, so critical to his
well-being and prestige, stolen from him.
This symbolic theft leads to his madness
and death. Influenced by German
Expressionism and reminiscent in theme
of *The Last Laugh* (1924), the picture is
characterized by elongated shadows and
distortions and stylized performances.

HANDS UP!

January 11, 1926. U.S.A.
Famous Players-Lasky (Paramount). Directed by Clarence Badger. Script by
Monty Brice, Lloyd Corrigan, based on
a story by Reginald Morris. Photographed by H. Kinley Martin. With
Raymond Griffith, Marion Nixon, Mack
Swain.
65 min. B&W. Silent. 24 fps.

The feature comedy of the twenties, of
which this is an outstanding example,
was more carefully planned, more subtle and complex, and had a sounder plot
construction than the earliest slapstick
comedy shorts. Most important, it had
the developed talents of the great comics. In this pointed parody of Civil War
films and the western epic, Raymond
Griffith demonstrates that he deserves
comparison to Keaton, Chaplin, and
Lloyd. Two emissaries from opposing
sides of the war strive to get their hands
on a shipment from a Nevada mine of
gold that may help determine the outcome of the conflict. Griffith wears the
uniform of a Confederate soldier at first,
but soon trades it for his spy disguise of
formal clothes and tall silk hat, which
turns out to be his more typical cos-

tume. The legacy of Mack Sennett
training is present in every bit of violence and in each visual gag, of which
there is an endless parade. The ending
recalls the superb touch of Chaplinesque pathos.

THE LATE MATTHEW PASCAL (FEU MATHIAS PASCAL)

March 1926. France.
Albatros-Cinegraphic. Directed and
written by Marcel L'Herbier from the
novel by Luigi Pirandello. Art Direction
by Alberto Cavalcanti. With Ivan Mozhukhin, Michel Simon, Lois Moran.
English titles.
159 min. B&W. Silent. 18 fps.

Based on a Pirandello novel, this is a
comedy about a man trapped in an unhappy marriage who wins his freedom
when he is mistakenly assumed dead but
finds it does not bring him what he had
expected. The Pirandellian spirit of irony
and illusion is reflected in the film's visual translation. Marcel L'Herbier belonged to the Impressionist school of
Louis Delluc. The film's rapid cutting
rhythms, kaleidoscopic images in montage sequences, out-of-focus impressions of speed, camera movements, subjective viewpoints, and double exposures
belong to Impressionism, in which the
creation of atmosphere and psychological depth are significant. Begun in 1924,
this is, however, a late manifestation of
Impressionism and is related as well to
German Expressionist art, particularly
by Alberto Cavalcanti's famous sets with
their dominant lines, curves, and diagonals.

THE GENERAL (1927)

THE LODGER

September 1926. Great Britain.
Gainsborough Pictures. Directed by
Alfred Hitchcock. Produced by Michael
Balcon. Script by Hitchcock, Eliot Stan-
nard from a novel by Mrs. Belloc-
Lowndes. Photographed by Baron Ven-
timiglia (Hal Young). With Ivor Novello, Marie Ault.
87 min. B&W. Silent. 18 fps.

Hitchcock's third film was, he has said,
"the first time I exercised my style." Mrs.
Belloc-Lowndes's novel about the sadis-
tic Victorian murderer, Jack-the-Rip-
per, adapts itself well to the suspense
film formula that Hitchcock made his
own. Elements from German Expressionism help to create the mood of terror and guilt that he casts over his characters: the mysterious lodger, the
landlady and her daughter, and the police detective. The film's rhythm, its
cutting, its use of light and shadow, isolated glances, and gestures, suggest ambiguous, dramatic relationships without
the need for extensive subtitles, and even
create suggestions of sound in such
scenes as the lodger's footsteps heard
on the ceiling. Hitchcock's implication
of the spectator as voyeur is already
present in this first thriller.

THE MAGIC CLOCK (L'HORLOGE MAGIQUE. HISTOIRE DE LA PETITE FILLE QUI VOULAIT ÊTRE PRINCESSE)

1926. France.
Produced and directed by Ladislas
Starewicz. French titles.
46 min. B&W. (Also available in a color
version.) Silent. 18 fps.

Ladislas Starewicz, the creator of early
Russian puppet animation films (see
Revenge of a Kinematograph Camera-
man [1912]), worked also in feature film
production. After the revolution he
joined other émigrés in Paris. From 1923
onward, he devoted himself to the independent production of puppet films.
Using a combination of live action and
animation, Starewicz created this
charming fantasy about the clockmak-
er's daughter who falls in love with one
of the medieval knights decorating a
magnificent clock and who, in dreams,
enters the fantasy world of the clock.
Starewicz's imaginative work is a forerunner to the Czechoslovakian puppet
films by Jiří Trnka.

MOTHER (MAT')

October 11, 1926. U.S.S.R.
Mezhrabpom-Russ. Directed by Vsevolod I. Pudovkin. Script by Nathan Zarkhi from a novel by Maxim Gorky. Photographed by Anatoli Golovnya. With
Vera Baranovskaya, Nikolai Batalov.
English titles.
104 min. B&W. Silent. 18 fps.

With the simple theme of a working-class
mother growing in political consciousness through participation in revolutionary activity, this film established Pudovkin as one of the major figures of
the new Soviet cinema. A student of
Kuleshov and an admirer of Griffith's
films, he was writing his first book of
film theory at the same time he was
making **Mother**. His expert cutting on
movement and his associated editing of
unrelated scenes to form what he called
a "plastic synthesis" are amply demonstrated here. Although in direct opposition to Eisenstein's shock montage,
Pudovkin used a linkage method advanced far beyond Kuleshov's theories.
A planned variation in cutting rhythms
for the various sections comes to its climax in the famous rush of images comparing the spring thaw and breaking up
of the ice to the coming of the revolution. Where Eisenstein strove to portray
the class structure through types, Pudovkin depicts individual human beings
and personal relationships.

THE SORROWS OF SATAN

October 12, 1926. U.S.A.
Famous Players-Lasky (Paramount). Directed by D. W. Griffith. Script by Forrest Halsey adapted by John Russell and
George Hull from a novel by Marie
Corelli. Photographed by Harry Fischbeck. With Adolphe Menjou, Carol
Dempster, Ricardo Cortez, Lya de Putti.
84 min. B&W. Silent. 24 fps.

The same Marie Corelli novel on which
this film is based provided the starting
point for Dreyer's **Leaves From Satan's
Book** (1921). Bought by Paramount for
Cecil B. De Mille, it was assigned to
Griffith after De Mille left the company. After a series of financial difficulties, Griffith was now working under
contract. This story of Satan's role in
human affairs following his expulsion
from heaven gave the director opportunity to try some special effects. The
nightclub sequences, including erotic
dances, were lavishly produced but much
cut in the final version, which was not
prepared by Griffith. The tender love
scenes in the shabby rooming house
where the young couple live and work
in opposite rooms are more typical of
Griffith's work. Adolphe Menjou, then
at the height of his career, gives a suave
and sophisticated performance as Satan. In the final sequence, Griffith suggests his evil nature by showing just the
shadow of a monster devil, its awful
reality seen only by the hero's eyes.

WHAT PRICE GLORY

November 23, 1926. U.S.A.
Fox Film. Directed by Raoul Walsh.
Script by James T. O'Donohoe based on
the play by Maxwell Anderson, Laur-
ence Stallings. With Victor McLaglen,
Edmund Lowe, Dolores Del Rio.
122 min. B&W. Silent. 24 fps.

This archetypal celebration of war as a
game played by roistering comrades was,
in its time, a step toward a more realistic treatment of the subject of war.
World War I literature had not yet made
its most forceful appearance. The film's
advance in honesty is based on showing
war heroes that swear, get drunk, whore,
and fight among themselves. Its baw-
diness is typical of Raoul Walsh, as is the
expert, fast-paced direction of action
scenes. Its comedy is emphasized at the

expense of some of the bitterness and irony of the play, a big success in 1924. The battle scenes are excitingly mounted and dramatically photographed, using contrast lighting, with flares of light in the darkness revealing long shots of soldiers advancing and falling. The dying Mother's Boy stumbling down the steps, crying out to "stop the blood," provides at least one moment when the horrors of war are fully felt. The film's popularity centered on the characters of Captain Flagg and Sergeant Quirt, and the actors repeated these roles in *The Cockeyed World* (1929), again under Walsh's direction.

BERLIN: SYMPHONY OF A GREAT CITY (BERLIN, DIE SINFONIE DER GROSSTADT) (1927). *See* Documentary Film

THE CAT AND THE CANARY

March 31, 1927. U.S.A.
Universal-Jewel. Directed by Paul Leni. Script by Robert F. Hill, Alfred Cohn, adapted from a play by John Willard. Photographed by Gilbert Warrenton. With Laura La Plante, Creighton Hale, Tully Marshall, Gertrude Astor, Flora Finch, Forrest Stanley.
78 min. B&W. Silent. 24 fps.

The serials and their combination of suspense and thrills gave way in the late twenties to the mystery film well-laced with comedy. This is one of the best examples of the genre, derived, as many of them were, from a successful Broadway play. It is the first American film by Paul Leni, German stage-designer and artist, and director of the film *Waxworks* (1924). The relatives gather to read a will at midnight in a weird mansion. The heiress is required to be sane to inherit, and somebody else is determined to drive her crazy with fright. The Gothic-looking sets and dramatic lighting contrasts contribute to an atmosphere of foreboding. The oblique camera angles reflect the fashion not only for German directors but *any* director in Hollywood in the late twenties. The mystery-comedy genre of the late silent period was superceded in its turn by the horror film of the early thirties.

THE END OF ST. PETERSBURG (KONYETS SANKT-PETERBURGA)

December 13, 1927. U.S.S.R.
Mezhrabpom-Russ. Directed by Vsevolod I. Pudovkin. Script by Nathan Zarkhi. Photographed by Anatoli Golovnya. Art Direction by Sergei Kozlovsky. With Vera Baranovskaya, Ivan Chuvelev. English titles.

95 min. B&W. Silent. 18 fps.

Pudovkin was commissioned to make this film for the tenth anniversary of the October Revolution of 1917, as Eisenstein was for *October* (1928). Pudovkin's film, completed first, was the more intensely dramatic of the two films. It tells of the fall of the city, which would be renamed Leningrad, in part through the experiences of a young peasant who comes to understand the need for revolution. As an exercise of Pudovkin's montage theories the film is worth extended study. He goes further than in *Mother* (1926) to create symbols by associated shots, some of which rise to the realm of visual poetry. The horrors of war are graphically contrasted with the joy of stock market speculators over their war profits. The stone equestrian statue of Peter the Great is made, through montage, to play an active role in the events.

THE GENERAL

February 5, 1927. U.S.A.
Art Cinema (United Artists). Directed by Buster Keaton and Clyde Bruckman. Script by Joseph A. Mitchell, C. Bruckman. Photographed by J. D. Jennings. With Keaton, Marion Mack, Glen Cavender.
79 min. B&W. Silent. 24 fps.

A locomotive shares the honors with the deadpan comic, Buster Keaton, in this adventure suggested by a historical incident of the Civil War. Keaton loves his engine and his girl equally, and in saving one and impressing the other he ends up a hero. This is a masterpiece

of the Golden Age of silent film comedy, and may well be Keaton's greatest film. It is a model of clarity and coherence. The gags are completely visual, the comic situations built up through the technique of analytical editing. In Keaton films, machinery has a will and a destiny of its own, and he, uncomprehending, must follow it. He pursues a steady course that is entirely logical to him even if it runs counter to the rest of the world. It is difficult to analyze the comedy implicit in Keaton's performance—his stance, his stiff gestures, and his unblinking gaze—but it is unique.

HOTEL IMPERIAL

January 9, 1927. U.S.A.
Famous Players-Lasky (Paramount). Produced by Erich Pommer. Directed by Mauritz Stiller. Script by Jules Furthman from a story by Lajos Biro. Photographed by Bert Glennon. With Pola Negri, James Hall.
78 min. B&W. Silent. 24 fps.

During World War I, an Austrian officer behind the Russian lines is saved by a chambermaid in the hotel the Russians have made their headquarters. Designed as a star vehicle for Pola Negri when her Hollywood career was faltering, this film was an attempt to change her image from femme fatale to an innocent, wide-eyed young girl who sacrifices her reputation for the man she loves. The distinguished Swedish director Mauritz Stiller and the famous German producer Erich Pommer were assigned to work the transformation. When Negri's subdued performance is permitted a chance to show her fiery

THE ITALIAN STRAW HAT (1927) (p. 70)

Brigitte Helm (on stairs) in METROPOLIS (1927)

personality, it is still nothing short of electrifying. Although there are flashes of first-rate filmmaking, Stiller soon realized he was not at home in the American studios and went back to Sweden. The moving camera, mounted on rails constructed above the sets, is evidence of German production methods imported to Hollywood.

THE ITALIAN STRAW HAT (UN CHAPEAU DE PAILLE D'ITALIE)

July 1927. France.
Albatros. Directed by René Clair. Script by Clair adapted from the comedy by Eugene Labiche and Marc Michel. Photographed by Nicolas Rudakoff, Maurice Desfassiaux. With Albert Préjean, Olga Tschekova. English titles.
114 min. B&W. Silent. 18 fps.

René Clair's sparkling version of the 19th-century farce by Labiche and Michel turns the fast-stepping dialogue of the original into purely visual wit and into a satire of the bourgeoisie. A bridegroom is on the way to his wedding when his horse eats a hat belonging to a woman who is involved in an adulterous affair. His efforts to replace the hat and save the lady are interwoven with the family's simultaneous attempts to hold the wedding. These story elements constitute the components of a slapstick chase. The comedy is constructed in the manner of a well-wrought machine. A series of objects, including the famous hat, a lost glove, an ear trumpet, and several clocks provide material for visual gags, represent characters, and serve as symbols of bourgeois respectability. Clair, a journalist and an actor, entered directing with experimental films before turning to commercial filmmaking. This was his first big critical success.

THE LOVE OF JEANNE NEY (DIE LIEBE DER JEANNE NEY)

December 1927. Germany.
Ufa. Directed by G. W. Pabst. Script by Ladislaus Vajda, Ilja Ehrenburg from Ehrenburg's novel. Photographed by Fritz Arno Wagner, Walter Robert Lach. Art Direction by Otto Hunte. With Edith Jehanne, Uno Henning, Brigitte Helm, Fritz Rasp. English titles.
139 min. B&W. Silent. 18 fps.

The New Objectivity, which replaced Expressionism in German cinema, found its greatest eloquence in this film. It concerns a pair of young lovers inextricably and tragically entangled with corrupt and sordid characters in postwar Europe. They are in the midst of the Crimean War and then in Paris, embroiled in the intrigues of the Soviet Revolution. The film has a complicated, melodramatic plot. Its sense of realism comes from the graphic depiction of the low social milieu and the feeling that the action is taking place outdoors. Yet almost every shot was made inside the Ufa studios in specially constructed sets, the camera mounted on overhead rails for the utmost in fluidity. While many shots are made with the moving camera and the film appears to be seamless, it is in fact a powerful demonstration of the art of editing: the isolation of relevant details and objects and the recombination of them to express the psychology of the characters and subtleties of personal relationships. A particularly instructive example of Pabst's use of montage in this film is available as an excerpt (see Film Study).

METROPOLIS

January 10, 1927. Germany.
Ufa. Directed by Fritz Lang. Script by Lang, Thea von Harbou. Photographed by Karl Freund, Günther Rittau. Art Direction by Otto Hunte, Erich Kettelhut, Karl Vollbrecht. With Brigitte Helm, Alfred Abel, Rudolf Klein-Rogge, Gustave Fröhlich. English titles. 135 min. B&W. Silent. 18 fps.

Metropolis is a science fiction film, a grim view of a future world in which mechanization has succeeded in dehumanizing the human race. Its design is firmly rooted in the twenties aesthetic, with its emphasis on the city and the machine. Images of the modern urban landscape appear frequently in the decade's art forms. In *Metropolis*, these images are filtered through German Expressionism, Piscator's theater craft casting its influence on the geometrical patterns and massed composition of crowds of extras. Expressionism gives the picture its mystical emotional atmosphere by contrasting light and shadow. A robot is constructed to replace human workers, and yet the crowds of workers are themselves already as mechanized as the robot, assembling themselves into monumental architectural compositions. The function of the machinery is of secondary interest; it is its forms and movements, its pistons and gears, its geometrical abstraction that interest the designers of this film. Eugene Schufftan's mirror matte process was used for the first time in this film, making possible a greater degree of illusionism.

LA P'TITE LILIE (LITTLE LILIE)

1927. France.
Neó-Film-Braunberger. Directed by Alberto Cavalcanti. Music by Darius Milhaud. With Catherine Hessling, Jean Renoir. Original French intertitles with English subtitles.

10 min. B&W. Sound. 24 fps. (music score).

The Brazilian Cavalcanti was educated in Europe as an architect and became set designer for a number of notable French films of the twenties. He is identified with the French avant-garde (see *Rien que les heures* [1926]), to which this film belongs, as well as with the commercial cinema, and later, in the thirties, with the British documentary movement. This lyric little film was based on a popular song about a young girl led into prostitution by the man she loves. It is a fantasy, highly stylized, and charged with irony. In some sense it is also a satire of early film style. The film's special visual effect was achieved by filming through a veiled lens. Its cast is of special interest: the young director Jean Renoir and his wife.

SEVENTH HEAVEN

May 6, 1927. U.S.A.
Fox Film. Directed by Frank Borzage. Script by Benjamin Glazer from a play by Austin Strong. Photographed by Ernest Palmer, J. A. Valentine. With Janet Gaynor, Charles Farrell.
120 min. B&W. Sound. 24 fps. (music score).

The elements of German cinema were incorporated into the Hollywood technique by 1927: the recreation of different milieus inside the artificial world of the studio, Expressionist lighting, and above all, tracking shots. Here, they are applied to a pure love story. The story takes place in an imaginary Paris in 1914; the hero works in the sewers but looks "to the stars"; before he is married to the girl he loves, he is sent to war and reported killed, but returns to her, blinded. The director, Frank Borzage, specialized in films of sentiment. This very popular film exists in the realm of instinct and blind emotion, the powerful forces underlying human behavior. Its young lovers, Gaynor and Farrell, had a freshness and appeal that made them a famous co-starring team following the success of this film. *Seventh Heaven* won almost all the major Academy Awards in the first year they were presented.

SUNRISE. A SONG OF TWO HUMANS

September 23, 1927. U.S.A.
Fox Film. Directed by F. W. Murnau. Script by Carl Mayer based on the story "A Trip to Tilsit" by Herman Sudermann. Photographed by Charles Rosher, Karl Struss. With George O'Brien, Janet Gaynor.

95 min. B&W. Sound. 24 fps. (music score and sound effects).

Murnau's first American film is an allegory set in no particular time or place, about a man who is temporarily overruled by his passions, inflamed by the power of evil as personified by the city woman, and who finally returns to his senses and the orderly family life of the country. It is a virtuoso exercise representing the expressiveness of the silent film as it neared its end. Murnau brought with him from Germany his method of unified set construction that permitted the camera to move continuously to produce the subjective viewpoint that such a fluid camera made possible. The film is filled with visual symbols: moonlight, swamp, mud, and water representing the lure of illicit love; sun, flowers, and orderly domestic interiors for married love. Two sequences in particular have been widely admired. The first is the long tracking shot of the man drawn into the moonlit swamp, the camera turning and twisting with his passage. The second is the ride of the husband and wife on the trolley, the landscape slipping past unseen by them, because they are frozen in the tension of horror, guilt, and fear, until they find themselves at last in the very midst of the frightening city.

UNDERWORLD

August 20, 1927. U.S.A.
Paramount Famous Lasky. Directed by Josef von Sternberg. Script by Robert N. Lee, adapted by Charles Furthman from a story by Ben Hecht. Photographed by Bert Glennon. Art Direction by Hans Dreier. With George Bancroft. Evelyn Brent, Clive Brook.
83 min. B&W. Silent. 24 fps.

A forerunner to the gangster films of the 1930s, *Underworld* is not concerned with social problems but with the forces of destiny and human emotions. It has more action, suspense, quick cutting, and dazzling montage sequences than other Sternberg films, but it is equally filled with his characteristic dense compositions, tightly framed, loaded with meaning and emotion. The protagonists are gangsters, living a dangerous life, but the typical Sternberg drama is played out between two men and the girl they both love. With an economy of means, he creates a world of expression compacted into a few gestures and details. Born in Vienna, Josef von Sternberg learned his craft in American studios, and if this film bears traces of European influences, so did all of American cinema at the end of the si-

Evelyn Brent in UNDERWORLD (1927)

lent period. Above all, Sternberg was an artist concerned with total control of his medium.

BLUEBOTTLES

April 1928. Great Britain.
Angle Pictures. Directed by Ivor Montagu. Script and Art Direction by Frank Wells based on an H. G. Wells story. Photographed by F. A. Young. With Elsa Lanchester, Charles Laughton.
25 min. B&W. Silent. 24 fps.

One of a series of three short films made by Ivor Montagu in 1928 and written specifically for the actress Elsa Lanchester (*Day Dreams* was the second, *The Tonic* was the third), this is a slapstick comedy in which she innocently gets involved with the police when she picks up a whistle on the street. She blows it and sets off a police raid, and a parody of a chase, like the later one in *Duck Soup* (1933), involving a montage of planes, tanks, ships, and militia. Charles Laughton has only a small role here, as one of the gangsters. Ivor Montagu was a leader of the British avant-garde movement.

DAY DREAMS

May 1928. Great Britain.
Angle Pictures. Directed by Ivor Montagu. Script and Art Direction by Frank Wells based on a story by H. G. Wells. Photographed by F. A. Young. With Elsa Lanchester, Charles Laughton.
23 min. B&W. Silent. 24 fps.

The second in the series of low-budget avant-garde films made by Ivor Montagu, this is a comedy in which Elsa Lanchester dreams about the Countess Pornay, the famous actress, who began her career as a midinette, carrying hatboxes through the streets. When she falls in the mud, she is helped to her feet by the wealthy count and launched on a series of fantastic adventures. The same actors play both the characters in a lowly boardinghouse and in the fantasy. In the end, Elsa comes to the conclusion she should get a job carrying boxes. Ingenious cutting gives the illusion of a much more lavish production.

THE FALL OF THE HOUSE OF USHER (LA CHUTE DE LA MAISON USHER)

1928. France.
Les Films Jean Epstein. Directed by Jean Epstein. Script by Epstein from stories by Edgar Allan Poe. Photographed by Lucas and Hebert. With Jean Debucourt, Marguerite Gance, Charles Lamy. French titles.
62 min. B&W. Silent. 18 fps.

Jean Epstein's last film before he broke with the avant-garde movement is based on the tales of Edgar Allan Poe. The mysterious house of Usher is visited by a friend who finds Roderick following the family tradition of painting his wife's portrait with such passion that he draws the life from her to put it into his picture. Refusing to accept her death, he declines to have her coffin nailed shut. Everything in this film is subordinated to the creation of atmosphere.

OCTOBER (1928)

Misty, fog-shrouded scenes, slow-motion filming, low angles, lighting, and camera tricks lend themselves to eerie supernatural effects. Epstein was a cinema theoretician, and the maker of the important Impressionist film *Coeur Fidèle* (1923). After this film, he launched a series of lyric documentaries among the fishermen of Brittany, and found a new use for slow-motion in drawing emotional performances from nonactors.

THE GAUCHO

January 1, 1928. U.S.A.
Elton Corporation (Douglas Fairbanks). Directed by F. Richard Jones. Script by Lotta Woods from a story by Elton Thomas (pseudonym of Fairbanks). With Douglas Fairbanks, Lupe Velez, Gustav von Seyffertitz.
100 min. B&W. Silent. 24 fps.

In this Argentinian western, Douglas Fairbanks is an outlaw with a Robin Hood complex. He saves a holy shrine from desecration, falls victim to leprosy, lusts after women, experiences religious conversion. These elements are untypical of Fairbanks but do not prevent *The Gaucho* from being an exciting action film or Fairbanks from performing quite impossible acrobatic feats. The cattle stampede, coming at the climax of the picture, is one of the best ever filmed. Over and again the screen is filled with the massed animals; they surge through the streets; all the ensuing shots are filled with clouds of dust through which we half see the action. Characteristically for Hollywood films in the late twenties, the director favors unusual camera angles, tracking shots, and pictorial compositions and lighting. Mary Pickford plays a brief uncredited role as Our Lady of the Shrine.

THE LAST COMMAND

January 21, 1928. U.S.A.
Paramount Famous Lasky. Directed by Josef von Sternberg. Script by John F. Goodrich from a story by Lajos Biro. Photographed by Bert Glennon. With Emil Jannings, Evelyn Brent, William Powell.
90 min. B&W. Silent. 24 fps.

A former Russian general is discovered as an extra on a Hollywood lot by a director who was formerly a Communist leader whom the general had humiliated. The general is assigned the part of a Russian general in a movie about the revolution. This Pirandellian story is as much about Hollywood as a factory for the creation of illusion as it is about the Russian revolution; the relationship

between two men and a girl, as in the other Sternberg films, is its chief theme. Through dense, crowded compositions, profuse with movement and rich in lighting effects, Sternberg relates an imaginary Russia to Hollywood, creating endless visual parallels. By the time of this film, Sternberg had made the prolonged tracking shot and the dissolve intrinsic to his style. Long, slow tracking shots slide past close-ups of faces or advance around corners, and with Sternberg's economy of means, tightly-packed shots of crowds suggest infinite extension beyond the frame.

THE LITTLE MATCH GIRL (LA PETITE MARCHANDE D'ALLUMETTES)

1928. France.
Production Jean Tedesco. Directed by Jean Renoir. Script by Renoir and Tedesco from the story by Hans Christian Andersen. Photographed by Jean Bachelet. With Catherine Hessling. French titles.
40 min. B&W. Silent. 18 fps.

The artists of the French avant-garde were as intrigued by camera tricks and illusionism as any of the earliest filmmakers. This version of the Andersen fairy tale about the fantasies of a poor little street urchin dying in the cold was created in a little attic studio in Le Vieux-Colombier, an avant-garde film theater managed by Jean Tedesco. The little girl enters a dream world of a kingdom of toys, which come to life with the assistance of camera magic. Renoir has said that the film was made primarily to explore the possibilities of the newly developed panchromatic stock. It remains among his best-loved silent films, capturing the childlike innocence and magic of the fairy tale.

OCTOBER (TEN DAYS THAT SHOOK THE WORLD)

March 18, 1928. U.S.S.R.
Sovkino. Directed and written by Sergei Eisenstein and Grigori Alexandrov. Photographed by Eduard Tisse. With Nikandrov, N. Popov, B. Livanov, Eduard Tisse. English titles.
149 min. B&W. Silent. 18 fps.

Eisenstein was already at work on *Old and New* (1929) when called upon to make this film about the events of the October 1917 revolution in time for the tenth anniversary celebrations. Eisenstein's ambitious film was not completed in time, though he and Pudovkin, who was making *The End of St. Petersburg* (1927) for the same occasion, were firing off salvos at the Winter Palace for their productions at the same time. The film has no single hero but the masses. Eisenstein's intent was to force intellectual comprehension of the revolutionary events through his montage methods. Where others tried to achieve a seamless illusion of reality, Eisenstein called attention to his cuts, with many shots only a few frames each. Among the many famous examples in this film is the opening of the bridge, extended in time by some forty shots, increasing tension and building an emotional force. During the production, the open split between Stalin and Trotsky occurred, and some scenes had to be cut out.

THE PASSION OF JOAN OF ARC (LA PASSION DE JEANNE D'ARC)

April 21, 1928. France.
Société Générale de Films. Directed by Carl Theodor Dreyer. Script by Dreyer, based in part on a novel by Joseph Delteil. Photographed by Rudolph Maté. With Marie Falconetti, Eugene Silvain, Michel Simon, Antonin Artaud. English titles.
119 min. B&W. Silent. 18 fps.

The trial and death of Joan of Arc, her sufferings and her ecstasy, form the subject of Dreyer's great film at the end of the silent period. Basing it on contemporary documents of the trial, Dreyer here has created a work of transcendental power. The sets are austere. There is little historical background. Huge close-ups dominate, sometimes without the context of establishing shots. Oblique camera angles express a subjective point of view, distorting facial expressions. The texture of human skin, of hair, cloth and metal, mouths and eyes are emphasized. The pace is slow and relentless. Marie Falconetti's intense performance as Joan is one of the most famous in all film history.

SPIES (SPIONE)

March 22, 1928. Germany.
Ufa. Directed by Fritz Lang. Script by Lang and Thea von Harbou based on a novel by Thea von Harbou. Photographed by Fritz Arno Wagner. Art Direction by Otto Hunte and Karl Vollbrecht. With Rudolf Klein-Rogge, Willy Fritsch, Gerda Maurus, Lupu Pick. English titles.
85 min. B&W. Silent. 24 fps.

After the monumental styles of his two previous films, **Die Nibelungen** (1924) and **Metropolis** (1927), Lang returned to the adventure-film serial form of **Dr. Mabuse** (1922). Master criminal Haghi is a banker who is also a spy. Govern-

ment agents try in vain to identify and capture him, until one is successful because one of Haghi's spies falls in love with him. Haghi and the agents appear in innumerable disguises. Lang's avoidance of the establishing shot and emphasis on objects, details, expressions, and movement places the film in a paranoid fantasy context. Haghi sits like a spider in his web in a chaotic and violent universe filled with machinery in motion, while in his underground headquarters all is ordered, calm, and rational. Lang's earlier films emphasized the supernatural and mysticism, but here he moves toward a psychological realism built of gestures and expressions. The film retains the episodic form of the serial, and therefore this version, though abridged by half for the American release, still contains the original flavor.

STORM OVER ASIA (POTOMOK CHINGIS-KHAN)

1928. U.S.S.R.
Mezhrabpomfilm. Directed by Vsevolod I. Pudovkin. Script by Osip Brik based on a story by I. Novokshonov. Photographed by Anatoli Golovnya. With Valeri Inkizhinov, A. Christiakov, A. Dedintsev. English titles.
105 min. B&W. Silent. 18 fps.

A fable and an epic poem about revolution among the Mongolians in 1920 against the British occupiers, this follows the adventures of a nomadic fur hunter when he runs up against the British, who discover he wears an amulet identifying him as a direct descendent of Ghengis-Kahn. They set him up as a puppet ruler to quiet the revolt, but as he comes to political consciousness, he turns to lead the rebels to victory. Pudovkin gave weight to editing which was equal to that given by Eisenstein, but preferred to follow the more intuitive line of Griffith. This film depends on cutting, using camera movement only when necessary to follow action. Parallel editing is used for ironic contrast and metaphor. Slow motion is used for what Pudovkin calls "close-ups in time," as in the low angle shot of the soldiers doing a slow-motion about face, giving the impression of a mighty army. The wind storm at the end, like the breaking up of the ice in **Mother** (1926), is an emotionally charged allegory of revolution and a brilliant example of the power of disjunctive editing. This picture also has ethnographic interest: it represents the first time the life of the Mongolian people had been documented on film. This is the abbreviated American release version.

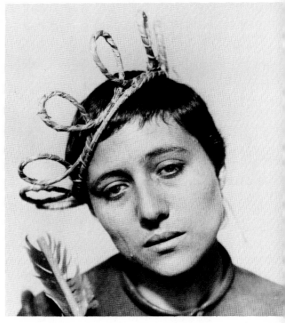

Marie Falconetti in
THE PASSION OF JOAN OF ARC (1928)

TWO TARS

1928. U.S.A.
Hal Roach. Directed by James Parrott. Photographed by George Stevens. With Stan Laurel and Oliver Hardy, Edgar Kennedy.
22 min. B&W. Silent. 24 fps.

In this example of the best work of Laurel and Hardy, about all that happens in terms of plot is that two sailors on leave have trouble with a rented car, pick up two girls who are fighting a recalcitrant chewing-gum machine, and encounter a traffic jam where they start a fight of colossal proportions in which the cars are all demolished. It is, however, quite enough for the special talents of this pair. The peculiarly slow rhythm of their performance, their emphasis on dignity upset, trust betrayed, and frustration expressed makes them unique among comics. And absolutely hilarious. Their frustrations are those we all meet in daily life and we experience vicarious satisfaction in the orgy of destruction by which they resolve them. Their destruction of the machine, totem of American life in the twenties, made this comedy of special significance for the period.

ARSENAL

February 25, 1929. U.S.S.R.
Vufku. Directed and written by Alexander Dovzhenko. Photographed by Danylo Demutsky. Art Direction by Isaac Shpinel and Vladimir Muller. With Semyon Svashenko, Nikolai Nademsky, Ambrose Buchma. English titles.
95 min. B&W. Silent. 18 fps.

Hailed as the first masterpiece of the Ukrainian cinema and a forceful ideological statement, this film continues to live because of its remarkable reflection of the equality between man and nature, and because of its substitution of poetic continuity for the usual story structure. The flow of ideas and emotions, rather than conflicts between individual characters, determines the structure. It covers the events in the Ukraine from World War I, through the February and October Revolutions in Russia, to the suppression of a revolt of workers barricaded in a Kiev munitions factory in January 1918. It shows the struggles of the separatists versus the Ukrainian workers who supported the Bolsheviks. Its richly assorted imagery has a cumulative effect. The film's concepts and symbols are diverse and complicated enough to demand repeated viewing for a full appreciation.

BIG BUSINESS

June 27, 1929. U.S.A.
Hal Roach. Directed by J. Wesley Horne. Photographed by George Stevens. With Stan Laurel and Oliver Hardy, Jimmy Finlayson.
20 min. B&W. Silent. 24 fps.

This Laurel and Hardy comedy confidently dispenses with all but one gag. The illustrious innocents are trying to sell Christmas trees in a sunny California suburb. At Jimmy Finlayson's house, they meet their match. He angrily cuts up the trees; they destroy his house; he takes their truck apart. The entire two reels are spent in the slow, rhythmic orgy of destruction. Crowds gather to watch, joined by a policeman who does nothing but stare in disbelief and write it all down. Laurel and Hardy's chief contribution to the Sennett slapstick tradition

was their recognition of the time needed for an audience to react to a gag before it is topped by another, or, in this case, by its repetition and extension.

BROTHERS (BRÜDER)

1929. Germany.
Produced, written, and directed by Werner Hochbaum. With a cast of non-professionals. German titles only.
63 min. B&W. Sound. 24 fps (music score and sound effects).

Brothers is a recreation of the events of the Hamburg dock strike in the winter of 1896–97 and their effect on the lives of one of the workers and his family. Forgotten for forty years, this remarkable film was rediscovered through the restoration work of the Staatliches Filmarchiv der DDR. It is an outstanding representative of the handful of socialist or leftist films made in Germany in the shadow of the approaching Nazi regime. Even in its own time, it was not widely known, and received only a limited circulation by the Social Democrat Party. This was the first feature film by Werner Hochbaum, best known until recently for his **The Eternal Mask** (Switzerland, 1935). **Brothers** is filled with strikingly composed images, its opening sequence of the wakening of a city on a winter morning ranking with the best of the city symphony films in its lyricism. It is an example of the International Style, that confluence of many national styles at the very end of the twenties, with a special link to the early Eisenstein films not only in its theme but also in the metaphoric or satiric images of statues and the use of

nonactors. Viewers of the film today also see in it a forecast of the Neo-Realism of the forties, in its warm humanistic portrayal of the docker's life with his family in their poor tenement flat. The German titles, few in number, should not prove a serious obstacle to understanding the film. The soundtrack with music and sound effects was added in 1973.

CHINA EXPRESS (BLUE EXPRESS; GOLUBOI EKSPRESS)

December 20, 1929. U.S.S.R.
Sovkino. Directed by Ilya Trauberg. Screenplay by Sergei Tretyakov. Photographed by B. Krennikov, Yuri Stilianudis. With Sun Bo-Yang, Chou Hsifan, Chang Kai, Sergei Minin. Available with Russian or English titles: please specify.
90 min. B&W. Silent. 18 fps.

In this Soviet film, a train crossing China is a powerful metaphor for political forces. The first class contains foreigners and Chinese war lords, the second middle-class merchants and professionals, the third class peasants. An attack on a young peasant girl launches a peasant revolt, and they take over a shipment of firearms and the train. Attempts to halt the train fail, and it speeds on as a revolutionary force, in the last shot rushing directly up the screen. In director Ilya Trauberg, the youthful Soviet cinema had a second generation. He had worked as an assistant on Eisenstein's **October** (1928). With this film he makes a practical application of Eisenstein's montage theories in a less abstract manner, and in an adventure genre patterned after American cinema.

FRAGMENT OF AN EMPIRE (OBLOMOK IMPERII)

October 28, 1929. U.S.S.R.
Sovkino. Directed by Friedrich Ermler. Screenplay by Ermler, K. Vinogradskaya. With Fyodor Nikitin. English titles.
103 min. B&W. Silent. 18 fps.

Through the parable of a man who loses his memory in World War I and regains it ten years later in the new world of the Soviet Union, Ermler's last silent film dramatizes the social problems and conflicts arising from the imposition of the revolutionary order on the old Czarist culture. The famous sequence during which the hero regains his memory remains one of the finest examples of associative editing. The first part of the film concerns the return of memory, and the war scenes in which

Oliver Hardy and Stan Laurel in TWO TARS (1928) (p. 73)

the hero, left for dead, has lost his sense of the past. The second half is really a comedy in the style of *Bed and Sofa* (1926), as the hero encounters the human aspects of the reconstruction of society, its working relationships, its mass culture, and its modern concept of marriage.

THE IRON MASK

February 21, 1929. U.S.A.
Elton Corporation (Douglas Fairbanks). Directed by Allan Dwan. Screenplay by Elton Thomas (pseudonym of Fairbanks) from Alexandre Dumas's novel *The Man in the Iron Mask*. Photographed by Henry Sharp. With Douglas Fairbanks, Marguerite de la Motte, Nigel de Brulier.
98 min. B&W. Silent. 24 fps.

This sequel to *The Three Musketeers* (1921) is much closer to the spirit of the romantic adventures by Alexandre Dumas than the first film, which was dominated by the exuberant Fairbanks screen personality. This is the story of the twin sons born to the queen during the reign of Louis XIII, the first-born hidden away and his identity concealed behind an iron mask. Cardinal Richelieu intrigues for power, and D'Artagnan, Athos, Porthos, and Aramis join in the effort to restore the prince to the throne. Each of the comrades, some of them played by the same actors as in the earlier film, dies in turn in the service of France. At the end they march off together in a bank of clouds. It is as though Fairbanks bid farewell to his career as a swashbuckler. The production values are lavish, and Allan Dwan's direction of big crowd scenes in vast sets is very effective. The film was issued in both sound and silent versions in 1929; this is the silent one.

THE MAN WITH THE MOVIE CAMERA (CHELOVEK S KINOAPPARATOM) (1929). *See* Documentary Film

SUCH IS LIFE (TAKOVY JE ZIVOT; SO IST DAS LEBEN)

1929. Czechoslovakia/Germany.
Kavalirka. Directed by Carl Junghans. With Vera Baranovskaya, Theodor Pištěk, Valeska Gert. Made without intertitles (a few German titles announce the days).
74 min. B&W. Sound (music score). 24 fps.

The various currents of national film styles flowed together at the end of the twenties to form an international style. Ideas and filmmakers moved freely across borders. Certain films like *Such is Life* appeared at the conflux of currents to sum up the contributions of a decade of vigorous investigation into the art of the film. This film tells of the events in the life of a washerwoman and her family in Prague; the vitality of life in the Czech capital reflects its rhythms, as in the city symphony films. The shots of a statue seeming to fling its arms upward recalls Eisenstein's famous roaring lion statues in *Potemkin* (1925). The sequence of shots on the death of the washerwoman, her face dissolving in water, the flapping of her laundry, the soaring flight of birds, recalls the moment of death in Dreyer's *The Passion of Joan of Arc* (1928). None of this takes away from the originality of Junghans's imaginative work, which sums up the expressiveness of silent film as it reached its end.

ÜBERFALL (ACCIDENT)

1929. Germany.
Directed by Ernö Metzner. Script by Metzner and Grace Chiang. Photographed by Eduard von Borsody. With Heinrich Gotho, Sybille Schmitz, Eva Schmidt-Kayser.
22 min. B&W. Silent. 18 fps.

An experimental film related to the "street films" and the New Objectivity, this tells what happens as a consequence of a man picking up a counterfeit coin in the street. First gambling with it, he is then pursued and beaten by a thief for his winnings. He wakes up in a hospital, and the film's only title asks "Who is the guilty one?" It makes a remarkable use of subjective camera and mirror images to create an atmosphere of emotional intensity. It was banned by the Nazis as "brutalizing and demoralizing," and the original negative was burned.

THE WHITE HELL OF PITZ PALU (DIE WEISSE HÖLLE VOM PIZ PALÜ)

November 15, 1929. Germany.
H.R. Sokal-Film. Directed by Arnold Fanck and G. W. Pabst. Screenplay by Fanck and Ladislaus Vajda. Photographed by Sepp Allgeier, Richard Angst, Hans Schneeberger. With Leni Riefenstahl, Gustav Diessl, Ernst Petersen, Ernst Udet, Mizzi Götzel, Otto Spring. English titles.
75 min. B&W. Sound. 24 fps. (music score and sound effects).

One of Germany's most enduring film genres during the twenties and continuing into the sound period was the mountain-climbing epic. These films celebrate the mystic forces of nature and mankind's heroic efforts in combat with them, a theme that Siegfried Kracauer relates to the mysticism in the Nazi spirit. Fanck was a specialist in the mountain films, and Leni Riefenstahl began her film career starring in Fanck's films. For this outstanding example of the genre, Fanck was joined by Pabst, an unlikely collaboration. It is difficult to discover what Pabst, the realist filmmaker, contributed to this romanticism. A couple on their honeymoon in the mountains encounter the stern Dr. Krafft (Gustav Diessl), who lost his bride on the same mountain a year before, and join their fates to his in an attempt to conquer the North Wall, an irrational decision since thawing conditions make it the most dangerous time. The camera work of Sepp Allgeier, Richard Angst, and Hans Schneeberger created images of a terrifying and mysterious beauty, snow-covered mountains, clouds, icy slopes, and the torch-light search for the mountain's victims in an ice-covered crevice. The airplane is flown by Ernst Udet, the real-life stunt flier who later committed suicide as an ace of the Nazi Luftwaffe, and whose story is told in the film *The Devil's General* (Germany, 1955). The soundtrack was added in 1935.

A COTTAGE ON DARTMOOR

January 17, 1930. Great Britain.
British Instructional Films. Directed and written by Anthony Asquith. With Norah Baring, Uno Henning, Hans Schlettow.
74 min. B&W. Silent. 24 fps.

This late silent film was made with a synchronized music score and one dialogue sequence—when the couple goes to see the new talkies—but the sound was on separate discs, now lost. It is an example of the international film style, in which all the expressive devices of the silent film are called upon and the use of intertitles avoided. The story line of the film is in the genre of the suspense thriller. Told as a prolonged flashback by an escaped convict who shows up at a lonely cottage in Dartmoor, it is about the growing jealousy of a barber's assistant over the love of the manicurist for a Dartmoor farmer, and his arrest for attempted murder. Subjective camera devices make a chilling scene of the barber's assistant poised with a razor over the waiting throat of the farmer. A talkative customer is visually compared to a rooster; a sports newsreel is cut in to show the topic of conversation; an image jumps up and down to show the viewpoint of a client receiving massage.

GOLD DIGGERS OF 1933 from AMERICAN MUSICALS:
FAMOUS PRODUCTION NUMBERS (1929–35)

Sound Fiction

ANNOTATIONS

Lucy Fischer, Herbert Reynolds,
Marita Sturken

THE COMING OF SOUND

1927–28. U.S.A.
Total Program: 39 min. B&W. Sound.

THE JAZZ SINGER (Homecoming sequence and Finale)

October 6, 1927.
Warner Bros. Directed by Alan Crosland. Screenplay by Alfred A. Cohn, from the play by Samson Raphaelson. Photographed by Hal Mohr. With Al Jolson, Eugenie Besserer.
11 min. and 3 min.

SHAW TALKS FOR MOVIETONE NEWS

June 25, 1928.
Fox Movietone. With George Bernard Shaw.
6 min.

THE SEX LIFE OF THE POLYP

1928.
Fox Movietone. With Robert Benchley.
11 min.

STEAMBOAT WILLIE

November 18, 1928.
Walt Disney. By Ub Iwerks.
8 min.

These four films, all made prior to Hollywood's first "full" year (1929) of conversion to sound, are major examples of the principal competing motion picture sound systems and the varied uses they served at the dawn of the talking era. Warner Bros.' sound-on-disc (Vitaphone) system required the simultaneous playing of separate sound discs along with the film. The public premiere of this process in August 1926 presented demonstration shorts and the feature-length **Don Juan** with recorded orchestral accompaniment. *The Jazz Singer*, released in October 1927, was primarily "silent," with recorded music, but it also contained four talking sequences, each with singing and two with short sketches of dialogue. The first excerpt here shows the transition from silent portions (with intertitles and accompaniment that includes bits of Tchaikovsky's *Romeo and Juliet*) to talking ones: returning home, the jazz singer (Al Jolson) is reunited with his mother; he sings "Blue Skies" for her before suffering the disapproval of his father,

an orthodox Jew who had resolved that his son should become a cantor. The second excerpt is the finale of the movie, where Jolson performs "My Mammy" in blackface on stage before an enthralled crowd. (Warner Bros. followed this triumph with the first all-talking feature; see **Lights of New York** [1928].) Despite the revolution that Warner Bros. precipitated, the constant problem of synchronization posed by the sound-on-disc process caused it to be abandoned within a few years in favor of its rival, the clearly superior sound-on-film (Movietone) system introduced early in 1927 by Fox. The prototype of soundtracks used ever since, the Movietone system integrated sound and picture by printing the track directly onto the film strip, adjacent to the picture frames; sound was thus picked up simultaneous to the projection of the film. This process was used to provide music and sound effects for Murnau's **Sunrise** (1927); but for live recording—notably, of speech—Fox limited it at first to newsreels and short subjects such as **Lindbergh's Flight From N.Y. to Paris** (1927), Bernard Shaw's appearance (what title, if any, the film originally bore is uncertain), and **The Sex Life of the Polyp**. Shaw had already been recorded on Lee De Forest's Phonofilm system in the early 1920s, when he agreed to be filmed by Fox Movietone, provided that he could supervise the filming himself. The recent Nobel Prize playwright affects his good-humoredly self-conscious public pose, pretending to be surprised

by the camera on a walk through his garden. Then he speaks directly to his audience, hamming it up and adding an imitation of Mussolini. In **The Sex Life of the Polyp**, comic Robert Benchley's nervous confusion with speech forms the basis for his clowning; already the apprehension about sound recording has become something suitable to joke about. Walt Disney, who always liked to be at the vanguard of technical innovation, contributed enormously to the transition period with **Steamboat Willie**, the first sound cartoon, drawn by Ub Iwerks. Recorded on the "independent" Cinephone system (also sound-on-film) of P. A. (Pat) Powers, the film used a simple rhythm—two beats per second—to synchronize its animated and audible effects. Mickey and Minnie Mouse both make their debuts to the tune of "Turkey in the Straw." The cartoon received as much acclaim and accomplished as much toward the acceptance of the talking medium as any other work.

—

LIGHTS OF NEW YORK

July 8, 1928. U.S.A.
Warner Bros. Directed by Bryan Foy. Screenplay and dialogue by Murray Roth, Hugh Herbert. Photographed by Ed DuPar. With Helene Costello, Cullen Landis, Mary Carr, Wheeler Oakman, Gladys Brockwell, Eugene Pallette.
56 min. B&W. Sound.

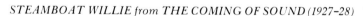

STEAMBOAT WILLIE from THE COMING OF SOUND (1927-28)

Nine months after **The Jazz Singer** (1927), Warner Bros. released the first all-talking feature-length sound film. Its favorable public reception kept the door open for the talking era. A Prohibition melodrama warning of the evils of the big city, **Lights of New York** is a fine example of the problems and solutions behind early sound films. Like most, it includes song and dance routines among stodgy dialogue scenes where actors deliver their lines slowly and carefully to insure clear sound recording. Each performance rests on the actor's ease with speech. Particularly instructive is the visible awkwardness of early microphone placement. (Later, booms were introduced out of camera range over the heads of the performers.) Hidden mikes necessitate actors' always speaking in the same spots within rooms, maintaining silence while crossing to other positions. In the movie's best-remembered scene, a pack of mobsters hover around a desk phone while receiving orders to "take him [the hero] for . . . a ride." The script's brand of over-written dialogue (in contrast to the improvisational quality of **The Jazz Singer**) would become a Hollywood trademark, but the film's frequently cliché-charged language and emotions provide sufficient entertainment.

ST. LOUIS BLUES

1928. U.S.A.
R.K.O. Written and directed by Dudley Murphy. Photographed by Walter Strenge. Music arrangements by W. C. Handy and Rosamond Johnson. With Bessie Smith, Isabel Washington, Jimmy Mordecai.
15 min. B&W. Sound.

Short, all-talking subjects like this one were considered novelty items in the American film industry (especially before the sound era fully blossomed), but because this is the only extant film of Bessie Smith, it represents a good deal more than a novelty today. It tells a simple fictional story as a pretext for Bessie to sing the blues: arriving home, she discovers her man with another woman, who has brought him luck in a crap game. Disconsolate over his infidelity, Bessie sings "My man's got a heart like a rock" ("The St. Louis Blues") and the scene changes to a bar at a nightclub. Bessie is joined by a band and chorus, grouped at tables scattered around the floor. One more confrontation with her no-good lover occasions a reprise. Belying the difficulties of sound recording, the direction of the musical number is notable for its blend of naturalness and high style, with the camera roaming around the club. The

director, Dudley Murphy, also made the companion film **Black and Tan** (1929) with Duke Ellington. The black stereotypes (which Murphy celebrates rather than ridiculing) for the most part add historical interest to this film, which would have played widely on the black theater circuit.

AMERICAN MUSICALS: FAMOUS PRODUCTION NUMBERS

1929–35. U.S.A.
Total program: 38 min. B&W. Sound.

SUNNY SIDE UP ("Turn On the Heat" number)

1929.
Fox. Written and directed by David Butler. Dances choreographed by Seymour Felix. Photographed by Ernest Palmer. Songs by Buddy DeSylva, Lou Brown, Ray Henderson.
8 min.

42ND STREET ("Shuffle Off to Buffalo" and "Young and Healthy" numbers)

1933.
Warner Bros. Directed by Lloyd Bacon; musical sequences directed by Busby Berkeley. Photographed by Sol Polito. Songs by Harry Warren and Al Dubin. With Ruby Keeler, Clarence Nordstrom, Una Merkel, Ginger Rogers, Dick Powell, Toby Wing.
10 min.

GOLD DIGGERS OF 1933 ("The Shadow Waltz" number)

1933.
Warner Bros. Directed by Mervyn LeRoy; musical sequences directed by Busby Berkeley. Photographed by Sol Polito. Songs by Harry Warren and Al Dubin. With Dick Powell, Ruby Keeler.
6 min.

GOLD DIGGERS OF 1935 ("The Words Are in My Heart" number)

1935.
Warner Bros. Directed by Busby Berkeley. Photographed by George Barnes. Songs by Harry Warren and Al Dubin. With Dick Powell.
8 min.

FLYING DOWN TO RIO (First part of "The Carioca" number)

1933.
R.K.O. Directed by Thornton Freeland. Dances choreographed by Dave Gould, Hermes Pan. Photographed by Roy Hunt. Songs by Vincent Youmans, Gus

Kahn, Edward Eliscu. With Fred Astaire, Ginger Rogers.
5 min.

The musical film sprang up immediately with the movies' acquisition of the soundtrack. Although many early examples were hopelessly static, other musicals were among the first films to explore the imaginative possibilities of the new medium (see **The Love Parade** [1929], **The Blue Angel** [1930], **Le Million** [1931], and the shorts **St. Louis Blues** [1928] and **Black and Tan** [1929]). The addition of sound to the already realistic photographic component of the film persistently challenged the movie musical: how should song and dance, so natural to the recognizably artificial province of the theater, be achieved with the believability which the commercial cinema strove to maintain? A common answer was to present musical numbers precisely as if they were taking place as part of a performance before an audience. This convention allowed cinematic invention while superficially bowing to the demands of verisimilitude. The five examples here use this method, but to varying degrees. On one hand, the musical numbers in the Astaire-Rogers series for R.K.O. concentrate on the dancing or singing and do not allow excessive camera work or editing to interfere. In **Flying Down to Rio**, their first film together, the basic integrity of Astaire and Rogers's dancing is largely maintained and this procedure was to become a dictate of Astaire so that the wholeness of a dance would not be fragmented. On the other hand, Busby Berkeley's choreography took every liberty imaginable in his brilliant sequences for Warner musicals. Whereas **42nd Street**'s "Shuffle Off to Buffalo" routine might well be approximated in a real stage presentation, the "Young and Healthy" number which follows is already a sequence for the cinema alone, with its kaleidoscopic, overhead views and final tracking shot through the legs of chorus girls. That Berkeley's sequences are given theatrical settings becomes an even more fantastic joke with the extensive camera cranes and the lighted violins in "The Shadow Waltz" from **Gold Diggers of 1933**. Some of his most elaborate trickery occurs in **Gold Diggers of 1935** in "The Words Are in My Heart," where a sylvan glade turns out to be a miniature atop a piano—which itself introduces even further metaphysical conceits. A predecessor that surely inspired Berkeley in design if not execution was "Turn On the Heat" from Fox's **Sunny Side Up**, which introduces a female chorus in arctic wraps who demonstrate that "the hottest girls in the world are Eskimos." While it lacks Berkeley's cinematic eye, the number has hardly been surpassed for outrageous sexual imagination.

—

APPLAUSE

October 1929. U.S.A.
Paramount. Directed by Rouben Mamoulian. Produced by Monta Bell. Story by Beth Brown, adapted by Garrett Fort. Photographed by George Folsey. With Helen Morgan, Joan Peers, Fuller Mellish Jr., Henry Wadsworth.
79 min. B&W. Sound.

Produced at Paramount's Long Island studio in Astoria, Queens, N.Y., *Applause* was the East Coast's response to the challenge of using the new sound medium artistically. (In Hollywood, Ernst Lubitsch was simultaneously producing *The Love Parade* [1929].) Monta Bell, recently named to head production at Astoria, had been a conscious visual stylist in the silent period, inspired by Lubitsch and by Chaplin's *A Woman of Paris* (1923), which he worked on. For his part, Rouben Mamoulian proved a fine choice in his debut as a film director, both because of and in spite of his background in theater. With Bell's encouragement, Mamoulian made stylish and inventive use of this melodrama about a washed-up burlesque queen (Helen Morgan) who sacrifices herself for her daughter. The sequences of theatrical performance, with their searching camera movement and varied cutting, combined with the overlay of hubbub on the soundtrack, convey a vital sensation of the bristling activity on both sides of the curtain. Some actual location shooting around New York City adds a sense of realism and period interest to the film.

BLACK AND TAN (BLACK AND TAN FANTASY)

December 8, 1929. U.S.A.
R.K.O. Written and directed by Dudley Murphy. Photographed by Dal Clawson. With Duke Ellington and his Cotton Club Orchestra, Fredi Washington, the Hall Johnson Choir.
19 min. B&W. Sound.

Duke Ellington's first film, **Black and Tan**, like **St. Louis Blues** (1928), is the work of Dudley Murphy. After returning from France, where he contributed technical assistance to Fernand Léger's *Ballet mécanique* (1924), Murphy wrote and directed both features and short films throughout the 1920s and 1930s. (In the 1940s he worked in the Mexican cinema.) His films demonstrate special interests in dance, the avant-garde, and in black performers. (He also directed Paul Robeson in **The Emperor Jones** [1933].) As with **St. Louis Blues**, **Black and Tan** opens with racial stereotypes of its period: two lackeys who come to repossess Duke Ellington's piano are bought off with a bottle of booze. The story centers on Duke's girlfriend, played by the lovely Fredi Washington, who risks her bad heart condition to dance (in a slinky costume styled after Josephine Baker) because the couple needs money. She sacrifices her life, hearing Duke's "Black and Tan Fantasy" in a final expressionistic reverie. More visually audacious than **St. Louis Blues**, the film includes multiple imagery to represent Fredi's dizziness, and an Art Deco nightclub number that might have inspired choreographers of 1930s musicals from Astaire to Busby Berkeley (see **American Musicals: Famous Production Numbers** [1929–35]).

BLACKMAIL

November 25, 1929. Great Britain.
British International Pictures. Directed by Alfred Hitchcock. Screenplay by Hitchcock, Benn W. Levy, and Charles Bennett, from a play by Bennett. Photographed by Jack Cox. With Anny Ondra (voice dubbed by Joan Barry), John Longden, Sara Allgood, Cyril Ritchard.
86 min. B&W. Sound.

One of the most fascinating of Hitchcock's entire oeuvre, this film is unusually frank, and ironic several times over. A young woman kills an attempted rapist and then is divided between concealing her involvement in the ugly incident and disclosing the truth in order to clear herself from the suspicion of murder. Her dilemma is exacerbated when she becomes a target of further threats—from a blackmailer, and from the police investigator, who happens to be her boyfriend. In addition to the complex moral ambiguities that it poses, *Blackmail* is an example of experimentation during the period of transition to sound. As shooting neared completion, the studio decided to release the film as a part-talkie; Hitchcock retained the essentially silent visual rhythms of many sequences while revising others, adding live dialogue as well as asynchronous sound, and even dubbing in a new voice for the German lead actress.

THE LOVE PARADE

November 19, 1929. U.S.A.
Paramount. Produced and directed by Ernst Lubitsch. Screenplay by Ernest Vajda and Guy Bolton from Leon Xanrof and Jules Chancel's play "The Prince Consort." Photographed by Victor Milner. Music by Victor Schertzinger, lyrics by Clifford Grey. With Maurice Chevalier, Jeanette MacDonald, Lupino Lane, Lillian Roth, Eugene Pallette, Ben Turpin.
107 min. B&W. Sound.

Maurice Chevalier is the new prince

Jeanette MacDonald and Maurice Chevalier in THE LOVE PARADE (1929)

consort who finds he resents having to play housemate to his spouse, the queen (Jeanette MacDonald); their squabble over sexual dominance yields curious observations about conventional marital roles. Lupino Lane and Lillian Roth are the low comic counterparts who mimic the goings-on of the royal household. Many important filmmakers were skeptical of the coming of sound; Lubitsch put skepticism to use with comic invention: *The Love Parade* presents his cheering prescription for learning to love the new talking film. We eavesdrop on voices from out-of-sight, watch people talking whom we cannot hear, or listen to foreign speech or gibberish which we cannot understand; and the talk is all the more intriguing as it is often full of sexual innuendo. Lubitsch frequently built visual sequences silently, adding sound later in order not to restrict the flexibility of the camera. Instead of patiently attending each speaker, the camera was freed to cut away playfully, and the film thus retained much of the jaunty spirit and rhythm of the mature silent cinema. No other filmmaker attained such bouyant results so early in the sound period, and Lubitsch immediately became the critical standard by which others were measured or inspired. (Working independently, René Clair achieved comparable success; see *Le Million* [1931].)

THUNDERBOLT

June 22, 1929. U.S.A.
Paramount. Produced and directed by Josef von Sternberg. Screenplay by Jules Furthman, dialogue by Herman J. Mankiewicz, from a story by Charles and Jules Furthman. Photographed by Henry Gerrard. Sets by Hans Dreier. With George Bancroft, Fay Wray, Richard Arlen, Eugenie Besserer, Tully Marshall.
90 min. B&W. Sound.

Josef von Sternberg's first sound film was so fully overshadowed by his second—*The Blue Angel* (1930)—that it has been largely forgotten. His direction contributed to the success of the watershed gangster film *Underworld* in 1927, but the same genre yielded quite different results in *Thunderbolt*. George Bancroft plays the title character, a proud and tough king of crime who loses his moll (Fay Wray) to an innocent-faced boy-next-door (Richard Arlen). Thunderbolt frames his rival so that the two men wind up in opposite jail cells on Death Row, but eventually the gangster reveals a heart of gold. During the first half of the film—set in nightclubs, tenements, on city streets—Sternberg was toying, on a modest Paramount budget, with the expressionistic shadows, cluttered decor, and jumble of incidental sound that the huge Ufa studio would later provide for *The Blue Angel*. For the second half, in the prison, he concentrated on the archly emotional tone that would dominate his late style.

THE BLUE ANGEL (DER BLAUE ENGEL)

April 1, 1930. Germany.
Ufa. Directed by Josef von Sternberg. Produced by Erich Pommer. Screenplay by Sternberg (uncredited) from Heinrich Mann's novel *Professor Unrat* (1905). Photographed by Gunther Rittau, Hans Schneeberger. Sets by Otto Hunte, Emil Hasler. Songs by Friedrich Hollaender. With Emil Jannings, Marlene Dietrich, Kurt Gerron, Rosa Valetti, Hans Albers. German language version, no English titles.
114 min. B&W. Sound.

With the coming of sound, Emil Jannings returned to Germany in 1929 after a successful stretch in Hollywood that won him the first Academy Award given to an actor, in part for his role in *The Last Command* (1928). Josef von Sternberg, his director on that film, received an invitation from Ufa to guide Jannings's talking debut in a film based on the famous novel by Heinrich Mann (Thomas Mann's elder brother). The subject seemed tailored to challenge Jannings: an authoritarian teacher's fall into degradation in pursuit of a temptingly amoral cabaret singer, Lola-Lola. Virtually unknown when Sternberg cast her as the leggy seductress, Marlene Dietrich easily matched Jannings and defined the elemental sexuality of the story which has given the work an archetypal dimension. Her song "Ich bin von Kopf bis Fuss auf Liebe eingestellt" ("Falling in Love Again") has become an ironic, universal refrain for casual liaisons. The film's atmospheric sets, in the tradition of German studio production of the 1920s, suggest a link between Sternberg's work and *Kammerspiel* style. (The film was produced in both German and English language versions—each with a deemphasis on dialogue—of which this is the German.)

WESTFRONT 1918

May 23, 1930. Germany.
Nero-Film. Directed by G. W. Pabst. Screenplay by Ladislaus Vajda, Peter Martin Lampel, from the novel *Four from the Infantry* by Ernst Johannsen. Photographed by Fritz Arno Wagner, Charles Métain. Design by Erno Metzner. With Gustav Diessl.
Originally 98 min.; cut to 89 min. in this English version. German dialogue with occasional English intertitles.
89 min. B&W. Sound.

G. W. Pabst was not only the central figure in the German cinema's shift toward the New Objectivity starting in the mid-1920s, but also the leading proponent of political liberalism in the film community before Hitler came to power in 1933. *The White Hell of Pitz Palu* (1929) was Pabst's first experience with sound, but the ensuing *Westfront 1918* is far more indicative of his ideas for the use of sound, just as its realistic and pacifist subject is closer to his own philosophical interests. Foreswearing music altogether, Pabst concentrated on natural sounds and a minimum of dialogue to heighten this depiction of the futility of war. The story is told through the intersecting lives of four German soldiers stationed on the Western Front in France during the First World War. Pabst's camera style, which combined brilliantly graphic montage sequences and long, often mobile shots, was the model for what contemporary critics called the International Style. International critics preferring *Westfront 1918* to *All Quiet on the Western Front* (released the same year), long considered it one of the greatest films ever made about war. Unfortunately, this slightly cut English language release version was produced with only a few intertitles to interpret the action instead of full subtitles to translate the dialogue.

AROUND THE WORLD WITH DOUGLAS FAIRBANKS (AROUND THE WORLD IN 80 MINUTES WITH DOUGLAS FAIRBANKS)

1931. U.S.A.
Elton Corporation; released by United Artists. Produced and narrated by Douglas Fairbanks. Directed by Victor Fleming and Fairbanks. Script by Robert E. Sherwood. Photographed by Henry Sharp. With Douglas Fairbanks, Victor Fleming, Henry Sharp, Chuck Lewis, Duke Kahanamoku of Hawaii, Sessue Hayakawa, Dr. Mei Lim-Fang in China, Gen. Emilio Aguinaldo of the Philippines, King Prajadhipok of Siam, Mickey Mouse.
78 min. B&W. Sound.

One of the genuine curiosities of the early sound period, this film was released in the wake of a six-month tour through the eastern hemisphere by Douglas Fairbanks and his production team. As well as extensive location shooting, they recorded live sound of the star speaking with representatives of many of the places they visited: Hawaii, Japan, Hong Kong, China, the Philippines, Cambodia (stunning views of Angkor Wat), Siam, and India. Part travelogue, part well-intentioned jape, the film uses Fairbanks's thesis that "the world is a great place for laughs" to poke fun while introducing distant and, for most of his audience, unreachable cultures. In addition to an unrelentingly humorous narration and his own sporting antics, Fairbanks peppers the show with special effects: the Indian rope trick is rendered cinematically, Mickey Mouse dances to Siamese music, the circumnavigation is completed in requisite time via magic carpet back to Hollywood. The naïveté of the film recalls the very first years of the medium, yet many of its scenes continue to fascinate—a testament to the documentary power of cinema.

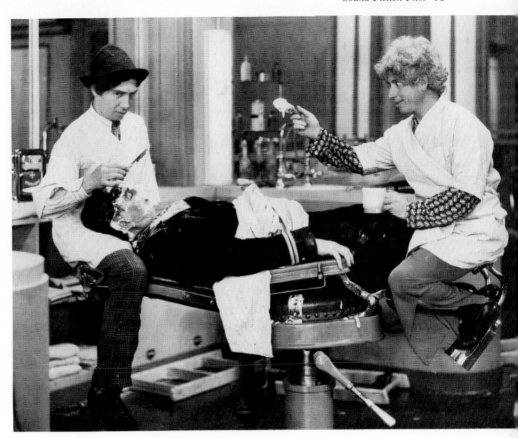

Chico and Harpo Marx in MONKEY BUSINESS (1931)

LE MILLION

1931. France.
Tobis. Written and directed by René Clair. Based on a comedy by Georges Berr and M. Guillemaud. Photographed by Georges Périnal and G. Raulet. Art Direction by Lazare Meerson. Music by Armand Bernard. With René Lefèvre, Annabella, Louis Allibert, Paul Olivier, Odette Talazac, Constantin Stroesco. In French; no English titles.
80 min. B&W. Sound.

Le Million is Clair's second sound film. His first, *Sous les toits de Paris* (1930), had been essentially a silent film with a scored musical track. Clair had vigorously protested the coming of sound, claiming that speech and sound effects would destroy the poetry of the silent film medium. He conceded, however, that music offered aesthetic possibilities for cinematic form. In *Le Million* Clair attempts to infuse the entire structure of the film with a fundamentally musical conception. Thus, dialogue is largely replaced by choral singing; actors' gestures and the editing pattern itself seem determined by musical rhythms; and narrative elements are connected through the continuity of the melodic line. Because of this formal rigor, *Le Million* is far more ambitious than many other "operettas" of the early sound period, and represents a major attempt to explore the potentials of the new medium. As in all Clair films, the plot of *Le Million* is whimsical, involving an artist's fantastic pursuit of a misplaced lottery ticket worth a million francs. Coincidences abound, and the narrative circles back on itself in perfect symmetry. What becomes apparent is that for Clair a plot is not an opportunity to delineate realistic events, but rather an excuse to create a complex formal design.

MONKEY BUSINESS

September 19, 1931. U.S.A.
Paramount. Directed by Norman Z. McLeod. Screenplay by S. J. Perelman and Will B. Johnstone; additional dialogue by Arthur Sheekman. Photographed by Arthur Todd. With Groucho, Harpo, Chico, and Zeppo Marx, Thelma Todd, Rockliffe Fellowes, Tom Kennedy, Ruth Hall, Harry Woods.
77 min. B&W. Sound.

Years of vaudeville finally led the Brothers Marx to three big successes on the Broadway stage. Two of these plays became their first commercial films, *The Cocoanuts* (1929) and *Animal Crackers* (1930), both shot at Paramount's Astoria studio in New York. *Monkey Business* was their first movie made in Hollywood from an original screenplay; with the subsequent *Horse Feathers* (1932), it was also the only Marx Brothers script credited to S. J. Perelman, and bears some influence of his own comic sarcasm. The Brothers emerge from four barrels labelled "Kippered Herring" as stowaways in the hold of an ocean liner. In their later attempt to pass U.S. Customs *sans* passport, they each pretend to be Maurice Chevalier. Even before arriving in the States, however, they have been thoroughly prepared for American life, all becoming henchmen for rival gangsters, one of whom is retiring into polite society. Highlights are Groucho's amorous inclinations with Thelma Todd, playing the wife of the still-active con-man; Chico and Harpo's stint as barbers; and Harpo's slapstick eluding of ship's officials to the amusement of an audience of children at a Punch and Judy show. The musical numbers include Harpo and Chico at harp and piano, entertaining the guests just before the final, glorious disassembly of a large high-society affair. (See also *Duck Soup* [1933].)

THE ROAD TO LIFE (PUTYOVKA V ZHIZN)

June 1, 1931. U.S.S.R.
Mezrabpomfilm. Directed by Nikolai Ekk. Screenplay by Ekk, Alexander Stolper, R. Yanushkevich. Photographed by Vasili Pronin. With Nikolai Batalov, Mikhail Zharov, I. Kyrla.
99 min. B&W. Sound.

One of the first Soviet sound films, *The Road to Life* dramatizes, with a mixture of realism and sentiment, the rehabilitation of homeless and delinquent Russian boys orphaned during the period

Cary Grant and Marlene Dietrich in BLONDE VENUS (1932)

of World War I and the Revolution. The subject was based on real events that posed a great challenge to the new Soviet state; Vertov had reported these children's plight in **Kino Pravda** (1922). The intent of **The Road to Life** was to inform and interest a mass audience—a strategy shared by many documentaries of the same decade. Batalov, the handsome leading man of the Soviet screen, plays the social worker who leads the model experiment. Most interesting as a rare social document, the film attempts a free and poetic use of natural sound that makes it a telling example of the transition period. (It was released just after Vertov's **Enthusiasm** [1931].) The film is the major achievement of Ekk as a filmmaker; he had acted for Meyerhold and directed documentaries prior to this work.

BLONDE VENUS

September 16, 1932. U.S.A.
Paramount. Directed by Josef von Sternberg. Screenplay by Sternberg, Jules Furthman, S. K. Lauren, from a story by Sternberg. Photographed by Bert Glennon. With Marlene Dietrich, Herbert Marshall, Cary Grant, Dickie Moore, Gene Morgan, Rita LaRoy, Sidney Toler, Sterling Holloway, Hattie McDaniel.
88 min. B&W. Sound.

Susan Sontag has described Sternberg's films with Dietrich as defining the essence of camp. **Blond Venus**, fifth in their series, is probably the most entertaining example of the outré sensibility that the star brought out in her director. Dietrich plays a one-time nightclub performer, now quietly settled as wife and mother, who must resume her profession in order to raise the money necessary for a rare, life-saving operation for her husband (Herbert Marshall). Once back in her former life, however, she is captivated by another man (Cary Grant); her infidelity brings threats from her husband, including the loss of custody of her little boy. (One of the film's curiosities is that sympathies go with the "other" man.) She flees incognito with the child on a journey through the American South. The movie's famous apogee is Dietrich's "Hot Voodoo" act, during which she climbs out of a gorilla costume as a white jungle goddess in a shimmering skin-tight suit and blond Afro hair-do. (See also **The Blue Angel** [1930] and **The Devil is a Woman** [1935].)

THE LOST SQUADRON

1932. U.S.A.
R.K.O. Directed by George Archainbaud. Produced by David O. Selznick. Screenplay by Wallace Smith from the story by Dick Grace; additional dialogue by Herman J. Mankiewicz, Robert S. Presnell. Photographed by Leo Tover, Edward Cronjager. With Richard Dix, Mary Astor, Robert Armstrong, Joel McCrea, Erich von Stroheim.
79 min. B&W. Sound.

During his short, brilliant directing career, Erich von Stroheim had so often cast himself in his own films as an obsessive, autocratic Prussian military officer (see **Blind Husbands** [1918] and **Foolish Wives** [1921]) that studio publicity promoted him as "The Man You Love to Hate." This persona stuck indelibly with von Stroheim after he was forced to rely on acting roles starting in the late 1920s, when Hollywood self-portraits had become rife. This one, about four ex-World War I fighter pilots who take jobs as movie stunt flyers, tries incredibly to rivet our attention to its themes of comradeship and brotherly self-sacrifice. Most of our interest, however, centers on von Stroheim's performance as the legend of himself: a murderous, seductive, and fanatically realistic movie director who (coincidentally) emblazons his name on stunt planes with a swastika-like insignia.

THE MAN I KILLED (BROKEN LULLABY)

January 19, 1932. U.S.A.
Paramount. Produced and directed by Ernst Lubitsch. Screenplay by Samson Raphaelson and Ernest Vajda, from the play L'Homme que j'ai tué by Maurice Rostand and its English adaptation by Reginald Berkeley. Photographed by Victor Milner. Sets: Hans Dreier. With Lionel Barrymore, Nancy Carroll, Phillips Holmes, Louise Carter, Lucien Littlefield, ZaSu Pitts.
77 min. B&W. Sound.

The most startling anomaly in Ernst Lubitsch's career, **The Man I Killed** was the director's first and, with **Angel** (1937), only dramatic film of the sound period. A Frenchman, motivated by remorse for the German soldier he killed in the First World War, seeks out his victim's family, but is drawn so close to them—and to the dead man's fiancée—that he cannot bring himself to tell them the truth of his visit. This intriguing material, from a French play, moved the German director enough to set aside his gift for comedy to plead against national prejudices and the waste of war. Released after a spate of antiwar films, however, and at a time when patriotism was again gathering force, **The Man I Killed** failed commercially in spite of a sentimental retitling to **Broken Lullaby** (which this print bears). The film stunned audiences of its period and does not fail to rivet attention today. Forty minutes into the film are a group of scenes that identify Lubitsch's best and most familiar stylistic devices, concluding with the spread of gossip through the small German town as the young couple walk its streets. The opening sequence, including the original title and credits, is available separately as an excerpt (see Film Study).

MILLION DOLLAR LEGS

July 8, 1932. U.S.A.
Paramount. Directed by Edward Cline. Produced by Herman J. Mankiewicz. Screenplay by Joseph L. Mankiewicz, Henry Meyers. Photographed by Arthur Todd. With W. C. Fields, Jack Oakie, Andy Clyde, Ben Turpin, Dickie Moore, Billy Gilbert, Lyda Roberti, Susan Fleming.
66 min. B&W. Sound.

This delightful bit of nonsense humor suggests how the great American screwball comedies of the 1930s were derived in part from the classic tradition of silent comedy: it carries over some of the frenetic slapstick and adds colloquial dialogue that contributes an irreverence all its own. The result has affinities to both Mack Sennett and the Marx Brothers. Many wonderful silent comics appear in this film along with some others who established themselves with the coming of sound. W. C. Fields is the president of Klopstokia, a little nation hoping not to disgrace itself in the upcoming Olympic Games; Jack Oakie is an enterprising American youth with eyes for the president's daughter.

MR. ROBINSON CRUSOE

September 22, 1932. U.S.A.
Elton Corporation; released by United Artists. Produced by Douglas Fairbanks. Directed by Edward Sutherland. Story by Elton Thomas (pseudonym of Fairbanks), adapted by Tom Geraghty. Photographed by Max Dupont. Music by Alfred Newman. With Douglas Fairbanks, William Farnum, Maria Alba, and native South Sea Islanders. No dialogue: intertitles and soundtrack.
70 min. B&W. Sound.

Fairbanks had trained on the stage but always relied more on his puckish good nature and acrobatic enthusiasm than on any strengths of acting or elocution. Like the great silent comics, he was less at home in talking pictures, and his popularity declined in the early sound period. Because of this, and for increased distribution abroad, as late as 1932 he made **Mr. Robinson Crusoe** in both talking and nontalking versions. His last personal production and next-to-last film, it benefits from the lack of dialogue, accompanied by a track with music, sound effects, and two distinct forms of gibberish. Eddie Sutherland, having worked with Chaplin and W. C. Fields, directed. Fairbanks plays a modern romantic who yields to the urge to spend a month marooned on a tropical island. Murau's *Tabu* (1931) might have put the idea into his head, but several of his adventures, and his aplomb for devising solutions to daily tasks, are reminiscent of Buster Keaton's in **The Navigator** (1924). His most joyful inventions are a treetop penthouse supplied with fresh water by a tortoise-powered aquaduct, a jungle tramway that would have solved Tarzan's grocery needs, a snare counterbalanced by coconuts that traps the island beauty, and a catapult equally suited to dragnet fishing or escaping irate natives.

DUCK SOUP

November 17, 1933. U.S.A.
Paramount. Directed by Leo McCarey. Story, music, and lyrics by Bert Kalmar and Harry Rubin; additional dialogue by Arthur Sheekman and Nat Perrin. Photographed by Henry Sharp. With Groucho, Harpo, Chico, and Zeppo Marx, Margaret Dumont, Raquel Torres, Louis Calhern, Edgar Kennedy.
70 min. B&W. Sound.

This, the funniest, most uninhibited of the Marx Brothers' movies, is their best. With a measure of thanks to director McCarey, they appear to be completely in control (if that's a proper word for their unbridled demolition) in **Duck Soup**. Without the burden of a romantic story line strung out with musical numbers, the Marx Brothers for once are involved in all plotting and command every song. The film combines their most inspired comic turns with the most rewarding of their scripts. Produced in the year that the Nazis came to power, this manic parody of nationalism and militarism is just beyond the reach of precise satire, but it binds the comedy into a masterpiece of slapstick absurdity. Groucho, with Zeppo as his lackey, takes control of Freedonia; its jingoistic Parliament sings "All God's Chillun Got Guns." Harpo and Chico are spies for an enemy ambassador, but by the end, when war erupts, they have joined forces against all forms of bourgeois propriety. On anyone's list of great moments are Groucho's and Chico's mirror reflection routine, Harpo's assaults with blow torch and scissors, and his Paul Revere-like seduction that upholds the demands of the Production Code.

1860 (I MILLE DI GARIBALDI)

1933. Italy.
Cines. Directed by Alessandro Blasetti. Produced by Emilio Cecchi. Screenplay by Blasetti and Gino Mazzucchi, based on a story by Mazzucchi. Photographed by Anchise Brizzi, Guilio De Luca. With Aida Bellia, Giuseppe Gullino, Gianfranco Giachetti, Toto Maiorana. In Italian with English subtitles.
73 min. B&W. Sound.

According to film scholar Carlo Lizzani, *1860* "marks the highest summit of the Italian cinema of the fascist period," an era traditionally disregarded by film historians. The film concerns the triumphant conquest of Sicily and Naples by Giuseppe Garibaldi in May of 1860, a theme that clearly reflects the nationalist ideology of the Mussolini period. Blasetti chooses not to examine Garibaldi's campaign for Italian unification as a distant historical event, but renders it through the experience of a patriotic Sicilian peasant who bravely leaves his bride to join Garibaldi's forces. Blasetti's concentration on the personal aspect of social phenomena, his use of natural locations and lighting sources, and his employment of nonprofessional actors, all prefigure the blossoming of Italian Neo-Realism in the 1940s. Beyond that, however, *1860* is characterized by plush visual beauty. Most notable are the graceful tracking shots scanning the body-strewn battlefields and following the path of moving characters. The photographic style is starkly arresting and borrows from the Soviet school of the 1920s a propensity for dramatic, low-angle compositions.

HITLERJUNGE QUEX

September 19, 1933. Germany.
Ufa. Directed by Hans Steinhoff. Screenplay by K. A. Schenzinger, B. E. Lüthge, from the novel by Schenzinger. Photographed by Konstantin Irmen-Tschet. With Heinrich George, Berta Drews, Hermann Speelmans, Rotraut Richter, Claus Clausen. In German; no English subtitles. This print contains annotations, in the form of intertitles, added by the anthropologist Gregory Bateson in 1943. These intertitles appear in the first reel of the film.
102 min. B&W. Sound.

This work is an excellent example of the Nazi propaganda film of the 1930s. The

HITLERJUNGE QUEX (1933) (p. 83)

narrative concerns a young boy, Heini, who is faced with the dilemma of choosing allegiance between the Communist and Nazi youth organizations. He counters the leftist leanings of his parents, and not only joins the Nazi youth group but eventually becomes a martyr to its cause. In 1943 the anthropologist Gregory Bateson engaged in a study of **Hitlerjunge Quex** at The Museum of Modern Art. The purpose of his analysis was to reveal the manner in which the plot and character relationships of the film were mere pretexts for the dissemination of Nazi attitudes and values. As Bateson himself noted: "The motion picture camera can lie freely about whatever passes in front of the lens, but inasmuch as the film was made by Nazis and used to make Nazis, we believe that at a certain level of abstraction the film must tell us the truth about Nazism." Portions of Bateson's unpublished study are incorporated into the film in the form of intertitles, which interrupt and comment on the dynamics of propaganda within the narrative. Bateson concentrates largely on the family relationships depicted. He notes, for example, how the father's "degenerate" qualities (drunkenness and violence) are identified with the Communists, and how Heini's love for his victimized mother is transferred to an allegiance to the Nazi Party. Though Bateson's analysis seems at times naive from the vantage point of contemporary film scholarship, it does serve as an early model for psychologically and anthropologically informed criticism.

LA MATERNELLE (CHILDREN OF MONTMARTRE)

1933. France.
Directed and written by Jean Benoît-Lévy and Marie Epstein; from a novel by Léon Frapié. Photographed by Georges Asselin. Music by Édouard Flament and Alice Verlay. With Madeleine Renaud, Mady Berry, Paulette Elambert, Alice Tissot, Henri Debain. In French with English subtitles.
83 min. B&W. Sound.

An exemplary work of French poetic realism, *La Maternelle* is a sensitive portrayal in fictionalized form of the plight of children in the urban ghetto. Specifically the narrative revolves around the character of Rose (Madeleine Renaud), whose experiences as maid and teacher at a public school form the basis of the story. The directors were concerned with communicating a sense of authenticity in the *mise-en-scène*. Consequently, for several months prior to shooting, they visited Parisian schools and ultimately used amateurs for many of the children's roles. In this respect the film clearly prefigures the Italian Neo-Realism of the 1940s. But *La Maternelle* is distinguished not only for its realism, but for its style. The film evinces a rig-

orous compositional sense, a sophisticated use of sound for the period, and many innovative narrative techniques. A visual theme is developed throughout the work by repeatedly showing the hands of characters, thus making literal the metaphor in the opening title, which instructs us that the fate of children "rests in our hands."

THUNDER OVER MEXICO

September 22, 1933. U.S.A.
Produced by Sol Lesser. Edited by Harry Chandlee from footage shot for **Que Viva Mexico!**, directed by Sergei Eisenstein in collaboration with Grigori Alexandrov, photographed by Eduard Tisse. With nonprofessional actors. Music by Hugo Riesenfeld, synchronized sound effects added.
60 min. B&W. Sound (may be run silent, 24 fps.).

After fruitless proposals to Paramount for various American film projects, Sergei Eisenstein finally obtained backing from Upton Sinclair and others to make a film in Mexico. Eisenstein, Alexandrov, and Tisse worked throughout 1931 to amass over fifty hours of footage, shooting five of the six sections of their envisioned epic when Sinclair ordered filming to cease. Misunderstanding the business of filmmaking, wary of the growing length of the material, and mistrustful after a number of contretemps with Eisenstein, Sinclair refused to permit him to finish shooting or to edit his completed material. Sinclair eventually signed over to producer Sol Lesser the job of assembling a film from the raw footage. **Thunder Over Mexico** is the result. Drawn from one of the six sections ("Maguey") in Eisenstein's original plan, the film tells the story of a young peon in an early 20th-century feudal hacienda who is moved to rebellion following the rape of his fiancée and his lack of recourse to justice. Despite the betrayal of Eisenstein's specific intentions, the subject and the beautiful images in the finished work testify to the great Russian's gifts, certainly at the height of their power. Additional footage from **Que Viva Mexico!** survives in **Time in the Sun** (1939) and in **Eisenstein's Mexican Film: Episodes for Study** (1955); both further reveal the special genius of Eisenstein's unfinished masterpiece.

OUR DAILY BREAD

1934. U.S.A.
United Artists. Produced and directed by King Vidor. Screenplay by Elizabeth Hill from a story by Vidor; dialogue by

Joseph L. Mankiewicz. Photographed by Robert Planck. Music by Alfred Newman. With Karen Morley, Tom Keene, Barbara Pepper, Addison Richards, John Qualen.
74 min. B&W. Sound.

During the 1930s, if the harsh facts of the Depression were ever mirrored on American movie screens, it was mostly by conspicuous omission since films of serious social conscience were boxoffice poison for Hollywood producers. King Vidor, then at the height of his esteem, bravely sought to counter this reluctance toward truly contemporary subjects, and to respond in his own personal way to the poverty and misery he witnessed around him. Refused by every potential backer, Vidor had to finance **Our Daily Bread** himself, and therefore to limit himself to only half the funds of an average Hollywood production. The picture's abrupt transitions and occasional weak motivations betray its tight budget, but (partly as a result) on the whole it compellingly delivers the mood of the Great Depression with all its human waste. The rather utopian idea of the plot—the establishment of a "back to the land" cooperative farm—is a reflection of the emotional climate of the period, not the outgrowth of reasoned economic theory. The depiction of the irrigation ditch in the final minutes of the film, however, is a marvel of cinematic achievement, and is available separately as an excerpt (see Film Study).

THE PRESIDENT VANISHES

November 17, 1934. U.S.A.
Paramount. Directed by William Wellman. Produced by Walter Wanger. Screenplay by Carey Wilson, Cedric Worth; dialogue by Lynn Starling, from the novel of the· same name. Photographed by Barney McGill. With Edward Arnold, Arthur Byron, Janet Beecher, Osgood Perkins, Rosalind Russell, Andy Devine.
83 min. B&W. Sound.

Produced five years before the start of World War II, this remarkably prescient political fiction opens with Europe already embroiled in war (the antagonists are unspecified) and the U.S. divided over the question of entering the conflict. Conspiring to bring the country into the war for their pecuniary or political gain are the bosses of American capital—big oil, steel, banking, a newspaper chain—as well as an ambitious judge and a powerful lobbyist. Public opinion is calculatedly manipulated by the bosses' rallying slogan, "Save America's Honor!," and solidified

THE PRESIDENT VANISHES (1934)

through the agitation of a fascist group called the Grey Shirts (which mirrored domestic Nazi organizations of the time). Congressional support weighs increasingly toward a declaration of war, so the main hope for peace rests on the elderly president—wise and compassionate, but with doubtful powers of persuasion. Can he deter Congress from war? An hour before his important address on the crisis, the President mysteriously disappears, possibly the victim of the ruthless Grey Shirts. The film's stand, openly opposing American participation in any European conflict, was in harmony with the pervasive national opinion (shared by the Roosevelt Administration prior to 1939). Still, Hollywood rarely broached political subjects as topical and sensational as this film's, which director William Wellman whips into successful entertainment using the thriller devices and emotionalism of 1930s gangster movies. A key work of its period, and an instructive precedent to Frank Capra's best-known films later in the decade.

REVOLT OF THE FISHERMEN (VOSTANIYE RYBAKOV)

October 5, 1934. U.S.S.R.
Mezhrabpomfilm. Directed by Erwin Piscator. Screenplay by Georgy Greb-ner, from Anna Segher's novel *Revolt of the Fishermen of St. Barbara* (1929). Photographed by Pyotr Yermolov, M. Kirillov. With Alexei Biky, Emma Tsesarskaya. In Russian with English (sometimes Danish) titles.
85 min. B&W. Sound.

Erwin Piscator was, following Max Reinhardt, one of the most important directors of the German stage of the 1920s and, like Bertolt Brecht, a leading advocate of epic theater. He often used film in his experimental theatrical production. In 1931, amid the economic and political collapse in Germany, he left for the Soviet Union with specific plans to make a feature film from Anna Segher's famous German novel. The story of a general strike against ship merchants is complicated by division among groups of fishermen, dockworkers, and sailors, some of whom oppose the strike until they are persuaded by an example of heroic sacrifice. Piscator knew and admired the great works of Eisenstein and Pudovkin and shared their commitment to agit-prop art, so it is no surprise that his film owes much to Soviet film style while incorporating many of the Expressionist and realist elements of German theater and cinema—notably of Murnau and Pabst. Thus, Piscator employs bold close-ups, parallel editing, and rapid montage as well as atmospheric lighting, camera movement, and special effects. He also adds Brechtian songs and a musical treatment akin to Lubitsch's and Clair's. Recommended for those with special interest in the German or Soviet cinemas or their interconnection, this print has been restored from various sources and includes one fifteen-minute portion with Danish but no English subtitles.

THE DEVIL IS A WOMAN

May 3, 1935. U.S.A.
Paramount. Directed by Josef von Sternberg. Screenplay by John Dos Passos and Sternberg, from Pierre Louÿs's novel *The Woman and the Puppet* (1898). Photographed by Sternberg and Lucien Ballard. With Marlene Dietrich, Lionel Atwill, Caesar Romero, Edward Everett Horton.
80 min. B&W. Sound.

The Devil is a Woman is the last, and the most extreme, of the seven films that Sternberg and Dietrich made together (see also numbers one and five: *The Blue Angel* [1930] and *Blonde Venus* [1932]). The director had often resisted continuing their professional relationship, but now that his contract with Paramount had come to an end, he knew this film

would be their last. The film mirrors the romantic psychology and ambiguous relationship that the two created: the Pierre Louÿs novel it is drawn from depicts the male myth of the vampire who leads men to ruin for her pure enjoyment; in the movie, the two men who destroy themselves over Dietrich (Atwill and Romero) both resemble Sternberg himself. Whether under the pressure of the Production Code or by Sternberg's own design, the femme fatale undergoes an apparent change of heart at the end. Sternberg took an obsessive involvement in the film, designing the claustrophobic Spanish carnival settings with Hans Dreier and taking screen credit for photography for the first time. The cold, hazy, impressionist surface of this film is the consummate manifestation of his visual style during the 1930s. Buñuel based his mocking **Obscure Object of Desire** (1977) on the same novel.

THE LIVES OF A BENGAL LANCER

January 12, 1935. U.S.A.
Paramount. Directed by Henry Hathaway. Screenplay by Waldemar Young, John L. Balderston, Achmed Abdullah; adapted by Grover Jones and William Slavens McNutt from the novel by Francis Yeats-Brown. Photographed by

Charles Lang, Ernest Schoedsack. With Gary Cooper, Franchot Tone, Richard Cromwell, Sir Guy Standing, C. Aubrey Smith, Kathleen Burke, Douglas Dumbrille, Monte Blue, Akim Tamiroff.
108 min. B&W. Sound.

Set in British India, where a few stalwart colonial troops must maintain the peace over the feudal rumblings of the imperial subcontinent, this film represents the standard of Hollywood knockabout adventure. Confronting the 41st Bengal Lancers is a crafty chieftain named Mohammed Khan, who uses his Oxford education and decorous manners to smooth over the most brutal designs, which include intercepting an ammunition convoy to instigate an uprising. Deterring Khan requires an end to the bickerings between two officers: the mischievous but affable Franchot Tone (who at one point inadvertantly charms a cobra with a rude flute) and the headstrong but true-blue Gary Cooper, who disapproves of the old colonel's strict adherence to duty that makes him cold even to his own son, a fledgling with the regiment. Henry Hathaway, having recently begun a long career of directing action movies, lingers over every moment of the story. The film was one of the largest commercial successes of its day.

RUGGLES OF RED GAP

March 6, 1935. U.S.A.
Paramount. Directed by Leo McCarey. Screenplay by Walter DeLeon, Harlan Thompson; adapted by Humphrey Pearson. Photographed by Alfred Gilks. With Charles Laughton, Mary Boland, Charlie Ruggles, ZaSu Pitts, Roland Young, Leila Hyams.
85 min. B&W. Sound.

A rough-mannered, *nouveau riche* Midwesterner (Ruggles) claims an impeccably refined British gentleman's gentleman (Laughton) in a poker game and brings him home to Red Gap, U.S.A., where his socially ambitious wife (Boland) can display him to full advantage. This wildly popular comedy exploits the polarities of English and American character types, then resolves the differences with a display of patriotic sentiment when Laughton admiringly recites the Gettysburg Address from memory. Nearly as famous—and more deservedly so—is the scene in which Leila Hyams endeavors to instruct Roland Young on playing the drums. The film unconsciously anticipates the future theme of a common heritage which would link the U.S. and Britain so strongly through the coming war.

Jean Arthur, Edward Arnold, and Mary Nash in EASY LIVING (1937)

DESIRE

February 21, 1936. U.S.A.
Paramount. Directed by Frank Borzage. Produced by Ernst Lubitsch. Screenplay by Edwin Justin Mayer, Waldemar Young, Samuel Hoffenstein, from a play by Hans Szekely and R. A. Stemmle. Photographed by Charles Lang. With Marlene Dietrich, Gary Cooper, John Halliday, William Frawley, Akim Tamiroff.
99 min. B&W. Sound.

Reunited six years after **Morocco** (1930), Dietrich plays an almost rock-hard European jewel thief and Cooper a wealthy, but average Joe American—naive yet good-at-heart. They meet in Spain, where, vacationing, he winds up with the pearl necklace she has stolen from Paris. He pursues her to the Riviera in hopes of winning her heart; her initial inclination is simply to get back the pearls. Ernst Lubitsch, Paramount's new head of production in 1935, chose this fairly promising material for Dietrich himself. The beginning of the movie shows Lubitsch's touch when the camera observes Cooper and his boss in heated argument out of our earshot on the other side of a window (a visual joke right out of **The Love Parade** [1929]) or when Dietrich convinces each of two men that she is married to the other. Once the romancing begins, however, the tone shifts into the hands of the director, Frank Borzage, who specialized in boldly sentimental love stories (such as **Seventh Heaven** [1927]). This is a telling example of Hollywood piecework.

SABOTAGE

December 1936. Great Britain.
Gaumont British. Directed by Alfred Hitchcock. Screenplay by Charles Bennett, from Joseph Conrad's novel *The Secret Agent* (1907). Photographed by Bernard Knowles. With Sylvia Sidney, Oscar Homolka, John Loder.
79 min. B&W. Sound.

This is the darkest film from Hitchcock's British period; in it, the director's calculated sacrifice of innocent victims evidences the cruelty which lurked beneath the ironic surface of much of his suspense. An insidious foreigner, married to an Englishwoman and operating a movie house in London, becomes an enemy agent in a terrorist bombing campaign. Joseph Conrad's original tale dealt with anarchist bombings that took place around the turn of the century, but Hitchcock's film clearly suggests a contemporary enemy power: Oscar Homolka is the evil central character and his accent is German. Having repu-

ALEXANDER NEVSKY (1938) (p. 88)

diated the Treaty of Versailles, Hitler was rearming Germany, and had remilitarized the Rhineland in March of the year **Sabotage** was released. The British government backed off from supporting France's call for countermeasures. In contrast, Sylvia Sidney as an average British housewife in the film, summons courage to act against her murderous husband. An unusual feature of **Sabotage** is its inclusion of Walt Disney's Silly Symphony cartoon **Who Killed Cock Robin?** (1935) in a memorable scene in the movie theater. The sequence suggests the sinister power of the cinema to gloss over reality and redirect our conscious emotions.

THE WAVE (REDES) 1936. *See* Documentary Film

EASY LIVING

July 7, 1937. U.S.A.
Paramount. Directed by Mitchell Leisen. Screenplay by Preston Sturges, from a story by Vera Caspary. Photographed by Ted Tetzlaff. With Jean Arthur, Edward Arnold, Ray Milland, Luis Alberni, Mary Ball, Franklin Pangborn, William Demarest.
88 min. B&W. Sound.

Angry with his wife's extravagance, a millionaire capitalist (Edward Arnold) throws her sable coat out of their high-rise apartment window. It lands on an innocent working girl (Jean Arthur), and she's off on a madcap adventure that is about as perfect as any screwball comedy of the 1930s. When word gets around, unbeknownst to her, that she is wearing a fur given her by "the Bull of Broad Street," she encounters a few upturned noses. More often, though, she finds herself the unwitting beneficiary of a shower of further riches and attention—her polite, unsuspecting refusals notwithstanding— from all those who'd like an inside track with her powerful new "friend." To complicate matters, she takes under her wing a nice young man (Ray Milland) who appears to be down on his luck, but is really the son of her supposed benefactor. A fast-paced film by Mitchell Leisen with the best script by Preston Sturges before he began directing his own, **Easy Living** treats the Depression era as a blind-luck treasure hunt through terrain that's as charmed as it is unpredictable. The satire includes characteristic Sturges parodies of the acquisitive impulses behind the American Dream, from a stock market panic to a food riot in the Automat—itself a classic sequence in Hollywood comedy.

MAKE WAY FOR TOMORROW

April 30, 1937. U.S.A.
Paramount. Produced and directed by Leo McCarey. Screenplay by Viña Delmar, based on a novel by Josephine Lawrence and a play by Helen and Nolan Leary. Photographed by William C. Mellor. With Victor Moore, Beulah Bondi, Fay Bainter, Thomas Mitchell, Porter Hall, Barbara Read.
92 min. B&W. Sound.

Through most of the 1930s, Leo McCarey directed vehicles for a procession of comics who included Laurel and Hardy, Eddie Cantor, the Marx Brothers (see **Duck Soup** [1933]), W. C. Fields, Mae West, and Harold Lloyd. **Make Way for Tomorrow** marks a sharp reorientation for the director as he began producing and often contributing to the scripts of a number of seriously single-minded and earnestly sentimental film projects. (In part, the industry would follow his turn to less frivolously funny material as the Second World War came and went.) The subject of **Make Way For Tomorrow** is the loneliness facing the lives of the aged; if its moral, "Honor Thy Father and Thy Mother," seems unusual for Hollywood, its handling is less so: it is a very effective tearjerker. A retired couple, their home repos-

sessed, are forced into the care of their own children, now middle-aged, who separate them and begrudge them their upkeep. The film does concede the upsetting nuisance that parents sometimes cause, though sympathy is naturally with the old couple. Victor Moore's lifelong experience in comedy and musical theater helps him maintain a light-heartedness as the father, which helps mollify an excess of contrived emotionalism.

YOU ONLY LIVE ONCE (Bank robbery sequence) 1937. See *You Only Live Once: Production Takes from a Film in the Making* (1937) in Film Study

ALEXANDER NEVSKY

November 23, 1938. U.S.S.R.
Mosfilm. Directed by Sergei Eisenstein. Screenplay by Pyotr Pavlenko and Eisenstein. Photographed by Eduard Tisse. Music by Sergei Prokofiev. With Nikolai Cherkasov. In Russian with English subtitles.
109 min. B&W. Sound.

Eisenstein was unable to complete a sound film until 1938, by which time many of his earlier ideas for joining sound and image had altered or developed, yet in his fruitful collaboration with Prokofiev he saw the realization of plans he had envisioned many years before. Together they produced a unique

film opera; **Alexander Nevsky** is perhaps Prokofiev's finest film score, and the work itself is increasingly seen as one of Eisenstein's greatest. Often jubilant and playful in its interaction between image and music, it displays more humor and gaiety as well as a greater degree of abstraction than the body of his other work. Eisenstein's subject is a retelling of the 13th-century invasion of Russia by Teutonic armies from the west and their expulsion by Russian forces under the command of Prince Alexander Nevsky. The film's climax, the Battle on the Ice, ranks among the superlative sequences in cinema. Challenged by the growing threat of Nazi Germany, Eisenstein completed the film far ahead of schedule. An unmistakable fable for its time (Eisenstein decided it was unnecessary to place swastikas on the helmets of the Germanic invaders as he had once planned), **Alexander Nevsky** nevertheless ends with a warning, lest any potential invader fail to comprehend its message. For this film, Eisenstein shrewdly adapted his usual theme of the mass as hero in order to center upon an individual hero, one molded by historic moment (Nevsky is, at least, summoned by the masses). Stalin appreciated this adumbration of his own leadership, and the film was a success for its long-troubled maker. It was, however, withdrawn from distribution after the Russo-German non-aggression pact of August 1939, but rereleased after Germany's unexpected attack on the Soviet Union in June 1941.

THE STARS LOOK DOWN (1939)

PRISON TRAIN

1938. U.S.A.
Equity Pictures. Directed by Gordon Wiles and (uncredited) Shepard Traube. Screenplay by Spencer Towne (pseudonym of Traube); story by Matthew Borden. Photographed by Marcel Picard. With Fred Keating, Clarence Muse, Linda Winters (pseudonym of Dorothy Comingore).
63 min. B&W. Sound.

In the 1930s and 1940s, Hollywood—and especially the Warner studio—made successful gangster melodramas by presenting charismatic underworld figures (often played by Bogart, Cagney, or Edward G. Robinson) who were ultimately revealed to be doomed or little men, hopelessly trapped in the web of their own folly. With this formula, the films could claim social responsibility and satisfy the Production Code. Small, "independent" studios which aped this strategy on low budgets often couldn't reconcile these extremes. In **Prison Train** a decidedly uncharismatic, small-time racketeer is bound for Alcatraz by transcontinental rail and learns that the father of the man he killed is out to have him murdered on board. Are our sympathies being elicited at last for the life of this gangster when he begins to have delirious flashbacks and when his good kid sister comes along to accompany him on the trip? Intertitles and newspaper headlines are inserted to help carry the plot and build characterizations; the train motif proves fairly effective for conveying a cramped, claustrophobic milieu on limited production funds.

THE STARS LOOK DOWN

December 1939. Great Britain.
Grafton. Directed by Carol Reed. Screenplay by J. B. Williams, from an adaptation by A. J. Cronin from his own novel. Photographed by Mutz Greenbaum, Henry Harris. With Michael Redgrave, Margaret Lockwood, Emlyn Williams, Nancy Price, Edward Rigby, Cecil Parker.
103 min. B&W. Sound.

The first famous work of Carol Reed, *The Stars Look Down* paved the way for Reed's becoming one of the preeminent masters of the British cinema. The film itself ranks among the finest British features of the 1930s. Throughout that decade, the British documentary movement had championed the dignity of the working man, and in adapting A. J. Cronin's novel about life in a poor mining community, Reed followed the lead of his documentary predecessors, rejecting the sentimentalism that John Ford relied upon two years later in *How Green Was My Valley* (1941). Michael Redgrave contributes a beautifully modulated performance as David Fenwick, the bright son of a mining family whose father led an unauthorized strike against an unsafe mine in defiance of the owners and complaisant union leaders. The young man leaves home to get an education so he can better the lot of his people. An advocate of public ownership of mines and stronger political representation for mining communities, he is thwarted from his aims when he is lured into a hapless marriage to a pert, pettily ambitious young woman (Margaret Lockwood). Emlyn Williams brings menace to the role of the lout who betrays his fellows for his own gain by abetting the reopening of the dangerous mine shaft—the event which portends a tragic end. Reed's direction uses a sharp-focused realism to etch detailed observations of the divergent environments of the working-class village, university town, and comfortable haunts of the well-to-do.

THE FORGOTTEN VILLAGE (1941)

TIME IN THE SUN

October 1939. U.S.A.
Produced by Marie Seton. Screenplay and editing by Seton with Paul Burnford, from footage shot for *Que Viva Mexico!*, directed by Sergei Eisenstein in collaboration with Grigori Alexandrov and photographed by Eduard Tisse. With nonprofessional actors. Music by Carlos Tarin and Ponce Espino; sound effects and narration added.
59 min. B&W. Sound.

The release of *Thunder Over Mexico* (1933) seemed to signal an end to any hope that Eisenstein's aborted *Que Viva Mexico!* would appear in a form that respected the director's original plan. In an effort to salvage a greater remnant of Eisenstein's work, however, Marie Seton, his eventual biographer, corresponded with Eisenstein and negotiated with Upton Sinclair to obtain footage that had not already been used to produce *Thunder Over Mexico*. Seton followed the general order Eisenstein had established for the film, including material from each of the five sections he shot, but worked it into a single narrative thread tracing the history of Mexico from the times of Mayan and Aztec predominance, through the Spanish conquest and continuing suppression of the Indian population, up to the start of the 1910 Revolution (lacking only the revolutionary section "La Soldadera," which was never filmed), then concluding in the happy celebration in the present of Death Day. Accompanying these scenes, Seton used Mexican musicians and narrators to contribute folk melodies and native legends from various periods. Her film necessarily lacks Eisenstein's own dramatic editing, and he remained unhappy with the fate of his footage. What Seton does accomplish, interestingly, is to turn the material into a documentary overview of 400 years of Mexican cultural heritage and (implicitly) a suggestion of the grandeur of Eisenstein's conception, with even more examples of his visual brilliance. (See also *Eisenstein's Mexican Film: Episodes for Study* [1955].)

THE FORGOTTEN VILLAGE

1941. U.S.A.
Produced by Herbert Kline and Rosa Harvan Kline. Directed by Herbert Kline and Alexander Hackenschmied [Hammid]. Story and screenplay by John

Orson Welles and Jeanette Nolan in MACBETH (1948)

Steinbeck. Photographed by Hackenschmied [Hammid]. Music by Hanns Eisler. Narration by Burgess Meredith. With nonprofessional actors.
68 min. B&W. Sound.

Set in Santiago, Mexico, **The Forgotten Village** is about a young boy's attempt to bring modern science and medicine to his village and the resistance of his people to new ideas. Using the village people to tell a story very close to their own experience, Steinbeck and the filmmakers made a sensitive film that never condemns the ignorance that is the story's real villain. The film opens with a scene establishing the spiritual and medical culture of the village: a young pregnant woman is taken to the wise-woman to discover the future of her unborn child. When the children of Santiago become sick and begin to die despite the elaborate cures of the wise-woman, young Juan Diego goes to the city on the advice of a local teacher and brings back a rural medical team. Their efforts to purify the contaminated well that is causing the sickness and to innoculate the sick children are thwarted by the wisewoman's influence and the fears of the villagers. Juan Diego is ex-

pelled from the village in disgrace, but he returns to the city to study medicine in hopes of returning to Santiago with new skills and knowledge. Exquisitely photographed by Alexander Hammid, who later made **Meshes of the Afternoon** (1943) with Maya Deren, **The Forgotten Village** is an observant, informative drama.

L'ÉCOLE BUISSONNIÈRE (I HAVE A NEW MASTER; PASSION FOR LIFE)

1948. France.
U.G.C.—C.G.C.F. Directed by Jean-Paul Le Chanois. Screenplay by Le Chanois, Elise Freinet. Photographed by Marc Fossard, Maurice Pecqueux, André Dumaitre. With Bernard Blier, Juliette Faber, Dany Caron. In French with English subtitles.
84 min. B&W. Sound.

Based on a true story of Provence after World War II, this sincere, humane drama by Jean-Paul Le Chanois, who went on to make **Sans laisser d'adresse** (1950) and **Les Misérables** (1958), is about a young teacher revolutionizing education in the village of Salezes. Played by Bernard Blier, this ambitious educator takes over a school from a strict,

uncompromising old man and brings an entirely new method of learning. He encourages the students to talk, write, and learn about the crafts of their village, winning their trust but gaining the resistance of the older villagers. After the students organize a press, print a book, and build an electrical conductor in the town river, the stodgy town leaders organize against the new teacher. Ultimately, when the most difficult student makes a moving speech in his favor at the examination, the teacher is accepted by the community. With humorous dialogue and convincing characters, this film, whose title means "playing hookey," is both an affectionate portrait of life in a small provincial French village and a convincing educational statement.

MACBETH

October 1, 1948. U.S.A.
Mercury Productions for Republic. Produced, written, and directed by Orson Welles, based on the play by William Shakespeare. Photographed by John L. Russell. Music by Jacques Ibert. With Orson Welles, Jeanette Nolan, Dan O'Herlihy, Roddy McDowall.
85 min. B&W. Sound.

Welles's **Macbeth** is a moody and visually fascinating film made on a significantly low budget at Republic Studios. This experimental interpretation is distinctly visual, with a primitive, craggy Scottish set and exceptional camerawork. Welles portrays the tragic figure as a tormented and unsteady man, creating a tension which is heightened by Jeanette Nolan's icy Lady Macbeth. Many scenes are altered for the screen, and the battle scenes that were offstage in the original play are added. The most successful of these alterations, such as the banquet scene in which Macbeth is haunted by the ghost of Banquo, are exceptionally imaginative cinematic renderings of Shakespeare's study of a tortured conscience. This, the shortened release version, has the English soundtrack that replaced the original Scottish brogue that many viewers found incomprehensible when the film was released.

UNDER CAPRICORN

1949. Great Britain.
Transatlantic Pictures. Directed by Alfred Hitchcock. Screenplay by James Bridie, adapted by Hume Cronyn from the novel by Helen Simpson. Photographed by Jack Cardiff. Music by Richard Addinsell. With Ingrid Berg-

man, Joseph Cotten, Michael Wilding, Margaret Leighton, Cecil Parker. 117 min. Color. Sound.

Hitchcock made *Under Capricorn* after *Spellbound* (1945) and *Rope* (1948) and before the well-known *Strangers on a Train* (1951). The film is set in New South Wales in 1831, a raw territory of ex-convicts with an odd transplanted version of English protocol. Michael Wilding plays Charles Adare, a charming Irish dandy who has just arrived in town with his cousin, the newly-appointed governor. Naive and trusting, Adare finds himself being entertained by Sam Flusky, played with dignity and force by Joseph Cotten, an expatriate exconvict who has amassed a considerable fortune. There Adare meets Flusky's wife, Lady Henrietta, played with a graceful, quivering instability by Ingrid Bergman, who is not only a long-lost friend but an unhappy and disillusioned alcoholic. Adare's attempts to help Henrietta step back into the world and change her life provide the film's intrigue and ensuing drama, revealing the truth of her relationship with Flusky, complete with a Mrs. Danvers-like housekeeper and menacing thunderstorms. Hitchcock weaves his atypical plot through a series of complex revelations in a style which is melodramatic and well-saturated, from the elaborate hues of the Australian sunsets to the rich costumes. Only Hitchcock's second film in color, *Under Capricorn* is a fine example of Technicolor at its richest and most lavish.

WHITE MANE (CRIN BLANC)

1953. France.
Directed by Albert Lamorisse. Screenplay by Denys Colomb de Daunant, from a story by Lamorisse. Photographed by Edmond Séchan. Music by Maurice Le Roux. Commentary by Lamorisse; English version by James Agee. With Folco. Sparse French dialogue, English narration.
38 min. B&W. Sound.

White Mane is a children's fable par excellence, brimming with the strength and wonder of a child's active imagination. A young boy finds and wins the trust of an untamed white stallion in the marshes of the Camargue region of Provence in Southern France. The brave and exhilarating world they share together is threatened by professional cowboys whose business is capturing wild horses. The gifted filmmaker, Albert Lamorisse (famous as well for his later *The Red Balloon* [1956]), has captured the feelings and rhythms that are essential to true fairy tales. The film achieved re-

nown when French critic André Bazin cited its realist photography in discussing his theory of realism in the cinema. Avoiding opportunities to fake scenes by relying on the tricks of film editing, Lamorisse exposes the risks involved in action sequences between the boy and the horse using stunts that are not simulated but actually performed before the camera. The music score for the film is based on authentic folk songs from the region.

SALT OF THE EARTH

1954. U.S.A.
Directed by Herbert J. Biberman. Produced by Paul Jarrico in association with Local 890 of the International Union of Mine, Mill, and Smelter Workers. Screenplay by Michael Wilson. Music by Sol Kaplan. With Rosaura Revueltas, Juan Chacon, Will Geer, David Wolfe, and members of the union.
94 min. B&W. Sound.

This unusual and moving cooperative project brought together a union of Chicano mine workers and three blacklisted film professionals—director Biberman, screenwriter Wilson, and composer Kaplan. (One of the Hollywood Ten, Biberman had served a six-month jail term for contempt of Congress after his refusal to cooperate with the HUAC investigations in 1947.) Based on the 1951–52 strike by Mexican-American miners against the Empire Zinc Company of Silver City, New Mexico, the film depicts not one but two timely struggles, both decades in advance of American commercial filmmaking: the Chi-

cano miners' fight for equal pay and living conditions with "Anglo" (white) miners, and the concomitant battle within the union by the women of the community for social and political equality with the men. In fact, it is this latter confrontation which gives the film its special value as an enduring social drama. The many nonprofessionals in the cast include the actual union president (Chacon), who portrays the central character, with the crucial role of his wife heightened by the performance of the Mexican actress Rosaura Revueltas. (Will Geer also contributes an important small part.) Appearing at the climax of the McCarthy era, the film's support of unionism and civil equality caused it to be roundly attacked as communist propaganda, a charge which reflects the attitudes of the period more than those of the film itself.

AMELIA AND THE ANGEL

1958. Great Britain.
British Film Institute production. Directed and photographed by Ken Russell. Produced by Anthony Evans. Screenplay by Russell and Evans.
27 min. B&W. Sound.

Amelia and the Angel is one of the most seminal of Ken Russell's early films, exploring the themes of religion, guilt, faith, and redemption that are central to most of his work, which includes *Women in Love* (1969) and *The Boyfriend* (1971). Simply and beautifully photographed, the film tells of Amelia, a young girl proud of playing an angel in a school play, who takes home her

Monica Vitti and Alain Delon in ECLIPSE (1962) (p. 92)

angel wings only to find them ruined by her little brother. Her search for new wings before the play's performance takes this film from realism to a more elusive and sometimes humorous world of enigmatic characters and discovery. While this is a children's story, it is also an innovative religious parable.

LA PREMIÈRE NUIT

1958. France.
Argos Films. Directed by Georges Franju. Screenplay by Marianne Oswald and Remo Forlani, adapted by Franju. Photographed by Eugen Shuftan. Music by Georges Delerue. With Pierre Devis, Lisbeth Persson. No dialogue.
20 min. B&W. Sound.

The Paris Métro is the setting for a fantasy of distanced romantic encounters. Franju, who made this film after his documentaries and prior to his narrative features, is concerned with the first experiences of love and separation. The story involves a young boy who attempts to follow an enchanting companion on the Métro, and culminates in a dream sequence of phantom Métro cars and brief encounters. The camera explores the subway with extraordinary sensitivity, creating a child's image of a machine of automatic closing doors with people riding in its maze. With a strong sense of Paris and its time, **La Première Nuit** is a parable of the unpredictability of human encounters, reflected in watching a face go by on an adjacent subway train.

ECLIPSE (L'ECLISSE)

April 1962. Italy.
Interopa Film—Cineriz—Paris Films. Directed by Michelangelo Antonioni. Screenplay by Antonioni, Tonino Guerra. Photographed by Gianni Di Venanzo. Music by Giovanni Fusco. Produced by Robert and Raymond Hakim. With Monica Vitti, Alain Delon, Francisco Rabal. In Italian with English subtitles.
123 min. B&W. Sound.

Following **L'Avventura** (1960) and **La Notte** (1961), **Eclipse** represents a further progression of style for Antonioni, from a reliance on elongated dialogue to an effective language of images—epitomized in this film by opening and closing sequences of considerable length which contain almost no conversation. Set in the barren milieu of Italy's upper bourgeoisie, **Eclipse** is permeated with restless, ominous overtones. It opens with the end of an affair between Vittoria (Monica Vitti) and her distant lover (Francisco Rabal) in which the filmmaker successfully evokes the tired, frustrated mood of separation. Vittoria wanders rather aimlessly through much of the film—she takes a plane ride, dresses up in African garb, and goes to the *borsa* (stock exchange), where her mother is caught up in the frenzy of bidding. These scenes of the *borsa*—presented as a chaotic theater—provide a central image in the film. "The Roman *borsa* is unlike any other stock exchange in the world," Antonioni has said. "I wanted the petty bourgeois world and not that of high finance." The *borsa* also provides the context for Vittoria's encounter with Piero (Alain Delon), a shrewd, mercurial broker. Their relationship develops yet the mistrust between them remains, and the final sequence of the film defines not only a pessimism but the inability of the two lovers to come together—the spot they have chosen to meet remains deserted. Antonioni couples images that hint of destruction and the precariousness of peace in a conclusion which is filled with a feeling of finality and mortality. With exceptional performances and an elusive, tightly controlled style, he made this film elegant, pitiless, and succinct.

HALLELUJAH THE HILLS (1963). See Experimental Film

THE GOSPEL ACCORDING TO ST. MATTHEW (IL VANGELO SECONDO MATTEO)

1964. Italy.
Arco Film—C.C.F. Lux. Directed by Pier Paolo Pasolini. Produced by Alfredo Bini. Screenplay by Pasolini, based on the New Testament book of Matthew. Photographed by Tonino Delli Colli. With Enrique Irazoqui. In Italian with English subtitles.
136 min. B&W. Sound.

The Gospel According to St. Matthew is Pasolini's most ambitious and complex work, dedicated to the memory of Pope John XXIII, whom Pasolini credits with establishing a religious climate in which making the film was possible. It was shot almost entirely in exteriors in Southern Italy, an arid, expansive landscape that acts as an enormous stage for Pasolini's drama. In this historical epic, Christ is an intellectual in a world of revolutionaries, a bohemian ever wandering and ever confronting his stubborn people. At times harsh, arrogant, and demanding, and at others gentle and forgiving, Pasolini's Christ is always a self-reflective enigma. The director captures the visual effect of a highly charismatic figure through his strong use of facial expressions. In a close-up style reminiscent of Eisenstein's unfinished **Que Viva Mexico!** or Dreyer's **The Passion of Joan of Arc** (1928), the stirring, strong gaze of Christ is set against the barren landscape, as are the hypnotized responses of those who see him. Pasolini uses a combination of cinematic styles to tell his story, from hand-held shots to formal setups reflective of Italian paintings. A collage of musical styles, from Gospel to African to classical, complements the visuals and helps to project a universal tale.

THE GOSPEL ACCORDING TO ST. MATTHEW (1964)

A BALLAD OF LOVE (CVOYE; TWO PEOPLE)

1965. U.S.S.R.
Riga Films. Directed by Mikhail Bogin. Screenplay by Mikhail Bogin and Yuri Chulyukin. Photographed by Richard Pieck and Heinrich Pilipson. Music by Romuald Grinblatt. With Victoria Fyodorova, Valentin Smirnitsky. In Russian with English subtitles. Scanned version; originally in scope.
36 min. B&W. Sound.

A Ballad of Love is an early Russian film by Mikhail Bogin, the Soviet director who later emigrated to the United States and went on to make *A Private Life* (1980). It is a touching, well-crafted story of a young music student who falls in love with a deaf woman who is studying the circus and works in a pantomime theater. Their tentative approach toward each other and attempts to communicate their different worlds are portrayed with gentleness. The use of sound to isolate and recreate the silence of the young deaf woman (played by the well-known Soviet actress Victoria Fyodorova, who also emigrated to the U.S.), is exceptional, centering on her war-related memories of the hearing world. Charming and cleverly made, *Ballad of Love* is an excellent example of Bogin's early work.

A BORING AFTERNOON (FĀDNĪ ODPOLEDNE)

1965. Czechoslovakia.
Directed by Ivan Passer. Screenplay by Ivan Passer and Bohumil Hrabal from a story by Hrabal. Photographed by Jaroslav Kučera. In Czech with English subtitles.
15 min. B&W. Sound.

A Boring Afternoon is the first film of Czech director Ivan Passer, who is now directing in the United States and whose later films include *Intimate Lighting* (1966), *Born to Win* (1971), and *Cutter's Way* (1981). The scene of this sensitive, elusive film is a cafe on a normal, "dull" afternoon. In one corner several old women are playing cards and singing a low, melodic tune which serves as the background of the action. A young, arrogant man reads and smokes at one table, and at another an old man reminisces about his early soccer-playing days. A strange, mysterious woman appears from time to time in the window. The characters interact and evolve in this brief portrait of the passage of one day. It is a subtle, ironic film.

TWO (A PARABLE OF TWO)

1965. India.
Written, directed, and with music composed by Satyajit Ray.
12 min. B&W. Sound.

This short parable by India's foremost director is a universal story of impenetrable social and economic barriers. Two young boys encounter each other; one is a bored, Americanized child who is surrounded by expensive toys, and the other, in rags, stands before a solitary hut. They compete, and their confrontation produces a victory for neither. A story of the extremes of the Indian caste system and of the social structures begun in childhood, *Two* has a biblical sense of simplicity and wisdom.

THE RISE OF LOUIS XIV (LA PRISE DE POUVOIR PAR LOUIS XIV)

November 1966. France.
ORTF. Directed by Roberto Rossellini. Screenplay by Jean Gruault, Jean-Dominique de La Rouchefoucald (uncredited) from a story by Philippe Erlanger. Photographed by Georges Leclerc, Jean-Louis Picauet. With Jean-Marie Patte. In French with English subtitles.
93 min. Color. Sound.

The Rise of Louis XIV is the first of Rossellini's historical and didactic films that filled the last phase of his career. It concentrates on a key historical figure, and sets the detached style that the director would pursue further in films like *Socrates* (1970) and *Pascal* (1975). Still the most widely acclaimed of this series, *The Rise of Louis XIV* emphasizes the everyday details of Louis's court life with an overlying theme of transition. It begins with the death of Cardinal Mazarin, who ruled the country during the young king's childhood, and explores the tactics used by Louis to gain and retain control over the court. He has the powerful Minister of Finance arrested, removes his mother and other members of the royal family from their spheres of government influence, builds Versailles, and creates a court in which the nobility is not only privileged, pampered, and extravagantly dressed but continuously under his immediate scrutiny. Louis's routine is relentlessly detailed, from the initial scene of his awakening with a room full of noblemen for the morning benediction to the central image of his elaborate multicourse meal, consumed before the entire court. The ritual, the importance of appearance, and the lack of privacy in the court are consistently reiterated by Rossellini's exacting approach. Using detached long shots which depersonalize the action and a low-key acting style, Rossellini portrays all this ceremony in remote tableaux. The film ends with Louis, alone for the first time before the camera, removing his frills and trappings and settling down to read La Rochefoucald's maxim "Neither the sun nor death can be faced steadily."

A MIDSUMMER NIGHT'S DREAM

September 1968. Great Britain.
Directed by Peter Hall. Executive producer: Martin Ransohoff. Produced by Michael Birkett. Photographed by Peter Suschitzky. Music by Guy Woolfenden. Text by William Shakespeare. With the Royal Shakespeare Company, including Derek Godfrey, Barbara Jefford, David Warner, Diana Rigg, Michael Jayston, Helen Mirren, Paul Rogers, Sebastian Shaw, Bill Travers, Ian Richardson, Judi Dench, Ian Holm.
119 min. Color. Sound.

Peter Hall's experimental production of Shakespeare's gentle comedy is a classic which combines an intriguing array of sets and costumes (an amalgam which includes both contemporary and medieval attire, as well as some nudity) with some of the most exceptional Shakespearean players to work in film. Filmed in the lush countryside of Sherwood Forest in Warwickshire, near Stratford, the film contrasts the green, mysterious world of the fairies with the world of foolish and lovelorn mortals. Aided by special effects, Ian Holm's Puck is strong and amusing, Ian Richardson's Oberon powerful, and Judi Dench's Titania both comic and vivacious. The young lovers, well executed by Diana Rigg, Helen Mirren, David Warner, and Michael Jayston, follow the intricate web of Shakespeare's plot to the hilarious scene of Bottom and his acting troupe's mottled version of Pyramus and Thisby. Faithful to the original play and elaborately staged, this well-acted production is a fine example of cinematic Shakespeare.

FIVE EASY PIECES

September 12, 1970. U.S.A.
B.B.S. Productions. Directed by Bob Rafelson. Produced by Bob Rafelson and Richard Wechsler. Executive producer: Bert Schneider. Screenplay by Adrien Joyce (pseudonym of Carol Eastman) from a story by Rafelson and Joyce. Photographed by Laszlo Kovacs. Songs sung by Tammy Wynette. With Jack Nicholson, Karen Black, Susan Anspach, Lois Smith, Ralph Waite, Fannie Flagg, Sally Ann Struthers, Billy "Green" Bush.
97 min. Color. Sound.

Five Easy Pieces, like *Easy Rider* (1969) and *Midnight Cowboy* (1969), was one of the films made in the late 1960s and early 1970s that successfully explored the road-as-panacea theme in American culture. Jack Nicholson plays Bobby Dupea, a drifter from a family of distinguished musicians living on an island in Puget Sound. Bobby has fled this isolated intellectual atmosphere. When the film opens he is living in defiance of his past—working as an oil rigger, living with Rayette, a waitress (played by Karen Black), and hanging around cheap cafes and bowling alleys. He is the quintessential rootless character who, in rejecting one lifestyle, has failed to replace it with another that he can abide for long. His father's illness returns Bobby to the family's island, where he becomes infatuated with his brother's fiancée (Susan Anspach), a serious pianist. Ultimately rejected by her, Bobby is caught between the extremes of his life when Rayette shows up. *Five Easy Pieces* is remarkable in its skepticism and understated complexity. While the viewer naturally identifies with Nicholson's character to a certain extent, the film does not provide us with a hero but with a nomadic figure whose way of life seems to doom him to permanent exile.

ALONE AND THE SEA

1971. U.S.A.
Directed by Sean Malone. Assisted by Ed Dupres. Music by Diane McGrew. With Gilbert Strachan.
12 min. Color. Sound.

Alone and the Sea is a touching story of a fisherman who struggles to make his living solely from the sea on the Oregon coast. Stoic and weathered, he sees the sea as his adversary, saying "I've always felt that I didn't get anything from the sea that I didn't take. I had to either outsmart it or drown, and I didn't care much which." This portrait of an authentic American character culminates in the destruction of his boat by storm, ending a lifelong battle of this man and sea. Accompanied by a haunting soundtrack with whale sounds, the Oregon coast is richly photographed in this sad and lonely tale.

RED PSALM (MÉG KÉR A NÉP)

1972. Hungary.
Mafilm I. Directed by Miklós Jancsó. Screenplay by Gyula Hernádi. Photographed by János Kende. With Andrea Drahota, Lajôs Balázsovits, András Balint, Gyöngyi Bürös. In Hungarian with English subtitles.
88 min. Color. Sound.

Set in 19th-century Hungary, this richly symbolic and political film presents socialist doctrine through the story of an agrarian revolt. The foremost figure in Hungary's cinematic renaissance, Miklós Jancsó has consistently produced works that employ an aesthetic of extensive single takes to construct pageantlike parables of historic and doctrinal reflection. Composed of long tracking shots, the film is a choreography of actors and camera, at once a positive view of revolutionary movement and a scene ridden with death. The peasants struggle against the army with dance, songs, children, and sheer numbers, as the action unfolds in a series of ritualistic scenes: three young women disrobe and confront the army like sacrificial virgins; a church and religious effigies are burned; a large dancing crowd is encircled and killed by soldiers; a river runs red with blood. Throughout this complex of action and symbol, a song is constantly reiterated: "We are workers; we have no freedom. Whatever happens, we're the losers. Long live the worker's society."

WEDDING IN WHITE

1972. Canada.
Dermet Production. Written and directed by William Fruet. Produced by John Vidette. Photographed by Richard Leiterman. Music by Milan Kymlicka. With Donald Pleasance, Carol Kane, Doris Petrie, Leo Phillips, Paul Bradley, Doug McGrath.
103 min. Color. Sound.

Wedding in White is a richly photographed, harrowing story of a young girl destroyed by a society that idolizes its males and glories in military bravado and violence. Set in a poor Canadian village in 1944, it is exceptionally accurate in its details, from the Union Jack in the parlor to the wartime slang. Jeannie (played by Carol Kane, who later starred in *Hester Street* [1975]) is a scrawny, naive girl who is intrigued by her daring, lascivious friend Dolly, and papers her room with romantic movie stills. Jeannie is raped by her brother's friend when the two soldiers come home for a one-night stay, and her unlucky pregnancy is worsened by her mother's shame and father's violent anger. Ultimately married off to her father's drinking buddy three times her age, Jeannie is effectively played by Kane as a combination of naive helplessness and tragic determination. Donald Pleasance is excellent as Jeannie's boozing, bragging father, and Doris Petrie is convincing as her thin-lipped, worn mother. The film portrays a culture in which the men go drinking while their women huddle in fear in the kitchen—a society riddled with hypocrisy and fearfully unjust to its victims. *Wedding in White* is exceptionally well crafted, and explores not only the intricate relationships in this father-dominated family but also the society that fostered these actions.

MATCHLESS

1974. Australia.
By John Papadopoulos. Screenplay by Sally Blake.
54 min. B&W. Sound.

A story of social outcasts, *Matchless* examines the friendship of three characters: two young women, one an epileptic and one a suicidal schizophrenic, and an older man who is an alcoholic. The action centers on their inner struggles, strong bond of friendship, and communal living situation—all of which are juxtaposed against the dry, clinical diagnosis of a group of psychiatrists. Not only a portrait of an unlikely threesome, this is a film about a society's inability to accept misfits and those living on the margin of our established social structure. Its ending is both haunting and inevitably tragic.

THE PRICE OF A UNION (LA RANÇON D'UNE ALLIANCE)

1974. Republic of the Congo (now Zaire). Congo Films Production. By Sebastien Kamba. Based on the novel *La Legende de Mpfoumou Ma Mazono* by Jean Malonga. French head titles and Congolese dialect with English subtitles.
68 min. Color. Sound.

Set in the early 1900s, *The Price of a Union* was the first feature film from the Republic of the Congo (now Zaire). Based on the novel *La Legende de Mpfoumou Ma Mazono* by Jean Malonga, it tells the story of a marriage between two tribes, the Tsoundi and the Tsembo. The film is an elaborate study of the social customs and rituals of these two tribes as well as a story of fallen hopes, guilt, and social upheaval. The organization of the clans, the nonhuman status of the slaves, and the powerless condition of the women are social issues intricately woven in this convincing parable.

A PINT OF PLAIN

1975. Ireland.
By Thaddeus O'Sullivan and Derrick O'Connor. Photographed by Dick Perrin.
41 min. B&W. Sound.

Executed in twelve fluid shots, *A Pint of Plain* follows several characters throughout London, each of them paralleling and occasionally intersecting the episodes of one another. The two central characters travel from Ireland to go on a weekend tour of the city, and through their experiences in pubs and on the street expose the tensions of these two opposing cultures. The filmmaker creates an effective reality in these scenes, most of which use improvised dialogue. When this is combined with the seemingly random coincidences of its episodic structure, the film is reminiscent of Buñuel's narrative style. Thaddeus O'Sullivan went on from this first film to make **On A Paving Stone Mounted** (1978), which takes the experience of emigration as a theme.

DOWN THE CORNER

1977. Ireland.
By Joe Comerford. Produced by Ballyfermot Community Arts Workshop and the British Film Institute. Screenplay by Noel McFarlane. Edited by Joe Commerford and Bob Quinn. With nonprofessional actors. In English with some subtitles.
53 min. Color. Sound.

Down the Corner is a realistic drama about the experiences and lifestyles of young, working class boys in urban Ireland. The film effectively shows the restless and rather empty lives of the boys through the use of nonactors, naturalistic sound, and a loosely structured narrative. We see their community almost entirely through their own eyes, as they fight in school, clash with their families, and finally go on a spree to raid a local orchard. A central scene, in which the grandmother of one of the boys recounts a story about the repression by the British Black and Tans during her youth, defines the enormous gap between the youths' aimlessness and the political struggles of Irish history. Along with Bob Quinn's **Poitín** (1978), **Down the Corner** represents an emerging, realistic Irish cinema.

JOG'S TROT

1978. Australia.
Directed by John Papadopoulos. Screenplay by Sally Blake.
60 min. Color. Sound.

Jog's Trot is a surreal, cinematic fantasy that follows the character Henry Wilburforce Jog on his life-after-death journey. The world Jog encounters is an eerie one, complete with strange animals, mocking people in masquerade costumes, symbolic objects, and human

Lotte and Paul Andor in A PRIVATE LIFE (1980)

figures who transform into beasts. With his top hat and mournful face, Jog is reminiscent of characters in Samuel Beckett's *Waiting For Godot* as he encounters these figments of his imagination. **Jog's Trot** culminates in a haunting twist on all reincarnation fantasies.

POITÍN (POTEEN)

1978. Ireland.
Directed by Bob Quinn. Screenplay by Colm Bairéad. Photographed by Seamus Deasy. With Cyril Cusack, Donal McCann, Niall Toibín. In Gaelic with English subtitles.
65 min. Color. Sound.

Made in the rugged terrain of Connamara, **Poitín** is notable as the first Gaelic-language feature film. It is a sensitive portrayal of the lifestyle and people of western Ireland, and is described by director Bob Quinn as an attempt to counter the stereotypical view of that Irish territory established in John Ford's **The Quiet Man** (1952). The story of **Poitín** concerns an old poteen-maker, played by Cyril Cusack (of **Odd Man Out** [1947], **Taming of the Shrew** [1967], and **Day of the Jackal** [1973]), who employs two men to sell his illegal native brew. Waylaid by the police, who confiscate their goods, the two steal back the brew, go on a spree, and return to terrorize the old man and his daughter. In the end, the poteen-maker has his revenge.

A PRIVATE LIFE

1980. U.S.A.
Directed by Mikhail Bogin. Produced by Peter Almond; coproduced by Stephen Brier. Screenplay by Nancy Musser and Peter Almond. Photographed by Alicia Weber. Edited by Charles Musser. Music performed by Evelyne Crochet. With Lotte and Paul Andor.
30 min. Color. Sound.

Mikhail Bogin, the distinguished Soviet director, has joined his talents with a group of American filmmakers to produce this sensitively developed drama on the themes of aging, love, and immigration. **A Private Life**, set in present-day New York, focuses on Margot Lerner (Lotte Andor), a German-Jewish émigré, and her attempts to establish a lasting relationship with Karl (Paul Andor), a man of similar age and background. Margot is a vital woman who enjoys exploring her adopted city, works part-time as an accountant, and looks forward to a fulfilling future. Karl, on the other hand, while appearing to value Margot's proffered friendship, is incapable of sharing her interest in the future, and dwells instead on his projected memoirs of life in pre-World War II Germany. The story of these two people attempting to find love is a universal one that takes on special poignancy because of their age and the dislocations they face in adapting to a new land.

Joris Ivens filming POWER AND THE LAND (1940)

The Documentary Film:
Trends in the Nonfiction Tradition

by William J. Sloan

The roots of the documentary film spring from the first works of realist cinema of the late 1890s and early 1900s, particularly in the work of the French pioneers Louis and Auguste Lumière. Their simple vignettes of workers leaving the factory, Auguste Lumière feeding his baby, and a train arriving at a station were, in fact, proto-newsreels and proto-documentaries. On the heels of their first successes with scenes shot in France, Lumière cinematographers were soon traveling throughout the world recording public events and creating short travelogues. (A selection of thirty-two Lumière films circulate as LUMIÈRE PROGRAM I: FIRST PROGRAMS [1895–96] and LUMIÈRE PROGRAM II: EARLY LUMIÈRE FILMS [1895–98].) In America the Edison Company and other producers made similar brief films (available on FILMS OF THE 1890s [1894–99]) such as *Feeding the Doves* and *New York Street Scenes*. Later, newsreels were much influenced by these early works in their objective, reportorial style, as is illustrated by THE PATHÉ NEWS-REEL, which ran from 1910 until the 1940s (see THE PATHÉ NEWSREEL [1917–31]), and *Lindbergh's Flight From N.Y. to Paris* (1927) by Fox Movietone News.

The nonfiction film was brought a significant step further in its development by the Soviet filmmakers after the Russian Revolution of 1917. Their journalistic reports, usually quite short, on the progress of the new Soviet society were inspired by revolutionary social and political ideas and achieved an intensity hitherto unknown in films. Working with realist images, they brought a point of view, sympathy for their subjects, and political commitment for the first time to nonfiction filmmaking. A documentary tradition was beginning to evolve. The principal filmmaker who contributed to this development was Dziga Vertov. This young poet-filmmaker, with government backing, produced the newsreel series KINO PRAVDA. Cameramen-correspondents from around Russia sent news footage to Vertov in Moscow where, with great editing skill, he put together journalistic reports of life in the Soviet Union. The KINO PRAVDA project lasted from 1922 to 1925. The Museum's circulating reel contains scenes from several programs produced in 1922.

In the late 1920s Vertov moved stylistically far beyond the newsreel concept of KINO PRAVDA to create one of the most complex documentaries in the history of cinema, *The Man With the Movie Camera* (1929). On the surface the film simply records a day in the life of the Soviet Union. But through

NANOOK OF THE NORTH (1922)

its innovative use of montage, its special effects, its moving camera, and its playing with discontinuity, it stands as a challenge and an inspiration to filmmakers of today. Film historian Erik Barnouw has called it "an avant-garde determination to suppress illusion in favor of a heightened awareness."[1]

Two years later, in 1931, Vertov made his first sound documentary, *Enthusiasm, Symphony of the Don Basin*, on the contribution of miners to the Soviet's Five Year Plan. It extends Vertov's fascination with experimental film structure that he had developed in *The Man With the Movie Camera*. Unfortunately, because the printing materials for *Enthusiasm* have deteriorated during the years since it was completed, today we see and hear only a faded remnant of the original work. Even so, it reveals one of the most original figures in film history.

It was the American filmmaker Robert Flaherty, however, who began to develop the documentary as a distinct cinematic genre with his great classic *Nanook of the North* (1922). This film was the first work in the realist tradition to emerge as a coherent, thoughtful, fully realized work of art. Until Flaherty, the nonfiction film was little more than simple reportage, as exemplified by the newsreels of the period. *Nanook*, on the one hand, explores an entire way of life as it studies human character, and on the other, expresses Flaherty's own vision of mankind. This does not obscure the fact that Flaherty exploited the artifices of conventional moviemaking: he worked carefully with his subjects, staged at least some of his shots, and, when necessary, reshot material. It is Flaherty's special contribution to take realist images and shape them into a unified, significant work unlike anything seen before. Because of this he is generally considered the "father" of the documentary film.

The widespread success and critical recognition of *Nanook* made it possible for Flaherty to get backing from Paramount Pictures to make another film on a similar theme. The result was *Moana*, released in 1926, an idyllic picture of native life on the South Pacific islands of Samoa. It has a more conventionally developed story line than *Nanook*, but like *Nanook*, uses native nonactors in the cast. While *Moana* did not achieve the heroic proportions of *Nanook*, it nevertheless demonstrates Flaherty's distinctive exploratory photographic style and his uncanny ability to capture the essence of an exotic way of life.

Although *Nanook* received widespread recognition, the documentary canon did not really begin to develop until the late twenties. One of the transitional documentaries of the mid-twenties that presaged the greater activity of the next decade, and at the same time kept alive interest in the film on faraway places, was *Grass* (1925). This impressive work on the migrating tribesmen of the remote mountain areas of Iran was made under extremely harsh conditions by the team of Merian C. Cooper and Ernest Schoedsack (who together later directed *King Kong* [1933]).

Walter Ruttmann, working in Germany toward the end of the decade with a distinguished team that included the cinematographer Karl Freund and the scriptwriter Carl Mayer (who later withdrew from the project when he realized Ruttmann would not incorporate social issues into his film), directed *Berlin: Symphony of a Great City* (1927). This beautiful, poetic work, which takes its form from musical composition, has intrigued filmmakers ever since it was made and is largely responsible for establishing a virtual sub-genre of the documentary: the "city film." Other films in the Circulating Film Library that develop city themes are *Manhatta* (1921), *Rien que les heures* (1926), *The Man With the Movie Camera* (1929), *Rain* (1929), *A Bronx Morning* (1931), *City of Contrasts* (1931), *The City* (1939), *Notes on the Port of St. Francis* (1952), and *N.Y., N.Y.* (1957).

In the late twenties, a new figure emerged whose influence was to dominate the documentary movement for the next generation. It was John Grierson, with a background in labor, journalism, and the social sciences, who brought political conscience to the documentary film. Grierson was moved both by the strong political commitment in the work of the Soviet directors (he said of Vertov's *Enthusiasm*, "I have never set eyes on a film that interested me more"[2]) and by the humane feeling in the films of Robert Flaherty. Although he expressed a degree of hostility toward the apolitical nature of Flaherty's work, Grierson's best films shared with Flaherty a similar artistic vision and a humanitarian sensibility. Grierson summed up the two main paths—the social and the humanist—that the documentary would take in the thirties, and indeed on to the present, in his essay "First Principles of Documentary," which he wrote in 1932:

This sense of social responsibility makes our realist documentary a troubled and difficult art, and particularly in a time like ours. The job of romantic documentary is easy in comparison: easy in the sense that the noble savage is already a figure of romance and the seasons of the year have already been articulated in poetry. Their essential virtues have been declared and can more easily be declared again, and no one will deny them. But realist documentary, with its streets and cities and slums and markets and exchanges and factories, has given itself the job of making poetry where no poet has gone before it, and where no ends, sufficient for the purposes of art, are easily observed. It requires not only taste but also inspiration, which is to say a very laborious, deep-seeing, deep-sympathizing creative effort indeed.[3]

Grierson's use of "romantic," an intentionally pejorative reference to Flaherty's humanistic documentaries, is indicative of the uneasy alliance not only between the political and the apolitical paths within the documentary movement, but also between the two men themselves.

One of Grierson's special gifts was his ability to enlist government support for his film production ideas. In 1927 he persuaded the head of the British government's Empire Marketing Board to make him its Film Officer, and by the following year he was actively involved in film production. In 1933 his unit, which had grown to a staff of over thirty, was transferred to the General Post Office. The films made under his supervision at these two government agencies brought respect and dignity to the working man and explored broad issues of social justice. By no means revolutionary, the films aimed to bring about progressive change within the framework of existing democratic institutions. Grierson's role within his production unit was that of mentor-producer who guided, cajoled, and bullied his directors, often to superhuman efforts. The Grierson "school" spread into several film units, working for both government and commercial sponsors in the latter half of the decade. Films in the collection that illustrate the development of the British documentary are: *Housing Problems* (1935), directed by Arthur Elton and Edgar Anstey, which investigated the evils of slum housing; *The Smoke Menace* (1937), directed by John Taylor, which examines the danger of air pollution; *Children at School* (1937), directed by Basil Wright, which took a look at the problems of public education; *North Sea* (1938), directed by Harry Watt, which dealt with ship-to-shore radio; and *To-Day We Live* (1937), directed by Ralph Bond and Ruby Grierson, which reported on public works in British villages. Grierson himself directed and photographed *Granton Trawler* (1934); influenced in style by the Soviet directors, it is a stirring film study of fishermen engaged in dragnet fishing off the coast of Scotland.

Another filmmaker who worked briefly under Grierson and who has been much admired for the poetic sensibility that he brought to documentary is Humphrey Jennings. His *Spare Time* (1939), on the theme of leisure, is a good example of Jennings's early development, in which he carries on in film the spirit of the British personal essayists.

From the period of Grierson's leadership, two acknowledged classics have emerged. *Song of Ceylon* (1934), directed by Basil Wright, is a richly textured, complex work, which in the brief span of forty minutes interprets Ceylonese history, religion, culture, and present-day commerce. Historian of the documentary Richard Barsam writes: "With its juxtaposition of traditional customs against modern methods, the film builds an intelligent and sensitive impression of a changing culture."[4] But the British documentary of greatest stature in the pre-World War II period, produced under Grierson's close supervision, is *Night Mail* (1936). Directed by Harry Watt and Basil Wright, its subject is the nightly run of the "Postal Special" between London and Glasgow. The contrast between the train's surging power and the intimate scenes of the men at work, supported by the lyrical poetry of W. H. Auden and the music of Benjamin Britten, makes it an achievement rarely equaled in the documentary tradition.

Grierson left Britain shortly before World War II for Canada, where he set up the National Film Board of Canada and guided the production of documentary films in support of the Canadian war effort. (The history of the Film Board is described in this catalog under "The National Film Board of Canada," and Grierson's career itself is reviewed in the NFB film *Grierson* [1973].)

In the United States the social documentary movement had its beginnings in the Workers Film and Photo League (soon to drop "Workers" from its title) established in 1930. Its aim was to document and promote the workers' struggle for jobs, unions, and other rights that grew out of the economic upheavals of the Great Depression. Begun in New York, Leagues also flourished in several large cities. The newsreels that its filmmakers assembled were in opposition to the newsreels produced in Hollywood, where, as Erik Barnouw states, "avoidance [of controversy] became hallowed principle."[5] In the late 1970s, Leo Seltzer, who had been a cameraman and editor on many of the League's films, restored six of them, available now from the Circulating Film Library in two programs (FILM AND PHOTO LEAGUE PROGRAM I [1931–32] and PROGRAM II [1931–34]).

In 1934 a breakaway group led by Leo Hurwitz, Ralph Steiner, and Irving Lerner left the Film and Photo League to found the production co-operative Nykino (New York Kino). Its first production was not a documentary but the experimental comedy *Pie in the Sky* (1935) directed by Ralph Steiner, with Elia Kazan playing a leading role. Paul Strand joined the group shortly after its inception, and was followed by Willard Van Dyke, Sidney Meyers, and Ben Maddow. Joris Ivens, who visited New York in 1935, was a major influence on the group.

Nykino reconstituted itself into Frontier Films, a production cooperative dedicated to producing militant political films. It produced a number of impassioned documentaries, among them *Heart of Spain* (1937), photographed by Herbert Kline and Geza Karpathi and edited by Paul Strand and Leo Hurwitz, on the work of Dr. Norman Bethune during the Spanish Civil War. Film historian William Alexander describes it as "perhaps the finest Frontier film."[6]

In 1941, Hurwitz and Strand directed the only feature to come out of Frontier Films, *Native Land* (1942). Part documentary and part narrative, it depicts in a series of vivid episodes the violation of civil rights in the United States. A film of towering stature, it has come to be recognized as one of the major works in the history of the documentary tradition.

Leo Hurwitz has continued to make independent documentaries up to the present time. Two of these later works are *Strange Victory* (1948), a study of racism in post-World War II America, and *The Museum and the Fury* (1956), which explores man's search for dignity against the background of the horrors of the Holocaust.

The work in the thirties of the Film and Photo League, Nykino, and Frontier Films supported left-wing causes and was outside the mainstream political establishment. The leading figure working within that establishment in the United States was Pare Lorentz, who carried on the liberal film tradition of John Grierson. Like Grierson, he worked within government, eventually heading the U.S. Film Service under the Roosevelt Administration, and like Grierson he used the best artists and technicians he could find. He was himself a gifted writer and he wrote the scripts for his major works. His first film was *The Plow That Broke the Plains*, made in 1936. The exceptionally brilliant crew included Leo Hurwitz, Paul Strand, and Ralph Steiner. *The Plow That Broke the Plains*, with its sweeping photography of the Great Plains, contained seeds of the grandeur and majesty that were to find full flower in Lorentz's second film, *The River* (1937), on the history of the despoliation of the Mississippi River Basin. Virgil Thomson composed the score, as he had for *Plow*. It was the American documentary masterpiece of the prewar period, and fully the equal to Britain's *Night Mail*. However, even the support of President Roosevelt was not enough to save the documentary unit, and in 1940 Congress curtailed its activities.

Another major classic from this period, made in the U.S. but outside of government sponsorship, was *The City* (1939), directed by Ralph Steiner and Willard Van Dyke with a memorable score by Aaron Copland. (Van Dyke had been a cameraman on *The River*.) This film is especially note-

*THE PLOW THAT BROKE
THE PLAINS (1936)*

worthy for the way the scenes shot in New York capture the dynamism and rhythm of a modern metropolis. Thousands saw the film at the New York World's Fair of 1939. The following year Van Dyke went on to direct *Valley Town* (1940), which examines the harsh consequences of unemployment in an industrial city during the Depression. To underline the starkness of the images, Van Dyke employed a voice-over musical recitative (composed by Marc Blitzstein) in combination with spoken narration. Contemporary audiences were not, on the whole, prepared to accept the unconventional use of sound in the film, and by the time the film was completed America was weary of the Depression and not interested in seeing painful scenes of its recent past. Thus it is only in recent years that the film has come to be recognized as the impressive work that it is, rightfully taking its place among the major works of the period.

Robert Flaherty's *The Land* (1942), begun for the U.S. Film Service at the invitation of Pare Lorentz, has suffered a fate not unlike that of *Valley Town*. Its gentle, reflective portrayal of the dispossessed of rural America was out of step with the interests of a nation at war. Also, it did not reflect the concerns of a wartime government and for a considerable time was withheld from circulation. Currently, the film is undergoing reevaluation. Andries Deinum, the eminent American film scholar, introducing *The Land* at the twenty-fifth annual Flaherty Film Seminar in 1979, said, "I believe that in *Nanook* and *The Land* Flaherty was intimately involved with the lives of the people he filmed. In these two films Flaherty shows that he was profoundly moved by the experience." Richard Corliss, editor of *Film Comment*, is another scholar who considers that *Nanook* and *The Land* are Flaherty's two finest films. He describes *The Land* as "a great document," and writes, "The film's very lack of cohesion reflects, in the splinters of a broken economic mirror, a human catastrophe too overwhelming to be shoehorned into the microcosm of a narrative scenario."[7]

Another aspect of the documentary—indeed one could term it a subgenre—that developed in the pre-World War II years was the documentary-as-entertainment, exemplified by the MARCH OF TIME series, produced by Louis de Rochemont for Time Inc. Although in keeping with its aim for mass appeal it often skirted the political commitment of the social documentary tradition, as war threatened America it increasingly took an anti-fascist position. Examples in the Circulating collection are *Arms and the League* (1938) and *The Movies March On!* (1939).

Continental Europe between the world wars also produced a great social documentarian in the Dutch filmmaker Joris Ivens. His output has been prodigious. Ivens's first films were poetic documentaries—*The Bridge* (1928) and *Rain* (1929). However, beginning in the 1930s he soon went on to make political and social issue films for a Dutch labor union, for Grierson at the National Film Board of Canada, for the U.S. Government, and for private political groups concerned with issues of fascism and war. (His editor during these years was Helen van Dongen, who later edited *The Land* and *Louisiana Story* [1948] for Flaherty.) Ivens's *New Earth* (1934), on dual themes of land reclamation (of the Zuider Zee) and the waste of resources in a capitalist system, exemplifies the social documentary tradition at its best. In 1936 he got an assignment to make a film in support of the Spanish Loyalist cause against Franco. *The Spanish Earth* (1937) is a stirring, stark report on the Spanish Civil War, containing many scenes of horror that were soon to become recurring motifs in the films of World War II. Virgil Thomson and Marc Blitzstein worked together on the musical track. For the U.S. Film Service and the Rural Electrification Administration, Ivens directed *Power and the Land* (1940). As was typical of productions of this period, he collaborated on the film with other artists—the poet Stephen Vincent Benét wrote the commentary and Douglas Moore composed the score.

Paralleling the work of Ivens in Holland was that of Henri Storck in Belgium. Like Ivens he made experimental films at first but soon turned to documentary. Storck has played a central role in the Belgian documentary movement since the thirties. A fine example of his early work is *L'Histoire du soldat inconnu* (1930), which uses a montage of newsreels to make an antiwar statement. He also edited John Ferno's beautifully photographed *Easter Island*, produced in 1934.

In Spain, Luis Buñuel, following his own unique vision, made the stark *Land Without Bread (Las Hurdes)* (1933) on an isolated, poverty-stricken village in Spain. He says of it, "I made *Las Hurdes* because I had a Surrealist vision and because I was interested in the problem of man. I saw reality in a different manner from the way I'd seen it before Surrealism."[8]

Meanwhile in this same prewar period, Nazi Germany also produced a major figure in the documentary movement, Leni Riefenstahl. Her glorification of the Nazi ideal was the direct antithesis of the Griersonian school, with its concern for issues of justice and social welfare. Riefenstahl's best-known film is *Triumph of the Will* (1935), a work much praised and much damned, which documents the Nazi Party Rally of 1934 in Nuremberg. It presents Hitler as a godlike figure, his followers as a vast, disciplined machine of frightening proportions. Considered too powerful a propaganda weapon by the enemies of fascism, it was banned in the West until long after the fall of Nazi Germany.

Nazi propaganda is a subject of endless fascination today because of the role it played in molding the values and attitudes of an entire nation that committed some of the worst crimes against humanity in recorded history. The propaganda films, because they form a vivid record of the Nazi effort, are especially compelling. While Riefenstahl is the acknowledged master of Nazi filmmakers, other films that provide a solid cross-section of image manipulation in the Nazi cause are NAZI PROPAGANDA FILMS (1933–37), GERMAN NEWSREELS (1933–40), and *Campaign in Poland (Feldzug in Polen)* (1940). (A work related to these films is the postwar documentary on the use of film propaganda in the Third Reich by Erwin Leiser, *Germany, Awake!* [1968]. It is a compilation of excerpts from narrative feature films that were produced under Nazi government supervision.)

During World War II documentary production received a major push, especially in the United States, Britain, and Canada. In the U.S., the WHY WE FIGHT series (1942–45), produced under the direction of Frank Capra for the U.S. War Department, was among the most effective group of propaganda films to support and explain U.S. participation in the war and was seen by millions of civilians and armed service personnel. The first film in the series, *Prelude to War* (1942), which discusses the causes of the war on a global scale, serves as a model of excellence for film exposition, combining an abundance of stock footage (including some from *Triumph of the Will*) and a minimum of new material—in a variety of cinematic techniques. Indeed, all the films in the WHY WE FIGHT series are impressive examples of films used for the purposes of information and persuasion.

In addition to the millions of feet of film shot by the armed forces, the U.S. Office of War Information, Overseas Branch, also produced films on American life for showing abroad. Representative of OWI wartime propaganda is *The Town* (1944) by the Hollywood director Josef von Sternberg, which examines life in a typical midwestern town in order to reveal the strength and integrity of the American people and American institutions. It has the solid production values that characterize OWI films and a direct, simple handling of the message that overlooks any shadings or subtleties that might obscure the film's basic purpose. Other OWI films in the Circulating collection are *The Autobiography of a "Jeep"* (1943), produced and written by Joseph Krumgold, which provides a whimsical justification of the military jeep; and *Window Cleaner* (1945), a bright and humorous account of the workman who cleans the windows of the Empire State Building.

But it was John Huston who produced the most famous American wartime film, *The Battle of San Pietro* (1945). It follows a U.S. Army infantry and tank assault on German positions in the mountains of central Italy with a ferocity that has rarely if ever been matched in documentary. Indeed, the original version was so overpowering the military insisted on cuts (from a total running time of fifty to thirty minutes), added an explanatory foreword by General Mark Clark, and then held up its release until the war was almost over. It remains, in spite of the enforced changes, a monumental work. Later, in 1945, Huston directed *Let There Be Light* (1946), on the rehabilitation of veterans with emotional and psychiatric disorders brought on by their combat experience. The film suffered an even crueler fate than *The Battle of San Pietro*—it was considered so controversial that it was banned from all public circulation until 1980.

Britain also developed extensive documentary production during the war under the direction of men who had gotten their start with John Grierson, including Harry Watt, Basil Wright, Arthur Elton, Edgar Anstey, Humphrey Jennings, and Paul Rotha. One of the most vivid British films showing the war in action is *Desert Victory* (1943), directed by David MacDonald, which follows Britain's Eighth Army as it pursues Rommel's Afrika Corps across Libya. Turning to the home front, Ruby Grierson directed *They Also Serve* (1940), on the role of women in wartime. She was one of the small group of women who were given directing assignments in the U.S. and Britain during the war. One of Humphrey Jennings's films made during this period is *The Silent Village* (1943), a remarkable work that reenacts the Nazi takeover of Lidice, Czechoslovakia, using the setting and the people of a small Welsh town.

In the period immediately after the war, documentary production continued, but at a much slower pace. Pare Lorentz directed *Nuremberg* (1948) for the U.S. Army on the Nuremberg War Crimes Trials. Also on the theme of war is the deeply moving *Le Retour* (1946), by the renowned French photographer Henri Cartier-Bresson and the American Richard Banks, on the return of inmates from Nazi concentration camps. However, on the whole, the postwar years were difficult ones for the documentary movement. In Britain the government closed down most of its production. In the U.S. there were jobs in the emerging television industry, but it was not a period that welcomed the socially and politically aware film, with many filmmakers soon to be blacklisted during the McCarthy years.

One of the very few independently produced American documentaries of this period is *In the Street* (1952), by the distinguished team of Helen Levitt, James Agee, and Janice Loeb. It is a sensitive, poetic study of street life, principally of children, in a New York slum. It was made on such a low budget that it has never had a "wedded" sound track—one either shows it silent or with a separate audio cassette prepared by the filmmakers. This is indicative of the problems of financing independent films at that time.

A major documentary filmmaker to emerge at the same time as *In the Street* was George Stoney. His *All My Babies* (1952), a film made in Georgia for the training of midwives, received acclaim as one of the few films of that period to treat blacks with understanding and sympathy. Stoney went on to a distinguished career as a film teacher and producer. In 1978, he independently produced *The Shepherd of the Night Flock*, very much in the humanistic tradition of Robert Flaherty. It portrays a Lutheran pastor who ministers to the needs of the jazz community in New York City, among whom he is a beloved figure. It combines with unusual skill the spontaneity of *cinéma vérité* shooting and the more traditional aspects of controlled documentary.

In Britain during the early fifties documentary production waned, much as it did in the U.S. In the mid-fifties, however, a small but significant movement developed, called Free Cinema, which drew together talented and original young filmmakers such as Lindsay Anderson, Karel Reisz, and Tony Richardson (all of whom soon left documentary for theatrical film production). A film like *Every Day Except Christmas* (1957), one of the foremost works associated with this short-lived movement, shows that Free Cinema nevertheless planted the seeds for strong independent documentary to flower in Britain in the sixties and seventies, parallel to the independent movement in the United States during the same period. (Free Cinema, as well as the subsequent growth of British documentary, is described in this catalog in the essay "Contemporary British Independent Film.")

Throughout the latter part of the fifties and the early sixties, many documentary filmmakers were becoming dissatisfied with the prevailing technique of photographing in the field with a silent camera and later adding music, sound effects, and narration in the studio. New lightweight, high-quality tape recorders introduced during that period gave them the promise of capturing sound simultaneously with image, and by the end of the fifties filmmakers were solving the problems of precise synchronization of sound and picture. Among the first to use the technique successfully was Jean Rouch in France, and as a result of its French roots the style has come to be called by the name he gave it, *cinéma vérité*. Later, many American directors preferred the term "direct cinema." Film historian Lewis Jacobs describes the coming of *cinéma vérité* as follows:

Another kind of documentary began to emerge. It showed a revolutionary technique, a distinctive style, and a commitment to subject matter that ranged from an intimate form of journalism to a heightened form of theatricality.[9]

In the U.S., Drew Associates, working for Time Inc. during the early sixties, produced a large number of *cinéma vérité* documentaries, and the group is generally credited with establishing the style in America. The best known and most influential of the Drew Associates filmmakers are Richard Leacock, D. A. Pennebaker, Al Maysles, and Terence Macartney-Filgate (who also worked with the National Film Board of Canada). Other directors who came to be identified with the style in the sixties are the Americans William Jersey and Frederick Wiseman, and the Canadians Allan King and Michel Brault. In fact, major contributions to the form of *cinéma vérité* were sponsored in Canada by the National Film Board; Brault and Macartney-Filgate are among the leading figures represented in the NFB collection.

Among the young directors who emerged in the late sixties, and one of the few independents who worked in the *cinéma vérité* style, was Ed Pincus. In 1968 he coproduced with David Neuman a quintessential work of this form in *One Step Away*, which captures the life of a commune in California. At the height of the hippie period, the film's *cinéma vérité* style seems particularly suited to record the freewheeling, bizarre, and ultimately sad behavior of these alienated youths. Paul Ronder's sympathetic and intimate documentary *Part of the Family* (1971) reflects as well a feeling for the radical impact of the sixties on the traditional structure of the nuclear family.

Another of the new independents who works in this style in some of his films is Danny Lyon. A masterful example of his use of *cinéma vérité* technique is *Los Niños Abandonados (The Abandoned Children)* (1974), a warm, caring look at the harsh lives of street children in Colombia, South America. His uncanny ability to enter into the lives of his subjects is strongly reminiscent of Flaherty's relationship with the Eskimos. Other films by this artist, who handles film in a very personal way, are *Soc. Sci. 127* (1969), *Llanito* (1971), *El Mojado (The Wetback)* (1974), *Little Boy* (1977), and *El Otro Lado (The Other Side)* (1979).

On the international scene, an outstanding example of *cinéma vérité* in the service of political ideals is *Ireland Behind the Wire* (1974), made by a British political group, the Berwick Street Collective. It is a violently anti-establishment film in a raw, hand-held style, so outspoken that the footage of its last few minutes was seized by the British authorities because of its inflammatory interpretation of events in Northern Ireland. Although incomplete, it is still a powerful work.

While *cinéma vérité* is an influential technique, few filmmakers strictly adhere to it throughout their films. Rather, they combine it with other more conventional forms. This has been particularly true with the public service television documentary. Here *cinéma vérité* techniques have opened up and enhanced a style of screen journalism that had depended previously upon strict adherence to a written script. Through the sixties, television networks and the Public Broadcasting Service produced a large body of journalist-filmmakers, among them Edward R. Murrow, Morton Silverstein, Jack Willis, Martin Carr, Jay McMullen, Peter Davis, Arthur Barron, Albert Wasserman, and Frederick Wiseman.

Perhaps the most interesting television documentary of the early sixties, and one of the most controversial, was Robert M. Young's and Michael Roemer's *Cortile Cascino* (1961). It is a warm, sympathetic, yet uncompromising look at the slums of Palermo, Sicily, and the people who live there.

The film was among the first to combine *cinéma vérité* effectively with more controlled methods of filmmaking. It is imbued with the spirit of Robert Flaherty, and like Flaherty, Young and Roemer felt free to employ theatrical film devices. The film was never shown on television—its content as well as its style appeared at the time too unconventional—and it has only now been put into release. From the perspective of twenty years it seems a very fine film indeed, and one of the best from that period of television documentaries.

A decade later one of the most controversial documentaries in the history of television was produced and, unlike *Cortile Cascino*, broadcast. It was *The Selling of the Pentagon* (1971), directed by Peter Davis for CBS. During the heated national debate over the Vietnam War, it brought to light the practice in the U.S. Department of Defense of spending large amounts of public funds to promote the federal government's war policy. Not unexpectedly, the film came under virulent attack both from the government and the war lobby. It still stands as a high point of investigative television journalism.

A more recent independently produced film, *Portrait of an American Zealot* (1982) by Alan and Marc Levin, is remarkable for the skillful way it combines several documentary traditions. It uses the filmed profile of an individual to explore an issue—in this instance the religious right wing in America. It is part of the investigative tradition in that it probes and reveals its subjects, but at the same time it shares the original spirit of *cinéma vérité* in that it does not take an openly partisan position but aims simply to tell a straightforward story and let the audience make up its own mind about the issues. Moreover, it has the comforting appearance of a television net-

THE SHEPERDS OF BERNERAY (1981)

work documentary to a sufficient degree (it was broadcast on public television) that the mass audience can accept its controversial message.

Since the beginning of documentary filmmaking, there have been a few artists who have tried to enrich its canon by creating new cinematic forms. They often have been inspired by ideas within the avant-garde, but they differ from the experimental filmmakers in that their primary purpose is to make a political statement. They are, in effect, carrying on a tradition begun by Dziga Vertov. Such an artist is the American independent Paul Brekke. His *Outtakes—Paysage de Guerre* (1979) attacks the concept of war. His title, *Outtakes*, is a reference to the raw material for his film, newsreel footage of actual bombing runs. By processing the footage, altering its color, changing its speed, and using repetition, he underlines the horror of war; at the same time, he also ritualizes it, thereby creating a more reflective and philosophical antiwar statement.

One of the most accomplished films among current documentaries is *The Shepherds of Berneray* (1981), by Allen Moore and Jack Shea. The cinematic elements of structure, editing, photography, and sound are masterfully interwoven with the story, recorded over the course of a full year, of daily life and the winds of change in a Gaelic-speaking community on a remote island off the coast of Scotland. Evoking both a poetic spirit and a conscience, it represents the best of many strands that make up the documentary tradition.

Looking back on the history of the nonfiction film, these two principal directions seem clear: the social and political documentary, exemplified by John Grierson, and the humanistic tradition, reflected in the films of Robert Flaherty. Parallel to these two mainstreams is the work of artists whose primary concern has been the search for new forms, as in the work of Dziga Vertov. Moreover, throughout the growth and development of the documentary movement, technical innovations have been important in giving the documentary its shape, especially advances in synchronous sound recording. Equally determinant has been the impact of film financing by sources as diverse as the government, commercial and public television, grant-giving organizations, and private donors. As we move into the eighties, it is the independents who are expanding and extending the scope and meaning of the documentary film.

Notes

[1]Erik Barnouw, *Documentary: A History of the Non-Fiction Film* (New York: Oxford University Press, 1974), p. 63.

[2]John Grierson, in *Grierson on Documentary,* ed. Forsyth Hardy (New York: Praeger 1971), p. 128.

[3]*Ibid,* p. 151.

[4]Richard Meran Barsam, *Nonfiction Film* (New York: Dutton, 1973), p. 55.

[5]Barnouw, *Documentary,* p. 111.

[6]William Alexander, *Film on the Left* (Princeton, N.J.: Princeton University Press 1981), p. 162.

[7]Richard Corliss, "Robert Flaherty: The Man in the Iron Myth" (1973), in Richard Meran Barsam, ed., *Nonfiction Film Theory and Criticism* (New York: E. P. Dutton 1976), p. 236.

[8]Luis Buñuel, interviewed by André Bazin and Jacques Doniol-Valcroze, *Cahiers du cinéma* 36 (June 1954), pp. 2–14. Reprinted in Francisco Aranda, *Luis Buñuel: A Critical Biography,* ed. and trans. David Robinson (New York: DaCapo, 1976), pp. 90-91.

[9]Lewis Jacobs, *The Documentary Tradition,* 2nd ed. (New York: Norton, 1979), p. 375

ANNOTATIONS
Herbert Reynolds, William Sloan,
Marita Sturken

FILMS OF THE 1890s (1894–99). *See*
Silent Fiction

EARLY FILMS OF INTEREST
(1895–1918). *See* Silent Fiction

LUMIÈRE PROGRAM I: FIRST
PROGRAMS (1895–96). *See* Silent
Fiction

LUMIÈRE PROGRAM II: EARLY
LUMIÈRE FILMS (1895–98). *See*
Silent Fiction

THE PATHÉ NEWSREEL

1917–31. U.S.A.
Pathé News.
Total program: 19 min. B&W. Silent and
Sound. (16 min. Silent. 18 fps. plus 3
min. Sound. 24 fps. for the final two
subjects.)

WILSON SIGNS DECLARATION OF
WAR

1917.

SUFFRAGETTES RIOT AT WHITE
HOUSE

1918.

WILSON SPEAKS FOR TREATY

1919.

BATTLESHIP "MARYLAND"
LAUNCHED

1920.

DESTRUCTION OF HOMEMADE
STILLS

1920.

SAN LUIS OBISPO OIL FIRE

1926.

RUDOLPH VALENTINO FUNERAL

1926.

SIOUX ADOPT COOLIDGE

1927.

JOE POWERS SITS ON FLAGPOLE
FOR SIXTEEN DAYS

1928.

ITALY'S LEGIONS MASS FOR
MUSSOLINI

1931.
Sound.

BILLY SUNDAY BURNS UP THE
BACKSLIDING WORLD

1931.
Sound.

In France in 1909 or 1910 the Pathé
Frères Company, then the world's largest film producer, introduced the first
weekly newsreel, the *Pathé Journal*. Soon
thereafter Pathé subsidiaries introduced newsreel production in England
and, on August 8, 1911, in the United
States. Less than three years later, U.S.
Pathé began supplementing its weekly
issues (*Pathé Weekly*) with daily ones
(*Pathé Daily News*), which continued until the First World War. Thereafter, its
weekly releases were called *Pathé News*;
these ran until their acquisition by Warner Bros. in 1947. For a good part of
its life, the Pathé newsreel was America's foremost. This program offers
eleven issues, covering the decade and
a half following the nation's entry into
World War I. These titles indicate the
variety of subjects, both historic and entertaining, covered by the newsreel, and
the newsreel's reporting styles. (The
1917 example constructs a story using
a cause-effect relationship: President
Wilson signs the war order, this is "telegraphed" with animated effects, and the
naval militia is called out. Thereafter,
the newsreels are more straightforward, adding voice-over and live recording after the start of the sound period.) Highlights include Wilson's
heartbreaking exhaustion while pleading for American participation in the
League of Nations, the Valentino funeral, and the oratory of the leading
fundamentalist evangelist of the era.
(Compare Vertov's Soviet newsreel, **Kino**
Pravda [1922].)

MANHATTA

1921. U.S.A.
Directed and photographed by Paul
Strand and Charles Sheeler. Titles from
Walt Whitman.
9 min. B&W. Silent. 18 fps.

Half a decade or more before major
filmmakers around the world were undertaking "city symphonies" (see *Rien*
que les heures [1926, France], *Berlin:*
Symphony of a Great City [1927, Germany], *The Man With the Movie Camera* [1929, U.S.S.R.], and *Rain* [1929,
Holland]), two of America's leading artists might be said to have inaugurated
the genre in New York. The painter
Charles Sheeler had taken up photography to support himself during the
decade after 1910 when his new geometric, planar canvases were not selling. He grew interested in the expressive, artistic use of the camera and
enlisted photographer Paul Strand to
join him in making a film. Their collaboration on this impressionistic representation of Walt Whitman's lyric hymn
to the city evidences a much less realistic, more "photo-secessionist" mode
than these men's respective later styles
might suggest. *Manhatta* was only the
beginning of a brilliant career in cinematography for Strand, whose sharply
drawn images for *The Wave* (1935) and
The Plow that Broke the Plains (1936)
are examples of his mature film work.

KINO PRAVDA (Selections)

June to August, 1922. U.S.S.R.
Kultkino. By Dziga Vertov. Photographed by various cameramen, including Mikhail Kaufman. Edited by Yelizaveta Svilova. With Anatoli
Lunacharsky. English intertitles.
17 min. B&W. Silent. 18 fps.

The Soviet filmmaker and theorist Dziga
Vertov is now recognized alongside
Robert Flaherty as a major progenitor
of the documentary. Appropriately, it
was 1922, the same year *Nanook of the*
North was released, that Vertov launched
his **Kino Pravda** series and issued a
group of manifestos proclaiming his
nonfiction goals. This followed four
years' training with short films on daily
life and compilations of historical actualities. Long drawn to Russian Futurism and charged by the spirit of the
Revolution (born Denis Kaufman, his
artistic name connotes a whirl of energy), Vertov renounced the theatrical
film with its studio sets, scripts, and actors and dedicated his aims to depicting
reality on the screen. **Kino Pravda** ("Film
Truth," after the Bolsheviks' party
newspaper) appeared in twenty-three
issues over three years. These selections
from the initial year of his radical newsreel indicate many of Vertov's interests
and the inventiveness that led to *The*
Man With the Movie Camera (1929) and
Enthusiasm (1931). They begin with the
projectionist unpacking and spooling up
the reel we are "about" to see (a playful
touch, and instructive to viewers unacquainted with the technology of the film
medium). A split screen effect announces the dateline: Moscow. Dynamic intertitles accompany some specific subjects: reconstructing the trolley
system, tanks leveling a new airport, organizing peasants' communes, a new
sanitorium, the horror of abandoned
children. "Save the starving children,"
pleads the intertitle. Vertov sought to
exhort his audience, especially to make

them aware of social ills, but he invited their participation without explaining or interpreting events for them as did conventional newsreels—even when his subject is a trial of social revolutionaries. Honoring Vertov's example, Jean Rouch translated "kino pravda" into French to give us the term *cinéma vérité*.

NANOOK OF THE NORTH

1922. U.S.A.
Produced by Revillon Frères, released by U.S. Pathé. Written, directed, and photographed by Robert Flaherty. Music track for the restored version by Stanley Silverman, performed by Tashi (Peter Serkin, Ida Kavafian, Fred Sherry, Richard Stoltzman).
64 min. B&W. Sound (music track).

Nanook of the North was the second film about Hudson Bay Eskimo life that Robert Flaherty made. The first, photographed during his mining expeditions of the mid-1910s, was irrecoverable after Flaherty accidentally burned up the negative with a lighted cigarette. Dissatisfied with the straightforward, "travelogue" approach he had taken, Flaherty determined upon a more dramatic narrative for his second effort; and once he had obtained financing, used it so successfully that he commanded the future of the documentary form. To give the work a human intimacy, Flaherty used his understanding of the Eskimos' customs and his personal sympathy to

MOANA (1926)

enlist their participation, centering the film on one family, that of Nanook and Nyla. A consummate film craftsman, he borrowed the fluid style of commercial movie fiction and the story-telling techniques perfected by Hollywood features. He had scenes acted out over and over until he was satisfied with results, striving to build and then release the emotional tension of his audience. He sought to recapture a traditional way of life, before the intervention of the modern era, and he struck upon a great universal theme—man's struggle to live against the most inimical forces of nature. For all his devising, he attained his ends: a passionate and recognizable truth about the human spirit. *Nanook* is a fresh and exciting film, warmly humanist, romantic, visionary. This, the original release version of the film, preserves Flaherty's very special intertitles, which were unfortunately cut out of the 1947 reissue. The film was restored by David Shepard in 1975, and includes a specially composed modern score.

GRASS. A NATION'S BATTLE FOR LIFE

April 12, 1925. U.S.A.
Released by Paramount. Directed and photographed by Merian C. Cooper and Ernest B. Schoedsack, with Marguerite Harrison. Edited and titled by Terry Ramsaye and Richard P. Carver.
86 min. B&W. Silent. 18 fps.

One of the the most celebrated early documentaries, *Grass* was also the first important film to record an American travel expedition. Shot on location under the most primitive circumstances (a feat for which its makers never cease to be self-congratulatory), the film recounts the annual migration of over fifty thousand Bakhtiari tribesmen as they brave violent rivers with their animals and supplies and cross on foot the mountain ranges of Turkey and Persia—all in search of grasslands where their flocks can graze. Capturing both thrills and breathtaking vistas, while evidencing the proclivity for exotic fiction that Cooper and Schoedsack would develop further in their most famous collaboration, *King Kong* (1933), *Grass* shares something of the epic side of Flaherty's romantic sensibility.

MOANA. A ROMANCE OF THE GOLDEN AGE

1926. U.S.A.
Famous Players-Lasky (Paramount). Written, directed, and photographed by Robert Flaherty, with the assistance of Frances Hubbard Flaherty and Bob

Roberts.
85 min. B&W. Silent. 18 fps.

Hollywood had shown no interest in distributing *Nanook of the North* (1922), but after that film's overwhelming commercial success the Paramount organization offered to finance Flaherty's next film. Choosing to depict the life of Samoan islanders in the South Pacific, the filmmaker undertook a challenge at odds to that of filming *Nanook*: how to adapt his great theme of man's survival against the elements to a beneficent tropical climate. The measure of Flaherty's success in *Moana* lies in his mastery of the most difficult problem facing a documentary filmmaker, that of finding his way to the emotional heart of his subject. Flaherty sought out the Samoan cultural tradition within his beautiful images of their everyday activities—fishing, hunting, feasting, dancing—and one that he resurrected for them, the ritual of the tattoo. John Grierson first used the term "documentary" in reference to this work.

BERLIN: SYMPHONY OF A GREAT CITY (BERLIN, DIE SINFONIE DER GROSSTADT)

1927. Germany.
Fox-Europa. Directed by Walter Ruttmann. Scenario by Ruttmann and Karl Freund, from an idea by Carl Mayer. Photographed by Freund and others. Made without intertitles.
53 min. B&W. Silent. 24 fps.

Just after mid-decade in the 1920s, the German cinema was beginning a transition away from its heavy Expressionist leanings and toward more realistic subjects, the latter movement known as the New Objectivity. Significantly, two leading figures, the outstanding screenwriter, Carl Mayer (*The Cabinet of Dr. Caligari* [1920], *The Last Laugh* [1924]), and fine cinematographer, Karl Freund (*The Golem* [1920], *The Last Laugh* [1924], *Variety* [1925], *Metropolis* [1927]), each sought release from the restrictions of studio artificiality and agreed to a project suggested by Mayer: to film a city symphony drawn from the reality of Berlin itself. Mayer left the film early over a difference of opinion with Walter Ruttmann, its director and a former abstract filmmaker (see his **Opus** films [1921–24]), who Mayer felt was emphasizing surface appearance at the expense of meaning. Ruttmann's *Berlin* does indeed exult in formal visual properties and what a glory of stunning photography and editing! Curiously, it is strongly influenced by, and a close approximation of, Dziga Vertov's symphonic style of visual imagery, and it is undoubtedly the greatest city film outside of Vertov's *The Man With the Movie Camera* (1929), which it preceded. Yet where Vertov endeavors constantly to convey an implicit, often highly complex, message about life, work, and filmmaking, Ruttmann larks in the pure lyric flow or comic juxtaposition of the images themselves. *Berlin* opens at dawn on a late spring day and proceeds to midnight: empty streets fill up, a morning's multitude of work gives way to noontime lunch, more commercial bustle until evening, then a new world of recreational pursuits—sports, night spots, socializing, an automobile ride, a concert, dance halls, and trysts. Unique in the German cinema, *Berlin* is a marvel of documentary montage, wedding avant-garde style to feature filmmaking.

THE MAN WITH THE MOVIE CAMERA (1929)

THE FALL OF THE ROMANOV DYNASTY (PADENIYE DINASTI ROMANOVIKH)

March 11, 1927. U.S.S.R.
Sovkino. Written and edited by Esther Shub. English intertitles.
101 min. B&W. Silent. 18 fps.

This is the premier example of the compilation film, assembled from earlier footage and often without new material. Sponsored for the tenth anniversary of the 1917 Revolution, *The Fall of the Romanov Dynasty* is one of the most engrossing reenactments of history, covering Czarist Russia from 1912 through World War I and the revolutions of February and October 1917. Its maker, Esther Shub, had years of experience as a film editor on a variety of fictional works, but developed a greater interest in documentary. *Potemkin*'s account of the 1905 Revolution reputedly inspired her to make a history film of her own, but one that would utilize actual film records of events. She located newsreels of the pre-revolutionary period, and, after a successful struggle to obtain production approval, uncovered home movies of Czar Nicholas II taken by the court cinematographer. By her positioning of regal celebrations, boating parties, croquet and tennis games adjacent to contemporary strikes, breadlines, arrests, munitions factories, and war, and with the use of pointed intertitles, Shub reaffirmed Kuleshov's principle of imbuing each shot with new meaning by dialectical montage. Her heirs in the compilation genre, including Frank Capra in the **Why We Fight** propaganda series (1942–45), would profit by Shub's example. She followed *The Fall of the Romanov Dynasty* with

corresponding films on the periods 1917–27 and 1896–1912 to form a trilogy.

LINDBERGH'S FLIGHT FROM N.Y. TO PARIS

1927. U.S.A.
Fox Movietone Entertainments. Produced by Jack Connolly. With Charles A. Lindbergh, Calvin Coolidge.
12 min. B&W. Sound.

Produced from 1919 to 1963, the Fox newsreel began in January 1927 to play an important part in introducing sound to the film medium. The year before, the parent Fox Film Corporation purchased the sound-on-film system developed by Theodore Case, Earl Sponable, and Lee De Forest and founded the Fox-Case Corporation to release the process commercially. Fox Movietone was the name chosen for the new sound newsreel. Its biggest early triumph was its live recording of Charles Lindbergh's takeoff on May 20, 1927, from Roosevelt Field, Long Island, for the first transatlantic flight. The expectation of the crowd gathered for "Lindy's" sendoff is evident in the hushed silence followed by its cheers as the Spirit of St. Louis disappears into the gray overcast as it taxies down the runway. Apparently victims of the haste to issue the newsreel, the title cards misspell the aviator's name and misidentify his takeoff site. After Lindbergh's return, Fox Movietone recorded the welcoming home ceremony held June 12 in Washington. The momentous occasion moved President Calvin Coolidge to deliver an uncharacteristically long address (five minutes), reportedly the most extensive since his inaugural. Following a flush of birds released as Lindbergh steps up to the

microphones, the hero himself speaks. Uneasy with public appearances, he usually refused to be filmed thereafter. Other landmark newsreels from Fox Movietone are **Shaw Talks for Movietone News** (1928; see **The Coming of Sound** [1927–28]) and *Assassination of Alexander and Barthou* (1934; see *Assassination of King Alexander of Jugoslavia* [1934]).

THE BRIDGE (DE BRUG)

May 1928. Netherlands.
Capi-Amsterdam. By Joris Ivens. Made without intertitles.
12 min. B&W. Silent. 24 fps.

For his first significant film, Ivens assigned himself an exercise in form and motion, photographing the operation of a railroad drawbridge over the Maas River in Rotterdam. A cinematic essay on the functional dynamics of man and machinery, *The Bridge* achieves a purely visual narrative as a train waits for the bridge to be raised and lowered so a boat can pass, and then accelerates across. Interestingly, Ivens introduces *The Bridge* with a short of himself filming with a Kinamo camera, the year before Vertov's similar depiction in *The Man With the Movie Camera* (1929).

SHAW TALKS FOR MOVIETONE NEWS (1928). See **The Coming of Sound** (1927–28) in Sound Fiction

THE MAN WITH THE MOVIE CAMERA (CHELOVEK S KINOAPPARATOM)

January 8, 1929. U.S.S.R.
Vufku. Written, directed, and edited by Dziga Vertov. Photographed by Mikhail Kaufman. Assistant editor: Yelizaveta

RAIN (1929)

Svilova. Made without intertitles.
89 min. B&W. Silent. 18 fps.

In many ways, **The Man with the Movie Camera** is not only Vertov's masterpiece and final film of the silent era, it is a work which notably exemplifies the montage aesthetic of the Soviet avant-garde of the twenties. Filmed in Moscow and Odessa, it belongs to the "city symphony" genre—documentaries of the period that depicted a day in the life of an urban metropolis (e.g., Ruttmann's **Berlin: Symphony of a Great City** [1927] and Cavalcanti's **Rien que les heures** [1926]). **The Man with the Movie Camera** presents the city in a visually exuberant way. Vertov uses his assertive editing style to cut among various forms of labor, instructing the viewer about the interrelationship of each worker's task. Central to his vision of socialist production is the role of the filmmaker whose labor is compared to that of other workers. Vertov accentuates this conceptual parallel with formal similarities: thus a rotating machine part is compared to a camera crank, and fabric passing through a sewing-machine gear to a film strip moving through the editor's fingers. **The Man with the Movie Camera** is both a documentary on the nature of socialist society and an investigation of the filmmaking process itself. In particular it seeks to reveal cinematic illusions to the spectator, and as part of that project utilizes all the extravagant visual devices of the twenties avant-garde: superimposition, split-screen effect, slow and accelerated motion, as well as freeze-frame.

RAIN (REGEN)

December 1929. Netherlands.
Capi-Amsterdam. Directed and edited by Joris Ivens with Mannus Franken. Photographed by Ivens. Made without intertitles.
15 min. B&W. Silent. 24 fps.

Rain is a famous and lyrical impression of a rain storm in Amsterdam. This model "city poem" observes, as Ivens put it, the changing face of the city during the rain. Filmed at moment's notice over four months' time—inclement weather permitting—but edited into a single passing shower, the film is wonderfully simple and conceals Ivens's meticulous care. (Its reliance on a bare minimum of light was a virtuoso achievement in itself.) More spontaneous than *The Bridge* (1928), and subtler in evoking emotion than *Breakers* (1929), it is Ivens's finest gem of the twenties, before he turned to social and political documentary. He compared its embodiment of a mood to the verse of Paul Verlaine: "Il pleure dans mon coeur/ Comme il pleut sur la ville" (It weeps in my heart as it rains on the town). But Ivens's film is filled with joy.

L'HISTOIRE DU SOLDAT INCONNU
(1930). *See* Experimental Film

SALT FOR SVANETIA (SOL SVANETII)

1930. U.S.S.R.
Goskinprom (Georgia). Written and directed by Mikhail Kalatozov, from an idea by Sergei Tretyakov. Photographed by Kalatozov and M. Gegelashvili. English intertitles.
54 min. B&W. Silent. 24 fps.

The Soviet Georgian Mikhail Kalatozov was trained as a cameraman and brought an eye for strong formal imagery to his films. His best-known film is the 1957 fiction feature **The Cranes are Flying**, but his earlier **Salt for Svanetia** is more important. It reports on life in Svanetia, an isolated section of the Caucasus between the Black and Caspian Seas that was cut off from the world by mountains and glaciers except for one narrow footpath through the mountains. At the time of the Russian Revolution, its inhabitants were still living in the most primitive conditions, intensified by ignorance and superstition. Typifying the plight of the region was its lack of salt, without which the herds could not produce milk. The salt thus had to be hand-carried up the footpath from the lowlands. The climax of the film shows the difficult construction of a road that will bring salt (communications, nutrition, medicine, education, assimilation) to Svanetia; but the scenes which make it unforgettable are those of the too-recent past: a cow lapping human urine for salt; a crazed horse galloping until it drops dead; a woman dripping the milk from her breast onto a recent grave in this region so poor that each new life is a curse and death the only consolation. While incorporating much of Eisenstein's angular compositions and some of Dovzhenko's themes and lyricism, the film often imbues its images with a biting clarity akin to Surrealism. As a result, it resembles in power as well as subject Buñuel's later **Land Without Bread** (1933). Despite its champions, among them the perceptive American critic Harry Alan Potamkin, this unusual masterwork has just recently become generally available outside the Soviet Union.

A BRONX MORNING

1931. U.S.A.
By Jay Leyda.
11 min. B&W. Silent. 24 fps.

"The Bronx does business . . . and the Bronx lives . . . on the street." So read the three intertitles in young Jay Leyda's fond glimpse of the borough in the early thirties. Signs in storefront windows ("Prices Down") hint at the times but unlike the contemporary **City of Contrasts** (1931) or **Film and Photo League** news films (1931–34), Leyda's film concentrates on the perseverance of daily life rather than its disruption by economic collapse. The views of elevated trains, tenements and shops, and the varieties of street life are linked by motion and visual motifs. They are photographed in fragmented detail but with the clear focus that marks the common ground between documentary and the avant-garde of this period. **A Bronx Morning** served its maker as portfolio when he won a scholarship to study with Eisenstein.

CITY OF CONTRASTS

1931. U.S.A.
By Irving Browning. Released by Sol Lesser.
18 min. B&W. Sound (may be shown silent, 24 fps).

When Irving Browning shot this modest portrait of New York City with a portable camera in the early part of the Depression, he could have been inspired by *Rien que les heures* (1926). Images of glamour and high life are contrasted with barkers, beggars, and street performers hustling to get by; handsome and resolute apartment houses on Riverside Drive overlook a squatters' shanty town on the banks of the Hudson River. But like prosperity itself, the silent film had newly been eclipsed, and the narration added to the film for theatrical release mitigated and exploited its visuals. The result is a "city symphony" transformed to commercial use, perhaps reminding us of the sort of condescending travelogue Buñuel parodied in *Land Without Bread* (1933).

ENTHUSIASM, SYMPHONY OF THE DON BASIN (ENTUZIAZM, SIMFONIA DONBASSA)

April 2, 1931. U.S.S.R.
Ukrainfilm. Written and directed by Dziga Vertov. Photographed by Zeitlin. Edited by Yelizaveta Svilova. Music by N. Timofeyev. Russian head titles and sparse voice-over, plus one synchronized speech; no English subtitles, but not difficult to follow.
67 min. B&W. Sound.

In this film about the Don Basin, the extensive region lying between Moscow and the Black Sea, Vertov's object was ostensibly to celebrate the coal miners' achievement in only four years of their part in the first Five Year Plan. It was his first sound film, however, and like Eisenstein, Vertov had revolutionary ideas about employing the new medium. Natural sounds of machinery and men at work, voices, music, and songs were recorded separately from the picture and edited freely and dissociatively, sometimes even superimposed like the visuals. Soviet montage had demonstrated the dynamic variety of editing visual images: why shouldn't the soundtrack be as creatively structured as well? (For a few synchronous passages, Vertov also used a portable sound recorder that he himself helped develop.) Vertov's result is a novel and exhilarating concerto—by his own title, a

"symphony"—of sight and sound, and an exploration further along the path of the silent *The Man With the Movie Camera* (1929). *Enthusiasm* begins with a cinematic recapitulation of recent Russian history to indicate the transformations in society that accompany the gearing up of mine, factory, and mill production. At the end, Vertov links industrial progress with agricultural growth, but throughout the film his dominant theme is the feverish enthusiasm underlying the new Soviet life—not only for work, but for rallying, marching, dancing, singing. Eisenstein himself would be unable to complete a sound film to equal it before *Alexander Nevsky* (1938); his brilliance, like Vertov's, often perplexed general viewers and worried the Stalin regime, which condemned both as "formalist." This print of *Enthusiasm* has been restored from surviving materials by Peter Kubelka.

FILM AND PHOTO LEAGUE PROGRAM I

1931–32. U.S.A.
Produced by the Film and Photo League of the Workers International Relief.
Total program: 32 min. B&W. Silent. 24 fps.

WORKERS NEWSREEL UNEMPLOYMENT SPECIAL 1931

1931.
Photographed by Robert Del Duca, Leo Seltzer. Edited, with original still photos by Seltzer.
7 min. (or 9 min. at 18 fps.)

DETROIT WORKERS NEWS SPECIAL 1932: FORD MASSACRE

1932.
Photographed by Jack Auringer, Robert Del Duca, Joseph P. Hudyma (Dearborn attack), Leo Seltzer, John Shard. Edited by Lester Balog, Hudyma.
7 min. (or 9 min. at 18 fps.)

HUNGER: THE NATIONAL HUNGER MARCH TO WASHINGTON 1932

1932.
Photographed by Sam Brody, Robert Del Duca, Leo Hurwitz, C. O. Nelson, Leo Seltzer. Edited by Del Duca, Hurwitz, Seltzer, Norman Warren.
18 min.

The Workers Film and Photo League (later known simply as the Film and Photo League) was begun in New York in 1930 by a dedicated group of leftist

and left-liberal photographers, filmmakers, and critics. Branches opened in other cities as the Depression lengthened, and League members undertook to photograph with still and moving images the breadlines and Hoovervilles, hunger and unemployment marches, restless protests and labor disputes. In short, their intent was to bear witness to the effects of economic and social (perhaps political) collapse and lend support for a progressive working-class movement in the U.S. Films produced by the League were shown directly to workers' groups, in union halls or strike headquarters or even outdoors at night. Many viewers recognized themselves or their friends on screen, so the presentations were frequently lively and exhortative. But beyond the specific events they had participated in, workers often knew little of similar struggles occurring around the country or abroad, nor of the widespread results of economic crisis and class conflicts. The Film and Photo League films thus became solidifying agents in political education, aiming to inform, to build morale, to agitate. The Hollywood entertainment industry, which controlled commercial newsreel production and theatrical exhibition, generally expunged controversy. In their own *Workers Newsreel*, League members sometimes captured and included material shot but unreleased by their counterparts in the industry—scenes the producers considered too sensitive for public consumption. The first film on this program shows the first mass demonstration against unemployment and hunger, in Union Square, New York City, on March 6, 1930. Hundreds were injured when the crowd, estimated at 100,000, was rushed by 1,000 policemen in an attempt to break up the rally. As severe hardship increased, authorities became more ruthless toward such demonstrations. The Detroit Film and Photo League filmed the march to Grand Circus Park through bitter cold and snow to petition for unemployment relief and oppose President Hoover and Mayor Murphy's "starvation program"; at the River Rouge Ford Motor plant, Dearborn police joined with Ford guards to attack protesters with clubs, tear gas, and guns. Of the four young men murdered, the film observes, "They asked for food and jobs. . . . They got bullets!" *Hunger* reports the December 1932 march to Washington by 3,000 delegates from the National Unemployment Councils (an animated map depicts their convergence on the capital). After being held at the outskirts of the city by a squadron of police for two days and three nights and denied a permit to march and a hall to assemble in, the marchers pressed on at last to the Capitol building. Running throughout these demonstrations are the common demands for unemployment insurance, cash relief, jobs, food, and housing, issues that have persisted up to our time. More than important works in the history of the cinema, these films are often the only surviving visual history of the social and political upheaval of the Depression era. (See also **Film and Photo League Program II** [1931–34].)

———

FILM AND PHOTO LEAGUE PROGRAM II

1931–34. U.S.A.
Produced by the Film and Photo League of the Workers International Relief.
Total program: 35 min. B&W. Silent. 24 fps.

THE NATIONAL HUNGER MARCH 1931

1931.
Photographed by Sam Brody, Robert Del Duca, Kita Kamura, William Kruck, Leo Seltzer, Alfred Valenti. Edited by Lester Balog, Del Duca, Seltzer.
11 min. (or 15 min. at 18 fps.)

AMERICA TODAY and THE WORLD IN REVIEW

1932–34.
Photographed and edited by Leo Seltzer.
11 min.

BONUS MARCH 1932

1932.
Photographed and edited by Leo Seltzer; opening montage edited by Lester Balog.
12 min.

Like the **Film and Photo League Program I** (1931–32), these valuable works are rare visual documents of some of the most historically dramatic yet little-seen events of their turbulent period. All have recently been restored and reassembled by Leo Seltzer, a regular among League members in the early 1930s. Through the youthful energy of Seltzer, Lester Balog, Robert Del Duca, and others, the Film and Photo League attempted the most wide-ranging program of grassroots filmmaking in the course of American documentary. Its scope is suggested in the film on the National Unemployment Council Hunger March of November and December 1931. Concentrating on the ground swell of

activity as 1,650 men and women, black and white, set out from disparate parts of the U.S. to represent twelve million unemployed, League filmmakers assembled views of various groups as they passed through ten different American cities bound for Washington: Boston, Providence, New Haven, Buffalo, New York City, Philadelphia, Pittsburgh, Cleveland, Detroit, and St. Louis. In addition to such special reports on single events, the League issued roundups on news across the country and overseas, often incorporating suppressed commercial newsreels. *America Today* features protests against the first U.S. envoy from Nazi Germany, against the jailing of striking workers in New York, and against the framing of the Scottsboro Boys (we see Seltzer arrested while filming the demonstration). It also depicts farmers' action against scab milk shipments in Wisconsin and a vicious armed attack on striking steel and metal workers in Ambridge, Pennsylvania. *The World in Review* depicts world leaders (Mussolini, Hitler, FDR) preparing for war, Nazi stormtroopers enforcing the anti-Jewish boycott, and the French Popular Front opposing fascism in France. A cardinal aim of the League's field team was to be able to show their work as soon as possible after an event, so speed was a higher priority than polish. Yet, with experience, the filmmakers learned to anticipate for editing while shooting, and to structure their material for greater effect. *Bonus March 1932*, for instance, ironically recalls the heroism of the First World War and Congressional legislation to provide a future service bonus for veterans. When a "Bonus Expeditionary Force" of unemployed ex-servicemen arrived in Washington to demand immediate payment of their bonus money, President Hoover called out the regular army, under the command of MacArthur, Patton, and Eisenhower, which burned and gassed the vets out of the capital. The impact of these scenes is devastating, but the film sounds a final note for renewed struggle, reflecting the League's conviction that the film medium could serve as a weapon in political and economic struggle.

———

PHILIPS-RADIO (INDUSTRIAL SYMPHONY)

1931. Netherlands.
Capi-Amsterdam for Philips Eindhoven. Written and directed by Joris Ivens. Photographed by Ivens, John Ferno, Mark Kolthof. Edited by Ivens and Helen van Dongen. Music by Lou

Lichtveld. English intertitles (one in French).
36 min. B&W. Sound (music track).

In 1930, Joris Ivens accepted an offer from the Philips Company to make a film of its radio factory at Eindhoven in southern Holland. He was granted a substantial budget and the freedom to choose his subject as long as he did not venture beyond the gates of the plant— a restriction that prevented his examining the living conditions of workers in the company town. Ivens and his crew concentrated on the methods of work in a modern factory, developing a polished, well-crafted account of the stages involved in the assembly of radios, including the manufacture of components such as blown-glass amplifier tubes, receivers, transmitting valves, and loud speakers, until the finished products are packaged and shipped for distribution. The film's flow of images accompanied by music inspired the epithet "Symphonie Industrielle" when the film was presented in Paris. With its central theme of men at work (compare Ivens's treatment with Flaherty's in **Industrial Britain** [1933]), *Philips-Radio* represents the interval between 1929 and 1933 in Ivens's career, as he turned from his early works of purer formal beauty (*The Bridge* [1928] and *Rain* [1929]) toward ones with preeminent social and political subjects (as in *New Earth* [1934] and *The Spanish Earth* [1937]).

———

THE EARTH SINGS (ZEM SPIEVA)

1932. Czechoslovakia.
Directed and photographed by Karel Plicka. Edited by Alexander Hackenschmied (Alexander Hammid). Czech intertitles only.
67 min. B&W. Sound (music track).

The new Czechoslovakian republic, formed out of the First World War, generated a wave of nationalism that had helped to shape a growing film industry by the 1930s (see also *Such is Life* [1929]). How to include the constituent region of Slovakia, however, was a problem for the government and the cinema alike. At the easternmost stretch of the country, divided by the Carpathian Mountains, and harboring a strong separatist movement, Slovakia had its own ethnic tradition—rural, folkloric, strongly Roman Catholic. *The Earth Sings* honors the indigenous character of Slovakia, beginning with scenes complimenting its modern capital, Bratislava, but moving quickly to the alpine beauty of the Carpathians. The film's sponsorship came both from a Slovak cultural group and President T. G. Masaryk, father of the Czech state. The director, Karel Plicka, had studied Slovak folklore and was acquainted with avantgarde film style, which he borrows in constructing this lengthy cinematic hymn filled with ennobling views of the people in customary dress set against the majesty of the natural world. (Some of its imagery derives from Dovzhenko's *Earth* [1930], which advocated the incorporation of another integral region, the Ukraine, within the U.S.S.R.) Plicka used some intertitles and a music score derived from popular melodies of the region to accompany the age-old customs of farming and harvesting, herding, craftwork, religious festivals, and dancing. Affirming the profound loveliness of the land and the people's life within this realm of nature, *The Earth Sings* makes a striking contrast to contemporary anthropological documentaries such as *Salt for Svanetia* (1930) and *Land Without Bread* (1933).

GERMAN NEWSREELS

1933–40. Germany.
In German; no English titles.
Total Program: 23 min. B&W. Sound.

NATIONAL SOCIALIST PARTY DAY IN NUREMBERG (PARTEITAG DER N.S.D.A.P. IN NÜRNBERG)

1933.
Fox Tönende Wochenschau.
4 min.

YOUNG GERMANY CHEERS THE FÜHRER (DAS JUNGE DEUTSCHLAND JUBELT DEM FÜHRER ZU)

1933.
Ufaton.
2 min.

FRONT-LINE REPORTS OF THE PROPAGANDA COMPANIES (FRONT-BERICHTE DER PROPAGANDA-KOMPANIEN)

1940.
Die Deutsche Wochenschau.
17 min.

These newsreels, both fascinating and awesomely fearful, present Adolf Hitler in 1933 and 1940 on occasions of his greatest personal triumph. The first two subjects—one produced by Ufa, the other from the German corporate counterpart of Fox Movietone—record scenes from the 1933 Nazi Party Rally in Nuremberg. In January of that year, following impressive (though by no means decisive) electoral gains and con-

siderable political intrigue, Hitler was appointed Germany's Chancellor. With the power of state at last in their hands, the Nazis celebrated with their first rally in four years and the largest to date, officially named the Party Day of Victory. Hitler's speeches (recorded live) and the enormous scale of human columns marching down the streets and in the stadium adumbrate the next year's rally and its depiction in *Triumph of the Will* (1935). Seven years later, in 1940, Hitler gloried in a year of unbounded military successes. An annual roundup of events by **Die Deutsche Wochenschau,** the Third Reich's greatest newsreel (see *The Camera Goes Along!* [1936]) offers scenes from the newly conquered territories—northern France, Brussels, Amsterdam. Hitler sports conspicuously in the railway car where the Treaty of Versailles was signed in 1918. A remarkable sequence shows crowds of Parisians listening in silence to the announcement of the fall of France; abandoned automobiles and refugees line country roads. The most famous and familiar scenes are also set in Paris, as Hitler pays a surprise visit to the subjugated city: in a mobile shot from a passing vehicle, the newsreel camera sweeps across the facade of the Madeleine and down to street level to reveal an official car pulling to a stop in front, then in a breathless instant Hitler is out and up the stairs to the building, his entourage hurrying to keep pace. The effect is absolutely chilling, and the shot is followed by others scarcely less so—the car passing through the Place de la Concorde and Hitler, with Albert Speer at his side, reviewing the Eiffel Tower from the Palais de Chaillot. The events of 1940 lead up to a segment ridiculing the British military (including a clip from a fiction comedy) and a German U-boat heading across the Channel toward England.

—

INDUSTRIAL BRITAIN

November 1933. Great Britain.
Empire Marketing Board. Released by Gaumont British Picture Corporation. Produced by John Grierson and Robert Flaherty. Photographed by Flaherty, with additional photography by Basil Wright, Arthur Elton, and Grierson. Edited by Edgar Anstey and Grierson. Narrated by Donald Calthrop.
21 min. B&W. Sound.

Robert Flaherty was a major inspiration to John Grierson as Grierson built his government-supported British documentary unit at the Empire Marketing

Board beginning in 1929. And Flaherty brought great prestige to that unit when, two years later, he accepted an assignment that was to include a finished film. The theme for *Industrial Britain*—that the spirit of individual craftsmanship has not been lost in Britain, despite the modern industrial world coal has created—is borne out in Flaherty's images of the faces and occupations of a variety of workmen. Weavers and potters continue their traditional crafts; glassblowers and steel workers find increasing applications for their skills; precision machinists and inspectors take up new tasks that no machine alone can accomplish. (Increased mechanization was frequently cited as a major cause of unemployment during the early Depression years.) Flaherty himself never got beyond photographing these scenes, however. By 1932 the film unit had grown to include Basil Wright, Arthur Elton, Edgar Anstey, Harry Watt, Paul Rotha (briefly), Stuart Legg, John Taylor, and others—all young men who worked as a tight-knit team under Grierson's coaching. Grierson's interests lay in producing a wide range of films for the public benefit and not in supporting individual artists; he relieved Flaherty rather than allow him to exceed the budget for the project. Grierson and others completed and edited the film (it carries the single credit title: "Production: Grierson-Flaherty"). Further, because theatrical presentation was important for the promotion and dissemination of the group's work, the film was licensed for distribution by Gaumont-British, which added the commentator and the music track (Beethoven's *Coriolan* Overture). This mixed production history has caused *Industrial Britain* generally to be deemphasized, yet it is an unusually handsome film, and likely the finest to come from the EMB. Much admired by Basil Wright in particular, it may well have helped motivate the British school toward its great works of human and aesthetic dimension as it moved to the General Post Office: *Song of Ceylon* (1934) and *Night Mail* (1936).

LAND WITHOUT BREAD (LAS HURDES; TERRE SANS PAIN)

1933. Spain.
Directed and edited by Luis Buñuel. Written by Buñuel and Pierre Unik. Photographed by Eli Lotar. English narration.
27 min. B&W. Sound.

One of the facets of Luis Buñuel's genius is to confound expectation; it is no surprise, then, that his one documentary is as startlingly original as his fiction. Financed by a friend's lottery winnings, Buñuel's uncompromising revelation of the desperately poor Las Hurdes region in northwest Spain, near the border with Portugal, anticipated the social documentary movement in Western Europe; but it is so unusual a work that it resists inclusion in any mainstream. Buñuel's Spanish Surrealist tradition, more than its French counterpart, emphasized social and moral as well as aesthetic revolution. Rather than merely report on the plight of an oppressed people, or on the educational and religious systems that maintain that oppression, Buñuel used a controversial method to arouse his audience beyond the unmotivating emotions of pity and dread. The lush majesty of Brahms' Fourth Symphony underscores a voice-over narration that is so condescendingly academic, so impertinently aloof to its subject that we are driven to react with the horror and outrage Buñuel desires—for these responses precipitate action.

90° SOUTH

1933. Great Britain.
Produced, photographed, and narrated by Herbert G. Ponting.
72 min. B&W. Sound.

Before the rise of the Griersonian documentary, Britain was nobly represented by this devoted account of Captain Robert F. Scott's spellbinding and ultimately tragic expedition to the South Pole from 1910 to 1912. Recognizing the

advantage of photography and film, Scott commissioned Herbert Ponting to accompany the expedition and record its scope. Thus, years before Flaherty began to experiment with filmmaking under arctic conditions, Ponting had successfully completed all the historic shooting on this great late-romantic adventure: life aboard the high-masted *Terra Nova* that carried the party to Cape Evans on Ross Island, at the edge of the Great Ice Barrier; the remarkable animal life and fearful beauty of the Antarctic wilderness; preparations for and the start of the climactic assault on the South Pole. Still photos taken by Scott himself after the final team had pressed ahead, maps, and full explanation complete the heroic saga. Scott reached the Pole January 17, 1912, just one month after the Norwegian team led by Roald Amundsen. On their return journey the party of five perished. Ponting dedicated much of his life to preparing various films of the famous expedition (the earliest, **With Captain Scott, R.N., to the South Pole**, was issued in 1912); he completed this final sound version more than twenty years after the death of his esteemed commander, who once had exclaimed, "What fun it will be when we are home again and see this at the cinema!"

NAZI PROPAGANDA FILMS

1933–37. Germany.
All in German; no English subtitles.
Total program: 27 min. B&W. Sound.

BLUTENDES DEUTSCHLAND (BLEEDING GERMANY) (Concluding sequence)

March 30, 1933.
Deutscher Film-Vertrieb (Defi). Directed by Johannes Haüssler.
5 min.

HANS WESTMAR, EINER VON VIELEN. EIN DEUTSCHES SCHICKSAL AUS DEM JAHRE 1929 (HANS WESTMAR, ONE OF THE MULTITUDE. A GERMAN DESTINY OF THE YEAR 1929) (Concluding sequence)

December 13, 1933.
Volksdeutsche Film GmbH. Directed by Franz Wenzler. Screenplay by Hanns Heinz Ewers, from his book *Horst Wessel*.
8 min.

FÜR UNS (FOR US)

1937.
Produced by the National Socialist Party.
14 min.

How the Nazis used the commemoration of "martyrs" as propaganda for their cause is shown in these three penetrating examples from both documentary and fiction films. In 1933 Hitler was consolidating his power as head of the government and needed to build popular support. The excerpt from **Blutendes Deutschland**, released that year, shows footage taken at the funeral of Horst Wessel, who was eulogized after his death in February 1930 as a murdered Brownshirt and supposed author of the Party Anthem, commonly called the "Horst Wessel Song." The event was staged by the Nazis to suggest the largest possible mass following. The film ends with the superimposed slogan, "Hear the Dead Ones' Warning!" The same funeral was reenacted to climax the feature **Hans Westmar**, a fictionalized biography of Wessel made at the end of the year. The hero appears, apotheosized among the clouds, and some apparent actuality footage shows marching columns of the faithful singing their anthem. This film also adds an unruly Communist counterdemonstration at the funeral, but by the end of the sequence even the Communists are converted by the experience they witness: their clenched fists of protest turn to outstretched Nazi salutes. Wessel is also inserted anachronistically into the 1937 documentary short **Für Uns**, made by the Nazis to record a ceremony honoring other loyal dead. In this case, those who sacrificed their lives were participants in the failed Beer-Hall Putsch led by Hitler in Munich on November 9,

90° SOUTH (1933)

1923. (While in jail for his role in that insurrection, Hitler wrote *Mein Kampf*.) Clearly inspired by the architectonic monumentality of *Triumph of the Will* (1935), the film incorporates such persistent Nazi symbols as the eagle and eternal flames. The final title proclaims to these dead, "And yet you have been victorious."

—

EASTER ISLAND (L'ÎLE DE PÂQUES)

1934. Belgium.
Cinéma Edition. Directed and photographed by John Ferno. Produced and edited by Henri Storck. Commentary by Henry Lavachery. Music by Maurice Jaubert. French narration; no English subtitles.
25 min. B&W. Sound.

John Ferno (born Fernhout) was a young Dutch prodigy and protégé of Joris Ivens, with whom he photographed from the time he was fourteen (notably, on *Philips-Radio* [1931], *New Earth* [1934], and, later, *The Spanish Earth* [1937]). Ivens provided liaison with Belgium's great documentarist, Henri Storck, who produced and edited Ferno's own *Easter Island*, shot during a Franco-Belgian expedition while Ferno was still a teenager. His remarkable portrait of this entrancing island, well off the coast of South America in the South Pacific, is representative of the romantic humanist tradition of Flaherty, but Ferno and Storck add a political fillip for their decade: witnessing a lost civilization, the island's giant stone heads stand as monuments (like Ozymandias's statue in Shelley's sonnet) to great peoples who destroyed each other in past wars; now the inhabitants live under colonial domination, in dire poverty, plagued by leprosy. Another real attraction of the film is its score by the gifted Maurice Jaubert. Ferno's later work includes *And So They Live* (1940).

GRANTON TRAWLER

1934. Great Britain.
Empire Marketing Board. Produced and photographed by John Grierson. Edited by Edgar Anstey. Sound by Alberto Cavalcanti.
11 min. B&W. Sound.

Edgar Anstey joined John Grierson at the Empire Marketing Board Film Unit in 1930. Together there they made *Granton Trawler*, about dragnet fishing off the east coast of Scotland. Grierson had earlier done a much longer, silent film about fishing, *Drifters* (1929), and *Granton Trawler* is a very conscious re-finement, with sound. The problems posed by the sound film were a real challenge for low-budget filmmaking, and Grierson used *Granton Trawler* as a textbook example for his school of documentary, to demonstrate perfect juxtaposition between visual and aural components. The film had been photographed silent by Grierson, its compositions set against a backdrop of sky and sea, and skillfully edited by Anstey. The soundtrack was added by Alberto Cavalcanti after the film unit moved to the General Post Office. It abjures narration in favor of the natural sounds of waves, wind, and men (reputedly talking about soccer). Following his work with Grierson, Anstey made two landmark social documentaries for the British gas industry, *Housing Problems* (1935) and *Enough to Eat?* (1936).

NEW EARTH (NIEUWE GRONDEN)

1934. Netherlands.
Capi-Amsterdam. Written and directed by Joris Ivens. Photographed by Ivens, John Ferno, Joop Huisken, Helen van Dongen, Eli Lotar. Edited by Ivens and van Dongen. Sound effects by van Dongen. Music by Hanns Eisler. Dutch narration and titles; no English subtitles. (The English release version of the film was considerably censored.)
30 min. B&W. Sound.

During the early thirties, including the time he spent on *Phillips-Radio* (1931), Ivens felt an increasing need to present social truth in his work. *New Earth* identifies the cutting edge in his career as he faced the social crises of the decade. Off and on since 1929 he had been filming the Netherlands' massive land reclamation project in the Zuider Zee, where the sea was dammed off and land drained for homes and crops. This heroic national effort was completed in 1933, and Ivens had soon edited his footage into an exciting battle of men and machines against the traditional Dutch archenemy, the sea. In *New Earth*, the visual drama is heightened by Hanns Eisler's brassy and percussive music score, incorporated with the droning of gasoline motors and the onslaught of the waves. The waters conquered and pumped away, telephone and electric lines link new houses, and wheat fields are sown on the new fields of earth. But the beauty and optimism we anticipate were not in fact the immediate outcome of these progressive labors, for the worldwide economic disaster struck hardest just as the harvest was being reaped. The beauties of the initial section of the film are abruptly reversed by the bitter politics of the second, for which Ivens used stock newsreel footage, newspaper headlines, and a voice track to report the calamity of the unemployed and hungry. To support falling wheat prices on international commodity markets, the world's financiers dictate that grain be destroyed. In Holland, ironically, it was thrown back into the sea. Ivens concludes with a Brechtian ballad, its final verses reading, "One bagful [of wheat] brings too small a price./Throw half the harvest into the water;/Throw it in my boy./What a winter it will be." After *New Earth* Ivens elected to sacrifice formal quality when necessary for the sake of direct political statement. His rededication soon was rewarded by a masterpiece, *The Spanish Earth* (1937).

SONG OF CEYLON

1934. Great Britain.
Empire Marketing Board (later GPO) Film Unit for Ceylon Tea Propaganda Board. Directed, photographed, and edited by Basil Wright. Assistant: John Taylor. Produced by John Grierson. Commentary, taken from a 1680 travel account by Robert Knox, spoken by Lionel Wendt. Music by Walter Leigh.
39 min. B&W. Sound.

With the dissolution of Britain's Empire Marketing Board as a government agency, the Grierson film unit transferred to the sponsorship of the General Post Office in 1934. Almost immediately it produced its early masterpiece, *Song of Ceylon*, begun under the auspices of the EMB for the Ceylon Tea Propaganda Board. The film at once honors Flaherty's *Moana* (1926), yet finds a style of its own. Very much the personal work of Basil Wright, the sunny rhythms of its photography made him famous as a lyricist. Adopting a four-part structure ("The Buddha," "The Virgin Island," "The Voices of Commerce," "The Apparel of a God"), Wright respects the almost timeless beauty of the island (now Sri Lanka) and its native culture, conveying the tranquility of its Buddhist heritage, the people's self-reliance, and the continuity of their traditions in the face of British imperial interests. As with *Granton Trawler* (1934), the film's soundtrack crystallizes its genius. With the move to the GPO, Grierson's group acquired its first sound equipment (for earlier soundtracks, works such as *Industrial Britain* [1933] had to be entrusted to an outside distributor). Not coincidentally, Grierson brought in the ingenious Alberto Cavalcanti to advise on the use of sound. In a brilliant stroke, Wright used a seventeenth-century travel book on Ceylon

Basil Wright filming SONG OF CEYLON (1934) (p. 117)

for most of the narration; the book's old-fashioned language reinforces the theme that old customs still remain on the island. Walter Leigh's fine score adds further to this evocation of the East. In "The Voices of Commerce" section, Cavalcanti's assistance is felt in the abstracted, contrapuntal sounds of radio and telegraph which punctuate the general quietude. (Len Lye would repeat the effect in *Trade Tattoo* [1937].) This section most of all leaves the impression that commercial exploitation can hardly fail to disrupt Singhalese life; surely not the intention of the sponsoring agency. At the same time (and this is one of the artful complexities of the work), the film reassures with the changeless serenity of its images.

THE WEDDING OF PALO (PALOS BRUDEFAÈRD)

March 5, 1934. Denmark.
Palladium Films. Director of expedition and screenplay: Knud Rasmussen. Directed by Friedrich Dalsheim. Photographed by Hans Scheib and Walter Traut. Music by Emil Reesen. Some Inuit dialect, English intertitles.
72 min. B&W. Sound.

Though the worldwide Depression brought the social documentary to the fore, the romantic tradition was never wholly eclipsed. The work of Dr. Knud Rasmussen, the prominent Danish explorer and anthropologist, *The Wedding of Palo* is an affectionate account of Eskimo life, played out by natives of the Angmagssalik district of eastern Greenland. As a prelude, the filmmak-

ers are shown arriving in Greenland during their expedition of 1931–33; thereafter, the film follows its own narrative sequence, without reference to external observation (compare *Dance Contest in Esira* [1936]). The film is an obvious successor to *Nanook of the North* (1922) and embraces Flaherty's model, yet it provides even more spectacular, polished views of the arctic regions—sometimes even rivalling *90° South* (1933). As sympathetic to its subjects as Flaherty's film, it also invents a plot-line for them. In spite of the title (actually "Palo's Courtship" in Danish), there is no wedding ceremony; instead we follow the rivalry between Palo and Samo for Navarana, and her growing affection for Palo in the face of her brothers' opposition to giving up their only cook and housekeeper. In addition to this rather winning tale, the film raises a number of interesting cross-cultural issues in its portrayal of the life of these people.

HOUSING PROBLEMS

1935. Great Britain.
A.R.F.P. for the British Commercial Gas Association. Directed by Arthur Elton and Edgar Anstey, assisted by Ruby I. Grierson. Photographed by John Taylor.
17 min. B&W. Sound.

From the mid-1930s, the British documentary movement was expanding into different units, with a number of commercial sponsors in addition to the government. With this variety came new styles and emphases. *Housing Problems*, made by Arthur Elton and Edgar An-

stey, both of whom had trained with Grierson, introduced a new documentary of social urgency emphasizing direct, interpretive reporting rather than Grierson's earlier, more artful and less editorial approach. Produced to explain and engender broad popular acceptance for urban renewal projects, whereby decaying and overcrowded slums were replaced by well-designed, publicly financed housing units, the film offers its information quite directly, crediting its audience with seriousness, and thus making no provisions to entertain in order to arouse concern. Its makers introduce a novel device—direct, on-camera talks by slum dwellers themselves, who address their troubles with candor and some humor, and similar reports from relocated residents who speak happily of their new quarters and how it will now be possible to clean and maintain them. The British Commercial Gas Association was evidently persuaded to fund the film by the argument that modern housing would bring increased consumption of gas. The influence of *Housing Problems* on the Griersonian school was immediately felt: see *Enough to Eat?* (1936), *Children at School*, *The Smoke Menace*, and *To-Day We Live* (all 1937).

PIE IN THE SKY (1935). *See* Experimental Film

TRIUMPH OF THE WILL (TRIUMPH DES WILLENS)

March 28, 1935. Germany.
Produced by Leni Riefenstahl for the National Socialist Party; distributed by Ufa. Directed and edited by Leni Riefenstahl. Opening titles by Walter Ruttmann. Photographed by Sepp Allgeier and a reported 47 others. Music by Herbert Windt. Architecture: Albert Speer. In German; no English subtitles.
120 min. B&W. Sound.

Leni Riefenstahl's notoriously great propaganda epic has, from its inception, been the stuff of legend. In the heart of Bavaria, Nuremberg had served as the site for Nazi Party Rallies since 1923. The official Sixth Congress, September 4–10, 1934, fell a month after President Hindenburg's death and the August 19 plebiscite confirming Hitler as Führer. Recognizing the persuasive power of motion pictures, Hitler commissioned *Triumph of the Will* from Riefenstahl, the fetching 31–year-old actress (see *The White Hell of Pitz Palu* [1929]) and sometime director who had also filmed the prior year's event at his invitation. The film's intention was to demonstrate the strength of the party, point out its leaders, and identify Hitler's own command over German destiny—for both domestic and foreign audiences. (Hitler's choice of title for the work corresponds to the domination of will over intellect in Nazi ideology.) No costs or production details were spared; by Riefenstahl's own account, published in 1935 as *Behind the Scenes of the Reich Party Day Films*, she was provided with thirty cameras, four sets of sound equipment, twenty-two chauffeured automobiles, SA and SS bodyguards, and field police. The authorization of the Führer secured her command over her male crew of 120. Extensive camera positions included lifts, towers, tracks laid along and above the ground, and cranes improvised atop extension ladders on fire engines and service trucks. The population of the city swelled to over one million, and the rally was coordinated to facilitate the filmmaking. Riefenstahl collected about sixty hours of footage and reedited the events to achieve her two-hour structure. The famous opening depicts Hitler descending from the clouds like an airborne demigod to be spirited by motorcade to the tumultuous hosannas of his faithful. Parades honor him day and night; geometric hoards decorate vast architectural vistas; policy speeches exhort every gathering. Herbert Windt's music builds upon themes from the "Horst Wessel Song" and *Die Meistersinger von Nürnberg*. Even in the off hours when these boyish legions are at play, the film never ceases to be a chilling portrait of fascism. Thus, though banned in English-speaking countries (a subtitled version exists only in abridgement), the film proved just as effective for anti-Nazi propaganda (see particularly **Prelude to War** [1942] and **The Nazis Strike** [1942] in the **Why We Fight** series).

TRIUMPH OF THE WILL (TRIUMPH DES WILLENS) (Abridged version)

1935. Germany.
(For credits, see entry for full-length version.) In German with English subtitles.
42 min. B&W. Sound.

This condensed version of **Triumph of the Will**, on the Nazi Party Rally in Nuremberg, Germany, in 1934, was prepared in association with The Museum of Modern Art Film Library to contribute to the U.S. World War II effort as an important example of Nazi propaganda. Speculation that Luis Buñuel worked on the editing while employed at the Museum in the early forties has never been confirmed. The film follows the structure of the original version,

opening with the complete sequence showing Hitler's arrival by air and his enthusiastic reception in the streets of Nuremberg. There are numerous parades by the uniformed party members throughout the city, scenes of the Hitler Youth in the great arena, and a torchlight parade. The speeches by the Nazi leaders included here all have English subtitles (an important feature, as the full-length version has never been titled in English; the original German introductory titles have simply been translated and placed in subtitles over the opening shots of Hitler's plane amid the clouds). The principal sections that have been omitted are the behind-the-scenes activities of the men in their encampment and several lengthy orations and formal assemblies.

THE CAMERA GOES ALONG! (DIE KAMERA FÄHRT MIT . . .!) and FLIEGER, FUNKER, KANONIERE! (PILOTS, RADIO OPERATORS, GUNNERS!) (excerpt)

1936–37. Germany.
Both in German; no English subtitles.
Total program: 23 min. B&W. Sound.

THE CAMERA GOES ALONG! (DIE KAMERA FÄHRT MIT . . .!)

1936.
Tobis-Kulturefilm. Written and edited by Hans Schipulle. Photographed by Walter Brandes, Bernhard Juppe, Hans Kluth.
12 min.

FLIEGER, FUNKER, KANONIERE! (PILOTS, RADIO OPERATORS, GUNNERS!) (excerpt)

1937.
Ufa. With Hermann Göring.
11 min.

Goebbels's Ministry of Propaganda oversaw all film production in the Third Reich, fictional or documentary, including the introduction of a new and unusually effective newsreel, **Die Deutsche Wochenschau** ("The German Newsreel"). Like its U.S. contemporary, **The March of Time** (see **Arms and the League** [1938]), the **Wochenschau** was longer and more compellingly structured than previous newsreels. *The Camera Goes Along!* is an instructional short subject designed to acquaint German audiences with the newsreel and to explain its production methods, from on-location shooting through the final editing process. Most notable are its views of Nuremberg Party Rallies, the 1936 Winter Olympics, aerial daredeviltry, fires, and miscellaneous news events. (A stunning roundup of **Deutsche Wochenschau** subjects from 1940 is included in **German Newsreels** [1933–40].) More clearly geared toward propagandizing among domestic cinema patrons, *Flieger, Funker, Kanoniere!* is personally hosted by Field-Marshall Göring, who proudly presents the German Luftwaffe, and assures viewers that no German need fear any threat of air attack, their Führer and the Party having created a new and insuperable air force (in defiance of the Treaty of Versailles). The film is peppered with

TRIUMPH OF THE WILL (1935)

exciting aerial photography and features a military exercise pitting antiaircraft ground troops against the Luftwaffe. Göring does not explain why such emphasis is placed upon the attacking capacity of his air force when its stated purpose is "as a defense for peace and a protection of our Fatherland." (The actual role of these planes is more accurately glimpsed in **Campaign in Poland** [*Feldzug in Polen*] [1940] and **The Battle of Britain** [1943].)

DANCE CONTEST IN ESIRA (DANSTAVLINGEN I ESIRA)

1936. Denmark.
Nordisk. Directed by Paul Fejos. Photographed by Rudolf Frederiksen. English narration.
11 min. B&W. Sound.

The mercurial Paul Fejos despaired of feature filmmaking after contributing to it in Hollywood, France, Austria, Denmark, and his native Hungary. Thereupon he undertook a long career in anthropology that began with several short ethnographic subjects, among them **The Bilo** and **Dance Contest in Esira** (both 1936). These were made for Nordisk, the leading Danish production company, during an expedition to Madagascar. (Never released publicly in Denmark, the series were given Swedish titles.) **Dance Contest in Esira** maps the course of the journey there in such a way as to congratulate the expedition for its tenacity. The dance contest of the title, we are told, is an event held every five years among several tribes in the village of Esira in the southern wilderness of the island. Beyond its superficial explanation of the meaning of the dances, the narration—at least in this English version—often belittles the natives in its striving for jaunty entertainment, as has been typical of anthropological films that aim at a broad commercial market. With similar motive, however, **The Wedding of Palo** (1934) succeeded with a sympathetic approach. Technically, the film exhibits another fashion—a fancy assortment of wipes between shots—that was all the rage in the mid-1930s.

ENOUGH TO EAT? THE NUTRITION FILM

1936. Great Britain.
A.R.F.P. for the Gas Light and Coke Company. Directed by Edgar Anstey. Assistant: Frank Sainsbury. Photographed by Walter Blakeley, Arthur Fisher. Commentary presented by Julian Huxley.
22 min. B&W. Sound.

The work of the General Post Office filmmakers brought offers from sponsors outside of the British government which the GPO unit, being government-supported, could not accept. So, late in 1935, the main group of Griersonians set up Associated Realist Film Producers. (The organization quickly evolved into Film Centre.) A.R.F.P. could facilitate production opportunities for the filmmakers beyond the limitatons of the Post Office. For example, with the favorable reception of **Housing Problems** (1935), the British gas industry had become interested in funding public service documentaries. **Enough to Eat?** is the second important result of that series. It addresses the serious problem of malnutrition in Britain in the characteristic form of a filmed lecture. It might be said to have contributed to the format of the present-day television news special. Julian Huxley, the renowned biologist and author (and elder brother of Aldous Huxley), greets us and appears throughout as correspondent. Direct testimonies are given by experts and by mothers trying to feed their families properly; charts and animated diagrams illustrate particular points for emphasis or clarification. The film deliberately avoids any harrowing pictures of the worst cases of malnutrition, presenting instead the less obvious but more widespread problems. Recent nutrition studies showed that because of insufficient or misguided diet, as many as half the population of Britain were undernourished. Furthermore, with precise figures, **Enough to Eat?** draws a direct correlation between personal income and proper feeding, suggesting that a complete solution must answer the need for an adequate income level for the entire population. The reins of government or commercial sponsorship always limited the political expression of the British documentary movement, yet, of all the works it produced, **Enough to Eat?** makes the most radical implication about the need to transform society. (The issues it presents continue to grow ever more grave in today's world.) The fame of the film landed Anstey a job with **The March of Time** in London and New York until the eve of World War II. The thrust of the film's message was taken up by the daily press, which lobbied for legislation from Parliament.

NIGHT MAIL

1936. Great Britain.
GPO Film Unit. Directed by Harry Watt, assisted by Basil Wright and W. H. Auden. Production, script, and dialogue by Basil Wright. Photographed by Henry E. (Chick) Fowle, Pat Jackson, Jonah Jones. Sound direction: Alberto Cavalcanti. Verse by W. H. Auden, spoken by Stuart Legg and John Grierson. Music by Benjamin Britten.
23 min. B&W. Sound.

Working for the General Post Office largely restricted the Grierson unit to topics concerning communications, but to Grierson this was a major theme of the modern era. Certainly **Night Mail** vindicated his enthusiasm by setting alive the nightly run of the marvelous mail train, the Postal Special, from London to Glasgow, Edinburgh, and Aberdeen. Few subjects have proved more splendidly suited to cinematic ingenuity. The intricate scheduling of operations along the route, the working together of professionals and machines (epitomized by the train's ability to snatch up or drop off mail pouches at full speed), contribute to the fascination and excitement we share with the men involved. As a result, the persistent theme of the film unit—the working man's pride in his skills—was never more persuasive or vibrant. Much credit goes to Harry Watt, the most accomplished director of the lot, and to Basil Wright, who conceived it, oversaw production, and wrote the script and dialogue. Yet, more than any other film, **Night Mail** also displays the zest in collaboration that the unit was able to attain. Like most of Grierson's principal recruits, Watt and Wright were no older than their mid-twenties when they started work in documentary, and except for short educational subjects or a unique achievement like **90° South** (1933), there were no precedents in Britain. These young men shaped a form for documentary within the broadest scope of Grierson's definition, "the creative treatment of actuality." Each new work was a new experiment, a fresh adventure. For the problems of adding sound, new inspiration came in the mid-1930s from Cavalcanti and, for a time, even from W. H. Auden and Benjamin Britten (to say nothing of the brilliant avant-garde work of Len Lye). The wonders of **Night Mail** are attributable to no fewer than a handful of spirited artists, all engaged in an experimental enterprise, incorporating live dialogue and using sound as inventively as images. While much of the thrust of British documentary in the later 1930s would shift outside government sponsorship and toward more immediate social purpose (led by **Housing Problems** [1935] and **Enough to Eat?** [1936]), the film suggested anew the potential of documentary for rousing entertainment. And, as Cavalcanti succeeded Grierson as head of the GPO unit the following year, it would continue to experiment (see *North Sea* [1938] or *Spare Time* [1939]). But there was never again as extraordinary a work as *Night Mail*.

THE PLOW THAT BROKE THE PLAINS

May 28, 1936. U.S.A.
Resettlement Administration. Written and directed by Pare Lorentz. Photographed by Paul Strand, Ralph Steiner, and Leo Hurwitz. Music by Virgil Thomson. Narrated by Thomas Chalmers.
28 min. B&W. Sound.

When Pare Lorentz came to the attention of Rexford Guy Tugwell in the Roosevelt administration, he had a lifetime interest in film and politics and had written on both, but he had never made a film. Nevertheless, for under $20,000 from the government and his own pocket, Lorentz made *The Plow That Broke the Plains*, and it transformed U.S. government film production. Lorentz enlisted three exceptional photographers in Strand, Steiner, and Hurwitz (Strand had just finished *The Wave* [1936]), who contributed images to rival the Farm Security Administration (FSA) photographs of Walker Evans, Dorothea Lange, and others. They also brought a social militancy to the work, which, in the end, Lorentz softened. In his productive collaboration with composer Virgil Thomson, he developed an original film ballad, combining narrative verse with an independent, contrapuntal score. *The Plow*'s subject, the tragedy of the Dust Bowl—productive land lost through ruinous management for short-term gain—is reviewed while subtly and poetically advertising the conservation policies of the New Deal's farm program. Despite political, legal, and economic opposition (Hollywood was antagonistic to providing major studio distribution), the widespread popular appeal of the film netted it commercial engagements in thousands of movie theaters across the country. This success opened the way for Lorentz to head an important, though short-lived, government film unit. His subsequent productions included his own *The River* (1937), Ivens's *Power and the Land* (1940), and Flaherty's *The Land* (1942).

THE WAVE (REDES; literally, "Nets")

1936. Mexico.
Secretariat of Education. Produced, supervised, and photographed by Paul Strand. Directed by Fred Zinnemann

THE WAVE (1936)

with Emilio Gomez Muriel. Scenario by Strand, Velasquez Chavez, Henwar Rodakiewicz.
60 min. B&W. Sound.

The great photographer Paul Strand had bought his own movie camera and worked periodically with film during the 1920s (beginning with *Manhatta* [1921]), but in the politicized Depression era he took a predominant interest in the medium and joined in founding Frontier Films (see *Heart of Spain* [1937]). In the early 1930s, he also acquired a fascination for Mexico, photographing there in the summers, admiring its progressive social reforms, and becoming friends with the composer Carlos Chavez. Through Chavez's influence, Strand was invited by the Mexican government to make a series of films reflecting the concerns of most Mexicans, and particularly the country's eighteen million Indians. Strand accepted, producing and photographing *The Wave* from a draft by Chavez's nephew. Because of a change in governments in 1934, more films in the planned series were never realized, but the film played an enormous role in subsequent Mexican filmmaking, as well as in U.S. documentary. A dramatized documentary set in the fishing village of Alvarado on the Gulf of Veracruz, *The Wave* recounts a fishermen's strike against an exploitative merchant. Strand left the direction of the nonprofessional cast to a recent Viennese immigrant, Fred Zinnemann, who became a strong Hollywood director in the 1940s. (His best known films remain *High Noon* [1952] and *A Man For All Seasons* [1966].) *The Wave*'s finest component is Strand's exceptional photography, matched but not surpassed even by *The*

Plow That Broke the Plains (1936), and comparable to Eisenstein's *Que Viva Mexico!* in the heroic strength of its compositions (see *Thunder Over Mexico* [1933], *Time in the Sun* [1939], and *Eisenstein's Mexican Film: Episodes for Study* [1955]).

THE CATCH OF THE SEASON

1937. Great Britain.
Gaumont-British Instructional. Directed by Mary Field. Photographed by Percy Smith.
10 min. B&W. Sound.

Short educational documentaries, like their feature counterparts, have frequently aimed at entertaining as much as instructing. This successful example from British Gaumont's **Secrets of Life** series is quite comparable to the later Walt Disney subjects of the same name. Employing exacting close-up live-action photography, it brings to human perspective the world of the brook trout—egg laying, fertilization, embryonic development, hatching, and early life—and then humanizes the fish with good-natured British humor by pitting the aquatic protagonist in a contest of wits with a dedicated dry-fly fisherman! Mary Field and Percy Smith were pioneers in instructional filmmaking, winning plaudits for their **Secrets of Nature** series produced by British Instructional Films in the 1920s—well before the advent of John Grierson.

CHILDREN AT SCHOOL

1937. Great Britain.
Realist Film Unit for British Commercial Gas Association. Directed by Basil Wright. Assistant: Patrick Moyna. Pro-

duced by John Grierson (Film Centre). Photographed by A. E. Jeakins and Erik Wilbur. Commentary by H. Wilson Harris, editor of *The Spectator*.
24 min. B&W. Sound.

In the diversification of the General Post Office Film Unit into a multiplicity of groups, Basil Wright formed the Realist Film Unit in 1937. By then more non-fiction films were being made outside the British government than within; and Grierson himself left the GPO in June to set up Film Centre, an independent research and advisory organization that undertook no production itself, but permitted him continued oversight of the documentary movement. *Children at School* was made by Wright's unit with Grierson acting as producer from his new post. The film's financing came from the British gas industry, and this is evident in its production, for it shares the unembellished reportorial quality of its predecessors, *Housing Problems* (1935) and *Enough to Eat?* (1936). Artistically, the film displays warmth and ebullience, but the fact that Wright, the great lyricist of *Song of Ceylon* (1934) and *Night Mail* (1936), would move toward asceticism to such a degree is a mark of the extent to which the Depression and attendant social concerns had militated for a direct, insistent style of editorial journalism. (Not that the "classics" were suddenly without value: a classroom here is shown watching *Night Mail*.) The film assesses the current state of British public education (called "private" there and initiated in 1870): its basic organization and methods and its strengths and serious obstacles, chiefly poor facilities and overcrowding. To urge swift action toward meeting Britain's educational needs, the film contrasts the systematic indoctrination of many young people under fascist governments and asks whether the democracies can afford not to keep pace. (Under the same sponsorship, the Realist Film Unit also made *The Smoke Menace* [1937]).

HEART OF SPAIN

1937. U.S.A.
Frontier Films. Documented in Spain by Herbert Kline and Geza Karpathi. Material scenarized and edited by Paul Strand and Leo Hurwitz. Commentary written by David Wolff [Ben Maddow] and Herbert Kline; narrated by John O'Shaughnessy. Principle photography: Geza Karpathi. Music arranged by Alex North with the assistance of Jay Leyda; sound effects by Irving Lerner. Produced with the cooperation of the Canadian Committee to Aid Spain and the American Medical Bureau to Aid Spanish Democracy.
30 min. B&W. Sound.

Early in 1937, several independent left-wing filmmakers, many from the New York Film and Photo League and from Nykino, formed Frontier Films. The group's name suggests its ideals: to pioneer a new kind of film in America, more artful than its political predecessors but just as firmly committed to social justice and an egalitarian society; to set its goals within the practical, "popular front" framework of mainstream American progressivism; and thereby to seek a wider audience. As it happened, Frontier's first completed production focused on a ringing political struggle overseas, the Spanish Civil War, which became a touchstone of its era for progressive opposition to the rising threat of fascism (see also Joris Ivens's *The Spanish Earth* [1937]). *Heart of Spain* was begun, not as a Frontier project, but by three international volunteers for the Loyalist cause in Spain. Geza Karpathi, a Hungarian still photographer, and Herbert Kline, an American leftist journalist, were urged to make the film by the Canadian physician Norman Bethune, who hoped to use it to raise funds for the blood transfusion service he was operating. Lacking previous filmmaking experience, Karpathi and Kline later entrusted their script and footage to the Frontier group back in the U.S., where Paul Strand, Leo Hurwitz, Ben Maddow, and others completed the work. (Hereafter Kline turned professionally to filmmaking, later directing *The Forgotten Village* [1941].) *Heart of Spain* is compelling both for its shrewd formal aesthetics and as a sympathetic human document of the war. In a long introductory sequence, its clipped, imaginatively editorial narrative charges the intervention of Germany and Italy for the destruction we witness in a fortified Madrid and the battle-scarred countryside. The final section presents Dr. Bethune and his American colleague, Dr. Edward Barsky. Their heroic blood donation operation serves as a symbol of resilient civilian support for the Loyalist army—most memorably in the meeting of a Spanish woman donor and the wounded young fighter who has received her blood. *Heart of Spain* was a major initial success for Frontier Films. Important works ahead for the group included *People of the Cumberland* (1938) and *Native Land* (1942). (See also the National Film Board of Canada production *Bethune* [1964].)

THE RIVER

October 29, 1937. U.S.A.

U.S. Farm Security Administration. Written and directed by Pare Lorentz. Photographed by Willard Van Dyke, Floyd Crosby, and Horace and Stacey Woodard. Music by Virgil Thomson. Narrated by Thomas Chalmers.
30 min. B&W. Sound.

With the commercial and critical success of *The Plow That Broke the Plains* (1936), Pare Lorentz's ensuing project received generous production funds from the Roosevelt Administration and eventual major studio distribution (from Paramount, which had warmed up to Flaherty a decade earlier and backed *Moana* [1926]). Even more importantly, the strengths and experience of the first film enabled Lorentz to perfect his model. *The River* chronicles the crisis in the Mississippi River Basin—the rapacious lumbering and careless tilling that promoted soil erosion, washing away fertile topsoil and flooding the alluvial plain downstream. The subject embraced many issues central to the New Deal, and particularly to its bold and controversial Tennessee Valley Authority: soil and water conservation, erosion and flood control, hydroelectric power, and rural electrification. A disastrous flood in January 1937 supplied the calamity that cemented the film's argument. As in *The Plow*, Lorentz chose cameramen of merit (Van Dyke had apprenticed with Edward Weston, Crosby shot *Tabu* [1931] for Flaherty and Murnau). *The River*'s photography, less grandstanding than *The Plow*'s, is stronger for its narrative flow. Once again, Lorentz composed a narrative in ballad form, shaping free verse with cadenced repetitions that are heightened by Thomas Chalmers's sturdy baritone and enhanced by Virgil Thomson's majestic score. Of excessive lumbering in the north woods: "Black spruce and Norway pine; Douglas fir and red cedar; scarlet oak and shagbark hickory—we built a hundred cities and a thousand towns, but at what a cost!" Rather than point an accusing finger, the film acknowledges America's proud if reckless frontier drives. Because it accepts the course of economic history as inevitable, its disclosure of history's lessons becomes all the more emphatic. *The River* swells with a vigor and confidence that define a native American documentary style. As an individual work of art, it is the equal of Flaherty's finest or the best of the British school. As the crowning achievement of American documentary in the 1930s, its voice is heard throughout much of the work of Lorentz's generation, from Frontier Films to **The March of Time**. Regrettably, Lorentz's own brilliant future was cut short by Congress's elimination of funding for the U.S. Film Service, which Roosevelt instituted in response to *The River*. With Lorentz at its helm, this government-backed production unit might have challenged its British counterparts.

THE SMOKE MENACE

1937. Great Britain.
Realist Film Unit for the British Commercial Gas Association. Directed by John Taylor. Produced by John Grierson and Basil Wright. Photographed by A. E. Jeakins. Commentary by J. B. S. Haldane.
14 min. B&W. Sound.

Like *Children at School* (1937), *The Smoke Menace* was made by Basil Wright's Realist Film Unit for the British Commercial Gas Association. Wright and Grierson (at Film Centre) both served as producers, with John Taylor receiving his first credit as director. Taylor had been a disciple of Grierson since he left school at 15 to work at the Empire Marketing Board in 1930. (His older sister, Margaret, married Grierson the same year.) Taylor's education with the British school, primarily as a cameraman, was supplemented by a photographic assignment on Flaherty's *Man of Aran* (1934); but his most recent work on the gas industry series (see *Housing Problems* [1935]) was the immediate influence on the style of this film. A forward-looking essay on the dangers of air pollution from the burning of raw coal, *The Smoke Menace* holds considerable topical interest today. Broaching the issue of coal soot was a serious and difficult subject, since coal and the energy it provided were bedrocks of the British economy. The film recognizes this fact and actually speaks of some industries served by pollution before weighing its graver costs against property and public health (including the deprivation of Vitamin D). Besides its undeniable contribution to public awareness, the film enabled its sponsor to advertise its own cleaner, safer alternative of treating raw coal to produce gas and other useful by-products.

THE SPANISH EARTH

July 19, 1937. U.S.A.
Contemporary Historians, Inc. Scenario and direction by Joris Ivens. Commentary written and spoken by Ernest Hemingway. Photographed by Ivens and John Ferno. Music compiled by Marc Blitzstein, arranged by Virgil Thomson. Edited by Helen van Dongen.
53 min. B&W. Sound.

THE SPANISH EARTH (1937)

Joris Ivens made this classic anti-fascist documentary on the Spanish Civil War (1936–39) to enlist support in the West, and especially in the United States, for the Spanish Loyalist cause against Franco. Ivens's growing reputation had brought him an invitation to visit the U.S. just at the outset of the war. While there, he received financial support for *The Spanish Earth* from a number of American progressives (among them Lillian Hellman, Archibald MacLeish, Dorothy Parker, Herman Schumlin) under the banner of "Contemporary Historians." The film was shot in and around Madrid and in the village of Fuenteduena, forty miles southwest of the city. It develops two parallel themes: the building of an irrigation project by farmers in order to grow food for the troops and civilians, and the defense of the Spanish democracy by the people's civilian army. There are vivid battle scenes on the outskirts of Madrid and the shelling and bombing of civilians by the rebels. We see the wreckage of a downed German Junkers bomber. The Loyalist troops are shown successfully holding back their attackers, but their largely obsolete armaments and lack of heavy artillery indicate weaknesses that foretell their ultimate defeat. A sequence showing the Spanish leadership includes the woman leader "La Pasionara." Although the young Orson Welles receives screen credit as narrator, Hem-

ingway disliked the tone of Welles's voice and rerecorded the commentary himself.

TO-DAY WE LIVE. A FILM OF LIFE IN BRITAIN

1937. Great Britain.
Strand Film Company for the National Council of Social Services. Produced by Paul Rotha. Directed by Ralph Bond and Ruby I. Grierson. Scenario by Stuart Legg. Photographed by S. Onions, Paul Burnford.
24 min. B&W. Sound.

Well remembered as a major film historian, Paul Rotha worked briefly for John Grierson at the Empire Marketing Board in 1931 and later set up his own independent productions. In 1936 he joined the Strand Film Company, the first established to make documentaries for hire, and also published his important critical history, *Documentary Film*, in which he emphasized the importance of social commitment. In the book he praised Grierson's sister Ruby, who had directed the interviews in *Housing Problems* (1935), and Rotha recruited her to direct part of *To-Day We Live*. First explaining the socio-economic background to industrial unemployment during the Depression, the film then shifts to its immediate subject—two public works projects organized by the National Council of Social Services. Unemployed miners in the Rhondda Valley of southern Wales were directed by Ralph Bond, villagers in the Cotswolds in the west of England by Ruby Grierson. Both groups were encouraged to raise funds and construct community centers, and they portray their activities for the camera. The work does not restore lost jobs, but it does combat the demoralization caused by unemployment and helps repair the spirit of community. In some respects *To-Day We Live* effects a stylistic synthesis: it addresses real social concerns and deals directly with working-class citizens, as had *Housing Problems*, yet it does this with an experimental aesthetic like the General Post Office films. Its experiment, a successful one, was to have the workers and townspeople reenact the events they experienced and thus develop a storyline much as in a fictional film. Ruby Grierson carried this technique even further in *They Also Serve* (1940).

ARMS AND THE LEAGUE (from **THE MARCH OF TIME**, Vol. IV, No. 8; reissued as *The League of Nations*.)

March 18, 1938. U.S.A.
Time Inc. Produced by Louis de Rochement. Narrated by Westbrook Van Voorhis. With Anthony Eden, Neville Chamberlain, Ramsay MacDonald, Gustav Stresemann, Aristide Briand, Haile Selassie.
8 min. B&W. Sound.

In February 1935, Time Inc. introduced a new form for the newsreel—in its words, "a new kind of pictorial journalism": **The March of Time**. Running through August 1951, the series caught notice for its fresh approach and captivating style. Appearing about once a month instead of twice weekly like other newsreels (see **The Pathé Newsreel** [1917–31] and Fox Movietone subjects *Lindbergh's Flight From N.Y. to Paris* [1927] and *Assassination of Alexander and Barthou* [1934]), **The March of Time** was able to devote far greater care and financing to each issue. Each issue also usually ran twice as long as its contemporaries and concentrated on a limited number of topics (allotting the entire issue to a single subject as early as January 1938). Where other newsreels sought to be noncommittal, avoiding or soft-peddling most hard news for fear of stirring controversy, **The March of Time** frequently broached sensitive subjects and in fact exploited public attention by taking opinionated editorial stances. The producer of the series, Louis de Rochement, a former newsreel photographer, developed a keen gift

for editing and dramatic construction. This gave each issue a stamp of recognition. By the late 1930s, the newsreel's audience surpassed twenty million, about the same number of viewers as the most popular television series have today. *Arms and the League* was the first of two subjects contained in the issue of March 1938. The previous February 20, British Foreign Secretary Anthony Eden had resigned his post in opposition to Prime Minister Neville Chamberlain's appeasement policy toward the Axis powers. Eden had attacked their aggression on the floor of the League of Nations. A segment of the May 1936 **March of Time** (partly shot by Edgar Anstey) criticizing the League's impotence had been censored in Britain; now with the virtual collapse of the organization, the series is unflinching in its support as it recounts the League's history: Woodrow Wilson's first proposal; its propitious beginnings as forty-three nations pledged to disarmament and non-aggression; the devastation after Japan's attack on China, Italy's invasion of Ethiopia, Germany's rearmament, the interference of the latter two in the Spanish Civil War; and the walkout of all three powers. **The March of Time**'s frequent practice of staging scenes where actual events could not be filmed nor stock footage located—today the most troubling characteristic of the series—is evident here in the one shot, faked in the New York studio, of "Italian delegates" jeering down Haile Selassie. (See also *The Movies March On!* [1939].)

NORTH SEA

1938. Great Britain.
GPO Film Unit. Directed by Harry Watt. Produced by Alberto Cavalcanti. Photographed by Henry E. (Chick) Fowle, Jonah Jones, Pat Jackson, Ralph Elton. Edited by Cavalcanti and R. Q. Macnaughton. With Mattie Mair and other trawlermen and townspeople of Aberdeen, and Post Office radio operators.
31 min. B&W. Sound.

Alberto Cavalcanti was already esteemed as a member of the French avant-garde of the 1920s, having made the remarkable *Rien que les heures* (1926), when he joined the General Post Office Film Unit in 1934. His fame and inventiveness immediately made an impression on his younger colleagues there, but his mark became more visible after he succeeded Grierson as head of the unit in 1937. *North Sea* demonstrates a resurgence of creativity in the wake of direct social documentary (from *Housing Problems* [1935] through *The Smoke Menace* [1937]). An exceptional

film by any standard, it uses a forceful narrative to dramatize the importance of the Post Office's ship-to-shore radio service. It was directed by Harry Watt, who had also directed *Night Mail* (1936). Like Cavalcanti, Watt had a penchant for fiction and followed him into feature filmmaking at the Ealing Studios, where Cavalcanti became a producer in 1940. Representing the liberties of fiction more than the restrictions of the straight documentary, *North Sea* anticipates the path of its makers, whose hopes that it would be a big box office hit were amply rewarded. The story follows a fishing crew as they leave their wives and homes and become endangered in a severe storm off the north coast of Scotland. Their pumps break down after they have lost radio contact with the mainland; the tense anticipation matches that of a successful studio thriller, yet the story is resolved without the pat contrivances so common in commercial movies. Watt shot the interiors on a moving studio set, the exteriors on a rented trawler with a carefully selected crew of nonactors. The photography and editing are first-rate. Even after World War II necessitated the production of wartime propaganda, British documentary filmmakers continued to rely on the use of dramatic narrative; see Ruby Grierson's *They Also Serve* (1940) and Humphrey Jennings's *The Silent Village* (1943).

OLYMPIA (Diving sequence) (1938).
See Film Study

PEOPLE OF THE CUMBERLAND

1938. U.S.A.
Frontier Films. Directed by Robert Stebbins [pseudonym of Sidney Meyers] and Eugene Hill [pseudonym of Jay Leyda], assisted by Elia Kazan and William Watts. Photographed by Ralph Steiner. Edited by Helen van Dongen. Commentary written by Erskind Caldwell, assisted by David Wolff [Ben Maddow]. Music by Alex North and Earl Robinson. Narrated by Richard Blaine.
21 min. B&W. Sound.

Following works like *Heart of Spain* (1937) and *China Strikes Back* (also 1937), which alerted viewers to the importance of political struggles abroad, the Frontier Film group redirected its attention to crucial issues at home, particularly to the need for unionization. *People of the Cumberland* was the first of this latter group. It publicized the efforts of Miles Horton's Highlander Folk School to provide practical and political education among the poor Cumberland mountaineers of southern Tennessee.

Unionizing enabled them to work for better wages in the region's textile mills and also gave them greater social and recreational opportunities. The film supplements its direct reporting with several enacted scenes, such as "interviews" with local workers, to add variety and a feeling of spontaneity; these experiments within the documentary form culminated in Frontier Film's *Native Land* (1942).

THE CITY

1939. U.S.A.
American Documentary Films, Inc. for the American Institute of Planners. Directed and photographed by Ralph Steiner and Willard Van Dyke. Scenario by Henwar Rodakiewicz and commentary by Lewis Mumford from an outline by Pare Lorentz. Narrated by Morris Carnovsky. Music by Aaron Copland.
43 min. B&W. Sound.

Ralph Steiner and Willard Van Dyke, accomplished photographers who had worked for Pare Lorentz (see *The Plow That Broke the Plains* [1936] and *The River* [1937]), brought their own sense of poetic rhythm to this American classic, drawn from a plan by Lorentz and produced for the 1939 New York World's Fair. Spurred by personal and political differences and hungry for artistic autonomy, Steiner and Van Dyke had left Frontier Films the previous year to start their own film unit, American Documentary Films, Inc., which was inspired by contemporary British models. The one fruit of this brief collaboration is *The City*. The film traces the historic stages in the growth of cities in the U.S., ending in a prescription for the future by the group of city planners who sponsored the film: that urban development could be decentralized to eliminate congestion and relieve health and safety hazards. This theme remained central in the writing of Lewis Mumford, the outstanding architectural critic who contributed the narration. But the heart of the film lies in its lively (and somewhat antithetical) celebration of contemporary Manhattan life. Candid scenes of bustling city dwellers, traffic snarls, and a climactic montage sequence at a frenetic lunch counter introduced a delightful satiric humor to the American documentary; and Aaron Copland's score adds an unmistakable native flavor. *The City*'s combination of a freely developed personal style with an added commercial message established one direction for sponsored documentaries in the U.S. for at least two decades.

THE ISLANDERS

1939. Great Britain.
GPO Film Unit. Directed by Maurice Harvey. Assistant: Stewart McAllister. Produced by J. B. Holmes. Music by Darius Milhaud.
17 min. B&W. Sound.

A little-known General Post Office film from Cavalcanti's stewardship (but not credited to his direct supervision), *The Islanders* is an interesting contrast to *North Sea* (1938). Both stress the importance of radio communication to span the seas (a service of the GPO), but whereas *North Sea* employs dramatic thunder in a clever and sophisticatedly conceived short-story form, *The Islanders* is a quietly engaging essay that flows with an easy grace reminiscent of the early works of the GPO unit. Its photographic beauty is evocatively underscored by the lovely music of Darius Milhaud, punctuating a subtle narration that recounts the economic development of three islands. The first, Eriskay in the Outer Hebrides off Scotland, is agriculturally based and enjoys gradually increasing trade with the mainland. Guernsey in the English Channel is more advanced, with established industries and thriving commerce. Inner Farne, once inhabited but lacking ties to the world beyond, now lies desolate in the North Sea, indicating that if an island's economic links are severed, its hospitality may collapse. In short, people must live on the means available on an island, but the conduct and quality of their lives depend upon communications and trade beyond their shores: a subtle thought for Britain, the unstressed fourth island, on the threshold of wartime isolation.

MEN IN DANGER

1939. Great Britain.
GPO Film Unit. Produced by Alberto Cavalcanti. Directed by Patrick Jackson (begun by Harry Watt). Assistant: W. J. R. Lee. Photographed by Henry E. (Chick) Fowle. Narrated by Sir Henry H. Bashford.
35 min. B&W. Sound.

This is the first directorial effort of Pat Jackson, one of the youngsters who had nearly grown up with the General Post Office unit, which he joined after finishing high school in 1934. The film was begun by Harry Watt (who accepted an offer around this time to do second-unit direction of Hitchcock's *Jamaica Inn* [1939]) and produced by Cavalcanti. At two points in particular, one is reminded of their inclination for dramatic fiction (see *North Sea* [1938]): the

booming music over the opening credits and an early montage sequence that climaxes in a frightful accident with machinery. Jackson himself turned to feature filmmaking following the Second World War, but for the most part, *Men in Danger*, despite its melodramatic title, is a handsome but straightforward report on a subject of social concern: health and safety in the workplace. The General Post Office, proud of its own record of medical protection for its employees (the film is narrated by its chief medical officer), was obviously motivated by the gas industry's series of public interest films, which this one closely resembles in its journalistic mix of offscreen narration and on-camera interviews (see *Housing Problems* [1935], *Enough to Eat?* [1936], *Children at School* [1937], and *The Smoke Menace* [1937]). Industrial protection was costly. *Men in Danger* describes government regulations, safety classes, and emergency drills that guard against physical injury. Some detail is also devoted to preventative measures against four serious industrial diseases—lead poisoning, anthrax, epithelioma (skin cancer), and silicosis—and one psychological problem—monotony. *Men in Danger* is among the last of the social documentaries of the 1930s; with the arrival of war and the rise of Humphrey Jennings (see *Spare Time* [1939] and *The Silent Village* [1943]), British documentary would synthesize propaganda and art.

THE MOVIES MARCH ON! (THE MARCH OF TIME, Vol. V, No. 12)

July 1939. U.S.A.
Time Inc. Produced by Louis de Rochemont. Narrated by Westbrook Van Voorhis. With prominent figures of the American movie industry and The Museum of Modern Art Film Library.
22 min. B&W. Sound.

Beginning March 1939, **The March of Time** examined a single subject in every issue (see *Arms and the League* [1938]). During its first four years, the newsreel had been celebrated for its unflinching examination of issues of great national and international importance, such as Depression problems and the threats to peace by the Axis powers. (War would be declared following Hitler's invasion of Poland September 1.) But **The March of Time** was by no means inattentive to the entertainment of its audience nor ungrateful to the film industry (then the nation's fifth largest), which made possible its success. *The Movies March On!* runs through the first four decades of American movie history and affords a contemporary glance at the Hollywood community, from major production heads to the Hays Office (all presented in complimentary terms). The newsreel was occasioned by the work of the new Museum of Modern Art Film Library, begun in 1935. The Film Library assisted with the film's assembly, and visible are some of its early facilities and staff, including curator Iris Barry and director John Abbott. The view of film history that emerges represents only the most cursory approach of its period, but the newsreel itself is a fine display of the booming grandiloquence (for example, the title: "A sideshow curiosity in 1903, the moving picture was destined in a few short years to build a city, found a dynasty and establish an art") so immortally parodied in 1941 by the "News on the March" sequence from *Citizen Kane*.

SPARE TIME

1939. Great Britain.
GPO Film Unit. Written and directed by Humphrey Jennings. Assistant: D. V. Knight. Produced by Alberto Cavalcanti. Photographed by Henry E. (Chick) Fowle. Commentary: Laurie Lee.
15 min. B&W. Sound.

Humphrey Jennings joined the GPO unit in 1934, but only after the start of World War II did he solidify the genius that establishes him in many critics' minds as the finest of British documentarists. *Spare Time*, the first important film Jennings directed, was finished before the war and just hints at the great works ahead: *Listen to Britain* (1942), *Fires Were Started* (1943), *The Silent Village* (1943), and *A Diary for Timothy* (1945). Yet it is a wonderfully cheerful film and serves well to introduce the skills of its maker. A literary scholar and occasional painter of easygoing and poetic temperament, Jennings was inclined not so much to declare or explain as to observe subtly. This placed him somewhat at odds with Grierson's explicit prescription for instruction and public service. One of Jennings's major interests in the late 1930s was the Mass Observation movement, begun by anthropologist Tom Harrison and poet and political scientist Charles Madge. The movement espoused a methodology for investigating public behavior that involved candidly watching and listening to people going about their daily lives. *Spare Time* is a Mass Observation film on the way many Britishers spend their off hours. Jennings chose workers from three industries in different parts of the country—steel, textiles, and coal. The film is simplicity itself; it is so objective and has such an impartial narration that the result is most informal and playful.

Whether pigeon-keeping or sporting, reading a newspaper or drinking beer, going to carnivals or making music, these citizens fulfill Jennings's unassuming observance, "As things are, spare time is a time when we have a chance to do what we like, a chance to be most ourselves." (See also *Return Journey* [1981].)

TRANSFER OF POWER. THE HISTORY OF THE TOOTHED WHEEL

1939. Great Britain.
Shell Film Unit. Produced by Arthur Elton. Directed by Geoffrey Bell. Animated diagrams by Francis Rodker.
21 min. B&W. Sound.

On a report from Grierson, a film unit had been set up in 1934 under Edgar Anstey for Shell Oil in London. When Anstey left for **The March of Time** (see *Enough to Eat?* [1936] and *Arms and the League* [1938]), Arthur Elton began a lifelong association with the Shell Unit, which grew to become one of the world's most active. A unique production group, it was staffed, housed, and financed by the oil company, which nevertheless permitted the Film Centre to plan operations. Elton was interested in the history of technology, and he took special pleasure in the realization of *Transfer of Power*, an outstanding demonstration of the workings of levers and gears. Capturing some of the charm of live-action educational predecessors like *The Catch of the Season* (1937), the film uses precise animated drawings in such inventive fashion that an illustrated lecture about a sophisticated technical subject, the development of the toothed wheel, is transformed into a rewarding treat. As such, it anticipates another animated instructional classic, the National Film Board of Canada's *An Introduction to Jet Engines* (1959).

AND SO THEY LIVE

1940. U.S.A.
Written and directed by John Ferno and Julian Roffman. Commentary by Edwin Locke. Music by Lee Grön.
25 min. B&W. Sound.

This social documentary centers on the educational system of a Kentucky mountain community. It portrays a school system that teaches irrelevant and antiquated material to children who live in a poverty-stricken environment where a knowledge of the land and agriculture is essential. Classroom scenes where an 11th-century legend and European geography are taught are juxtaposed with scenes of daily life in the community, including scenes that illustrate ignorance of nutrition and bad farming techniques that deplete the soil. The film ends on a more optimistic note as a new system of education, an experiment conducted by the local university, is to be initiated whereby the children will be taught the basics of agriculture.

CAMPAIGN IN POLAND (FELDZUG IN POLEN)

February 8, 1940. Germany.
Directed by Fritz Hippler. Music by Herbert Windt. English narration.
34 min. B&W. Sound.

One of the most infamous vehicles of political propaganda produced by the Third Reich, *Campaign in Poland* presents the official Nazi explanation of Germany's devastation of Poland and the circumstances that provoked the war. The film's highly manipulative retelling of history is an eye-opening, frequently arresting record of documentary subterfuge, for its falsification of recent events is narrated directly over actual news footage, including substantial coverage of the *blitzkrieg* across Poland. The detailed Nazi account is itself most compelling: the alleged Polish atrocities against the "German" people of Danzig (now Gdansk); Germany's long efforts toward a peaceful solution met by repeated Polish refusals and military threats; Danzig's proclamation of its independence from Poland and unity with the Reich on the same day (September 1, 1939) on which the German military is left no recourse but to begin its "countercharge" against the Polish forces; the reasonableness yet firm invincibility of German troops, welcomed wherever they go by those who seek no hostility. In the absence of decisive views of military victories, the film substitutes animated maps showing the disintegration—coolly abstracted—of Polish divisions, then pictures the aftermath of destruction on buildings or machinery. Fritz Hippler, the director, was a principal figure among Nazi filmmakers, in charge of the film section of Goebbel's Ministry of Propaganda for most of the war after having worked there in newsreel production since 1935. Herbert Windt's score is as notable as his earlier contribution to *Triumph of the Will* (1935). Versions of the film were prepared in several languages, not just to disseminate the Nazi rationalization of these events, but to frighten potential combatants into submission. (A recurring motif is that those who oppose German might are annihilated.) This English language version is a good deal shorter than the domestic release and was perhaps intended as much for Americans, whom Hitler still hoped to win to his side, as for the British, who had declared war at the start of the invasion of Poland.

POWER AND THE LAND

1940. U.S.A.
U.S. Film Service for the Rural Electrification Administration (REA) of the U.S. Department of Agriculture. Directed by Joris Ivens. Photographed by Floyd Crosby and Arthur Ornitz. Edited by Helen van Dongen. Commentary by Stephen Vincent Benét. Music by Douglas Moore.
38 min. B&W. Sound.

Power and the Land is the first American film by Dutch documentarian Joris Ivens, who made *Rain* (1929), *New Earth* (1934), and *The Spanish Earth* (1937). The film is remarkable for its sensitive portrayal of American ideals and lifestyles. Made for the Department of Agriculture to explain and promote its program of rural electrification, the film acclaims America's hardworking farmers who love the land: "They know, and their children know, the work that goes into raising food for a nation," says Benét's poetic commentary. Filmed on the farm of Bill and Hazel Parkinson in St. Clairsville, Ohio, the film first shows the hardship of a nonelectrified farm and then the progress and profit brought by electricity. It admonishes the private electric utilities for their reluctance to bring power to rural areas and proves its point through specific, scripted events: milk that is not properly cooled going sour and Mrs. Parkinson watching her children reading by kerosene lamp as the commentary says, "Wouldn't be so hard with a good light on your work." The hardship of the farm is replaced by "kilowatt hours that don't get tired," irons, incubators, washing machines, running water, and more. With elegant photography and a complementary score, Ivens has created a calm, respectful portrait of the American farmer as the essence of our country.

THEY ALSO SERVE

1940. Great Britain.
Realist Film Unit for the Ministry of Information. Directed by Ruby I. Grierson.
8 min. B&W. Sound.

The heroine of this simple and touching tribute is the average British homemaker during World War II. These women quietly assumed all the burdens of daily living to free soldiers and defense workers for their jobs. The subtle, fictional narrative, which deemphasizes the fact of war itself, is suggestive of the work of Humphrey Jennings, especially in its quiet focus on the peaceful continuity of British life in the course of "seeing it through." Ruby Grierson was an influential force in the British documentary movement, though credited only modestly. She was known to be remarkable in conducting personal interviews and working with nonprofessional performers, and was largely responsible for the British shift toward the personal in films like *Housing Problems* (1935) and *To-Day We Live* (1937). She was drowned later in 1940 while crossing the Atlantic.

VALLEY TOWN

1940. U.S.A.
Directed by Willard Van Dyke. Photographed by Roger Barlow and Bob Churchill. Edited by Irving Lerner. Music by Marc Blitzstein.
35 min. B&W. Sound.

Immediately following the outstanding success of *The City* (1939), Willard Van Dyke directed *Valley Town*. This film provides a remarkable picture of urban poverty in the Great Depression, and today stands as one of the most powerful portrayals of that period. It is a study of the effects of unemployment upon a steelworker's family when the father is thrown out of work by a new automated steel strip mill. It was shot in New Castle, Pennsylvania (not named in the film, it could be "anywhere" U.S.A.); the steelworkers and their families play themselves. Van Dyke's skillful use of nonactors prefigures a similar device used in the Italian Neo-Realist movies following World War II. The hallmark of all of Van Dyke's work is the clarity and beauty of the images, and *Valley Town* is very much in that tradition. The film did not receive the wide exposure and recognition that it deserved at the time it was made, largely because America was tooling up for World War II and unemployment was no longer a central issue. In addition Van Dyke employed a musical recitative (composed by the eminent American composer Marc Blitzstein) to express the inner thoughts of his principal characters, a device that proved too avant-garde for some audiences of that period. Thus, it is only in the last decade that the exceptional qualities of the film have come to be appreciated, first by film scholars and gradually by an ever-widening general audience.

A SUMMER SAGA (EN SOMMARSAGA)

1941. Sweden.
Produced by Svensk Filmindustri. Directed and photographed by Arne Sucksdorff. In Swedish; no English subtitles.
12 min. B&W. Sound.

An early film by this major figure in Swedish cinema, *A Summer Saga* is a unique example of Sucksdorff's depiction of the beauty and cruelty of nature. Photographed in a natural style against the rich Swedish landscape, two foxes are followed on their adventures on a summer's afternoon. This was an enormously popular film when it was released, establishing Sucksdorff as a gifted nature photographer whose films are strong textural and sensuous studies of his environment.

THE BATTLE OF MIDWAY

1942. U.S.A.
U.S. Navy. Directed, written, and photographed by John Ford. Narrated by Donald Crisp, Henry Fonda, Irving Pichel, Jane Darwell.
18 min. Color. Sound.

It has been said that the purest form of documentary is the home movie. Despite the all-inclusive ring of its title, John Ford's film is anything but an exhaustive account of the pivotal U.S. naval victory that reversed the course of the Pacific War. Instead, it is as personal and idiosyncratic as its maker, a wartime photographer who boldly picked up a camera and filmed in 16mm Technicolor the bombardment he witnessed from his own base on the island. Ford padded his unabashed one-man's view with additional aerial and ocean footage, shots of our boys and the island's native birds, voice-overs of Henry Fonda and Jane Darwell as if out of *The Grapes of Wrath* (1940), and sentimental renditions of American standards, from patriotic and service anthems to "Onward Christian Soldiers," "Red River Valley," and "Over There." Because of Ford's high esteem in Hollywood at the time, the film was released commercially by his long-time studio, 20th Century-Fox, and was awarded one of the four Oscars given in patriotic zeal to war documentaries that year. (Major Frank Capra's *Prelude to War* [1942] got another.)

THE LAND

April 1942. U.S.A.
U.S. Film Service and the Agricultural Adjustment Administration. Directed,

written, and narrated by Robert Flaherty in collaboration with Frances Flaherty. Editorial supervision by Helen van Dongen. Contributing photography by Irving Lerner, Douglas Baker, Floyd Crosby, and Charles Herbert. Music by Richard Arnell.
51 min. B&W. Sound.

Robert Flaherty made **The Land**, his most controversial film, at the invitation of Pare Lorentz and the U.S. government. Stunningly photographed, the film is an essay on the destructive nature of machines that displace workers by replacing them. It begins with the erosion problem, explores the deserted towns of the West, and ends by lauding irrigation systems and a nationwide network of granaries as government projects that will resolve poverty and unemployment. An effective combination of New Deal propaganda, keen insight, visual beauty, and Flaherty's lyrical romanticism, **The Land** is the most atypical of Flaherty documentary classics.

NATIVE LAND

1942. U.S.A.
Frontier Films. Directed by Leo Hurwitz and Paul Strand. Photographed by Paul Strand. Edited by Leo Hurwitz. Written by David Wolff [Ben Maddow], Leo Hurwitz, and Paul Strand. Commentary by David Wolff [Ben Maddow]. Narrated by Paul Robeson. Associate directors: Alfred Saxe and William Watts. Music by Marc Blitzstein.
88 min. B&W. Sound.

Native Land was the most important film made by Frontier Films, the film collective that produced social documentaries from 1936–42, including **Heart of Spain** (1937) and **People of the Cumberland** (1938). The epitome of the collective's style, which successfully combined fictional scenes with documentary information, **Native Land** focuses on the fascist forces existing within the U.S. democratic structure. Based on the U.S. Senate's LaFollette Committee findings concerning union busting and the tactics of massive corporate labor spying, it is a significant pro-labor statement that begins by saying "the American people have had to fight for their freedom in every generation." The film outlines several incidents—the killing of a Michigan farmer who spoke up at a farmer's meeting, the death of an anonymous union organizer in a Cleveland hotel, the dramatic killing of black and white sharecroppers in Arkansas who wanted ten cents more for their cotton, and the terrorizing of a shopkeeper in Tennessee who gave money to the union. With forceful and moving commentary spoken by Paul Robeson, these scenes combine to show the web of conspiracy that comprised the anti-labor movement, emphasizing the public's ignorance of these events. The central dramatic scene concerns a labor spy, Harry Carlisle, who becomes trapped in a never-ending cycle of union betrayal under the grip of corporate bosses. The film uses footage from the Film and Photo League of actual protests and strikes to root the dramatic sequences in a documentary context. **Native Land** also outlines the immense task of piecing together the shredded documents that were the evidence used by the Senate Committee and ends with a touching scene of the funeral of a young worker who was killed in a Memorial Day massacre at a steel plant in Chicago in 1937. Three years in the making, the film was released right after Pearl Harbor, a time when national unity was of utmost importance. Thus, the film was not widely shown. Its funders removed it from distribution during the McCarthy era and only returned it to the filmmakers for circulation in the early 1960s. It remains today one of the finest examples of the radical social documentary.

WHY WE FIGHT

1942–45. U.S.A.

The **Why We Fight** series of seven films is renowned as the most effective American propaganda produced during World War II. These dramatic, informative documentaries were produced by Frank Capra (who had never previously directed a documentary) for the U.S. War Department. Looking back on these films in his autobiography, *The Name Above the Title*, Capra wrote: "The **Why We Fight** series became our official, definitive answer to: What was the government policy during the dire decade 1931–1941? For whenever State, the White House or Congress was unable, or unwilling, to tell us what our government policy had been (and this happened often) I followed General Marshall's advice: 'In those cases, make your own best estimate and see if they don't agree with you later.' By extrapolation, the film series was also accepted as the official policy of the allies. . . . Thus it can be truly said that the **Why We Fight** series not only stated, but, in many instances, actually created and nailed down American and world prewar policy." Capra was selected for the project and made a Major by Gen. George C. Marshall because of considerable confusion, division, and ignorance about the war among American troops bound overseas. The films are based on a series of lectures prepared

NATIVE LAND (1942)

for the troops intended to reduce their isolationist views, build up a self-image of strength and bravery, and give the troops a thorough explanation of military strategy. The style of these films is forceful and persuasive. It combines extensive combat footage from both allied and enemy sources (Capra studied Leni Riefenstahl's *Triumph of the Will* [1935] and incorporated much of its footage and technique) with fiction films and animation. The superb graphics add an even more dramatic flair to the punctuated style of the narration: Germany is an amorphous blob of black ink oozing across Europe, radio towers send out rings of "lies" (propaganda), and swastika termites invade the castle of France. Each film ends with the ringing of the Liberty Bell and a "V" for victory. These films were shown to thousands of American troops as well as British, Canadian, and Australian soldiers. *The Battle of Britain* was widely shown in England on Churchill's orders, as was *The Battle of Russia* shown throughout Russia on Stalin's orders. Several of the films were released commercially and shown to the American people in movie theaters; *Prelude to War* was voted an Academy Award for Best Documentary of 1942.

PRELUDE TO WAR (1942)

PRELUDE TO WAR

1942.
Produced and directed by Major Frank Capra for the U.S. War Department. Script by Major Eric Knight and Captain Anthony Veiller. Edited by Major William Hornbeck. Narration by Walter Huston.
54 min. B&W. Sound.

This first film of the **Why We Fight** series is based on the principle that all countries are divided into "free" and "slave" worlds, and establishes the enemy trinity of Germany, Japan, and Italy. An exceedingly patriotic and prowar film, its purpose is to answer the **Why We Fight** question and explain the causes and events leading up to our entry into the war. The film analyzes the creation of a totalitarian government, describing the abolition of free press, public congregation, and freedom of religion; the indoctrination of children; and the creation of secret police. It contrasts this to the history of democracy and freedom of the press, religion, and education. The powerful graphics and maps underline the extensive documentary footage. With a brief summation of the Japanese attack on Manchuria in 1931 and on Shanghai in 1933 and of Italy's move into Ethiopia, *Prelude to*

War ends on the note of "It's us or them. The chips are down."

THE NAZIS STRIKE

1942.
Produced and directed by Lieutenant Colonel Frank Capra and Major Anatole Litvak for the U.S. War Department. Script by Major Eric Knight, Captain Anthony Veiller and Corporal Robert Heller. Edited by Major William Hornbeck. Music by Dimitri Tiomkin. Narrated by Walter Huston and Captain Anthony Veiller.
41 min. B&W. Sound.

A documentary of the growth of Nazi zeal and German history leading to Hitler's regime, this second of the **Why We Fight** series is a fervent anti-Nazi film that centers on Germany's "maniacal urge to impose its will on others." It analyzes Hitler's plan for world conquest, including his "pagan pageantry," secret manufacturing of arms, creation of a strong military force, and systematic indoctrination of youth. Footage compiled from the Nazi conquests of Austria, Czechoslavakia, and Poland and from Britain's declaration of war on Germany is used to emphasize the extensiveness of the threat.

DIVIDE AND CONQUER

1943.
Produced and directed by Lieutenant Colonel Frank Capra and Major Anatole Litvak for the U.S. War Department. Script by Captain Anthony Veiller and Corporal Robert Heller. Edited by Major William Hornbeck. Music by Dimitri Tiomkin. Narrated by Walter Huston and Captain Anthony Veiller.
57 min. B&W. Sound.

This third film of the **Why We Fight** series documents the completion of the Nazi strategy to divide and conquer the wall of Allied forces to Germany's west through the use of war propaganda. Explanations of war strategy include the use of underground caves by the French, the German tactic of landing thousands of troops via parachute, the use of refugees as weapons of war to block advancing Allied troops, and the plane-tank infantry team of Germany's new warfare. The conquests of Norway, Holland, Belgium, and France are recorded and explained, with France defined as "cynical and disillusioned" before Hitler's arrival. The final footage showing the surrender of France, its weeping people, and Hitler riding through an empty Paris, contains some of the most powerful and touching images of World War II.

THE BATTLE OF BRITAIN

1943.
Produced by Lieutenant Colonel Frank Capra for the U.S. War Department. Written and directed by Captain Anthony Veiller. Edited by Major William Hornbeck. Music by Dimitri Tiomkin. Narrated by Walter Huston and Captain Anthony Veiller.
54 min. B&W. Sound.

This fourth film of the **Why We Fight** series centers on the blitz of London and Coventry, after the battle at Dunkirk, and ends with the Christmas firebombing of London in 1940. Employing many scenes from fictional wartime films, it describes in a heart-wrenching and very pro-British style the lives of British civilians and how they survived the onslaught of Nazi bombs. The role of the

British women, the day-to-day routine of living underground, and descriptions of British industry are coupled with a thoroughly reverent portrait of the Royal Air Force and its ability to keep the Germans from landing. *The Battle of Britain* is credited with reducing anti-British sentiment among American forces.

THE BATTLE OF RUSSIA

1943.
Produced by Lieutenant Colonel Frank Capra for the U.S. War Department. Directed by Lieutenant Colonel Anatole Litvak. Script by Captain Anthony Veiller and Corporal Robert Heller. Edited by Major William Hornbeck. Music by Dimitri Tiomkin. Narrated by Walter Huston and Captain Anthony Veiller.
80 min. B&W. Sound.

Considered perhaps the most successful of the **Why We Fight** series, this fifth film begins with a comprehensive description of Russian history. It uses clips from Eisenstein's *Alexander Nevsky* (1938) and other early films and makes a thorough analysis of Russia's size, industry, culture, and cities. It documents the massive Nazi strike on Russia beginning in 1941, stressing the strength of Russia's numbers, the vastness of its territory, and the bitterness of its weather. Heavily ironic and exceptionally laudatory of the Russian people, *The Battle of Russia* effectively explains the complexities of this specific campaign through diagrams and exceptional footage of the seige of Leningrad and the battle of Stalingrad.

THE BATTLE OF CHINA

1944.
Produced by Colonel Frank Capra for the Army Pictorial Services. Directed by Colonel Frank Capra and Lieutenant Colonel Anatole Litvak. Script by Major Anthony Veiller and Sargent Robert Heller. Edited by Major William Hornbeck. Music by Dimitri Tiomkin. Narrated by Walter Huston and Captain Anthony Veiller.
67 min. B&W. Sound.

Like *The Battle of Russia*, this sixth film of the **Why We Fight** series begins with a review of China's history, and is designed to win sympathy for China's struggle. China is presented as an inventive, hardworking country with a vast population capable of building the Great Wall, yet militarily unprepared for war. Starting with the Japanese conquest of Shanghai and movement westward, it documents the decision of the Chinese to slowly yield territory while building an army and embarking on the "greatest mass migration ever recorded" as 30 million Chinese burnt their factories and moved 2,000 miles eastward to Chunking. Showing extraordinary respect for the unusual methods of defense used by the Chinese, it also documents the building of the Burma supply road. Ending with a speech on U.S. aid to China and the war in the South Pacific, *The Battle of China* concludes with the firm statement that "China's war is our war."

WAR COMES TO AMERICA

1945.
Produced by Colonel Frank Capra for the Army Pictorial Service. Directed by Lieutenant Colonel Anatole Litvak. Script by Major Anthony Veiller and Lieutenant Colonel Anatole Litvak. Edited by Major William Hornbeck. Music by Dimitri Tiomkin. Narrated by Walter Huston and Major Anthony Veiller.
67 min. B&W. Sound.

This final film of the **Why We Fight** series is a unique patriotic statement designed to eliminate any possibility of U.S. reluctance to enter the war. It emphasizes U.S. democracy and a national portrait to stress a unified war effort. The American soldier is seen as a conglomeration of various states and backgrounds, and civilians are portrayed as well-educated and inventive, with a love of sports and travel. All Americans, declares the narration, say "Let our freedoms be endangered and we will fight." The quiet peacefulness and isolation of American streets is juxtaposed with war footage as Americans listen to war reports on the radio. A thorough history of American sentiment toward the various stages of the war is documented through polls, which are referred to as "we the people" and are effectively made to look like actual voting booths. Ending with Pearl Harbor and Roosevelt's declaration of war, this film asserts the prevailing sentiment that the U.S. was the symbol of the free world and the only means to stop the Nazis.

———

THE AUTOBIOGRAPHY OF A "JEEP"

1943. U.S.A.
Office of War Information. Produced and written by Joseph Krumgold. Directed by Irving Lerner. Photographed by Roger Barlow.
10 min. B&W. Sound.

Autobiography of a "Jeep" is a humorous and informative film about army jeeps. Along with *The Town* (1944) and *Window Cleaner* (1945), this film is part of a group of successful short films made by the Office of War Information (OWI). The film is narrated in the first person by the jeep itself in a rather jocular, old-boy's voice. It explains the testing that was necessary to make it an army success, and jokes about posing with celebrities while reassuringly proclaiming that it is "my pal the soldier" who matters most. Interesting details are revealed, such as the origin of its name (from GP, which stood for general purpose) and all the possible uses for the vehicle. This affectionate short was quite popular when shown with army feature films during the war.

DESERT VICTORY

1943. Great Britain.
Produced by the British Army Film and Photographic Unit and the Royal Air Force Film Production Unit. Directed by Lieutenant Colonel David MacDonald. Commentary by J. L. Hodson. Music by William Alwyn.
60 min. B&W. Sound.

Desert Victory is one of the finest documentary films of World War II. It was made as a routine British War Office assignment to cover General Montgomery's brilliant African campaign against Rommel's Afrikan Korps. The Eighth Army's campaign moved from El Alamein over 1,300 miles to Tripoli in what was a turning point in the war. Director David MacDonald, a Scotsman with Hollywood training, effectively reconstructs the intensity and drama of actual combat in scenes of night fighting and intimate details of the infantry's daily life. In addition, there is highly charged footage taken from Royal Air Force planes on bombing runs. Twenty-six cameramen photographed this film with a realism and intimacy that is remarkable for the period. MacDonald reportedly outfitted his cameramen with guns as well as cameras, telling them that if ever they were near enough to the enemy to use their guns, they should use their cameras instead. Four were killed, seven wounded, and six captured in the film's making. Concise and dramatic, *Desert Victory* is an exceptional combat documentary.

THE SILENT VILLAGE

1943. Great Britain.
Crown Film Unit, British Ministry of Information. Produced and directed by Humphrey Jennings. In English and Welsh.
33 min. B&W. Sound.

The Silent Village is one of several films by Humphrey Jennings during World War II that stressed the courage and perseverance of the British (others were **London Can Take It** [1940], **Listen to Britain** [1942], and **Fires Were Started** [1943]). It is a very effective version of the "it could happen here" approach designed to show the English what it would be like to live in occupied territory. Made in the Welsh mining town of Cwmgiedd, the film reenacts the events that took place in the Czechoslavakian mining town of Lidice, which resisted the Nazis in subversive ways and was eventually obliterated. Jennings begins by establishing a romantic portrait of quiet town life. This is interrupted by the arrival of an ominous official car carrying a megaphone announcing the suspension of civil rights and the supremacy of the German Reich. Details of life under occupation—instructions over the radio, the banning of Welsh in the schools—are coupled with a miners' strike and their organized resistance. With haunting photography and a very effective portrayal of an anonymous enemy—we never see the Germans' faces, we only hear their instructions—this film was a warning to the British people of the possible consequences of their failure to resist the German forces.

L'AMITIÉ NOIRE

1944. France.
Conceived and narrated by Jean Cocteau. Photographed and edited by François Villiers. In French; no English subtitles.
20 min. B&W. Sound.

This French portrait of the changing black African culture, specifically in the Congo, is remarkably sensitive, showing great respect for the customs and rituals of the Congolese. While simultaneously depicting the economic progress and modernization of Africa, *L'Amitié Noire* also documents aspects of the African culture which are very removed from Europe. Cocteau is fascinated by the gestures of this culture, as well as by its dances and masks. His commentary is directed to those who lack his respect, saying "Don't laugh at strange customs." Cocteau's poetic and insightful approach is unique for anthropological films of the time.

THE BRIDGE

1944. U.S.A.
Foreign Policy Association. Directed by Willard Van Dyke and Ben Maddow.
30 min. B&W. Sound.

Made for the Foreign Policy Association, **The Bridge** is an assessment of the effects of World War II on the trade and transportation problems of South America. It is a continent defined by Van Dyke's wartime camera as hardworking, unchanging, and isolated from the war, rich with natural resources, but hindered by a lack of industry. A thorough documentation of South American surpluses of corn, cotton, and minerals, and its foreign blockades, widespread disease, and social problems, this film is an affirmation of the importance of air transport as a solution to the backward state of transportation. Most of all, it is a portrait of how Americans viewed this continent during the war.

THE NEGRO SOLDIER

1944. U.S.A.
Special Services Division, Army Service Forces, U.S. War Department. Directed by Captain Stuart Heisler and Colonel Frank Capra. Script by Carlton Moss. Music by Dimitri Tiomkin.
40 min. B&W. Sound.

This U.S. War Department film that followed the **Why We Fight** series was made to defend segregation in the armed forces. In true propaganda style, it glosses over issues like segregation and racism and tells a glowing history of the blacks in the United States, with no mention of slavery. Segments of Jesse Owens and other blacks winning at the Berlin Olympic Games in 1936 are highlighted, as well as a portrait of boxer Joe Louis as a soldier. A minister's sermon about blacks in the military and their contribution to American life sets the tone for this film, which centers on one black soldier's experience in basic training and military life. *The Negro Soldier* was acclaimed on its release for its dignity and sincerity; it now offers a historical perspective of the stereotypes and condescending racial attitudes held by the military and the public during the war.

THE TOWN

1944. U.S.A.
U.S. Office of War Information, Overseas Branch. Directed by Josef von Sternberg. Produced by Philip Dunn. Script by George Milburn. Photographed by Larry Madison.
13 min. B&W. Sound.

Like **The Autobiography of a "Jeep"** (1943), **The Town** was a production of the Office of War Information. Rare in its employment of a major Hollywood director, it is nonetheless most indicative of the usual purpose and patriotic thrust of OWI's quiet propaganda, designed for use abroad. One of **The American Scene** series, *The Town* showed foreign audiences how a number of social and architectural traditions brought from Europe were still serving America well in her everyday life, as exemplified by the community of Madison, Wisconsin. Typical Americans were depicted in OWI films as easy-going small-town citizens and church-goers, leading lives with values held in common with other free peoples—values worth defending in the Allied war against the Axis powers.

TRUT! (SEA HAWK)

1944. Sweden.
Svensk Filmindustri. Directed and photographed by Arne Sucksdorff. In Swedish; no English subtitles.
18 min. B&W. Sound.

Sucksdorff's powerful documentary of the sea hawk, a specific species of gull, is distinguished by its superb photography of the Swedish coast. One of the most feared predatory birds, the sea hawk plunders the nest of other gulls and steals their eggs. This wartime film, though produced in neutral Sweden and seemingly detached from the war, was widely interpreted as a parable about Nazism.

THE BATTLE OF SAN PIETRO (SAN PIETRO)

1945. U.S.A.
U.S. Army Pictorial Service. Written, directed, and narrated by Major John Huston. Photographed by Captain Jules Buck and U.S. Army Signal Corps cameramen.
30 min. B&W. Sound.

The Battle of San Pietro was commissioned by the U.S. Army to explain why the conquest of Italy had been so long and costly. The army's prologue explains: A military goal in 1943 was to isolate a maximum of German troops on the Italian peninsula, away from the Russian front and the French coast, while directing the bulk of supplies to Britain for the pending Allied invasion of France. Liberating Italy in the process, with limited forces and materiel (in the winter and with severe casualties) was a secondary aim. That the Italian campaign required superhuman effort is demonstrated in John Huston's filmed chronicle of the winning of the little village of San Pietro in the central mountains. Completed in 1944, the film realized its objectives so penetratingly that the army ordered cuts and delayed its release until the last days of the war. Huston presents drawing-board military strategy with maps and designs, then provides an unsurpassed account of the ground fighting, photographed alongside the foot soldiers throughout the battle. The result shows how uncertain victory was and the extreme losses that made it possible. The sense of uncertainty is aided by the ironic and skeptical tone of Huston's narration. Even more than a great, humane statement of the horror and devastation of war, the film captures the very ambivalence of war itself—its reasons and calculated rewards. At the conclusion of this exceptional work we see the villagers returning to the rubble of their homes; children smile at the camera, and we ponder the price and meaning of their new freedom.

SHADOWS ON THE SNOW (SKUGGOR ÖVER SNÖN)

1945. Sweden.
Svensk Filmindustri. Directed and photographed by Arne Sucksdorff. In Swedish; no English titles.
10 min. B&W. Sound.

Sucksdorff tells the story of a man stalking a bear that frightens his child, continuing his portrayal of the enchantment and cruelty of nature. Using a combination of documentary nature footage and fictional scenes, this film depicts the harshness and beauty of the Swedish landscape, where men are helpless in comparison to the animals and must traverse with cross-country skis. Like *Trut!* (1944), this film can be considered a metaphor of the events of its time.

WINDOW CLEANER

1945. U.S.A.
Office of War Information. Directed and photographed by Jules Bucher. Written by Joseph March.
6 min. B&W. Sound.

Window Cleaner is a charming Office of War Information (OWI) short designed to present the common man of America. Like *The Town* (1944) and *The Autobiography of a "Jeep"* (1943), this is a fine example of the OWI's quiet propaganda. Following a window cleaner on his rounds of skyscrapers in New York City, the film combines his chummy narration with dizzying views from the uppermost stories of Manhattan. He tells his history as a window cleaner, describing how he graduated from street-level to ladder work to per-

ilous upper windows, where he hangs with the support of a single strap. Amiable and humorous, he defines OWI's jingoism well when he states "I remember a customer said to me one day, 'My dear fellow, you're as much a part of the American scene as the skyscrapers themselves.'"

BAMBINI IN CITTA

1946. Italy.
Directed by Luigi Comencini. Produced by Gigi Martello. Photographed by Plinio Novelli. Narrated by Mario Amerio. In Italian; no English subtitles.
15 min. B&W. Sound.

This early portrait of street children in Milan is a distinct example of early realist cinema, predating *cinéma vérité*. Comencini's camera is unobtrusive and effective in capturing these children whose playground is the postwar ruins of World War II. The delicacy and smallness of the children is contrasted with the massive machinery and destitution of the city, as the children are portrayed as the essence of the street and observers of its destruction. *Bambini in Citta* is a remarkably sensitive and unmanipulated film for the documentary tradition of its time.

DEATH MILLS

1946. U.S.A.
Produced by the U.S. War Department.
21 min. B&W. Sound.

This is a straightforward news documentary on the Nazi concentration camps in Europe as they were liberated by the U.S. Army at the end of World War II. The tone of the voice-over commentary is one of barely repressed rage as it tells how 20 million men, women, and children were murdered by the Nazis. There are scenes of troops entering the death camps, including a distressed General Eisenhower. We see the emaciated survivors, the stacked corpses of the prisoners, cremation furnaces, gas chambers, Zyklon "death gas" tanks, a torture device, and the last remnants of the executed, which had been carefully stacked by the Germans into categories for future use: human hair, clothing, toys, jewelry, wedding rings, gold teeth, eye glasses. There are also scenes showing the Nazi men and women guards, including Joseph Kramer, commander of Bergen-Belsen. In one sequence horrified German civilians are forced by American soldiers to march through a recently liberated death camp. The film was shot at Dachau, Buchenwald, Ohrdruf, Ebensee (Aus-

tria), Ravensbrueck, Majdanek, and Auschwitz.

LET THERE BE LIGHT

1946. U.S.A.
Army Pictorial Service. Directed by John Huston. Written by Huston and Charles Kaufman. Photographed by Stanley Cortez, George Smith, Lloyd Fromm, John Doran, and Joseph Jackman. Narrated by Walter Huston. Music by Dimitri Tiomkin.
58 min. B&W. Sound.

After completing *The Battle of San Pietro* (1945), John Huston went on to make a final film for the U.S. Army that dealt with the aftermath of the war and the rehabilitation of returning soldiers. To make *Let There Be Light*, Huston brought a team of Signal Corps cameramen to Mason General Hospital on Long Island to film the intensely personal moments of psychiatric treatment for veterans suffering psychotic and psychosomatic disorders from their war experiences. The result was a film that was banned by the army and not released until 35 years later, in December 1980. The paradox of that suppression is one that is heightened by time. While it was withheld for a variety of reasons, including the invasion of the patients' privacy and the obvious fear that the film would scare off potential recruits, *Let There Be Light* is, in fact, an extremely positive view of psychiatric treatment. Soldiers who cannot walk or talk, who stutter, and who suffer from amnesia and melancholia are all shown getting progressively well and regaining confidence. The treatment of these men, which includes hypnosis and truth-inducing drugs, is presented as effecting near-miracle cures. The strength of the film stems from Huston's unfailing realism and compassion for these veterans. The unobtrusive camera documents a spectrum of uninhibited, powerful emotions as well as astonishing moments of self-revelation. In his intent to break through the myth of the heroism of warfare and the stereotypically triumphant American soldier, Huston was, in fact, far ahead of his time.

LE RETOUR

1946. France.
Photographed by Henri Cartier-Bresson, André Bac, U.S. Signal Corps and Air Force cameramen. Edited by Cartier-Bresson and Richard Banks. Commentary by Claude Roy. Music by Robert Lannoy. In French; no English

subtitles.
34 min. B&W. Sound.

One of the most moving documents of human agony and joy to emerge from World War II, *Le Retour* follows the liberation and homeward journey of French prisoners from Nazi concentration camps from August to October 1945. From their disbelieving, sunken faces to their hospital recoveries and finally to their journey home by foot, truck, and plane, the camera captures their profound expressions of fear, anticipation, and bliss. Confrontations at border checks, the U.S. airlift over France, and the tentative smiles on the men's faces as they arrive by train and search for familiar faces are rendered unforgettably by Cartier-Bresson's adroit camera. By concentrating on this single event, he has said more about the separation and destruction of war than hours of combat footage. "In the face of great catastrophe and human tragedy," says film historian Richard Barsam, "the artist is often mute; in reflection he finds that simplicity is the only technique by which to capture the magnitude of the events before him. Henri Cartier-Bresson is such an artist."

LOUISIANA STORY (Opening sequence) (1948). See **Louisiana Story Study Film** (1962) in Film Study

NUREMBERG (NÜRNBERG)

1948. U.S.A.
Civil Affairs Division, U.S. War Department. Compiled by Pare Lorentz and Stuart Schulberg. Edited by Joe Zigman.
70 min. B&W. Sound.

Nuremberg was initiated by Pare Lorentz and later completed in Germany by Stuart Schulberg, a member of the Official Strategic Services (OSS) postwar evidence-gathering teams. It was shown in American and British occupied areas of Germany before being withdrawn from circulation in 1950. The film combines footage of the Nuremberg trials with German war footage to explain and clarify the crimes of the Nazi defendants. Subtitled "its lesson for today," the film's premise is to offer answers to a confused postwar audience, and its style continues the forceful, punctuated style of Frank Capra's **Why We Fight** series. Quotes from Hitler are isolated for irony, and footage is used to prove each accusation and counter each defense. The opening and closing speeches by the officials from France, the U.S., England, and Russia are as compelling as the cross examination is

fascinating. Unique in its historical and political context, *Nuremberg* exemplifies the ideology that the trials "constitute judicial action of a kind to insure that those who start a war will pay for it personally."

THE PHOTOGRAPHER (1948). *See* Films on the Arts

STRANGE VICTORY

1948. U.S.A.
Target Films Production. Directed, written, and edited by Leo Hurwitz. Produced by Barnet L. Rosset Jr. Narration written by Saul Levitt. Photographed by Peter Glushanok and George Jacobson. Narrated by Alfred Drake, Gary Merrill, and Muriel Smith. Music by David Diamond.
75 min. B&W. Sound.

When Frontier Films was dissolved after the making of **Native Land** (1942), Leo Hurwitz and Barnet Rosset, who later founded Grove Press, formed Target Films. Their only production and collaboration, *Strange Victory* is a strong statement on racism. Amidst the high hopes of the postwar frenzy and baby boom, this film was a provocative questioning of the discrepancies between the ideals of the allied victory and the lingering aspects of fascism in U.S. society. In a cyclical style, Hurwitz juxtaposes scenes of the war's destruction with the complacency of postwar America. The extremely forceful narration begins by asking "Remember? Remember how it

was?" referring to the motives for defeating Nazism and then questioning "Why does Hitler's voice remain?" Scenes of newborn babies—the archetypal symbols of peacetime promises—are accompanied by a poetic narration which suddenly reverts to realism: "Nigger, kike, wop," the narrator addresses them, "take my advice and accept the facts— the world is already arranged for you." The film culminates with a scenario of a veteran black fighter pilot who cannot get work, a series of interviews with businessmen who reveal their racist attitudes, and a survey of employment statistics which show startlingly low percentages of blacks in skilled jobs in comparison to those who served in skilled professions during the war. "Nobody knows where the victory is," concludes the narration. "It certainly isn't here." With the collaboration of Peggy Lawson, Hurwitz added the present epilogue to **Strange Victory** when it was re-released in 1964, detailing the civil rights movement until that date, including the March on Washington.

ALL MY BABIES

1952. U.S.A.
Georgia State Department of Public Health. Produced, written, and directed by George Stoney. Photographed by Peaslee Bond.
54 min. B&W. Sound.

All My Babies is the best-known film by major film documentarian George Stoney, who also made **You are on In-**

IN THE STREET (1952) (p. 134)

dian Land (1969) and *Shepherd of the Night Flock* (1978). It is a sensitive and direct film on effective midwife training, and it represented a breakthough in candidness at the time it was made. The film centers on Miss Mary, a knowing and dedicated midwife in Albany, Georgia. It opens with a meeting in which the town's midwives are chastised for the recent death of a baby and prompted to review the fundamentals of their work. The film follows two parallel stories, one of an experienced and confident expectant mother and the other of a young woman who comes close to losing her child out of ignorance. Stoney juxtaposes scenes in a home that is dirty and unprepared with one that is properly set up for childbirth and postnatal care. Miss Mary's gentle narration carries the action and adds a reassuring touch. An actual birth, which is both instructive and moving, provides the film's dramatic climax. *All My Babies* remains both a vital training film and an impressive example of a powerful yet very accessible documentary approach.

IN THE STREET

1952. U.S.A.
Photographed by Helen Levitt, Janice Loeb, and James Agee. Music (on cassette) by Arthur Kleiner.
16 min. B&W. Silent. 18 fps.

The focus of this urban documentary is the children of a neighborhood on Manhattan's Upper East Side. For them, the street is a playground, battleground, and theater. Still photographers Levitt, Loeb, and Agee, who had previously worked together on *The Quiet One* (1949), have captured the feeling of street energy with a series of gestures—young children parade, wear masks, and fight; old women observe the world from their front stoops; and young girls wait nervously on steps for their dates. The photography is surprisingly candid, which is due in part to the use of angle viewers so that photographers could remain inobtrusive. A cassette recording of Arthur Kleiner's music is available.

THURSDAY'S CHILDREN

1953. Great Britain.
Written and directed by Guy Brenton and Lindsay Anderson. Photographed by Walter Lassally. Music by Geoffrey Wright. Commentary spoken by Richard Burton.
21 min. B&W. Sound.

A documentary of the Royal School for the deaf in Margate, England, **Thursday's Children** is an innovative film in its style and intimacy. Anderson, who went on to use this human approach in *Every Day Except Christmas* (1957), portrays both the difficulty and successes in teaching deaf children. Using sound and silence to recreate cinematically how these children perceive the world, the film shows them learning speech by using flags to see sound, balloons to sense speech, and touch to visualize speech. The school's community and daily routine are also presented to show how the communal spirit gives the children the confidence they lacked in regular schools. Richard Burton's superb reading of the lyrical commentary emphasizes the special world of these children who, according to the nursery rhyme, "have far to go."

THE MUSEUM AND THE FURY

1956. Poland.
A Film Frontiers production for Film Polski. Produced, directed, and edited by Leo Hurwitz. Associate director: Peggy Lawson. Narration by Thomas McGrath. Music from Dimitri Shostakovich, and from Witold Lutoslawski and other Polish composers.
60 min. B&W. Sound.

The Museum and the Fury was made by Leo Hurwitz for Film Polski, which was aware of his background in making social documentaries like *Native Land* (1942) and *Strange Victory* (1948). Hurwitz was asked to make a film on the concentration camps and worked in New York with access to the Film Polski archive, out of which he integrated this compilation of wartime footage with images of the reconstruction of Poland and various works of art. Centering on the museum of the concentration camps at Auschwitz, this film begins as a historical survey that explores the function of a museum, establishing the kinship of art, stating that "art is man's way of remembering his experience." The art contained in the Auschwitz museum is related to scenes of the Warsaw ghetto, the deportation of Jews and Poles, and the horror of the camps. "This is what the museum remembers," the narration reiterates. Images of the war, the liberation of the camps, and the laughing Nazi offenders on trial at Nuremberg are interwoven with works of art that heighten the intense emotions of these scenes. The film also documents the socialist reconstruction of Poland with optimistic scenes of the rebuilding of Warsaw that are offset by a warning not to forget the past. This study of the war, museums, and memory is one of Hur-

witz's most concise and powerful films. Its skillful pacing and complex weave of information combine in an effective tribute to the war's victims and in the threat to survival of art and memory posed by the postwar world of nuclear arms. So forceful in its view of the Cold War era, the film was apparently never released in Poland, and is only now being released in the U.S. for the first time.

EVERY DAY EXCEPT CHRISTMAS

1957. Great Britain
Graphic Films for the Ford Motor Company Ltd. Written and directed by Lindsay Anderson. Produced by Leon Clore and Karel Reisz. Photographed by Walter Lassally. Music by Daniel Paris.
37 min. B&W. Sound.

In this poetic documentary of the market of Covent Garden in London, Lindsay Anderson creates a portrait, not only of the workings of a complex center of commerce, but also of the lives and ideals of many of its workers. The film has an unhurried style that was part of the Free Cinema movement in Britain that caused a stir because its films made intimate observations and had a heightened awareness of sound. *Every Day Except Christmas* establishes the nighttime domain of the market workers with its striking opening scene showing a lorry being loaded and driven through empty towns as the national anthem signs off the local radio station. The day begins for these people as it ends for most others. Anderson follows each stage of the production with a thoroughness that brings the marketplace alive. He is concerned with the feelings of people rather than with social issues. With a powerful sense of appreciation for the commonplace, this film is a portrait of the interaction of the Covent Garden vendors in their late-night flower-fresh world as well as of their actual work. Beyond that intent, *Every Day Except Christmas* is an exquisitely photographed, lyrical film.

INDIAN SUMMER

1960. U.S.A.
A Folkfilms Production. Produced and directed by Jules Victor Schwerin. Scenario by Peggy Lawson and Schwerin. Photographed by Julius Tannenbaum. Edited by Peggy Lawson. Narrated by Jared Reed. Music composed and performed by Peter Seeger and Michael Seeger.
28 min. B&W. Sound.

Indian Summer is a sensitive portrait of a man whose life and land are displaced by a government dam project in the Catskill region of New York State. Like

Flaherty's **The Land** (1942), the film takes a distinctive anti-machine stance that condemns the insensitivity of industry to the people whose land is taken from them. The old man of **Indian Summer** is robbed of his last precious scrap of pride when forced to move, and he responds by walking through the valley, talking to other evicted landowners and finally to the local judges. An excellently photographed example of a lyrical, nostalgic documentary style, **Indian Summer** concludes "the needs of the country change, and change becomes part of the land."

CORTILE CASCINO

1961. U.S.A.
Produced, directed, and written by Robert M. Young and Michael Roemer. Photographed by Young. Edited by Young, Roemer, Dena Berger, and Robert Ferren.
46 min. B&W. Sound.

A long-suppressed and controversial documentary, produced in 1961 for network television but never broadcast, **Cortile Cascino** broke new ground in the use of *cinéma vérité* techniques. The film is a sensitive but excoriating look at the slum called Cortile Cascino in the middle of Palermo, Sicily, where poverty and death are in constant competition with the church, the Mafia, and a rigid social structure. Directed by the team of Young and Roemer, who later made **Nothing But a Man** (1964), the film was almost lost: the original negative was destroyed, but a positive print and the sound elements were smuggled out, allowing the filmmakers to assemble a final mix seven years later. **Cortile Cascino** is a powerful indictment of an oppressive political system. It is also the human story of what the film calls "extraordinary lives . . . begun in love." The controversy surrounding the film was provoked both by its cinematic techniques and its subject matter. The established church seems to ignore the plight of its parishioners, while a faith healer, condemned by the church, draws large crowds to his ceremonies. The Mafia—"like death, they will always be with us"—run an illegal slaughter house and control the concession for funerals, but they also are shown distributing free food to the hungry residents of the district. Cortile Cascino is a society where women, in the face of a relentless absence of human and material resources, provide the only continuity that keeps the fabric of family life from unraveling. Perhaps the strongest and most moving sequence depicts the burial of a baby who died from malnutrition. The

father carries the little casket to a truck that collects wooden coffins and delivers them to a cemetery where bodies are exhumed after eight years to make room for more. The caskets are stacked in a long trench, some with the tops not even nailed down, and we hear the heartbreaking sound of dirt and rocks being thrown over the shallow grave. Despite its affinities with *cinéma vérité*, **Cortile Cascino** adopts narrative techniques to tell this story. Some scenes are reenacted, others edited together from footage taken at different times. Using this dramatic structure, the film is both accurate and insightful. The visual quality of the film is exceptional, filled with emotionally moving shots of small moments: a mother gently brushing the hair of a child, the vacant faces of men listening to a street singer, the premature aging of children hunched over the rag piles they must sort. The soundtrack is composed mostly of comments by the people of Cortile Cascino, recorded and translated by the filmmakers. We listen to people describing their lives in brief and observant statements: the women ("our lives are mostly work—work and children"), the men ("who like their fathers always find something to pass the time, but inside feel they are nothing"), and the children (wanting to join the Mafia "just to be somebody"). The final image is of a high-speed train rushing past the segregated but not forgotten world of Cortile Cascino, a world on the other side of the tracks.

THE INNOCENT FAIR

1963. U.S.A.
Written and produced by Ray Hubbard. Narrated by Walter S. Johnson.
25 min. B&W. Sound.

The Innocent Fair is a "nostalgic visit to the Panama Pacific International Exposition" held in San Francisco in 1915. Comprised almost entirely of footage taken during the fair, it is a document not only of the exposition but of San Francisco and the U.S. prior to World War I, called "innocent" by Hubbard because "by May 1915 the *Lusitania* had been sunk and the world would never be innocent again." The San Francisco depicted in the film is one that is recovering from its major earthquake and fire. The Exposition includes "Wonders of the Age," with baby incubators, airplanes, and an automatic post office, and appearances by Charlie Chaplin, Fatty Arbuckle, Mabel Normand, and Teddy Roosevelt. Excellent footage of airplane tricks, car races, and a horse exposition are included in this thorough picture of this colossal event. The film ends on a

sad note with the ruins of the Palace of Fine Arts, which still stand in San Francisco as a symbol of the lack of innocence in the intervening fifty years.

RICE

1964. U.S.A.
Directed by Willard Van Dyke and Wheaton Galentine. Written by Howard Enders. Narrated by John Connell. Music by Irwin Bozelon.
27 min. Color. Sound.

In this beautifully photographed film, Van Dyke and Galentine document the important role of rice in Asia, its harvest, and the customs associated with it. Included are Japan's crowded hillside rice fields, ceremonies in Bangkok, and the work of the Rice Research Institute in the Phillipines. The message is clear: in this part of the world, where rice is the essential staple of the diet, it is grown and harvested "slowly, laboriously, and wastefully" with ancient, primitive methods. Affirming the value of the Rockefeller Foundation-funded Rice Research Institute, the film shows how science is working to educate peasants and to discover new methods of rice cultivation to help alleviate world hunger.

NAVAJOS FILM THEMSELVES

1966. U.S.A.

In 1966 Sol Worth and Jon Adair conducted an experiment in Pine Springs, Arizona, "to determine whether it is possible to teach people with a technically simple culture to make motion pictures depicting their culture and themselves as *they* see fit." At the conclusion of the project, the films were premiered on the Navajo reservation. In their book *Through Navajo Eyes*, Worth and Adair have since analyzed the "cultural context" in which the films were made—the learning situation, choice of students, choice of subjects, manner of working, and relations with the community, and the "code" of the films, which they find is culturally specific. The following films were made by the Navajo as part of this project:

INTREPID SHADOWS

By Al Clah.
18 min. B&W. Silent. 24 fps.

One of the most complex films and least understood by other Navajos, this film has been called by Margaret Mead "one of the finest examples of animism shown on film." Unlike the other films, this one deals with subjective rather than objective aspects of Navajo life. In the film Al Clah attempts to reconcile the Western notion of God with his traditional Navajo notion of gods.

THE NAVAJO SILVERSMITH

By Johnny Nelson.
27 min. B&W. Silent. 24 fps.

This film traces the creation in silver of some small Yebitchai figures, from mining the silver to the finished figure.

A NAVAJO WEAVER

By Susie Benally.
22 min. B&W. Silent. 24 fps.

Susie Benally depicts her mother weaving at the loom and includes all of the necessary steps prior to the actual weaving.

OLD ANTELOPE LAKE

By Mike Anderson.
11 min. B&W. Silent. 24 fps.

This film shows the source of the lake, then moves around the lake portraying the unity of natural things and human beings in the environment.

SECOND WEAVER

By Mrs. Benally.
9 min. B&W. Silent. 24 fps.

This film is the result of Susie Benally teaching her mother to use the camera. Similar in theme to her daughter's film, it depicts Susie weaving a belt.

THE SHALLOW WELL PROJECT

By Johnny Nelson.
14 min. B&W. Silent. 24 fps.

This film is very different in style and approach from the craft films. It illustrates the building of a shallow well to replace an open pond once used for water supply.

THE SPIRIT OF THE NAVAJOS

By Maxine and Mary J. Tsosie.
21 min. B&W. Silent. 24 fps.

The film begins with an old medicine man looking for roots to use in a curing ceremony. He prepares for a sand painting, and part of the actual ceremony is featured.

———

KYOTO

1968. Italy.
Produced by Seiichiro Eida for the Olivetti Corporation. Directed by Kon Ichikawa. Written by Shuntaro Tanikawa. Photographed by Naoyuki Sumitani. Supervised by Kenzo Tange, Yusaku Kamekura, Tadashi Ichikawa. Music by Tohru Takemitsu. Narrated by Michael Redgrave. In English with Italian opening titles.
38 min. Color. Sound.

Kyoto is a stunning portrait of Japanese history and culture through a cinematic exploration of the city of Kyoto. It was made by Kon Ichikawa, one of Japan's leading filmmakers, known for both his narrative films, such as *Fires on the Plain* (1959), and his documentaries, including *Tokyo Olympiad* (1966). To set the tone of tradition, the film begins with an evocative scene of an ancient gong ringing in a misty forest. The camera skillfully explores a rock garden and several temples, including the Ryoanji and Saihoji temples, and the Katsura Imperial Villa, to explain the fluid aesthetics of these structures and the philosophy of Japanese architecture. To give an impression of the complexity and delicacy of his country, Ichikawa sensitively documents the daily ritual of a Zen Buddhist monastery and the details of a young woman dancer dressing in layers of clothing. From the quiet of these isolated scenes, the film ends with a festival of extraordinary floats in a city street, revealing the interweaving of old and new cultures.

ONE STEP AWAY

1968. U.S.A.
Produced and directed by Ed Pincus and David Neuman. Edited by Eden Williams, Alan Jacobs. Additional camera by Peter Adair. Music by The Hallucinations.
54 min. Color. Sound.

Filmmakers Pincus and Neuman study the changing relationships within a commune of young people in California in the late 1960s, at the height of the free-wheeling life style of the "hippie" craze. Their skillful handling of observational cinema techniques creates a compelling series of portraits. In concentrating on one particular couple, they raise basic questions about family relationships, child rearing, and drug use. A landmark in the development of the *cinéma vérité* documentary.

T'AI CHI CH'UAN

1968. U.S.A.
By Tom Davenport. Sound by Tom Johnson. Performed by Nan Huei-Jin.
10 min. B&W. Sound.

Tom Davenport, who went on to make *It Ain't City Music* (1973), uses an unobtrusive, respectful approach in this study of the Chinese art of t'ai chi ch'uan. This martial art, which developed in China more than a thousand years ago, is based on the philosophy that

Al Clah and Sam Yazzie making a sandpainting for use in
THE SPIRIT OF THE NAVAJO from NAVAJOS FILM THEMSELVES (1966)

cyclic change occurs in the universe. Inspired by the movements of a crane and snake in combat, its gestures are related to self-defense. Nan Huei-Jin performs these graceful movements on a rocky coastline cliff in Taiwan overlooking the ocean. Sensitively photographed and enhanced by this natural setting, the fluid movements of t'ai chi ch'uan become powerfully evocative.

SOC. SCI. 127

1969. U.S.A.
Directed by Danny Lyon.
21 min. Color. Sound.

Danny Lyon's first film was made in Houston, Texas, and is a portrait of the late tattoo artist Bill Sanders and his "painless" tattoo shop. We see Sanders at work and teaching. Social Science 127 is a course he taught on "Tattoos: History, Myth, and Legends" at a local school. His tattoo shop is plastered with outrageous photographs of the great tattoos of his career, and while working, he talks an incredible streak on a variety of diverse subjects including gays, "wetbacks," and Vietnam.

YOU ARE ON INDIAN LAND (1969).
See National Film Board of Canada

HIROSHIMA—NAGASAKI, AUGUST 1945

1970. U.S.A.
Produced by Erik Barnouw for the Center for Mass Communication of Columbia University Press. Photographed (1945) by Akira Iwasaki. Written by Paul Ronder. Narrated by Paul Ronder and Kazuko Oshima.
16 min. B&W. Sound.

In August 1945, the United States dropped two atom bombs on Japan. The first, on August 6, destroyed Hiroshima. The second, on August 9, destroyed Nagasaki. Shortly thereafter a crew of Japanese cameramen recorded the unparalleled horror of these explosions in the two cities. Their film was confiscated by the U.S. Army and labeled "Secret." Only in recent years was it declassified and finally returned by the Department of Defense to Japan. From this footage Erik Barnouw and Paul Ronder created their film, an authentic report of what happened in Japan nearly forty years ago, a catastrophe we have yet to fully comprehend. Barnouw's subsequent production *Fable Safe* (1971) takes a satiric view of nuclear proliferation, while Ronder went on to make *Part of the Family* (1971).

FABLE SAFE

1971. U.S.A.
Center for Mass Communication, Columbia University Press. Written and directed by Erik Barnouw. Animation by John Osborn. Photographed by Ted Nemeth. Music composed and performed by Tom Glazer.
9 min. Color. Sound.

Fable Safe is an animated film essay that probes and satirizes military rhetoric and the escalation of the arms race. The cast of characters, including birdlike generals, fat atom bombs, and sharklike missiles, is used by political cartoonist Osborn to create a colorful, chaotic image of our world's weaponry. Glazer's talking-blues soundtrack exposes the paranoia behind military strategy within such terms as "intercontinental ballistic missiles," "deterrent credibility," and "bargaining through strength." An atomic explosion predicts a somber, horrid end to this folly. Applying the intellectual humor of political cartoons, *Fable Safe* is an informative anti-nuclear statement for arms control.

LLANITO

1971. U.S.A.
Directed and photographed by Danny Lyon.
51 min. B&W. Sound.

Lyon uses a sharply realistic *cinéma vérité* style to document the people of Llanito, New Mexico. Juxtaposing different aspects of the culture, he describes a town of extremes and hardship. The poverty and abandonment of the Chicanos is sensitively presented in a scene where a group of men sing and dance to Mexican songs that seem incompatible with their environment and then get drunk at the local bar. The Chicanos and Indians are contrasted with a group of patients in the local mental institution, one of whom gives a remarkable falsetto sermon on Christ. Starkly photographed in black and white, this is the first of a group of political films done by Lyon in New Mexico that explores discordant and misplaced aspects of American society.

PART OF THE FAMILY

1971. U.S.A.
Produced and directed by Paul Ronder. Photographed by Mark Obenhaus. Edited by Geof Bartz. Music by Marc Ling and Clarke Meyer.
77 min. Color. Sound.

This fine example of *cinéma vérité* is a portrait of three families who lost someone in the bitter struggles of the late 1960s: in the Vietnam War, at Jackson State College, and at Kent State University. Interweaving intimate scenes of these families with home movies, reminiscences, and footage from these three events, Ronder, who collaborated on *Hiroshima—Nagasaki, August 1945* (1970), delves into personal aspects of that era. One family, whose son was killed in Vietnam, talks about their loss and political awareness. The end of the film shows them driving to Canada, where they are contemplating moving to prevent the drafting of their other sons. The sister and young, pregnant wife of a student shot at Jackson State College while crossing the courtyard are seen visiting his grave in a segregated cemetery and talking about their anger and their plans for the future. The father of a young woman shot at Kent State University is compelling and forceful before Ronder's trusting camera. His anger very clearly expresses the frustration and feelings of helplessness of many at that time. His wife reads the examples of condolences and hate mail that they received from all over the country. This sensitive film has many powerful and moving moments when the camera seems to disappear and we are allowed glimpses into people's emotions. Not only an excellent example of the extraordinary moments this style of filmmaking can capture, *Part of the Family* is also a compelling document of the turmoil of the late 1960s.

THE SELLING OF THE PENTAGON

1971. U.S.A.
CBS News Production. Produced and written by Peter Davis. Correspondent: Roger Mudd. Photographed by William Wagner, Walter Dombow, James Kartes, Robert Clemens, Richard Francis. Edited by Dina Levitt. Executive Producer: Perry Wolff.
50 min. Color. Sound.

The high-water mark in the history of the public affairs television documentary came on February 23, 1971, with the nationwide broadcast of *The Selling of the Pentagon*. The investigative documentary in the 1960s had established a strong tradition within broadcast journalism. But *The Selling of the Pentagon* marked the first time a concerned documentarian, Peter Davis, was given the opportunity to question on a major television network the policies of the most powerful and best-financed department of the United States government. The film examines how the Department of Defense was spending vast amounts of public monies (at least $30 million annually) to propagandize its

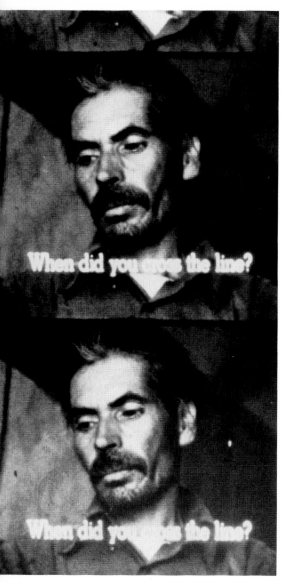

EL MOJADO (1974)

program and especially to influence the print and broadcast media nationwide. The Department of Defense is also shown using other means to influence public opinion, such as large displays of military equipment and the distribution of an extensive library of propaganda films. Excerpts from these films, which feature Jack Webb, James Cagney, Chet Huntley, and others, provide an unusual look into the process of propaganda and form a subtext to the film itself. *The Selling of the Pentagon* is presented within a conventional television format with an on-camera commentator. Its landmark status derives not from its style, but from its defiance of the central government during a period of national unrest and from the impact this had upon public opinion and public policy. As the 1970s progressed, television network programming changed, and the hour-long, single-issue, big-budget documentary was largely superseded by other formats. Thus *The Selling of the Pentagon* marks the end of an era of investigative broadcast journalism. The circulating version of the film contains some deletions: faced with litigation by some of the people who appeared in the film, the producers made cuts to facilitate its release, including an interview with former Louisiana Congressman Hébert.

CHESTER GRIMES

1972. U.S.A.
By Herbert Di Gioia and David Hancock.
30 min. Color. Sound.

Chester Grimes is a crusty old Vermont logger who is one of the last practitioners of a dying lifestyle. He uses horses to haul his lumber and myriad primitive, yet effective tools to do his work. Filmmakers Di Gioia and Hancock have used an understated and trusting camera style to portray Grimes's life and his views on his surroundings. He talks about his love for the land, examines some ruins of good old farmsteads, and angrily comments on the infringement by newcomers and summer people on the territory he knows well. What emerges is a portrait of a true loner, one who is unwilling to change with the times or to associate with society. The film is a sensitive portrait of a character of the Northeast, and of a life-style doomed to extinction.

IT AIN'T CITY MUSIC

1973. U.S.A.
Directed by Tom Davenport.
14 min. Color. Sound.

Filmed at the National Country Music Contest in Warrenton, Virginia, the oldest country music contest in the U.S., *It Ain't City Music* is an affectionate film on the roots, culture, and people of country music. Rather than concentrating on the competition, Davenport, who also made *T'ai Chi Ch'uan* (1968), shows the communal, get-together aspect of the festival. He interviews the participants, most of whom have been coming to Warrenton for years. This slice-of-Americana approach portrays how country music is changing as many of its creators have moved from the hills to towns, suburbs, and cities, altering not only the themes of country songs, but increasing the importance of contests like this one.

IRELAND BEHIND THE WIRE

(1974). *See* Contemporary British Independent Film

KENTU

1974. Republic of the Congo (now Zaire). Congo Film Production. By Herbert Risz. In French with English narration. 28 min. Color. Sound.

Kentu is an anthropological film documenting the lives of five Congolese women as they struggle to change their social roles. It gives an overall impression of the situation of black African women in the 1970s, and of African culture, kinship roles, and the importance of family. The five women in this film are from diverse economic levels, all of them in the city of Brazzaville. They are, for the most part, the sole supporters of their children and are disillusioned with men as providers. "African women are using the old family organization to their advantage," says Risz. "They maintain the forms but subvert the spirit of the institution to gain a new position in society."

EL MOJADO (THE WETBACK)

1974. U.S.A.
Directed and photographed by Danny Lyon. Produced by J. J. Meeker. Edited by Paul Justman. Sound by Ed Bevan and James Blue. In Spanish and English with English subtitles.
20 min. Color. Sound.

El Mojado is a short portrait about undocumented Mexican workers and their border crossing into U.S. territory. Contrasted with the humor and the remarkable determination of the workers (personified in a long, eloquent scene of a man building a house with adobe bricks) is the border patrol's activity of arresting, harassing, and confiscating goods from the workers. "It's like hunting an animal," says one patrolman, "but you're stalking a human being and that makes it a helluva lot more fun." This film is Lyon's political statement on the unjust and unresolved situation facing these Mexican workers.

MUKISSI

1974. Republic of the Congo (now Zaire). Congo Film Productions. By Herbert Risz. In English and Congolese dialect with English subtitles.
25 min. Color. Sound.

This documentary is a study of the subservient roles of women in a tribal Congolese society, centering on one woman who has a nervous breakdown under the strain of her responsibilities. She is treated as a victim of the Mukissi, a water spirit that personifies nature in its most raw state. The antithesis of culture and civilization, this spirit can control those who have difficulty coping with everyday life and society. The anthropological approach of this film shows the daily life of the tribal women, who do all of the planting and provide most of the tribe's food but are restricted in their diets and activities. Administrations of herbal medicine and the ritual in the long, elaborate treatment of the Mukissi-possessed woman is followed in great detail, showing the support and solidarity of the tribe as it helps her re-emerge in society. This is a fascinating study of African psychological treatment and of the intricate details of a society in which women are "needed and exploited."

LOS NIÑOS ABANDONADOS (THE ABANDONED CHILDREN)

1974. U.S.A.
Directed and photographed by Danny Lyon. Edited by Paul Justman. In Spanish with English subtitles.
63 min. Color. Sound.

This intimate portrayal of street children in a small coastal town in Colombia is singular in its view of the inside of these abandoned children's small, desolate world. An extensive social problem in Latin America, these children survive by begging or stealing food, prostituting themselves, sleeping in the streets, and looking out for each other. Lyon's film captures them so closely that they appear uncommonly at ease with the camera, always singing sad, melodic songs. With exquisite photography, the film documents details like the children assuming adult postures and crawling into the nooks and crannies of a church to sleep. Filmed in three weeks under dangerous conditions (a grip was stabbed and a cameraman was shot at), **Los Niños Abandonados** is a rare glimpse at a troubling and unresolved social problem.

ITALIANAMERICAN

1975. U.S.A.
By Martin Scorsese. Produced by Saul Rubin and Elaine Attias.
45 min. Color. Sound.

This first documentary film by Martin Scorsese, well-known for his feature films **Mean Streets** (1973), **Taxi Driver** (1976), **New York New York** (1977), **Raging Bull** (1980), and **The King of Comedy** (1983), is a touching and humorous portrait of his parents, Charles and Catherine. Scorsese uses an open *cinéma vérité* approach to create this portrait of his father and mother, their culture, and their relationship to him. On the pre-

text of documenting his mother making tomato sauce, he prods them to talk about their parents and childhoods on Manhattan's Lower East Side and Staten Island. He adds to their anecdotes with the use of old photographs and juxtaposition of new and historical footage of Orchard and Delancy Streets. More than a portrait of a marriage, **ItalianAmerican** is about the merging of two cultures. It shows a strong respect for family, for the gestures, humor, and energy of the Italian culture, and for the struggle of immigrants in this country. The recipe for Mrs. Scorsese's tomato sauce with meatballs is included.

TIME AND DREAMS

1976. U.S.A.
By Mort Jordan. Produced by Temple University.
53 min. B&W. Sound.

Time and Dreams is a questioning portrait of the effect of time and change on a community in Greene County, Alabama. Using an approach that is at times lyrical and at times condemning, Jordan explores the theme of time—how the stability of tradition and heritage hold the community together, yet the persistence of social change and segregation produce conflict and confusion in a set society. The film is harsh on those who refuse to admit how cruel "the way things were" really was, and admiring of those who choose to dream of the possibilities of social change. With consistent juxtaposition of black and white worlds, the filmmaker shows the results of transition, segregation, and an upwardly mobile black society, including the problems white children have in predominantly black schools and other very candid views of the racial situation. Ultimately, the film is a reminder of the detrimental effects of a resistance to social change, concluding that "to live in the past is to deny time's wisdom."

LITTLE BOY

1977. U.S.A.
Directed and photographed by Danny Lyon. Edited by Paul Justman. In Spanish and English with English subtitles.
54 min. Color. Sound.

Little Boy is about the difficult contrasts in Southwest U.S. life, epitomized in the title shots of Chicanos digging coal and sheep grazing in the shadow of a nuclear power plant. The "little boy" is embodied in many themes: the child whose funeral opens the film, the first atomic bomb built and detonated in New Mexico, and a troubled young Chicano,

Willie Jaramillo. Also portrayed are a solar inventor condemning nuclear power, a Chicano activist directing his anger into politics, and the protests and struggles of the Navajo Indians. Lyon's camera remains consistently unobtrusive as it observes these diversified aspects of the Southwest.

THE SHEPHERD OF THE NIGHT FLOCK

1978. U.S.A.
Directed and photographed by George Stoney and James Brown.
58 min. B&W. Sound.

The Shepherd of the Night Flock is an affectionate portrait of Pastor John Garcia Gensel and a glimpse of a unique aspect of New York's jazz community by George Stoney, who had established a reputation as a social documentarian with **All My Babies** (1952) and **You Are On Indian Land** (1969). Gensel, as pastor of St. Peter's Church in Manhattan, befriended many jazz musicians and later became their pastor, holding jazz vespers in his church. The musicians, in turn, see him as a "shepherd of modern time . . . helping to educate people to their own music." Jim Hall, Ruth Brisbane, Howard McGee, Frank Foster, Zoot Simms, and Billy Taylor are among the many jazz personalities featured in the film. Duke Ellington's fu-

Duke Ellington and Pastor John Garcia Genzel in THE SHEPHERD OF THE NIGHT FLOCK (1978)

neral is a central scene and includes a touching sermon by Gensel. Culminating with the temporary move of the congregation to a neighboring church after the sale of their church to Citicorp, **The Shepherd of the Night Flock** is a unique portrait of music and modern religion.

TATTOOED TEARS

1978. U.S.A.
By Nicholas Broomfield and Joan Churchill. A Guyo Films Production.
88 min. Color. Sound.

Tattooed Tears, one of the first films by the documentary filmmaking team of Nicholas Broomfield and Joan Churchill, who went on to make **Soldier Girls** (1981), is a relentless study of a California youth training school. In a revealing opening statement, an official explains that "our primary concern is not rehabilitation, our primary concern is the safety and welfare of the public." The school is the scene of never-ending anger and conflict; arguments about food escalate into fights, and the ceaseless room "shake down" and bodily searches reinforce an ever-present tension. Graphic portrayals of the brutality and obscenities of prison life are juxtaposed with scenes of guards training with clubs and gas masks and of a panel that determines the terms of each inmate's sentence by centering on his infractions, ignoring the relevant facts, such as one's inability to read or write. A few moments of genuine compassion alleviate the sense of hopelessness and despair when a woman guard deals sensitively with an inmate who suffers from delusions, and when we see inmates learning new skills. This disturbing and powerful film ends with an attempted suicide and the authorities' use of force and debasement to keep the inmate alive.

EL OTRO LADO (THE OTHER SIDE)

1979. U.S.A.
Directed by Danny Lyon. Sound by James Blue and Michael Becker. In Spanish with English subtitles.
60 min. Color. Sound.

Lyon concludes his series of films on New Mexico with this portrait of illegal Mexican workers. "El Otro Lado" is the workers' name for the U.S. The filmmaker follows them from their Mexican homes across the border and into the vast citrus orchards where they make their living. While documenting the injustices and discrimination they experience as they participate in the American economy, which both abuses and

needs their cheap labor, Lyon also films his subjects very poetically. Scenes of diffused sunlight and of hands picking branch upon branch are accompanied by the men's constant, calm singing. Caught between two cultures, the workers are filmed with respect and fondness.

OUTTAKES—PAYSAGE DE GUERRE

1979. U.S.A.
By Paul Brekke.
26 min. Color. Sound.

Outtakes is a meditation upon war and at the same time an attack upon the concept of war. The film is comprised largely of World War II combat news footage. The images consist of bird's-eye views of bombing runs, usually from the pilot's or bombardier's seat, and aerial views of bombed-out landscape. The rich color, overlays, multiple exposures, repetitions, and chiaroscuro effects beguile us with their beauty. At the same time the viewer recoils in the horrible knowledge that the expanding bomb bursts are wreaking death and destruction on people, cities, and countryside. The film reaches a climax in flames and burnt flesh. The surreal, dreamlike atmosphere is enhanced by the dissonant, dirge-like musical accompaniment. This is an altogether original work that introduces avant-garde technique and sensibility into the genre of the social documentary film. The filmmaker, Paul Brekke, says of **Outtakes**, "I made this film to show that the detachment from tragic events is a form of violence."

THE BATTLE OF WESTLANDS

1980. U.S.A.
Produced and directed by Carol Mon Pere and Sandra Nichols. Written by Carol Mon Pere. Cinematography by Jon Else. Edited by Irving Saraf.
59 min. Color. Sound.

In **The Battle of Westlands**, Carol Mon Pere and Sandra Nichols explore the complex problems of land use in California's Central Valley. Their film shows how the small family farmer is fighting to regain control of the land now in the hands of giant agribusiness units owned by corporate conglomerates such as Standard Oil, Southern Pacific Railroad, and Tenneco. Supporters of the large landholders claim that the vast farms make possible economies that are passed on to the consumer in lower prices. The small farmers claim that their direct, traditional involvement with the land makes for even greater economies and other advantages. They also claim

that the corporate farmers' monopolistic control over production enables them to set artificially high prices for food. The United States government has spent billions of dollars on irrigation to create 600,000 acres of some of the richest farmland in the world, but the film points out that the intent of the federal land-use program was that the land be used for small farms. The film reveals how the large landholders have succeeded in subverting the law's intent. The outcome of the struggle between the large and small farmers in the Central Valley will probably establish a precedent for solving similar land-use problems in other parts of the country and may well influence the prices that Americans pay for food for generations to come. The film identifies some of the critical issues facing the American public today. It makes a major contribution to the study of the American economy and values, and is at the same time an outstanding example of investigative film reporting. Structured to follow the seasons, the film beautifully captures the vast sweep of the land and the epic nature of the confrontation.

FAREWELL ETAOIN SHRDLU

1980. U.S.A.
Produced and directed by David Loeb Weiss. Photographed by Phillip Messina and Richard Adams. Technical advisor and narrator: Carl Schlesinger.
29 min. Color. Sound.

"Etaoin shrdlu" are the first two rows of letters on a linotype machine keyboard. **Farewell etaoin shrdlu** is a tribute to those machines. The film documents the changeover at the *New York Times* from the hot-type linotype production process to a cold-type computerized system. With striking visuals of the linotype machinery at work, the film thoroughly documents the final day of hot type at the *Times*, including typesetting, proofing, final make-up, and metal casting, and the page editors working on the first and second edition deadlines. As they watch the machines run one last time, the machine operators discuss their feelings about the replacement of this traditional printing process and training in a new electronic system. Stating that "phototechnology has conquered hot metal," the film documents the new electronic system with precision, a system that increased production from 14 to 1,000 lines per minute. **Farewell etaoin shrdlu** is a vivid document of an intricate profession stepping forward from an age-old process to a modern technological system.

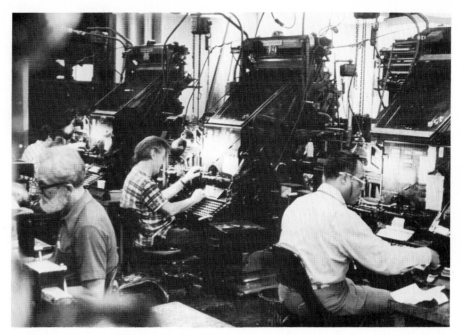

FAREWELL ETAOIN SHRDLU (1980)

STATIONS OF THE ELEVATED

1980. U.S.A.
By Manfred Kirchheimer. Streetwise Film Production. Music by Charles Mingus.
45 min. Color. Sound.

Stations of the Elevated is a poetic, visually eloquent study of subway trains and the graffiti which covers their surfaces. The film begins in the switching yards, where the trains are kept, as they rouse and change position in early morning. Kirchheimer photographs them as stunning works of art: we see them hurtle through the urban landscape, as canvases for the graffiti voices of the city and as the instruments that define the city's pulse. They are juxtaposed with images of billboards and advertisements, which the filmmaker calls "sanctioned vandalism" and "strange artifacts of 20th-century American culture." Faces are glimpsed through subway windows, a billboard is painted by a figure dwarfed by its huge features, a lone car sits on a scaffold above a highway, and subway trains read "Heaven is life, Earth is hell." With an urban, jazz soundtrack by Charlie Mingus and exceptionally beautiful photography, **Stations of the Elevated** is a political film exploring the lyrical possibilities of the medium of cinema and the visual textures of urban life.

WE ALL KNOW WHY WE'RE HERE

1980. U.S.A.
By Nicholas Holmes. Photographed by Kent Moorhead. Music by Harold Seletsky.
30 min. B&W. Sound.

We All Know Why We're Here is a portrait of a vital educational experience in an inner-city school. Leslie Stein is a teacher at Central Park East Elementary in New York City's East Harlem. Her open classroom is an extraordinary example of trust, self-expression, inquiry, and a sense of community. Believing that "children learn from each other," Stein teaches the basics through art, journals, games, storytelling, and studies of different cultures. The voices of the children form the commentary of this sensitive film as they describe their teacher and classroom activities. Glimpses of the school's desolate urban neighborhood reinforce the importance of the children's opportunity to learn in this exciting classroom and to take their lessons into the street with them. This film challenges traditional educational techniques by presenting an alternative that works.

THE SHEPHERDS OF BERNERAY

1981. U.S.A.
University Film Study Center, Harvard University. Photographed and edited by Allen Moore. Conceived, produced, and recorded by Jack Shea. Executive producer: Robert Gardner. In Gaellic and English with English subtitles.
55 min. Color. Sound.

The Shepherds of Berneray is a sensitive and visually astonishing portrait of the lives and craft of the shepherds and fishermen on one of the smallest inhabited islands of the Outer Hebrides. The film progresses through the yearly cycle of the sheep-tending tradition. Through each season we follow the sheep's herding, their transport from one island to another, their birth, breeding, shearing, and slaughter. The island is full of contrasts: both harsh and stunningly beautiful, it is fiercely loved by these people, yet owned by an absentee landlord; its treasured, traditional way of life is dying as children leave the island and the population decreases. Weaving visually arresting scenes of daily life with interviews and Gaelic songs, the film reveals the texture of life on Berneray, where the yearly cycle and the stability born of tradition are of utmost importance.

PORTRAIT OF AN AMERICAN ZEALOT

1982. U.S.A.
Produced and directed by Marc and Alan Levin. Executive producer: Alvin H. Goldstein. Photographed by Mark Benjamin. Edited by Marc Levin and Peri Muldofsky. Sound by Alvin Krinsky.

55 min. Color. Sound.

Ed McAteer, the American zealot this engaging film portrays, is an architect of the Moral Majority movement and president of the Religious Roundtable, a national organization which conjoins religion with conservative politics. McAteer is an effusive, talkative, and convincing subject, and the filmmakers provide a complex picture of this "beaming, Bible-quoting grandfather who has probably done more than anybody to bring the Bible into the voting booth." The film documents McAteer in myriad roles—at home with his family, traveling across the country raising money, convening with his fellow Roundtable members, giving speeches, and meeting with corporate leaders like Nelson Bunker Hunt, political leaders like Senator Jesse Helms, and conservative leaders like the Reverend Jerry Falwell. He elaborates on his views of the Equal Rights Amendment, sex education, abortion, prayer in the schools, nuclear war, poverty, and religious salvation. "I am, in the truest sense of the word, a religious political activist," says McAteer. "The part I play in the religious political movement began with a deep concern in my heart concerning the moral drift of the country." The film goes beyond a single portrait, though, in its riveting portrayal of the workings of the Moral Majority's political and religious machine. It captures the strength of the religious movement by documenting the religious broadcasters and the new cable television preachers, including Richard Hogue, who McAteer calls the "Christian Phil Donahue." **Portrait of an American Zealot** is a comprehensive portrayal of America's new conservatism.

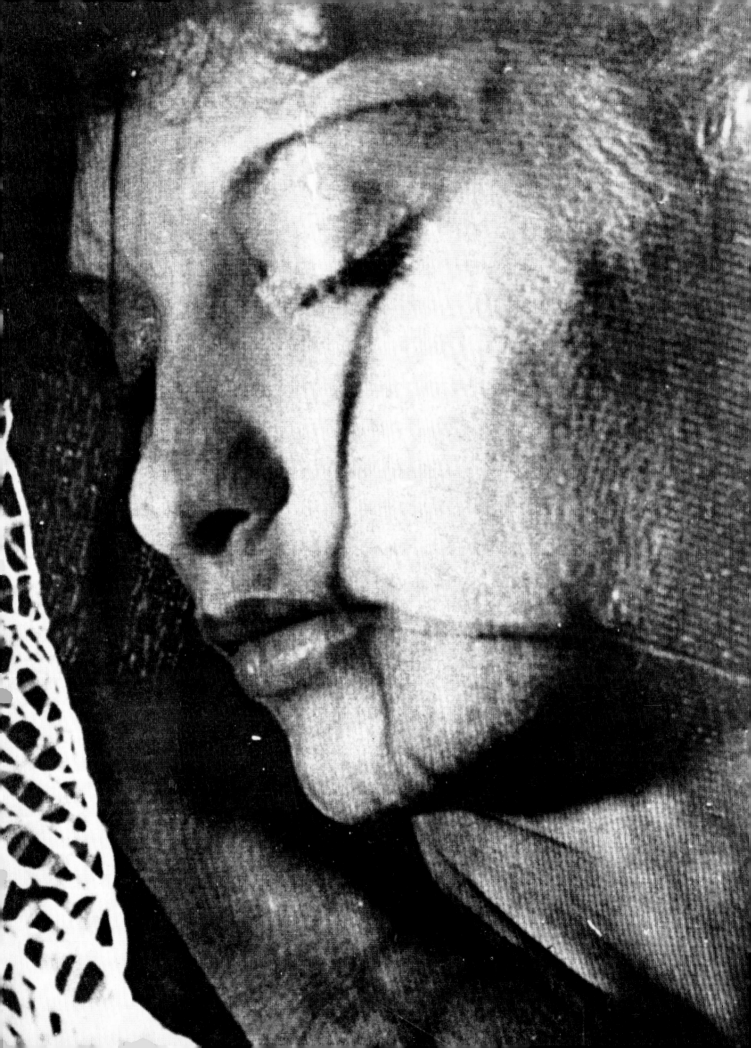

American Experimental Cinema: Breaking Away

by Lucy Fischer

I. The Movement in Context

Every breaking away from the conventional, dead, official cinema is a healthy sign. We need less perfect but more free films. If only our younger film-makers . . . would really break loose, completely loose, out of themselves, wildly, anarchically! Jonas Mekas, February 4, 1959, *The Village Voice*[1]

The American experimental cinema has long resisted definition, and even naming. Consider the wealth of labels it has amassed over the years: the art film, independent cinema, visionary film, the underground movie, new American cinema, the avant-garde.[2] The descriptive elusiveness of the genre cannot be attributed to critical indolence or inadequacy, but rather to the highly complex nature of the art form, whose boundaries and postures are difficult to fix. Though no single term has ever proven adequate to encompass the mode (or corner the critical market), all have shed light on its nature. Thus, a review of the "lexicon" of the avant-garde can clarify certain issues of definition.

The term "experimental," perhaps the most comprehensive, has historically referred to films that test new artistic hypotheses. Experimental cinema has, thereby, been identified with innovation—on both a formal and technical level. Similarly, the epithet "avant-garde" has been used to imply a commitment to change, to breaking new aesthetic ground. Thus, the experimental film has placed its faith in the inventive possibilities of the future, not the static repetition of the past.

The term "new" American cinema, on the other hand, has served to distinguish the movement from "traditional" film—the legacy of Hollywood. Experimental cinema has thereby declared itself independent of the corporate system—of its production-line work style, its marketplace aesthetics. It is this opposition to mainstream cinema that explains the notion of the "art" film as well. Rather than locate its roots solely in the commercial movies, experimental film asserts its connections to other modernist forms: painting, music, sculpture, dance, literature, and performance.

The term "visionary" film reveals yet another side of experimental cinema—its emphasis on personal expression, a trait that has linked it to the other arts. Finally, the label "underground" connotes a sense of things hidden, or illicit. Thus, experimental film has often been associated with social

Maya Deren in MESHES OF THE AFTERNOON (1943)

challenge, with the subversion of established culture.

A reading of these terms reveals a basic principle: that experimental film presupposes a norm, a bottom line against which its formal innovations, cultural critiques, and economic rebellions can be measured. Experimental cinema does not exist in isolation, for it constitutes the cinematic "other."[3] Though a breaker of codes, it nonetheless presumes an official language. As Germaine Dulac remarked in 1932: "The avant-garde and the commercial cinema . . . form an inseparable whole."[4]

First Wave

In the United States . . . England, France, Denmark, Holland, Belgium, experimental film groups of individual artists . . . have taken up the work begun by the avant-garde of the 1920s. . . . In that way, a tradition, temporarily interrupted by the stormy political events in Europe has been taken up by a young generation, here and abroad. It is obvious today that this tradition will not be eradicated again but will grow. Hans Richter, 1955[5]

The American experimental film movement came of age in two phases, each reflecting aesthetic developments in Europe. The first American avant-garde filmmakers—Ralph Steiner, James Sibley Watson, Melville Webber, Robert Florey, and Herman Weinberg—worked in the late twenties and early thirties. Their sense of the medium had been formed by an awareness of the European experimental cinema: the works of Dziga Vertov and Sergei Eisenstein in the Soviet Union; Germaine Dulac, Jean Cocteau, Luis Buñuel, and Salvador Dali in France; and Hans Richter and Viking Eggeling in Germany. Attuned to the lessons of modernism, they saw their work as part of a tradition—spanning Dadaism, Surrealism, Cubism, Constructivism, and Expressionism.

Some early experimental filmmakers came to the medium with experience in other arts. *Manhatta* (1921), one of the first avant-garde films made in America, displays this rich aesthetic heritage. Based on a poem by Walt Whitman, it was the joint project of the painter Charles Sheeler and the photographer Paul Strand. Among other prominent figures in the movement of the late twenties was Ralph Steiner, first known for his photographic work.

Parallels between the American and European avant-gardes are revealed by an examination of some early films. *The Fall of the House of Usher* (1928) pursues a brand of Expressionism forged in Germany in the late teens. And its fascination with Poe reflects the writer's privileged position in the Surrealist pantheon. Robert Florey's *The Life and Death of 9413—A Hollywood Extra* (1928) transfers continental Expressionism to the California shores; and Herman Weinberg's *Autumn Fire* (1931) pays stylistic homage to Walter Ruttmann in Germany and Dimitri Kirsanov in France. Finally, the documentary abstractions of Ralph Steiner's *H₂O* (1929) and *Surf and Seaweed* (1930) bear comparison to the work of Joris Ivens, a contemporary in Holland.

Some of the filmmakers of this generation had (or were to have) direct ties to Hollywood. Robert Florey, an immigrant from Yugoslavia, worked as a professional screenwriter in the early twenties, and Slavko Vorkapich (one of the filmmakers of *Hollywood Extra*) later became a master of commercial film montage. In 1934 Ralph Steiner collaborated with future Hollywood director Elia Kazan on *Pie in the Sky* (1935), an improvised satire on the Protestant ethic. Historian David Curtis notes that most filmmakers of this first experimental wave worked in standard 35mm gauge and hoped for access to traditional channels of film distribution and exhibition.[6] In 1935 artist Mary Ellen Bute achieved great success when her short film *Rhythm in Light* was premiered at Radio City Music Hall.

Second Wave

There seems to be a post-war revival of interest in experimental film. . . . More and more independent artists and intelligent amateurs are exploring the infinite resources of the film as a medium of personal expression, trying to catch flashing across the screen that ephemeral moment when light and shadow fuse with movement to release an emotion that could arise from no other art. Richard Foster and Frank Stauffacher, 1947[7]

The second wave of the American experimental cinema took shape in the late forties. Again, its history was tied to the European avant-garde. The political upheavals of World War II had brought Hans Richter and Oskar Fischinger to the United States in the mid-thirties; and by 1944 Len Lye was living in New York City, working for the MARCH OF TIME newsreel. With these European artists residing on native shores, the spiritual link between the American and Continental avant-gardes became more concrete. This sense of a Euro-American community is apparent in the writing of Richard Foster and Frank Stauffacher, who describe the 1946 film scene in international terms:

> In Paris, Jean Cocteau has finished . . . *La Belle et la bête.* In New York Hans Richter is putting the finishing touches on *Dreams That Money Can Buy,* with scenarios by Fernand Léger, Marcel Duchamp, Man Ray, Max Ernst, and Alexander Calder. In San Francisco, Sidney Peterson and James Broughton have completed their psychological fantasy, *The Potted Psalm.* The films of Maya Deren . . . are evoking the praise of critics and public wherever they are shown.[8]

Foster and Stauffacher were also responsible for creating an atmosphere of cultural exchange. In 1947 they organized a film series entitled "Art in Cinema," exhibited at the San Francisco Museum of Modern Art. Consisting of ten programs ranging from "Experiments in the Fantastic and the Macabre" to "Fantasy into Documentary," the series intermixed historic works of the European avant-garde with their American counterparts. Thus an evening of "Poetry in Cinema" presented Cocteau's *Blood of a Poet* (1932), Richter's *Ghosts Before Breakfast* (1928), and Watson and Webber's *Lot in Sodom* (1933).

Simultaneously, on the East Coast another experimental group, Cinema 16 Film Society, was founded at the Provincetown Playhouse in New York City. According to Amos Vogel, one of the organization's founding members, the society's goal was to present works that "comment on the state of man, his world, and his crises, either by means of realistic documentation or through experimental techniques."[9]

Other factors encouraged the growth of an American experimental cinema in the late forties. The Museum of Modern Art's Circulating Film Library, established in 1935, had been distributing works of the European avant-garde for a decade—raising the general level of cinematic consciousness. Furthermore, the movement had by then spawned several articulate spokespersons. Hans Richter, as director of the Institute of Film Techniques at the City College of New York, was an avid lecturer on the medium. Maya Deren frequently traveled with her films, leading discussions on experimental cinema. In short, a sense of "film culture" was rapidly developing.

During the postwar years, advances in portable 16mm equipment gave avant-garde artists a more economically viable technological format and freed them from rigid studio-bound restrictions. The turn away from 35mm also marked a realization that the experimental cinema was not fated for the standard commercial circuit, and that, as Jean Cocteau once stated, "The cinema will only become an art when its raw materials are as cheap as pencil and paper."[10]

In the early fifties distribution networks for avant-garde film also developed—including one associated with the Cinema 16 group. With production, distribution, and exhibition channels forged, the experimental filmmakers could finally propose an alternate model for cinema in America. This sense of a "second" cinema formed the goals of Cinema 16, which sought to bring "outstanding social documentaries, controversial adult screen fare, [and] advanced experimental films" to the public.[11]

II. Toward an Experimental Film Style

More and more filmmakers are realizing that there is no one single way of exposing (seeing) things; . . . that, really, the cinema language, like any other language and syntax, is in a constant flux, is changing with every change of man. Jonas Mekas, 1963[12]

Beginning in the late forties, the American experimental cinema set out to reinvent film language. In a radical gesture, it sought to take the cinema back to its roots, creating anew the shape in which it might grow. In so doing, the avant-garde filmmakers reconsidered the very "givens" of the classical medium: its claims to representation, its bonds to narrative, its obsession with external action, its illusionistic bias, its conventional values. Each artist posed the challenge in different terms, questioning one or another aspect of traditional film form. And, over the course of avant-garde history, each challenge was raised many times—with varying thrust and intensity.

Thus, an overview of The Museum of Modern Art's experimental film collection reveals certain patterns, or organizing principles of theme and form.

The Seventh Art

The motion-picture medium has an extraordinary range of expression. It has in common with the plastic arts the fact that it is a visual composition projected on a two-dimensional surface; with dance, that it can deal in the arrangement of movement; with theater, that it can create a dramatic intensity of events; with music, that it can compose in the rhythms and phrases of time and can be attended by song and instrument; with poetry, that it can juxtapose images; with literature generally, that it can encompass in its sound track the abstractions available only to language. Maya Deren, 1960[13]

One of the ways experimental film has traditionally defined itself has been through its interest in various art forms as models for the cinema. While commercial film has depended largely on the novel or the well-made play, experimental cinema has found inspiration in a wide range of sources: music, painting, sculpture, dance, and performance. Concurrent with this investigation of the other arts, avant-garde filmmakers have attempted to forge an aesthetic identity for film by exploring its unique formal capabilities. As Germaine Dulac wrote in 1925, the cinema was to be "freed from its chains and . . . given its true personality."[14]

This force-field between cinema and the other arts has attracted many filmmakers. Maya Deren, while borrowing from dance in *Meshes of the Afternoon* (1943) and other films, relished the cinema's special capacity for "creative geography," for transporting bodies through time and space impossible in the normal (or theatrical) world. Years later, Shirley Clarke renewed the dance/film metaphor in works like *Dance in the Sun* (1953), *Bullfight* (1955), *A Moment in Love* (1957), and even *Bridges-Go-Round* (1958).

Other experimental filmmakers have pursued the links between cinema and painting—a trend initiated in the European avant-garde by such graphic artists as Hans Richter, Len Lye, and Viking Eggeling. In the early forties, the illustrator Douglass Crockwell used an oil-on-glass technique to animate abstract images in *Glens Falls Sequence* (1946). And in the latter part of the decade, painter Jim Davis explored light, reflection, and tonal hue in works like *Light Reflections* (1948), *Analogies #1* (1953), and *Evolution* (1955). Artist Robert Breer began making abstract animated films in the late fifties. In *Blazes* (1961), *69* (1968), and *70* (1970), he employed painted imagery to realize his cinematic canvases, and in *Jamestown Baloos* (1957) and *77* (1977) he harnassed collagist techniques. More recently, in films like *Gulls and Buoys* (1972), *Fuji* (1974), and *Rubber Cement* (1976), he has incorporated the rotoscope process (tracing from live-action) into his animation work. Another artist in the field of experimental graphics is David Ehrlich, who in films like *Vermont Étude* (1977) and *Robot* (1977) has created optical effects through the use of prisma color and ink on tracing paper.

Music has also served experimental filmmakers as an archetype for cinematic form. Much of the critical literature on experimental cinema has, in fact, been peppered by references to that art. Germaine Dulac, writing in 1928, compared the visual impact of film to a musical chord.[15] And Bruce Baillie described *Castro Street*, made in 1966, as a "lesson from Erik Satie."[16] In the same year, Stan Brakhage said that the more "silently-oriented" his film work had become, the more "inspired-by-music [had been his] photographic aesthetics."[17]

A central figure to explore the cinema/music parallel was Oskar Fischinger, a German animator who came to the United States in the mid-thirties. In works like *Composition in Blue* (1935) he pursued the relationship of abstract forms to classical music, and in *Allegretto* (1936) and *An American March* (1941) he used more popular pieces to accompany his visual animation. Even certain live-action works of the experimental cinema have aspired to musical organization. *Moods of the Sea* (1942), for instance, made by Slavko Vorkapich and John Hoffman, synchronized ocean imagery with a rendition of Mendelssohn's "Fingal's Cave." Other filmmakers have pursued the cinema/music analogy in more structural terms. Bruce Baillie's *Mass for the Dakota Sioux* (1964) is clearly modeled on liturgical form, and James Broughton's *The Golden Positions* (1970) is described as "a cantata in seven parts."[18]

Avant-garde filmmakers have also embraced poetry as a source for their cinematic art. Ian Hugo's *Bells of Atlantis* (1952) is based on a prose poem by Anaïs Nin, and James Broughton's *Testament* (1974) incorporates his own verses into his filmic work. Likewise, theater has attracted experimental artists: Broughton's *Mother's Day* (1948) and *The Bed* (1968), for example are strongly influenced by a sense of stage tableaux, and Ken Jacobs's *Blonde Cobra* (1963) is marked by a tone of Hollywood "camp."

In addition to mining other aesthetic forms for their riches, American experimental filmmakers have often paid tribute to particular artists as influences upon their work. Sidney Peterson "quotes" Magritte in *The Petrified Dog* (1948), and Anita Thacher constructs an elaborate cinematic *Homage to Magritte* (1975).[19] In similar gestures, Robert Breer invokes Kandinsky in *LMNO* (1978) and Michael Snow honors Cézanne in *La Région Centrale* (1971).[20] Finally, in *Cornell, 1965* (1978), Larry Jordan creates a documentary paean to his friend and mentor, the renowned collage artist Joseph Cornell.

A Cinema of Consciousness

On the screen we can sit inside and outside ourselves at the same time. The veil between dream and reality, when suffused with light, is capable of yielding the modulations of the spirit which animates all life. Henry Miller, 1947[21]

Experimental cinema has often distinguished itself from the traditional film in its emphasis on the tension between the interior and the exterior worlds. Rather than focus on concrete, visible human actions (in what Dulac disparagingly deemed "gestures . . . comings and goings, races, [and] battles"),[22] the avant-garde film has sought to explore the intangible realms of the human mind: dream, memory, hallucination, meditation, and perception.

This trend emerged early on in the American experimental cinema with Deren's *Meshes of the Afternoon*—a psychodrama that cast the filmmaker as somnambulist/protagonist. As Deren explained, her goal was to capture interior reality: "to put on film the *feeling* which a human being experiences about an incident, rather than to accurately *record* the incident."[23]

The dream mode was also embraced by Sidney Peterson, an artist influenced by the Surrealist aesthetic. In films like *The Potted Psalm* (1946) and *The Cage* (1947), he used various image-distorting techniques to emulate mental realms. Ian Hugo, another pioneer of the cinema of consciousness, sought to embody the "multiple dimensions of our inner world."[24] In his trance film *Bells of Atlantis*, he elaborates a parallel between the origins of consciousness and the lost island of Atlantis, a site that functions as a metaphor for the subconscious.[25]

Another artist to work in the psychological tradition was Stan Brakhage, who later forged his own, more lyrical style. Profoundly influenced by psychoanalytic theory, he once envisioned a project called *Freudfilm*, which never reached fruition.[26] In the mid-fifties, however, he did make several films in a psychodramatic vein. *Desistfilm* (1954) is an expressionistic exploration of a teen-age party that focuses on the tensions of eroticism and desire. *Daybreak* (1957), a first-person narrative seen from a young woman's point of view, communicates a sense of alienation and anguish. More recently, filmmakers like Stan VanDerBeek have continued in this psychological mode. In *Mirrored Reason* (1980), for example, a woman whose face is optically bisected spouts a stream-of-consciousness monologue that is haunted by the doppelgänger theme.

In addition to the domain of dream and desire, the experimental cinema also examined other states of consciousness. Primary in its investigation was the realm of vision—not normal quotidian perception, but sight unbridled by optical and cultural conventions. This theme appeared early on in Sidney Peterson's *The Cage*, a picaresque adventure of an artist's escaped eyeball, and was elaborated in the work of Stan Brakhage, who articulated his aspirations in both his filmic and critical work. In *Metaphors on Vision*, published in 1963, Brakhage wrote:

Imagine an eye unruled by man-made laws of perspective, an eye unprejudiced by compositional logic, an eye which does not respond to the name of everything but which must know each object encountered in life through an adventure of perception.[27]

With this sense of personal vision, Brakhage created a body of cinematic work that P. Adams Sitney has labeled the "lyrical film." This genre "postulates the film-maker behind the camera as the first-person protagonist of the film. The images of the film are what he sees, filmed in such a way that we never forget his presence and we know how he is reacting to his vision."[28] This aesthetic is evident in such early Brakhage works as *The Wonder Ring* (1955), *Anticipation of the Night* (1958), and *Window Water Baby Moving* (1959), and characterizes later films like *Sluice* (1978), *@* (1979), and *Sexual Meditations #1: Motel* (1980). Bruce Baillie emerged in the sixties as another practitioner of the lyrical film, and works like *Castro Street* and *Roslyn Romance* (1977) present the world inflected by the artist's vision.

Because the goal of much experimental cinema is to present visual *experience*, and not visual *record*, it frequently dispenses with traditions of classical representation. Perspective is eliminated in a flattening of the visual plane; extreme close-ups and swish pans obliterate any clear sense of figure or ground; painting on film annihilates any sense of realistic photography;

and synthetic editing eludes any sense of a navigable space.

Avant-garde film artists have also used the medium to portray states of altered consciousness. Through its heavily layered superimpositions and intricately matted photography, Baillie's *Castro Street* emulates "the essential of *consciousness*."[29] In *Serene Velocity* (1970), Ernie Gehr dissolves the three-dimensional world into an animated pattern of geometric lines and pure shape and color "for spiritual purposes."[30] Standish Lawder's *Corridor* (1970) employs stroboscopic light fluctuations to induce heightened sensations in the viewer. In these films, the powers of cinema are seen as analogous to those of the mind: capable of transforming "objective" reality.

In recent years, the American experimental cinema has turned to yet other realms of consciousness: cognition and perception. In *Print Generation* (1974), J. J. Murphy constitutes and decomposes the soundtrack and image, testing the audience's sense of what they see and hear. Michael Snow in *Wavelength* (1967) expands this phenomenological mode by using a 45-minute zoom shot to suggest the very "movement of consciousness."[31]

Narrative Innovations

The future belongs to the film that cannot be told. . . . The cinema can certainly tell a story, but you have to remember that the story is nothing. The story is a surface. Germaine Dulac, 1928[32]

American experimental filmmakers inherited from the European avant-garde a certain distrust for narrative, and a resistance to classical story-telling modes. To these artists, the traditional structures of the novel or well-made play were seen as arbitrary and repressive grids, imposed on the cinema for their commercial value. Furthermore, they were felt to lure the viewer into a hypnotic spell, precluding more active modes of film viewing. As Amos Vogel wrote in his Cinema 16 notes, the avant-garde saw its audience as "the intellectually curious who want stimulation, not . . . the mentally tired who require routinized entertainment."[33]

So from the early years, the American experimental cinema voiced an opposition to conventional narrative form. In some films it was engaged, then subverted. In others it was studiously ignored. In some, alternative narrative structures were forged through the adoption of mythic, ritualistic, or autobiographical models. In all cases, there was an aspiration toward Dulac's ideal of the film that could not be narrated, that simply could not "be told."

This drive toward undermining logical narrative appears initially in the work of such artists as Maya Deren and Sidney Peterson. Through its dream-like structure, *Meshes of the Afternoon* presents a highly paradoxical "story"—where actions are inexplicably repeated and freed of causal constraints. Similarly, Peterson's *The Potted Psalm*, *The Cage*, and *The Petrified Dog* are highly disjointed, picaresque tales displaying the kind of liberated narrative pioneered by the Surrealists in *Un Chien Andalou* (1929). For both Deren and Peterson the tool of film editing is central to the creation of disjunctive narrative lines.

Other avant-garde artists chose to dismantle classical narrative through techniques of film collage. In *A Movie* (1958), for example, Bruce Conner combines found footage from various westerns, and pornographic and military films to advance a view of commercial cinema as fueled by the joint powers of eros and violence. In *Permian Strata* (1969) he employs a "mismatched" collision of sound and image to mock religion and its screen embodiment. In a similar vein, Ken Jacobs, in *The Doctor's Dream* (1978), has created a work entirely based on restructuring a sentimental "B" western film. Scott Bartlett and J. J. Murphy have also used assemblage techniques in films like *Heavy Metal* (1978) and *Science Fiction* (1979).

MOTHER'S DAY (1948)

In addition to tangling story lines and employing collagist techniques, experimental filmmakers have taken other approaches to narrative form. James Broughton's *Mother's Day* virtually stops narrative dead in its tracks with its frozen, atemporal tableaux. Ken Jacobs reprocesses conventional narrative in *Tom, Tom, The Piper's Son* (1971)—a revision of a 1905 Biograph film. Peter Rose laces his abstract films with teasing narrative fragments, like the man running down the hallway in *Analogies: Studies in the Movement of Time* (1977). Some filmmakers strip narrative down to its basic core. For example, the "action" of Snow's *Wavelength* has been read by Annette Michelson as simply the movement of the camera itself.[34] Other American experimental filmmakers have been strongly influenced by the Brechtian strategies of modernist European *cinéastes* like Jean-Luc Godard. Central to this group is Yvonne Rainer, who in such works as *Kristina Talking Pictures* (1976) and *Journeys From Berlin/1971* (1980) creates highly distanced, reflexive, dramatic texts that comment on the process of narration and performance.

Still other artists have attempted to supplant conventional narrative with alternative structural forms. Early on, Sidney Peterson and Maya Deren displayed interest in ritual and myth, themes apparent in *The Lead Shoes* (1949), *Mr. Frenhofer and the Minotaur* (1948), and *Meshes of the Afternoon*. In later years, the mythic impulse reappeared in the work of Ian Hugo, whose *Apertura* (1970) enacts a "myth of birth," and in the films of Scott Bartlett, whose *Serpent* (1971) "embodies the primal chaotic life force in mythic symbology."[35] On a different note, Kenneth Anger revels in pop-culture ritual in *Scorpio Rising* (1963).

Stan Brakhage has sought to modify classical mythology by formulating a personal "mythopoeia." In *Dog Star Man* (1964) he elaborates a myth of "the birth of consciousness, the cycle of the seasons, man's struggle with nature, and sexual balance in the visual evocation of a fallen titan bearing the cosmic name of the Dog Star Man."[36] This concern continues in such recent works as *The Stars Are Beautiful* (1974), where he invents comic legends for the origin of the universe. Filmmakers have invoked other primal narrative forms as source material for their art. Brakhage subtitles *The Shores of Phos* (1972) a "fable," and Bruce Baillie in *Mass* and *Quixote* (1965) draws on ancient epic form.

Autobiography is yet another narrative model that has served experimental filmmakers. Many of the early artists appeared as "characters" in their own works: Deren in *Meshes of the Afternoon*, and Brakhage as the Dog Star Man. But as the genre developed, more overtly self-referential structures took precedence. Brakhage alluded to an emotional crisis in *Anticipation of the Night*, and documented the birth of his first child in *Window Water Baby Moving*. In later works, like *Hymn to Her* (1974), he constructed filmic tributes to his wife and their domestic drama. With a similar impulse James Broughton reviews both his life and work in *Testament*. Jonas Mekas, in *Notes for Jerome* (1978), simultaneously creates an elegy for a friend and a meditation on eight years of his existence.

Optical Options

By deliberately spitting on the lens or wrecking its focal intention, one can achieve the early stages of impressionism. . . . One may over- or under-expose the film. One may use the filters of the world, fog, downpours, unbalanced lights, neons with neurotic color temperatures, glass which was never designed for a camera, . . . or one may photograph an hour after sunrise or an hour before sunset, those marvelous taboo hours when the film labs will guarantee nothing. . . . One may become the supreme trickster, with hatfuls of all the rabbits listed above breeding madly. Stan Brakhage, 1963[37]

Whereas classical film has favored realistic representation, the experimental cinema has sought to undermine cinematic illusion. Over the course of American avant-garde history that challenge has been addressed in various ways. In a work like *Blue Moses* (1962), Brakhage acknowledges the presence of the filmmaker through reflexive direct-address to the audience. In a film like *A Movie*, Bruce Conner's collage of found footage exposes the synthetic nature of filmic construction. In *Sky Blue Water Light Sign* (1972), J. J. Murphy intentionally confuses the audience about the "reality" of a pictorial landscape. Though conventional cinema usually masks its illusionistic techniques, experimental film flaunts its "hatfuls of rabbits breeding madly." So, it is no surprise that many works of the avant-garde have been openly concerned with the theme of magic: Kenneth Anger's *Rabbit's Moon* (1970 and 1978), Ian Hugo's *Through the Magiscope* (1969), and Broughton's *Testament*.

Some artists reveal the artifice of the film image by radically "disintegrating" the cinematic shot. Thus, in *Tom, Tom, The Piper's Son*, Ken Jacobs rephotographs an early Biograph short, decomposing the realistic image into abstract, amorphous shapes. In a similar vein, J. J. Murphy in *Ice* (1972) rephotographs a film through a fifty-pound block of ice, and in *Print Generation* contact-prints a film strip fifty times, diluting the image with each successive version. Will Hindle in *Watersmith* (1969) optically reprocesses footage of Olympic swimmers, and Scott Bartlett in *Metanomen* (1966) employs a catalog of optical strategies (negative imagery, polarization) to achieve an abstract effect. Adopting yet another stylistic stance, Ernie Gehr in *Serene Velocity* annihilates the depth of the photographic image by single-framing a series of zoom lens shots.

Some artists, like Anita Thacher in *Homage to Magritte*, use complex matting techniques to "embed" one shot in another, reorganizing the spatial relations of the visual world. And Bruce Baillie in *Castro Street, Roslyn Romance, Mass,* and *Quixote* utilizes intricate superimpositions to lend a viscosity to the atmosphere of the external world. Filmmakers such as Francis Thompson in *N.Y., N.Y.* (1957) employ prismatic lenses and other optical effects to transform the photographic image. And others, like David Rimmer in *Surfacing on the Thames* (1970), use the freeze-frame and dissolve to achieve a similar metamorphosis. Certain artists have used a radical repetition of imagery to produce a disorienting effect. In *Analogies*, Peter Rose generates multiple frames of the same shot, and mounts them simultaneously on the screen. Filmmakers such as Jane Aaron have also combined animated and live-action footage to create their own bizarre synthetic terrains. In *Interior Designs* (1980), for example, cartoon characters on a painted canvas move about a real three-dimensional room.

Other avant-garde artists dispel cinematic illusionism by avoiding entirely the photographic shot. In John Whitney's films—*Catalog* (1961), *Permutations* (1968), *Experiments in Motion Graphics* (1968), *Matrix* (1971), *Arabesque* (1975)—computer-generated imagery replaces conventional cinematography as the basis of film content. And in Larry Jordan's collage works, *Duo Concertantes* (1964) and *Our Lady of the Sphere* (1969), nineteenth-century engravings constitute the primary cinematic material. Finally, such abstract animators as Robert Breer and Howard Danelowitz replaced the realistic photographic image with a tapestry of painted and drawn iconography.

Another way filmmakers have challenged cinematic illusionism is to focus on the concrete materials of film itself. In Michael Snow's ⟷ *(Back and Forth)* (1969) the assertive pan shots call attention to the camera as mechanical instrument; and in *Breakfast* (1976) the tabletop dolly literally "consumes" the filmic *mise-en-scène*. Finally, in *La Région Centrale* the shadow of the camera-machine reveals it as the true filmic *auteur*.

Film Culture

We are not only for the New Cinema: we are also for the New Man. . . . We are for art, but not at the expense of life. We don't want false, polished, slick films—we prefer them rough, unpolished, but alive; we don't want rosy films—we want them the color of blood. Statement of the New American Cinema Group, 1961[38]

In addition to formal exploration, the experimental cinema has historically challenged the reigning social, psychological, and political mores of the culture. After all, the formal disjunctions of *Un Chien Andalou* and its bold imagery of sliced eyeballs were not solely advanced in the name of Surrealist aesthetics, but rather to shock the complacent French bourgeoisie.

This tendency informs the American experimental cinema as well. Many of its filmmakers have identified with an artistic counterculture—be it the "beat" movement of the fifties or the antiestablishment groups of the sixties. Others have been more directly political in their orientation. The New American Cinema Group, formed in 1960, declared itself "concerned with what is happening to Man," and rejected the purely "aesthetic school that constricts the film-maker within a set of dead principles."[39] Some of its founding members—like Emile de Antonio—remain involved in political cinema today.

The cultural critique advanced by the American experimental cinema has, however, taken many forms. Satire has historically served as a favored aggressive stance, dating back to *Pie in the Sky*. In more recent years, Bruce Conner has amassed a body of work skeptical of the American system. *Mongoloid* (1977), an assemblage of found footage set to a rock-and-roll lyric by

Devo, advances the notion of the average American as hopeless automaton. Similarly, Robert Nelson mocks racism in *Oh Dem Watermelons* (1965), an irreverent avant-garde comedy, and Stan VanDerBeek ridicules the cold war space-race in the collagist *Science Friction* (1959). Sometimes experimental filmmakers confront political issues in a more serious vein. Yvonne Rainer's *Kristina Talking Pictures* raises the issue of political concern and commitment in a generation haunted by the Holocaust.

Experimental filmmakers also critique society by breaking certain cultural and cinematic taboos. Many of the films of Stan Brakhage depict the erotic in a manner incompatible with "community standards." As he wrote in 1966: "I've many times risked jail sentences for showing films of mine which were, at the time, subject to sexual censorship laws, and will do so again if the occasion arises."[40] Ironically, even his birth film *Window Water Baby Moving* shocked audiences unprepared for its bold presentation of a natural process. James Broughton also challenges sexual taboos in his cinematic work. *The Golden Positions* relishes in explicit nudity, and *The Bed* pairs couples in homosexual as well as heterosexual arrangements.

Experimental filmmakers also attack the sacred sphere of religion. In *Scorpio Rising*, Kenneth Anger juxtaposes images of Christ with the rock-and-roll song "He's a Rebel." And in *Permian Strata*, Bruce Conner synchronizes biblical footage of a martyred apostle with Bob Dylan's lyric "Everybody Must Get Stoned."

Since the city has traditionally been the site of cultural counterrevolution in America, it holds a special fascination for avant-garde filmmakers. Specifically, they have paid homage to the two centers that spawned the experimental movement—New York and San Francisco. Thus we find, in the canon of the avant-garde, a virtual subgenre of "city symphonies"—a form originally forged in Europe with such works as *Berlin: Symphony of a Great City* (1927) and *The Man with the Movie Camera* (1929). One thinks of such east-coast eulogies as *City of Contrasts* (1931), *A Bronx Morning* (1931), *N.Y., N.Y.*, *Bridges-Go-Round*, and *Skyscraper* (1959), and of such west-coast tributes as *The Cage* and *Notes on the Port of St. Francis* (1952). For the avant-garde artist, the city is seen as a privileged site, the locale in which societal change first takes place. And it is this cultural ferment that the experimental artist wishes to generate. James Broughton writes:

Poets are not moral examples of society. Their value is in being obstreperous, outlandish and obscene. Their business is to ignite a revolution of insight in the soul.[41]

Roots

The early history of film is studded with archetypal figures: Theda Bara, Mary Pickford, Marlene Dietrich, Greta Garbo, Charles Chaplin, Buster Keaton, etc. These appeared as personages, not as people or personalities, and the films which were structured around them were like monumental myths which celebrated cosmic truths. Maya Deren, 1960[42]

Having begun this essay with the premise that experimental film defines itself in relation to the traditional cinema, let us consider further that dynamic. While it is true that the American avant-garde movement has charted a course divergent from mainstream cinema, the notion of opposition does not adequately characterize their relationship. Throughout its history the experimental movement has also been *drawn* to the classical film, and their relationship has been a decidedly love-hate affair. Richard Foster and Frank Stauffacher touch on this in their introduction to the *Art in Cinema* catalog when they characterize the avant-garde as suffering from an aesthetic "neurosis": "It exists on the back of the commercial film, and if there had not been the commercial film, there could not have been the Avantgarde."[43]

But it is the artists themselves who most poignantly communicate great affection for the classical film, albeit for certain privileged moments in its evolution. In this light, we can understand Maya Deren's fascination with such luminaries as Dietrich or Garbo, actresses the filmmaker herself rivaled in her own magnetic film performances.

This love for traditional cinema has been expressed in many ways throughout the history of the American avant-garde. Robert Breer in *Rubber Cement* affectionately recalls the cartoon character of Felix the Cat. James Broughton in *Loony Tom the Happy Lover* (1951) pays his respects to Chaplin's Tramp, and Stan VanDerBeek in *Breathdeath* (1963) dedicates his film to the comedies of both Chaplin and Keaton. Kenneth Anger in *Scorpio Rising* conjures the celluloid auras of James Dean and Marlon Brando, while Bruce Conner in *A Movie* evokes the anonymous "B" world of westerns and macho action films. Scott Bartlett in *Heavy Metal* creates an abstract, pseudo "film noir," and characters in Ken Jacobs's *Blonde Cobra* dance to an Astaire-Rogers routine, "Let's Call The Whole Thing Off." On a more ambitious level, Hollis Frampton has organized his entire filmic work to constitute a virtual "metahistory" of the cinema, paying allusive homage to figures as diverse as Sergei Eisenstein and Orson Welles.

In recent years this fascination with the classical cinema has turned toward an interest in early film as the source of all celluloid art. So, many avant-garde artists are exploring the "primitive" cinema as an inspiration for new aesthetic forms. Ken Jacobs in *Tom, Tom, The Piper's Son* transforms a naive Biograph short into a sophisticated modernist essay. And Kenneth Anger in *Rabbit's Moon* recollects the magical world of Georges Méliès. James Broughton in *The Golden Positions* invokes the 1897 filmed dance of Fatima, and in *Testament* harkens back to the trick film and melodrama in his re-creation of "The Follies of Dr. Magic." Thus these "advance guard" filmmakers have come back full circle to the very roots of cinema, in their exploration of modernist film art. For as Sidney Peterson once noted:

Film has the problem of divesting itself of much that it has accomplished, . . . starting over from scratch, returning to a time when it still had choices in the directions it might take.[44]

Notes

[1]Jonas Mekas, *Movie Journal* (New York: Collier Books, 1972), p. 1.

[2]See David Curtis, *Experimental Cinema* (New York: Dell, 1971); P. Adams Sitney, *Visionary Film* (New York: Oxford University Press, 1974; revised 1978); Sheldon Renan, *An Introduction to the American Underground Film* (New York: E. P. Dutton, 1967); P. Adams Sitney, ed., *The Avant-Garde Film* (New York: New York University Press, 1978).

[3]John Hanhardt discusses this concept in "The Medium Viewed: The American Avant-Garde Film" in *A History of the American Avant-Garde Cinema*, Marilyn Singer, ed. (New York: American Federation of Arts, 1976), p. 21.

[4]Germaine Dulac, "The Avant-Garde Cinema," *Avant-Garde Film*, p. 44.

[5]Hans Richter, "The Film as an Original Art Form," in P. Adams Sitney, ed., *Film Culture Reader* (New York: Praeger, 1970), pp. 19–20.

[6]David Curtis, *Experimental Cinema*, p. 71.

[7]Richard Foster and Frank Stauffacher, "Introductory Notes," in *Art in Cinema*, Stauffacher, ed. (San Francisco: San Francisco Museum of Art, 1947; reprinted New York: Arno Press, 1968), p. 2.

[8]*Ibid.*

[9]Amos Vogel, "Cinema 16: A Showcase for the Nonfiction Film," *Hollywood Quarterly*, vol. 4 (1949–1950), p. 420.

[10]Jean Cocteau, cited by Curtis, *Experimental Cinema*, p. 57

[11]Cinema 16 announcement, cited by Curtis, *Experimental Cinema*, p. 67

[12]Mekas, *Movie Journal*, p. 92.

[13]Maya Deren, "Cinematography: The Creative Use of Reality," *Avant-Garde Film*, p. 62.

[14]Germaine Dulac, "The Essence of the Cinema: The Visual Idea," *Avant-Garde Film*, p. 37.

[15]Germaine Dulac, "From 'Visual and Anti-visual Films,' " *Avant-Garde Film*, pp. 31–35.

[16]Bruce Baillie, *Castro Street* description, *Film-Makers' Cooperative Catalogue*, no. 5 (New York: 1971), p. 23; cited in Sitney, *Visionary Film* (1974), p. 208.

[17]Stan Brakhage, "Letter to Ronna Page (On Music)," *Avant-Garde Film*, p. 135.

[18]The Museum of Modern Art program note (January 1974).

[19]Sitney, *Visionary Film* (1974), pp. 66–67.

[20]Snow mentions Cézanne in an interview with Charlotte Townsend, "Converging on *La Région Centrale*," *ArtsCanada*, no. 152/153 (February/March 1971), p. 46.

[21]Henry Miller, "Introduction: The Red Herring and the Diamond-backed Terrapin," *Art in Cinema*, p. 5.

[22]Dulac, "From 'Visual and Anti-visual Films,' " p. 33.

[23]Deren, "Writings of Maya Deren and Ron Rice," *Film Culture*, no. 39 (Winter 1965) p. 1. Italics mine.

[24]Ian Hugo, cited in Stuart Liebman, "Program 2," *A History of the American Avant-Garde Cinema*, p. 89.

[25]*Ibid.*

[26]Sitney, *Visionary Film* (1974), p. 175.

[27]Stan Brakhage, "From *Metaphors on Vision*," *Avant-Garde Film*, p. 120.

[28]Sitney, *Visionary Film* (1974), p. 180.

[29]Baillie, *Film-makers' Cooperative Catalogue*, p. 24.

[30]Jonas Mekas, "Ernie Gehr Interviewed by Jonas Mekas, March 24, 1971," *Film Culture*, no. 53–54–55 (Spring 1972), pp. 26–27.

[31]Annette Michelson, "Toward Snow," *Avant-Garde Film*, p. 175.

[32]Dulac, "From 'Visual and Anti-visual Films,' " p. 34.

[33]Vogel, Cinema 16 program note (October 1955).

[34]Michelson, "Toward Snow," p. 175.

[35]George Amberg, cited in *Recent Acquisitions* (New York: The Museum of Modern Art, 1979), p. 41.

[36]Sitney, *Visionary Film* (1974), p. 211.

[37]Brakhage, "From *Metaphors on Vision*," p. 123.

[38]"The First Statement of the New American Cinema Group," *Film Culture Reader*, p. 83.

[39]*Ibid.*, p. 81.

[40]Brakhage, "Letter to Ronna Page," p. 138.

[41]James Broughton, *Seeing The Light* (San Francisco: City Lights Books, 1977), p. 13.

[42]Deren, "Cinematography," pp. 66–67.

[43]Foster and Stauffacher, "Introductory Notes," p. 2.

[44]Sidney Peterson, "Cine Dance and Two Notes," *Avant-Garde Film*, p. 75.

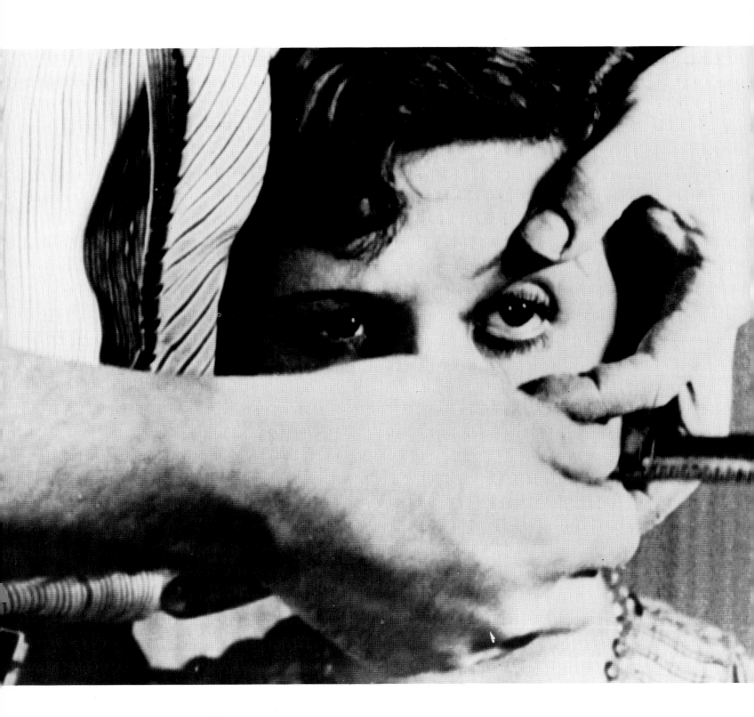

UN CHIEN ANDALOU (1929)

International Avant-Garde Film:
Scattered Pieces

by Larry Kardish

Lucy Fischer writes in her essay that American experimental cinema has "resisted definition." This is not surprising given the wide range of aesthetic and social concerns of its filmmakers and the equally diverse strategies and techniques by which these are expressed. The international titles within this experimental section are somewhat easier to categorize both because of their historic distance and Continental remove. The films in this listing reflect the chronology of the international avant-garde; as a result, someone interested in the relationship between the cinema of one period and that of another may trace how French and German filmmakers of the twenties and thirties influenced American independent film artists of the forties and fifties—artists whose successors during the sixties in turn inspired some of the European avant-garde of the seventies.

The earliest experimental films were tied inextricably to certain painters, collagists, and photographers living principally in Paris, Berlin, and Munich during the twenties. These innovative figures were working within a loose network of new and unorthodox ideas about artistic endeavor and art itself. As modern artists ("modern" meaning both a historical period and an aesthetic), they came to cinema impressed by film's seemingly limitless capacity for plasticity and eager to animate through a motion medium what in art had been "frozen" in space. The technology of cinema permitted the visual arts a new kineticism, and the first avant-garde filmmakers were anxious to explore ideas of motion and change. Among the filmmakers in this "first wave" were Viking Eggeling, the Swedish painter; Hans Richter, the German painter; Walter Ruttmann, the German painter and architect; Fernand Léger and Francis Picabia, both French painters; Man Ray, the American painter and photographer who worked in Paris, as did Alberto Cavalcanti, the Brazilian set designer; Marcel Duchamp, the French painter and collagist; Oskar Fischinger, the German painter; Salvador Dali, the Spanish painter; and Len Lye, the painter from New Zealand who began his film work in London.

Richter, looking back on the beginnings of the experimental cinema, commented in 1947 that,

In the ten years between '21 and '31 there developed an independent artistic movement in cinematography. This movement was called Avantgarde. It was the only independent artistic movement in the history of cinematography until today. This

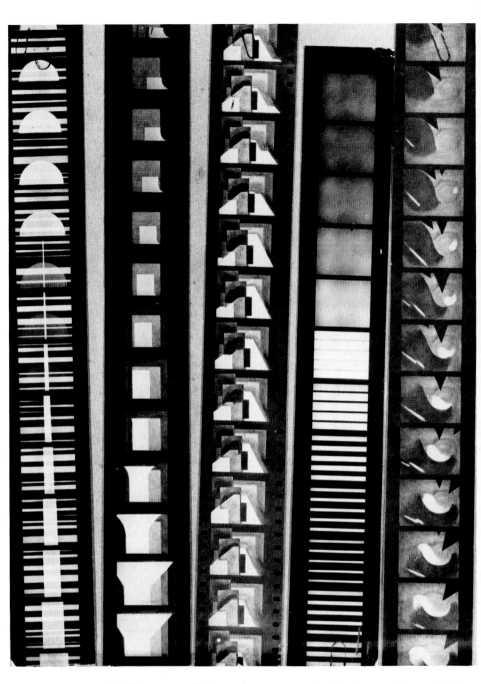

OPUS FILMS II, III, IV (1921-24)

art movement in film was parallel to such movements in plastic art as Expressionism, Futurism, Cubism and Dadaism. It was non-commercial, non-representational, but international.[1]

Because Richter was both a seminal artist and eloquent spokesperson, his description of the alliance between the graphic arts and the cinema is of particular interest. Richter's use of the term "nonrepresentational," however, does not correspond precisely to the contemporary sense of the word that now refers to an image that is wholly abstract, and complete in and of itself. Richter suggests that the avant-garde cinema grew out of "Expressionism, Futurism, Cubism and Dadaism," at a time when these movements sought to liberate themselves from traditional imagery and Renaissance perspective. The first films are indeed nonrepresentational, and are easily recognized as such: Eggeling's *Symphonie diagonale* (1924), Richter's *Rhythmus 21* (1921), and Ruttmann's OPUS series (see OPUS FILMS II, III, IV [1921–24]). Each of these is a silent, elegant orchestration of abstract forms that include lines, circles, and squares—all simple and pure.

These nonobjective works are also known by the positive name applied to them by Richter: the Absolute film. Given that Absolute films are about the motion of abstracted forms, these works are primarily animations, carefully hand drawn by the artist/filmmaker. The images mutate: the films are artificial and precise.

Preferring to work from photographed reality, Richter abandoned the Absolute film by 1926, but both Fischinger (who had been an assistant to Ruttmann) and Lye continued to investigate and enrich this form throughout their careers.

Fischinger's inspired abstractions (see OSKAR FISCHINGER PROGRAMS I–V [1923–53]) derive in part from his having photographed in stop-motion (one or more frames exposed at a time) a host of materials on variegated bases: charcoal on paper, oil on glass, wax dripped on various surfaces. On the other hand, Lye drew on the film itself, at times etching through the emulsion. As a pioneer of the "direct" film technique, in which an image is applied to the film without the aid of a camera and developer, Lye was a definite influence on Norman McLaren, who was later to become the master animator of the National Film Board of Canada.

In contrast to Absolutism, the movements cited by Richter—Expressionism, Futurism, Cubism, and Dadaism—need the quotable image, a representation no matter how abstract, to modify and elaborate. *The Cabinet of Dr. Caligari* (1920), the Expressionist classic in cinema history, gains nightmarish power primarily from its distortion of decor: sets, costumes, makeup, and lighting all working in grotesque emotional synchronism. Unlike many of the films in this experimental category, *Caligari* is not the work of one man, but a collaboration among its designers, writers, director, performers, and producer. Although stylistically daring, it is also distinct in that it was specifically made as a commercial enterprise intended for major theatrical release.

Cubism, to a large extent, is based on variations in perspective and on how the surface of a given object, whether moving or at rest, appears from different points of view. The sightline possibilities are seemingly infinite, and the impetus is usually formal and architectonic. Several alternatives may be presented within or upon a single plane.

Ballet mécanique (1924), created by Fernand Léger in collaboration with Dudley Murphy, is regarded as a Cubist film partly because it was made by Léger, one of the most celebrated Cubist painters. The visual tension of Cubist painting derives from the competition of various perspectives on a two-dimensional surface. In film this competition is neither as dramatic nor dynamic as in painting. Instead of appearing within the stationary confines of a single frame, in film these perspectives are spread out in time and obey a chronological succession. While some of the images in *Ballet mécanique*, particularly those of mechanical objects, are manipulated for form's sake, others, like the famous sequence in homage to Duchamp of a woman forever ascending a staircase, have a provocative intent. Duchamp, himself principally a Dadaist, used letters as a kind of abstract word play in his animated, spiral-infested, anagrammatic *Anemic Cinema* (1926). Although Cubism suffers in translation to film, the bridge-and-horse sequence in Eisenstein's kinetic visualization of history, *October* (1928), is both Cubistic and cinematically powerful.

Hans Richter's useful anthology film, FROM DADA TO SURREALISM: 40 YEARS OF EXPERIMENT (1961), actually journeys from Absolutism to Cubism to Surrealism and back to Dada. Nevertheless, Richter's title does make a distinction between Dada and Surrealism, and since these modern movements are particularly influential on the course of experimental cinema, it is instructive to look at them more closely.

Dada preceded and in a way was absorbed by Surrealism: both connect images of familiar objects and events in unfamiliar ways. Conventional notions of causality and landscape do not apply: everything is unexpected. Strangeness and unorthodoxy reign; the spectator is forced constantly to reorient himself. How and why the images disconnect distinguish Surrealism from Dada.

Dada is a reaction, originally an angry one. Born of the First World War in 1916 Zurich, its artist-agitators held attitudes that were antimilitaristic, anticlerical, and antiaesthetic. By the time experimental cinema assumed the pose of Dada eight years later, its bite was less pained and ferocious. Latecomers to what could then barely be called a movement, these filmmakers wanted to provoke, upset, and generally *épater le bourgeois*. Anarchic and subversive, Dada cinema is a mischievous rebellion against the unagitated, a lively response to the stultifications of middle-class life.

Dada is also the imagination run riot, and the result is stirring, absurd, and comically outrageous. All this describes René Clair's *Entr'acte* (1924), probably the most mirthful example of Dada. Made as an intermission piece for the Ballets Suédois, *Entr'acte* was filmed from a scenario jotted down by Francis Picabia and accompanied by an orchestral score composed by Erik Satie. Man Ray, Marcel Duchamp, Picabia, Jean Borlin, Rolf de Maré of the Ballets Suédois, and Satie appear in this nonnarrative succession of amusing and unpredictable events. Richter's *Ghosts Before Breakfast* (1928) also enjoys sabotaging expectations. Ordinary appliances and vestments proclaim their own laws of gravity in this merry pixillation that passes itself off as a model of sobriety. Playfulness also marks Duchamp's *Anemic Cinema*, in which verbal and visual puns hypnotically draw the viewer into the vortex of its revolving images.

In films of Dada there is a madcap sense of the fantastic. There is little madcap about Surrealism. Indeed, where Dada may laugh, Surrealism takes itself seriously. Dada may be rebellious, but it is not cruel—Surrealism can be. Because it is basically absurd, Dada cinema often makes it impossible to read sensible connections between the events in its film. However, in Surrealism connections may be discerned.

Surrealism is an investigation of the unconscious. While Dada recognizes that social and sexual repression exist, Surrealism attempts to express these submerged feelings through Freudian or poetic symbology. While Dada attacks the bourgeoisie for its sensibility, Surrealism reveals what that sensibility hides: sexuality and power. Surrealism focuses on the pre-language mind, on pictures not words, on forbidden ideas clandestinely visualized.

In the history of experimental film, the key transitional work between Dada and Surrealism is the Luis Buñuel-Salvador Dali collaboration, *Un Chien Andalou* (1929). Buñuel admitted making *Un Chien Andalou* in part as a reaction to those contemporary avant-garde films created as "art for art's sake," such as Jean Epstein's hauntingly beautiful *The Fall of the House of Usher* (1928) on which the young Buñuel himself had worked as an assistant. Buñuel and Dali did not want *Un Chien Andalou* to be beautiful, but rather a "despairing call to murder." *Un Chien Andalou* is a belligerent film; it opens with one of the most visually threatening sequences in cinema history, and sustains its pugnacity throughout. It is scabrous, wicked, and shockingly funny. Like the original Dada, it is antiaesthetic and anticlerical; like a Surrealist work, it moves as if in a dream. The peculiar disjunctions of *Un Chien Andalou* are made even more disconcerting by being framed in rather conventional narrative strategies: proper intertitles locating time and place, performances that are straight-faced. No less disturbing is *The Seashell and the Clergyman* (1928), a definitive work of Surrealism made by Germaine Dulac from a scenario by Antonin Artaud. Although *The Seashell*

THE FALL OF THE HOUSE OF USHER (1928)

and the Clergyman is not explicitly sexual, it is unsettlingly erotic. The film is overgrown with mysterious ciphers (what is the seashell of the title?) by which the eponymous churchman deals with the "ugly" aspects of his subconscious.

The coming of sound in 1929 was not necessarily a blessing for the independent filmmaker. Experimental film artists decried sound as an impure addition to an already fully expressive art; several simply did not have the financial and technological means to explore the expanded medium. Others adapted more easily to these changes. René Clair, who had returned to the making of feature-length films, completed three narratives within the French commercial film industry, *Sous les toits de Paris* (1930), *Le Million* (1931), and *À Nous la liberté* (1931), each of which is distinguished by its fresh and original use of music and dialogue. In 1929 Richter completed a three-reel burlesque of a fair, the sound film *Everything Turns, Everything Revolves!* (an excerpt is included in FROM DADA TO SURREALISM); Walter Ruttmann, having finished his first sound documentary, *Melody of the World*, in the same year, went on in 1930 to complete a symphonic film without images, *Weekend* (now believed lost).

Oskar Fischinger never hesitated about exploring sound, and his earliest films in the STUDY series (dating from the late-twenties) were absolute abstractions that moved in rhythm to jazz or classical music. Supporting himself by making theatrical commercials like *Muratti Gets in the Act!* (1934) and *Muratti Privat* (1935?), Fischinger was virtually the only filmmaker on the Continent to work continually through the mid-thirties on a personal experimental cinema.

By the time Fischinger left for America in 1936, the only major experimental filmmaker working in Europe was Len Lye. Lye worked in England for the General Post Office and the Ministry of Information, where he made the brilliant "message" animations, *A Colour Box* (1935), *Trade Tattoo* (1937), *Swinging the Lambeth Walk* (1939), and *Musical Poster No. 1* (1940). Lye's protege at the GPO, Norman McLaren, moved to New York (*Dots* [1940]), and then to the National Film Board of Canada, working under wartime commissions and practicing his own art while making films of persuasion. Even considering the mildly propagandistic intents of the Lye films and McLaren's *V for Victory* (1941) and *Keep Your Mouth Shut* (1944), these works are among the most plastic and endearing animations ever made.

In 1944 Lye, too, came to America and worked for the film newsmagazine THE MARCH OF TIME. Fischinger had earlier had a discouraging experience with the Disney studio; he had worked on an episode for *Fantasia* (1940) that was subsequently excised. Richter, who came to the U.S. in 1941, concentrated for the next several years mainly on his scroll-paintings. With the transplantation of its major figures to the New World, European experimental cinema was virtually extinguished.

During the late thirties a number of American painters, including Mary Ellen Bute, Douglass Crockwell, Dwinell Grant, and James Davis, turned to film for reasons similar to those of the first generation of French and German painters. However, the America independent cinema was ultimately not to be characterized by a formal quest for plasticity. In 1943 a young woman, Maya Deren, made the signal film of what became the New American Cinema, *Meshes of the Afternoon*, and three years later, Sidney Peterson and James Broughton completed *The Potted Psalm*. Both these films, and Deren's later work, established the major direction that independent American filmmaking was to take, and it was not that of the European graphic artists. Deren and Broughton came to film as self-taught filmmakers, as original artists determined to use film for its very own expressive properties. That their early works have surreal elements and express an interest in the subconscious experience is notable; if a link can be made between the earlier European avant-garde and the New American Cinema, it is here.

Hans Richter, who had taken a brief sabbatical from filmmaking, returned with a new enthusiasm. Over a period of three years he produced and directed *Dreams That Money Can Buy* (1947), a feature-length film that is as comfortable in the company of Germaine Dulac's *The Seashell and the Clergyman* as it is with Maya Deren's *Meshes of the Afternoon*. Richter collaborated with Max Ernst, Fernand Léger, Man Ray, and Alexander Calder on this episodic film in which a poor poet offers his listeners a series of dreams appropriate to each individual. Each dream is shaped after the vision of the contemporary artist who created the episode. In retrospect, this film turned out to be the poignant transatlantic swan song of the first generation of European avant-garde filmmakers.

During the fifties and into the mid-sixties there seemed to be little experimental filmmaking activity in Europe. What did emerge in the late-sixties was inspired to a modest extent by the American avant-garde filmmakers whose work began to be circulated in Europe. A number of young people, particularly in the Federal Republic of Germany and in England, unattached to the earlier avant-garde filmmaking tradition, began making films according to their own original and often rigorous aesthetic: American-born Steve Dwoskin and Malcolm LeGrice working in Britain; Klaus Wyborny, Wim Wenders, Werner Nekes, and Brigit and Wilhelm Hein in West Germany. At first without any financial encouragement or showcases for their work, these filmmakers, like their earlier American counterparts, made films for the sake of making films. Soon after, however, they began

RIDDLES OF THE SPHINX (1977)

to receive some minimal support from public funds. Although not too much should be made of these subsidies, they did allow avant-garde filmmaking to develop again in Europe.

The contemporary international films in The Museum's Circulating Library are for the most part from England, Germany, and Australia. However, today there is also considerable avant-garde activity in Japan, Holland, Italy, and a growing movement in France. The Museum's collection is formed around the work of certain key international filmmakers. Each is a leading independent filmmaker in his/her country with a significant body of original work of international significance: from Britain, Peter Greenaway and the filmmaking team of Laura Mulvey and Peter Wollen; from the Federal Republic of Germany, Klaus Wyborny; and from Australia, Paul Winkler.

Laura Mulvey and Peter Wollen are exploring new approaches to narrative in cinema. Their three films, *Penthesilea* (1974), *Riddles of the Sphinx* (1977), and *Amy!* (1979), employ explicit formal strategies in dealing with the narrative aspect. In *Riddles of the Sphinx* the story is straightforward and familiar, but the manner in which it unfolds is ingenious and effective. The narrative comments upon itself through a myriad of devices, including the rotation of the camera and the use of silence. Like *Riddles of the Sphinx, Amy!* is "committed to feminist politics . . . to problems of desire and self-construction, which inflect and disturb the whole course and nature of social practice."[2] *Amy!* is as much about the society that broke her spirit as it is about the once celebrated aviatrix Amy Johnson. It uses biography as base material, but is structured like a collage, comprised of different kinds of film material (newsreels, "acted" moments, actual interviews) that have particular meaning in themselves yet when edited together create a rough, elliptical, and barbed perspective. Mulvey-Wollen collaborations are richly nuanced and they must be listened to as carefully as they are watched.

Peter Greenaway and Mulvey-Wollen make very different kinds of experimental films. However, they do share a canny use of soundtrack. That language is important for Mulvey and Wollen is not surprising, given that each is a noted writer. Mulvey is known in Britain for her essays on film criticism and feminism, and Wollen for his book on the semiological theory of cinema.[3] Greenaway, however, came to filmmaking through his employment with the Central Office of Information in London. In addition to developing a valuable sense of paranoia, his work with the COI taught Greenaway that with regard to information, what is said is often of less interest than what is unsaid. Although a lot is said, or rather imparted solemnly, in Greenaway's hilariously oddball films, the humor resides in the lacunae—in all the delicious information that is left out. This information may be about defenestration in Wardour (*Windows* [1975]), the ornithologist Tulse Luper's preoccupation with the number 11 (*A Walk Through H* [1978]), a domestic argument conducted over the telephone (*Dear Phone* [1977]), or about the limited activities of the Institute of Reclamation and Restoration (*Vertical Features Remake* [1979]) or the ninety-two victims of VUE, the otherwise unexplained Violent Unknown Event (*The Falls* [1980]). The ordered knowledge of the soundtrack is married to images that are at once spontaneous, romantic, and seemingly indefinite. The way the images, some of which are quite beautiful, relate (or don't) to each other and to the soundtrack is original and funny; that Greenaway sustains the humor, particularly with the visual complexities of *Vertical Features Remake*, is remarkable. Whether the work is appreciated as parody or not, Greenaway's irony is sly and unmistakable; it continually subverts us—not in any devastating way, but just to the point where we can't rest too assured that we know what is coming next. Greenaway is part Dada.

Paul Winkler, born in Germany, is now a mason in Australia. He takes pride in his craft, and his earnings make his filmmaking possible. Lucy Fischer has observed that his artisanship "is apparent in the technical care and skill with which he assembles his cinematic work."[4] His films are intense kinetic experiences: striking, pulsating, and rich. Composed of brief shots, some with multiple exposure, some on a screen split with the precision and elegance of architecture, Winkler's films are made patiently and precisely incamera. His soundtracks are just as exactingly "composed" of natural sound pieces that are repeatedly played back in an insistent aural symmetry. Winkler's images are everyday subjects—trees, flowers, cars, bridges, and people—in a backyard, on a beach, over the harbor. The films begin as neutral, abstracted landscapes, but gradually, with the quick play of images that with slight variation are similar to one another, and the play of afterimages that are left in the mind's eye after the image itself has actually left the screen, those abstracted landscapes become abstractions in themselves. The screen becomes a blaze, both pacific and furious, of colored shapes choreographed in sharp, compelling rhythm. *Brickwall* (1975) is a celebration of texture, and although at first it seems to be undifferentiated surface, Winkler's clean, syncopated editing entices our eyes into noticing the difference between the individual bricks and into savoring the irregular facade—knobs, plaster, holes, and all.

It is with Klaus Wyborny that the collection comes, so to speak, full circle. His work is visually startling, staccato, and bare: Wyborny is perhaps the most rigorous of all German filmmakers. Although trained as a mathematician, he has also worked as a long-distance truck driver and his films are marked by the logic, discipline, and planning that a complicated delivery schedule might demand. However, into his pre-shooting "score" Wyborny also orchestrates chance. This rigor gives his work its toughness; the sense of creeping unknown gives his films their lyricism. *Six Little Pieces on Film* (1979) raises its unexceptional landscape images to a kind of musicality. Although the few shots that constitute this work are unremarkable, they form a visual unit, with a theme played in so many variations that the shots are freed from their materiality and rise like so many notes. The oddly titled *Unreachable Homeless* (1978) seems to create a strangely placid and aqueous zone somewhere between the screen and the viewer. Wyborny cites Ken Jacobs as an American influence, and Jacobs's *Tom, Tom, The Piper's Son* (1971) also seems to have inspired his 1973 film *Die Geburt der Nation (The Birth of a Nation)*. However, unlike *Tom, Tom, The Piper's Son* which uses found footage, Wyborny's film is staged. The two-sectioned *Die Geburt der Nation* begins with an announcement that it takes place in 1911. A kind of narrative follows in which a group of men living in a barren landscape attempt societal cohesion. As soon as the idea of narrative is established, Wyborny at once starts to perform a dazzling reduction. The story shots are repeated so abruptly, persistently, and discursively, and with such tearing overlays, that their content dissolves into the colored illumination of the projector's light. The images, subject to the force of the filmmaker's energy, become so much shadow, scratch, emulsion, and grain. Meaning disappears and Wyborny leads us back with exultant simplicity to an Absolute Cinema.

Notes

[1]Hans Richter, "A History of the Avantgarde," in Frank Stauffacher, ed., *Art in Cinema* (San Francisco Museum of Art, 1947; reprinted New York: Arno Press, 1968), p. 6.

[2]Laura Mulvey and Peter Wollen, "Synopsis of *Riddles of the Sphinx*," *Catalogue of British Film Institute Productions 1977–1978* (London: BFI, 1978), p. 49.

[3]See Peter Wollen, *Signs and Meaning in the Cinema* (London: Secker and Warburg, and Bloomington: Indiana University Press, 1969).

[4]Lucy Fischer, "The Independent Cinema of Paul Winkler," Circulating Film Library brochure (New York: The Museum of Modern Art, 1978).

ANNOTATIONS
Lucy Fischer, Larry Kardish, Herbert Reynolds, Ron Rollet, Marita Sturken

THE CABINET OF DR. CALIGARI (DAS CABINET DES DR. CALIGARI)
(1920). *See* Silent Fiction

MANHATTA (1921). *See* Documentary Film

OPUS FILMS II, III, IV

1921–24. Germany.
By Walter Ruttmann.
Total program: 10 min. B&W. Silent. 18 fps.

OPUS II

1921.
2 min.

OPUS III

1924.
5 min.

OPUS IV

1924.
3 min.

ENTR'ACTE (1924)

Walter Ruttmann's **Lichtspiel Opus I** (1921) is thought to be one of the first abstract, animated films seen by a general audience. Ruttmann, who was an architect, painter, and musician as well as a filmmaker, continued his work in abstract film for the next few years, and his **Opus II**, **Opus III**, and **Opus IV** were widely shown in Europe. The techniques for producing these early films are not fully understood, though it is known that Ruttmann used clay forms molded on sticks which, when turned, changed their visible shapes and that he painted directly on glass. The simple, studied images of these **Opus** films are highly evocative: geometric shapes converge; forms resemble waves, comets, and swimming motions; bands of black and white pulsate in and over one another. One of Ruttmann's primary objectives was to fuse sound and image, so that tones of music would be made visible in light and color. To this end he had musical scores specifically composed for his films. The opening German title on this compilation, added recently, states that although the **Opus** films had been originally produced in color, Ruttmann returned to black and white later in his work.

—

RHYTHMUS 21

1921. Germany.
By Hans Richter.
3 min. B&W. Silent. 18 fps.

Rhythmus 21 is Hans Richter's first film, made simultaneously with Viking Eggeling's **Symphonie Diagonale** (1924), the earliest version of which was completed in 1921. Richter went on to make **Rhythmus 23** (1923) (see **From Dada to Surrealism** [1961]) and **Rhythmus 25** (1925). In this first of the series, originally known as **Film ist Rhythmus**, he experiments with square forms. These forms appear in very simple to very complex compositions—from the beginning shots where the squares occupy the entire screen, to compositions with squares within the frame. The effect is a subversion of the cinematic illusion of depth. Richter creates a precise rhythm with the movement of these shapes. "The simple square of the movie screen could easily be divided and 'orchestrated,'" wrote Richter in 1952. "These divisions or parts could then be orchestrated in *time* by accepting the rectangle of the 'movie canvas' as the form element . In other words, I did again with the screen what I had done years before with the canvas. In doing so I found a new sensation: *rhythm*—which is, I still think, the

chief sensation of any expression of movement."

—

OSKAR FISCHINGER PROGRAM V

1923–27. Germany.
By Oskar Fischinger.
Total program: 18 min. B&W and color. Silent. 18 fps.

WAX EXPERIMENTS

1923.
6 min. B&W.

THE BOXER

ca. 1925.
30 sec. B&W.

CHARCOAL STUDY FOR SPIRITUAL CONSTRUCTIONS

ca. 1925.
10 sec. B&W.

IRENE DANCES (IRENE TANZT)

ca. 1925.
30 sec. B&W.

SPIRALS (SPIRALE)

ca. 1926.
2 min. B&W.

R1

1927?
5 min. Part color.

MUNICH-BERLIN WALKING TRIP (MÜNCHEN-BERLIN WANDERUNG)

1927.
4 min. B&W.

This program of films by the animation pioneer Oskar Fischinger (see **Oskar Fischinger Program I** [1930–34]) is a collection of his early experiments in a variety of media. It provides an insight to his working process and the diversity of his films. Fischinger worked with wax in the early 1920s but most of these films have been lost. *Wax Experiments* shows fragments of several different versions of this early footage, in which wax slicing techniques are combined with other kinds of animation. *The Boxer*, the only remaining example of Fischinger's wax modelling, shows two fighters beating each other out of shape while two waterboys look on. *Charcoal Study for Spiritual Constructions* is an initial study for his silhouette film *Spiritual Constructions* (see **Oskar Fischinger Program IV** [ca. 1927–42?]), which was finally executed in wax on glass. *Irene*

Dances is an example of cutout animation, which Fischinger described as "Circus: Foxtrot." *Spirals* is an early example of Fischinger's experiments with radiating concentric and spiralling shapes that create the optical illusion of depth and an infinitely distant vanishing point. *R1* was composed by Fischinger as a compilation of his various experiments from the early 1920s, containing samples of sliced wax, cutouts, liquids, and hand-drawn shapes. Some footage is tinted, and originally the film was shown with multiple projectors to make a multicolor image. *Munich-Berlin Walking Trip* was made in the summer of 1927 when, because of financial and legal difficulties, Fischinger moved to Berlin, where the film business was more profitable. He walked to Berlin from Munich and recorded his journey in a visual diary composed of single-frame images of people and scenes. The film is both comic and a fascinating document of pre-World War II rural Germany.

LE RETOUR À LA RAISON

1923. France.
By Man Ray.
3 min. B&W. Silent. 18 fps.

Man Ray, an avant-garde artist known for his innovative work in photography, has made in this film a series of visual and kinetic experiments in the cinematic form. Weaving abstract and concrete images, positive and negative exposures, static and moving objects, Ray creates a catalog of techniques—including his own "rayographs," cameraless contact prints of objects on paper and film—that later filmmakers working in the experimental genre would explore and define. See also Man Ray's *Emak-Bakia* (1927) and *Les Mystères du Château du Dé* (1929).

RHYTHMUS 23 (1923). See **From Dada to Surrealism** (1961) in Film Study

BALLET MÉCANIQUE

1924. France.
By Fernand Léger. Photographed by Dudley Murphy.
15 min. B&W. Silent. 18 fps.

This film remains one of the most influential experimental works in the history of cinema. The only film made directly by the artist Fernand Léger, it demonstrates his concern during this period—shared with many other artists of the 1920s—with the mechanical world. In Léger's vision, however, this mechanical universe has a very human face. The objects photographed by Dudley Murphy, an American photographer and filmmaker, are transformed by the camera and by the editing rhythms and juxtapositions. In *Ballet mécanique*, repetition, movement, and multiple imagery combine to animate and give an aesthetic *raison d'être* to the clockwork structure of everyday life. The visual pleasures of kitchenware—wire whisks and funnels, copper pots and lids, tinned and fluted baking pans—are combined with images of a woman carrying a heavy sack on her shoulder, condemned like Sisyphus (but through a cinematic sense of wit) to climb and reclimb a steep flight of stairs on a Paris street. The dynamic qualities of film and its capacity to express the themes of a kinetic 20th-century reach a significant level of accomplishment in this early masterpiece of modern art.

ENTR'ACTE

1924. France.
Directed by René Clair. Script by Francis Picabia. With Erik Satie, Francis Picabia, Marcel Duchamp, Man Ray, Jean Borlin, Rolf de Maré.
14 min. B&W. Silent. 18 fps.

Entr'acte is a veritable encyclopedia of the cinema of magic: the image plastic and kinetic, the sensibility comic, inventive, charming, and absurd. Made as intermission entertainment for the *Ballets Suédois*, from an impromptu scenario by Francis Picabia and accompanied originally by an orchestral score by Erik Satie, the film stars a who's who of the Dada movement in Paris at the time. The plot, a series of improbable adventures, is inconsequential except as an excuse for Clair to explore the limits of the medium: the camera is run forward and in reverse, tipped side to side and upside down; the film is single-framed, undercranked, and run at high speed; the resulting action is animated, sped up, slowed down; the visuals are superimposed and transformed through various matte frames; the viewer is caught up and assaulted by the frenetic pace of the recorded and edited image. The sum of these parts is a charming but challenging vision of Paris as a world of the imagination and the Dadaist intellectual conceit.

SYMPHONIE DIAGONALE

1924. Germany.
By Viking Eggeling.
7 min. B&W. Silent. 18 fps.

Throughout the development of the experimental film there has existed a common interest in the relationship between cinema and music. A direct line of continuity can be defined from the work of Hans Richter (*Rhythmus 21* [1921]), Walter Ruttmann (**Opus II, III, IV** [1921–24]), and Viking Eggeling to that of contemporary filmmakers like John Whitney (whose theory of "Digital Harmony" is expressed in *Permutations* [1968] and detailed in *Experiments in Motion Graphics* [1968]). Viking Eggeling was concerned with the discovery of visual analogs to parallel musical composition. In *Symphonie Diagonale* he has created a feeling of orchestration, and of simultaneity and rhythm, through graphic alternation and variations on a theme. There is an almost three-dimensional quality given to the film medium in his technique of progressive emergence and withdrawal of abstract forms. Pattern, tone, contrast, tempo—all find animated counterparts in this example of "pure cinema."

MÉNILMONTANT (1925). *See* Silent Fiction

ANEMIC CINEMA

1926. France.
By Marcel Duchamp, assisted by Man Ray and Marc Allégret.
7 min. B&W. Silent. 18 fps.

This is the only film by the Dada artist Marcel Duchamp, and one of the central works of what P. Adams Sitney calls the "graphic cinema." The title itself—"anemic" is an anagram of "cinema"—gives a clue to the sardonic wit that pervades the film. It consists entirely of a series of rotating, spiral-like images intercut with spinning disks of words strung together in elaborate and nonsensical puns. (Duchamps links *ecchymoses* [welts], *esquimaux* [eskimos], and *mots exquis* [exquisite words], in one sentence.) The power and significance of *Anemic Cinema* lies in the visual tension between the optical illusion of depth in Duchamp's roto-reliefs and the word plays which, even though laid out in a spiral form similar to the graphic designs, are perceived as "text" and thus two-dimensional. Man Ray (see *Le Retour à la raison* [1923], *Emak-Bakia* [1927], *L'Étoile de mer* [1928], and *Les Mystères du Château du Dé* [1929]), and Marc Allégret, who became an an important French feature director (*Fanny* [1932] and *L'Arlésienne* [1942]), worked with Duchamp in the making of this classic experimental film.

FILM STUDY (FILMSTUDIE) (1926).
See **From Dada to Surrealism** (1961)
in Film Study

RIEN QUE LES HEURES

1926. France.
By Alberto Cavalcanti. French titles only.
45 min. B&W. Silent. 18 fps.

One of the most famous of a genre referred to as "city symphonies," **Rien que les heures** is an interweaving of documentary, experimental, and narrative elements that provides a vivid image—really a series of images—of Paris in the mid-1920s. The director, Alberto Cavalcanti, who went on to become a major force in John Grierson's GPO Film Unit, made this film without sponsorship; as such and because of its length it represents an early and major independent production. Following a progression over the period of a day, the camera concentrates on the human side of the city—its workmen, shopkeepers, concierges. But what distinguishes Cavalcanti's film is the social conscience of his camera's eye: he satirizes the life-styles of the rich (like those who return from a late night on the town, carefully stepping from their cab across a water-filled gutter but dropping a fancy doll which is swept away down the drain); he also sympathetically tells the story of a prostitute (who is used by her pimp to cover the robbery and murder of a young woman who sells newspapers). The narrative sequences are developed with a surprising amount of detail, including the intercutting of a scene where the fated papergirl's death is foreseen by a fortune teller. There is, as well, a sense of wit in the carefully shot sequence of a man dressing a woman—complete with sexual innuendo, extended by using only details until the camera reveals in full shot that the model is a mannequin in a store window, while the man casually stuffs a feather duster in her arm and begins work on another figure. Throughout the film, Cavalcanti was exploring experimental cinema techniques. A series of contrasting shots of fresh fruit and vegetables in a public market with shots of garbage cans full of rotting leftovers are connected by a diagonal splicing technique where one image appears to "wipe" another off the screen. The multiple exposures and spinning camera movement in shots from a carousel capture effectively the frenetic life of city entertainments, while the hand-painted and manipulated frames of the murdered girl heighten the viewer's feeling of shock and horror. In the end, **Rien que les heures** achieves its significance by virtue of its myriad of glimpses into the life and appearance of this particular city at one specific time: the traffic beginning to clog the main thoroughfares, the back alleys and side streets with their shuttered windows and narrow passageways, a cat perched on a low rooftop, a series of cinema handbills that advertise the same types of film—thrillers, romances, adventures—that fill movie theaters now, a sardonic sequence that documents the process of slaughtering a cow inserted over a plate of meat in a fancy restaurant, two old women walking down the sidewalk and talking comfortably to each other, a young boy on his tiptoes kissing a taller girl. This was Paris in 1926.

BERLIN: SYMPHONY OF A GREAT CITY (BERLIN, DIE SINFONIE DER GROSSTADT) (1927). *See* Documentary Film

EMAK-BAKIA

1927. France.
By Man Ray.
18 min. B&W. Silent. 18 fps.

Man Ray, an American artist living in Paris, named this provocative film for the Basque villa where some of the material was shot. ("Emak-Bakia" means "Leave me alone" in Basque.) Exhibiting Man Ray's early Dada affiliations, **Emak-Bakia** combines a series of visual metaphors in a nonlinear structure. Juxtaposing images that evoke the elements of cinema—a multieyed camera, neon and street lights projecting into darkness, prisms reflecting light—with Dada emblems, such as dice, and introducing a fragmented narrative, Man Ray uses "all the tricks that might annoy certain spectators." He described **Emak-Bakia** in *Close-Up* in 1927: "A series of fragments, a cinepoem with a certain optical sequence make up a whole that still remains a fragment. Just as one can much better appreciate the abstract beauty in a fragment of a classic work than in its entirety, so this film tries to indicate the essentials in contemporary cinematography. It is not an 'abstract' film or a story-teller; its reasons for being are its inventions of light-forms and movements, while the more objective parts interrupt the monotony of abstract inventions or serve as punctuation."

OSKAR FISCHINGER PROGRAM IV

ca. 1927–1942?
By Oskar Fischinger.

Total program: 19 min. B&W and color. Silent. 24 fps.

SPIRITUAL CONSTRUCTIONS (SEELISCHE KONSTRUKTIONEN)

ca. 1927. Germany.
7 min. B&W.

LOVE GAMES (LIEBESSPIEL)

1931. Germany.
3 min. B&W.

SQUARES (QUADRATE)

1934. Germany.
5 min. Color.

RADIO DYNAMICS

1942? U.S.A.
4 min. Color.

This program of films by animator Oskar Fischinger (see **Oskar Fischinger Program I** [1930–34]) is composed of early films that were intended to be pure, abstract animation and do not include Fischinger's usual musical accompaniment. **Spiritual Constructions** is the only substantial Fischinger silhouette film which remains today. It begins with the phrase "Mir ist so merwürdig, als sei die Welt betrunken" ("How very strange—as if the world were drunk!") and uses silhouettes to transform two drunks into fantastic creatures of each other's imaginations. **Love Games** is the only intentionally silent film that he made during his **Study** series. It is a meditation on love and reproduction and on positive and negative particles in space, in which cometlike figures perform, merge, and procreate. **Squares** is an example of Fischinger's silent color work. The film consists of 271 tempera drawings which Fischinger loop-printed to create colorful multiple squares that advance and recede. Fischinger prepared **Radio Dynamics** as a silent tool for meditation. As Fischinger scholar William Moritz has written in *Film Culture* (1974), "I believe this to be Fischinger's best film, the work in which he most perfectly joined his craftsmanship with his spiritual ideas into a meaningful and relatively faultless whole. No music distracts from the visual imagery which moves with sufficient grace and power of its own."

———

L'ÉTOILE DE MER

1928. France.
By Man Ray. Assisted by J. A. Boiffard.
Based on a poem by Robert Desnos.
With Alice (Kiki) Prin, André de la Rivière and Robert Desnos.

15 min. B&W. Silent. 18 fps.

L'Étoile de mer illustrates the diverse quality of Man Ray's work, from its disjunctive narrative and verbal puns to its numerous visual metaphors. The film is based on a poem by Robert Desnos that Man Ray described as containing "no dramatic action, yet all the elements of possible action." It begins with an encounter between a man and a woman on a road where they will meet again several times throughout the film. Disparate, elusive images are juxtaposed: still lifes, masked faces, a woman mounting a flight of stairs with a knife, a starfish reflected in a revolving device, and glimpses of Paris. Dreamlike, intriguing, and playful, *L'Étoile de mer* (which translates as "starfish") does not construct a story as much as provide clues to an imaginative sequence of events. "Narrative itself," writes P. Adams Sitney in *Visionary Film*, "seems to exist within *L'Étoile de mer* only to be fractured or foiled."

THE FALL OF THE HOUSE OF USHER (LA CHUTE DE LA MAISON USHER) (1928). *See* Silent Fiction

THE FALL OF THE HOUSE OF USHER

1928. U.S.A.
Produced, directed, and photographed by James Sibley Watson. Screenplay and art direction by Melville Webber. Music by Alec Wilder. With Melville Webber, Herbert Stern, Hildegard Watson.
12 min. B&W. Sound.

This is a haunting visual interpretation of the Poe short story. Constructed of layers of imagery through superimpositions, animation, and the use of expressionistic sets, this film is in the experimental tradition of *The Cabinet of Dr. Caligari* (1920). Equal credit and emphasis is placed on photography and art direction. The angular look to the film, with its art deco quality, gives a stylized sense of ominousness. The visual transpositions, objects floating through black space, actors crossing the scene at disconcerting levels, effectively conjure up a feeling of being pursued. The supporting soundtrack, with music by Alec Wilder, was added later.

GHOSTS BEFORE BREAKFAST (VORMITTAGSSPUK)

1928. Germany.
By Hans Richter. With Richter, Paul Hindemith, Darius Milhaud.
9 min. B&W. Silent. 18 fps.

GHOSTS BEFORE BREAKFAST (1928)

This delightfully absurd Dada comedy defies all conventions, social and cinematic alike. Through pixillation derbies fly through the air, pistols are fired and no one dies, and bearded men (among them Paul Hindemith, Darius Milhaud, and Richter himself) advance heavily toward the camera. Originally created for the 1928 Baden-Baden music festival (with a Hindemith score now lost) it remains a continually surprising burlesque of objects that are literally in revolt.

INFLATION (excerpt) (1928). See From Dada to Surrealism (1961) in Film Study

THE LIFE AND DEATH OF 9413—A HOLLYWOOD EXTRA

1928. U.S.A.
Written and directed by Robert Florey. Photographed by Gregg Toland and Slavko Vorkapich. Art direction and editing by Slavko Vorkapich.
11 min. B&W. Silent. 24 fps.

This classic American experimental film is a critique of the industrialized society that makes numbers of its members and of the mass media forms—in this case, Hollywood movies—that create an artificial and often cruel "star system" of absolute success or abject failure. The plot involves an "artist" who wants to become a "motion picture player." He is branded on the forehead with the number 9413 and begins the vicious cycle of dreams of glory and success contrasted with the reality of "No Casting Today" signs. The actor who puts on a cardboard face in place of his real, human one, becomes a star. 9413 can't bring himself to accept fully the necessity of living behind a false mask; in the end, he dies, still a number instead of a star, and is transported to heaven where the brand on his forehead is wiped clean and he flies away through a celestial landscape. The film is especially noteworthy for the cinematography—much of it involving table top models and animation by Gregg Toland, who went on to photograph Orson Welles's *Citizen Kane* (1941)—and for the art direction and montage sequences by Slavko Vorkapich, who became a master of special montage effects and a leading theorist on the visual structure of the filmed image.

LA MARCHE DES MACHINES

1928. France.
By Eugène Deslaw. Photographed by Boris Kauffman.
7 min. B&W. Silent. 18 fps.

Ukrainian-born Eugène Deslaw was a film journalist and theorist who lived in France. His few short films share similarities with the avant-garde of the 1920s, including the fascination with mechanization evidenced in other films of that period, such as *Ballet mécanique* (1924). *La Marche des machines* explores the world of machinery through form and movement and not through its social reality. Deslaw creates a choreography of movement in this graceful montage that removes the machines from the context of their functions and presents them as both delicate and powerful objects. Conveyor belts, pulleys, pounding steel instruments, and wooden saws blend together to form a unified image of a modern machine. In its concern with the dramatic visuals of mechanical form and motion, the film is evocative of another significant portrait of a machine at work made the same year, Joris Ivens's *The Bridge* (1928).

RENNSYMPHONIE (RACE SYMPHONY)

1928. Germany.
By Hans Richter.
5 min. B&W. Silent. 18 fps.

Made as an unconventional opening for the conventional feature narrative *Ariadne in Hoppegarten* (1928), *Rennsymphonie* is a quick-paced, explosively-cut impressionist sketch about horse racing. Inventive in its brief construction, this film reflects an image of European society at play during the late 1920s.

THE SEASHELL AND THE CLERGYMAN (LA COQUILLE ET LE CLERGYMAN)

1928. France.
By Germaine Dulac. Written by Antonin Artaud. Photographed by Paul Guichard. With Alix Allen.
39 min. B&W. Silent. 18 fps.

This famous early Surrealist film is packed with Freudian references, and at the same time represents a spirited attack on the Church. Originally a drama critic, always a feminist, the filmmaker Germaine Dulac employed a fantastic symbolism to probe the mind of a cleric whose religious vows deny his normal sexual impulses. Nevertheless, it was originally banned by the British Board of Censors, which issued the statement that "The film is so cryptic as to be almost meaningless. If there is a meaning, it is doubtless objectionable."

BREAKERS (BRANDING)

February 1929. Netherlands.
By Mannus Franken and Joris Ivens. Photographed and edited by Ivens. Script by Franken and Jef Last, from an idea by Last. With Jef Last. English intertitles.
23 min. B&W. Silent. 24 fps.

During his career as a documentary filmmaker, Joris Ivens has periodically been drawn to fictional films. As early as the completion of *The Bridge* (1928), his first major work, Ivens joined with Franken to make this simple melodrama (their next collaboration was *Rain* [1929]). An unemployed Dutch fisherman, confounded in his search for work, becomes torn from his fiancée by his growing poverty and his frustration in choosing between a life of the land and one of the sea. The film shares many characteristics of the avant-garde of its time. Although they used a few intertitles, the filmmakers endeavored to tell their story in purely visual terms, and Ivens's photography, punctuated by the recurrent visual motif of breakers on the shore, suggests the psychology of the protagonist with brooding, melancholic images.

UN CHIEN ANDALOU

October 1, 1929. France.
Directed by Luis Buñuel. Screenplay by Salvador Dali and Buñuel. With Pierre Batcheff, Simone Mareuil, Luis Buñuel.
16 min. B&W. Silent. 24 fps.

One of the seminal works of the avant-garde cinema and perhaps the most fully realized Surrealist film, this is Luis Buñuel's first directorial effort after assisting others, including Jean Epstein on *The Fall of the House of Usher* (1928). Buñuel and Salvador Dali collaborated on the script, which was intended as an expression of automatism, André Breton's concept of art produced directly from the subconscious mind without reference to rational explanations or conscious symbolism. The film is a cinematic assault on the eye of the viewer—literally illustrated in one celebrated shot where a straight razor is drawn across the surface of an exposed cornea. The dream-like quality of the film's logic and the striking originality of the images combine to create a series of memorable visual metaphors, the reflections of which can be seen in the subsequent history of cinema, especially in the later work of Buñuel himself (see *Land without Bread* [1933]).

EVERYTHING TURNS, EVERYTHING REVOLVES! (ALLES DREHT SICH, ALLES BEWEGT SICH!) (excerpt) (1929). See **From Dada to Surrealism** (1961) in Film Study

H₂O

1929. U.S.A.
By Ralph Steiner.
14 min. B&W. Silent. 18 fps.

An early and well-known experimental film composed around the theme of water in all its forms. As a type of cinematic tone poem, it emphasizes rhythm and alteration through the visual qualities of the images and the structure of the editing. When the filmmaker moves the camera closer to the reflective surface, the images become more abstract and visually dramatic. This concentration on patterns of movement, shading, and texture would appear in later films such as *Analogies #1* (1953) by James Davis and *Sea Travels* (1978) by Anita Thacher.

THE MAN WITH THE MOVIE CAMERA (CHELOVEK S KINNOAPPARATOM) (1929). See Documentary Film

LES MYSTÈRES DU CHÂTEAU DU DÉ

1929. France.
By Man Ray. With Man Ray and J. A. Boiffard. French titles only.
25 min. B&W. Silent. 18 fps.

Although Man Ray was an American artist, most of his films were made as part of the French avant-garde movement, including *Retour à la raison* (1923) and *Emak-Bakia* (1927). *Les Mystères du Château du Dé* was filmed at the modern villa of the Vicomte de Noailles, which was designed by Robert Mallet-Stevens. Although the Vicomte was prepared to continue to finance Man Ray's films, the artist was nearing the end of his interest in the medium. This film is permeated with an atmosphere of mystery and doom as well as playfulness. The camera explores the structure and the dramatic light effects created by the villa's forms, and anonymous characters play within its walls—rolling dice, swimming, and creating shadow plays and puns. While the tone of these ritualistic scenes is seriously intellectual, the film seems to have been, above all, an amusing project for the guests at the Vicomte's villa.

TWOPENCE MAGIC (ZWEIGROSCHENZAUBER [ZWISCHENGROSCHENZAUBER(?)])
(1929). See **From Dada to Surrealism** (1961) in Film Study

ÜBERFALL (ACCIDENT) (1929). *See* Silent Fiction

L'HISTOIRE DU SOLDAT INCONNU

1930. Belgium.
By Henri Storck.
17 min. B&W. Silent. 24 fps.

Like many other experimental filmmakers of the period, Storck turned from avant-garde methods to straight documentary reportage and yet retained much of the freedom of the earlier manner. This is a montage of newsreel clips satirizing ceremonies commemorating the war dead and indicting world rearmament. It is an ancestor of many subsequent compilation films.

OSKAR FISCHINGER PROGRAM I

1930–34. Germany.
By Oskar Fischinger.
Total program: 15 min. B&W and color. Sound.

STUDY NO. 6 (STUDIE NR. 6)

1930.
Music by Paul Hindemith.
2 min. B&W.

STUDY NO. 7 (STUDIE NR. 7)

1931.
Music from "Hungarian Dance No. 5" by Brahms.
3 min. B&W.

STUDY NO. 8 (STUDIE NR. 8)

1931.
Music from "The Sorcerer's Apprentice" by Dukas.
5 min. B&W.

STUDY NO. 11 (STUDIE NR. 11)

1932.
Music from a Divertimento by Mozart.
4 min. B&W.

STUDY NO. 11A. A PLAY IN COLORS (EIN SPIEL IN FARBEN, STUDIE NR. 11A)

1934.
Music from a Divertimento by Mozart.
2 min. Color.

Experimental filmmaker Oskar Fischinger (1900–67), considered the champion of absolute film, worked in his native Germany until he came to the United States in 1936. This program includes four of Fischinger's most famous black and white film studies and an example of his color work. His **Study** series were shown before first-run features and brought Fischinger his first popular success. Made with thousands of separate charcoal drawings, the films are closely synchronized with music, and consist of figures of pure light whose importance lies in the actions they describe. *Study No. 6* was originally choreographed to Jacinto Guerrero's "Los Verderones," but when a dispute over rights prevented the music from being transferred onto the film, German composer Paul Hindemith and his students composed a new score for it. The film is a study of movement that interweaves a flow of flying objects and a target-like shape that gives off waves of vibrations. *Study No. 7*, the first of Fischinger's films to gain wide popular acceptance, creates illusions of depth with hard-edged shapes flickering, curving, and twisting through a dark space. Set to Dukas's "The Sorcerer's Apprentice," *Study No. 8* explores the textures of the music with a multiplicity of forms that emphasizes simple vs. complex structures, and random grouping vs. ordered patterns. The film ends abruptly because Fischinger could not afford the rights to the second half of the music. In *Study No. 11*, Fischinger simplified and abstracted a series of rococo sketches into geometric swirling forms. *Study No. 11a* is Fischinger's experiment in coloring *Study No. 11*. He never considered it a success, because the introduction of color compromised the pure abstraction of the figures. It is, nevertheless, an indication of the dynamic quality of Fischinger's work in color (see **Oskar Fischinger Program II** [1930–41]).

———

OSKAR FISCHINGER PROGRAM II

1930–41.
By Oskar Fischinger.
Total program: 14 min. B&W and color. Sound.

STUDY NO. 5 (STUDIE NR. 5)

1930. Germany.
Music: "I've Never Seen a Smile Like Yours."
3 min. B&W.

CIRCLES (KREISE) (Abstract version)

1933. Germany.
Music from *Tannhäuser* "Venusberg Music" by Wagner and "Huldigung's March" by Grieg.
2 min. Color.

COMPOSITION IN BLUE (KOMPOSITION IN BLAU)

1935. Germany.
Music from *The Merry Wives of Windsor* Overture by Nicolai.
4 min. Color.

ALLEGRETTO

1936. U.S.A.
Music by Ralph Rainger.
3 min. Color.

AN AMERICAN MARCH

1941. U.S.A.
Music from "Stars and Stripes Forever" by Sousa.
3 min. Color.

This program of Oskar Fischinger's important color works begins with one of his early black-and-white study films for comparison. *Study No. 5* sets abstract dancing figures to a popular foxtrot with Fischinger's distinctive style. *Circles*, made originally as a commercial for the Tolirag Theater (see **Oskar Fischinger Program III** [1932–53] for the advertising version), was redone by Fischinger to add a purely abstract ending in place of the theater slogan. The film, a free-form composition of radiating circles, caused a sensation on its release because it was the first film made with a three-color separation process and its colors were much more brilliant than previous color films. *Composition in Blue*, a highly sophisticated blend of diverse animation techniques including pixillation, is a virtuoso exercise in the musical manipulation of marching squares, swimming circles, and dancing cylinders. Both *Allegretto* and *An American March* were made by Fischinger after his immigration to the United States in 1936. *Allegretto* was originally made for Paramount in 1936 as "Radio Dynamics" (a title which Fischinger later assigned to another film), but when the studio insisted on using the footage as a background for representational imagery, Fischinger withdrew the film and later released it with this new title. It was Fischinger's first experiment with cel animation and celebrates America as seen through the eyes of an immigrant— bursting forth with skyscrapers, stars, and California colors. *An American March*, with a patriotic message and dynamic imagery, is Fischinger's exploration of America as a melting pot. It begins with the stars and stripes; these gradually transform into a variety of geometric shapes, the red, white, and blue blending until they form a rainbow of colors.

—

SURF AND SEAWEED

1930. U.S.A.
By Ralph Steiner.
11 min. B&W. Silent. 18 fps.

Ralph Steiner began as a still photographer and his experimental films, including *H₂O* (1929), *Mechanical Principles* (1931), and *Surf and Seaweed*, all share in a strong graphic sensibility. The repetition of the rhythmic motion of the waves casts a kind of cinematic spell heightened by the reflection of sunlight on the water and surface wrack that lingers with an eerie glow like phosphorescence among the seaweed. Steiner went on to an illustrious career in documentary films, including photographic contributions to Pare Lorentz's *The Plow that Broke the Plains* (1936) and codirecting, with Willard Van Dyke, *The City* (1939).

AUTUMN FIRE

1931. U.S.A.
By Herman G. Weinberg.
20 min. B&W. Silent. 18 fps.

Subtitled "A Film Poem (1930–33)," this personal narrative illustrates the story of two estranged lovers, separated through some unexplained misunderstanding, who in the end are reunited. The film is told through the symbolism of the change of seasons from winter to spring and the contrast of city and rural settings. Crosscutting from the woman, isolated in a country house, to the man, silhouetted against the urban skyline, the filmmaker has composed the action as a sequence of fragmented shots of details of the larger scene, building in increased rhythm to the lovers' final meeting together in Grand Central Station.

HANS AND OSKAR FISCHINGER PROGRAM

1931–32. Germany.
By Hans and Oskar Fischinger.
Total program: 12 min. B&W. Sound.

STUDY NO. 10 (STUDIE NR. 10)

1932.
Music from *Aida* by Verdi.
4 min.

STUDY NO. 9 (STUDIE NR. 9)

1931.
Music from "Hungarian Dance No. 6" by Brahms.
3 min.

STUDY NO. 12 (STUDIE NR. 12)

1932.
Music from "Torch Dance" from Anton Rubinstein's *Bride of Corinth*.
5 min.

Hans Fischinger, the younger brother of the well-known animator, worked on several films with Oskar in the early 1930s, when he was an art student and Oskar was becoming known in Germany. The three films on this program are presented in the order in which they reveal Hans's style. He preferred hard-edged figures, symmetry, and emphasis on the two-dimensionality of the picture frame, whereas Oskar preferred asymmetry and creating the illusion of three-dimensional space. *Study No. 10* was begun by Oskar at about the same time that he made *Study No. 8* (1931) (see **Oskar Fischinger Program I** [1930–34]), and then put aside until later, when Hans was assigned to fill out and execute the rest of the film. Hans photographed poster colors and inks in black and white to give a more distinct line than Oskar's use of charcoal. In *Study No. 9* the basic forms were designed by Oskar, and Hans completed all of the sequences. Set to Brahms's music, the film is gracefully choreographed with infinite gradations of gray. *Study No. 12* was apparently designed and executed by Hans alone, while still under Oskar's supervision. This abstract visual dance shows clearly his distinctive style with its emphasis on a flat surface and its streamlined figures.

—

IDYLLE SUR LE SABLE (IDYLLE À LA PLAGE)

1931. Belgium.
By Henri Storck. Music by Manuel Rosenthal. With Gwen Norman and Raymond Rouleau.
22 min. B&W. Sound.

Described by the Belgian filmmaker as "a fiction film, rather poetic—not very structural," this film is an evocative and tender visual reverie using abstract patterns of sea, sand, shells, and bodies to tell of two lovers meeting on the beach. Storck, influenced by René Clair, established his reputation with a series of short surreal films like this one, and later became a leading documentary filmmaker.

MECHANICAL PRINCIPLES

1931. U.S.A.
By Ralph Steiner.
11 min. B&W. Silent. 18 fps.

A visual clockwork mechanism celebrating the details of gears, rods, pistons, hinged levers, eccentric wheels, and screwthreads. Ralph Steiner's film, like the objects he photographs lovingly, is intricate and fascinating to watch.

PORTRAIT OF A YOUNG MAN

1931. U.S.A.
By Henwar Rodakiewicz.
48 min. B&W. Silent. 18 fps.

This is a "portrait" in an indirect, oblique sense. A film composed entirely of images of objects ("above all—the sea"), it is a view of a young man in terms of the things he likes. The film is divided into three "movements," the musical structure of which is evoked through the rhythmic patterns of motion and editing and the visual variations in the play of light on reflective surfaces. There is a kind of youthful, obsessional quality here, a sense of cycle—of approach and pull back, obscure and reveal. The visual pleasure of the images (white smoke in long, thin veils pulled across the screen) was recognized by Alfred Stieglitz, who launched Rodakiewicz as a filmmaker when he showed *Portrait of a Young Man* at his An American Place Gallery.

L'IDÉE (THE IDEA)

1932. France.
By Berthold Bartosch. Based on woodcuts by Frans Masereel. Music by Arthur Honegger. French opening titles.
25 min. B&W. Sound.

An animated narrative on the theme of humanity's response to ideals, this film traces the story of an artist who sends his abstract ideal out into the world. His artistic conception (symbolized by the figure of a nude woman) is rejected and exploited by the ruling powers of business, religion, and the military. As the titles make clear, Bartosch's conclusion is that "men live and die for an idea . . . the idea is immortal. You can persecute it, judge it, forbid it, condemn it to death. But the idea continues to live in the minds of men." Despite its heavy didacticism, the film is interesting for its unique style of animation. Bartosch utilizes two-dimensional figures posed at varying distances in relation to the painted backgrounds for diverse depth effects. The lighting creates a soft-focus halo around the figures and produces an overall muting of the painted decor. The history of the film's inception dates back to 1930, when Bartosch met Masereel in Berlin and agreed to make an animated version of the latter's book, *Die Idee*. The collaboration fell through, however, and Bartosch proceeded alone. The music was written expressly for the film by Honegger and added in 1934. It makes use of a new electrical instrument, "Les Ondes Musicales," played by Martenot. The female figure representing the artist's idea is always announced and accompanied by notes from this instrument.

OSKAR FISCHINGER PROGRAM III

1932–53.
By Oskar Fischinger.
Total program: 10 min. B&W and color. Sound.

COLORATURA (KOLORATUREN)

1932. Germany.
Music from "Was kann so schön sein wie deine Liebe" by Nikolaus Bridsky. Sung by Gitta Alpar. In German.
1 min. B&W.

CIRCLES (KREISE) (Advertising version)

1933. Germany.
Music from *Tannhauser* "Venusberg Music" by Wagner and "Huldigung's March" by Grieg.
2 min. Color.

MURATTI GETS IN THE ACT! (MURATTI GREIFT EIN!)

1934. Germany.
Music from the ballet *Die Puppenfee* by Josef Bayer.
3 min. Color.

MURATTI PRIVAT

1935? Germany.
Music from Piano Sonata No. 11 ("Alla turca") by Mozart.
3 min. B&W.

OKLAHOMA GAS

1952. U.S.A.
Music from *Gayne* Ballet "Sabre Dance" by Khachaturian.

1 min. B&W.

MUNTZ TV

1953. U.S.A.
1 min. B&W.

Throughout his career Oskar Fischinger made animated commercials to support his work. Uncompromising in their imagery and use of music, these ads were some of his most popular and imaginative films. *Coloratura* was commissioned by Carl Froelich as a trailer to his feature *Gitta Entdekt ihr Herz (Gitta Discovers her Heart)* (1932), starring the popular operetta singer Gitta Alpar. In Fischinger's teasing trailer, we hear Alpar singing to abstract designs. Originally the film ended with a question mark to get the audience to guess the name of the film and singer, but after the film rights reverted to him, Fischinger removed it. *Circles* was commissioned by the Tolirag Theater. Using the slogan "Alle Kreise erfasst Tolirag" ("Tolirag Reaches all Circles"), Fischinger explored the myriad movements of circles in this brilliantly colorful film. It was the first color film to use a three-color separation process (for the abstract version see **Oskar Fischinger Program II** [1930–41]). *Muratti Gets in the Act!* is the most famous of Fischinger's commercials. Made for Muratti cigarettes, it is a tour de force of pixillation composed of marching, dancing, and ice-skating cigarettes. The black-and-white *Muratti Privat* was probably made after *Muratti Gets in the Act!*. In it Fischinger purposefully avoids having the cigarettes walk, but uses them primarily like the abstract figures in the **Study** series. They perform layered, geometric choreography to Mozart's music, including a chorus line whimsically reminiscent of a Busby Berkeley routine. Lacking a original head title, it has been supplied with one reading "Muratti greift ein." During the 1940s and 1950s, in the United States, Fischinger undertook a variety of commercial work for television, of which two commercials are represented here. *Oklahoma Gas* features special effects, drawings, moving objects, and animated designs. *Muntz TV* uses an oil-on-plexiglas technique of which Fischinger's *Motion-Painting I* (1947) is the best example. It is, in effect, a title that moves as an invisible painter continuously writes the words "Muntz TV."

JOIE DE VIVRE

1934. France.
By Hector Hoppin and Anthony Gross.
11 min. B&W. Sound.

Joie de vivre is a lively, animated fairy tale. It follows two female dancers through an entire spectrum of environments from high-tech industrial wires to pastoral scenes overflowing with flowers. They are pursued by a mysterious man on a bicycle, a chase which ends at a complex of train tracks in a dizzying visual collage. Hoppin and Gross developed an animated style, combining both dance and abstract imagery, considered very innovative for its time. As an example of matching music and visuals, the film is exceptional.

LA PÊCHE À LA BALEINE

1934. France.
Directed by Tchimoukoff. With Jacques Prévert. In French; no English subtitles.
4 min. B&W. Sound.

This comic Surrealist short is narrated in song by poet Jacques Prévert in a delightfully expressive voice. The story, told in isolated, static shots in a very small room, is about the tragic plight of a whale fisherman. Leaving his angry son in the closet, Cousin Gaston at the table with a bowl of water, and his wife at home, the fisherman goes off fishing and returns from a long day with a blue-eyed whale in tow. In the ensuing conflict, the whale kills the fisherman and bids the widow adieu. The odd humor of this skit, whose title translates as "whale fishing," is a good example of the comic yet sophisticated charm the Surrealists brought to film.

THE FILMS OF LOTTE REINIGER

Recently acquired by the Circulating Film Library is a collection of animation films by Lotte Reiniger (1899–1981). One of this century's major animation artists, Reiniger pioneered a distinctive style of black-and-white silhouette animation in her interpretations of classic myths and fairy tales. She began working in her native Germany in the late 1910s, eventually moving to Britain in the mid-1930s and settling there after the war. (Her classic **Carmen** [1933] is available on the **Animation Program** [1908–33].) Included in this collection is the *The Art of Lotte Reiniger* (1970), in which the artist demonstrates her animation techniques. The following titles are now available:

PUSS IN BOOTS (DER GRAF VON CARABAS)

1934. Switzerland.
11 min. B&W. Sound

THE STOLEN HEART (DAS GESTOHLENE HERZ)

1934. Germany.
11 min. B&W. Sound.

GALATHEA

1935. Switzerland.
11 min. B&W. Sound

THE LITTLE CHIMNEY SWEEP (DER KLEINE SCHORNSTEINFEGER)

1935. Switzerland.
11 min. B&W. Sound.

ALADDIN

1953. Great Britain.
14 min. B&W. Sound.

SNOW WHITE AND ROSE RED

1953. Great Britain.
13 min. B&W. Sound.

THE CALIPH STORK

1954. Great Britain.
11 min. B&W. Sound.

THE FROG PRINCE

1954. Great Britain.
11 min. B&W. Sound.

THE GALLANT LITTLE TAILOR

1954. Great Britain.
11 min. B&W. Sound.

THE GRASSHOPPER AND THE ANT

1954. Great Britain.
11 min. B&W. Sound.

THE SLEEPING BEAUTY

1954. Great Britain.
11 min. B&W. Sound.

CINDERELLA

1955. Great Britain.
11 min. B&W. Sound.

THUMBELINA

1955. Great Britain.
11 min. B&W. Sound.

THE ART OF LOTTE REINIGER

1970. Great Britain.
Directed by John Isaacs.
17 min. Color. Sound.

A COLOUR BOX

1935. Great Britain.
General Post Office (GPO) Film Unit.
By Len Lye. Produced by John Grierson. Music performed by Don Barretto and his Cuban Orchestra.
3 min. Color. Sound.

New Zealand-born animator Len Lye made his early films in England, sponsored by the GPO Film Unit under John Grierson's supervision. *A Colour Box*, the work that actually convinced Grierson to give Lye a job there, was his first cameraless, direct animation and is largely credited as the first film made in this manner. (While Man Ray and others are said to have made direct films before *A Colour Box*, none of these films seem to have survived.) Lye is considered to be the pioneer of this technique, which consists of drawing, painting, and scratching directly on the surface of the celluloid to create abstract images and textures. *A Colour Box* is an exquisite example of the energetic, vibrant, and flawlessly-paced effects that Lye perfected. Set to lively Cuban music, colors and lines dance on the screen in a rhythmic celebration. The slogan "G.P.O. Cheaper Parcel Post" is stenciled on these colors along with a few dancing prices, an addition required by Grierson for the sponsorship of the film. Unlike most other government-sponsored films, *A Colour Box* is an example of spontaneous, innovative animation.

PIE IN THE SKY

1935. U.S.A.
Nykino. By and with Ralph Steiner, Irving Lerner, and Group Theatre members Elia Kazan, Ellman Koolish, Molly Day Thatcher, Russell Collins.
16 min. B&W. Silent. 24 fps.

In the depths of the Depression, a band of leftist friends put together this off-hand satire about the dichotomy between the illusory promises of religion and the stark prospects of an actual life of poverty. The film introduced the work of Nykino, a group dedicated to creating a new agit-prop cinema. The result is a bit of light-hearted political humor, featuring Elia "Gadget" Kazan and Ellman Koolish as a couple of knuckle-headed down-and-outs clowning around in a Long Island dump. At the turn of the century, Joe Hill had written new lyrics to the old Salvation Army hymn, "In the Sweet By and By." These lyrics provide the title of this film and appear at the very end: "You will eat/by and by/in that glorious/ land above the sky./Work and pray,/live on hay./ You'll get pie/in the sky/when you die."

TRADE TATTOO

1937. Great Britain.
General Post Office (GPO) Film Unit.
By Len Lye. Produced by John Grierson. Music played by the Lecuona Band.
6 min. Color. Sound.

After making *A Colour Box* (1935), Len Lye continued to make films for the GPO Film Unit. Experimenting in various techniques, including color printing and puppet animation, Lye also explored the use of live-action footage in combination with direct animation. In *Trade Tattoo*, he took outtakes from GPO Film Unit documentaries to make an animated film about "the rhythm of the work-a-day," also known as *In Tune With Industry*. Lye transformed the black-and-white footage by colorizing it in an elaborate process of color separation, and then added stencil patterns, handpainting, and cartoon animation. Images of workers are juxtaposed with colorful imagery and catchy slogans in this fine example of Lye's witty visual ideas and use of words with images. Inserted in rhythmic bursts, slogans such as "The Rhythm of the Trade is Maintained by the Mails" blend effectively with the scenes of people at work.

SWINGING THE LAMBETH WALK

1939. Great Britain.
By Len Lye. Tida Film production.
4 min. Color. Sound.

With the same direct images that he used in *A Colour Box* (1935), Lye made this interpretation of several versions of the tune "Lambeth Walk." Made with a British Council grant, this is one of his few early films that was not an exercise in combining government slogans with animation. Designed simply to achieve pure, rhythmic animation, *Swinging the Lambeth Walk* is a colorful, fast-paced tumble of abstract images that reflects the spontaneity and exuberance of the accompanying jazz music.

DOTS (POINTS)

1940. U.S.A.
By Norman McLaren. Produced by the Guggenheim Museum of Non-Objective Art.
3 min. Color. Sound.

Scotsman Norman McLaren began his filmmaking career in England with animator Len Lye at the GPO. Later he moved to the U.S. and, in 1941, to Canada, where he became a leading pioneer in animation at the National Film Board of Canada. While in New York, he sold a thirty-second holiday greeting film to the fledgling Guggenheim Museum. The museum subsequently financed his production of several color, abstract shorts, including *Dots*, that used cameraless animation and hand-drawn sound. The geometric abstractions of *Dots* were drawn directly on film with pen and ink. For the soundtrack, McLaren drew a percussive rhythm of clicking sounds along the edge of the film, creating music that ranges over several octaves. This integrates perfectly with the blue and white dots flipping across a red background. The film is a fine example of how McLaren synchronized visuals with a synthetic soundtrack, and reveals how early in his career he achieved sophisticaton with this method.

MUSICAL POSTER NO. 1

1940. Great Britain.
By Len Lye. Produced by the British Ministry of Information.
3 min. Color. Sound.

Len Lye made several films for the British Ministry of Information during World War II, the first of which was *Musical Poster No. 1*. Set to wartime jazz tunes, including "Bugle Call Rag," it opens and closes with an animated bugle. Using direct animation, Lye combined abstract, colorful imagery with a warning against gossiping. Lively images yield to the stenciled message "Careful! The enemy is listening to you," and the film ends with an admonishing "Shh!" and a forboding swastika. This film was a precursor to Norman McLaren's animated propaganda film, *Keep Your Mouth Shut* (1944).

MOODS OF THE SEA (FINGAL'S CAVE)

1942. U.S.A.
By Slavko Vorkapich and John Hoffman. Music: Mendelssohn's "Hebrides" ("Fingal's Cave") Overture.
10 min. B&W. Sound.

Slavko Vorkapich was famous for his imaginative montage sequences in such films as *Crime without Passion* (1934: the Furies) and *San Francisco* (1939: the earthquake), and for his work on *The Life and Death of 9413—A Hollywood Extra* (1928). He was a stubborn advocate of cinema's potential as an independent form of art that could rise to great heights of visual poetry. *Moods of the Sea* is a stunning montage of music and imagery. The film is an interpretation of Mendelssohn's "Fingal's Cave," and combines images of rolling waves and graceful birds along a seacoast in a contrapuntal style to portray the infinite subtlety of nature's motion. Dramatic waves break over a crescendo of music, a bird alights on a rock at a central chord, crashing waves are punctuated by powerful rhythms, and the moon's reflection on dark, calm waters harmonizes with the final note. *Moods of the Sea* is a fine example of Vorkapich's ability to create cinematic poems.

MESHES OF THE AFTERNOON

1943. U.S.A.
By Maya Deren with Alexander Hammid.
18 min. B&W. Silent. 24 fps.

This film is one of the most influential works in the American experimental canon. Made by the wife and husband team of Maya Deren and Alexander Hammid, *Meshes of the Afternoon* established the independent avant-garde movement in the U.S. and inspired its initial course in works such as Kenneth Anger's *Fireworks* (1947) and Stan Brakhage's *Daybreak* and *Whiteye* (1957). P. Adams Sitney has referred to this tradition in experimental cinema as the "trance film." It is characterized by a somnambulistic arising out of a highly subjective focus. In *Meshes*, Deren—playing the central figure—is caught in a web of dream events that in the final scene appear to spill over into reality. The woman character experiences a series of symbolic images and actions: a knife falls and reappears on the stairs, in the bed, in her hand; a key is dropped, cascades down the stairs, is passed around a dining table, emerges from her mouth, becomes the instrument of suicide; other figures walk up the street, past the window, disappear around corners, have mirrors for faces. Throughout the film, the filmmakers use the conventional vocabulary of the fiction feature to indicate the dream state, to simulate special effects (such as the movement of the camera to create a sense of earthquake), and to separate for the viewer the subjective world from the apparently objective one. For instance, the transition from waking to dream is accomplished by having the eye close and a shadow line pass over the eye itself and the open window before it. Credit for the exceptional use of the camera—both in quality of the images and in their fluid continuity—must be given to Hammid, who shot the entire film himself. (As Alexander Hackenschmied he had worked on many documentaries and fiction films; see *The Earth Sings* [1932] and *The Forgotten Village* [1941].) Deren went on to become the preeminent woman avant-garde film artist of the 1940s and 1950s (she died in 1961), partly through her films and partly through her extensive lectures and writings.

GLENS FALLS SEQUENCE

1946. U.S.A.
By Douglass Crockwell.
8 min. Color. Silent.

Douglass Crockwell was a well-known cover illustrator and designer for the *Saturday Evening Post* and other popular magazines. Crockwell painted mostly with plastic paint on several layers of glass, but he also experimented with clay and cutout animation. *Glens Falls Sequence*, named after Glens Falls, New York (where Crockwell lived most of his life), is a compilation of short animations that represent diverse aspects of his work. These scenes originally had titles, such as "Parade" and "Frustration," that were ultimately omitted from the film by the filmmaker for the sake of unity. The result is a sampler of metamorphosing, elongated shapes and scenes of organic landscapes evocative of geological formations, interspersed with imaginative pixillation of objects. *Glens Falls Sequence* is an interesting prelude to Crockwell's later animation, *The Long Bodies* (1947).

THE POTTED PSALM

1946. U.S.A.
By Sidney Peterson and James Broughton. With Beatrix Perry, Harry Honig, Joyce Geary, Donald Nelson, Ann Whittington, Bernice Van Gelder, Janice Dieckman, Victoria Vineros.
18 min. B&W. Silent. 24 fps.

Made in collaboration with James Broughton, *The Potted Psalm*, Sidney Peterson's first 16mm film, was inspired by works of the European avant-garde cinema which the filmmaker had seen in Paris. As Peterson states: "We were aware of the European avant-garde, and we wanted to make film as art." *The Potted Psalm* is a disjunctive, Surrealist narrative, which progresses from the site of a graveyard, to a strange indoor social gathering, and finally back to the original locale. A coherent dramatic structure is avoided, and, as Peterson notes, "All scenes are susceptible of a dozen different interpretations based on visual connections." The film however, has a distinct psychological bent—with the *mise-en-scène* reminiscent of a dream. Strange and suggestive images fill the screen: mannequins, masked figures, boxes of keys, all of which hold mythic and symbolic overtones. Technically, Peterson employs a variety of experimental visual techniques—blurred imagery, anamorphosis, superimposition—to achieve what he has termed "the necessary ambiguity of the specific image." *The Potted Psalm* was shown during the premiere season of the "Art in Cinema" film society, and its success led to the inclusion of a filmmaking course at the California School of Fine Arts in San Francisco.

THE CAGE

1947. U.S.A.
By Sidney Peterson. Workshop 20 production, California School of Fine Arts. Photographed by Hy Hirsh. With Joseph Brusberg, James Keeney, Anne Hopkins, Beverly Campbell, Rex Mason, Charles Campbell, Harlan Jackson, and Merle Jenson.
28 min. B&W. Silent. 24 fps.

After Sidney Peterson and James Broughton made **The Potted Psalm** (1946), the success of the newly opened "Art In Cinema" film society in San Francisco prompted the director of the California School of Fine Arts to initiate an avant-garde filmmaking course and to hire Peterson to teach it. **The Cage** is the first of four films that Peterson made as workshop projects (the others were **Mr. Frenhofer and the Minotaur** [1948], **The Petrified Dog** [1948], and **The Lead Shoes** [1949]). **The Cage** "uses every trick in the book and a few that weren't" to describe the adventures of a deranged artist. The protagonist, whom we come upon painting in his studio, removes his eye in an act of self-mutilation, whereupon it escapes his studio into an open field and roams the streets of San Francisco. The artist then appears in a cage and becomes schizophrenic, alternating with a double (a device necessitated by the disappearance of Peterson's first actor). Soon, the artist's girlfriend, a doctor, and the two protagonists chase the eye around the city. Peterson uses a variety of techniques to give **The Cage** its visual dynamism and innovation. The traveling eye's perspective is captured with an anamorphic lens that creates a circular, distorted view, and the disorientation of other perspectives is created with pixillation, reverse action, superimposition, and slow and fast motion. After numerous adventures, the wandering eye is recovered, and the schizophrenic becomes the original protagonist, triumphing over the doctor who had been scheming to destroy his eye. **The Cage** ends on a note of parody when, as the artist and his girl walk off in a happily-ever-after shot, she flies out of his arms into a tree as he embraces her.

CLINIC OF STUMBLE

1947. U.S.A.
By Marian Van Tuyl, Sidney Peterson, Hy Hirsh. Choreographed by Marian Van Tuyl. Decor: Arch Lauterer. Music by Gregory Tucker. Dancers: Beth Osgood, Barbara Bennion, Edith Wiener.
13 min. Color. Sound.

An early work in the experimental dance film genre, **Clinic of Stumble** is based on a performance piece by Marian Van Tuyl. Three women, in rather formal attire, appear on a set that resembles a small city street. They enter the scene on scooters and the camera focuses on their feet peddling along. They take off their capes and begin to dance, frequently interrupting their choreography to sit on a bench and read fashion magazines. Peterson's primary visual trope in the film is superimposition, which he employs in almost all of the shots. The dancers interact in hazy layers: one figure in close-up, the other in long-shot; one moving laterally, the other horizontally. Color is also a crucial aesthetic tool in the film, with the dancers garbed in brightly hued frocks. Finally, as images of the dancers appear superimposed over magazine pages, they seem like female models come to life.

DREAMS THAT MONEY CAN BUY

1947. U.S.A.
By Hans Richter in collaboration with Max Ernst, Fernand Léger, Man Ray, Marcel Duchamp, and Alexander Calder. Photographed by Arnold Eagle. With the participation of Paul Bowles, John Latouche, Libby Holman, Josh White, Darius Milhaud, John Cage, David Diamond, Louis Applebaum, Jack Bittner, Julien Levy.
80 min. Color. Sound.

Probably the first feature-length avant-garde film produced in America, **Dreams that Money Can Buy** is an omnibus work in which seven dreams are offered for sale by Joe, a poor young poet with a rich imagination. The dreams are tailored to the unconscious of seven different people; each dream episode is shaped by one of the contributing visual artists: Max Ernst, Fernand Léger, Man Ray, Marcel Duchamp, Alexander Calder, and of course, Hans Richter, who directed the entire remarkable adventure. **Dreams that Money Can Buy** is a truly original work that remains what *Sight and Sound* called, "the most startling film of the year."

THE LONG BODIES

1947. U.S.A.
By Douglass Crockwell.
4 min. Color. Silent. 24 fps.

Experimenting with a grab bag of materials and techniques in his animation, Crockwell has made a fascinating study of physical change, growth, and mutation. Beginning with images painted on glass and including clay figure manipulation, he settles on the process of

THE CAGE (1947)

filming thin slices of blocks of colored wax. The effect is graphic, and the eye is mesmerized by the gradual evolution of the two-dimensional forms.

MOTION-PAINTING I

1947. U.S.A.
By Oskar Fischinger. Music from "Brandenburg Concerto No. 3" by Bach. 11 min. Color. Sound.

Motion-Painting I, which was commissioned by the Guggenheim Foundation, is perhaps the most ambitious of Oskar Fischinger's works (see **Oskar Fischinger Programs I–V** [1923–53]) and his longest film. Created with oil on plexiglas, it is, as its title suggests, a study of the motion of painting and music. Fischinger made the film over a nine-month period as one continuous "take," photographing a single frame of each brushstroke as it was made. As an ever-changing painting, it documents the creative process with its progression of shapes from soft, amorphous figures to more defined forms. *Motion-Painting I* is the most purely abstract of Fischinger's films.

Oskar Fischinger making MOTION-PAINTING I (1947)

LIGHT REFLECTIONS

1948. U.S.A.
By James Davis. Photographed by John A. Stewart. Music by Edward Muller. 14 min. Color. Sound.

This film is an experiment in capturing the color and movement of light transmitted from the artist's mobiles. What emerges on film is a pure and ethereal form of floating, almost three-dimensional, light shapes. Like specters, the images appear against a black background and move off into space. The mysterious and absorbing effect of the visuals is set off by the effective modern piano score by Edward Muller.

MR. FRENHOFER AND THE MINOTAUR

1948. U.S.A.
By Sidney Peterson. Workshop 20 production, California School of Fine Arts. Based on "Le Chef-d'oeuvre inconnu" by Honoré de Balzac. Music by Frederic Daunic. With Harold Bronstein, Albert Dadian, Walter Degen, William Heick, Al Joyce, Leslie Turner, Ramon Vega. Voice: Beatrix Perry. 21 min. B&W. Sound.

Focusing on the archetypal role of the artist, Peterson bases his film on three sources: Balzac's story "Le Chef-d'oeuvre inconnu," Picasso's engraving "Minotauromachia" and James Joyce's

interior monologue style. The bizarre, disjunctive narrative loosely sketches a tale of an older artist who tries to idealize female beauty in his painting. As P. Adams Sitney comments, however, the film has broader overtones that express the conflict between "the model in the flesh and the illusion on canvas . . . between a man's work and his love." While a woman's free-associative monologue is heard on the soundtrack, highly abstract images appear, transposed by various distorting techniques. A cat and mouse are seen in anamorphosis, people dance on a mattress in hazy slow-motion, and a man repeatedly climbs a ladder in loop printing reminiscent of Léger's *Ballet mécanique* (1924). At points the mythological beast/man minotaur appears literally in the *mise-en-scène*, a reference to Picasso's engraving. As in all Peterson films, the world created shares little with objective reality, but rather is infused with a sense of symbolism, ritual, and dream. As Peterson remarks, the structure of the film is not formulated "as though one were writing an essay," but instead is organized in terms of resonant "thematic material."

MOTHER'S DAY

1948. U.S.A.
By James Broughton. Assisted by Kermit Sheets. Photographed by Frank Stauffacher. With Marion Cunningham, Donald Pidgeon, Hal Goldman, Donald Nelson, Beatrix Perry, Betty Lee Baldes, Elaine Mitchell, Marion Farquhar, Jack W. Stauffacher. 23 min. B&W. Sound.

In this film, Broughton creates a world of recollected childhood, a "country of emotional memory" in which the adult recalls his youth. Central to this nostalgic vision is the primordial figure of Mother—seen as awesome and forbidding from the perspective of a man-child. *Mother's Day* is an avant-garde Oedipal drama, staged in the realm of the psyche, rather than the domain of real time and space. Broughton's style in the film is one of arch theatricality, with scenes deployed in characteristic tableaux. In a radical gesture, adults play the roles of youths to emphasize a sense of the child that remains perpetually within us. On a pictorial level, the film is abstract and composed, with static images of Mother in silhouette, seen through a veil of hazy lace. Linear chronology is disrupted and events flow forward and backward simultaneously. Mother is young at one moment and old the next. In one scene she is in a 1940s outfit and then Victorian garb. Broughton's aim is to emulate human consciousness which commutes fluidly among the spheres of past, present, and future.

THE PETRIFIED DOG

1948. U.S.A.
By Sidney Peterson. Workshop 20 production, California School of Fine Arts. Sound by Carl Austen, Leslie Turner, Hal Bronstein, Harry Reminick. With Gail Randall, Marie Hirsch, Jo Lander, Ian Zellick, Leslie Turner, Carl Austen, William Heick, Charles Mather, Hal Bronstein.
19 min. B&W. Sound.

An abstract and disjunctive narrative, in the tradition of Peterson's earlier *The Potted Psalm* (1946), *The Petrified Dog* has been compared to Lewis Carroll's *Alice in Wonderland*. The central protagonist of the "story" is a young girl in Victorian dress who crawls out of a hole in the ground. What follows is a subjective rendition of the strange world she sees: an artist painting an empty frame, men wrestling with a skeleton, a woman obsessively eating her lipstick, and a man recurrently running down a street making no apparent progress. To communicate the girl's interior vision, Peterson continually returns to close-up shots of her blinking, and employs a catalog of disorienting visual tactics: anamorphosis, distorted mirror imagery, slow and accelerated motion, and magical stop-motion appearances and disappearances. The soundtrack of the film, an early example of concrete music, is comprised of traditional instrumentation, as well as of piano strings being plucked and beaten. *The Petrified Dog* thus creates a world of surrealistic dissonance, or what Stan Brakhage has termed Peterson's "studied ambiguity," or "articulate chaos."

SAUSALITO

1948. U.S.A.
By Frank and Barbara Stauffacher.
10 min. B&W. Sound.

This film is part "city symphony" and part "outtakes for an experimental film." Sausalito is the picturesque waterfront town across the Golden Gate Bridge from San Francisco and has functioned, during times of low rent, as an artists' colony. It is the kind of place that produces postcard-perfect images from practically any visual perspective: point the camera and the result will be ocean bay, fog, sailboats, waves, seashells, rocky beach, inclined streets, wooden piers, antique shops, dancer's legs, and California shore birds. Stauffacher has combined these elements through a technique of abrupt visual and audio crosscutting and juxtaposition that helps transcend the clichéd material. Along the way he experiments with slow motion, split screens, and superimposition, all of which are lightened by a constant thread of whimsicality and wit. (In the same year, Stauffacher was the cameraman for James Broughton's first film, *Mother's Day*; see also the filmmaker's portrait of San Francisco, *Notes on the Port of St. Francis* [1952].)

THE LEAD SHOES

1949. U.S.A.
By Sidney Peterson.
18 min. B&W. Sound.

Sidney Peterson scrambles two ballads—"Edward" and "The Three Ravens"—to create a highly disjointed Oedipal narrative about a mother and her son. This basic "plot," however, is obfuscated by a style of radical ellipsis, and as Parker Tyler notes, the film contains "numerous stories unfolding at one and the same time." Contributing to this narrative confusion are the abstract visual techniques that Peterson uses. We witness reverse-motion images of a hand chalking the ground, accelerated shots of a girl playing hopscotch, and magical stop-motion transformations by which a bone becomes a piece of bread. The soundtrack is a work of experimental dissonance—combining phrases from the ballads with shouts, chants, howls as well as a cacophonous instrumental jam session. Ultimately, as Parker Tyler remarks: "Every attempt at symbolic or historical understanding of *The Lead Shoes* is bound to destruct against the multiplicity of meanings, leaving the thoughtful viewer with scattered wits—though *not* at wit's end."

AI-YE

1950. U.S.A.
By Ian Hugo. Music by Ozzie Smith.
24 min. Color. Sound.

Ian Hugo came to filmmaking from a background in painting and printmaking. *Ai-ye*, his first film, was made in Mexico, Cuba, and Puerto Rico, and interprets the simplicity of Indian life and the brooding mystery of the jungle. Cecile Starr in *The Saturday Review* has called it, "A beautiful film with unique musical accompaniment! . . . outstanding among experimental films . . . a film those of vastly different background and interests can enjoy."

LOONY TOM THE HAPPY LOVER

1951. U.S.A.
By James Broughton. With Kermit Sheets and Gertrude Harris. Music by Ralph Gilbert.
10 min. B&W. Sound.

In *Looney Tom the Happy Lover* James Broughton has created a witty and nearly perfect homage to the silent comedy tradition and to the films of Chaplin in particular. The Tramp figure, played by Kermit Sheets, dances through a series of escapades with charm and enthusiasm, overcoming all physical obstacles and female objections to end in amorous embraces. These comic hijinks are performed with a combination of graceful movements and tongue-in-cheek asides and are set off by marvelous details, such as the dallying wife who proffers her face to the unexpectedly returned husband and promptly scratches off his kiss while the Tramp peers from behind the bushes. There is also a brilliant chase scene when the Tramp surprises five young girls in a farmyard and merrily sets off to catch them as they fly away—only not too far—in different directions. The Tramp finally conquers the matron of the house as he advances through a torrent of china cups she hurls in his path and subdues her with a single kiss. Meanwhile, in a metaphor for the proper balance of love and art in life, we watch the progression of an artist and model: from his arranging her in a pose, to an exchange of roles, to both painting the picture together, to a passionate embrace in which the Tramp throws the canvas away and strews flowers over the oblivious lovers. Accompanied by the nursery-like rhymes of Broughton's poem and the silent-film music accompaniment of Ralph Gilbert, the film's action occurs in a number of wonderful fairy tale settings with accompanying Victorian period costumes. The total effect is magical and light hearted, leaving the viewer with a lingering smile as the Tramp disappears in the distance.

BELLS OF ATLANTIS

1952. U.S.A.
By Ian Hugo. Abstract color effects by Ian Hugo and Len Lye. Music by Louis and Bebe Barron. Performed by and with commentary spoken by Anaïs Nin.
9 min. Color. Sound.

Based on Anaïs Nin's prose poem *The House of Incest*, and particularly the line "I remember my first birth in water," *Bells of Atlantis* evokes the watery depths of the lost continent of ourselves, and the images suggest the aqueous beauty of that lost world. It is a lyrical journey into another time, an imaginative film exploration of a poet's world. Abel Gance wrote of the film: "Upon viewing Ian Hugo's *Bells of Atlantis* I had just as powerful an impression as I had received reading "Une Saison en enfer" or "Le Bateau ivre" of Rimbaud. In my opinion, this is the first cinematic *poem* worthy of that name. The fusion of image, text, and sound is so magical that it is impossible to disassociate them in order to explain the favorable reactions of the unconscious, which is at once disoriented and delighted. And when a work of art offers to the teeth of analysis only its impenetrable marble, it is very close to being a masterpiece."

BLACKTOP

1952. U.S.A.
By Charles and Ray Eames. Music from "Goldberg Variations" by Bach, played by Wanda Landowska.
11 min. Color. Sound.

This celebration of the powers of invention is pure delight in its visual and aural combination. Deceptively simple, it is subtitled "a story of the washing of a school play yard" and it is, like the "Goldberg Variations" to which it plays counterpoint, an intricate weaving together of texture, motion, and the play of light. This film could teach the Zen art of patience, as the camera waits for water to flow across the frame, carrying flotsam and jetsam ahead of it and revealing patterns of water and soap suds more captivating and diverse than the uninitiated ever expected. (See also: *Parade* [1952], *A Communications Primer* [1953], *House* [1955], and *Powers of Ten* [1968 and 1978].)

COLOR CRY

1952. U.S.A.
By Len Lye. Music by Sonny Terry. Produced by Ann Zeiss for Direct Film Company.
3 min. Color. Sound.

After his early prolific period of filmmaking during the 1930s and World War II, including *A Colour Box* (1935) and *Trade Tattoo* (1937), Len Lye was forced to give up experimental filmmaking for a while because of financial problems. He emigrated to the United States and became a director of the **March of Time**, the documentary series by Time Inc. Lye began to work in animation again in the early 1950s, and his first film of this new period was *Color Cry*, also known as *The Fox Chase*. It proved once again his talent for innovation and experimentation. Inspired by Man Ray's "rayographs," *Color Cry* was made with what Lye called a "shadowcast." This consists of placing objects directly on film and then exposing the film to create elusive shadow images of the original objects. An extension of Lye's

direct animation techniques, these "shadowcast film stencils" create complex textures and abstract shapes that are evocative of organic cells and tissues. Lye collected materials and experimented with them for several years. Eventually he set these fragments to a powerful tune called "Fox Chase." Written and played on the harmonica by blind blues musician Sonny Terry, the tune simulates a fox hunt ("more like a lynch chase," according to Lye). See also **Len Lye's American Films** (1952–80).

LEN LYE'S AMERICAN FILMS

1952–80. U.S.A.
By Len Lye.
14 min. B&W and color. Sound.

After an eight-year hiatus in making animated films, Len Lye, who produced such classics as *A Colour Box* (1935) and *Trade Tattoo* (1937) under the sponsorship of the GPO in Great Britain, began to make experimental films in the United States in 1952. Characterized by Lye's movement from color to explorations in black and white, these films include *Color Cry* (1952), *Rhythm* (1957), *Free Radicals* (1979), *Particles In Space* (1979) and *Tal Farlow* (1980). Please see individual titles for descriptions: *Color Cry* rents individually; *Rhythm* and *Free Radicals* rent together (see 1957); *Particles in Space* and *Tal Farlow* rent together (see 1979).

NOTES ON THE PORT OF ST. FRANCIS

1952. U.S.A.
By Frank Stauffacher. Assisted by Hy Hirsh, Allan Schoener, Herb Gleitz, and Gene Tepper. Narration from an 1882 text by Robert Louis Stevenson, spoken by Vincent Price.
21 min. B&W. Sound.

Frank Stauffacher, together with Richard Foster, organized a film series beginning in 1947 at the San Francisco Museum of Art called "Art in Cinema." The series combined European avant-garde works with American experimental films. He was deeply aware, then, of the tradition of "city symphony" films: portrait films that often straddle both the documentary and the experimental traditions (see also *Rien que les heures* [1926], *Berlin: Symphony of a Great City* [1927], *The Man with the Movie Camera* [1929], *The City* [1939], and *N.Y., N.Y.* [1957]). Stauffacher, who directed *Sausalito* (1948), also worked with other Bay Area filmmakers, notably James

Broughton, as cameraman. In this film, the visual strength outweighs any formalistic explorations, and what emerges is a kind of travelogue with historical value for capturing images of a city unrecognizable when set against its contemporary skyline. The camera is in constant motion—up hills, across streets, along building silhouettes—giving a kinetic life to the film. The narration, spoken by Vincent Price and credited to Robert Louis Stevenson, calls San Francisco a city of contrasts and so it appears: particularly in the mixture of people who call it home, a veritable United Nations of a city and an appropriate birthplace for that organization. The fog, of course, drifts over Golden Gate Bridge and the sea waves submerge rocks on the coast. As in his earlier portrait of Sausalito, Stauffacher reveals a sense of humor as he follows the labor of a car that can't quite get up one of the city's famous vertigo-inducing hills.

PARADE

1952. U.S.A.
By Charles and Ray Eames. Music by John Philip Sousa.
6 min. Color. Sound.

Drawing from their extensive collection, the Eameses have staged for this playful film, subtitled "Here They Come Down the Street," a parade of toys of every design and national origin—Hopi kachina dolls, puppets from India, tin soldiers, mechanical figures, Mexican papier-mâché animals, a huge robot. The camera pays close attention to the marvelous detail of the toys and the setting of fanciful cutouts, while the John Philip Sousa music keeps the action marching briskly to the final image of a single red balloon floating away into the sky. The filmmakers' sense of appreciation for the toys' design and the form their careful editing gives the film leaves the audience with only one regret at the conclusion: *Parade* is all too brief.

ANALOGIES #1

1953. U.S.A.
By James Davis.
10 min. Color. Sound.

The artist James Davis has chosen a formal structure separating two sequences involving images of color and motion—one photographed from nature (objects mirrored on water) and the other created in the studio. His expressed purpose is to explore the "analogy: between effects of moving forms of color which are observed in highly reflective surfaces—both natural and artificial." The film is most striking when the natural reflected images are not recognizable as objects but become kinetic visual patterns, as the ripples pour like thick paint across the water. The success of **Analogies #1** is demonstrated in the seamless blending of the two parts and the ease with which one can be unaware of the transition.

A COMMUNICATIONS PRIMER

1953. U.S.A.
By Charles and Ray Eames. Music by Elmer Bernstein.
22 min. Color. Sound.

It is difficult to conceive, from the current perspective of microscopic processing units more powerful than the original Univac computer which filled rooms of space, of the futuristic quality of this 1953 film by the creative team of Ray and Charles Eames. That it still has relevance—perhaps even more so three decades later—is an enormous testament to the ability of these multi-talented designers, who have made, with powerful graphic impact, a visual interpretation of some of the most influential and complex ideas that challenge society today. The narration speaks of "entering the era of communication" and offers a broad and human-scaled—not technological—definition of communication as "that which links any organism together." The Shannon-Weaver communication model forms much of the introductory base of the film. The Eameses chose to emphasize the fact that communication technology has a fundamental human metaphor and that it must constantly be reviewed and corrected by human supervision. The concluding statement is both a challenge and a warning: "Communication means responsibility of decision all the way down the line." The final image is the brush stroke of a Chinese character, the essence of which, according to the classical brush painting masters, is strength learned through the accord of heart and hand.

DANCE IN THE SUN

1953. U.S.A.
By Shirley Clarke. Music by Ralph Gilbert. With Daniel Nagrin.
6 min. Color. Sound.

Shirley Clarke performed as a modern dancer before she made this first film. Two motives drew her to filmmaking: she wanted to preserve that which she and her colleagues had spent months in achieving, and more immediately, she wanted to discover how to take a stage dance and turn it into a good dance film. She chose for her first try Daniel Nagrin's "Dance in the Sun." She photographed the artist performing his dance at Jones Beach on Long Island, but discovered that the appearance of nature in the sun, sand, and sea overwhelmed the motions of the dancer. Still determined to preserve the dance and to chronicle this in a distinctly cinematic manner, Clarke devised an elegant, but simple method. She cut Nagrin's dance outside by the sea together with the same choreography performed in a rehearsal hall. Nagrin would then leap from the shore and land on a stage floor. Thus, Clarke invested the dancer's motions with a new dimension: the choreography of the body, free and graceful, not only in time, but now also through space. Even though this technique may now appear familiar to those exposed to contemporary television commercials, this pioneer film still elicits in its audience a true kinetic exhilaration for the dance.

DESISTFILM

1954. U.S.A.
By Stan Brakhage. With Austin Benson, Fair Jordan, Newcomb Tenney.
7 min. B&W. Sound.

This very early film in Brakhage's development uses both sound and narrative cinema techniques to explore a teenage party. The camera moves actively around the room, drawing relationships between the five boys and one girl through its restless pursuit from face to face. The film, compact in its structure, manages to evoke a range of feelings from the setting and the characters. It captures their isolation, sexual tensions, boredom, flirting, awkwardness, frustration, competitiveness, as well as the sense of veiled threat. P. Adams Sitney in *Visionary Film* cites the combination of realism and expressionism as characteristic of Brakhage's first works, and calls the liberated camera style a formal advance for the filmmaker.

IN PARIS PARKS

1954. U.S.A.
By Shirley Clarke. Music by Lanoue Davenport.
12 min. Color. Sound.

Clarke has captured the daily rhythm of the Luxembourg Gardens in Paris with a documentary quality and a playful sense of humor not unlike the Punch and Judy show performed for an enchanted audience. This is a park and a film for both adults and children. The music is a calliope of sound that serves as an effective transitional element from scene to scene.

JAZZ OF LIGHTS

1954. U.S.A.
By Ian Hugo. Music by Louis and Bebe Barron. With Anaïs Nin, Moondog.
16 min. Color. Sound.

The lights of Times Square at night take on new, fresh meanings in this film. Abstracted from their gaudy signs, divorced from their function of selling, they create intricate patterns of form and color with a beauty of their own. Like haunted figures moving through the colors are Moondog, a blind poet, and the writer Anaïs Nin, who describes the film: "The basis is imaginative realism, that is, realism transmuted into fugitive impressions, an ephemeral flow of sensations. [Hugo] manipulates with skill the elements which dislocate or blur objects and faces and reveals new aspects of them as they are revealed in emotional states. Ian Hugo has added to the phantasmagorical qualities of film images, special effects which have caused the images to meet together as if they were notes in musical composition, to flow into one another and become pure image and pure rhythm."

ROBERT BREER PROGRAM II

1954–68. U.S.A.
By Robert Breer.
Total program: 17 min. Color. Sound.

UN MIRACLE

1954.
Made in collaboration with Pontus Hultén.
30 seconds.

CATS

1956.
Sound by Frances Breer.
1 min.

JAMESTOWN BALOOS

1957.
5 min.

BLAZES

1961.
3 min.

66

1966.
5 min.

PBL 2

1968.
1 min.

This survey of films by animator Robert Breer, whose films *Horse Over Teakettle* (1962), *Fist Fight* (1964), *TZ* (1979), and others are also in the collection, represents a broad span of Breer's work. *Un Miracle*, Breer's first collage animation, is a humorous 30-second parody of Pope Pius XII as he stands on the Vatican balcony. In what Breer calls "a Kafka-like metamorphosis of a human being," the pope juggles a series of balloons as well as his head. When he sprouts wings and flies away, a hand appears with a sign to signal the "Fin du Miracle." *Cats*, one of Breer's earliest cartoons, is a fine example of his technique of transforming line. Cutout cat shapes are interspersed with an enticing string and a bevy of felines which grow, ooze, and metamorphose into different shapes and sizes. *Jamestown Baloos* is divided into three movements that incorporate a satiric collage of Napoleon with the instruments of warfare. Two sections are set to military drum rhythms and frame a silent section of watercolor images that are blurred in a frenzy of movement. Although the film returns repeatedly to satiric military images, Breer consistently subverts the viewer's urge to fix this as the film's central theme. *Blazes* is Breer's well-known exploration of rapid single-frame animation. To construct the film, he painted 100 cards with bold color lines and shapes, and then he shuffled and photographed these cards in irregular alternations of one or two frames each, varying the duration and spacing of these explosions of color with sections of black leader. The result is a mesmerizing deluge of color that creates the effect of kinetic painting. In *66*, Breer explores the problem of color in terms of spasmodic perception, using Matisse-like cutout shapes. The central strategy of the film is to create a play of afterimages by presenting a series of colored shapes on a white background that are then interrupted by a smaller shape on a color background. These shapes flash back and forth and on and off the color background, forming afterimages, creating depth and flattening it, and presenting color and interrupting it. *PBL 2* is an imaginative cartoon in which a line becomes two opposing characters, one a red-nosed redneck and the other a black with an earring. They fight, the black character plays a drum, and the white character is transformed into symbols of his position: a U.S. flag, a noose, a gun, and a dollar sign. The dollar sign spews smoke into the black man's face, and in the end, the enraged black rises up, triumphant over the cowering redneck.

—

TREADLE AND BOBBIN

1954. U.S.A.
By Wheaton Galentine. Music by Noel Sokoloff.
8 min. Color. Sound.

Treadle and Bobbin is an intricate study of the mechanics and movements of an early model Singer sewing machine. Using close-ups to isolate the details of the machine, Galentine creates a rhythm that echoes the tempo of the machine in a style reminiscent of the fascination with machines in Fernand Léger's *Ballet mécanique* (1924) and Eugène Deslaw's *La Marche des machines* (1928). The simplicity and logic of the machine's design is revealed by the fresh observations in this loving portrait.

BULLFIGHT

1955. U.S.A.
By Shirley Clarke. Photographed by Bert Clarke, Shirley Clarke, Peter Buckley. Music by Norman Lloyd. Danced and choreographed by Anna Sokolow.
9 min. Color. Sound.

Working with the modern dancer Anna Sokolow, Clarke parallels the sense of theater and the real violence of an actual bullfight with a dance interpretation of the experience. Sokolow creates her movement out of a distillation of the ritual gestures we see photographed in the Spanish bull ring. In her intense performance, she embodies both the matador and the bull, both the executioner and the sacrifice. The evocative music by Normann Lloyd underscores the filmmaker's effective joining, through careful editing, of both elements.

EVOLUTION

1955. U.S.A.
By James Davis. Film Images production.
9 min. Color. Sound.

Deep, saturated colors emerge out of a highly polished surface as if from the primordial ooze. The film seems to grow—as do the viscous images—organically, from the center of the forms. At times sparks of light are struck off the patterns of reflected shapes, lifting the eye of the imagination outward from the depths.

HOUSE

1955. U.S.A.
By Charles and Ray Eames. Music by Elmer Bernstein.
13 min. Color. Sound.

The contributions to modern design of the team of Charles and Ray Eames span fields as diverse as multimedia, furniture design, architecture, and film. This film, which is subtitled "After Five Years of Living," is a celebration of the modular structure they built in 1949 on a cliff overlooking the Pacific Ocean. The emphasis in the film and in the house is not on architecture but rather on the sense of space and the feeling of interrelationship between building and site. Using exclusively a series of still images, the filmmakers have chosen to create a kind of kaleidoscope of brief, individual fragments that blend together on the screen into a harmonious whole. Color, reflections, light, and shadow patterns are motifs captured by the Eameses' choice of visual style for the film. It is significant that the designers let five years elapse between construction and filming, because this is a house that is very much lived in—it is a stage set for their numerous collections of folk art and everyday objects, all transformed by arrangement and juxtaposition into a gallery where even the breakfast table gives an aesthetic pleasure to the eyes. (See also *Parade* [1952], another Eames film that highlights their collecting "enthusiasms.") The meditative and perfectly fitted score is by the gifted Hollywood composer Elmer Bernstein, who wrote music for *A Communications Primer* (1953).

THE WONDER RING

1955. U.S.A.
By Stan Brakhage.
4 min. Color. Silent. 24 fps.

This gemlike visual ring around the Third Avenue elevated train in New York City was suggested and financed by Joseph Cornell, who wanted a film made about the El before it was torn down. It is a breakthrough work for Brakhage, marking the beginning of his lifelong emphasis, for the viewer as well as the filmmaker, on film as vision. There is a loving attention in the way the camera lingers on the details of the stations and a documentary sense not only of the architectural and engineering qualities but also of the kinetic experience of riding on the El itself. The cinematography and editing styles prefigure techniques widely adopted by filmmakers some two decades later.

ROBERT BREER PROGRAM I

1956–74. U.S.A.
By Robert Breer.
Total program: 17 min. B&W and color.
Sound.

RECREATION

1956.
Text written and spoken by Noël Burch.
In French. 2 min. Color.

A MAN AND HIS DOG OUT FOR AIR

1957.
2 min. B&W.

69

1968.
5 min. Color.

FUJI

1974.
8 min. Color.

This program of some of animator Robert Breer's most accomplished works illustrates the diversity of his techniques. **Recreation** is a fast-paced collage that incorporates colored paper and numerous objects, including a mechanical mouse, the animator's hand, and a crumpled piece of paper expanding outward. Accompanying this barrage of images is a pun-ridden, nonsensical French monologue by Noël Burch (who made **Correction Please, or, How We Got Into Pictures** [1979]). The chaos of the soundtrack complements the playful mix of the visuals. **A Man and His Dog Out for Air** is a masterpiece of metamorphosing line. It begins with elusive images of the wind, a bird, swirls, and movement, and ends with an amorphous image of an enormous man walking his dog around the circumference of the frame. "I can describe it as a sort of stew," says Breer. "Once in a while something recognizable comes to the surface and disappears again. Finally at the end you see the man and his dog and it's a kind of joke. The title and the bird songs make you expect to see the man and his dog and it's the absurdity that makes audiences accept what is basically a free play of lines and pure rhythms." In **69**, Breer deals directly with depth illusions. The central image of the film is a horizontal bar which sweeps through the frame as though it is slicing through it in a circular movement. This bar also sets the pace of the geometric movements. Breer creates a dialogue between the depth of receding forms and a series of simple, colorful, interacting shapes. **69** is a stunningly orchestrated study of elegant movement and flashing colors, and culminates in an onslaught of sound and visuals. **Fuji** represents an advanced stage in Breer's use of the rotoscope technique. The film is an abstract recreation of a train ride past Mt. Fuji in Japan, in which Breer characteristically mixes modes of representation. Besides rotoscope imagery, Breer utilizes live-action footage and simple line drawing, and shifts between them with a fluidity that blurs perceptual distinctions. In abstracting the original photographic material, Breer emphasizes its compositional form. Mt. Fuji becomes a giant triangle and the passing landscape becomes a series of rectangles punctuated by the vertical lines of electricity poles. **Fuji** transforms the visual imagery of a train ride into an experience of kinetic geometry.

—

DAYBREAK and WHITEYE

1957. U.S.A.
By Stan Brakhage.
10 min. B&W. Sound.

This pair of films contrasts the two camera points of view: in **Daybreak** the objective camera records a woman as she sleeps, awakes, brushes her hair and applies her makeup, leaves her apartment, walks anxiously down the street, finally ending up at dusk on a bridge where she has a brief and unresolved exchange of glances with a man as they both look out toward the water. **Whiteye** uses the subjective camera entirely to assemble the visual pieces as a man attempts to write a letter to his love, and captures the persistent distractions of the writer as he gazes out the window at the winter landscape beyond. Brakhage has called these films investigations of the "frustrations of loving."

8 × 8 (8 MAL 8)

1957. Switzerland.
By Hans Richter in collaboration with Jean Cocteau. Photographed by Arnold Eagle. Sound direction by Richter in collaboration with Robert Abramson, Bebe and Louis Barron, John Gruen, Douglas Townsend. Lyrics by John Latouche. Sung by Oscar Brand. With Jean Arp, Jacqueline Matisse, Yves Tanguey, Julien Levy, Richard Huelsenbeck, Alexander Calder, Ceal Bryson, Willem de Vogel, W. Sandberg, Dorothea and Max Ernst, Jean Cocteau, Eugene Pellegrini, Paul Bowles, Achmed el Yaccoubi, Jose L. Sert, Frederick Kiesler, Paul Weiner.
70 min. Color. Sound.

8 × 8, subtitled "A Chess Sonata in 8 Movements," is the second of Hans Richter's elaborate cinematic collaborations with other artists, following **Dreams That Money Can Buy** (1947) and preceding **Dadascope** (1961). Taking the title, **8 × 8**, from the dimensions of a chess board, the film pays homage to Lewis Carroll's use of chess in *Through the Looking-glass*. It begins with the statement by Richter that "We use chess, as did Carroll, as the plane, the board on which all things which happen in life are also happening . . . transformed, symbolic—but not less real." Using humor and chance, Richter creates a heavily symbolic, surreal world where kings, queens, and other players on the chess board act out some of life's episodes. Included are sculptor Alexander Calder constructing mobiles and setting them to motion, painter Max Ernst pursuing his wife, Dorothea, through the canyons of lower Manhattan and a rocky western landscape in an overplayed domestic struggle, and writer Jean Cocteau playing a pawn who whimsically becomes a queen. **8 × 8** is an imaginative journey through the symbols and satire of Surrealism.

A MOMENT IN LOVE

1957. U.S.A.
By Shirley Clarke. Photographed by Bert and Shirley Clarke. Choreographed by Anna Sokolow. Music by Norman Lloyd. Danced by Carmela Gutierrez and Paul Sanasardo.
8 min. Color. Sound.

The performer in Shirley Clarke's **Dance in the Sun** (1953) makes a leap through time and space through the matching of two different shots so that they appear to be one unbroken motion in space. In **A Moment in Love** double images of the same movement, sometimes placed in different parts of the frame, sometimes placed one after the other with a slight time delay, are used to recreate the intensity of mood and tensions in a passionate relationship of two lovers. A boy and a girl meet in clouds, take off into a brief and rich dance designed for the camera by Shirley Clarke choreographed by Anna Sokolow. **A Moment in Love** is an experiment in "cinedance," a term used to describe a dance film that is not merely a record of an existing stage dance but actually extends dance choreography to a further dimension. Movements and images physically impossible to perform on a stage become the very essence of this new choreography where dreams and fantasies become visual realities through the truth-magic of a camera. There is a particular moment in which a superb use of multiple images and a streak of blazing color turn the two lovers into a blossoming flower.

N.Y., N.Y.

1957. U.S.A.
By Francis Thompson. Music by Gene Forrell.
15 min. Color. Sound.

Subtitled "A Day in New York," Francis Thompson's *N.Y., N.Y.* makes a major contribution to the genre of "city symphony" films represented by works such as Cavalcanti's *Rien que les heures* (1926), Ruttmann's *Berlin: Symphony of a Great City* (1927), and Steiner and Van Dyke's *The City* (1939). *N.Y., N.Y.* is a series of surreal urban images that, taken together and in large doses, force the viewer to see the everyday in a new light. Thompson has combined the visual elements of the kaleidoscope, prism, hall of mirrors, and fisheye lens into a cinematic technique the cumulative impact of which is wonderful. Through a variety of lenses, reflectors, special optical effects, and brilliant editing, Thompson distorts and recreates a city that defies superlatives. One of the reasons for Thompson's successful integration of this menagerie of techniques is the sense of organic development created by the film's underlying diurnal structure. When the clock shatters at 8 a.m. and sounds 12 p.m.—it *feels* like morning and noon. The transition to night follows a slowing down of the frantic pace as if a gathering of strength for the bright lights to come is a natural rhythm of change. The musical score by Gene Forrell is every bit as complex and effective as the imagery, moving from concrete sounds to abstract jazz, alternating tempos to evoke both time and place. The director's juggling act of all these ingredients reminds us of the complexity in good filmmaking that is usually taken for granted.

RHYTHM and *FREE RADICALS*

1957–79. U.S.A.
By Len Lye.
Total program: 5 min. B&W. Sound.

RHYTHM

1957.
Produced by Direct Film Company for the Chrysler Corporation.
1 min.

FREE RADICALS

1979. U.S.A.
Assisted by Paul Barnes and Steve Jones.

Produced by Direct Film Company.
Music by the Bagirmi Tribe (Africa).
4 min.

These two American films by Len Lye are fine examples of Lye's various experiments in the latter part of his filmmaking career. Although he was unable to interest American advertisers in his work, Lye did make *Rhythm*, a remarkable trial commercial for the Chrysler Corporation. It is an extraordinary attestation to his ability to give a kinetic quality to fragments of live-action footage. Lye transformed stock footage of car assembly into a dramatically speeded version by using hundreds of jumpcuts. African drum music heightens the impression of activity. This one-minute motion composition was never used by Chrysler. Lye then made *Free Radicals* in 1958, which he revised into a tighter version in 1979. A departure from his experiments in color, the film is a stark black-and-white study of direct animation, made by scratching forms and patterns into black film leader. Lye described *Free Radicals* as "white zigglezag-splutter scratches in quite doodling fashion." Set to African music, the film is evocative of tribal art and of the particles of energy known in chemistry as free radicals. (See also **Len Lye's American Films** [1952–80].)

ANTICIPATION OF THE NIGHT

1958. U.S.A.
By Stan Brakhage.
42 min. Color. Silent. 24 fps.

This hauntingly powerful statement is one of the central works of Brakhage's career and a major contribution to the experimental film canon. *Anticipation of the Night* is a metaphor in vision, filled with beautiful imagery, that functions as a cinematic primer, teaching the viewer how to see: color, light, movement, objects familiar and unknown. It is also a meditation on the formal qualities of film structure: repetition, contrast, rhythm, progression in space and time. The screen is a flat plane of vision; objects and lights move across this plane in controlled and geometric patterns. Density is achieved more by a seamless compression of imagery through editing than by layers of superimposition. The artist offers the following "summary of the subject" for "identification purposes only": "The daylight shadow of a man in its movement evokes lights in the night. A rose bowl held in hand reflects both sun and moonlike illumination. The opening of a doorway onto trees anticipates the twilight into the night. A child is born on the lawn, born of water with its promissory rainbow, and the wild rose. It becomes the moon and the source of

BRIDGES-GO-ROUND (1958) (p. 184)

all light. Lights of the night become young children playing a circular game. The moon moves over a pillared temple to which all lights return. There is seen the sleep of the innocents in their animal dreams, becoming the amusement, their circular game, becoming the morning. The trees change color and lose their leaves for the morn, they become the complexity of branches in which the shadow man hangs himself." Light—its presence and absence—is the primary causal element of the film image. Brakhage moves from daylight and shadow to twilight to nightlight to dawn, traveling down an Odyssean path somewhere between the trance film (**Daybreak** and **Whiteye** [1957]) and the lyrical film (**Dog Star Man** [1964]). In the end, however, it is the strangely moving progress of the narrative "eye" of the "shadow man" that visually and emotively draws the viewer toward the inexorable conclusion of **Anticipation of the Night**.

BRIDGES-GO-ROUND

1958. U.S.A.
By Shirley Clarke. Music by Louis and Bebe Barron, Teo Macero.
8 min. (total of both versions) Color. Sound.

In this film Manhattan Island becomes a maypole around which its bridges, detached from moorings and land, execute a bewitched and beguiling dance. The filmmaker has freed these formidable structures from their everyday, pedestrian functions and has magically set them dancing to two different musical tracks—an electronic score by Louis and Bebe Barron and a jazz score by Teo Macero. Each track so affects the viewer's response to the imagery of the film that he imagines the content to have been altered.

BRUCE CONNER PROGRAM

1958–78. U.S.A.
By Bruce Conner.
Total program: 30 min. B&W and color. Sound.

PERMIAN STRATA

1969.
Music: "Rainy Day Women #12 & 35" by Bob Dylan.
4 min. B&W.

MONGOLOID

1977.
Music: "Mongoloid" by Devo.
4 min. B&W.

A MOVIE

1958.
12 min. B&W.

TAKE THE 5:10 TO DREAMLAND

1976.
6 min. Sepia tint.

VALSE TRISTE

1978.
5 min. Sepia tint.

Bruce Conner is one of the master satirists of American experimental cinema and the body of his work constitutes a wry, devastating portrait of contemporary America. Having begun his career as an assemblage artist in the mid-1950s, Conner was drawn to the avant-garde collage film. In 1958 he made **A Movie**, a work which juxtaposes clips from westerns, chase-films, pornography, and documentaries. The conjunction of images of sex and destruction establishes a clear link between the two forces, and advances the notion of the "movies" as fueled by the joint powers of eros and violence. **Permian Strata** also employs assemblage techniques for satirical purposes, although in this film it is the audio-visual disjunctions which are most bold. Taking religion as his ironic subject, Conner synchronizes imagery of a martyred apostle (from an old biblical epic) with the Bob Dylan lyric "Everybody Must Get Stoned." In **Mongoloid**, he uses a similar audio-visual strategy to mock the bourgeois way of life. As the punk rock group Devo sings on the soundtrack, images appear from advertising and science films: a television commercial whisks a man away from his living room; scientific footage shows people with electrodes in their brains. The average citizen emerges as automaton, a notion that Conner himself supports in his sly description of the film as exploring "the way in which a determined man [can overcome] a basic mental defect and become a useful member of society." The two other collage films on the program are less satirical in tone, and both use found footage to create a haunting sense of the past. **Valse Triste**, according to Conner, is a "nostalgic recreation of dreamland Kansas 1947," the environment in which he was raised. This sense is communicated poignantly by the imagery of the film, which intercuts shots of a young boy in bed with scenes of a rural landscape. **Take the 5:10 to Dreamland** shares a similar thrust. With its strange imagery of streams, rocket launches, plumb lines, and furrowed earth, it creates a cinematic dreamland express—precisely 5 minutes 10 seconds long.

—

MELODIC INVERSION

1958. U.S.A.
By Ian Hugo. With Anaïs Nin, Robert de Vries, James Leo Herlihy. Music from Quartet No. 4 by Schoenberg.
8 min. Color. Sound.

Howard Thompson, film critic for the *New York Times*, defines the theme of this film as: "Inversion—the process of reality unmaking itself as it makes itself—as in an hourglass. This film is a visual melodic study of transposal in which brilliantly diffused colors with fluid movements are constantly revealing moods embedded in its theme. With imaginative boldness it stands alone and proclaims its message—that which today appears strange is the spearhead of that which becomes comprehensible tomorrow. Through a glass, hypnotically, is perhaps the best way to describe the highly experimental entry by Ian Hugo. His strange, haunting footage uncoils in a special world of shimmering lights and color, weaving images, symbols, and, not inappropriately, Schoenberg's music. The total effect is original, striking, even startling."

WHEEEELS, OR, AMERICA ON WHEELS, PART 2

1958. U.S.A.
By Stan VanDerBeek.
4 min. B&W. Sound.

This extremely playful, madcap comedy is a collage animation portrait of America on wheels. Everything in the film is mobile: cars, bodies, motorbikes, and chaise lounges, while one couple watches the world go by through their car windshield. With a jazzy soundtrack that emits numerous car noises, **Wheeeels** is one of a series that VanDerBeek created about America's national passion to be on the move. This sophisticated animated farce is also referred to by its maker as "The Immaculate Contraption."

A LA MODE. AN ATTIRE SATIRE

1959. U.S.A.
By Stan VanDerBeek.
7 min. B&W. Sound.

This "attire satire" pokes fun at social conventions as expressed in the trappings of fashion. VanDerBeek reshapes and manipulates bodies in classic collage animation style to make a mockery of the material "objects" we wear. Dancing zippers and drawings which transform a face into a scene of Venice combine in this pop comedy to undress our perceptions of the role of clothing in our society.

CAT'S CRADLE

1959. U.S.A.
By Stan Brakhage.
9 min. Color. Silent. 24 fps.

In this sensuous film about the interplay of light and the relationships of two couples, Brakhage has created a diamond reflecting images from its many facets—700 shots lasting from $1/12$ of a second to two seconds. The film forms patterns out of the golden light falling on objects—a bedspread, wallpaper, the fur of a cat, a foot on a pillow. The brief glimpses of people—making love, dressing, washing dishes, writing—merge with the other elements of the film to make a web of intertwined images passed in rapid and rhythmic succession upon the screen.

SCIENCE FRICTION

1959. U.S.A.
By Stan VanDerBeek.
10 min. Color. Sound.

This fast-paced collage animation is a classic comment on the race to space between the U.S. and Russia in the 1950s. VanDerBeek cleverly turns symbols of western civilization and social paraphernalia into rocket ships, with the Statue of Liberty, the Eiffel Tower, and even the Tower of Pisa all blasting off into the stratosphere. Rockets are composed of the debris of American life, monkeys run the control boards, and the earth becomes a time-bomb which ends up as a fried egg. *Science Friction* is a social satire as well as a portrait of man and technology in combat.

SKYSCRAPER

1959. U.S.A.
By Shirley Clarke in collaboration with Willard Van Dyke, D. A. Pennebaker, Wheaton Galentine, and Kevin Smith. Music by Teo Macero. Lyrics by John White.
20 min. B&W and color. Sound.

This enthusiastic, sometimes comic musical salute to the collaborative effort of the building of a skyscraper is a fine collaborative effort in itself. Shirley Clarke directed the construction of this film from her editing table with Willard Van Dyke, D. A. Pennebaker, Wheaton Galentine, and Kevin Smith, and fashioned a dynamic, pulsating, rhythmic history of a major construction. The in-

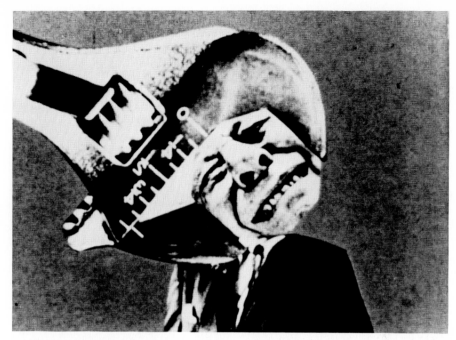

SCIENCE FRICTION (1959)

fectious energy expended in the building of 666 Fifth Avenue is translated into the building of a film that proceeds at the feverish pace that so characterizes life in New York. This film was a major breakthrough by turning a sponsored industrial documentary into a highly successful theatrical short. One of its major contributions is its original revolutionary concept of the soundtrack, in which Clarke uses actors' voices as if they were construction workers.

WINDOW WATER BABY MOVING

1959. U.S.A.
By Stan Brakhage.
12 min. Color. Silent. 24 fps.

Window Water Baby Moving is one of the most accessible of Brakhage's films. It is a lyrical and moving portrait of his wife as well as himself and the birth of their first child. Beginning with a scene of the mother bathing, illuminated by a bright window, and progressing through the entire childbirth process, including the expulsion of the placenta, the film combines the documentarian's innate sense of realistic sequence with the experimental filmmaker's transformation, through the eye of the camera, of the recorded images. The result is a recognized landmark in the history of the American avant-garde cinema.

THE DEAD

1960. U.S.A.
By Stan Brakhage.

11 min. Color. Silent. 24 fps.

The Dead is an intense vision based on Brakhage's experiences of a trip to Paris. Black-and-white views of the monumental tombs at Père Lachaise Cemetery and brief shots of Kenneth Anger in a cafe are combined in positive and negative images, superimposed, and intercut with color footage, photographed from a boat, of scenes along the Seine. The camera is always in motion, the editing frenetic, the effect—especially the use of solarization—is of strong graphic design. It is an eerie trip into a shadow world where normal visual senses are reversed—the disjuncture made more powerful by the seemingly ordinary pictures of Parisians going about their everyday business, pictures that flow through the imagination of the filmmaker in the city which contains cemetery and river both.

AN EVENT ON THE BEACH (HISTORIA DE PRAIA)

1960. Brazil.
By Fernando Amaral. Music by Luiz Bonfa.
15 min. B&W. Sound.

A predecessor of Brazilian "cinema novo," this mock documentary uses *cinéma vérité* techniques to record a staged incident on a Rio beach in which a man steals a watch. Four newsreel-type cameras were used to record the fight and subsequent chase. The composer also did the score for *Black Orpheus* (1958). Made at a time when the French New Wave was changing the direction of cinema, *An Event on the Beach*, with its then spontaneous mix of fact and fiction, may be seen as one of the earliest Latin manifestations of a "free" approach to narrative filmmaking.

HOMMAGE TO JEAN TINGUELY'S "HOMMAGE TO NEW YORK" (1960).
See Films on the Arts

A SCARY TIME

1960. U.S.A.
By Shirley Clarke and Robert Hughes. Produced by the United Nations Children's Fund. Music by Peggy Glanville-Hicks.
20 min. B&W. Sound.

Shirley Clarke's strong and touching plea for the United Nations Children's Fund is woven from both found and "improvised" footage. Shots of American children as they prepare to don spooky costumes for a Halloween celebration are intercut with shots of children starving around the globe. A boy in a skeleton's costume suddenly becomes a hungry baby whose skeleton is only too apparent. As the American children collect pennies for UNICEF, the children in the compilation footage begin to smile, laugh, and dance. The dance is taken up by children in various nations so that a circle that turns in Israel continues in China. At the height of this joyous dance of the children of the world the film changes into the shocking nightmare of the little "Halloween boy." He screams for help and on the screen appears the final image of a silent, still, accusing baby held tight to his mother's heart. An effective approach to film narration is the splendid use of the innocent voices of the American children that creates a reality and urgency that is emotionally devastating.

CATALOG

1961. U.S.A.
By John Whitney.
7 min. Color. Sound.

John Whitney, with his brother James, has helped to define the possibilities of abstract graphic animation. Working with an analog computer and an optical printer, he completed *Catalog* in 1961 as an exploration and meditation on the multiplying complexities of computer-generated visions and techniques. This is indeed like a salesman's sample book of images: spirals, dots, blocks of pure color, iris shapes that pulse and alternate, stroboscopic circles that set off sparks of color like fireworks. Whit-

ney's variations on the title and date of the film forecast future uses of this technique, particularly in television advertising and titling. The Indian music that accompanies the film is uncredited (see also *Permutations* [1968] and *Arabesque* [1975]).

DADASCOPE

1961. Switzerland.
By Hans Richter. Photographed by Arnold Eagle. Dadapoems written and performed by Jean Arp, Marcel Duchamp, Raoul Hasmann, Richard Huelsenbeck, Marcel Janco, Georges Robemont-Dessaignes, Walter Mehrig, Hans Richter, Kurt Schwitters, Tristan Tzara, Wladimir Vogel.
41 min. Color. Sound.

Dadascope is the third of Hans Richter's films made in collaboration with other artists (see *Dreams That Money Can Buy* [1947] and *8 × 8* [1957]). The well-known artists in the film include Marcel Duchamp, Jean Arp, Man Ray, and Tristan Tzara. What emerges from this delightful mix of episodes is a comprehensive portrait of the Dada movement with its specific techniques of sound and visual clash, word puns, chess, dice and other games of chance. "To these poems I made a film collage," said Richter. "To these Anti-poems, I have made an Anti-film. There is no story, no psychological implication except such as the onlooker puts into the imagery. But it is not accidental either, more a poetry of images built with and upon associations. In other words the film allows itself the freedom to play upon the scale of film possibilities, freedom for which Dada always stood—and still stands."

FILMS BY STAN BRAKHAGE: AN AVANT-GARDE HOME MOVIE

1961. U.S.A.
By Stan Brakhage.
5 min. Color. Silent. 24 fps.

Using the vocabulary of the home movie, Brakhage transforms the genre by combining its elements in unexpected ways—through superimposition, color abnormality, image distortion—while retaining and even heightening the feeling of direct contact with the daily life of his family. As P. Adams Sitney has noted, this film illuminates Brakhage's commitment to exploding "one of the most dominant [myths] of this century," that successful marriage is not possible for an artist. The filmmaker himself explains, "Where I take action strongest and most immediately is in reaching through the power of all that love toward my wife (and she toward me), and

somewhere where those actions meet and cross, and bring forth children and films and inspire concerns with plants and rocks and all sights seen, a new center, composed of action, is made."

FROM DADA TO SURREALISM: 40 YEARS OF EXPERIMENT (1960).
See Film Study

MR. HAYASHI

1961. U.S.A.
By Bruce Baillie.
3 min. B&W. Sound.

Originally made as a kind of newsreel for Canyon Cinema to help Mr. Hayashi get work as a gardener in Berkeley, this brief portrait film captures both a sense of the man and an Oriental feeling for the landscape he nurtures and inhabits. Baillie uses Japanese music and Hayashi's voice in counterpoint to each other, much as his camera discovers the figure and face of the man out of an enveloping fog. *Mr. Hayashi* is the first of his structural works.

OF STARS AND MEN

1961. U.S.A.
Directed by John Hubley. Adapted and produced by John and Faith Hubley. Based on the book by Harlow Shapley and narrated by Shapley. Animated by William Littlejohn and Gary Mooney. Musical direction by Walter Trampler.
53 min. Color. Sound.

Now over twenty years old, *Of Stars and Men* has come to be recognized as one of the major works in the history of the animated film and the magnum opus of the husband and wife team of John and Faith Hubley. With remarkable lucidity it explains, in terms that are understandable to older children as well as adults, man's place in the universe, giving an interpretation of the nature of the galaxies and stars, and of space, time, matter, and energy. A central figure in the film is a little boy who in his varying moods of arrogance and timidity is representative of man. The section on atoms and electrons is based on an amusing conversation between the Hubley children and was inspired by the earlier Hubley classic *Moonbird* (1959). (See also *The Hat* [1964] and *Cockaboody* [1973].)

BLUE MOSES

1962. U.S.A.
By Stan Brakhage. With Robert Benson.
11 min. B&W. Sound.

P. Adams Sitney writes that **Blue Moses** is unique in the filmmaker's output: "The existence of this film within Brakhage's filmography is very curious; there is nothing else like it in his work." It is a very polemical film that addresses the viewer directly in an obvious, Pirandellian fashion—thus calling on the theatrical origins of early dramatic cinema and questioning the theoretical structure of the realist cinema. Brakhage uses sound, an unusual element in his work, but extends himself even further by employing the technology of synchronous sound as well. Beginning with the visual analogy of Plato's Cave, the filmmaker goes on to challenge practically every narrative convention, undermining even the techniques of special filmic effects—by intentionally exposing the crude editing of the footage to simulate an eclipse: "manufactured, but not yet patented, for your pleasure." The actor's sign language and the pure white projected image at the end of the film reinforce Brakhage's concern with the visual as the primary force of his art.

HORSE OVER TEAKETTLE

1962. U.S.A.
By Robert Breer.
6 min. Color. Sound.

In this witty animation of brightly colored doodles, things are not quite what they appear to be. Disparate elements are juxtaposed and objects transform themselves only to reappear in new disguises—pigeon into man, woman into frog—while a boot flies across the screen and blobs blossom into a rainbow of hues, all done to a Keystone Cops timing. The filmmaker writes that "the pretext" for all these metamorphoses "is nuclear mayhem."

PAT'S BIRTHDAY

1962. U.S.A.
By Robert Breer.
13 min. Color. Sound.

Robert Breer's "home movie" documents the celebration of Pat Oldenburg's birthday, with much of the surreal humor and absurdist theatrical qualities of her husband Claes Oldenburg's sculptures. Scenes with no obvious connection are intercut: a man lying down on a bed of newspaper unbuttoning his jacket and shirt, people swimming fully clothed, others playing golf at a practice range in the pouring rain with strange objects as golf balls (a ball of twine, piece of pie). These visual oddities are brought to a climax in Claes's construction of a birthday cake,

Jack Smith in BLONDE COBRA (1963)

made of found ingredients (tires, rocks, children's toys), all painted white, set against a white background, and topped by a live white chicken. The entire creation appears to catch on fire as the party reaches full swing. The last image is of Oldenburg painting his hat white.

WARGAMES

1962. Japan.
By Donald Richie. Music by Donald Richie.
22 min. B&W. Sound.

This beautifully photographed, stark tale by Donald Richie, the noted authority on Japanese film, takes place on a deserted Japanese beach. A group of young boys find a goat and, out of curiosity, they begin to play with it. They gradually become more aggressive and fight with each other. In the midst of this the animal collapses and is gently washed by the waves like a relic left in the sand. Then the boys ritualistically carry the dead animal in a procession and bury it. **Wargames** not only explores the subtle aspects of the boys' interaction, but also is a metaphor for the rites of death and man's inability to coexist with his fellow man. The final image establishes a continuum as a solitary boy watches the water wash away the animal's grave, unearthing it as it would an artifact.

BLONDE COBRA

1963. U.S.A.
By Ken Jacobs. Photographed by Bob Fleischner. Edited by Ken Jacobs. With Jack Smith, Jerry Sims.
34 min. B&W and color. Sound.

Ken Jacobs edited **Blonde Cobra** out of film footage by Bob Fleischner and audio tapes by Jack Smith, the filmmaker of **Flaming Creatures** (1963). Both film and tapes had been abandoned because of a falling-out between the two. Jacobs had no idea of the original plan for the material (the pair had intended to create a "light movie-monster comedy, actually two separate stories," according to Jacobs) and he was given the freedom to develop the material as he wanted. The result is a very fragmented and complex weave of sound and visuals. Smith portrays a self-destructive personality playing many different characters, including Madame Nescience and Sister Dexterity and he performs and tells stories interrupted by false starts and long sections of black leader. Through his deliberate disarrangement of this "found" material, his undermining of the viewer's expectations regarding sound/visual coordination and narrative structure, Jacobs jolts the viewer out of a normal viewing situation. **Blonde Cobra**, writes P. Adams Sitney, "brackets dreams within stories, confuses a character with the actor playing it, and reveals a sexual despair while mocking sexual despairs. The folding over of guises and revelations deprives the film of a fixed point of reference, the solid presence of content, and makes it into a film object, which fitfully starts and after almost expiring several times, dies with an unanswered question, 'What went wrong?'" Instructions on the use of a radio with the soundtrack are included with the film.

BREATHDEATH. A TRAGEEDE IN MASKS

1963. U.S.A.
By Stan VanDerBeek. Soundtrack by Jay Watt.
15 min. B&W. Sound.

This dark comedy, using the technique of collage animation, was inspired by the vision of death in 15th-century woodcuts ("The Dance of Death")—to which the filmmaker compares modern man in a nuclear age. References to early cinema (Méliès peering out at the nuclear age) are combined with political commentary. VanDerBeek manipulates newsreel footage mocking social concerns about the end of the world and takes aim at Eisenhower, Nixon, Khrushchev, Hitler, and Charlie Chaplin. With juxtapositions of images of Hollywood and warfare, the film, VanDerBeek says, "superimposes Groucho Marx on a Karl Marx battlefield." *Breathdeath* still carries a powerful relevance today.

BREATHING

1963. U.S.A.
By Robert Breer.
6 min. B&W. Sound.

Breer's animation explores the theme and variation of the drawn line: a line in constant movement and transformation. With a very sketchy style, he demonstrates how a simple, abstract image can fill and satisfy the imagination of the film viewer. "Breer's unpredictable lines flow forth naturally with an assurance and a serenity which are the signs of an astonishing felicity of expression." (A. Labarthe, *Cahiers du Cinema.*)

HALLELUJAH THE HILLS

1963. U.S.A.
Written and directed by Adolfas Mekas. With Peter H. Beard, Sheila Finn, Martin Greenbaum, Peggy Steffans.
82 min. B&W. Sound.

Hallelujah the Hills, a whimsical and highly original romantic comedy, is one of the first feature films of the American independent cinema movement. Written, directed, and edited by Adolfas Mekas, it was one of the critical successes of the Cannes Film Festival of 1963. The nominal plot of the film concerns two men, Jack (Peter H. Beard) and Leo (Martin Greenbaum) who have met each other while courting the same woman—Vera—over the course of some seven years. The film begins in the autumn of the eighth year, when each man arrives at Vera's Vermont home to offer her a belated proposal of marriage. They find, however, that she has wed another man. The two men go off together on a camping trip in the woods, and their comic adventures are intermixed with recurrent memories of their respective relationships with Vera. A plot summary does not do justice to the film since the narrative line of *Hallelujah the Hills* is highly tenuous. Rather than presenting a coherent story, the film's structure offers a montage of vignettes. We slide fluidly from scenes, set in the present, of Jack and Leo frolicking in the woods to each man's remembered scenes of his beloved Vera. To complicate matters further, each man's recollected Vera is played by a different woman. Thus Jack's "winter Vera" is acted by Sheila Finn and Leo's "summer Vera" by Peggy Steffans. The film's temporal fluidity and use of ambiguity of identity caused one critic to refer to it wryly as "Last Year at Vermont." But this witty reference to Alain Resnais's *Last Year at Marienbad* (1961) is not totally gratuitous. For like the French New Wave films with which *Hallelujah the Hills* is contemporaneous, the latter is suffused with homages to moments in the history of cinema. In addition to specific filmic homages, *Hallelujah the Hills* also plays with more general cinematic conventions and devices. The film begins with a circular iris, a characteristic of the film style of the teens. At points within the film a rectangular frame, drawn within the larger frame formed by the screen, appears, emphasizing particular characters or elements within the *mise-en-scène*. At other times written words are superimposed over the image: characters' names (reminiscent of the title introductions of silent films); the word "breathless" over the image of Jack running (a reference to the title of Godard's seminal work); and Japanese titles placed at the side of the film frame (a reference to the popularity of foreign films in the early 1960s). *Hallelujah the Hills* is thus a work that is interesting from three perspectives: the

history of film comedy, the development of the new American cinema, and the international evolution of film form and style.

SCORPIO RISING

1963. U.S.A.
By Kenneth Anger.
31 min. Color. Sound.

An exploration of the myth of the American motorcyclist, or, as Anger puts it, "The Power Machine seen as tribal totem, from toy to terror. Thanatos in chrome and black leather and bursting jeans." Anger accomplishes his analysis of the myth primarily through his editing technique. Thus *Scorpio Rising* becomes a tour de force of montage, both in terms of purely visual relationships and the conjunction of sound and image. The film is divided into four sections. The first, "Boys and Bolts: (masculine fascination with the Thing that Goes)," presents the ceremonies of polishing and preparing the motorcycle. The lush sensuality of the imagery, as well as Anger's witty subtitle for the segment, clearly reveal the ritual's sexual connotations. The other sections are: "Image Maker," "Walpurgis Party," and "Rebel Rouser." Throughout the film Anger uses montage to make editorial statements about the motorcycle myth. Images of the cyclist, Scorpio, are intercut with footage of such cult figures as Marlon Brando in *The Wild One* (1954) and photographs of James Dean. The conjunction of rock-and-roll soundtrack and visual imagery also generates bold satirical comment. The song "Heat Wave," for example, accompanies shots of Scorpio snorting cocaine; "He's a Rebel" is linked to images of Jesus Christ from a low-budget education film. *Scorpio Rising* is not only one of the most important works of the American avant-garde, it is also one of the most illustrious. Because of its evocation of counterculture iconography and its celebration of mass media heroes (movie stars, rock-and-roll idols, comic-strip characters), it has been one of the few independent American films to achieve a degree of popular success.

TELEVISION COMMERCIALS

1963–76. U.S.A.
15 min. B&W and color. Sound.

Television commercials are essentially 30- to 60-second sponsored films. As films, they share in the technological and aesthetic possibilities of the medium, but economic exigencies and the blatant intention to sell a product often preclude creative use of that potential. Some commercials, however, have succeeded in achieving artistic, cinematic form. This reel represents a selection of such work. The style of television commercial cinematography both influences and reflects the tendencies of feature film production. The humor of the Alka-Seltzer or American Tourister luggage ads can be seen in relation to various modes of film comedy. Similarly, the Jamaica tourism spot can be viewed in terms of montage editing, and the earlier Volkswagen and Volvo ads are clever instances of long-take photography. Commercial cinematography also incorporates various styles of graphic design. The Pirelli tire ad, which seems like a magazine page come alive, is a noteworthy example. Commercials in this program are: General Telephone *Burning Egg*, Pirelli *Swing*, Qantas *Up a Tree*, Cracker Jack *Card Game*, Benson & Hedges *Dis-advantages*, Volkswagen *Keeping Up With the Kremplers*, Bic *Fruit*, Broxodent *200 Strokes*, American Tourister *Gorilla*, Jamaica *Waterfall*, Alka-Seltzer *Mama Magadini's Meatballs*, Volvo *Act of Congress*, Burlington Socks *Dancing Man*, Volvo *Attack of the Car Dogs*, American Lung Association *Rachel*, Qantas *Kangaroos*, and Volkswagen *Funeral*.

DOG STAR MAN

1964. U.S.A.
By Stan Brakhage.
74 min. Color. Silent. 24 fps.

One of the major works of the experimental cinema, **Dog Star Man** is an epic visionary challenge. Structured in a prelude and four parts, Brakhage has described the film as having a seasonal/diurnal form: "While it encompasses a year and the history of man in terms of image material . . ., I thought it should be contained within a single day." Working with one to four layers of images, adding other layers of direct manipulation through painting and scratching, Brakhage weaves a complex story of the mythical Dog Star Man. Sitney has compared the filmmaker's narrative in this film to the philosophy and art of William Blake, and this is perhaps the most accurate and insightful parallel for the viewer to understand the levels which Brakhage intends his work to embrace. There is a progression from innocence to experience, a fugal quality to the repetition of images, and an internal contrast in the respective meanings these images take depending on the stage within which they occur. The balance between earthy concerns in erotic visions and the spiritual quest of the Dog

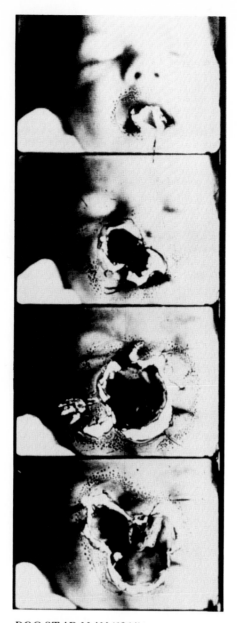

DOG STAR MAN (1964)

Star Man are intensely felt, and the alternation of Brakhage's interest in the childlike innocence of senses and the adult commingling of sexes is at once one of conflict and hopeful promise of union. **Dog Star Man** represents the distillation of Brakhage's focus on the "art of vision" and is perhaps the most compressed and articulate expression of his powerful art.

DUO CONCERTANTES

1964. U.S.A.
By Larry Jordan.
9 min. B&W. Sound.

Working with 19th-century engravings and a cutout animation style, Jordan has made a film in two parts: in one, "The Centennial Exposition," he conducts a visual tour of another time and place, while in the other, subtitled "Patricia

Gives Birth to a Dream by the Doorway," he creates a series of surreal images within the constraints of the door frame. A special highlight of the film is a spectacular fireworks scene.

FIST FIGHT

1964. U.S.A.
By Robert Breer. Music: "Originale" by Karlheinz Stockhausen.
9 min. Color. Sound.

Fist Fight is a rapid-fire onslaught of images in which animator Robert Breer uses myriad animation techniques including collage, cartoon, and punched holes. Set to the sound of the New York performance of Karlheinz Stockhausen's "Originale," which combines ambient sound and disparate instrumentation, **Fist Fight** is a chaotic barrage of single frame images that combine in a humorously sly way. Unlike any of Breer's other films, **Fist Fight** is also partly autobiographical. Breer scrambles still images—photographs of his family and friends—with fragments of cartoons, letters, fingers, mice, and other assorted objects. The film is articulated in bursts defined by sections of blackness, creating a strong tension between the lives depicted in the photographs and the brilliant explosions of imagery.

THE HAT

1964. U.S.A.
By Faith and John Hubley. Music and dialogue improvisation by Dizzy Gillespie and Dudley Moore.
18 min. Color. Sound.

In this effective animation about war and disarmament, two garrulous soldiers—played by jive-talking Dizzy Gillespie and cockney-accented Dudley Moore—patrol opposite sides of a boundary through an imaginative landscape. Their confrontation over the dropping of one's hat into the other's territory generates a lively discussion of issues like the nature of property, human relationships, the cold war, and the history of man's conflict from the Egyptians and Romans to feudal lords, centering on the concept that all wars are caused by lines just like the one which they patrol. Gillespie and Moore are funny, agile talkers who bring this film alive with a comic sense of logic and crystallize its serious message about peace in a world overpopulated with weapons and people willing to use them.

MASS FOR THE DAKOTA SIOUX

1964. U.S.A.
By Bruce Baillie.

20 min. B&W. Sound.

This film, conceived in the form of a Catholic Mass, is dedicated to the Dakota Sioux. Using the dramatic structure of a man dying on a crowded city sidewalk and following the procession of a motorcycle-led hearse/ambulance across the Bay Bridge, the film examines the visual landscape of modern American life replete with endless waves of tract houses and the omnipresent video eye. Baillie says of it, "*Mass* is a requiem tribute to the warrior, the poet, the best in man, by way of dedication to the original Americans—they who truly understood the *cycle*, or circle, the continuous flowing that is life."

LIFE

1965. Japan.
By Donald Richie.
5 min. B&W. Sound.

A witty and humorous morality play on a man's search—in an endless loop from youth to cemetery—for the symbols of life's pleasures: women and money. Drawn away from his first love by a trail of coins up a sharpening incline, he discovers an image—a photograph—of the perfect woman. His efforts to find her lead him down crowded streets, to the squandering of money, the surprise result of a child, and his panicked retreat at the reality of parenthood. When his frantic search ends in his collapse on the sidewalk, the child finds a coin on the road and the cycle begins again. With a sung and spoken score by the director.

OH DEM WATERMELONS

1965. U.S.A.
By Robert Nelson. Written by Nelson, Ron Davis, Saul Landau. Music by Stephen Foster and Steve Reich.
11 min. Color. Sound.

Oh Dem Watermelons is a crazy, anarchic spoof about watermelons—bouncing, exploding, and dancing watermelons. This satire begins with a watermelon posing as a football and with a watermelon rendition of the song, "Oh Dem Watermelons" ("Follow the Bouncing Watermelon!"), a biting but witty comment on racial stereotypes. Watermelons are chased through streets, hacked to pieces by ice skates, caressed by a naked woman, thrown out of a bus, and filled with animal guts until they become as demystified as they'll ever be. A riotous soundtrack by Stephen Foster and Steve Reich in a fabulous barrage of sound heightens the chaotic energy of the film.

QUIXOTE

1965. U.S.A.
By Bruce Baillie.
44 min. Color. Sound.

The filmmaker, as the visionary idealist bent on righting society's incorrigible wrongs, takes us on an American pilgrimage from California's vegetable farms to New York's Park Avenue, tilting against the windmills of exploitation (migrant workers bent over crops), injustice (civil rights marchers in the South), poverty (Native Americans on reservation lands), and imperialism (Vietnamese victims of a war that would soon mushroom). Along the way, the film stops to look at a small-town high school basketball game, the humor and spectacle of a circus performance, the billboard highways that cross the country, and a dozen varieties of work and work places. *Quixote* is filled with strong and memorable individual images and with superimposed and layered visual connections. Baillie spent over a year shooting this film, which was originally conceived for two screens and then reduced to one. He describes *Quixote*'s place in his development as "the last of the social-historical commentary works—(Western) man's relation to his world as *conquistador*."

ALL MY LIFE

1966. U.S.A.
By Bruce Baillie. Music written by Mitchell-Stept and performed by Ella Fitzgerald and the Teddy Wilson Orchestra.
3 min. Color. Sound.

A sunny summer film consisting entirely of camera movement—a long, continuous pan along a flower-covered fence in Caspar, California, lasting as long as it takes for Ella Fitzgerald, backed by Teddy Wilson's Orchestra, to sing "All My Life," and ending on a tilt up into an ethereal blue sky. Bruce Baillie says this is his favorite film and it is easy to understand his affection for this simple but perfectly satisfying combination of image and sound, which has come to be seen as a preeminent example of structural film.

CASTRO STREET

1966. U.S.A.
By Bruce Baillie.
10 min. Color. Sound.

Castro Street is a kinetic tour of a Richmond, California train yard and oil depot. Baillie reveals an industrial landscape in prismatic colors through selective matting of the frame, reversals, and superimpositions. The camera moves in the space with forward, up and down, sideways, and backward motions repeated in the locomotive movements, while layers of natural sound, jazz, and pop music amplify the total effect. A film of haunting images.

METANOMEN

1966. U.S.A.
By Scott Bartlett.
8 min. Color. Sound.

In this early Bartlett film, we see clearly the development of a personal cinema vocabulary. Experimenting with the techniques of film manipulation—high contrast, superimposition, negative image, polarization, and multiple matting—the film also tells a story about the relationship between two people viewed against the architecture of bridge and train.

PERMANENT WAVE and MANHATTAN DOORWAY

1966–80. U.S.A.
By Anita Thacher.
Total program: 5 min. Color. Sound.

PERMANENT WAVE

1966.
3 min.

MANHATTAN DOORWAY

1980. U.S.A.
Dance performed by Margot Colbert.
2 min.

Permanent Wave enacts a cinematic deconstruction of some pornographic film material. The original footage is tinted, abstracted, and set to Latin music. At points we see a close-up of a woman's face that seems to be "stitched" together from two original shots. Other sequences display a kind of "vertical roll" or "permanent wave." As the nude female model writhes in erotic ecstacy, the film image itself seems to pulsate—in a gesture of mock response. *Manhattan Doorway*, a film of a woman posed in the frame of a doorway, is simultaneously a study of space and movement and a vision of entrapment. Accompanied by rock-and-roll lyrics (which proclaim "Nowhere to run, Nowhere to hide") a woman performs exercises, both in real time and in pixillated fast motion. At points, the frame spins around or is turned upside down, so that the woman appears to dangle precipitously from the ceiling. Thacher has described the film as "movement and space perception turned inside out."

ATMOSFEAR

1967. U.S.A.
By Tom DeWitt.
6 min. Color. Sound.

It is possible to view this film as at once an indictment and a celebration of the urban environment. Colorized images, multiple matting, reversal, and solarization are all used to create a frenetic pattern of the cityscape with a feeling arising particularly out of its period—the 1960s. DeWitt describes the film as "The city scene: seen and unseen. Real and abstract. The fact without the figure, the figure without the fact."

DEAD YOUTH

1967. Japan.
By Donald Richie. Based on the poem "Shinda Shonen" by Mutsuro Takahashi. In English and Japanese.
14 min. B&W. Sound.

This contemplative film is both a homoerotic elegy and a meditation on death. With a rich sense of ritual and reflection, Richie explores the grief-stricken actions of several men in response to the death of a friend. Stunning images coalesce to form a universal elegy, reiterated by a reoccuring image of a young man's body washed by the sea on a solitary beach, an image which is both sensual and vulnerable, both a return to natural elements and a regeneration.

FIVE FILOSOPHICAL FABLES

1967. Japan.
By Donald Richie. Photographed by Makoto Yamaguchi. Music by Felix Mendelssohn.
47 min. B&W. Sound.

These five fables, performed by the Nihon Mime Kenkyukai, combine humor and morals in an unusual way. The stories are remarkable, eccentric tales of human interaction: two men vie for the affections of a young woman and become so consumed in their battle that they forget about her; a sculptor produces a statue which he brings to life for his constant sexual pleasure, until the tables are turned and he is used by her; three seemingly innocent picnickers devour their companion for lunch in an outrageous scene; a young man who walks everywhere on his hands falls

WAVELENGTH (1967)

in love with a young woman, who attempts to do the same to remain with him; and a lonely young man at a gathering is eventually disrobed by the insensitive guests and runs naked through the city into the countryside. Combining elements of both Japanese and American cultures with a style that embodies the rebellious spirit of the 1960s, Richie has fashioned fables that are both inventive and disarming.

THE GREAT BLONDINO

1967. U.S.A.
By Robert Nelson and William T. Wiley. Sound by Nelson with Moving Van Walters. With Wiley.
41 min. Color. Sound.

Inspired by the daredevil accomplishments of the highwire artist Blondin, who in 1859 crossed Niagara Falls pushing a wheelbarrow before him, the "Great Blondino," played by William Wiley, undergoes a series of picaresque experiences. Pursued throughout by a mysterious and ominous figure, "The Cop," and distracted momentarily from his path by "The Trollop," he finally arrives at the scene of his aerial performance and begins his dangerous crossing. Using the technique of intercutting action and reaction shots, the filmmaker builds a dramatic tension that leads inescapably to the tightrope walker's misstep and fall. The Great Blondino returns from his tragic end as we see him and his wheelbarrow profiled on the horizon against the sky. What Robert Nelson has done is to contrast the apparent narrative elements of the film with the seemingly random or illogical sequences from a dream structure. The film is characterized as well by a startling and humorous sense of disjunctive imagery—especially those images having to do with inversions of scale: Blondino "hot foots" it when he dances in diminutive size in an iron skillet or is caught in an *Alice in Wonderland* scene as he climbs upon a huge chair (built specially for the film) to watch the antics of a rhinoceros in a zoo. Nelson has dedicated his film to "Tightrope Walkers Everywhere."

OFFON

1967. U.S.A.
By Scott Bartlett, Tom DeWitt, Manny Meyer, Michael McNamee.
10 min. Color. Sound.

Bartlett and his co-filmmakers are experimenting here with a combination of film and video—the hard edge and the blurred. This film draws the viewer into a vortex of superimposed images that seem to pulsate with an electronic rhythm, while undergoing a transformation from what appears representative and naturalistic to a pure graphic form. Part of the mesmeric success of *OffOn* must be credited to the filmmakers' unerring sense of sound.

WAVELENGTH

1967. U.S.A.
By Michael Snow. With Hollis Frampton, Amy Taubin.

45 min. Color. Sound.

While it is accurate to state that *Wavelength* consists of a forty-five minute zoom from a wide angle at one end of a loft to a close-up of a photograph of a wave on the opposite wall—it is not accurate to conclude that the resulting film is simple, predictable, undramatic, and/or boring: it is none of these. Michael Snow has made perhaps the most complex structural film of that experimental sub-genre. Within the compass of the camera movement, four events transpire, including the moving of a bookcase, the playing of a Beatles song, a death, and the reporting on the phone of the discovered body. The screen flickers, pulsates, turns black, white, dark, colored; images are superimposed, repeated, blurred, inverted; action occurs within the frame, outside, beyond, and below it; sounds are synchronous, layered, natural, artificial, musical, mechanical, intentional, found, mysterious; time is stretched, compressed, abandoned, regulated, distorted, chopped up, endured. The filmmaker would continue this catalog of impressions for us—perhaps infinitely—for he says of the film: "I meant it as a summation of everything that I've thought about, everything."

THE BED

1968. U.S.A.
By James Broughton. Photographed by William Desloge. Music by Warner Jepson. With Alan Watts, Imogen Cunningham, Roger Somer, Grover Sales, James Broughton.
17 min. Color. Sound.

This film is a playful paean/homage to the bed as a site of daily (and nocturnal) living. Broughton has called it a "horizontal prayer," and a tribute to "affirmative eroticism." Shot in California's Muir Woods, the film begins with the entrance of a magically self-propelled bed. A man and woman appear, bearing the aura of a primordial Adam and Eve. Once the stage is set, the bed becomes the locus for a series of *tableaux vivants*: lovemaking, card-playing, reading, writing, sleepwalking, bed-making, and even dying. Broughton laces the film with characteristic humor: as an old lady reads to her sleeping dog, a foot fetishist relishes a woman's extremities, myriad people engage in an orgy, and repressed Victorian youths hover nervously around the headboard. But ultimately the film is a celebration of the diversity of daily living, with the bed seen as a microcosm for human existence. As Broughton has written: "All the world's

a bed . . . and men and women are merely dreamers."

BILLABONG

1968. U.S.A.
By Will Hindle.
9 min. Color. Sound.

Hindle explores elements of tension, frustration, and empty time in this film, which portrays the emotional states and anxiety of a group of young men who are divorced from society and waiting to be taken into the military. The title refers to a stagnant pool of water, and the opening shot of a road curving away from the camera, combined with train noises, establish a mood of anxious peering into the future. Hindle makes a collage of the isolated landscape and the solitary waiting figures. Using stark, grainy, black-and-white images to emphasize the sterility of their environment, he captures the gestures of tension, the expressions of frustration, and the subtle evidence of violence.

CHINESE FIREDRILL

1968. U.S.A.
By Will Hindle.
24 min. Color. Sound.

Chinese Firedrill is a personal, haunting vision of the breakdown of one man's mind. Using cinema to explore the psyche of this character, Hindle creates a complex scenario in which time elements are reversed and abstracted. The scene takes place in a small, claustrophobic room where we first see this character packing boxes of computer cards—which soon fall like leaves from the ceiling. As he interacts with objects in the room, a frenetic monologue of confused facts and distorted logic becomes an onslaught of sound that heightens the manic quality of his actions. Exploring themes of memory, closure, and disorientation, while creating extraordinary images, Hindle makes *Chinese Firedrill* a powerful study of the disintegration of thought.

EXPERIMENTS IN MOTION GRAPHICS

1968. U.S.A.
By John Whitney.
12 min. Color. Sound.

This film is intended as an illustrated guide to the process and potentials of computer assisted graphic animation, and accompanies John Whitney's *Permutations* (1968) as an explanation of the development and techniques employed in creating that final work. It is,

in addition, a prophetic film that calls for a future of "small, fast, cheap" computers to aid artists in the task of exploring the "elements of a structural system" of images as complex and ordered as language or music. (See Whitney's book *Digital Harmony* for his theory of the relationship between visual images and music.) Whitney expresses his own "agony of impatience" as he awaits an era of "home television sized computers" that will generate art that is a "regular part of television programming." So rapid is the climate of change within this technology that only a decade later his prediction has been fulfilled and many artists are today working on their own personal computers generating graphic motion art. The real goal, says the filmmaker, is to move beyond the level of "optical puzzles" and "to impinge on emotions *directly*." It is not easy, he reminds us, "to get emotionally involved at the computer"—but the potential and the rewards for creator and audience are clearly indicated in Whitney's own pioneering work. (See also *Catalog* [1961] and *Arabesque* [1975].)

PERMUTATIONS

1968. U.S.A.
By John Whitney. Music by Balachander.
8 min. Color. Sound.

A visual tour de force of constantly changing forms in color, motion, and variations of shape. This innovative work demonstrates that the digital computer as a graphic instrument can be used to create the fluid dynamics of a visual medium which Whitney sees as "analogous to the variational power of all musical instruments and the mathematical foundation of musical form." The filmmaker's concept of digital harmony developed out of the process of designing this film.

PLUTO

1968. U.S.A.
By James Herbert.
6 min. Color. Sound.

Herbert's last sound film is his first fully realized work: brief and pungent. Several of its aspects—including the technique of the rephotographed image—become incorporated into the artist's later works. The title suggests the underworld and the suggestion is apt. A sad and scruffy young man, as estranged as his disordered digs, gets out of and into bed. What is expressive is not that the figure moves, but how the filmmaker modulates those movements. The movements may be abbreviated, repeated, frozen, or slowed: the body is positioned in the frame not by its own will but through the intention of the filmmaker. *Pluto* is a quasi-animation, both haunted and haunting.

POWERS OF TEN (First version: A ROUGH SKETCH FOR A PROPOSED FILM DEALING WITH THE POWERS OF TEN AND THE RELATIVE SIZE OF THINGS IN THE UNIVERSE)

1968. U.S.A.
By Charles and Ray Eames. Music composed and performed by Elmer Bernstein.
8 min. Color. Sound.

Charles and Ray Eames's draft proposal for the film they would complete ten years later (see *Powers of Ten* [*Second version*] [1978]), this "rough sketch" gives us a "linear view of our universe from the human scale to the sea of galaxies." The film consists of a continuous zoom from a man sleeping on Miami Beach to the furthest known point in space, and back to the nucleus of a carbon atom in the sleeping man's hand. This provocative film at first seems to be a formal geometric exercise on elementary physics, but as the concept takes shape, disquieting questions about scale and time bombard the viewer. At the farthest remove from our planet, 10^{24} meters, nothing is recognizable and for every ten seconds in space 100 million years elapse on earth: history as we know it evaporates. At the other extreme, 10^{-14} meters, the electron, rather than being a terminus, opens instead a Pandora's Box of even more profound depths containing unseen quarks and more—as yet undiscovered—mysteries.

WAIT

1968. U.S.A.
By Ernie Gehr. With Gary, Sharon, and Kerlin Smith.
6 min. Color. Silent. 18 fps.

This film is an abstract study of domestic space. A couple is seated at a table: the man seems preoccupied, the woman reads. Through techniques of time-lapse photography, the sense of continuous motion is disrupted and the domestic scene becomes a jarring and disjointed barrage of images. The lighting continually switches from bright to dark, as though a lightning bolt had temporarily filled the room, then passed. At points, the picture abrasively changes in scale, as from a long-shot to a close-up view of a chandelier. By using these abstract techniques, Gehr creates not only an interesting visual fabric, but a charged psychic atmosphere of anticipation and weight—a space imbued with promise of drama.

⟷ (BACK AND FORTH)

1969. U.S.A.
By Michael Snow.
52 min. Color. Sound.

⟷ is Michael Snow's second major work, following *Wavelength* (1967). It was filmed in 1968 over a two-week period at Farleigh Dickinson University in Madison, New Jersey, where Snow participated in a seminar. ⟷ explores space through velocity and cinematic process, using an elaborate structure of camera pans in a classroom. As the camera movement accelerates, people wander through the room, a class is conducted, a large gathering appears, a fist fight breaks out, and other interactions peripheral to the frame occur. With a metronome-like soundtrack composed of the whirr of the camera and a slap at the end of each pan, the perspective changes from a back-and-forth pan to an up-and-down tilt over a single window, and then to a highly complex superimposition of numerous pans. In demystifying this space and emphasizing the camera movement, Snow transforms the room into myriad surfaces. "As a move from the implications of *Wavelength*," says Snow, "⟷ attempts to transcend through motion more than light. . . . It is more 'concrete' and more objective. ⟷ is sculptural. It is also a kind of demonstration or lesson in perception and in concepts of law and order and their transcendence. It is in/of/depicts a classroom. . . . ⟷ is sculptural because the depicted light is to be outside, around the solid [wall] which becomes transcended/spiritualized by motion-time."

MOON 1969

1969. U.S.A.
By Scott Bartlett.
15 min. Color. Sound.

Moon takes us on a voyage suspended between the sky and the sea, building to a final accelerated race through space. Bartlett creates a sense of mystery and drama through the sophisticated manipulation of picture and audio track, using synthesized images and sound to construct a film with multiple layers of abstraction. In his film, Bartlett combines both the disquieting and captivating feelings we harbor about extraterrestrial travel and allows us our own resolution of these conflicting emotions.

NUPTIAE

1969. U.S.A.
By James Broughton. Photographed by Stan Brakhage. Music by Lou Harrison. With Broughton, Alan Watts.
14 min. Color. Sound.

Nuptiae commemorates Broughton's 1961 wedding in a series of three different marriage ceremonies: secular, religious, and personal. Shot by Stan Brakhage, the first part of the film presents footage of the civil service held at the San Francisco City Hall. The second documents a religious ceremony, performed by Alan Watts. In the final segment, Broughton and bride are glimpsed by the ocean, enacting a ritual of their own creation. Accompanying these images is a soundtrack of music, liturgical chants, and dialogue fragments, which lends a mystical aura to the documentary footage. Favoring the mystical, Broughton also intercuts etchings, paintings, and drawings from oriental and alchemical sources with the autobiographical material. A central iconographic symbol reoccurs throughout the film: Yin and Yang locked in an oppositional embrace. As Broughton has noted, *Nuptiae* is "a film of ritual magic," celebrating the universal union of diverse bodies and souls.

ONE SECOND IN MONTREAL

1969. Canada.
By Michael Snow.
23 min. B&W. Silent. 18 fps. (May be projected at 24 fps, 17 min.)

One Second in Montreal, which Michael Snow completed after ⟷ (*Back and Forth*) (1969), is a film at the opposite extreme of the ceaseless motion of the earlier film. Silent and static, it is composed of stills of wintry park scenes in Montreal. The photographs were originally taken in 1965 to document potential locations for large sculptures and were sent to various artists, including Snow. *One Second in Montreal* is primarily about time, which is emphasized by the film's silence, its static quality, and its use of ambiguous, unexceptional images. During the first half of the film, the amount of time that each image is held on the screen increases in regular units, and in the second half that amount of time decreases (using a different mathematical formula) down to the single, last frame. The structure emphasizes the differences between viewing a photograph and a film (in which the viewing time is controlled by the filmmaker) and creates a contrast between the pictures as single images and combined to form a whole.

OUR LADY OF THE SPHERE (1969)

OUR LADY OF THE SPHERE

1969. U.S.A.
By Larry Jordan.
10 min. Color. Sound.

Larry Jordan, who made **Duo Concertantes** (1964) and **Cornell, 1965** (1978), has a distinctive style of collage animation that transforms old engravings by removing them from their context. Using Victorian engravings that are stunningly tinted in saturated colors, Jordan creates a classic example of innovative collage animation in **Our Lady of the Sphere**. The first section of the film follows the suspended figure of a young man who tumbles through a succession of scenes that involve acrobats, trapeze artists, and tour balloons. As spherical images dominate the action, a well-dressed Victorian lady with a balloon for a head wanders through intricate landscapes, meeting a similar woman and a man in a metal diving suit. The spherical forms create a central feeling of suspension, while the movement of the figures suggests a search. Jordan's imagery is elusive, fragile, and ethereal.

THROUGH THE MAGISCOPE

1969. U.S.A.
By Ian Hugo. Photographed by Bob Hanson. Music by David Horowitz. With Anaïs Nin.
10 min. Color. Sound.

Hugo conjures a forest of women by filming through "magiscopes"—crystal, plastic, and metal sculptures by Mexican artist Feliciano Bejar. Through the mottled, prismatic lenses of the sculptural piece, multiple images of woman are presented, creating a sense of life "on the other side of the looking glass." Within this mythical atmosphere, part of the birdlike sculpture erupts into a wild "dance" that ends the fiery holocaust.

WATERSMITH

1969. U.S.A.
By Will Hindle.
32 min. Color. Sound.

Watersmith is a striking visual exploration of swimmers in training for the Olympics. The film was shot entirely in and around a swimming pool, which is transformed by Hindle into a surreal, highly evocative realm with the use of a room-size optical printer which he designed himself. The swimmer's world becomes a series of abstract patterns, an orchestration of isolated gestures, and thanks to Hindle's brilliant color effects, an unreal, explosive environment. The rhythm of the swimmer's strokes, the intricate rotation of the training lanes, and the merging of bodies and water combine to create an eerie, graceful sensuality.

APERTURA

1970. U.S.A.
By Ian Hugo. Photographed by Bob Hanson and Lam Thanh Phong. Music by David Horowitz. With Anaïs Nin, Barbara Ward.
6 min. Color. Sound.

George Amberg, the noted American film scholar, has said of **Apertura**: "Here it is, the myth of birth, ritualistic ordeals through a labyrinthian underworld; and after primitive initiation, sacrifice, exit, and rebirth. The dominant quality is a ceremonial beauty for which the artist has powerful visual equivalents."

CORRIDOR

1970. U.S.A.
By Standish Lawder. Music by Terry Riley.
22 min. B&W. Sound.

Corridor is a complex exploration of depth and space, designed to bring about a change in the viewer's brain wave activity through the stimulation of alpha wave frequencies. The film begins with a long, slow zoom down a corridor, reminiscent of Michael Snow's **Wavelength** (1967), accompanied by an ever-increasing electronic pitch and producing an extremely tense and suspenseful effect. An elusive female figure appears, moving with a ghost-like effect, eventually merging in form with the corridor as it disintegrates, flattens, and expands. Lawder superimposes myriad images of this corridor in stroboscopic flashes to create an increasingly abstract, mesmerizing, cinematic pulse.

THE GOLDEN POSITIONS

1970. U.S.A.
By James Broughton and Kermit Sheets. Photographed by Fred Padula. Music by Robert Hughes. With James Brunot, Norma Leistiko, Ann Halpern.
32 min. Color. Sound.

Broughton writes that **Golden Positions** is "a poetic celebration and playful contemplation of the human body" and its characteristic stances: sitting, standing, and lying. For Broughton, the realm of human posture has not only practical value but spiritual power, and his title for the film derives from the Confucian notion of bodily "golden positions." Structured in the form of a seven-part cantata, Broughton presents diverse views of nude men and women arranged in sculptural tableaux. Some enact daily gestural rituals: washing, dressing, drinking tea. Others bear a more mythical aura: a man regards himself in a mirror (like Narcissus), and another stands Christlike, with arms outstretched, as though nailed on a cross. Other sequences present erotic poses, in heterosexual and homosexual groupings. Broughton's tone in the film is witty and humorous. For example, he accompanies an image of a man reclining with the statement that men "have made an art of lying." Throughout the work there are references to early cinema history. The nude figures remind us of Muybridge's human subjects and a belly-dancer suggests *Fatima* (1897). Thus a view emerges in the film of cinema as not only an art of movement, but an art in celebration of bodies in space.

LOVEMAKING

1970. U.S.A.
By Scott Bartlett.
14 min. Color. Sound.

Lovemaking, perhaps the subtlest of Bartlett's films, is a sensual, ambiguous interpretation of a couple making love. Through his use of close-ups, elusive lighting, soft focus, and spatial ambiguity, Bartlett abstracts the action so that it becomes a continuous choreography of movement, texture, and sound. Beautifully photographed and delicately constructed, *Lovemaking* is a personal, graceful statement.

THE MACHINE OF EDEN

1970. U.S.A.
By Stan Brakhage.
11 min. Color. Silent. 24 fps.

This tapestry film begins with shots of a loom and extends beyond it to the elements that are interwoven in the filmmaker's life: the Colorado landscape, the interior of a house, animals, plants, and his family. The colors are saturated and the footage of the scenery is spectacular, befitting a vision of Eden. There is an absorbing sense of detail—both small (parts of the loom, a child's sneaker, red and green leaves on a bush, microscopic tissues) and large (fields stretching to hills, multiple layers of mountains, dramatic skies, suns and moons). All of this is recorded and transformed by the machine of Eden: Brakhage's movie camera.

NECROLOGY

1970. U.S.A.
By Standish Lawder.
12 min. B&W. Sound.

This film is one continuous shot as people facing the camera pass, in reverse and slow motion, up a crowded escalator. It reminds us that the eye of the camera is nonobjective and transforming even when it does not change position or focal length. The faces on the screen seem to be looking back at us,

the audience, while we look at them. The filmmaker has added a long "cast list" to complete the sense of theatricality underlying his work.

NEUROSIS

1970. Australia.
Paul Winkler.
9 min. Color. Sound.

Paul Winkler makes **Neurosis** a powerful antiwar statement through its use of animated still photographs from the Vietnam war as well as live-action footage of a political demonstration. Thus images of wounded Vietnamese war victims, of American soldiers, and of world leaders like Nixon, Mao, and Ho Chi Minh flash percussively across the screen, intercut with scenes of an anti-conscription rally in Australia. At certain moments the animation of still photographs is so dynamic that it creates a sense of live-action footage, particularly in a sequence involving battle imagery. At other times it is the very stasis of that imagery that is so effective, as in the case of the haunting photograph of a maimed Vietnamese girl which poignantly ends the film.

PORCH GLIDER

1970. U.S.A.
By James Herbert.
25 min. Color. Silent. 24 fps.

Porch Glider, Herbert's most popular film, is unlike his others in that there is a story, fractured though it is, and there is also the use of image as sign or metaphor. *Porch Glider* is a complex and layered film that for the most part takes place on the front porch of a gracious ante-bellum southern home. Out of a loose community of skittish young people (the film also works as a document of its time), an attractive young couple barely out of adolescence find one another, and awkwardly, with more curiosity than passion, they make love. The structure of the film is giddy, and the entire work enjoys a plasticity that is as fresh as the sudden showers which are seen as a kind of visual chorus.

RABBIT'S MOON (LA LUNE DES LAPINS) (First version)

1970. U.S.A.
By Kenneth Anger. Photographed by Tourjansky. With André Soubeyran, Claude Revenant, and Nadine Valence.
15 min. Color. Sound.

Rabbit's Moon was shot by Anger in 1950 when he moved to Paris. The project was eventually abandoned for lack of funds,

and the film remained unavailable until 1970, when Anger edited this soundtrack. In 1978, he made a second version of this film (see **Rabbit's Moon [Second version] [1978]**). The poetic narrative employs the stock figures of *commedia dell'arte* (Pierrot, Harlequin, and Columbine) in what Anger calls a "Fable of the Unattainable." Essentially, though, **Rabbit's Moon** is a film about the nature of the cinema. ("Making a film," Anger has said, "is like casting a spell.") Throughout the work the magical powers of the moon (symbolized by the image of the rabbit—a magician's prop) are compared to those of a magic lantern. The lantern beam, after all, projects a luminous circle like the moon and has comparable magical powers. Furthermore, **Rabbit's Moon** seems a direct tribute to cinema's first magician, Georges Méliès, and shares imagery and characters with that director's **The Magic Lantern** (1903) and **Au Clair de la lune** (1904). Anger creates a bold formal disjunction between the images of 16th-century theater and the rock-and-roll soundtrack, reminiscent of *Scorpio Rising* (1963). The film is shot in blue-tinted stock and the stylized actors move through artificial sets like those of Reinhardt's *A Midsummer Night's Dream* (1935), the film that Anger appeared in as a child.

SERENE VELOCITY

1970. U.S.A.
By Ernie Gehr.
20 min. Color. Silent. 18 fps.

This film is an abstract study of space that transforms the three-dimensional world into an animated graphic pattern. Gehr sets up his camera in an empty, institutional building corridor. He then proceeds to shoot the film frame-by-frame, varying the zoom position of the lens every four frames. In the beginning, the lens is set around the middle zoom range; as the work progresses, the lens is moved toward the extreme points of the continuum. Though the film follows a highly structural, almost scientific plan, the viewer's experience of the work transcends its mathematical basis. The corridor is breathtakingly transformed, through the strict manipulation of formal elements, into a series of geometric lines and patterns. A sense of deep space is subverted and the image seems entirely flattened. Walls appear to move laterally and an exit sign seems to advance and retreat. At the ends of the zoom the corridor dissolves into a giant X, as identifiable objects meld into pure shape and color. Gehr's stated goal for the film is "a desire less to express myself and more of making something out of the film material itself relevant to film for spiritual purposes."

70

1970. U.S.A.
By Robert Breer.
5 min. Color. Silent.

Breer is moving toward a pure color vision in this film of emanating forms. The saturated images are seen in stroboscopic light while hard edges are transformed to soft. P. Adams Sitney writes in *Visionary Film*, "Here [Breer] used spray paint, which spreads over his white cards as a borderless affirmation of pure color . . . In [*66* (1966), *69* (1968), and *70*] Breer for the first time joined Harry Smith, Jordan Belson, and Bruce Baillie as one of the chief colorists of the American avant-garde film."

SURFACING ON THE THAMES

1970. U.S.A.
By David Rimmer.
7 min. Color. Silent. 18 fps.

In this structural film, David Rimmer has radically reduced the visual elements presented within the frame in order to challenge the concept of filmic "action." The effect of the film is to raise the question of what constitutes change: are the images on the screen in motion and is motion itself the subject matter of a "motion picture"? The use of still framing, the flattening of the image, and the emphasis on the film grain all lend a tension to the subtle, almost imperceptible progression of the film in the mind's eye of the viewer.

APHRODISIAC

1971. U.S.A.
By Ian Hugo. Photographed by Bob Hanson. Music by David Horowitz. With Barbara Ward.
6 min. Color. Sound.

This has been called "a modern painter's film." It is an abstract expression of human sensibilities created around the plastic and gemlike sculptures of Feliciano Bejar (see also *Through the Magiscope* 1969) and the sensuality of the female form. These elements combine with Hugo's rich patterns of color and light to create a beautifully textured film. This is a companion film to *Aphrodisiac II* (1972).

DEUS EX

1971. U.S.A.

By Stan Brakhage.
33 min. Color. Silent. 24 fps.

By concentrating his camera on the multitude of details that together assemble the larger reality, the filmmaker guides the viewer, through a process of indirection and accumulated impact, to a vision of what happens in a hospital. Based on his own hospitalization and on the work of the poet Charles Olson, Brakhage has made a film entirely of glimpses: things seen but not fully or for long. There is a documentary concern for specifics in the images of curtains, sheets, tubes, hands, and piles of white towels being folded; there is as well a dramatic building of impact from the seemingly endless shots of waiting (shoes pacing back and forth, rows of wheel chairs, faces staring upward from beds) to the intricate sequence in the operating room where finally the red of the blood—in color and quantity—seems to dye even the omnipresent green gowns. The stain of the image spreads across the screen and then is resolved into a patient's blood red flower backlighted against a window pane. The film ends in the subbasement of the building with the camera tracing in close-up the movement of pipes along the ceiling, like a pencil connecting the dots, and then pulling back for a brief moment to let us see the overall pattern that emerges.

FABLE SAFE (1971). *See* Documentary Film

FALL

1971. U.S.A.
By Tom DeWitt.
17 min. Color. Sound.

Fall, an abstract work, employs the myth of Icarus to comment on the dangers of war. The film begins with images of the sun, moon, and sky, transformed through tinting and other optical effects. Soon the figure of Icarus appears, his body a mass of clouds. Accompanying this archetypal imagery is a Greek chorus chanting: "Do not fly too close to the sun." The film then articulates a free-form vision of nuclear holocaust, seen as a punishment for mankind's hubris. In sharp counterpoint to grandiose images of birds in flight are such nightmare scenes as bombs exploding, men in gas masks, and the sounds of cavalry bugles and gun-shots. DeWitt uses myriad sophisticated optical techniques to transpose and deconstruct the film image. As he has stated, it "tells [its] story in an iconic language: simple symbols in a synthetic setting."

THE GONDOLA EYE

1971. U.S.A.
By Ian Hugo. Assisted by Leo Lukianoff. Music by David Horowitz.
16 min. Color. Sound.

The film focuses on the power of suggestion of the multiple images of that magical city, Venice. A gondola (from which all the scenes are filmed) weaves rhythmically past patterns of wedding gondolas, funeral gondolas, work barges, women, children, laborers, dogs, cats, refuse, and reflected light. Filmed in Venice over a period of three years, in all seasons, it is a striking example of Ian Hugo's film language. Howard Thompson, in the *New York Times*, writes: "*The Gondola Eye*, unlike any previous films of Venice, is a bold, beautiful, and haunting capstone to one of the most original and searching careers in movie experimentalism. This is Hugo's masterwork."

MATRIX

1971. U.S.A.
By John Whitney.
6 min. Color. Sound.

In this film of computer-generated images, rectilinear shapes and lines are patterned in a kind of Möbius strip of movement and return. The filmmaker describes how earlier experiments in *Permutations* (1968) led to the design of this film as a visual realization based on musical harmonic relationships: "The resonant moments of symmetry in the differential play of lines, squares and cubes are made to coincide with the exact harmonic resolves of a strict harmonist composer of the 18th century, Padre Antonio Soler."

MY NAME IS OONA

1971. U.S.A.
By Gunvor Nelson. Sound by Patrick Gleeson and Steve Reich.
10 min. B&W. Sound.

My Name is Oona is a celebration of a young girl's perception and self-awareness. With effective superimposition, pacing, and vibrant images, Nelson deftly captures Oona's energy and her exploration of her environment. The soundtrack is a complex reverberation of phrases associated with early childhood, such as Oona reciting her name and memorizing the days of the week. This montage of sounds reaches a crescendo as Oona rides a horse, dances, and is chased by the camera. These scenes are combined with striking images of nature to reinforce her liveliness. This interpretation of a young girl's coming into consciousness is both perceptive and inventive.

REAL ITALIAN PIZZA

1971. U.S.A.
By David Rimmer.
10 min. Color. Sound.

Shot between September 1970 and May 1971, with an unmoving camera apparently bolted to the window ledge, this film chronicles what takes place within the view of the lens at a typical New York pizza stand. The actors are the people who happened to be there during that half year; the plot is the aimlessness of life itself.

LA RÉGION CENTRALE (THE CENTRAL REGION)

1971. Canada.
By Michael Snow.
190 min. Color. Sound.

La Région Centrale is Snow's epic homage to the landscape tradition, "a movie of a completely open space." Set in a mountainous region of northern Quebec, Snow employs a complex camera/machine to execute an intricate series of movements: rolls, arcs, sweeps, figure eights, tilts, twirls, and pans. The film then presents a record of what the camera saw, as it moved fluidly through space. Images of sky, mountains, hills, and rocks whirl before us, abstracted by the camera's trajectory and speed. Accompanying these visuals on the soundtrack is a composition of sine-wave signals that actually controlled the camera/machine. Snow has noted that the sound-image relation in the film is "a whole world of conversation in itself." *La Région Centrale*, however, is not only a landscape documentary, but a perceptual experience as well. As Snow writes, it is "a source of sensations and ordering, an arranging of eye movements and of inner ear movements." But beyond that, the film is also a poignant comment on the nature of human existence. As the camera operates devoid of human intervention, the frame "emphasizes the cosmic continuity which is beautiful, but tragic: [which] just goes on without us."

SERPENT

1971. U.S.A.
By Scott Bartlett.
15 min. Color. Sound.

Serpent begins with a series of natural images—fields of grass, trees, seashore. There is a meditative quality to the slow motion, repetitious sequences. A television screen enters the film frame. It is only a part of the picture at first, but it introduces a discordant note of soldiers, cowboys, tanks. Then there is a radical break in the soundtrack, as rhythmic music replaces the om-like drone. The video images dominate the natural scenes. In the aftermath, the film returns to what appears to be a burned out landscape. The filmmaker is retelling a mythical story using contemporary technology and poetic imagery. He is tapping a kind of cultural memory. Of his award-winning film, Bartlett writes that "*Serpent* embodies the primal chaotic life force in mythic symbology. It uses natural and electronic imagery to particularize this creative force."

TOM, TOM, THE PIPER'S SON

1971. U.S.A.
By Ken Jacobs. Assisted by Jordan Meyers.
100 min. B&W and color. Silent. 18 fps.

Ken Jacobs based this film on a 1905 American Mutoscope and Biograph Company film, photographed by G. W. (Billy) Bitzer. The film was an illustration of the children's nursery rhyme of the same title and was one of the first chase films. Jacobs opens and closes his version with the original Biograph footage as a framing device and expands the film in a highly reflexive study which examines the nature of the film medium. Jacobs's *Tom, Tom, The Piper's Son* deals with issues involved in the film viewing experience—representation, narrative, abstraction, and illusion—and with the structuring of time and space. Jacobs used myriad strategies to break down and restructure this ten-minute Biograph: he rephotographs details of the images, introduces camera movement within the frame, creates sporadic imagery with sections of black leader, does shadow play on the screen, adds two color sequences, and even photographs the light of the projector. The result is a rich, visual vocabulary which Jacobs employs exhaustively to create a completely new film. "Seven infinitely complex cine-tapestries comprise the original film," says Jacobs, "and the style is not primitive, not uncinematic but the cleanest, inspired indication of a path of cinematic development whose value has only recently been discovered. My camera closes in, only to better ascertain the infinite richness, searching out incongruities in the story-telling, delighting in the whole bizarre human phenomena of story-telling itself and this within the fantasy of reading any bygone time out of the visual crudities of film: dream within a dream!"

APHRODISIAC II

1972. U.S.A.
By Ian Hugo. Photographed by Bob Hanson. Music by David Horowitz. With Barbara Ward.
6 min. Color. Sound.

In this film, a companion piece to *Aphrodisiac* (1971), Hugo explores the sensual implications of visual form. Beginning with the image of a female nude reflected in an anamorphic mirrored surface, Hugo moves toward creating a purely abstract sculptural field of light, texture, and color. As he describes it, the woman's "inner physical sensations are progressively expanded and transformed, culminating in the rich images of a filmic painting." Accompanying the highly fluid film imagery is an assertive electronic score by David Horowitz.

GULLS AND BUOYS

1972. U.S.A.
By Robert Breer.
8 min. Color. Sound.

In *Gulls and Buoys* Robert Breer creates an abstract vision of a seaside locale through a mixture of original line drawings and rotoscoped imagery (traced from live-action footage). The space Breer elaborates shifts continually between the borders of representation and fantasy. At one moment some moving lines suggest the recognizable figures of a seagull in flight, a workman painting, or a child playing in the waves. These images are underscored by a soundtrack of seaside noises. In the next instant, however, the tenuous illusion of spatial "realism" is violated by the appearance of a geometric shape, or a cat walking upside down, or a huge key floating through the sky. *Gulls and Buoys* is not simply an abstract and beautiful evocation of a coastal landscape. Like all Breer's films, it is a text on the nature and limits of graphic representation.

HIGHWAY LANDSCAPE

1972. U.S.A.
By J. J. Murphy.
6 min. Color. Sound.

The ostensible subject of this film is a close-up shot, from a single camera position, of an animal killed by the side of the road. At first, the viewer may watch out of the corner of his eye, but then with growing fascination as the wind blows across the hair of the animal and a car suddenly goes by. This event is repeated first in one direction and then another and becomes central to this quiet but somehow affecting film.

COCKABOODY (1973)

IAN HUGO: ENGRAVER AND FILM MAKER (1972). See Films on the Arts

ICE

1972. U.S.A.
By J. J. Murphy.
9 min. Color. Sound.

A projected beam of light is refracted through the crystalline structure of a fifty-pound block of ice with a flickering, stroboscopic intensity. The result is a concentrated, demanding film experience.

LEVITATION

1972. U.S.A.
By Ian Hugo. Photographed by Bob Hanson. Music by David Horowitz. With Japanese mime Yass Hakoshima, Renate Boué.
7 min. Color. Sound.

The subtitle to this film is a statement by Anaïs Nin: "The poet teaches levitation." Thus the attempt by the protagonist to fly is symbolic, as are the obstacles that he meets in his attempt to become a bird. Like Hugo's later work *Transcending* (1974), *Levitation* effectively combines the universal gestures of mime with special effects.

MATRIX III

1972. U.S.A.
By John Whitney. Music by Terry Riley.
10 min. Color. Sound.

Matrix III is a computer film by John Whitney, one of the pioneers of that genre. It is an abstract work in which pure geometric forms (triangles, polygons, spheres) are choreographed in a complex visual design. Colors in the film are reduced to the primary tones and black and white. Whitney plays particularly with the illusion of depth in film, organizing his forms so that their relative size, modes of overlapping, and relation to the black background create tensions between two- and three-dimensionality. The film also involves an interesting rhythmic structure which Whitney articulates through the pace of the forms in motion. Whitney himself compares the dynamics of *Matrix III* to musical form. He speaks of employing "visual harmonics" and of how the film's "introduction, growth, exposition and final resolution have an emotional impact like a Bach Invention or a Telemann Trio Sonata."

SCARS

1972. Australia.
By Paul Winkler.
15 min. Color. Sound.

Scars is a film which deals with the subject of ecology in an abstract and highly innovative manner. Rather than make a direct statement about the effects of urbanization on the natural landscape, Winkler communicates his ideas through a poetic montage of powerful visual and aural imagery. Filmed in Sydney, Australia, *Scars* begins with a shot of a small tree growing on a road divider between two lanes of traffic. Cars zoom by in opposite directions while on the soundtrack we hear the piercing noise of an engine's roar. Each time Winkler returns to this image, the tree has shed more of its leaves. Intercut with this scene are shots of street crowds, television antennae, and garbage tossed on the ground. Contrasted to this imagery of urban decay is that of a more pastoral nature—trees, flowering bushes, fallen leaves. The film climaxes with a dramatic scene of men sawing down a tree. Winkler's innovative zoom technique and assertive soundtrack invest the sequence with a tone of passion and a sense of its having been shot from the fallen tree's point of view.

THE SHORES OF PHOS: A FABLE

1972. U.S.A.
By Stan Brakhage.
10 min. Color. Silent. 24 fps.

This film is a cinematic meditation on the basic formative element in the creation of the filmed image: light. Brakhage has used a close-up camera to flatten the planes of depth and to focus attention on the seemingly infinite variation of visual pleasure that shifting intensities of natural light can give to a reflective surface. By shooting through the legs of various animals, the camera directs the eye to reduced images that delight by virtue of their sense of disclosure of what is alternately hidden and then found.

SKY BLUE WATER LIGHT SIGN

1972. U.S.A.
By J. J. Murphy.
8 min. Color. Sound.

A slow, continuous pan across a postcardlike transparency of "the land of sky blue waters," actually an illuminated beer advertisement with a shimmering background of light on lake and sky. Complete with sound effects of water falling, this filmic illusion has some of the unreal qualities associated with the video image, while never losing its power of fascination.

THE WOLD-SHADOW

1972. U.S.A.
By Stan Brakhage.
3 min. Color. Silent. 24 fps.

Beginning with a standardly exposed, fixed camera shot of a group of trees, the film progressively alters and manipulates that original scene. Brakhage uses variations in exposure levels, time lapse, filters, and particularly hand-colored frames to expand the viewer's definition of the normal image. Brakhage describes his choice of title: " 'Wold' because the word refers to 'forests' which poets later made 'plains,' and because the word also contains the rustic sense 'to kill'—this then my laboriously painted vision of the god of the forest."

COCKABOODY

1973. U.S.A.
By Faith and John Hubley.
9 min. Color. Sound.

The Hubleys enter the world of children through the tape-recorded conversation of their two young daughters. Drawn from the perspective of a child, the film explores this animated play world with its myriad emotions, a place where these two sisters can transform themselves into the animals of their imagination, where anger is a black, moody cat with a cavernous mouth, and where balloons can really make them fly. *Cockaboody* is an excellent portrayal of childhood role-playing and growth.

DIE GEBURT DER NATION (THE BIRTH OF A NATION)

1973. West Germany.
By Klaus Wyborny.
70 min. B&W and color. Sound.

A "deeply ecstatic film . . . possibly the most searching discourse on film language that any filmmaker has yet attempted," is what Tony Rayns in *Time Out* wrote of Wyborny's kinetic two-part feature. The first section begins with the title situating the action in a specific place (not the U.S.) and time (1911, three years before Griffith made his epic with the same title). What proceeds is an anecdotal, elliptical narrative about men in a desert (*Greed* [1924] deliberately comes to mind) trying to make some social order. In the second half, the plot collapses (or rather explodes) into colored air as the shots that more or less constitute the film's first half rather deliriously obliterate their content through optical transformation and repetition while rather proudly proclaiming the beauty of what these shots *really* are—emulsion and base. The film that begins as a narrative ends as a lyric to the birth not of a nation but of the cinema.

HOWARD DANELOWITZ PROGRAM

1973–79. U.S.A.
By Howard Danelowitz.
Total program: 21 min. Color. Sound.

KALEIDOFORM

1973.
Sound by Doug Lynner.
3 min.

THE FUNNIEST I KNOW IS MUD PUDDLES

1974.
Music by Howard Danelowitz and Doug Lynner.
3 min.

HEADSTREAM

1976.
Music by Jeff Franzel.
5 min.

INSIDE OUT

1979.
Sound by Norman Roger.
10 min.

This comprehensive program shows Howard Danelowitz's progression from simple animation to sophisticated and complex animated works. *Kaleidoform* is a short, colorful portrayal of a series of strange, long-nosed, two-legged characters that transform, ooze, and expand into different shapes and into each other in a highly imaginative fashion. *The Funniest I Know is Mud Puddles* was inspired by an eight-year-old girl's drawing. Uttering high-pitched, tittering sounds, three colorful characters stand in the rain until they are firmly planted in three sumptuous mud puddles. Immersing themselves and reappearing from the mud, they splash forth in an explosion of color, capturing the mischievousness of childhood. *Headstream* examines a young boy's self-perception. Laughing, and accompanied by a babbling soundtrack, he becomes many eyes and mouths. He reaches into a landscape where he finds the glasses of a small geometric character who seems inspired by Navajo art. In a delicate, small voice, this creature laments the loss of his glasses until they are returned. Funny and intriguing, *Headstream* represents Danelowitz's departure into more figurative territory. *Inside Out* is a more mature example of *Headstream*'s figurative and innovative techniques. Creating Cubist creatures that are reminiscent of Saul Steinberg's drawings, Danelowitz pushes the boundaries of line drawing further into abstraction. The film centers on a creature who contends with a roster of funny characters that keep springing forth from different parts of his person: a yapping dog, a carnivorous fish, and a Minotaur-like figure, among others. This portrayal of a world (and body) out of control culminates in the creature throwing all the characters out and becoming a multi-reeled projector that spews out film. Frustrated, he weeps forth clocks, demons, telephones, and other objects, until he looks inside himself a final time to discover sunlight and a calm landscape. An effective interpretation of artistic struggle and confused imagination, *Inside Out* is a beautifully crafted, fascinating animation.

—

TRANSMIGRATION

1973. U.S.A.
By Ian Hugo. Photographed by Bob Hanson. Music by David Horowitz. With Odelianna, Elena Vaughn.
6 min. Color. Sound.

Hugo continues his exploration of the mythic in this film (see also *Apertura* [1970] and *Levitation* [1972]). *Transmigration* is based on an ancient myth of human souls transformed after their life into animals.

APALACHEE

1974. U.S.A.
By James Herbert.
12 min. Color. Silent. 24 fps.

In reviewing Herbert's work for the *New York Times*, the critic Roger Greenspun wrote, "I have rarely seen movies so aware of the mortal sadness of young bodies." This is certainly true of *Apalachee*; posed by a clear stream, the film should be a light-dappled pastoral, but through the distancing of rephotography, it becomes something darker and more beautiful. In the filmmaker's use of rephotography the original movements of the nudes (a young man and woman) are substantially reshaped. A gesture is fashioned into an event, and a gaze (eyes are significant in a Herbert film) into a provocative mystery. *Apalachee* is rich, sensual, and unique.

DARK

1974. Australia.
By Paul Winkler.
19 min. Color. Sound.

In *Dark* Winkler confronts the subject of the Australian aborigine by intercutting footage from a contemporary aborigine political demonstration with traditional images of the past: primitive cave drawings, the sacred Ayers Rock, and, most particularly, the head of an old aborigine warrior. Through assertive zoom and pan shots of the rally, Winkler achieves a sense of extraordi-

INTERIOR DESIGNS (1980)

nary energy, of a generation of people coming out of oppression. As Winkler himself expresses it: "*Dark* is a visual explosion of pent up emotions coming out of the Australian aborigine from dream time to action time."

HYMN TO HER

1974. U.S.A.
By Stan Brakhage.
3 min. Color. Silent. 24 fps.

A celebration of the filmmaker's wife and of the light which grows the green plants that surround her and which transforms the raw film material into the images we see on the screen. Brakhage describes the film: "HER to me is always Jane, in the first place, but also Hera, goddess of women and marriage, naturally enough. Then too, as it is a hymn of light, and as he/me feels the self that way, it sings of and to itself."

JANE AARON PROGRAM

1974–80. U.S.A.
By Jane Aaron.
Total program: 10 min. Color. Sound.

A BRAND NEW DAY

1974.
Music by Richard Grando, Larry Packer.
3 min.

IN PLAIN SIGHT

1977.

Music by Richard Grando, Larry Packer, Steve Silverstein.
3 min.

INTERIOR DESIGNS

1980.
With the assistance of Chris Beaver, Skip Blumberg, Sandy Drooker, Andy Aaron, Nancy Calderwood, Judy Irving, Jerry Ross, Deborah Shaffer, Curtis Shreier, Karen Spangenberg.
4 min.

This program presents three animated films by Jane Aaron, a filmmaker with a background in drawing and sculpture. *A Brand New Day* renders in line-drawing a morning scene of a woman awakening. As she does her morning exercises, she repeatedly opens and closes her window shade, glancing out at the exterior vista. Each time the shade rises, however, a different locale appears: verdant landscape, barren desert, coastal horizon. The final time it reveals the wall of an urban apartment building and it is clear that this has been the real view throughout. *In Plain Sight* is a more experimental work which intermixes live-action and hand-drawn imagery. Aaron's technique for this process involves the implantation of animated drawings into real-life settings. As she has noted, "The drawings are actually part of the live-action frame and act as a comment on the environment." In one section of the film we peer out the windshield of a moving car on which cartoon drawings of a passing landscape are attached. Sometimes the real

and animated landscapes coincide; other times they depict diverse events. In another scene, an animated drawing of clouds is mounted on a post against the real sky. Through these complex visual paradoxes Aaron playfully questions the status of the film illusion. *Interior Designs* employs a similar conjunction of live-action and animated imagery. In one sequence, cartoon characters on a painted canvas move through a real room. In another, paper cutout cactuses grow magically out of the real desert terrain. As Aaron has commented, her primary interest is in "the relationship of animation to live situations," of "drawing to reality."

PRINT GENERATION

1974. U.S.A.
By J. J. Murphy.
50 min. Color. Sound.

Beginning with a pattern of abstract red dots reflecting off the screen and the sound of wind blowing against a microphone, the filmmaker begins an additive process: he returns through a series of copies of a sequence of filmed images until gradually the forms and colors are restored to the original projection material. The film then repeats the process, but in a reductive progression until the image is abstracted to its original starting point. A fascinating and arresting film. (See also *Sky Blue Water Light Sign* [1972] and *Highway Landscape* [1972].)

SKEIN

1974. U.S.A.
By Stan Brakhage.
4 min. Color. Silent. 24 fps.

This is a film of pure color in alternation with stained-glasslike frames varying separately and together in a visual jazz rhythm and intensity. Brakhage calls the film "A loosely coiled length of yarn (story) . . . wound on a reel—my parenthesis! This is a painted film (inspired by Nolde's 'unpainted pictures'): 'skins' of paint hung in a weave of light."

STAR GARDEN

1974. U.S.A.
By Stan Brakhage.
21 min. Color. Silent. 24 fps.

A cinematic summer's day, as Brakhage quotes Brancusi, "one of those days I would not trade for anything," that begins with the sun ascending across the screen and ends with a parallel sequence of the moon rising. In between the filmmaker has picked a bouquet of images from his garden of daily events and has made them glow with a starry luminosity. Scarlet colored watermelon, two girls walking along a dirt road, wildflowers in the breeze, a Turnerlike sky, the texture of rough wood siding and planked floors, a can of Babo on the bathroom sink—Brakhage makes us look at mundane objects differently and as a result we become suspicious of dramatic or exotic constructions in other films.

THE STARS ARE BEAUTIFUL

1974. U.S.A.
By Stan Brakhage.
19 min. Color. Sound.

Brakhage's only sound film in the last decade, *The Stars are Beautiful* alternates synchronous sound sequences—of chickens' wings being clipped, children playing outside—with images accompanied by voice-over commentary by the filmmaker. The general theme of the narration consists of theories of the origin and purpose of the heavenly constellations. "The Stars are the broken fragments of the mirror that reflects reality," says Brakhage.

TESTAMENT

1974. U.S.A.
By James Broughton.
20 min. Color. Sound.

This is Broughton's most overtly autobiographical film and a cinematic "testament" to his life and work. The occasion for the film is a ceremony in Broughton's honor, sponsored by his home town of Modesto, California. The film begins and ends with the image of Broughton in a rocking chair by the sea, contemplating the ocean's depths. On the soundtrack, the filmmaker's voice is heard, reciting lines from his own poetic works. Segments of the film recreate his childhood in a manner reminiscent of *Mother's Day* (1948), while others present family photographs or footage of the testimonial. Interwoven are excerpts from his earlier films: *Adventures of Jimmy* (1950), *Loony Tom The Happy Lover* (1951), *The Bed* (1968), *Nuptiae* (1969), *The Golden Positions* (1970), and *This Is It* (1971). Characteristically, Broughton also pays homage to the cineastes who have preceded him. His own childhood movies suggest Pathé magic films, or the productions of Méliès. Central to *Testament* is the issue of Broughton's poetic initiation, which he represents as occurring through the visit of a silver, glittering

angel. As Broughton recollects, "[he] told me I was a poet and always would be and never to fear being alone or being laughed at." The film ends with the specter of death, and Broughton's gesture of opposition to it. He reverses the direction of ocean waves, and photographs of himself dissolve in achronological order, from the present moment back toward childhood.

TRANSCENDING

1974. U.S.A.
By Ian Hugo. Choreography and mime by Yass Hakoshima. Technical associate: Bob Hanson. Produced at the Experimental Television Lab of WNET/13. Music by David Horowitz.
16 min. Color. Sound.

Ian Hugo uses video special effects and mime Yass Hakoshima to explore the subconscious in this innovative videofilm. It concerns the adventures of a young man in search of an idea who thinks he can capture it by splitting his two brains one from the other. The film is a kinescope transfer from the original video production.

VOYAGE TO NEXT

1974. U.S.A.
By Faith and John Hubley. Music by Dizzy Gillespie. Voices: Maureen Stapleton, Dizzy Gillespie, and Dee Dee Bridgewater.
10 min. Color. Sound.

Voyage to Next is an animated jazz allegory of the human condition as seen by Mother Earth (Maureen Stapleton) and Father Time (Dizzy Gillespie). Beginning with a scene in which the ever skeptical Father Time questions Mother Earth's new invention (human beings), the film touches on important peace issues using colorful, vibrant imagery combined with an energetic, brilliant soundtrack by Gillespie. The humans build boxes around themselves and create general turmoil as the jive-talking dialogue between the two continues. It ends on a note of optimism for human equality, compatibility, and the ability to share. "That's what I had in mind," comments Mother Earth.

ARABESQUE

1975. U.S.A.
By John Whitney. Music by Manoocheher Sadeghi.
7 min. Color. Sound.

John Whitney, whose pioneering work in computer generated graphic animation can be seen in *Catalog* (1961) and

Permutations (1968), turns his attention here to the form of design called arabesque: "an ornament or style that employs flower, foliage, or fruit and sometimes animal and figural outlines to produce an intricate pattern of interlaced lines." (Webster's). *Arabesque* is a lovely, meditative film.

BRICKWALL

1975. Australia.
By Paul Winkler.
22 min. Color. Sound.

In *Brickwall*, Winkler constructs a film which on one level simply records the process of bricklaying: the temporal experience of building a wall, the brick-by-brick construction process, the sounds of the mortar being mixed and applied. Thus it is a film which conjoins both sides of Winkler's life—his work as a bricklayer and his work as a filmmaker. On another level, however, *Brickwall* is a highly abstract film that transforms the structure of the brick wall into a virtual canvas. The film begins with panning shots across the wall's facade and then moves into static shots, rhythmically edited. The wall is seen as an expanse of rectangular forms created by the bricks and their white cement borders. Due to the continual shift in Winkler's camera perspective the pattern is varied and everchanging. Each individual brick is seen also to be unique in tone and texture. One also finds parallels between the frame-within-a-frame designs made by the bricks in this film and the elaborate matting patterns that Winkler utilizes to divide the screen in such works as *Backyard* (1976) and *Sydney Harbour Bridge* (1977).

CHANTS

1975. Australia.
By Paul Winkler.
15 min. Color. Sound.

Chants employs liturgical imagery to create an abstract and meditative visual experience. According to Winkler's own description of the work, "A church image is illuminated by candlelight on time lapse photography. From then on a new image takes over: an image of a highly elaborate Greek Orthodox golden cross. That cross is shown moving endlessly in the black void to the accompanying modes of the Gregorian chants. The film takes on a distinctly spiritual air and has a quieting effect upon one's senses and one's soul. Hopefully it will relieve one from looking at a film as film, but rather more create a beautiful calmness in your body and soul: a spiritual experience, a long prayer."

HOMAGE TO MAGRITTE

1975. U.S.A.
By Anita Thacher.
10 min. Color. Sound.

This film begins with the sense of juxtaposition and the absurd that are the basis of René Magritte's paintings, and then successfully makes its own contribution to the Surrealistic tradition through the careful and evocative manipulation of the filmed image. In **Homage To Magritte** we see the cinematic frame within the frame as objects and views are shifted, superimposed, reflected, and transformed. Simple actions of flower arranging and natural movements of water and sky are layered on the screen before our absorbed eyes. Magritte's super-realistic blue skies and white clouds are transposed through imagery, motion, and texture to form a visual context for the filmmaker's point of view.

STUDY IN DIACHRONIC MOTION

1975. U.S.A.
By Peter Rose.
3 min. Color. Silent. 24 fps.

This is a "notebook" for the development of a process the filmmaker calls "diachronic motion," the simultaneous presentation of several aspects of an action by means of multiple image techniques. Using simple gestures—a person entering a doorway, walking up steps—the movement appears to progress across the screen, magnified and divided into as many as twenty-five individual images within the projected frame of the film. This experiment is a precursor to the fully realized film **Analogies: Studies in the Movement of Time** (1977).

URBAN PEASANTS: AN ESSAY IN YIDDISH STRUCTURALISM

1975. U.S.A.
By Ken Jacobs. Photographed by Stella Weiss. In Yiddish and English on accompanying cassette tape with projection instructions.
45 min. B&W. Sound (both 24 and 18 fps).

This film, which involves a reworking of old home movies, might be thought of as an avant-garde venture into "ethnography." The material, shot by Stella Weiss (an aunt of the filmmaker's wife), presents typical scenes of Jewish, middle-class life in Brooklyn during the 1930s and 1940s. Mothers wheel car-riages in the park; boys play ball on the block; neighbors picnic in the country; families gather together for the Passover Seder. A sense of the ethnic milieu is further created by signs on the street for kosher butchers, and by the taped soundtrack, which replicates a Yiddish/English language lesson. The film is marked by a great sense of nostalgia—not so much for the times themselves as for the warmth and optimism that imbues these domestic scenes. Though the film is not autobiographical in a technical sense, in compiling the footage Jacobs creates a tableau of Everyfamily—as much the viewer's as his own.

WATER WRACKETS (1975). *See* Contemporary British Independent Film

WINDOWS (1975). *See* Contemporary British Independent Film

BACKYARD

1976. Australia.
By Paul Winkler.
15 min. Color. Sound.

Backyard is a film whose central structural principle involves successive panning shots across Winkler's backyard. Beginning with this basic formal concept the filmmaker elaborates a work of great complexity and stunning visual beauty. He achieves this by his subtle use of the matting technique. Thus only part of the image is presented on the screen while other areas of the frame remain black. Often Winkler divides the screen into multiple areas, presenting pan shots of the yard at different stages in the progression and from opposing directions. At one point the image is sectioned into fifteen such areas and produces an effect of screen "corrugation." Throughout the film a strong rhythmic sense is achieved by the regular, alternating left-to-right and right-to-left panning motions which serve to unify the complex visual transformations. Winkler's use of sound is also highly effective; he accompanies the muted imagery with the harsh sounds of steel cables. In his notes for the film he states that this unnerving sound was chosen to take away the "false beauty" of the backyard footage. In its use of both sound and image, **Backyard** seems forged in the tradition of Bruce Baillie's **Castro Street** (1966). **Backyard** involves the repeated camera-scan of a delimited landscape. Yet the complexity of the views presented defies our attempts to understand that geography in a conventional sense, and we surrender to Winkler's elaboration of an entirely cinematic space.

BREAKFAST (TABLE-TOP DOLLY)

1976. U.S.A.
By Michael Snow.
15 min. Color. Sound.

This film is a comic transposition of the pictorial "still life" to the realm of the moving camera. The film begins with a shot of a breakfast table, with objects arranged sedately on the table top: orange juice container, egg crate, milk carton, sugar box, fruit bowl. Off-screen, typical morning sounds are heard: radio music, a weather forecast, clanking dishes, fragments of a conversation. Suddenly, the objects on the table top begin to move, as though propelled by a supernatural force. The tablecloth mysteriously bunches up and objects inexplicably fall off the edge. By the end of the film it is revealed that the camera itself has "devoured" the *mise-en-scène*, executing a tabletop dolly shot that has nudged its subject out of the frame. As critic Regina Cornwell notes, **Breakfast** "is a kind of comedy without characters, where objects are taken over by the camera's action."

CAN CAN (1976). *See* Contemporary British Independent Film

A FILM

1976. U.S.A.
By Steve Gluck. Music: "The Gunfighter" by Pregadio and Micalizzi.
3 min. Color. Sound.

In a mock-heroic examination of food to the accompaniment of highly dramatic, western-genre music, images of such culinary delights as paella, noodles, and fresh lettuce emerge against a jet-black background. We witness the drama of butter melting on a hot skillet, and the landscape of a hero sandwich is accorded a majestic pan shot. **A Film** seems both an homage to, and an affectionate spoof of, the sensuality of commercial cinematography.

KRISTINA TALKING PICTURES

1976. U.S.A.
By Yvonne Rainer. Photographed by Roger Dean, Babette Mangolte. With Burt Barr, Frances Barth, James Barth, Edward Cicciarelli, Blondell Cummings, David Diao, John Erdman, Janet Froelich, Epp Kotkas, Kate Parker, Lil Picard, Ivan Rainer, Yvonne Rainer, Valda Setterfield, Sarah Soffer, Shirley Soffer, Simian Soffer.

92 min. Color. Sound.

Yvonne Rainer, who has had a notable influence on dance and performance art since the early 1960s, began making films in the early 1970s. Her earlier films were concerned with dance, but her work has progressed into complex narrative structures that subvert linear narrative form, undermine expectations of characterization, and explore political thought through unconventional strategies. *Kristina Talking Pictures* is, on the surface, about a young European woman lion tamer who comes to America and takes up choreography. The film diverges from a strict narrative line via reflections on art, love, and catastrophe by Kristina, the heroine-narrator, and her lover, Raoul. A constant dialogue based on works by Samuel Beckett, Simone de Beauvoir, John Cage, Susan Sontag, Albert Speer, and others is combined with scenes of Kristina and other characters, segments of choreographed movement, printed words, photographs, and film fragments. The central thought that emerges is the disparity between individuals' political ideology and their public action—the dichotomy between the semblance of political awareness and the reality of uncommitted, passive people. "Within its form of shifting correlations between word and image," says Rainer, "persona and performer, enactment and illustration, explanation and ambiguity, *Kristina Talking Pictures* circles in a narrowing spiral toward its primary concerns: the uncertain relation of public act to personal fate, the ever present possibility for disparity between public-directed conscience and private will."

RED CHURCH

1976. Australia.
By Paul Winkler.
17 min. Color. Sound.

Red Church opens with a lush, red-toned image of a church altar before a stained glass window, as seen from the perspective of the church aisle. On the soundtrack is an awesome roar. The rest of the film involves a complex transposition of that image through multiple exposures within the camera. Over the course of approximately 200 exposures the images become more abstract and blurred and attain an almost liquid quality. As the film emulsion wears down, the image becomes lighter and achieves a glowing, translucent quality. Although a structural film in the strictest sense of the word, *Red Church* joins a rigorous design with a strong sense of spirituality, for Winkler dissolves the material world into an aura of light and color.

RUBBER CEMENT

1976. U.S.A.
By Robert Breer.
10 min. Color. Sound.

Rubber Cement by Robert Breer is an extraordinarily eclectic film in both form and theme. Like most Breer films it is an aesthetic collage, employing animated geometric shapes, line drawings of figures, abstract color washes, and found material in the form of sales receipts and newspaper clippings. The style of figure drawing in the film marks an extension of Breer's use of the rotoscope process in *Gulls and Buoys* (1973) and *Fuji* (1974). His color technique, however, results from some new experimentation with Xerography. The space created in *Rubber Cement* is extremely complex. At various points shapes overlap or contain cutout windows through which other spaces are perceived. The iconography of *Rubber Cement* is equally complex. One segment (with titles like "Emily Plays Soccer" and "Amos Chases a Stick") is an animated transposition of the home movie genre. Another section offers advancing rectangles and squares reminiscent of Richter's *Rhythmus 21* (1921). Breer's artistic roots are in not only avant-garde animation, however; the film also contains an affectionate homage to Felix the Cat.

THE SIN OF THE POET

1976. U.S.A.
By Donald Hyams. Photographed by Amnon Soloman. Dancer: Arié Burstyn.
5 min. Color. Sound.

With a dance by Arié Burstyn that uses the choreography of the body's expanding and contracting motions as its theme, the filmmaker creates a parallel visual feeling through the multiple imagery of the optical printing process. The soundtrack combines voice and percussion to synthesize a musical score that reflects the film's photographic complexity.

33 YO-YO TRICKS

1976. U.S.A.
By P. White. Music by Robert Sheff. With Daniel Volk.
8 min. Color. Sound.

33 Yo-Yo Tricks is a comic short that consists of yo-yo aficionado Daniel Volk's repertoire of thirty-three extraordinary tricks. In a subtle match of action, P. White uses a minimal approach that outlines the precision and economy of the performance. The exact framing and timing, the seeming effortlessness of the tricks, the intensity of the action, and the detachment of the camera combine to create a unique film that is among the best of deadpan comic shorts.

ANALOGIES: STUDIES IN THE MOVEMENT OF TIME

1977. U.S.A.
By Peter Rose.
14 min. Color. Sound.

Analogies is a visual matrix of sequential motion, the logic of which is called into question by the use of time delays and multiple, staggered images that pulsate across the screen. Rose has constructed a film of simple themes and complex variations with a fugal quality that evokes both a musical and dancelike reaction. The setting is a sterile, high-tech space (actually a modern college classroom building) that has a "less is more" aesthetic that forces the viewer to look at and appreciate pure objects like a metal handrail leading down white tiled stairs. The whole experience is enlivened by the filmmaker's presence and spontaneous sense of humor.

BARK RIND

1977. Australia.
By Paul Winkler.
30 min. Color. Sound.

Bark Rind is a single-concept film that creates a unique audio-visual cinematic experience. Presented over the course of the work are gyrating, close-up images of various aspects of the landscape: flowers, bark, grass, leaves. Accompanying them on the soundtrack is the shrill, piercing shriek of insect sounds, repeated over and over through loop printing. The effect achieved is one of extraordinary kinetic energy; the images themselves seem to pulse and vibrate as though they were the source of the resonating, buzzing sounds issuing from the aural track. Winkler achieves this exceptional visual quality by shooting the entire film in single frames. Each frame, however, involves multiple superimpositions of the same flower, tree, or blade of grass in complex combinations of close-up, medium-shot, and long-shot. All effects were realized in-camera. The sense of visual and acoustic vibrancy created in *Bark Rind* is also clearly relevant to the film's thematic overtones. For as Winkler himself has stated: "My subject matter is trees—earth—grass—flowers—bark: to show eternal growth . . . a growth of images into polyphonic sounds."

ROBOT (1977)

DAVID EHRLICH PROGRAM I

1977–79. U.S.A.
By David Ehrlich.
Total program: 8 min. Color. Sound.

VERMONT ETUDE

1977.
3 min.

ROBOT

1977.
3 min.

ROBOT TWO

1979.
2 min.

This program of films by David Ehrlich explores the realm of abstract animation, creating optical effects through the use of prismacolor and ink on tracing paper. In *Vermont Étude*, a series of colored forms undergoes continual transformations, establishing a dialectic between geometric and biomorphic shapes. Ehrlich writes that his aim is to "express the tension of trying to hold on to the moment which forever passes behind us—the tension of remembering in sadness, yet looking forward in excitement—a tension between having been and becoming." In *Robot* and *Robot Two* Ehrlich fashions a universe of abstract animated "science fiction," with the figure of a robot assembling and disassem-

bling in an iconography of constant flux. As Ehrlich has commented, within the films "fragmentation and integration are simultaneous." *Robot* and *Robot Two* also explore the world of architectural form with the automaton frequently dissolving into the structure of a building or a room. According to the filmmaker, the films constitute "an introduction to a unique and logically consistent universe with its own rules of environment, perspective, behavior and interaction of life forms."

———

DEAR PHONE (1977). *See* Contemporary British Independent Film

THE GOVERNOR

1977. U.S.A.
By Stan Brakhage.
51 min. Color. Silent. 24 fps.

In an unusual break from his normal, immediately personal focus and subject matter, Brakhage turns his camera outward in this film on Richard D. Lamm, Governor of Colorado. The result is anything but an authorized film biography. Instead, it is a real Brakhage film—personal, idiosyncratic, and concerned above all with the interplay of power and light. *The Governor* captures the rhythm and pace of the hectic life of a politician, where so much is a smile, a nod, a wave of the hand; it also illu-

minates the patience, concentration, and responsiveness the job requires. The film is a visual pleasure to watch, though much of what is filmed is repetitious. Brakhage manages to cut through the trappings to look not only at this man but also through his eyes. What he sees are endless papers, meetings, phone calls, faces lining parade streets or sitting across from his desk, all in constant motion. It is, finally, a very moving film and a human one.

LUMINESCENCE

1977. U.S.A.
By Ian Hugo and Arnold Eagle. Music by David Horowitz.
9 min. Color. Sound.

Ian Hugo, whose earlier *Levitation* (1972), and *Transcending* (1974) also explore states of consciousness through cinema, describes this film: "After a life of turmoil a woman symbolically returns to the comfort and protection of the womb and her closeness to nature. In the end she attains fulfillment and her joy bursts forth in cosmic flames."

RIDDLES OF THE SPHINX (1977). *See* Contemporary British Independent Film

ROSLYN ROMANCE (IS IT REALLY TRUE?), INTRO I & II

1977. U.S.A.
By Bruce Baillie.
18 min. Color. Sound.

This film (the introduction to Baillie's epic work-in-progress, *Roslyn Romance*) is an avant-garde evocation of memory, a remembrance of things past. The central visual theme of the film consists of old photographs—family album stills and antique postcards. Baillie interweaves these images with rural domestic scenes as fall and winter come to pass. The soundtrack presents an aural pastiche of dialogue fragments, ethnic music, and ambient noise. *Roslyn Romance* creates a sense of diary and autobiography in its portrait of a family scene, but it is never clear whether the people portrayed (in photographs and live-action) have any relation to one another or to the filmmaker himself. It is the aura of memory and family history that concerns Baillie—a quality he achieves through the hazy visual style of the film and its radical use of superimposition. To quote Baillie's words from a journal entry included in the film, the work is a document "of what [he sees], like postcards to a dear aunt—a monument, an illumination, an attempt to reach a lost friend."

77

1977. U.S.A.
By Robert Breer.
8 min. Color. Sound.

Behind the childlike appearance of this combination of abstract and concrete images lies a very sophisticated sensibility. Breer's basic animation style has retained a continuity in the fifteen years that separate **Horse Over Teakettle** (1962) and **77** (1977), but his control of the material seems more assured and economical as he mixes a variety of media, including a brief on-camera debut of the filmmaker's hand.

SILK

1977. U.S.A.
By James Herbert.
25 min. Color. Silent. 24 fps.

Silk is rare in Herbert's work in that the longing apparent in his other work is answered by touch; the lovers make love, and the melancholy that is so pronounced, as in **Appalachee** (1974), is for the most part absent here. In **Silk** there is consummation and joy. Not only does Herbert work with that most venerated subject in art, the nude, but he absorbs the image of the nude into the camera so that through rephotography it emerges with a new quality. Rhythm, light, and color change; the figures move, at times away, at times into one another: an erotic patina is achieved, but the ordinary act of looking has been both dislocated and made voluptuous.

SIT DOWN SWEET SEPTEMBER

1977. U.S.A.
By Harry de Ligter.
21 min. Color. Sound.

This experimental narrative depicts a reclusive old man's reminiscences on his lost youth. In the setting of an antique store, he sinks into a deep reverie, inspired by old photographs and gramophone recordings. The film then erupts into a bizarre, expressionist parade of recollected scenes: a wartime battle, a love affair, a wedding, the birth of a child. To emphasize the disjunction between past and present, de Ligter alternates sepia and colored segments of the film. Ultimately, the past is seen as a giant carnival, and clown figures, circus barkers, and an ersatz Charlie Chaplin wend their way through the text. In the film's focus on the psychological past, and its stylized theatrical tone, it pays homage to the rhetoric of Ingmar Bergman and Federico Fellini, two masters of the European narrative cinema.

STYX

1977. U.S.A.
By Jan Krawitz and Thomas Ott. Produced by Temple University. Sound by Henry Faracs. Music by Mother Mallard's Portable Masterpiece Company.
11 min. B&W. Sound.

Styx is an early film by Jan Krawitz and Thomas Ott, who went on to make **Little People** (1982). It uses the Philadelphia subway as a metaphor for the underworld. Solitary figures ominously descend the stairs of a subway station and board a train. The camera isolates the riders' gestures and facial expressions as they ride with urban stoicism and anonymity. As the train speeds along, music permeates the soundtrack, transforming the tunnels into entrancing, endless rows of lights and making the train appear to float. When the train finally rushes through a station occupied by a solitary, lost figure, the image of passing to another state is complete. This impressionistic blend of sound and visuals gradually reveals the vulnerability of the passengers in the isolated subterranean environment.

SYDNEY HARBOUR BRIDGE

1977. Australia.
By Paul Winkler.
13 min. Color. Sound.

Sydney Harbour Bridge is a visually stunning virtuoso work, a tour de force in its exploitation of the in-camera matting technique. Winkler's conception of the film began with a panoramic view of Sydney Harbour Bridge popular in many tourist postcards. But the beauty of the film lies in his complex transpositions of that image. At points the screen is divided into myriad horizontal stripes, each containing pan shots of the bridge with movements in opposing directions. At another point a long-shot of the bridge is combined with shots of the glistening water. In another section of the film the screen is segmented into sixteen square images, each containing pans of the bridge's metal structure. The sense of movement created in the composite shots is of the bridge in dancelike animation, of its constituting a giant, fluid, slinky toy. The spirit of playful movement motivates the rest of the film, both in terms of the choreography of shots of the bridge and in the dance of light reflections off the water's surface. A soundtrack of tinkling belllike notes accentuates the film's rhythmic and musical conception.

BETWEEN NIGHT AND THE LIGHT OF DAY

1978. U.S.A.
By Donald Hyams. Assisted by Pierre Montant and Harriet Unruh.
10 min. Color. Sound.

Based on the paintings of Pierre Montant, this film is a progression of camera movements toward details of the artist's vision—through open doorways, out windows, across rooms, along roof tops, down a beach. The film begins with interior spaces filled with unattended musical instruments, with shadows, and reflections in a mirror, and then moves into the bright sunlight of a Côte d'Azur setting, pastel stucco houses, cabanas, sand, and the water beyond. Like the camera, the audience is a spectator, an inquisitive eye selectively focused on pieces of a larger image.

CHARMED PARTICLES (THE ADVENTURES OF THE EXQUISITE CORPSE: PART IV)

1978. U.S.A.
By Andrew Noren.
78 min. B&W. Silent. 18 fps.

Noren is one of America's most uncompromising and exciting filmmakers. His camera, having stalked, catches light. It is light and its ceaseless, refreshing manifestations that excite Noren's camera lens; his cinema is one of light mediated by a camera that either enhances or attenuates. It is light-blessed image sequences edited according to a sublime inner visual beat that is the percolating "subject" of a Noren film. Indeed, light so pulsates in this infinitely shaded black-and-white film that hued afterimages are experienced, and a ghostly color pervades. **Charmed Particles** is definitely not an abstract film, but it is Noren's most abstract. The recognizable has become less distinct but contours give space and shadow. The shots become briefer and briefer, and establish a rhythm in which the barely animate takes on a furious energy of its own. **Charmed Particles** gives the eye pleasure and the mind a dark enchantment.

CORNELL, 1965 (1978). *See* Films on the Arts

THE DOCTOR'S DREAM

1978. U.S.A.
By Ken Jacobs.
23 min. B&W. Sound.

In the same way that he restructured an early Biograph film in **Tom, Tom, The Piper's Son** (1971) by means of an optical printer, Ken Jacobs again creates a film about the nature of cinema by reediting a conventional short narrative film according to a precise system. The original film is a clichéd melodrama about the life of a kindly country doctor, centering on the illness of one of his favorite neighborhood children and her recovery due to a new vaccine. With Jacobs's subversion of the story, the narrative breaks down into a vocabulary of gestures, expressions, props, and plot devices. As the structure of the story dissolves, a subliminal subtext emerges, revealing the sexual overtones in the relationship between the doctor and his young patient.

FOUR JOURNEYS INTO MYSTIC TIME

1978. U.S.A.
By Shirley Clarke. Choreography by Marion Scott.
Total: 58 min. Color. Sound.

MYSTERIUM

Produced with David Cort. Photographed by Steve Conant. Dancers: Kathe Copperman, Gary Bates. Music by Paul Chihara.
14 min.

TRANS

Produced with David Cort. Photographed by Steve Conant. Dancer: Carol Warner. Music by Morton Subotnick.
7 min.

ONE TWO THREE

Produced with David Cort. Photographed by Wayne Orr. Dancers: Lynda Davis, Clay Taliaferro, Carol Warner. Music by Ernst Toch.
8 min.

INITIATION

Produced with David Miller. Photographed by Fuding Cheng, Chris Mohanna, Candace Reckinger. Danced by the UCLA Dance Company.
29 min.

Four Journeys Into Mystic Time is a four-part enigmatic study of dance and film by Shirley Clarke, whose earlier dance films include **Dance in the Sun** (1953), **Bullfight** (1955), and **A Moment in Love** (1957). Choreographed by Marion Scott, these four dances explore organic movement and video effects. **Mysterium** begins with two figures performing symmetrical movement as one form. Dramatic lighting isolates their movement in a dark space as it grows into a symbiotic encounter. **Trans** is a solo dance which expands and disinte-

grates through colorized video effects. Accompanied by a soundtrack of haunting whispers, its fluid movements become abstracted by the expanding color, which makes it seem to float in space. **One Two Three** presents three characters, a veiled man and two women, in a jazzy, upbeat dance in which their movements are governed in part by changing solid color backgrounds and pixillation. The soundtrack is a collage of chanting voices and amusing rhymes. In **Initiation**, a solitary figure dances alone in a misty, elusive space. She is surrounded by a line of dancers who move in ritualistic gestures. The initiate performs a dance of birth and growth until she becomes part of the group of dancers.

GOING HOME

1978. U.S.A.
By Dan Reder.
5 min. B&W. Sound.

This spirited animation imaginatively follows the journey back to nature of two city characters. Beginning with the grid structure of an urban apartment building, the scene focuses on two garbage-can-dwelling creatures. One of them creates a cloud that rains huge amounts of water, crumbling the cityscape. The creatures ride the crests of the waves through imaginative territory, finally arriving in a country landscape where they find a whole community of beings like themselves. **Going Home** ends with a celebration of nature and collective strength.

H IS FOR HOUSE (1978). See
Contemporary British Independent Film

HEAVY METAL

1978. U.S.A.
By Scott Bartlett. Music by Earl "Fatha" Hines and Tiny Parham.
12 min. B&W and color. Sound.

With a sense of humor and a feel for the American cultural melting pot, **Heavy Metal** juxtaposes the sound of early jazz and blues recordings by Earl "Fatha" Hines and Tiny Parham with video synthesized images of violent TV movies from the 1950s. Bartlett creates a film with a subtle tension between what is seen and what is evoked through the music. There is an economy of technique in the rearrangement of the movie sequences and the selective combination of scenes, as well as in the progressive abstraction of the manipulated

imagery, that shows the filmmaker working with complete control of the form.

LMNO

1978. U.S.A.
By Robert Breer.
9 min. Color. Sound.

In this collage animation, Breer demonstrates his special talent to reduce the representational image of an object to its essential form. The filmmaker is also exploring the idea of reflexive cinema: film referring to itself, reminding the audience—by allowing the animator's hand to enter the frame for example—of the process that lies behind the film. Breer states that "LMNO is a cartoon compilation of personal vision in which appear at different times goldfish, joggers, airplanes, a claw-hammer, croquet balls, milk cartons, bananas, Kandinsky abstractions and various versions of Emil Cohl's stick figure cop. The pace is hectic as usual with anxiety edging out whimsy, though what concerns me most is how the capsized boat looks with its bright red keel in the air."

NOTES FOR JEROME

1978. U.S.A.
By Jonas Mekas.
46 min. Color. Sound.

This film is both an abstract elegy for Jerome Hill (painter, cineaste, patron of the arts, and friend of Mekas) and a continuation of the filmmaker's work in the "diary" genre. The first and major section of the film recollects Mekas's visit to Hill's house in Cassis in the mid-1960s. Using assertive single-frame filming techniques, Mekas choreographs fleeting and fragmentary views of the French coastal town: the central square, the marketplace, Hill's home, the landscape, the painter at work, communal meals, and above all, the ocean. Intertitles give us Mekas's retrospective thoughts. He notes that "the evenings were full of silence" and that the beauty of Cassis reminds him of his homeland, Lithuania. The film's coda documents Mekas's return to Cassis after Hill's death some eight years later. Though the town is the same ("The trains still go thru the station at La Ciotat"), Mekas experiences a sense of loss: for Hill, for those days "long, long ago," for his own Lithuanian youth, and for life, which heedlessly and inexorably simply "goes on."

PASSAGES

1978. Canada.

By Nesya Shapiro.
29 min. B&W. Sound.

A provocative film about a young woman writer/taxi driver and her brief liaison with a musician. Set in Montreal, this poetic drama, part *cinéma vérité*, part dream, explores fate and free will; the autonomy of solitary living versus the compromise found in a romantic relationship. Like its jazz references, *Passages* is an improvisation, both free-wheeling and structured. In this way the structure of the film itself reflects on the dilemma of its heroine.

POWERS OF TEN (Second version: POWERS OF TEN: A FILM DEALING WITH THE RELATIVE SIZE OF THINGS IN THE UNIVERSE AND THE EFFECT OF ADDING ANOTHER ZERO)

1978. U.S.A.
By Charles and Ray Eames. Narrated by Phillip Morrison.
9 min. Color. Sound.

In this new and more colorful version of their film (see also *Powers of Ten* [*First version*] [1968]), the Eameses have dropped the provisional subtitle, "a rough sketch," and the point of origin has been changed to a picnic in Chicago near Lake Michigan. The comparison, within the frame, of earth and space time has been eliminated, and the image is less complicated and more graphically readable. The narrator pauses at 100 million light years distance to observe "this emptiness [of space] is normal—the richness of our own neighborhood is the exception," before plunging 40 powers of 10 to the microscopic scale of 10^{-16} meters where we enter a "vast inner space" not unlike that seen at 10^{24} meters.

RABBIT'S MOON (LA LUNE DES LAPINS) (Second version)

1978. U.S.A.
By Kenneth Anger. Photographed by Tourjansky. With André Soubeyran, Claude Revenant, Nadine Valence.
7 min. Color. Sound.

Rabbit's Moon was shot by Kenneth Anger in 1950 when he was living in Paris. The project was abandoned for lack of funds until Anger reedited it in 1970, adding a soundtrack of popular songs from the late 1950s and early 1960s (see *Rabbit's Moon* [*First version*] [1970] for a complete description.) This second version, made eight years later, differs from the first in length, soundtrack, and overall tone. Anger cut the film's length in half, accelerated the action at times,

substituted an image of the real moon, and used a mocking soundtrack that repeats the lyrics, "Things that go bump in the night give me a terrible fright," preceded by a werewolf howl. The effect is significantly different from Anger's 1970 version, which appears more serious and magical in comparison to this sarcastically humorous revision.

SEA TRAVELS

1978. U.S.A.
By Anita Thacher.
11 min. Color. Sound.

This is a film of memory, drawing on what Thoreau calls "the dreams of childhood," composed of spare and symbolic images and actions, and heightened by an accurate sense of the essential elements of the dream world. The filmmaker uses the optical printing and matting techniques to create layers of imagery and to insert one visual over part of another, combining the real and unreal within the same frame and inverting components of our normal landscape: a child rolls down a hill in the place on the screen where the sky should be above the sea, a powerboat races backward across the water, an orange moves along the horizon line. The filmmaker divides the film into five parts, progressing from the introductory "Sighting" through "The Chase" to a final "Landing." The last haunting image is of the young girl frozen in the midst of running up from the summer's beach—the journey continued in the mind's eye.

SELF PORTRAIT WITH RED CAR

1978. Ireland.
By Bob Quinn. Photographed by Joe Comerford. Music by Roger Doyle. With Brian Bourke.
17 min. Color. Sound.

This amusing early film by Irish filmmaker Bob Quinn is a portrait of an artist haunted by the sounds of the city. Played by Irish painter Brian Bourke, whose van Gogh-like painting *Self Portrait With Red Ear* opens the film, the main character is a pensive figure who stands solitary even in a crowd. When he takes his easel to the country, he draws a skyscraper while standing before a thatched cottage, and a car while sketching a horse. Bourke brings a brilliant sense of comedy to this character, who tries desperately to cross an empty country road yet hears roars of traffic whenever he steps forward. Ultimately, the artist is so maddened by aural delusions that he fails to see the real red

car coming toward him, driven, in appropriate irony, by the filmmaker himself.

SLUICE

1978. U.S.A.
By Stan Brakhage.
4 min. B&W. Silent. 18 fps. (Filmmaker designates that this film may also be shown at 24 fps.)

According to Webster's, a sluice is "an artificial passage for water, filled with a gate for regulating the flow." In this "filmic sluice," Brakhage creates an elegant vehicle for catching and modulating light. The screen is awash with luminous patterns that fade and grow in intensity. Tonal quality is varied by Brakhage's use of blurred focus and swish pans that transform the external world into a repository of dynamic light energy. Toward the end of the film, images of dripping liquid appear, recalling the root definition of "sluice."

UNREACHABLE HOMELESS (UNERREICHBAR HEIMATLOS)

1978. West Germany.
By Klaus Wyborny.
33 min. Color. Silent. 18 fps.

This fast-paced film by Klaus Wyborny makes use of brilliant color, deep space, and constantly changing focus to engage the viewer. Though crafted with mathematical precision, this structural film remains fluid and interesting. Since there are so many processes in getting a film from camera to editing table, there is always, for the filmmaker, an element of chance in the practice of his art. It is this risk, so to speak, that is incorporated into the otherwise analytical, very precise structure that Klaus Wyborny, trained as a mathematician, plots into his films. It is chance that gives Wyborny's otherwise rigorous film a surprising, even essential sensuousness. Fast on the eyes, staccato in rhythm, the film's action creates a deep, mysterious, and busy space that is as fluid as it is pleasurable.

A WALK THROUGH H (1978). See Contemporary British Independent Film

AMY! (1979). See Contemporary British Independent Film

@ (AT)

1979. U.S.A.
By Stan Brakhage.
7 min. Color. Silent. 18 fps. (Filmmaker

designates that this film may also be shown at 24 fps.)

In this film Brakhage continues his exploration of alternate modes of vision. Through blurred focus, the world is transformed into an abstract space of light, color, and texture. In the first part of the film, a trace of conventional representation remains; images of sky, clouds, airplane are recognizable, though amorphous. In the latter part, however, the external realm is metamorphosed into glowing, colored patterns of light and shape. At the end of the film a clear image of a face emerges. The eyes open and blink, recasting the previous images as a subjective vision. Like many Brakhage films, @ tends to defy verbal description. Brakhage himself has stated that it is "the first film of mine which is so very much there where it's **at** THAT it deserves visual symbol as title and no further explanation from me at/et? all."

BONDI

1979. Australia.
By Paul Winkler.
15 min. Color. Sound.

This film constructs a satirical and bizarre visual portrait of Bondi, a popular beach in Sydney, Australia. Winkler employs his signature—in-camera matting techniques—dividing the frame horizontally into multiple sections. Sometimes the composite vision is sharply ironic (as when a close-up of a discarded paper cup appears below a beach scene). At other times it is both comic and strange (as when ocean waves seem to lap up to a hotel entrance). Amos Vogel has commented on this quality of **Bondi** by noting that "the startling manipulation of pictorial space, the evocative absurdity of combinations are reminiscent of Max Ernst's surrealist collages."

CARS

1979. Australia.
By Paul Winkler.
15 min. Color. Sound.

Cars is a visual study of the automobile as both a symbol of 20th-century urban living, and a source of color, shape, movement, and design. The first half of the film is silent, allowing the viewer to study the pictorial qualities of the cars which Winkler choreographs in vertical, diagonal, and horizontal movement. Frequently images are matted together in various patterns—creating triangular shapes or boxes-within-boxes. Superimposition is employed as well to evoke the feeling of a hazy, lyric dreamscape. In the second half of the film,

automotive noises assertively emerge on the soundtrack and, as Winkler puts it, "a certain kind of shock reaction sets in which forces the viewer to 'rethink.'" Thus **Cars** is both a critique of the automobile culture and an homage to their kinetic beauty.

DAVID EHRLICH PROGRAM II

1979–80. U.S.A.
By David Ehrlich.
Total program: 8 min. Color. Sound.

VERMONT ETUDE, NO. 2

1979.
4 min.

PRECIOUS METAL

1980.
4 min.

In this program of films David Ehrlich explores the realm of abstract animation, creating optical effects through the use of prismacolor and ink on tracing paper. **Vermont Etude, No. 2** "was inspired by the changing of the seasons and by the wildlife of Vermont—by the mountain mists, the rising and setting of the sun, the bees." Visually, a series of colored forms and lines coalesce and decompose, suggesting alternately a landscape, the sun, an animal, or the horizon line. As Ehrlich states, his goal is to "break down the artificial boundaries between abstract and figurative design, line and mass, animal and human, life and death." **Precious Metal** presents a very different iconography—one of massive geometric forms, intersecting, piercing, and entwining one another in a choreography of transformations. According to Ehrlich, the repetitive structure of the film is based on the musical "crab (retrograde) canon, the fugal structure perfected by Bach in which the theme is played against itself going backwards."

—
—

EUCLIDEAN ILLUSIONS

1979. U.S.A.
By Stan VanDerBeek. Animated by Richard Weinberg. Music by Max VanDerBeek and Ferdinand Maisel.
9 min. Color. Sound.

This visual fantasy using computer animation was created by VanDerBeek while an artist-in-residence at NASA. Geometric shapes and forms are choreographed with precision and subtle complexity. Crystalline forms and cubes converge, expand, and revolve with a kaleidoscopic effect which continually

draws the viewer into the screen. **Euclidean Illusions** is an example of the myriad possibilities using computers in the visual arts.

PARTICLES IN SPACE and TAL FARLOW

1979–80. U.S.A.
By Len Lye.
Total program: 6 min. B&W. Sound.

PARTICLES IN SPACE

1979.
Assisted by Paul Barnes and Steve Jones. Music by the Bahamans, and the Yoruba of Nigeria.
4 min.

TAL FARLOW

1980.
Completed by Steve Jones. Music by Tal Farlow.
2 min.

Particles in Space and **Tal Farlow** are the last two films made by animation pioneer Len Lye. Like **Free Radicals** (1979), **Particles in Space** uses the direct animation technique of scratching on black film leader to explore energy. Lye created lightninglike scratches that echo the filmmaking process of shaping light out of darkness. The soundtrack combines the sound of his kinetic sculpture with African drum music. Calling this film "a smaller, more compact zizz of energy than I'd ever got before on film," Lye made **Particles in Space** an exuberant celebration of movement. Lye completed the drawings for **Tal Farlow**, his final scratch film, before his death in May 1980. The film was completed on Lye's instructions by his assistant, experimental filmmaker Steve Jones. **Tal Farlow** was also created by scratching on black film leader to create light shapes. In this brief and simple animation, white lines sway and dance to a jazz guitar solo. (See also **Len Lye's American Films** [1952–80].)

RE-BORN

1979. U.S.A.
By Ian Hugo. Photographed by Bob Hanson. Music by Teijo Ito. With: Gusti Bogok, Yass Hakoshima, and Anaïs Nin.
9 min. Color. Sound.

Re-born is an abstract, symbolic film with mythic overtones in which a man is driven to desperation by his mocking shadow. When he reaches the frontier of death, he is met by a madonna-like spirit (Anaïs Nin) who convinces him that he must cast aside his shadow if he is to survive. In rendering this archetypal narrative Hugo uses techniques of superimposition to achieve a doppelgänger effect, as well as a sense of a primal, magical atmosphere. The man seems, alternately, to fly or swim through space in his journey toward spiritual rebirth.

SCIENCE FICTION

1979. U.S.A.
By J. J. Murphy.
5 min. Color. Sound.

By reediting and eliminating the narration of an educational film, Murphy exposes the tenuous, taken-for-granted conventions of cinematic storytelling. In the process, the heavy moral lesson (on the sin of being late) and the unreality of filmic "simulation" (one can almost see the wires in the gravity-in-space scene) are playfully revealed, making us question the true impact of the instructional film on young audiences. The filmmaker reminds us that film is a manipulation—things are not what they appear to be, as in the sequence showing the camerawork required to fake the departure of an unmoving train—and a distortion—like the squeezed image recorded by an anamorphic lens. *Science Fiction* is a cautionary tale on the nature of film and the film experience.

SIX LITTLE PIECES ON FILM (SECHS KLEINE STÜCKE AUF FILM)

1979. West Germany.
By Klaus Wyborny.
37 min. Color. Silent. 18 fps.

Wyborny is one of the most impressive of the recent generation of European independent film artists. *Six Little Pieces on Film* is about as musical as a silent film can get. Each piece, a shot (of a house, harbor, etc.), is played like a note, over and over again, in different groupings, at various speeds, under various colors, in various superimpositions. Exactingly edited, both exhausting and refreshing to the eye, the film "plays" like a melody whose simple notes are familiar but whose score is so rich as to make the screen soar.

STEP BY STEP

1979. U.S.A.
By Faith Hubley. Music composed and performed by Elizabeth Swados. In French, Spanish, and English.
11 min. Color. Sound.

Centered on the image of a baby's first steps as representative of initial independence and separation, *Step by Step*

provides a historical and cultural view of childhood. Borrowing imagery from a variety of fine art sources, including Matisse, Picasso, Chagall, and Japanese and Flemish masters, Hubley's film begins with the violence of the abandonment, sacrifice, killing, and slavery of children, and then moves into warm images of the madonna and child from all cultures. The film's final section is a reinforcement of the rights of all children to health, love, education, and freedom. The fervent music composed by Elizabeth Swados includes French, Spanish, and English lyrics and adds a diverse cultural complement to Hubley's fluid, colorful imagery. This film was created in honor of the Year of the Child.

TZ

1979. U.S.A.
By Robert Breer.
8 min. Color. Sound.

In *TZ*, Robert Breer creates an abstract animated world of domestic imagery: ringing telephones, frying eggs, chairs and tables, light bulbs. New York film critic Amy Taubin calls it "an elegant home movie." The title of the film asserts this domestic theme as well, since it refers to the Tappan Zee Bridge which faces Breer's apartment building. The iconography of the film intermixes line drawing, still photography, and painted imagery—often juxtaposing "real" and "synthetic" realms. Thus a photograph of a sauce pan wends its way into a line-drawn kitchen and a sketch of the Tappan Zee Bridge follows its cinematographic image. Breer creates a fluid, dynamic space in the film, with objects whirling about as though caught in the eye of a hurricane. The soundtrack— with its concrete, material noises of pots clanking, phones ringing, fat frying— contrasts sharply with the sketchy, abstracted texture of the visuals and creates a resonant disjunction. Typically, Breer also plays with sound and language in the film: words heard on the track are converted into pictorial letters and a tension is established between alternate modes of discourse. Breer is highly reflexive in his imagery and stocks the film with various references to cinema. A film reel recurrently spins around and cartoon music is intermittently heard. Moreover, the animator's pen is revealed as a participant in the mad domestic drama.

VERTICAL FEATURES REMAKE

(1979). *See* Contemporary British Independent Film

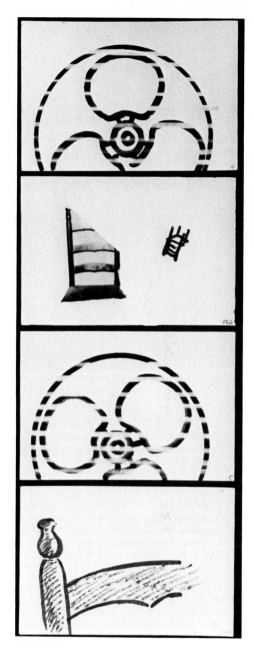

TZ (1979)

WINDOW

1979. Australia.
By Paul Winkler.
3 min. Color. Sound.

Window is structured as a visual variation on a theme. The scene is a window, looking out on tiled roofs; a woman stands in the foreground. With this basic material Winkler launches a series of visual permutations through sophisticated techniques of optical matting. In one segment, three windows seem to appear, then alternately fade in and out. In another sequence, the effect of a dizzying circular pan is achieved, though the space is entirely synthetic. In another section multiple prismatic images appear, organized on the diagonal; and elsewhere, the frame divides horizontally in two, with upper and lower images moving in opposing directions. Winkler likes to think of the film as a proto-narrative. He says the film progresses "like an average feature film, a slow introduction, a hectic middle part, and a surprise ending of ambiguous nature."

JOURNEYS FROM BERLIN/1971

1980. U.S.A.
By Yvonne Rainer. Produced in association with the British Film Institute and the Deutscher Akademische Austauschdienst. Photographed by Carl Teitelbaum, Michael Steinke, Wolfgang Senn, Jon Else, and Shinkichi Tajiri. Sound by Larry Sider, Helene Kaplan, Dan Gillham, Christian Moldt. With Annette Michelson, Ilona Halberstadt, Gabor Vernon, Chad Wollen, Amy Taubin, Vito Acconci, Lena Hyun, Yvonne Rainer, Ruth Rainero, Leo Rainer, Cynthia Beatt, Antonio Skarmeta.
125 min. Color. Sound.

Journeys From Berlin/1971 is Yvonne Rainer's fourth feature-length film. It furthers the political themes of her earlier work, such as **Kristina Talking Pictures** (1976), and continues to explore complex narrative structures. The film interweaves aural elements with visual elements such as printed information, letters, objects, and unusually orchestrated movement into a complex structure. Rainer's theme is the dichotomy of public and private action. She uses the political situation in Germany, specifically that involving the Baader-Meinhof group, to illustrate the private and social implications of violence. Paralleling this political theme is an extended psychiatric session in which the figure of the psychiatrist (played by several people) is placed with his back to the camera to enhance the relationship between the patient and the viewer. Artifacts of lives, ranging from letters, diaries, and mementos to aerial views of Stonehenge and the Berlin Wall, are strewn throughout the film, and factual information printed on the screen is contrasted with the media as seen in scraps of newspaper. Rainer effectively subverts cinematic convention by mixing visual and aural elements, playing off the viewer's expectations of sound synchronization, and creating choreographed movement through editing. *Journeys from Berlin* is an intricate, textured study of ambiguity as well as political thought.

MADE MANIFEST

1980. U.S.A.

By Stan Brakhage.
11 min. Color. Silent. 24 fps.

Brakhage's use of ocean imagery creates a homage to nature as well as to the aesthetics of light and movement. The film begins with delicate swirls of light set against a black background. Images of the sea emerge and his camera captures the light play upon the waves. Intermittently, flashes of brilliance erupt, punctuating the ocean view. Brakhage also manipulates the footage by editing shots of the sea upside down and sideways—creating his own form of geographic space. The title for the film comes from a passage in *I Corinthians 3:113*: "Every man's work shall be made manifest, for the day shall declare it, because it shall be revealed by fire and the fire shall try every man's work of what sort it is."

MIRRORED REASON

1980. U.S.A.
By Stan VanDerBeek. Edited by S. Fried. With Denise Koch. Music by Max VanDerBeek and Ferdinand Maisel.
10 min. Color. Sound.

Mirrored Reason is a dramatic performance about a schizophrenic by Denise Koch, who, in a monologue based on a Kafka tale, tells a story of losing her identity. A woman follows her and succeeds in taking over her life by living in her apartment, working at her job, and convincing other people that she is the real of the two. The real character loses her identity and becomes a void. VanDerBeek discovers a visual metaphor for this narrative through a stylized interpretation of reflections. Isolated on the screen, Koch's face fragmented by a mirror which at times makes her appear symmetrical and then seemingly ajar, she becomes the two figures combined. This parable about contemporary society is a study of the loss of individual reason and a sense of self.

SEXUAL MEDITATIONS #1: MOTEL

1980. U.S.A.
By Stan Brakhage.
7 min. Color. Silent. 18 fps. (Filmmaker designates that this film may also be shown at 24 fps.)

This film, the origin of Brakhage's entire 16mm **Sexual Meditation** series, has been described by the filmmaker as a "sexual dream piece in modern hermitcell." It begins suspensefully, with a survey of a motel room seen as the potential stage for action. Static images appear of the bathroom, a lamp, a wall plug, a chain-lock on the door. A color television plays to an empty room, displaying irrelevant images of cowboys. Brakhage suggests a narrative fragment: through a window a couple is seen in an embrace. The film progresses toward greater visual abstraction as the room and lovers are photographed through a plastic sheet, blending painted and cinematographic imagery.

SKY DANCE

1980. U.S.A.
By Faith Hubley. Music composed and performed by Elizabeth Swados.
10 min. Color. Sound.

Hubley uses primitive and prehistoric art to explore our historical search for the unknown. Subtitled "Reaching for Life in the Cosmos," this film travels from cave paintings to astronauts and aliens while drawing on mythology, cosmology, and astronomy. The lithe, dynamic figures of Hubley's art are joyous, dancing to the music of African drums, Asian chimes, Latin beats, and the chants and whispers of Elizabeth Swados's music. This film is a positive, whimsical view that effortlessly encapsulates some basic ideas of religion and philosophy.

SYDNEY=BUSH

1980. Australia.
By Paul Winkler.
14 min. Color. Sound.

This film explores, in complex visual form, contrasting views of urban and rural worlds through a study of Sydney, Australia versus the primitive bush. Through various in-camera techniques, Winkler creates a highly abstract tapestry, conjoining city and country iconography. At points panoramic shots of the Sydney skyline are matted into images of backland fauna; at other times, urban and rural footage are directly superimposed. Winkler also achieves an impressionistic quality for his landscapes through single-frame shooting, overlapping dissolves, and disorienting swish-pans. At one point, in fact, the entire image seems to spin around in concentric 360-degree turns—like a giant Catherine wheel. Accompanying the images on the soundtrack are lush sounds of native animals—parrots, kangaroos—further accentuating the dialectic of urban and primitive realms.

TAYLOR SQUARE

1980. Australia.
By Paul Winkler.
20 min. Color. Sound.

In *Taylor Square* Winkler creates an abstract portrait of a metropolitan area seething with energy and diversity. Matted and superimposed images of pedestrians, traffic, building facades, and commercial signs float by. The frame is continually segmented, and multiple shots coexist ambiguously in the same space. Through this technique Winkler alternately achieves the sense of a collage, or a prism, or even a metropolitan crazy quilt. To realize these effects Winkler's camera, as he puts it, "pans in semi-random movements in long telephoto shots over an area of 1½ miles of streetscrapers. The movements are shown in most cases four times, as four squares on the screen which bounce into each other on their edges." Through these visual strategies and Winkler's use of a pinball machine on the soundtrack, a sense of city life as a collision course ultimately emerges in the film.

SYDNEY=BUSH (1980)

TWO FIGURES

1980. U.S.A.
By James Herbert.
20 min. Color. Silent. 24 fps.

The eponymous two figures, both male, occupy a disturbing space that is in one sense particular and precise and in another placeless. They move within a defined territory, marked more by melancholy than exactitude; the space is alien—although not altogether unfamiliar—and alienating— seemingly unattached to the sensible world. Even the rooms that are open and windowed carry an unsettling feel of *huis clos*. There is a tension, palpably dramatic, between the cool location and the physical embrace of the figures in the space, but their touch conveys a separateness and a solitude not assuaged by passion. *Two Figures* is an exceedingly romantic work in the classic sense of the word: it has to do with the Ideal (the nudes, the space) and Loss (the aesthetic distancing through rephotography).

URBAN SPACES

1980. Australia.
By Paul Winkler.
27 min. Color. Sound.

In the avant-garde "city symphony" tradition, *Urban Spaces* is Paul Winkler's portrait of Sydney, Australia, the metropolis where he lives. Using his characteristic and extraordinary in-camera matting techniques, Winkler segments the frame to create striking geometric patterns out of the urban scenes. Winkler writes that one of the themes he articulates through this iconography is that of the "fragmentation of spaces be-

tween people and their immediate surroundings . . . the filmic images creat[ing] . . . a kind of surreal realism-claustrophobia." Other metaphors are suggested by the visual design. At points the matted strips of people and cars in motion look like arteries running through the interstices of the city, or like conveyor belts transporting objects through an urban machine. Finally, at times the matted sections look simply like a strip of film. *Urban Spaces* is useful not only for the study of experimental cinematic technique, but, as a catalog of metropolitan facades, it also constitutes a stimulating portrait of urban architecture.

THE BIG BANG AND OTHER CREATION MYTHS

1981. U.S.A.
By Faith Hubley. Music composed and performed by Elizabeth Swados.
11 min. Color. Sound.

The Big Bang is one of seven primal myths visualized by Faith Hubley in this imaginative ethnographic animation. The Bang is represented by a cosmic egg which explodes forth life in many masks of different cultures. In the creation myths from black Africa, Finland, China, Australia, and the Native American and Hindu cultures, the story of life's beginnings is told through fascinating characters and symbolism, including a fat god who vomits the sun and moon into the heavens, a duck whose shattered egg fragments create the sky, and a woman who bleeds a nation of people. Hubley creates a world perspective by using the art styles of many cultures

combined with multiethnic music by composer Elizabeth Swados.

MAN IN A BUBBLE

1981. U.S.A.
By Sidney Peterson. Assistant director: Marjorie Keller. Sound by Helene Kaplan.
16 min. B&W. Sound.

After completing *The Lead Shoes* (1949), Sidney Peterson worked in an array of commercial productions, including documentary, television, and animation. *Man in a Bubble*, which is dedicated to painter "Jerome Bosch," is an urban study that rejects the narrative structure of his earlier films for a subtle visual/aural collage. To set the theme, Peterson begins with the images of a young girl reading a bubble comic book, kids blowing bubbles, and paintings which encase figures in spherical shapes. He then takes this central image to the streets of New York and Chicago, where he constructs a vivid picture of the city as an urban bubble. Faces on the street, a newspaper headline that reads "What a Mess," mirrored windows, and subways coalesce, while the aural landscape is dominated by Walkmans and street radios. Isolated inside headphones and gliding fluidly on rollerskates, the urban performers are captured in exquisitely detailed shots. The claustrophobic, chaotic world is epitomized in the final shot by a young woman holding her ears, trying to keep the sound away. *Man in a Bubble* is an intriguing urban portrait which retains the dynamism and energy of Peterson's early films.

GALA DAY (1963)

Contemporary British Independent Film: Voyage of Discovery

by John Ellis

The story of British independent cinema is one of risk-taking arising from the bleakest possible circumstances. Young filmmakers in Britain in the late sixties and the seventies were faced with a drastic lack of opportunities. Instead of collapsing into despair, they set about making the best of the limited resources available. Theirs is a distinctive merging of both aesthetic and political tendencies, giving the term "independent cinema" a special meaning in Britain. The films distributed here are only a sample of the work created in British independent cinema over the last decade and more, but are a representative sample nonetheless.

The negative circumstances from which British independent cinema has grown are those of the declining British commercial cinema, and of what appears to be a very conservative and closed television industry. François Truffaut once remarked that there is incompatibility between the terms "British" and "cinema." Within the context of commercial cinema, this is largely true. There are two reasons for this. First, British film exhibition has been tightly controlled by two monopolistic companies that have been more concerned with the steady profits from showing American films rather than the risks of large-scale film production. Second, British directors have had no real context in which to develop a distinctive style. Apart from isolated examples like the team of Michael Powell and Emeric Pressburger or Robert Hamer and Alexander Mackendrick of Ealing Studios, the filmmaking of the fifties was resolutely aimed at a mass market and at the ever-present, never-realized dream of "breaking into the American market." The British "New Wave" at the turn of the sixties was more concerned with portraying the British working class than they were with turning cinema inside out like their French contemporaries. Then came the sixties, the boom in British film production, a flowering of British films. In retrospect, this flowering can be seen as a hothouse phenomenon, an artificial atmosphere produced by a massive influx of production finance from the United States. This money was chasing the then-fashionable myth of "Swinging London," a new youth culture around pop music that found its first expression in Richard Lester's Beatles films. When *The Graduate* (1967) and *Easy Rider* (1969) showed the way to doing similar (if not better) productions in the U.S., American investment was turned off overnight. British commercial production wilted and collapsed. For the whole of the seventies, there was essentially no British commercial cinema, no continuity of production. There have been the occasional British films, accompanied by much flag-waving; but a few films do not make a cinema.

The strange fact about British cinema is that, alone of European countries, it has not really developed an "art cinema." There are very few places in Britain where the films of François Truffaut, of Rainer Werner Fassbinder, or even the more exciting films of Robert Altman or Martin Scorsese can actually be seen. Commercial cinema exhibition was not interested in "continental" films, unless "continental" was a synonym for "explicit sex." Specialist art cinemas do exist, especially in London, with the distributors who service them scratching out a hand-to-mouth existence, often with only one 35mm print at their disposal. Exhibition outlets for art cinema outside London are even more limited. There are a few British Film Institute subsidized regional film theaters and some brave independent cinemas.

Also in Britain, no sympathetic ears were to be found in television. British TV has much stronger links with theater than it does with cinema, hence its principal export commodity is the historical drama. Standards are maintained by a ruthless traditionalism and an unwillingness to experiment. It is impossible to imagine a Ken Russell emerging from the British television of today, as he did in the sixties.

These are the impoverished circumstances from which independent cinema grew in Britain: a conservative commercial cinema, a hostile TV industry, and the lack of any real "art cinema" alternative. The earlier British films offered here show individual filmmakers coming to terms with these difficult circumstances. The small subsidies available from the British Film Institute's Production Board during the fifties and sixties helped some filmmakers at least to produce films that demonstrated their considerable talents. There is Ken Russell's *Amelia and the Angel*, showing the director's rich feeling for fantasy in this first tentative and typical expression. After making the film in 1958, Russell found work in television. Other filmmakers, like the Free Cinema group including Lindsay Anderson, Karel Reisz, Robert Vas, and the Swiss directors Alain Tanner and Claude Goretta (both working in Britain), sought first to make subsidized films for the BFI and, in Reisz's case, for the Ford Motor Company. However, they soon found that the only place in which they could hope to work was in the feature film industry (for those interested in fiction) or in television (for those, like the late Robert Vas, who were more interested in films of fact). The kind of filmmaking that grew out of the early years of Free Cinema is represented here by John Irwin's *Gala Day* (1963), a quasi-anthropological study of the Durham Miner's Gala. This Gala is a fairly obscure rite even to Londoners: it is a celebration of the tenacious culture of the northern working class and of its most enduring creation, the British Labour Party. Yet *Gala Day* is important because it does not fall into the condescending attitudes that marred some of the early films of the more well-known of Free Cinema's members. In other films, too, there are signs of filmmakers struggling with the weight of the problem of British class depiction. Paul Dickson's *David* (1951) opts for a fictionalized recreation of the life of a Welsh miner with literary leanings, and has the miner act out his own modest story. Paul Barnes's *Black Five* (1968) mourns the passing of steam trains but uses the reflections of train drivers and firemen themselves, which provide vivid descriptions of the texture of their work. But interesting as these films are individually, they are witnesses to a wasted potential. Barnes, Dickson, and Irwin are not household names, nor even respected figures within television documentary traditions. They are lost talents, people whose single films stand as signposts to the roads down which British cinema and

British television did not choose to travel.

Free Cinema was the last group of young directors who found careers in British commercial films; figures like Ken Russell or Peter Watkins were the last adventurous directors able to establish a career in television. Others fell by the wayside, or turned to alternate modes of expression. It took a very different set of positive circumstances to create an independent cinema in Britain. The independents were influenced decisively by the increasing opportunities for financing offered by the British Film Institute and the Arts Council of Great Britain.

The years 1966 to 1970 mark the real beginnings of British independent experimental cinema. Steadily through the mid-sixties a new cultural movement had begun to develop, a fresh avant-garde inspiration that produced a new group of filmmakers whose aspirations were very different from those of Free Cinema. Inspired by the work of American filmmakers like Stan Brakhage or Kenneth Anger, as well as more recent work from New York, a resolutely "anti-illusionist" aesthetic was taking root in London and elsewhere. In 1966 the London Film-makers' Co-op was founded, and soon involved filmmakers like Stephen Dwoskin and Peter Gidal (both Americans resident in London), Simon Hartog, Malcolm LeGrice, and Jeff Keen. The Co-op was and is still a crucial factor in the British independent scene. This represented the first time that British filmmakers had concentrated on creating new forms of cinema. In the case of the Co-op this was innovation from top to bottom. Films were made to explore concerns new to cinema in Britain: the materiality of the medium of film itself and the nature of film performance, offering a challenge to the overly presumptive claim of film to realistic representation. Films of this kind are represented here by Tony Sinden's *Can-Can* (1976), a witty use of a mundane event (a beer can rolling across the floor of a moving train) to reflect on framing and color combinations. This film exists in two versions in Britain: one for single-projector screenings, one for simultaneous projection on two screens.

Besides the Co-op, other filmmaking groups began to appear, some directly motivated by the political explosion that occurred in May 1968. Though the events in Britain that spring were not comparable to those on the streets of Paris, nevertheless a whole new political atmosphere rapidly developed. Unlike traditional leftist films, these new political films stressed the importance of many different changes in society, particularly at the level of personal behavior. A different rationale for filmmaking developed from this movement, a rationale that pervades almost the whole of British independent production even now. In the year 1968, a collective that called itself Cinema Action began to make agitational films for immediate showing to audiences beyond the confines of the traditional cinema: to political groups, to public meetings, to factory workers. In the eighties, Cinema Action is still making "working class films." Similarly, the Berwick Street Collective was founded in the early seventies by a group separating themselves from the commercial film industry. Their *Ireland Behind the Wire* (1974) was a courageous film to have been made in Britain. Though partly financed by the British Film Institute, the negative was confiscated by the laboratory, which considered the film treasonous. It offers a trenchant analysis of the situation in Northern Ireland in the mid-seventies, including accounts of British torture of political prisoners. Since the European Court of Justice has established that torture did indeed take place, the film has been tolerated, though occasional attempts are still made to withdraw it from distribution. Its importance is not only that it represents the Northern Ireland situation in a way that is taboo in Britain, but also that in doing so it reveals the distortions of the television reporting of events in the province. It is a

IRELAND BEHIND THE WIRE (1974)

film that comes from a political awareness of the importance of the media in the structuring of reality.

Other initiatives in the early seventies included the formation of the Newsreel Collective, of Liberation Films, and the foundation of a distribution and exhibition agency for radical films, the Other Cinema. These events caused profound changes in the British independent filmmaking scene. While the industry was in its death-throes, deprived of its flow of American capital, a whole new area of film activity was springing up, using 16mm equipment, and creating new audiences. A major readjustment of film financing in Britain seemed necessary. Until that point, the British Film Institute's Production Board had been trying to create a British "art cinema" on its inadequate funds. An indication of this change was Germaine Greer's involvement in making a short gag film for the BFI intended for showing in conventional cinemas. *Darling, Do You Love Me?* (1968) has Greer playing a satirically amusing part for the author of *The Female Eunuch*: a woman who insistently demands love and eventually smothers her lover to death.

It took pressure to convince the BFI that support for the growing sector of an independent, socially aware cinema was vitally needed. But once this argument had been won, the funds made available had a crucial galvanizing effect, both directly in that they enabled much more ambitious films to be made, and indirectly in that other sources of public funding began to develop: the Arts Council and Regional Arts Associations.

The BFI Production Board has also continued to explore the possibilities of a British "art cinema." Tony Scott's *Loving Memory*, coproduced in 1969 with Woodfall (the production company for the early sixties British New Wave), is a successful example that has received comparatively wide showings. It is a variant on the horror film: an old brother and sister run over a young boy, and the sister tends to the corpse as though it were a replacement younger brother. The film avoids the macabre by its meticulously ordinary action, with long silences, cups of tea, the rhythm of rural life and old age. It deliberately falls between two incompatible genres and thereby achieves a curious poignancy and realism. Equally, throughout the seventies, the BFI supported the slow gestation of Bill Douglas's autobiographical trilogy, *My Childhood* (1972), *My Ain Folk* (1973), and *My Way Home* (1978). These stunning films offer a child's vision of a complicated growing-up in a grindingly poor Scots village. We are presented with Jamie's attempt to understand who his parents are (from among the many men and women who take care of him and feud among themselves). Moments are frozen, as in the mind's eye; the elliptical dialogue pulsates with repressed meanings. Emotions erupt suddenly; their consequences endure. Douglas's images spring from a whole tradition of social realist still photography. Their explicit use as images of memory (rather than of truth or reality) casts a whole new light on the claims of social realism.

In addition to supporting the possibilities for a British art cinema, the BFI has also underwritten work that exists at the edges of what television sees as its domain. Films such as *Above Us the Earth* (1977), *Welcome to Britain* (1975), and *Who Cares* (1971) were made by the BFI simply because no television network was prepared to make them itself. However, once made by an outside producer, the BBC felt itself able to broadcast them, deflecting any public criticism onto the producers and away from itself. *Who Cares*, the first film by controversial documentarist Nicholas Broomfield, is about Liverpool's urban renewal, which consisted chiefly of laying waste to large areas of the city and then neglecting to put anything up as replacements. *Welcome to Britain* is a crusading, investigative documentary about the hostile reaction toward nonwhite peoples entering Britain. *Above Us The Earth* is challenging in a different way. It mixes semidocumentary with semifiction, so that the convenient dividing lines are blurred. South Wales miners fight a mine closing; prominent Labour politicians appear, make speeches, and disappear again; one miner's home life and his slow death from emphysema are chronicled. A bleak story from the grass-roots of the British labor movement, but handled in a fresh way, moving from fact to fiction with no apparent break.

One of the important products of British independent cinema has been the move toward new forms of programming films, and the creation of film workshops that integrate film production and film exhibition. Many of the films here were made with unconventional exhibition in mind. *The Song of the Shirt* (1979) reveals its meanings in discussions after a screening of one or more of its parts. It has an open structure that presents multiple forms of evidence—speeches, inquiries, declarations, fictions, imaginative art, and commercial engravings—about nineteenth-century seamstresses. This evidence is presented and juxtaposed in such a way that the viewer is not drawn (or driven) to a particular conclusion. Too many factors are in play. Instead, different viewers come to the film and find their own preconceptions disturbed. A viewing of the film followed by a discussion is a fascinating exercise in the exploration of ideas of history, of representation, of female labor, of fashion. Other films benefit from "structured programming," the creation of a series of screenings around a particular film or a particular issue that reveals a series of perspectives on one topic. Hence, *Amy!* (1979), about a heroic woman aviator trying to come to terms with "being a star," was shown with Dorothy Arzner's 1933 Hollywood feature *Christopher Strong*, in which a similar problem is dealt with in a startlingly different way.

A recent development in independent cinema has been the creation of a series of regional film workshops that have both cinemas and production facilities. This development, which allows audiences direct access to filmmakers and their work (and vice-versa), is the outgrowth of funds from Regional Arts Associations, whose purpose is to encourage local filmmaking activity. Regional Arts Associations have begun to offer limited financing to film production (both *Song of the Shirt* and *Amy!* were made partly with their funds), and have deliberately favored independent filmmakers working in loose groups who have set up filmmaking and exhibiting workshops. The scale of productions is currently very modest, but the development is significant because it is the first time since 1914 that there has been any substantial film production taking place outside London.

The effect of all the many influences outlined above has been the creation of a particular style, an invitation to the viewer to *read* images and sounds as being constructed rather than as illusions of a reality. It is also a matter of acknowledging the pleasure gained from watching—a pleasure that is examined in all its ambiguities in several films, notably *Phoelix* (1979). Commercial cinema exploits this pleasure, but attributes the effects of beauty and astonishment to the things that are shown rather than to the way they are shown. In traditional art cinema, the way of showing sometimes comes forward as an element in the pleasure of the film (Miklós Jancsó's camera movements, Bernardo Bertolucci's landscapes), but it is finally character and moral value that dominate. In British independent cinema, there is a cinema free from these constraints, a cinema that has learned from Jean-Luc Godard and from the London Film-makers' Co-op alike, a cinema that keeps a keen but wary eye on developments in film narrative.

Two films demonstrate this approach in different ways. *Riddles of the Sphinx* (1977) was a pioneering film, falling into sections. One section (the examination of the image of the Sphinx) could be said to draw directly on the work of the Co-op; others (the slow camera-revealing pan around a mirror-filled room) draw on areas of the art film. But it brings a distinctive attention to image and sound that marks it out from either of these cinemas. It is essentially a voyage of discovery, both of cinema and of the film's subject, the difficult contradictions in which a contemporary young mother is caught.

A Walk Through H (1978) and *Dear Phone* (1977) demonstrate the eclectic wit of Peter Greenaway. *Dear Phone* alternates images of telephone booths with handwritten stories of bizarre encounters with and attitudes toward the phone. A voice-over persuasively reads these stories, but makes significant alterations to them. The phone kiosks begin as illustrations, but soon become anthropomorphized as eccentric characters in their own right. *A Walk Through H* develops this comic attitude, talking of a mythical journey which is shown through fragments of maps, pictures of birds, and various ephemera. The disjunctions and accidental meanings that are created are the real pleasure of the film. To say that Greenaway's work is the encounter between Ealing comedy and the avant-garde is not as far-fetched as it might seem. (The Circulating Film Library also distributes five other Greenaway films: *Water Wrackets* [1975], *Windows* [1975], *H is for House* [1978], *Vertical Features Remake* [1979], and *The Falls* [1980].)

The feminist film movement, with its attention to how mediated representations construct individuality, has produced some fine independent films. *Rapunzel Let Down Your Hair* (1978) was Britain's first feminist feature, marking the movement away from documentary and campaign filmmaking toward a critical engagement with fiction. The Rapunzel fairy tale is told in a number of different ways, as animation, as detective story, as historical examination, and then finally as a modern perspective on liberation. *Riddles of the Sphinx* pushes the examination of women in representation much further; *Phoelix* examines the convoluted erotic attitudes of an old high-society voyeur and the young woman who in turn finds herself fascinated by him. Both demonstrate how women are caught in particular socio-sexual attitudes and the problems of escaping from them. *Mirror Phase* (1978) reveals one aspect of this construction. Carola Klein's own baby daughter is shown at the point in which her narcissistic self-image is being formed. The filmmaker reflects upon the perception women have of their own images and the difficulties of formulating images as a feminist filmmaker. *Amy!*, too, sees Amy Johnston unable to find herself in the star-image that her flying exploits gain for her; being a star-woman in a male world destroys her sense of identity rather than confirming it. *Angel In The House* (1979) is the delicately told story of a young woman whose decision to make a career in writing marks her out as strange in her conventional family. And Vera Neubauer's *Animation For Live Action* (1978), a mad dash through the problems of making an animated film while pregnant, is full of wry jokes and audacious puns.

The difficult political situation in Northern Ireland has also produced a series of independent films. Independent cinema is the only arena of the media in Britain that has tried to come to grips with the almost intractable problems of representing this situation. It has produced *Ireland Behind the Wire*'s political perspective, as well as a body of films dealing with the realities of life north and south of the border. Thaddeus O'Sullivan gives a personal account in *On A Paving Stone Mounted* (1978) and *A Pint of Plain* (1975); his is a calm voice that deserves more attention. Joe Comerford's *Down the Corner* (1977) shows ordinary life in the Republic: an independent film in Britain, in Dublin it was a decidedly commercial film, opening at a major cinema with press coverage declaring "God Bless the British Film Institute," which had partly financed it.

Finally, British independent cinema has created two films of exceptional breadth of vision. Phil Mulloy's *In The Forest* (1978) takes as its subject the history of Britain from the Dark Ages to the Industrial Revolution. Not the history of history books, but history from the bottom up. Following three peasants as they wander down the centuries, we see how they are constantly cheated by persuasive stories, or beaten by forces stronger than themselves, until they are swallowed up into the anonymous crowd working in a factory. Again, it is the images that speak, holding together history and poetry in a luminous whole. Edward Bennett's *The Life Story Of Baal* (1978), based on Brecht's earliest play, is about an anguished male artist. Bennett has converted it into a film that further distances Brecht's somewhat equivocal examination of his hero by tracing the sordid roots of Brecht's story. Baal's empty roaring and his purposeless outraging of bourgeois morals provide a fitting epitaph to an outdated conception of the artist. The image of the artist-as-genius still dominates the popular conception of the film director, but it is an idea that British independent cinema has rejected—at least for now.

ANNOTATIONS

Larry Kardish, Marita Sturken

DAVID

1951. Great Britain.
By Paul Dickson. British Film Institute
production.
38 min. B&W. Sound.

Made in Ammanford, Wales, **David** is a
film which, through its juxtaposition of
documentary and fictional techniques,
richly depicts a specific culture with
warmth and national pride. This true
story of David Reese is told as a reminiscence by a young man who in his
youth had known him. Reese is injured
in a coal mine explosion and becomes a
caretaker for the local school. Shocked
by the death of his only son, he writes
a poem which, finally, brings him the
reward of a tribute from an old, now-
famous friend. The power of the story
derives from the young boy's adoration
for the caretaker and Reese's quiet
dignity. Dickson uses a dramatic approach to get closer to the harsh reality
of life in a coal mining town. He combines these narrative scenes with documentary footage of the mines and
everyday life in the town. Only a few of
the characters are professional actors;
the rest of the roles are played by the
people of Ammanford, who are surprisingly unselfconscious before the
camera's eye. **David** is a regional film

DAVID (1951)

which effectively depicts an entire people and culture.

THURSDAY'S CHILDREN (1953). *See*
Documentary Film

EVERY DAY EXCEPT CHRISTMAS
(1957). *See* Documentary Film

AMELIA AND THE ANGEL (1958).
See Sound Fiction

GALA DAY

1963. Great Britain.
Directed by John Irwin. British Film
Institute production.
26 min. B&W. Sound.

This film documents a day in 1962 when
the city of Durham in northern England had a gala, complete with a miners' union parade, political rally, and
carnival. Both a political and social portrait, the subject is not only one day's
actual events, but also the almost ritualistic strength of the miners' union and
the frustrated energy of the working
class population, whose gala day ends in
a confrontation with the police. With a
sensitivity and attention to detail that is
reminiscent of Lindsay Anderson's *Every
Day Except Christmas* (1957), Irwin
chronicles the day's events from the early

morning preparations to the lonely calm
of the day's end as children stand in the
windblown garbage, alone and forgotten.

AN UNTITLED FILM

1964. Great Britain.
By David Gladwell. British Film Institute production.
9 min. B&W. Sound.

This film is shot entirely in slow motion
(at times up to 150 fps), an effect combined with fragmentary, close-up camerawork to isolate and magnify a series
of daily activities on a farm. A bucket
of water being thrown, a dog's tail wag-
ging, a horse's hooves being cleaned, and
a chicken being slaughtered are actions
that become eerie and suspenseful when
captured by Gladwell's stylized technique. These fragments are observed by
a young boy, whose distraught face expresses his horror at the death of an animal. The electronic musical score builds
a tension that underscores the disquieting beauty of this film.

BLACK FIVE

1968. Great Britain.
By Paul Barnes. British Film Institute
production.
24 min. Color. Sound.

This nostalgic essay on the disappearance of steam engines is a detailed and
lovingly photographed portrait of the
versatile Black Five, "one of the finest
engines ever built." Images of the train's
mechanisms and powerful movements
are overlaid with the reminiscences of
the engineers witnessing the replacement of this method of transportation
by diesel engines. The important mechanical features such as the reversing
gear and the brake, as well as the practical difficulties of working with steam,
are described by the railwaymen. "With
steam you had to make your power," one
of them says, "with diesel it's there at
your command," adding that working
with a steam engine gives a greater sense
of achievement upon arriving on time,
and a greater possibility of things going
wrong. Long, nostalgic discussions of the
merits of steam are balanced in the film
by the genuine respect of these men for
the new machinery that has replaced it.
Visually, however, the film remains in
awe of the powerful iron beauty of these
engines.

DARLING, DO YOU LOVE ME?

1968. Great Britain.
By Martin Sharp and Bob Whitaker.

British Film Institute production. With Germaine Greer and Alisdair Burke. 4 min. B&W. Sound.

In this humorous, campy short, feminist writer Germaine Greer plays a clown-faced vampire who assaults a resolute young man, desperately trying to get him to say he loves her. In a fast-paced collage, Greer plays a myriad of roles, from harpy to siren to distraught housewife—comically embodying the archetype of an insecure female figure who lives for the magical phrase "I love you." *Darling, Do You Love Me?* was made as a gag film to be shown in commercial movie theaters in Great Britain.

LOVING MEMORY

1969. Great Britain.
By Tony Scott. British Film Institute production.
53 min. B&W. Sound.

This mysterious tale takes place in rural Yorkshire, a moody landscape beautifully photographed in black and white. It tells the story of a young boy who is hit and killed by a car driven by a strange brother and sister. They take the body home to their secluded cottage, where the woman becomes increasingly attached to the corpse, creating a complex fantasy of it as her only companion and the incarnation of their dead brother. The film plays upon the tradition of psychological dramas and horror films through a style of sophisticated, formal parody. It is a melodrama rich with genre props—a worn photograph, an ancient Victrola, a cobweb-ridden attic—and classic settings which portray the subtle violence and barely contained madness inherent in everyday life.

WHO CARES

1971. Great Britain.
By Nicholas Broomfield. British Film Institute production.
18 min. B&W. Sound.

Who Cares is a sensitive approach to documenting the destructive effects of an urban renewal project in Liverpool, England. This early film of documentarian Nick Broomfield, who went on to make *Tattooed Tears* (1978) and *Soldier Girls* (1981) with Joan Churchill, has an understated style. As we see buildings being razed, we hear the residents talking about their old neighborhoods and the community that existed there. We see these same people move to large apartment complexes where the structure of the buildings makes it hard for them to meet and create a sense of

neighborhood. Their feelings of loss and social isolation are reinforced by Broomfield's imagery of solitary figures dwarfed by the scale of the tower apartment architecture. Conveying a full sense of the hardship of this kind of urban redevelopment by centering on individuals, *Who Cares* gives us the full dimensions of this social dilemma. It brings the social skepticism of its period to bear upon the optimistic view of urban renewal reflected in its classic predecessor, *Housing Problems* (1935).

MY CHILDHOOD

1972. Great Britain.
Written and directed by Bill Douglas. Produced by Geoffrey Evans. Photographed by Mick Campbell. British Film Institute production. With Stephen Archibald, Jean Taylor-Smith, Hughie Restorick, Bernard McKenna.
48 min. B&W. Sound.

My Childhood is the first film in an autobiographical trilogy by Bill Douglas which also includes *My Ain Folk* (1973) and *My Way Home* (1978). Set in the Scottish mining village of Newcraighill, south of Edinburgh, *My Childhood* deals unsentimentally with the poverty-stricken lives of two boys, Jamie and Tommy, who live with their grandmother in a bleak cottage. Structured on the subjective memories of childhood, the film provides information through specific details that were important to the boys. Many relationships are unclear (neither boy is sure of his parentage) and their lives are marked by absences—the absence of parents, family structure, comfort, and security. Caught between childhood and adult responsibilities, Jamie cares for his grandmother, leading her home when she gets lost; is taken to visit his mother in an insane asylum; and eventually befriends a German POW, to whom he teaches the alphabet. In the end, when the grandmother dies in her sleep and his German friend is sent home at the war's end, the distraught Jamie runs away and jumps a train. In a powerful shot, his huddled, grim figure is seen fading in the distance. Douglas uses a straightforward, brutally honest approach that reveals the action through the powerful emotions caught in minute gestures. Using a natural acting style with sparse dialogue, Douglas effectively portrays the confusion and mystery of a child's sense of the world. "The childhood of the title is literally my childhood," says Douglas, "and the incidents that I recount are, with a few variations, things that actually happened to me. This is not a dreamlike film composed of languid memories. It is a hard film made up of elementary contrasts: a few big events that have great importance and the silence and the sounds that surround them."

WHO CARES (1971)

WELCOME TO BRITAIN (1975)

MY AIN FOLK

1973. Great Britain.
Written and directed by Bill Douglas.
Produced by Nick Nascht. Photographed by Gale Tattersall. British Film Institute production. With Stephen Archibald, Hughie Restorick, Jean Talyor-Smith, Bernard Mckenna, Helena Gloag, Paul Kermack.
55 min. B&W. Sound.

My Ain Folk is the second in an autobiographical trilogy by Bill Douglas which begins with **My Childhood** (1972) and concludes with **My Way Home** (1978). Like **My Childhood**, the title of **My Ain Folk** is riddled with irony. Jamie, a young Scottish boy who was left homeless by the death of his maternal grandmother in the first film, now finds himself living with relatives who are strangers to him. In a horrifying web of family ties, Jamie's father is married to another woman and is dominated by his possessive mother, who grudgingly accepts responsibility for Jamie. The one sympathetic character who emerges is the grandfather who, after returning home from the hospital, attempts, if feebly, to befriend the boy. Driven to despair by his wife's bitter resentment and harshness, he finally gasses himself in the kitchen. Jamie, who in a depressive withdrawal has lost his ability to speak coherently, passively goes to a children's "home." A coherent portrait of Jamie's increasing confusions of identity, **My Ain Folk** is an unyielding and bitter recollection which is constructed in an elusive progression of memories. Ordinary childhood experiences take on revealing complexity in the context of Jamie's desolate circumstances. Like **My Childhood**, this film is a stark and moving portrait of the deprivation and isolation in the filmmaker's upbringing.

CHILDREN

1974. Great Britain.
Written and directed by Terence Davies. Photographed by William Diver. British Film Institute production.
46 min. B&W. Sound.

Children explores the theme of social and domestic violence through the story of an English boy. Robert Tucker's environment is permeated with irrational violence—he is subjected to cruel bullying in school, and his father beats his mother, filling their home with fear and anguish. The film is told as a series of flashbacks which combine to show the progression of Tucker's personality and psycho-sexual problems as he evolves from a helpless, alienated child to a young man who finds eroticism in violence. Never fully identifying with his character, the film remains distant and nonjudgemental of individuals while condemning of the social environment which condones and fosters violence.

IRELAND BEHIND THE WIRE

1974. Great Britain.
By the Berwick Street Collective. British Film Institute production.
110 min. B&W. Sound.

Ireland Behind the Wire is an uncompromising documentary that records the experience and attitudes of Catholic working-class people in the cities of Derry and Belfast in Northern Ireland between 1969 and 1973. The film explores the situation through extensive interviews combined with scenes of street violence, internment, and daily life, documenting the reality of the British army occupation and what it is there to suppress. The first section of the film chronicles the history leading up to the present struggle in Northern Ireland, the origins of Republicanism, and the resistance to British rule. The second part documents the army occupation, the internment of the community's men, and civil resistance. Footage of the "Free Derry" marches of 1969, with the barricading of the city, and the massacre of marchers in an anti-internment march in Derry are included, along with numerous scenes of the community organizing and wives visiting their interned husbands. The final section of **Ireland Behind the Wire** was censored by the British government, and the filmmakers chose to let the film end abruptly where it had been cut off, rather than fabricate a new ending.

WATER WRACKETS

1975. Great Britain.
By Peter Greenaway. Music by Max Eastley. Narrated by Colin Cantlie.
12 min. Color. Sound.

While quiet shots reveal a sensuous, apparently autumnal and closed marine landscape, a sober soundtrack describes a specific period—perhaps in the Arthurian past when ceremony counted for as much as deeds—of the tortured history of a bellicose but religiously observant waterside community. A wrack is wreckage or a ruin or even some vegetation cast ashore. All meanings are appropriate to the appreciation of **Water Wrackets**, in whose text unfamiliar words abound, and whose narration sounds as much like science fiction as historical surmise. Indeed, the whole strange and haunting work may be seen as a meditation on conjecture: the radical use of sound to image invites this explanation, and allows for many others. The brochure to the 1979 London Film Festival rightly saw **Water Wrackets** as "a commentary on a Tolkienesque civilization evoked by stunning and mystical lakeland imagery." (See also **Windows** [1975], **Dear Phone** [1977], **H is for House** [1978], **A Walk through H** [1978], **Vertical Features Remake** [1979], and **The Falls** [1980].)

WELCOME TO BRITAIN

1975. Great Britain.
Directed and edited by Ben Lewin. Photographed by Roger Deakins and Brian Huberman. British Film Institute production.
72 min. Color. Sound.

Welcome to Britain is a thorough, heartfelt study of the discrimination and injustices of the immigration system in Great Britain. The film is structured around the escalating confrontation of Reuben Davis, a self-styled controversial character known as the "Immigrants' Mr. Fixit," and Alex Lyon, the Minister for Immigration who represents the government bureaucracy at the other extreme. Lewin talks to visitors from Pakistan, India, and Bangladesh, among other places, who were placed in the Harmondsworth detention camp for many months because of government misunderstandings and abuse of policy. He documents legal proceedings and follows the story of Davis's "Ship of Wives," a massive transport of wives from India which, though never realized, was designed to embarrass the government. In a loose *cinéma vérité* style which allows him to interact with these people before the camera, Lewin explores the implications of Britain's reluctance to admit foreigners who are, in effect, the end product of that country's imperialistic heritage. "Above all," says the filmmaker, "**Welcome to Britain** is about the whole experience of immigration control, which is frequently humiliating and degrading for those who have to pass through it."

WINDOWS

1975. Great Britain.
By Peter Greenaway. Narrated by Colin Cantlie.
4 min. Color. Sound.

Peter Greenaway's cinematic examinations of cataloging and classification begin with a tidy selection of related incidents. *The* classic film on defenestration, it is about people who leave a room by its window, or at least about the large number of people who do so in a small but particular English country parish. While dogs bark and a clavichord is played, while daylight comes and goes through a window, statistics are read about who fell from windows in summer, how many fell into the snow, and so on: much interesting information is given. As the filmmaker notes elsewhere, statistics leave as much out as in, and **Windows** watchers are certainly tempted to imaginatively fill in the unspoken connecting links of this brief but illuminating report.

CAN CAN

1976. Great Britain.
By Tony Sinden. British Film Institute production.
10 min. Color. Sound.

Sinden describes **Can Can** as "a stretch printed film image of an empty beer can rolling back and forth across a table and floor area of a fast train traveling between London and Brighton. . . . Reflections and changes of light on the can's surface make up the central aspect of attention. . . ." Like Hollis Frampton's **Lemon** (1969), in which a familiar edible takes on sublime overtones, here a furiously moving object as banal and hackneyed as a man-made drinking cylinder assumes an unexpected beauty. **Can Can**, a very lively film, goes a long way toward answering the Socratic question on aesthetics: "Does good apply to the container as well as the contained?" It is a film about the ordinary seen in a new light and rhythm.

RESISTANCE

1976. Great Britain.
Directed by Ken McMullen. Produced by Chris Rodrigues. Music by Brian Eno. British Film Institute production.
75 min. B&W and color. Sound.

This film is a multilayered approach to the concept of political resistance which uses and analyzes both video and film footage. Interwoven with film fragments of wartime France, anti-fascist demonstrations, and figures such as Lenin and Trotsky is a psychodrama that was originally conducted by an analyst in 1948 with disturbed French resistance fighters and then reenacted in 1974 by a group of performance actors, artists, and an analyst. The resulting material is collaged, questioned, examined, and extended in this film to explore the idea in historical, political, and psychological terms as well as to examine the contradiction of filmic records and the controversial use of improvisational reenactment.

ABOVE US THE EARTH

1977. Great Britain.
By Karl Francis. Photographed by Roger Evans and Mike Fox. British Film Institute production.
86 min. Color. Sound.

Above Us the Earth tells two parallel stories about the miners of South Wales: one is the story of the closing of a pit and the subsequent reassignment of the miners to a new working place, and the other is concerned with the death of an old miner from the occupational disease emphysema. The film shows that a strong trust was created between the filmmaker and the miners of Rhymney Valley, South Wales, who are filmed in documentary style and who play themselves in certain dramatic scenes. The footage that records the closure of the pit reveals a community which is based on mining not only as an industry but also as a dominant social influence. The film examines the tension between the versions of the situation offered by the media, Parliament, and trade union officials and the reality of the miners' lives. By extending this realistic approach through narrative scenes involving the death of a miner, Francis has given the subject a personal context that is genuinely moving. The dignity and determination of these men, as well as the somber contradiction of their lives, make this film a convincing and informative record of a difficult and often tragic profession.

DEAR PHONE

1977. Great Britain.
By Peter Greenaway. Narrated by Colin Cantlie.
17 min. Color. Sound.

Telephones exert a tyranny in our everyday lives; although this cannot be denied, their power is certainly subverted, as is the progress of the fourteen stories in this wicked comedy that the filmmaker says masquerades as "an oblique consideration of narrative." Maybe the fourteen anecdotes are related: at first they are read by an off-screen voice; then they are also shown written out, smudges and all, but by the film's end they are neatly typed. There are pronounced tendencies toward the thriller, all brought up short, in this clever film in which the phone is much used and abused.

RIDDLES OF THE SPHINX

1977. Great Britain.
By Laura Mulvey and Peter Wollen.

ANIMATION FOR LIVE ACTION (1978)

British Film Institute production.
92 min. Color. Sound.

Shot in a series of virtuoso camera movements, the film weaves episodes from a woman's life with narration and music, conjoining a naturalistic story with an avant-garde form. When this feature work, probably the most celebrated of all British Film Institute productions, opened in New York, J. Hoberman of **The Village Voice** wrote, "Freud saw in the story of Oedipus 'the beginnings of religion, morals, society and art.' But the myth can be read another way—as a metaphor for the rise of patriarchy which displaced the 'primitive communism' of matriarchy. In this sense, the Sphinx who terrorizes Thebes but self-destructs when Oedipus correctly answers her riddle would be a representation of the preexisting matriarchal culture. It is used as such by Laura Mulvey and Peter Wollen in their elegant and erudite new film. . . . The film centers on the situation of Louise, a middle-class mother obsessively involved with her four-year-old daughter to the exclusion of the outside world. Initially the soundtrack is devoted to her rhyming, circular stream of consciousness; only as her husband announces that he is leaving her does it break into synch-sound. Throughout, Louise's oblique progress with motherhood is depicted in a series of thirteen 360-de-

gree panning shots. The effect is to rotate the boundaries of her world in a kind of slow delirium. As its title suggests, **Riddles of the Sphinx** is meant to raise questions. To that end, it succeeds admirably." After **Riddles of the Sphinx**, the filmmakers completed **Amy!** (1979).

ANIMATION FOR LIVE ACTION

1978. Great Britain.
By Vera Neubauer. Produced by Phillip Mulloy. Music by Alan Lawrence. British Film Institute production.
25 min. Color. Sound.

Animation for Live Action is an extremely imaginative combination of animation and live-action filming which explores themes of women's roles, artist's identities, and the tension between drawing and live-action photography. In the film, the filmmaker creates characters which she then does battle with—they attempt to break out of the film, fight back, and generally act as her unyielding artistic conscience. The animator also creatively destroys the feminine ideology of traditional women's roles—her muscle-men don't look right, and her knights in shining armor do battle and then impale her. Running a gamut of self-questioning and identity-exploring ideas, this film is also a fascinating example of cinematic self-reflection. Neubauer's characters troop through myriad filmmaking machines,

manipulating images on editors and examining the frames themselves. While this is delightful and serious exploration of women and artists, it is also a fine example of innovative contemporary animation.

H IS FOR HOUSE

1978. Great Britain.
By Peter Greenaway. Narrated by Colin Cantlie.
9 min. Color. Sound.

A curious, disturbing, and awfully funny film—in a very dry sort of way—of objects that are picture-book pretty: the idyllic outdoors, and various voices rhyming phrases like "half past four" that begin with "H." You must understand, of course, that this has to do with the world turning counter-clockwise, and that *H Is For House* is about as sensible and entertaining as other Dadaistic works. It is a lesson not only in the omnipresence of "H" but also in humor.

IN THE FOREST

1978. Great Britain.
By Phillip Mulloy. British Film Institute production.
80 min. B&W. Sound.

In The Forest is an inventive exploration and fictionalization of British history. Its three central characters move from their perilous existence as itinerant peasants to roles in an organized working class through a series of historical tableaux that span 400 years of British history, from the 14th to the 19th centuries. The density of the forest, where all images are the same, is a central theme of the film. As the travelers move out of this darkness, they meet death by plague, lives of poverty as landless peasants, and exploitation in industrial cities. In turn, two narrators, whose commentaries are taken from books and documents of the period, tell contradictory stories—one the romantic idealist position and the other a material analysis with a textbook style. Rich with landscape imagery, the film brings into focus the subjectivity of history and questions the possibility of a definitive history of any civilization.

THE LIFE STORY OF BAAL

1978. Great Britain.
Directed by Edward Bennett. From the play by Bertolt Brecht. British Film Institute production.
58 min. Color. Sound.

The Life Story of Baal is based on the play *Lebenslauf des Mannes Baal*, by Bertolt Brecht, which is an abridged and transformed version of *Baal*, Brecht's earlier, longer, and better-known play, first performed in Berlin in 1926. Baal is a magnetic and cruel character whose effect on others' lives, both through and in spite of his own actions, is traced in the play. He is a romantic, radical poet who is continuously trying to outrage and manipulate those around him. In his prologue to the play, Brecht wrote, "This dramatic biography shows the life story of the man Baal as it took place in the first part of this century. You see before you Baal the abnormality trying to come to terms with the twentieth-century world. Baal the relative man, Baal the passive genius, the whole phenomenon of Baal from his first appearance among civilized beings to his horrific end, with his unprecedented consumption of ladies of high degree, in his dealings with his fellow humans." Based on the story of a real figure known in Germany around the turn of the century, Brecht's Baal is a complex study and ultimately a critique of the myth of the romantic artist and rebel against cultural orthodoxy. A successful cinematic approach to a theatrical play, this film seeks to explore the possibility of showing on screen not only one man's life but also the mythology which gave it its meaning.

MIRROR PHASE

1978. Great Britain.
By Carola Klein. British Film Institute production.
47 min. Color. Sound.

This is an experimental, cinematic journal in which filmmaker Carola Klein documents her daughter Leonie's growth from seven months to two years, concentrating on her fascination with mirrors and her reflection. "The 'mirror phase'" says Klein, "is a stage held by French psychoanalyst Lacan to be important to the growth of subjectivity in a young child, and is a prelude to her or his ability to think symbolically and therefore to acquire language." The filmmaker places her daughter in various situations involving mirrors, using the reflected image as a metaphor throughout the film. The screen is divided into four juxtaposed images as parallels are drawn between Leonie and her mirror image, the filmmaker and the filmed image, and the roles of mother and filmmaker. Using a chorus of voices in the narration, Klein questions her roles as mother and filmmaker as well as her motivation in filming her daughter. Thus, *Mirror Phase* explores the issue of how the camera

THE LIFE STORY OF BAAL (1978)

affects its subjects in addition to documenting the first stages of recognition and language use in a young child.

MY WAY HOME

1978. Great Britain.
Written and directed by Bill Douglas. Photographed by Ray Orton. British Film Institute production. With Stephen Archibald, Joseph Blatchley, Paul Kermack, Gerald James, Jessie Combe. 80 min. B&W. Sound.

My Way Home is the final film of an autobiographical trilogy by Bill Douglas that also includes *My Childhood* (1972) and *My Ain Folk* (1973). Continuing in the sparse, unsentimental style of the two previous films, *My Way Home* is composed of two distinct parts—the first takes place in the boys' home where Jamie has been living and the second part in Egypt, where Jamie has gone with the British army. The film begins with a scene of Christmas at the boys' home as each boy waits for the donation of a single meager and identical present. Filled with inarticulate rage and becoming increasingly inert, Jamie leaves the home and returns to live with his neglectful father and then his now-decrepit and pathetic grandmother. Confused and despairing, he runs away and returns later to find the house boarded up as

the culmination of his displacement and lack of identity. The shift to Egypt is abrupt and fitting to suggest the beginnings of change and a reemergence for Jamie. Befriended by a self-assured boy named Robert who refuses to let him remain silent and indecisive, Jamie begins the slow, painful process of constructing an identity and coming to terms with his history. In a complex way, this trilogy of films is about the absolute necessity to speak a history, to uncover past events and the conscious and unconscious memories connected with them. It is also a profound exploration of social and familial structures. *My Way Home* ends with an image of the empty white rooms of the cottage in Newcraighill that began *My Childhood*, but the way home is not back to a home which never existed but a journey through a bewildered history to a sense of acceptance.

ON A PAVING STONE MOUNTED

1978. Great Britain.
Directed and photographed by Thaddeus O'Sullivan. British Film Institute production.
96 min. B&W. Sound.

Thaddeus O'Sullivan, whose first film, *A Pint of Plain* (1975), explored the Irish in Britain, brings to his second film the

AMY! (1979)

pain that goes with emigration to another country. This experience is translated through a series of images and subjective camerawork. The film introduces the Irish art of storytelling and then acts as an antithesis to that art by providing elusive and intriguing images that combine, not to tell a story, but to provide clues to the experience of an Irishman living in England. The film begins by contrasting the protagonist's romantic notions of England with the harsh life-style in Ireland. The memories of Ireland, brought out by the experience of ferrying across to England, provide images of Irish ritual in a combination of nostalgia and cynicism. The two most significant are a pilgrimage climb up a rocky mountain in an eerie mist and the vibrant Puck Fair. From these memories, the film moves into the emigrant's experience in England and his attempts to create situations that are reminders of Irishness. Ending with a storyteller's humorous account of Mick the Fiddler's return from a trip to America, *On a Paving Stone Mounted* is a refreshing exploration which uses the emigration experience as a metaphor for Irish history and provides a complex cinematic exploration of memory and imagination.

RAPUNZEL LET DOWN YOUR HAIR

1978. Great Britain.
By the London Women's Film Group.
British Film Institute production.
80 min. Color. Sound.

Rapunzel Let Down Your Hair examines the issues of women's identity and sexuality through the retelling and interpretation of this classic fairy tale. The story is told four times, each from a different character's point of view: the first is an extremely well-executed collage animation which emphasizes the erotic force of the myth and explores the imagery of women throughout art history; the second is a parody on the private detective genre with the witch-Rapunzel (stepmother-daughter) relationship presented with overtones of incest; the third is a soap-opera melodrama in which a young woman rebels against the overprotection of her mother; and the fourth is an affirmation of the political collective force of women in changing the images of this myth. A central section of the film discusses the background and popular misconceptions of witches and what witchcraft embodies in women's history. This unique cinematic study of the anthropology and mythology of women is one of the first films by a women's collective made in Great Britain.

A WALK THROUGH H

1978. Great Britain.
By Peter Greenaway. Photographed by John Rosenberg. Music by Michael Nyman. Narrated by Colin Cantlie. British Film Institute production.
42 min. Color. Sound.

Alternately titled ***The Re-incarnation of an Ornithologist***, this eccentric film is based on an ornithological treatise by Tulse Luper that describes a mythical journey through the land of H. As Tony Rayns wrote in *Time Out*, "Peter Greenaway's unique short feature is one of the best British movies of the decade. It defeats efforts at description. You could call it a cross between a vintage Borges 'fiction' and a Disney True Life Adventure, but that wouldn't get close to its humor or the compulsiveness of Michael Nyman's romantic score. It's

ANGEL IN THE HOUSE (1979)

nominally a narrative about an ornithologist following a trail blazed by the legendary Tulse Luper, but it's a narrative without characters."

AMY!

1979. Great Britain.
By Laura Mulvey and Peter Wollen.
British Film Institute production.
33 min. Color. Sound.

"We had in mind Maya Deren, Gertrude Stein, and Cubist portraits," co-maker Wollen says. In a way *Amy!* is a sketch, a very elliptical and apparently disjointed one, not so much about Amy Johnson, the British aviatrix who made a solo flight from England to Australia in 1930, but about what was then and is now the popular—or what was then and is now the popular—ideas of a heroine. Johnson was for a short while a symbol of feminine possibilities. She soon broke under the false pressures of a fame manipulated by the British media, which claimed a proprietary interest in her success. *Amy!* raises as many formal questions as it does social ones, and is continually inventive in its narrative strategies. Firmly set in a feminist context, the film, with its contemporary interviews, its various voice and visual portrayals of Amy Johnson, and its use of newsreels and superimposed titles, is a model of structure—rigorous and instructive. *Amy!* is Mulvey and Wollen's third collaboration; the directors, who are also film theoreticians and writers, previously completed two features, *Penthesilea* (1974) and *Riddles of the Sphinx* (1977).

ANGEL IN THE HOUSE

1979. Great Britain.
Written and directed by Jane Jackson. Photographed by Diane Tammes. Excerpts from Virginia Woolf read by Laura Mulvey. British Film Institute production. With Mary Maddox.
28 min. Color. Sound.

Angel In The House is the story of Lily, an aspiring young writer who has temporarily retreated to her parents' home on the English coast. She is there to work on her first novel, yet her visit triggers reminiscences and a self-questioning which incorporates itself into her writing. Scenes of Lily watching home movies with her mother and taking her grandfather for long walks are combined with flashbacks from her childhood to form a central thread of thought through which she reevaluates and expresses herself. The "Angel in the House" is a character defined by Virginia Woolf, in her essay "Professions for Women," as the ever-giving, com-

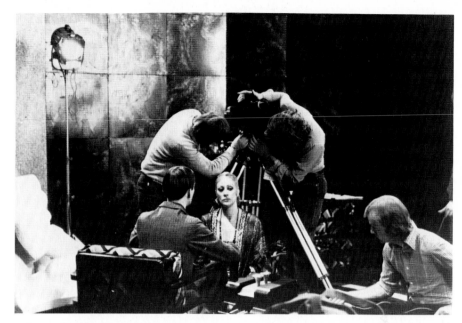

Filming CORRECTION PLEASE (1979)

placent female archetype "who never had a mind of her own but preferred to sympathize always with the minds and wishes of others." It is this image, recreated in the personalities of her relatives and mother, that Lily is battling in the film. She is the contemporary outgrowth of the women in Woolf's work. The film combines her modern struggle and family relationships with a sensitive study of the importance of one writer's work. Woolf's thoughts and writings permeate the film, from the influence of her writing on Lily to her position as an originator of feminist thought. The film employs Woolf's settings (the sea), character names (Lily, Ramsay, James), and biographical allusions (death by drowning). Well photographed with excellent performances, *Angel In The House* is a portrait of the barriers to creativity and self-confidence in all women writers.

CORRECTION PLEASE, OR, HOW WE GOT INTO PICTURES

1979. Great Britain.
By Noël Burch. Photographed by Les Young. Music by John Buller. Arts Council of Great Britain production.
52 min. Color. Sound.

Correction Please, or, How We Got Into Pictures is a unique exploration of early cinema and its evolution. The film opens with a statement that it will explore "how the mechanics of certain very primitive films (made prior to 1906) shed light on the nature of both the language of cinema, and the audience attitudes associated with it, as they came to be estab-

lished over the 25 years that followed." Yet the manner in which it pursues this goal is both inventive and unpredictable. Burch interweaves early films and anecdotes with a narrative that is reenacted numerous times using different cinematic conventions. As the scene progresses, each time incorporating new techniques such as close-ups, sound, point-of-view shots, parallel editing, and character voiceover, it is juxtaposed with several remarkable early films. These include: *Workers Leaving the Lumière Factory* (1895), *The Explosion of a Motor Car* (1900), *How it Feels to Be Run Over* (1900), *What Happened on Twenty-Third Street, New York City* (1901), *The Ingenious Soubrette* (1902), *The Gay Shoe Clerk* (1903), *The Bride Retires (Le Coucher de la Mariée)* (1904), *The Story the Biograph Told* (1904), *A Subject for the Rogue's Gallery* (1904), *Twins at the Theater* (1905?). (Several titles and dates are listed inaccurately in the film.) Noël Burch's rumination on early cinema is both informative and slyly entertaining.

PHOELIX

1979. Great Britain.
Written and directed by Anna Ambrose. British Film Institute production.
47 min. Color. Sound.

Phoelix is an inventive and intricate film that centers on the fantasies of an older British gentleman about the young woman who is his upstairs neighbor and his conversations with her. He lives in a timeless, museum-like room filled with objects collected over the years—sym-

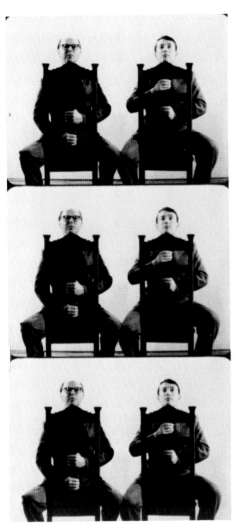

THE WORLD OF
GILBERT AND GEORGE (1980)

bols of his past life. She is an out-of-work actress who has taken a job as a stripper in a club. As she listens to him talk, the film moves into her fantasies, where she places herself in the role of a different woman from the past, who she thinks is a more fitting object of the man's attentions. The film oscillates between past and present, fantasy and fiction, exploring themes of voyeurism, obsession with appearance, and women as passive objects. It is only by confronting the gentleman with her actual life-style and shattering his dream image by making it concrete that the young woman can lose her position as victim. Ambrose has made a complex and very fluid film that explores fantasy and the rejection of passivity in a tightly woven, enigmatic structure.

THE SONG OF THE SHIRT

1979. Great Britain.
Directed by Susan Clayton and Jona-

than Curling. Music by Lindsay Cooper. Produced by the Film and History Project and the British Film Institute.
Part 1: 44 min. Part 2: 33 min. Part 3: 44 min. Postscript: 14 min. Total film: 135 min. B&W. Sound.

The Song of the Shirt grew out of a video project on women and the welfare state that examined why the status of working women had deteriorated since the Industrial Revolution, and why women working outside the home came to be seen as a threat to social order. The resulting film is a complex series of still photographs, graphics, and reenactments that provide context and information about dressmakers and women who worked in London's garment district sweatshops in the 1830s and 1840s. Directors Clayton and Curling employ an innovative use of several video screens, which eerily seem to bring 19th-century graphics to life. The film is concerned not only with the situation of these women in society but also the ways in which they were represented in several media—newspapers, romantic novels, cartoons, lithographs, and music. Several different accounts of the "needlewomen" are presented from different viewpoints to establish the tension between a specific ideology concerning women's roles and the notion of an open labor market. Part One includes scenes of women giving evidence before the Commission on the Employment of Women and Children, the upper and middle class response to the ongoing scandal of dressmakers, and several episodes from cheap novels and philanthropic journals concerned with the plight of the sewing women. Part Two examines the ready-to-wear trade with actors taking the roles of the Owenite and Charist leaders, debating whether it is best to form cooperatives or whether the central issue is the franchise for all and a more representative Parliament. Part Three returns to the historical impetus of philanthropy with scenes of servants reading from and satirizing a romantic novel and the plight of its heroine who in desolation turns to prostitution. It combines these fictionalized accounts with a debate between two officials on the effects of a proposed bill to limit the working hours of women. In the Postscript, many of the scenes of this intricate web of episodes reach a conclusion. This film is an informative historical document which, through a unique collage of accounts and a mixture of media, raises important issues about the history of working women and labor movements and also about the complex images presented by historical documents.

VERTICAL FEATURES REMAKE

1979. Great Britain.
By Peter Greenaway. Music by Brian Eno and Michael Nyman. Narrated by Colin Cantlie.
45 min. Color. Sound.

Vertical Features Remake is ostensibly an account of the fictitious Institute of Reclamation and Restoration's several attempts to reconstruct ornithologist Tulse Luper's study of the aesthetic and ecological significance of various trees, posts, and poles on the English landscape. Working outside any definable group, Greenaway, who is also a graphic artist, photographer, and writer, has created a distinct and distinguished body of films marked not only by a fresh use of sound-to-image and vice-versa, but by a wit that mixes sensible nonsense and earnest understatement. It is as if Lewis Carroll, A. A. Milne, and the National Film Board of Canada joined forces in a hilariously serious attack on the notion of institutional endeavor.

THE FALLS

1980. Great Britain.
By Peter Greenaway. Photographed by Mike Coles, John Rosenberg. Music by Michael Nyman, Brian Eno, John Hyde, Keith Pendlebury. Narrated by Colin Cantlie, Hilary Thompson, Sheila Canfield, Adams Leys, Serena Macbeth, Martin Burrows. British Film Institute production.
185 min. Color. Sound.

The Falls is an elaborate, absurd "investigation into biography" by Peter Greenaway, whose other films include *Dear Phone* (1977), *A Walk Through H* (1978), *Vertical Features Remake* (1979), and *The Draughtsman's Contract* (1982). *The Falls* is the culmination of Greenaway's obsession with documentation, information, cataloging, and classification. Rich with imaginary languages, eccentric personalities, and textured settings, it purports to document 92 of the victims of the "Violent Unknown Event" (VUE), a devastating incident which claimed nineteen million victims. Wittingly adapting a straightforward, narration-dominated documentary format, Greenaway meticulously details the VUE's effect on these victims, who comprise a block of names randomly chosen from the Event's Standard Directory, beginning with "Fall." From Orchard Falla, Musicus Fallanty, Cash Fallbaez, and Catch-hanger Fallcaster to Combayne Fallstoward, each of these characters has gained extraordinary new capabilities as the result of the VUE.

They speak new languages and their biographies are laced with numerous allusions to flight and birds. "An ideal history of the world is most perfectly told by a history of all its subjects," says Greenaway. "The impracticality of such a history, like a full-scale map of the world, mocks human effort—a compromise will have to do. . . . The 92 biographies are laid out end to end in the alphabetical order in which they appear in the Directory, and are presented with all the visual, literary, musical and aural material that is currently available. . . . Whenever possible the mode of cinematic presentation is tailored to fit the character, experiences or salient features of each successive individual—*The Falls* fully acknowledges the subjectivity of the history-maker." *The Falls* is Greenaway's triumph of apocalyptic cinema.

THE WORLD OF GILBERT AND GEORGE

1980. Great Britain.
Written and directed by Gilbert Proesch and George Passmore. Photographed by Martin Schafer. Produced by Phillip Haas for the Arts Council of Great Britain. With Gilbert and George.
69 min. Color. Sound.

Gilbert and George began performing in England in 1968 as living sculptures. They have created the personae of two very exact, stiff gentlemen, always impeccably dressed in tweed suits and always precise in their words and movements. While they first posed as living sculpture with bronze-painted faces, their work has extended into many different media, including large photographic murals, drawing and painting installations, postcard pieces, video sculpture, and film. *The World of Gilbert and George* is their first film, and it acts as an effective retrospective of their work to date as well as a new extension of their performances in the visual arts. Gilbert and George strive to render "all the world an art gallery." This means living the characters they use in performance. They bring the camera into their immaculate home, where they have tea and discuss the activities for the day ("Why don't we go out and buy a vase?") in excruciatingly well-chosen phrases. These polite conversations are juxtaposed with interviews of young street kids who are asked to describe themselves and what they like to do, and whose replies are reflections of seemingly pointless lives. These personal details and narratives are juxtaposed with extraordinary scenes of social commentary: religion is examined through re-

ligious iconography, rituals, and hymn singing; the military is represented by scenes of marching soldiers, brass bands, and memorials to the dead; the symbolic structures of the State are contrasted with images of urban decay; and everyday activities such as drinking a glass of water, dancing, or laughing are isolated in a performance context. Gilbert and George construct a unique and enigmatic world within this film. Obstinately neutral, purposefully baffling, and consistently intriguing, they present an inside view of their idiosyncratic world.

RETURN JOURNEY

1981. Great Britain.
Produced and directed by Ian Potts. Written by Potts and Peter Wyeth. Photographed by Russell Murray. Music by John Barker. Narrated by Ray Gosling. Arts Council of Great Britain production.
43 min. Color. Sound.

Return Journey traces the development and usage of documentary photography through the work of three British photographers: Humphrey Spender, Derek Smith, and Jimmy Forsyth. In 1937, Humphrey Spender joined an organization called "Mass Observation," which was making an anthropological study of working-class life in Bolton, Lancashire, in northern England. The organization recorded the daily life of the community in a direct, candid way, and when Spender joined *Picture Post* magazine in 1938, his stark photographs there exposed the living conditions and destitution in northern England. Derek Smith, a photographer whose pictures of the disintegration through redevelopment of his own northeastern community brought him critical success, rediscovered the photographs of Humphrey Spender and had them reprinted and exhibited. Smith then opened the Side Gallery, and in researching exhibitions, met Jimmy Forsyth, a local amateur photographer who had been photographing his own community of Scotswood since 1945. *Return Journey* weaves a fascinating story with these three photographers, tracing the events which brought them together, the similarities of their work, and aspects of documentary photography important to them, such as objectivity, context, intent, and exhibition alternatives. They discuss their methods and influences, such as the work of photographer Bill Brandt, in a meticulous way which attests to their respect for the photographic medium.

National Film Board of Canada: Four Decades of Documentaries and Animation

by Sally Bochner

Introduction

The National Film Board of Canada was founded in 1939 by an act of Parliament to initiate and promote the production and distribution of films in the national interest, and in particular, to interpret Canada to Canadians and to other countries.

To understand the need for such an institution, it is necessary to understand Canada in the thirties. A country more vast in area than the United States, it had a population approximately the size of greater New York City today. Most of these twelve million people lived in small pockets of settlement located along Canada's southern border. There was little communication among these scattered communities and little sense of what Canada was in terms of its art, its traditions, and its national image. To create a more tangible link from east to west called for imaginative measures to bring Canadians closer together.

The Canadian Government invited the pioneer documentary filmmaker John Grierson, who had already established his reputation working with film units in Britain, to take on this challenge. On the basis of his recommendations, the National Film Board of Canada was established. As the first Government Film Commissioner, Grierson's vision was that "the National Film Board of Canada will be the eyes of Canada. It will, through a national use of cinema, see Canada and see it whole . . . its people and its purpose."[1]

From its first production studio in a converted sawmill in Ottawa, the National Film Board of Canada (NFB) has grown to fill a twelve-acre complex in Montreal and employs almost 1,000 people working in Canada and abroad. Over 4,000 films have been produced since 1939, and in recent years production has averaged more than 100 new titles annually, in both French and English.

Documentary

Almost simultaneously with the birth of the Film Board, World War II broke out, and Grierson's work to disseminate information and promote national unity became critical. Grierson brought together a team of enthu-

John Grierson and Ralph Foster, Chief of the Graphics Division, against a backdrop of CANADA CARRIES ON posters.

siastic Canadians whom he introduced to the art of filmmaking. Names like James Beveridge, Tom Daly, Sydney Newman, Gudrun Parker, Evelyn Cherry, and Julian Roffman were signed up and trained on the job by some of the great figures in documentary film history: Stuart Legg, Stanley Hawes, Raymond Spottiswoode, and J. D. Davidson, all from Britain.

This small core of filmmakers brought their energy and talents together and laid the foundation of the Board's reputation as a leader in the production of documentary films. Their first contribution was the creative development of the "compilation film," a genre of filmmaking that combines newsreel and other existing stock with original footage and commentary. With this formula and virtuoso editing techniques, films could be produced quickly; and by using footage that had been shot all over the world, filmmakers were able to cover a range of subjects.

Two landmark series were developed during this period: CANADA CARRIES ON and THE WORLD IN ACTION. The CANADA series began in 1940 and was the Board's first wartime theatrical release. It brought all aspects of the war effort to movie screens across Canada and treated everything from training camp to the battle front itself. These films, averaging twenty minutes in length, were produced at the formidable rate of twelve per year and reached an estimated three million Canadians each month.

Made entirely from British and captured German footage, Stuart Legg's *Churchill's Island* (1941) is one of the best examples of a compilation film. It not only won the Board's first Academy Award, but was the very first documentary to receive an Oscar.

THE WORLD IN ACTION was the international sequel to CANADA CARRIES ON and informed Canadians of the global, economic, and political forces affecting them both during the war and later during the change-over to peace. This international series reached an estimated thirty million people in twenty-one nations. Stuart Legg made, or directly supervised, nearly all of these films. According to Canadian film historian Rodney James,

"Legg drew upon the work of V. I. Pudovkin, whose experiments in creating an 'intellectual' montage linked images by poetic visualization. He was also influenced by French Dada and Surrealist films that created continuity by connecting images on the basis of shape and movement alone, working toward ends rooted in the darker regions of psychoanalysis. From these disparate sources, Legg created juxtapositions of social, political, and economic images, playing off country against country, comparing social progress, military developments, and economic changes by use of aural-visual metaphors and similes."[2]

Thirty WORLD IN ACTION films were produced during the war, among them *Warclouds in the Pacific* (1941), which predicted the outbreak of war between the United States and Japan. This prophetic film was released in Canada just ten days before Japan attacked Pearl Harbor.

In addition to the English productions, there were French-language versions of CANADA CARRIES ON, called EN AVANT CANADA, and French news features. Grierson was firmly committed to making films in Canada's two languages, but with his entire teaching staff being English, most of the French productions were translations. This imbalance would change radically in the coming years.

Despite the pressures to keep war information flowing, Grierson also managed to produce nontheatrical films on a wide range of topics: Canadian industry, labor, agriculture, natural resources, native and immigrant peoples, health, frontier development, and many others. These films were distributed by a system of rural, industrial, and educational circuits staffed by traveling NFB projectionists—a system that played an important role in the Board's survival after the war.

By the end of the war, the NFB had produced 500 films and its staff had grown to over 700. During the relatively short period of six years, Grierson had formed a Canadian production-distribution unit that far surpassed the British Empire Marketing Board and General Post Office efforts he had directed earlier. Grierson left the Film Board in 1945. Legg, Hawes, Davidson, and Spottiswoode soon followed.

Rather than losing its momentum, as even Grierson feared it would, the NFB took on the challenge of surviving without the urgency of the war and without the leadership of Grierson. Theatrical distribution remained important, but the Board increasingly relied on its own distribution circuits throughout the country.

The trend was away from the hard news stories of war and toward social issues. A significant series to emerge was MENTAL MECHANISMS, sponsored by the Department of National Health and Welfare, of which *The Feeling of Rejection* (1947) is a skillfully made example. Developed by Robert Anderson and Stanley Jackson, these films examined a range of psychological and emotional problems. Documentary in format, scripts were based on actual case studies that were then reenacted by actors (or willing volunteers found in the NFB hallways).

Another important series, FACES OF CANADA, was designed to discover new talent through low-budget films with no other requirement to filmmakers than to find interesting Canadian characters in typical backgrounds. Colin Low and Wolf Koenig's *Corral* (1954) and Roman Kroitor's *Paul Tomkowicz: Street Railway Switchman* (1954) are typical of the series. *Corral*, a lyrical portrait of a cowboy breaking in a half-wild horse on the prairie, was the first film not to use commentary and is a fine example of the more subtle approach to film emerging at the NFB. *Paul Tomkowicz* shares the quiet tone. The camera simply follows its subject, a Polish immigrant, as he goes about his job of clearing snow from streetcar tracks in Winnipeg. The narration is Tomkowicz's own words and tells of his work and his life in Canada. Twenty-seven years later, *Corral* and *Paul Tomkowicz* are still actively in circulation and have become NFB classics.

City of Gold, combining the talents of Colin Low and Wolf Koenig, was released in 1957. This twenty-three-minute production, in Erik Barnouw's words, "virtually created a new genre and opened another century. . . . The use of camera movement in *City of Gold*—toward significant detail, from detail to larger context, from detail to detail—is one of the special triumphs of the film."[3] As basic visual material, the film used still photographs printed from 200 glass-plate negatives taken during the Gold Rush of 1898. *City of Gold* opened new vistas to film chroniclers and after its release filmmakers the world over began to ransack photographic files.

CANDID EYE, a series of half-hour documentaries made for television, was Canada's contribution to *cinéma vérité* filmmaking. Unlike previous NFB documentaries, CANDID EYE films were unscripted; events, rather than being orchestrated, were filmed as they happened. The filmmakers (Roman Kroitor, Wolf Koenig, William Greaves, Terence Macartney-Filgate, Stanley Jackson, John Spotton, Georges Dufaux, Michel Brault, and Gilles Gascon) found inspiration for this more "candid" approach in the films of the British Free Cinema. English works such as *Thursday's Children* (1953), by Lindsay Anderson and Guy Brenton, made a strong impression on the CANDID EYE team. The still photography of Henri Cartier-Bresson, and his book *The Decisive Moment*—a photographic exploration of life in the streets—inspired the NFB filmmakers to achieve a similar quality of immediacy and honesty in cinema.

CANDID EYE films include *The Days Before Christmas* (1958) and *The Back-Breaking Leaf* (1959). Standard film equipment was used in the earlier films, but by the time of *Lonely Boy* (1961), lightweight cameras and sound equipment, partly developed at the Board, permitted the filmmakers to capture scenes previously inaccessible. Crews of one or two men, for example, were able to accompany police on actual cases, or, as in *Lonely Boy*, to follow the young singing star Paul Anka through a crowd of fans. The mobility of this new equipment revolutionized the use of film for television and influenced filmmakers both in Canada and abroad.

The French production unit made several significant films in this style. In 1958 Gilles Groulx and Michel Brault produced *Les Raquetteurs*, a fourteen-minute film covering a snowshoe event. The humorous tone of this film is achieved without use of elaborate camera work or comic narration. In the true *cinéma vérité* style, events simply unfold.

In collaboration with Claude Jutra, Marcel Carrière, and Claude Fournier, Michel Brault also made *La Lutte (Wrestling)* (1961), an examination of the drama and artifice behind professional wrestling. Jean Rouch was prompted to say of Brault, "All that we've done in France in the area of *cinéma vérité* came from the National Film Board. It was Brault who brought a new technique of shooting that we hadn't known and that we have copied ever since."[4]

Art as a Hammer

In 1939 Grierson wrote,

"We are apt to think of art as something on the sidelines of life—pretty pictures on the walls—movies to while away the time on a dull night. But art is something deeper than that . . . they tell us that art is a mirror held up to nature. I think that is a false image, conceived of by men in quiet, unchanging times. In a society like ours, which is even now in the throes of a war of ideas and in a state of social revolution of the most profound nature, art is not a mirror but a hammer. It is a weapon in our hands to see and to say what is right and good and beautiful, and hammer it out as the mold and pattern of men's actions."[5]

In 1966 the NFB initiated, in cooperation with several government agencies, CHALLENGE FOR CHANGE. This unique program, perhaps more than any other at the Board, epitomized the Grierson tradition. It was formed to alert Canadians to the problems of poverty and related issues. Traditionally, films produced for government carried a one-way message from government to the people. CHALLENGE FOR CHANGE brought the people's message, whether it was about housing problems, unemployment, or native land rights, back to government.

The Things I Cannot Change (1966), by John Kemeny and Tanya Ballantyne, is considered the forerunner of the series. Shot in *cinéma vérité* style, the film looked at a family in trouble. For three weeks the camera became part of the family, recording problems with the police, the humiliation of begging for stale bread, and the birth of the tenth child.

Colin Low's *Fogo Island Project*, begun in 1967 and revealing the difficulties of unemployed fishermen off the coast of Newfoundland, and *You Are on Indian Land* (1969), produced by George Stoney, are typical of the CHALLENGE FOR CHANGE format as it finally evolved. The success of this series inspired similar film efforts in other parts of Canada.

It was not skillful filmmaking that made CHALLENGE FOR CHANGE significant (often the films consisted of talking heads giving a verbal account of a particular problem), but rather its social and political implications. Through film and video, CHALLENGE FOR CHANGE made it possible for people to express their concerns and complaints, and be heard by those in power. CHALLENGE FOR CHANGE was terminated in 1979. During the years it was in operation, it had clearly become Grierson's "hammer," driving home the problems affecting the country and performing the role of social catalyst.

Individual Styles

During the sixties and seventies, hundreds of documentaries were being produced outside the CHALLENGE FOR CHANGE program. Subjects included everything from how to fill out a tax return to covering the 1976 Montreal Summer Olympics. Although not directly involved in the process of social change, these films also took on human issues with candor, but with a renewed interest in the craft of filmmaking.

Two outstanding examples can be found in the work of Donald Brittain and Michael Rubbo. A police reporter from Ottawa, Brittain joined the NFB in 1955 and worked on staff until 1968. Brittain is perhaps best known for his perceptive profiles of people. These include such disparate subjects as Bernard Laufer, a Jewish glasscutter who makes a pilgrimage back to Belsen concentration camp, and Norman Bethune, the legendary Canadian doctor and humanitarian who served with the loyalists in Spain and with the Chinese Army during the Sino-Japanese War (*Bethune* [1964]).

A highly personal approach to filmmaking is evident in the work of Michael Rubbo. In almost all his films, Rubbo is on the screen collaborating with his subjects, provoking a range of emotions and ideas. His films have encompassed children's stories, portraits of France's intellectuals and of a political satirist from Quebec, and numerous international political issues. For Rubbo, *Waiting for Fidel* (1974) was a turning point in his career. "It was with *Waiting for Fidel* that I made an important discovery, namely that in documentary character is everything. . . . We [filmmakers] have been often too concerned with issues to notice that it is only when these issues are lived by a real person that they become interesting."[6] In the film, Rubbo, along with Joseph Smallwood (the former Socialist premier of Newfoundland), and Geoff Sterling (a radio-TV station owner from St. John's), travel to Cuba, where they are to meet Fidel Castro and to film the occasion. What unfolds from protracted waiting for yet another postponed meeting is a view of Cuba and insight into the three Canadians. *Waiting for Fidel* becomes not the film that was expected, but something completely different. It arises out of situations, as opposed to trying to control or dominate them. This is true of all of Rubbo's "diary" films. He finds what is there, not what he expects to see.

The Board has also produced a number of "special" documentaries, of which *Going the Distance* (1979) is an outstanding example. In this work, director Paul Cowan and a team of filmmakers looked at the Commonwealth Games from the perspective of eight of the athletes, as they trained at home and finally as they competed in Edmonton. The result is a mosaic of personal achievements and failures against the larger backdrop of the games. The film is internationally famous for its breathtaking scenes of the event and for its attention to detail.

Animation

The National Film Board's long and creative history in animation began in 1941, when John Grierson invited the young Scottish-born artist Norman McLaren to set up an animation unit. Since then, the NFB has developed two studios, for French and English production, which are renowned for their experimental work and their contributions to the art form. McLaren's personal role is legendary. He was one of the first to experiment with and popularize optical printing and drawing directly on film, he originated hand-drawn sound, and was a pioneer in 3-D animation.

236

*Norman McLaren draws
sound on clear film.*

For McLaren there has always been a connection between the small budget and the experimental approach to filmmaking; for him limited means stimulated the imagination. The source of his inventiveness and economy is directly attributable to the economic restrictions of the Second World War, when materials, time, and dollars were scarce and McLaren and his colleagues René Jodoin, Jean Paul Ladouceur, Grant Munro, Jim McKay, Colin Low, George Dunning, Evelyn Lambart, and Robert Verrall used what was readily available and developed a number of techniques: stark ink drawings on paper, chalk drawings that were erased and redrawn to create motion, painting on glass over a background of artwork on paper, jointed cutout figures, drawing or painting directly on the film stock, model animation (where three-dimensional objects were photographed with a traveling camera), and some cel animation.

During the war much of the animation studio's work was produced to support the war effort. Animated maps and diagrams were made for CANADA CARRIES ON and THE WORLD IN ACTION; and theatrical shorts carrying wartime messages were shown in commercial theaters.

McLaren's first NFB films include *Mail Early* (1941), a post office promotion; *V for Victory* (1941), a publicity message for a war-bond campaign; *Five for Four* (1942), which publicized a savings campaign; *Dollar Dance* (1943), dealing with wartime inflation and the role of price controls; and *Keep Your Mouth Shut* (1944), a warning against discussion of secret information in public places.

In addition to the studio's war films, two series were launched in 1944: CHANTS POPULAIRES and LET'S ALL SING TOGETHER, both animated interpretations of folksongs and popular tunes. The lyrics appeared on the screen and audiences would join in and sing along. Released theatrically and nontheatrically, these films provided a welcome moment of respite from the troubled times. They were one reel in length and were produced at the formidable rate of six per year. One of the best-known examples is *Cadet Rousselle* (1947), by George Dunning and Colin Low, which uses puppet animation. McLaren's paper cutout animation, *Alouette* (1944), was made with René Jodoin for this series.

More recently NFB's animators have shown particular fascination with Alexandre Alexeïeff's invention, the pinscreen, as seen in his *En Passant*

(1943). This painstaking technique used 240,000 pins, each about 1-1/2 inches long, imbedded in a screen 16 inches by 20 inches. Light is then directed at the pins, which are moved in and out, and the resulting shadows create the image. This method, used almost exclusively by Alexeïeff for forty years, was adopted by the young NFB artist Jacques Drouin in the early seventies. A fine example of Drouin's work can be found in *Mindscape* (1976).

Following World War II, the animation studio was free to explore a wide range of subjects. Films continued to be made for government, but more and more the studio produced films for use in the classroom.

While devoted to training other artists, McLaren continued to refine his own personal style of animation: drawing directly on film. In 1947 he finished work on the award-winning *Fiddle-De-Dee*, a film fantasy for which McLaren translated musical sound into a visual medium.

In 1953 the team of Colin Low, Robert Verrall, and Wolf Koenig joined forces for the first time and produced *The Romance of Transportation* (1953), a whimsical look at the trials and tribulations of travel in Canada. As Rodney James notes in his history of the NFB, *Film as a National Art: NFB of Canada and the Film Board Idea*, the film illustrates the Board's style of cel animation in which "content was given a higher priority, movements simplified, characters and backgrounds were abbreviated, resulting in a more graphic, less realistic style."[7] This simpler form of cel animation was inspired by the work of United Productions of America (UPA), in a move away from Disney's more elaborate animation. Another example of the Board's work can be found in *Huff and Puff* (1955), Grant Munro and Gerald Potterton's comic look at the serious problem of hyperventilation, produced for the Royal Canadian Air Force.

Norman McLaren also continued to break new artistic ground in the fifties. In *Blinkity Blank* (1955) he experimented with the use of intermittent animation and spasmodic imagery, playing with the laws relating to persistence of vision and afterimage. He was also working on animating live actors (a technique known as pixillation). The best-known example of this is *Neighbours* (1952), an eight-minute parable about two people who come to blows over the possession of a flower. *Neighbours* garnered eight international awards, including an Oscar.

Roman Kroitor and Colin Low brought their formidable talents and growing interest in special effects to the production of *Universe* (1960), one of the first film odysseys into outer space. The budget was $60,000, an enormous sum for the time. Through highly realistic animation, this twenty-six-minute film recreates the far regions of outer space. It was released just at the time the Russians launched Sputnik and nine years before man landed on the moon. The animation was so realistic, *Universe* became required viewing for astronauts and is still being used by NASA. Its technical effects were adapted by Stanley Kubrick for *2001: A Space Odyssey* (1968). (Even the narrator of *Universe*, Douglas Rain, was cast as the voice of HAL, the computer in Kubrick's film.)

A new generation of filmmakers came to the Board in the sixties, among them Arthur Lipsett and Ryan Larkin. In *Very Nice, Very Nice* (1961) by Arthur Lipsett, the artist abandoned the convention of story line and script and brought together fragments of stock sound to play against a subjective montage of images. News photos, magazine advertisements, and human faces flash across the screen, creating a disturbing portrait of modern society. *Very Nice, Very Nice* is an example of a highly personal form of filmmaking. Contrasting sharply with much of the other work being done at the NFB, Lipsett's work attracted a large underground following.

Ryan Larkin came to the Board in 1965 to participate in a training course given by Norman McLaren. In *Walking* (1968), a five-minute essay of people in motion, Larkin used colored ink on paper and animated the drawing without a background or the use of optical effects—a technique which, at the time, was an unusual departure. The film won five international awards, including an Oscar nomination.

McLaren's interest in music and dance found expression in two works in the sixties, *Canon* (1964) and *Mosaic* (1965). In the former, McLaren, in collaboration with Grant Munro, combined cutout figures, animated people, and a cat to demonstrate the musical structure of a canon. During the same period, McLaren produced his now-classic film *Pas de deux* (1967) in which he employed optical effects to record the ballet performances of two dancers. The dancers were filmed at various speeds against a black background. Frames were exposed as many as ten times and images printed over one another to create multiple stroboscopic figures. *Pas de deux* won sixteen awards, including an Oscar nomination.

During the past decade both the French and English animation studios have continued to encourage the individual artist and the use of a variety of techniques. Examples can be found in the productions nominated for Academy Awards in recent years. *The Street* (1976) was created by Caroline Leaf, internationally recognized as one of the leading talents in animation. To interpret a section of the short novel by Mordecai Richler, Leaf animated with paint and ink on glass. In Ishu Patel's *Bead Game* (1977), thousands of tiny beads were used to create the images for each frame. *The Sand Castle* (1977), Oscar winner in 1978, was made by Co Hoedeman, using foam rubber figures covered in sand. Other methods include computer animation (Peter Foldes's *Hunger* [1973]), pinscreen, puppets, plasticine, and multiple exposure.

This variety of animation techniques and the high level of expertise has attracted a number of artists to work at the Board through exchange programs or personal visits; these include Peter Foldes, Zlatko Grgić, Bretislav Pojar, and Alexandre Alexeïeff. Others such as Michael Mills and Gerald Potterton have worked at the Board and then gone on to build up their own studios in the private sector. In this way the Board has not only become a center for animation, but has encouraged the development of animation across the country.

Indeed, the NFB is generally recognized throughout the worldwide film community as one of the most important centers for the production of animation films.[8]

Notes

[1]John Grierson, "The Eyes of Canada," CBC Radio Broadcast, January 21, 1940.

[2]C. Rodney James, *Film As a National Art: NFB of Canada and the Film Board Idea* (New York: Arno Press, 1977), p. 79.

[3]Erik Barnouw, *Documentary: A History of the Non-Fiction Film* (New York: Oxford University Press, 1974), pp. 200–01.

[4]Jean Rouch, "Entretien avec Jean Rouch" by Erich Rohmer and Louis Marcorelles, *Cahiers du Cinéma*, vol. 24, no. 144 (June 1963).

[5]John Grierson, "Art in Action," quoted in James, *Film as a National Art*, pp. 81–82.

[6]Michael Rubbo, quoted by Piers Handling, *Cinema Canada*, no. 41 (October 1977), p. 36.

[7]James, *Film as a National Art*, p. 458.

[8]The annotations in the following section for films by Norman McLaren are taken in part from Maynard Collins, *Norman McLaren* (Ottawa: Canadian Film Institute, 1976). For other annotations, a major source was James, *Film as a National Art*.

ANNOTATIONS

CHURCHILL'S ISLAND

1941. Canada.
National Film Board production. Produced, directed, and written by Stuart Legg. Music by Lucio Agostini. Narrated by Lorne Green.
22 min. B&W. Sound.

Canada Carries On was the first of a series of wartime theatrical films produced by the NFB. It was aimed primarily at Canadian audiences and was the brainchild of documentarians John Grierson, who headed the NFB from its inception in 1939 to 1945, and Stuart Legg, who wrote and directed most of the early films in the series. *Churchill's Island* was the first of these films to attract critical attention outside of Canada when it received a special Academy Award in 1942. Composed entirely of British and captured German footage, the film combines the fast-cut newsreel style with a sense of British irony. Hitler's proclamation of Germany as a "peace-loving nation" is juxtaposed with scenes of British defense units. The film gives succinct and coherent coverage of the British defense plan, including the air war of 1940, the citizen army of fire fighters and antiaircraft gunners, the convoys and U-boats.

MAIL EARLY

1941. Canada.
National Film Board production. By Norman McLaren. Music played by Benny Goodman.
2 min. Color. Sound.

Norman McLaren, a native Scotsman, was invited by John Grierson in 1941 to set up an animation unit at the NFB. Upon arrival at the Film Board, McLaren made this initial film as a trailer for the post office to promote early Christmas mailing. Created in forty-eight hours, the film uses single-frame, cameraless animation in which symbols drawn in pen on clear 35mm film were superimposed on a painted, traveling background. Set to Benny Goodman's big band version of "Jingle Bells," the film is a fantasy dance of Christmas mail and packages rushing to reach their destinations in time for the holiday. (See also *Dots* [1940] in Experimental Film.)

V FOR VICTORY

1941. Canada.
National Film Board production. By Norman McLaren.
2 min. Color. Sound.

McLaren began his Film Board career by applying techniques that he previously worked with in abstractions for a more concrete purpose—wartime propaganda. In *V For Victory*, he used his single-frame animation to publicize Canada's wartime savings bonds, called Victory Bonds. In the film, the letter "V" is the main character, strutting across the screen to the beat of a military march, metamorphosing into Morse Code, marching feet, and finally the slogan "Come On Canada . . . Buy Victory Bonds."

WARCLOUDS IN THE PACIFIC

1941. Canada.
National Film Board production. Produced and directed by Stuart Legg.
20 min. B&W. Sound.

Warclouds in the Pacific, which was part of the wartime series **Canada Carries On** that also included *Churchill's Island* (1941) and *High Over the Borders* (1942), is a geopolitical analysis of the Japanese in Asia. The film discusses the U.S. bases at Pearl Harbor and the possibility of attack, a startlingly prophetic statement since the film was released just ten days prior to the actual attack on those American bases.

FIVE FOR FOUR

1942. Canada.
National Film Board production. By Norman McLaren. Music by Albert Ammons.
3 min. Color. Sound.

McLaren made this unpretentious animated short for the War Savings Committee. Subtitled "An Exercise in National Rythmetic," the film uses two archetypal Canadians, John Canuck and Jean Baptiste, to illustrate how four dollars invested in War Savings Bonds can become five dollars a few years later. The film uses two kinds of animation, combining conventional, realist renderings with the typical McLaren style of hand drawing—in this case, of money traveling across the background. It is set to a honky-tonk Ammons tune called "Pinetop Boogie."

HIGH OVER THE BORDERS

1942. Canada.
National Film Board production. By Irving Jacoby and John Ferno. Produced by Stuart Legg.
23 min. B&W. Sound.

Because the producers of the **Canada Carries On** series were required to deliver a film a month, several films with nonwar themes were included. One of these was *High Over the Borders*, by Irving Jacoby, who directed *Autobiography of a "Jeep"* (1943), and John Ferno, who earlier made *Easter Island* (1934) and *And So They Live* (1940). The film's theme of bird migration from Alaska to Argentina became a parable of unity among the nations of the West. Opening with a scene of a Canadian boy wondering where the swallows go in winter, the location shifts to Central America, where another boy watches them depart for the north. Asking "who can claim ownership?" the film explores the reasons and unexplained questions of migration, using maps to show the birds' routes and documenting their habits. It concludes with the image of these birds as an example of the possibility of overcoming the barriers of distance and national boundaries.

BATTLE IS THEIR BIRTHRIGHT

1943. Canada.
National Film Board production. Produced by John Grierson. Directed by Stuart Legg.
24 min. B&W. Sound.

The World in Action series was begun by the Film Board in 1942 and represented Grierson's major effort in international communications. Designed to function as a worldwide **Canada Carries On**, it was aimed at interpreting problems on a global scale, analyzing world events in a concise manner, and discussing the effects of the war in terms of all major world powers. *Battle Is Their Birthright* shows the rigorous training and toughening of both the Axis and the Allied soldiers. Juxtaposing the rigid military obedience of the Japanese recruits and Nazi youth with the practices of educating citizens in the U.S.S.R. and China, the film is an effective propaganda documentation of the different attitudes to the military and the war in these contrasting cultures. The film's emphasis is on the younger generation of all these countries who, born after World War I, have "battle as their birthright." **The World in Action** series was intended for theatrical screenings, and this segment ends with a "film forum" designed to promote audience discussion on the film's issues. Beginning with "Any questions?," it consists of a panel of Film Board and military officials who touch lightly on the questions of contemporary soldiers. Presumably in an effort to generate a similar discussion in movie theaters during the war, *Battle is Their Birthright* ends with the question "Why not start one here tonight?"

DOLLAR DANCE

1943. Canada.
National Film Board production. By Norman McLaren. Music by Lou Applebaum with lyrics by Norman McLaren and Guy Glover.
6 min. Color. Sound.

In **Dollar Dance**, McLaren featured an animated dancing dollar sign to encourage buying bonds, promote savings, and warn of the dangers of inflation. He drew directly on the film material itself, superimposed these images against a background of clouds, and wrote the lyrics to a short tune with Guy Glover, who was his assistant at the time. The song urged the implementation of price control to stop inflation and to "put the Axis in the coffin."

EN PASSANT

1943. Canada.
National Film Board production. By Alexandre Alexeïeff and Claire Parker. In French.
2 min. B&W. Sound.

Russian-born Alexandre Alexeïeff and his wife and collaborator Claire Parker are the inventors and nearly the sole exponents of the animation technique "l'écran d'épingles," the pinscreen. Consisting of a large board covered with pins which can be extended and withdrawn, the pinscreen is lit from the side so that the pins and their shadows combine to form a black-and-white image similar to an engraving. Although based in Paris, Alexeïeff and Parker lived in the U.S. during World War II and while there were approached by John Grierson to make a film for the NFB. **En Passant**, which is the only film this pair made between 1939 and 1951, is part of the Film Board series entitled **Chants Populaires (Let's All Sing Together)**, animations set to French Canadian folk songs. The pinscreen they built to make this three-minute short contained 240,000 pins, creating exquisite images of country scenes to illustrate this traditional song.

ALOUETTE

1944. Canada.
National Film Board production. By Norman McLaren and René Jodoin. In French; French titles only.
3 min. B&W. Sound.

As supervisor of **Chants Populaires (Let's All Sing Together)** McLaren also contributed to this series of animated French Canadian folk songs. In **Alouette**, he and Jodoin used paper cutouts to interpret a well-known song, using one of McLaren's favorite motifs, a little bird.

KEEP YOUR MOUTH SHUT

1944. Canada.
National Film Board production. By Norman McLaren. Animated by George Dunning.
3 min. B&W. Sound.

In this animated warning against wartime gossip that might aid the enemy, McLaren created a striking propaganda film which is chilling even today. The seemingly innocent idle chatter in the film takes on tragic meaning with the appearance of a glistening skull complete with swastikas gleaming in empty eye sockets. Creating a stark and sinister mood through a liberal use of black screen and dark shadows, McLaren shows how carelessness could bring death and destruction to the Allied Forces.

WHEN ASIA SPEAKS

1944. Canada.
National Film Board production. Directed by Stuart Legg. Produced by John Grierson.
19 min. B&W. Sound.

The World in Action series (which also included **Battle is Their Birthright** [1943]), unlike the **Canada Carries On** series, developed a cohesive form that remained consistent throughout all its programs. This was mainly owing to the fact that Stuart Legg made or directly supervised almost all of the films. The form evolved out of the need to describe problems, ideas, and situations spanning as much as half a century and several continents—in twenty minutes running time. Legg's films were built of interlocking blocks of history, sociology, and economics. **When Asia Speaks** examines the conditions in Asia as the background for growing nationalist movements. A study of the contrasts of the wealth of raw materials and extensive poverty, the film presents these socio-economic extremes as leading inevitably to political change.

A LITTLE PHANTASY ON A NINETEENTH CENTURY PAINTING

1946. Canada.
National Film Board production. By Norman McLaren.
4 min. B&W. Sound.

Using a reproduction of Arnold Böcklin's painting Isle of the Dead, McLaren animated parts of this work of art to create a mystical film of power and suggestiveness. Eerie shapes flicker to life, appear for a brief moment, and then mysteriously disappear, accompanied by brooding music. A distinct change from McLaren's usual lightness and visual wit, this film was originally intended to be part of a film on German culture through the ages by Stuart Legg, the director of numerous documentaries at the Film Board, including **Churchill's Island** (1941) and **Battle Is Their Birthright** (1943). **A Little Phantasy** is the only remaining completed sequence of that proposed film.

CADET ROUSSELLE

1947. Canada.
National Film Board production. Animated by George Dunning and Colin Low. Produced by James Beveridge. Music performed by Maurice Blackburn. In French; French titles only.
6 min. Color. Sound.

When the animated **Chants Populaires** series was terminated in 1944, a new series, now in color, called **Chansons de Chez Nous**, continued with the same concept of interpreting French Canadian folk songs. **Cadet Rousselle**, which was the first of these films, was made by Colin Low, who would later work with animating still photographs on **City of Gold** (1957). This film was one of the first experiments with metal cutouts, as opposed to paper, and the technical competence and artistic quality of **Cadet Rousselle** is notably more advanced than the Film Board's wartime animations. The story tells of the misadventures of a clownish Napoleonic soldier and his problems with disobedient dogs and tricky ladders. The animated figures act out these predicaments with color and verve.

THE FEELING OF REJECTION

1947. Canada.
National Film Board production. Produced and directed by Robert Anderson. Photographed by Dennis Gillson. Music by Robert Fleming. Written by Bruce Ruddick. Edited by Victor Jobin.
20 min. B&W. Sound.

The Feeling of Rejection was part of an ambitious project by the Department of National Health and Welfare called the **Mental Mechanisms** series. This series was designed as a set of educational films on psychology based on actual case histories and specific psychological problems. The film centers on Margaret, a young woman who is constantly giving in to other people's demands and whose lack of assertion brings on physical ills with no organic cause. When she goes to see a psychiatrist, we see her in a series of flashbacks as a silent "good girl" who was overprotected and discouraged from expressing herself. She is seen participating in group therapy at the film's end.

FIDDLE-DE-DEE

1947. Canada.
National Film Board production. By Norman McLaren. Music played by Eugène Desormeaux.
4 min. Color. Sound.

A fine example of McLaren's wit and visual humor, *Fiddle-de-dee* is a lively animated tumble of colors and forms. Like **Begone Dull Care** (1949), this film was made by painting directly on clear motion-picture celluloid in a process that involves no camera at all and is similar to an artist's working on canvas. Textures are achieved by using brushstroke effects, scratching off the paint, pressing cloths to the paint when still wet, and spraying on paint. In brilliant colors, **Fiddle-de-dee** reflects the gaiety of an oldtime fiddle, played by a Gatineau Valley fiddler. As he plays Alice Hawthorne's "Listen to the Mockingbird," lively abstract shapes frolic across the screen in a sparkling interpretation of the happy, toe-tapping music.

BEGONE DULL CARE

1949. Canada.
National Film Board production. Directed by Norman McLaren and Evelyn Lambart. Music composed by Oscar Peterson and performed by the Oscar Peterson trio.
8 min. Color. Sound.

One of McLaren's most famous works, **Begone Dull Care** is one of the best examples of his cameraless, frameless animation begun with **Fiddle-de-dee** (1947). McLaren and Lambart drew fluid lines and brilliant colors down the length of a piece of film, creating restless movement and shapes which converge, change, multiply, and recede to an original composition by jazz musician Oscar Peterson. This complex, eye-catching interpretation of a dynamic music score is as improvisational and melodious as the jazz it reflects.

HOW TO BUILD AN IGLOO

1950. Canada.
National Film Board production. Directed by Douglas Wilkinson. Edited by Neil Harris.
11 min. Color. Sound.

This classic short is a simple, straightforward illustration of man's ability to use the material at hand to satisfy his basic need for shelter. Two Eskimos in Canada's Far North give a step-by-step demonstration of igloo construction, showing how the site is selected and how, in an hour and a half of work, blocks of snow are used to make a snug, ventilated home.

LAND OF THE LONG DAY

1952. Canada.
National Film Board production. Produced by Michael Spencer. Written and directed by Douglas Wilkinson. Photographed by Jean Roy. Music by Lou Applebaum. Edited by Victor Jobin.
38 min. Color. Sound.

Land of the Long Day by Douglas Wilkinson, who had earlier made **How to Build an Igloo** (1950), follows the life of an Eskimo hunter and his family during the four months of summer when Baffin Island in Canada's Arctic North is exposed to continuous sunlight. Using a documentary approach, the film opens with the end of the cold season as the sun first appears on the horizon and the family moves out of their winter home, which has become too damp for comfort. When the weather warms and the land thaws, the Eskimos hunt seals and fish and harpoon whales, always intent on preparing for the following winter. The film concludes with the onslaught of September storms and October blizzards, while the sun moves away toward the Southern horizon.

NEIGHBOURS

1952. Canada.
National Film Board production. Produced, directed, and animated by Norman McLaren. Photographed by Wolf Koenig. Music by McLaren. With Koenig, Grant Munro, Jean Paul Ladouceur, Clarke Daprato.
8 min. Color. Sound.

Using the animation technique of pixillation which he pioneered, McLaren cast two Film Board animators to act out a parable of violence and brutality in this classic film. It begins with a picture of harmony as the two neighbors lie on lawn chairs contentedly reading their newspapers, although the headlines of these papers are ominous. A small flower sprouts through the grass between the two chairs and, attracted by its beauty, they succumb to the urge for possession. They grow quarrelsome and build fences to keep each other from trespassing. As they fight, they become more

NEIGHBOURS (1952)

and more violent until, with their faces hideously contorted by war paint, they batter each other to death. The film is powerful in all respects, from the simplicity and universality of the story and the technical virtuosity of the pixillation to the synthetic music composed and drawn on the film by McLaren. **Neighbours** was made in response to the outbreak of the Korean War. Upon release, it sparked an outcry of protest because of its graphic images of violence; McLaren reluctantly edited out the scenes of women and children being beaten to death. With the onset of the Vietnam War and changing attitudes, McLaren reinserted these scenes and restored the film to its original form.

THE ROMANCE OF TRANSPORTATION

1953. Canada.
National Film Board production. Directed and animated by Colin Low, Robert Verrall, Wolf Koenig. Produced by Tom Daly. Photographed by Lyle Enright. Commentary by Guy Glover. Music by Eldon Rathburn.
11 min. Color. Sound.

One of the first Film Board productions to use cel animation, *The Romance of Transportation* was tremendously successful on its release. A light-hearted history of the unique problems Canadians have faced in moving about their country since the days of Jacques Cartier, the film dramatizes how the vast distances and great physical obstacles were overcome. With tongue-in-cheek seriousness, it tells the story of transportation from early trailblazers to the aircraft of the present and future. Animators Low and Koenig would later use their animation experience in translating still photographs to film for the exceptional *City of Gold* (1957).

CORRAL

1954. Canada.
National Film Board production. Produced by Tom Daly. Directed by Colin Low. Music by Eldon Rathburn. Photographed by Wolf Koenig. With Wallace Jensen.
12 min. B&W. Sound.

Corral was made as part of the series **Faces of Canada**, a program designed to portray the common man of Canada. This picture of the Canadian West has a lyrical approach which combines movement and music to tell a dramatic story. Set in the foothills of Alberta, the film follows a cowboy as he rounds up a herd of wild horses. Working with a dog, he skillfully maneuvers the herd into a corral, and then struggles to rope a high-spirited, half-wild bronco. Finally, he masters the horse with patience and perseverance, and rides him off across the prairie. This film was the first non-animation film made for the NFB by Colin Low, who would later work with Wolf Koenig on *City of Gold* (1957).

PAUL TOMKOWICZ: STREET RAILWAY SWITCHMAN

1954. Canada.
National Film Board production. Produced by Tom Daly. Directed by Roman Kroitor.
9 min. B&W. Sound.

This personal and effective documentary, perhaps the most successful of the **Faces of Canada** series, has a subtle reportage that goes beyond simple portraiture. Paul Tomkowicz is a Polish-born Canadian whose job is to keep the trolleys of Winnipeg running, a job that in winter means clearing the tracks of frozen mud and snow. As the camera follows him on his rounds, he talks about his past—his persecution by the Germans in Poland and his eventual arrival in Canada. He emerges as a tough, stoic personality, and Kroiter's sensitive portrait emphasizes the contrast between his cold and harsh environment and the cozy, contained world of the passengers. *Paul Tomkowicz: Street Railway Switchman* is an important predecessor of the *cinéma vérité* style, which was to radically change documentary filmmaking beginning in the late 1950s.

BLINKITY BLANK

1955. Canada.
National Film Board production. Produced and animated by Norman McLaren. Executive producer: Tom Daly. Music by Maurice Blackburn.
5 min. Color. Sound.

Blinkity Blank represents one of McLaren's greatest technical achievements. He created the effect of intermittent animation and stroboscopic imagery by engraving on black celluloid with a penknife, sewing needle, and razor blades and then coloring the film with translucent dyes. McLaren left long sections of blank frames and drew his images on one frame or groups of two or three instead of drawing on each frame. The fascinating result takes advantage of the effects of persistence of vision and afterimages on the retina of the eye. The story of *Blinkity Blank* involves a bird escaping from a cage, meeting another bird, fighting, and then finally mating and producing offspring—a parable that is told not so much by the drawings but implied by the blank spaces between drawings.

HUFF AND PUFF

1955. Canada.
National Film Board production for the Royal Canadian Air Force. Story and animation by Grant Munro and Gerald Potterton. Directed by Graham Crabtree. Produced by Frank Spiller.
8 min. Color. Sound.

Huff and Puff is a comic animated look at the serious problem of hyperventilation. Produced for the Royal Canadian Air Force to inform air crews about the dangers of hyperventilation in high altitudes and its serious side effects, the film shows how to recover with appropriate respiration and emphasizes that this problem can occur in other situations, such as when under stress. Grant Munro, who later directed *The Animal Movie* (1966), made this informative short both lively and humorous.

CITY OF GOLD (1957)

A CHAIRY TALE

1957. Canada.
National Film Board production. Executive producer: Tom Daly. Directed by Norman McLaren and Claude Jutra. Production and chair animation by Evelyn Lambart. Music by Ravi Shankar, Chatur Lal, and Modu Mullick.
10 min. B&W. Sound.

In *A Chairy Tale* McLaren returned to the animation technique of pixillation that he used in *Neighbours* (1952). This charming film is typical of McLaren in that it speaks the universal language of pantomime, without dialogue or narration. The story involves a kitchen chair that revolts at being sat upon. A young man struggles with the chair, pouncing on it, pleading and cajoling without the least measure of success until the roles are reversed and the chair gets a chance to sit on the man for a moment. Then, "they sit happily ever after." More than a simple fairy story, *A Chairy Tale* is about friendship and understanding, a protest against inconsideration and oppression. As McLaren has explained, "I have sympathy for things that are sat upon—the exploited."

CITY OF GOLD

1957. Canada.
National Film Board production. Produced and edited by Tom Daly. Directed by Wolf Koenig and Colin Low. Storyline by Roman Kroitor. Commentary written and narrated by Pierre Berton. Animation photography by Douglas Roberts. Music by Eldon Rathburn.
22 min. B&W. Sound.

City of Gold is a nostalgic recollection of the period when Yukon gold fever was at its height. The film combines old photographs with contemporary footage of Dawson City to recreate and reanimate what was a bizarre moment in history. The NFB, says film historian Erik Barnouw, "virtually created a new genre" with *City of Gold*, adding that the film "opened new vistas to film chroniclers." This film represents the first extensive and successful use of still photographs shot in a cinematic way to make them come alive. The project began when Colin Low discovered a collection of 200 glass plate negatives of the Klondike gold rush of the 1890s, which were mostly the work of photographer A. E. Haig. Both filmmakers brought special skills to the project— Koenig was a still picture enthusiast who had wanted to experiment with their use in film, and Low was an animator who made *Cadet Rousselle* (1947) and *The Romance of*

LES RAQUETTEURS (1958)

Transportation (1953). Their technique of plotting camera movement was unparalleled at the time. This movement from details to full frame combines with the sensitive and informative narration by Pierre Berton, a native of Dawson City, to create a rhythmic, encompassing portrait. *City of Gold* is an important early example of the ability of cinema to bring photographs to life.

THE DAYS BEFORE CHRISTMAS

1958. Canada.
National Film Board production. Directed by Terence Macartney-Filgate, Stanley Jackson, Wolf Koenig. Photographed by Michel Brault, Georges Dufaux. Sound by Jack Locke, George Croll, Kay Shannon. Editing and production by Roman Kroitor, Wolf Koenig. Executive producer: Tom Daly.
29 min. B&W. Sound.

The Days Before Christmas was part of the **Candid Eye** series created by the NFB for television. These *cinéma vérité* films were made just before the documentary classics of Drew Associates in the U.S., and director Macartney-Filgate worked for Drew as a photographer on the well-known film *Primary* (1960). *The Days Before Christmas* sought to capture the last frantic week before the holiday in Montreal through an unscripted, improvisational style. With one final accelerated burst of preparation, spending, and merrymaking, the details

of holiday consumption are juxtaposed. The camera moves from department store Santas to crowds jamming airports and train stations, and captures the irony of a taxi driver describing both midnight masses and where the best bootleggers can be found. The visual excitement and immediacy of this early *cinéma vérité* example helped to bring a new form of documentary to television.

LES RAQUETTEURS

1958. Canada.
National Film Board production. Directed, photographed, and edited by Gilles Groulx and Michel Brault. Produced by Louis Portugais. In French.
15 min. B&W. Sound.

Michel Brault, who was an early pioneer of sync-sound experiments and *cinéma vérité* style, made this short with Gilles Groulx about the International Snowshoe Congress held in Sherbrooke, Quebec in 1958. The event unfolds, through the camera's sharp observance, complete with snowshoe races, parades with heavily bundled majorettes and dancers, and musicians competing in flair and ingenuity. The result is a film detailing some extraordinary moments of natural social satire.

THE BACK-BREAKING LEAF

1959. Canada.
National Film Board production. Di-

Filming UNIVERSE (1960)

rected by Terence Macartney-Filgate. Produced by Roman Kroitor and Wolf Koenig. Executive producer: Tom Daly. Commentary by Stanley Jackson. Edited by John Spotton. Music by Eldon Rathburn.
30 min. B&W. Sound.

In addition to *The Days Before Christmas* (1958), one of Macartney-Filgate's exceptional contributions to the **Candid Eye** series is *The Back-Breaking Leaf*. This graphic portrait of the tobacco harvest in southwestern Ontario is presented from the point of view both of the transient field workers, who move in for a brief bonanza when the leaves are ripe, and of the farmers, who depend solely on the crop. Using a jazz score blended with indigenous music played by the men working in the fields, the film captures the flow of work with its endless stooping, picking, and bundling in the airless, hot rows. Like the other films in the **Candid Eye** series, including *Glenn Gould: Off the Record* and *Glenn Gould: On the Record* (1959), this film is an example of Canada's pioneering *cinéma vérité*.

GLENN GOULD: OFF THE RECORD and GLENN GOULD: ON THE RECORD

1959. Canada.
National Film Board production. Executive producer: Tom Daly. Produced and directed by Wolf Koenig and Roman Kroitor. Assistant direction by Terence Macartney-Filgate and Gilles Gascon.
60 min. (Each part is 30 min.) B&W. Sound. (These films rent either as a single program or individually.)

This two-part film portrait of renowned pianist Glenn Gould, who died in October 1982, offers an intimate glance at Gould practicing and discussing his career at his country retreat north of Toronto, Canada. Twenty-seven years old at the time this film was made, Gould was an animated, articulate subject. He discusses the experience of performance versus aspects of recording, his desire to devote himself fulltime to composing, and his struggle for perfection. Scenes of Gould practicing and slowly, meticulously constructing the pacing of each work make this not only a portrait of one musician, but also a documentary of the artistic process. The second part of this film program concentrates on Gould recording his music in a studio in New York City. The collaborative aspect of Gould's working with the producers and engineers, his gestures while playing, and the process of attaining the "perfect take" combine to form an insider's view of the recording process.

AN INTRODUCTION TO JET ENGINES

1959. Canada.
National Film Board production for the Royal Canadian Air Force. Produced by Frank Spiller. Directed by René Jodoin.
Executive producer: Peter Jones. Design and animation by Kaj Pindal.
13 min. Color. Sound.

Using exceptional cutout animation, *An Introduction to Jet Engines* is a vivid view of the inside of a jet engine. Designed for the training of air force ground technicians, the film demonstrates clearly how a jet engine develops thrust and describes the workings of both centrifugal and axial flow engines, from the simplest form of ramjet to the more complex turbojet. Like *Huff and Puff* (1955), this film was produced for the Royal Canadian Air Force and is in scope and style much more than just an instructional film.

UNIVERSE

1960. Canada.
National Film Board production. Produced and edited by Tom Daly. Directed by Roman Kroitor and Colin Low. Storyline by Kroitor. Narrated by Douglas Rain. Music by Eldon Rathburn. Commentary by Stanley Jackson.
27 min. B&W. Sound.

Universe explores the solar system with the same delicate precision of Low's *City of Gold* (1957), using model animation combined with photographs and drawings to create an extraordinary interplanetary landscape. The study of the vastness of space begins on earth in the David Dunlap Observatory near Toronto, where an astronomer is preparing for the night's work. As the sun sets, the astronomer's work begins. He fixes his telescope on a distant star cluster; the scene dissolves through layer after layer of the visible part of the universe, through floating clouds of gas and dust, and through the stars of our galaxy to the limits of human vision, where particles of light are galaxies so distant they defy comprehension. This triumph of animation, accompanied throughout by Eldon Rathburn's excellent score, culminates with the dawn and the end of the astronomer's "day."

LONELY BOY

1961. Canada.
National Film Board production. Directed by Roman Kroitor and Wolf Koenig. Produced by John Kemeny. Executive producer: Tom Daly. Edited by John Spotten, Guy L. Coté.
27 min. B&W. Sound.

This *cinéma vérité* portrait of Ottawa-born singer Paul Anka was produced as part of the **Candid Eye** series. *Lonely Boy* shows Anka singing in Atlantic City to hysterical crowds of teenagers who hound him for autographs. Anka talks about his life and career, and his manager, Irvin Feld, speaks of "grooming Anka" and of "Paul's obligation to his talent." The film reveals Anka as a tenacious, determined personality and effectively captures the phenomenal attention devoted to this young man at the onset of his singing career.

LA LUTTE (WRESTLING)

1961. Canada.
National Film Board production. Directed by Michel Brault, Claude Jutra, Marcel Carrière, Claude Fournier. Produced by Jacques Bobet. In French and English.
28 min. B&W. Sound.

Cinéma vérité pioneer Michel Brault, who had earlier made **Les Raquetteurs** (1958), combined his talent with three other filmmakers to document the sport of professional wrestling. With tongue-in-cheek solemnity the cameras explore the activity in the Montreal Forum, where some of the biggest bouts are staged, and in the backstreet wrestling parlors, where the warriors practice their craft and are instructed in the arts of facial agony and mat choreography. Nothing escapes the probing cameras as well-muscled bodies grapple, punch, squirm, roar, and grimace, adding their own variations of showmanship to amuse and excite the crowd.

VERY NICE, VERY NICE

1961. Canada.
National Film Board production. Directed by Arthur Lipsett.
7 min. B&W. Sound.

Arthur Lipsett's first film, **Very Nice, Very Nice**, a cynical study of contemporary Western culture, defines his highly personal, underground style of filmmaking. The soundtrack was prepared first using sound fragments from stock footage of old Film Board documentaries, the images of which were then combined with magazine advertisements and news photos. This sociological diagnosis emphasizes all things that degrade the quality of human existence—children romp in parks as trash piles up in cities and junked aircraft lie in stacks as a fitting surrealist monument to human folly. The film has an intentionally disconcerting staccato rhythm that works well to evoke a strong sense of contemporary alienation.

BETHUNE

1964. Canada.
National Film Board production. Pro-duced and written by John Kemeny, Donald Brittain. Executive producer: Guy Glover. Photographed by Robert Humble, François Séguillon, Murray Fallen. Commentary by Brittain. Narrated by Lister Sinclair.
59 min. B&W. Sound.

This film biography of Dr. Norman Bethune marks an early period in the long career of documentary filmmaker Donald Brittain, who wrote the script for **Grierson** (1973), and went on to make **King of the Hill** (1974) and **Volcano** (1976). In **Bethune**, the filmmakers combined historical footage, reenactments, still photographs, and interviews to portray the legendary Canadian doctor who served with the Loyalists during the Spanish Civil War and with the North Chinese Army during the Sino-Japanese war. Bethune, who is also the subject of Frontier Films' **Heart of Spain** (1937), pioneered the world's first mobile blood transfusion service. This film is a probing document of a remarkable career.

CANON

1964. Canada.
National Film Board production. Directed by Norman McLaren and Grant Munro. Photographed by Ron Humble. Music by Eldon Rathburn.
10 min. Color. Sound.

Canon is an animated exercise in the form of a musical canon. The canon is a round in which each singer picks up the words and tune after an interval following the preceding singer. McLaren collaborated with Grant Munro (who also made **Huff and Puff** [1955]) to amusingly demonstrate this structure using blocks, humans, cats, and a butterfly. With the use of vertical splicing, the filmmakers divide the frame into four equal parts, two of which are upside down, to improvise upon and extend a visual parallel to the musical structure of the canon.

POUR LA SUITE DU MONDE (MOONTRAP)

1964. Canada.
National Film Board production. Written and directed by Michel Brault, Pierre Perrault, Marcel Carrière. Executive producer: Fernand Dansereau. Photographed by Brault and Bernard Gosselin. Edited by Werner Nold. Music by Jean Cousineau, Jean Meunier. Narrated by Stanley Jackson.
84 min. B&W. Sound.

Pour la suite du monde is the first of a trilogy of films by Pierre Perrault on Île aux Coudres, a small island in the St. Lawrence River, and the only one of the series in which he collaborated with Michel Brault, the noted *cinéma vérité* pioneer who made **Les Raquetteurs** (1958) and **La Lutte** (1961). Working in the tradition of Robert Flaherty, the filmmakers persuaded the French inhabitants of the island to reenact the old tradition of the porpoise hunt by sinking a corral of saplings into offshore mud at low tide. The debate of the is-

Paul Anka in LONELY BOY (1961)

landers as to whether or not the hunt should be revived, the construction of the trap, and the capturing of a white Beluga dolphin are documented with care by the filmmakers. With fluid pacing they transform a simple story into a rich and meaningful evocation of a self-contained environment and the tradition of a people.

HIGH STEEL

1965. Canada.
National Film Board production. Written, directed, and edited by Don Owen. Photographed by John Spotten. Produced by Julian Biggs. Music: "Mountains of Iron and Steel" by Bruce MacKay.
14 min. Color. Sound.

This early short by Don Owen, who is known for his dramatic features on contemporary youth, including **Nobody Waved Goodbye** (1964) and **The Ernie Game** (1967), is a fascinating portrait of the Mohawk Indians of Caughnawaga, near Montreal, who are famed for their skill in erecting skyscrapers. With dizzying views of Manhattan, the film effectively juxtaposes their nimble, high-risk work on the steel frames, stories above the pavement, with the quiet community life of the old Caughnawaga Reserve.

MOSAIC

1965. Canada.
National Film Board production. Directed by Norman McLaren and Evelyn Lambart. Music by Norman McLaren.

PAS DE DEUX (1967)

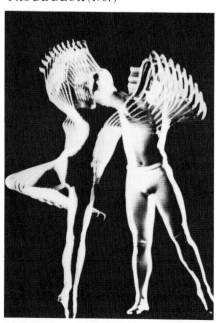

French and English titles.
6 min. Color. Sound.

Collaborating with Evelyn Lambart, who had previously worked with him on **Begone Dull Care** (1949), McLaren created this dance of dots and squares by sandwiching together two previous Mc-Laren-Lambart films called **Lines Vertical** (1960) and **Lines Horizontal** (1962). The film begins with a single dot that instantly takes life, dividing itself again and again until the entire screen is populated by dots that dance a spell-binding dance against a changing background of colors. "Being largely a play on the retina of the eye," the filmmakers wrote of **Mosaic** on its release, "**Mosaic** might be called an example of cinematographic 'op' art. Like most 'op' art it is strictly geometric and nonfigurative, making use of rapid fluctuations of complementary and contrasting colors, as well as afterimages."

THE ANIMAL MOVIE

1966. Canada.
National Film Board production. Directed and animated by Grant Munro and Ron Tunis. Photographed by Jacques Jarry. Produced by Sidney Goldsmith. Music by Pierre Brault, Kathleen Shannon, Malca Gillson.
10 min. Color. Sound.

Grant Munro, who made **Huff and Puff** (1955), collaborated with Ron Tunis on this animated cartoon, which is designed to help children explore why and how animals move as they do. Using ink on paper to achieve a luminous watercolor effect, the filmmakers depict a small boy learning about animal locomotion first hand and effectively capture the animals' point of view. A monkey helps the boy climb a tree, but he is unable to swing from branch to branch. He can ride on the back of a horse, but he is unable to gallop. A fall in the water gives him a chance to swim, but without the natural grace of a porpoise. In the end, he rides with another boy in a man-made vehicle which enables them to outdistance the animals in both air and water.

THE THINGS I CANNOT CHANGE

1966. Canada.
National Film Board production. Directed by Tanya Ballantyne. Produced by John Kemeny. Photographed by Paul Leach. Edited by Bill Brind.
56 min. B&W. Sound.

The Canadian Government Poverty Program, which became part of the **Challenge for Change** project, was be-

gun in 1966 as a cooperative effort of numerous government agencies, including the NFB. **The Things I Cannot Change** was the first of a significant number of films made under this program, and it remains an excellent example of the program's intent to arouse public interest and concern for the problems of the urban poor. The film examines three weeks in the life of Kenneth Bailey, an ex-seaman and unemployed cook, and his wife and nine children in Montreal. The film documents the grinding, frustrating poverty of an attempt to live a middle-class life with no means of support. To qualify for welfare, Bailey must sell the furniture, which he refuses to do. He is an articulate subject whose unselfconscious reminiscences of his wretched childhood, interspersed with his self-styled brand of socialism, give the film a unique personal touch. The film concludes with the birth of Bailey's tenth child, the continuance of the family's marginal existence, and the resignation of Bailey to "the things I cannot change."

PAS DE DEUX

1967. Canada.
National Film Board production. Directed by Norman McLaren. Photographed by Jacques Fogel. Special effects by Wally Howard. Choreography by Ludmilla Chiriaeff. Dancers: Margaret Mercier and Vincent Warren. Music adapted by Maurice Blackburn and played by Dobre Constantin and the United Folk Orchestra of Romania.
14 min. B&W. Sound.

Considered by many to be McLaren's masterpiece, **Pas de deux** uses dancers from Les Grands Ballets Canadiens to evoke a visual poem of form and movement. The white-clad dancers move before a black background, their bodies silhouetted by rear lighting. Employing an optical printer to extend, multiply, and reorchestrate their lyric kineticism, McLaren creates complex multiple imagery, which is heightened by the beautiful, melancholy Romanian music played on panpipes. A classic choreography of dance, cinema, and music, **Pas de deux** is a stunningly graceful achievement.

WALKING

1968. Canada.
National Film Board production. Conceived and animated by Ryan Larkin. Animation photography by William Wiggins and Raymond Dumas. Music by David Fraser, Pat Patterson, Christopher Nutter.
5 min. Color. Sound.

Walking is an animated study of human motion and the effects of rhythmic movement. Ryan Larkin, who is known for his earlier charcoal study, *Syrinx* (1965), used colored ink on paper to capture the movements of people on a street. The film begins with people waiting at bus stops and leaning out of windows. Walking figures appear. The springing gait of youth, the mincing step of a high-heeled woman, and the fragile amble of the elderly are all registered with humor and individuality in increasing speed until the screen is filled with imaginative figures rushing madly about. Larkin's use of ink washes creates a stunning watercolor effect that heightens this humorous film.

YOU ARE ON INDIAN LAND

1969. Canada.
National Film Board production. Produced by George Stoney. Location direction by Mort Ransen. Made in collaboration with Noel Starblanket, Mike Mitchell of the Indian film crew, and the people of the Akwesasne Mohawk Nation. Photographed by Tony Ianzelo. Edited by Kathleen Shannon.
37 min. B&W. Sound.

The **Challenge for Change** project aimed to "promote citizen participation in the solution of social problems," among which minority problems were considered crucial. As a result, Indian film crews were trained and equipped to document for themselves issues important in their lives. One such crew, led by Mike Mitchell, planned to film a demonstration to block traffic on the international bridge between the U.S. and Canada to protest the violation of a 1794 treaty which guaranteed them duty-free passage. George Stoney, whose social documentaries such as *All My Babies* (1953) had gained for him a reputation as a filmmaker who was sensitive to minority issues, was Executive Producer of **Challenge for Change** from 1968 to 1970. Upon hearing about the Mohawk demonstration plans, he sent additional crews to help cover the event. The result is a dynamic documentary of the confrontation between police and the Indians on a snowy, cold highway, culminating in the arrest of the Indian leaders. The film is constructed to examine the nature of the violence and the events that led up to it in order to form a complete portrait of what happened. When internal conflicts threatened to dissolve the unity of the tribe after the demonstration, Stoney sent down the rough footage at their request and the film was screened numerous times before it was finally edited. *You Are on In-dian Land* is credited with winning the Indians a government hearing and bringing a new solidarity to their movement.

HOT STUFF

1971. Canada.
National Film Board production. Directed by Zlatko Grgić. Produced by Robert Verrall and Wolf Koenig. Story by Don Arioli. Music by Bill Brooks.
9 min. Color. Sound.

This animated parody uses comic anecdotes to examine the basics of fire prevention. In retelling the history of its misuse from the beginning of creation, *Hot Stuff* proves that man has never treated fire with sufficient caution. From prehistoric times to the industrial present, fire is shown to be a hidden but active danger. Zlatko Grgić, who is known for his earlier Yugoslavian animations *The Musical Pig* (1965) and *Inventor of Shoes* (1968), uses lively cartoon personalities and humorous dialogue to make *Hot Stuff* an engaging, clever film.

NELL AND FRED

1971. Canada.
National Film Board production. Directed and photographed by Richard Todd. Produced by George Stoney and Colin Low. Edited by Malca Gillson.
28 min. B&W. Sound.

A fine example of the **Challenge for Change** films, *Nell and Fred* documents the decisions made by two elderly people on whether or not to live in an old people's home. Nell is a funny, garrulous woman who expresses her ambivalent feelings about leaving her own home and her worries about a regimented life in an institution. She and Fred, her ninety-year-old boarder, go to a meeting where officials explain the building and the routine. After much discussion, Fred moves in only to leave soon after because he cannot afford it. The natural, personal approach of this film can be attributed to a combination of Nell and Fred's ease before the camera and the fact that director Todd is Nell's grandson. This film is a portrait of the friendship between two elderly companions as well as an examination of the pros and cons of old age institutions.

ANIMATION FROM CAPE DORSET

1973. Canada.
National Film Board production in collaboration with the Department of Indian and Northern Affairs and the Government of the Northwest Territo-ries. Produced by Joanasie Salamonie and John Taylor. By Solomonie Pootoogook, Timmun Alariaq, Mathew Joanasie, Itee Pootoogook, Pitaloosie. Music by Aggeok, Peter Piseolak. In English and Inuktitut.
19 min. Color. Sound.

This film is a collection of short animated sequences produced by the Inuit Eskimos of the Cape Dorset (Baffin Island) Film Animation Workshop. The workshop was established to teach the Eskimos this new form of creative expression, and the results reveal an easy adaptation to the medium, a keen sense of observation, and an underlying sense of humor whether the subject be fact or fantasy.

GRIERSON

1973. Canada.
National Film Board production. Produced and directed by Roger Blais. Photographed by Eugene Boyko, Lewis McLeod, Michel Thomas-D'Hoste, Magi Torruella, Jacques Fogel. Commentary by Donald Brittain. Narrated by Michael Kane. Executive producer: David Bairstow.
58 min. Color. Sound.

This is an expansive tribute to film pioneer John Grierson, who headed the NFB from 1939 to 1945. Through a combination of film clips, interviews, and footage of Grierson, he emerges as a dynamic, demanding, and sometimes difficult personality. The film begins with Grierson's Scottish origins, his explorations of Hollywood, and then his "invention of the documentary" and influence in the early days of independent British cinema. Scenes from his first film, *Drifters* (1929), examples of early British documentaries like *Night Mail* (1936), and interviews with noted filmmakers Joris Ivens and Basil Wright among others combine to form a picture of British cinema in the 1930s. Grierson's leadership of the NFB during its inception is well documented, emphasizing his difficult role as mediator between filmmakers and government bureaucracy. Descriptions of early working methods during Grierson's directorship of the NFB are given by Lorne Green and Stuart Legg, and scenes from the **Canada Carries On** series, including *Churchill's Island* (1941) as well as Norman McLaren's *V for Victory* (1941), illustrate the Film Board's wartime production. The tribute to Grierson at the twenty-fifth anniversary of the NFB, and his life after stepping down from it—which included surveillance by the U.S. government, work for

Geoff Stirling, Joseph Smallwood, and Michael Rubbo in WAITING FOR FIDEL (1974)

UNESCO, producing a Scottish television program, and teaching at McGill University—provide the complete portrait of this important figure in the history of cinema. The far-ranging collection of biographical material in *Grierson* serves to create a complex image of Grierson, an image that is both critical and laudatory, and is a revelation of the drive and magnetism of a documentary pioneer.

HUNGER

1973. Canada.
National Film Board production. Directed by Peter Foldes. Produced by René Jodoin. Edited by Pierre Lemelin. Music by Pierre Brault.
12 min. Color. Sound.

Hunger is a computer-assisted animated satire of self-indulgence in a hungry world. The director is Peter Foldes, a Hungarian who worked mostly in England and France making films such as *A Short Vision* (1955) about the atomic bomb, and *Appetit Oiseau* (1965). Working in computer animation at the Film Board, Foldes made *Meta Data* (1971) and then *Hunger* using computer graphics to rapidly dissolve and reshape images, creating a stark contrast between abundance and want. The film involves a man who eats, at first sparingly, but then with an appetite that grows to gluttony, greed, and gratifi-cation of every desire. In this allegory of the hunger and extremes of the world, the glutton is subjected to a nightmare in which he is devoured by the starving people of the world.

CAT'S CRADLE

1974. Canada.
National Film Board production. Directed by Paul Driessen. Produced by Gaston Sarault. Photographed by Jacques Avoine, Pierre Provost. Sound by Normand Roger.
11 min. Color. Sound.

Beginning with a spiderweb instead of a string, the cat's cradle of this animated film involves images and transfigurations which are provocative, mystifying, and both humorous and ominous. The fable uses Gothic characters like witches and cloaked riders to tell its unusual tale. With a mysterious, effective soundtrack, Driessen, who went on to make the imaginative *An Old Box* (1975), plays havoc with the theme that one thing leads to another.

THE OWL WHO MARRIED A GOOSE: AN ESKIMO LEGEND

1974. Canada.
National Film Board production with the cooperation of the Department of Indian Affairs and Northern Development. Directed and animated by Caro-line Leaf. Produced by Pierre Moretti. In Inuktitut.
8 min. Color. Sound.

Caroline Leaf is one of the most respected of the new generation of Film Board animators. Exploring new techniques like the sand animation in *The Owl Who Married a Goose* and the pioneering use of paint applied directly on a glass surface in *The Street* (1976), Leaf has continually expanded the possibilities of the animated film. The story of this film is based on Eskimo legend, and the soundtrack is a combination of sound effects and dialogue recorded by three Inuit Indian collaborators. An owl falls in love with a goose, though this relationship violates the natural code of species separation. Awkward and unsuited to raising goslings that must be taught to swim and forage for food, the owl watches from the edge of the water. When fall signals the geese to fly south, the owl tries gamely to keep up with their migration. The geese alight on the surface of a pond and the owl, exhausted from the journey, lands beside them and sinks to the bottom. Though most viewers find this story tragic in its conclusions, Eskimo audiences, who do not anthropomorphize wildlife, find the results of the owl's fatal slip in judgment very humorous—after all, owls should know better.

WAITING FOR FIDEL

1974. Canada.
National Film Board production. Directed and edited by Michael Rubbo. Photography by Douglas Kiefer. Produced by Michael Rubbo, Tom Daly. Executive producer: Colin Low.
58 min. Color. Sound.

Michael Rubbo, known for his personal style of documentary filmmaking, made *Waiting for Fidel* after completing two films on war-ravaged Southeast Asia—*Sad Song of Yellow Skin* (1970) and *Wet Earth and Warm People* (1971). Rubbo's style is characterized by his interaction and collaboration with the subjects before the camera. In *Waiting for Fidel* he went to Cuba with Joseph Smallwood, the former socialist premier of Newfoundland, and Geoff Stirling, a millionaire owner of radio and television stations, with the intention of filming them interviewing Fidel Castro. "There was Cuba laid out for us with tours here and there to schools and mental hospitals," says Rubbo, "while we waited for Fidel to drive through the gates of the mansion where we were lodged. Within a day I knew that life could not have handed me a more intriguing drama.

So Fidel or no Fidel, I began to film our antics." Castro never appeared, but, more because of than in spite of this, the resulting film is a unique and humorous document.

JEAN CARIGNAN, VIOLONEUX

1975. Canada.
National Film Board production. Directed and photographed by Bernard Gosselin. Produced by Louise Carré and Paul Larose. Edited by Monique Fortier. In French.
88 min. Color. Sound.

Bernard Gosselin made this affectionate portrait of fiddler Jean Carignan during a *grande veillée*—a party lasting two days—at the home of the Gosselin family. Carignan plays a dozen songs from his repertoire of several thousand, talks about his music, and shares some of the secrets of his skill with violinist Paul Gosselin. He tells how he was sent to reform school for playing the violin in the streets to earn some money. Charming and dedicated to his craft, Carignan makes this film a musical document as well as a personal portrait.

AN OLD BOX

1975. Canada.
National Film Board production. Directed by Paul Driessen. Produced by Gaston Sarault. Photographed by Alan Ward, Raymond Dumas.
10 min. Color. Sound.

This imaginative animation by Paul Driessen, who also made *Cat's Cradle* (1974), uses the barest of lines, flashes of color, street sounds, and the tinkling of music to tell a story of loneliness and joy, old age and human values, and imagination and the spell of Christmas. An old bum catches sight of an empty, beat-up box in the alleyway trash; he snatches it up and takes it home to his tiny shack to decorate. Cutting a slot on its top and dropping a coin in it, he makes the box come to life with music. Cold, with nowhere to go, the old man climbs inside; the magic begins as the box reels in space, turns, flips inside out, and opens into richly colored Christmas scenes that emerge and then dissolve. In the end, the box is back where it began, in the garbage, but the bum has created his Christmas fantasy.

MINDSCAPE (LE PAYSAGISTE)

1976. Canada.
National Film Board production. Directed by Jacques Drouin. Animated by Alexeïeff-Parker. Produced by Gaston Sarault. Music by Jean Denis La Ro-

chelle.
8 min. B&W. Sound.

The Alexeïeff-Parker pinscreen, which Alexandre Alexeïeff and Claire Parker pioneered and used almost exclusively for forty years (see *En Passant* [1943]), is an elaborate technique used by only a few other animators. One of these, Jacques Drouin, made this film about a painter who steps inside the world of his painting for a journey through fascinating landscapes peopled with symbols. These scenes transform and metamorphose into one another in the fluid, evocative style unique to the pinscreen. A house becomes a box of toys, a tree becomes a face and a clock, and a maze envelops the screen. The film culminates with an image of the creative process, as the artist pictures himself in the painting and then steps out.

THE STREET

1976. Canada.
National Film Board production. Directed and animated by Caroline Leaf. Produced by Guy Glover and Wolf Koenig. Based on the book by Mordecai Richler.
11 min. Color. Sound.

Caroline Leaf, who established her reputation as a talented animator with *The Owl Who Married a Goose* (1974), received an Academy Award nomination for *The Street*, a poignant film from the book by Montreal author Mordecai Richler. In an unusual technique involving the use of soft, simple washes of watercolor and ink, she paints directly on the glass stage of the animation camera. Leaf interprets the reactions of a young boy in a poor Jewish family to a dying grandmother, capturing his feelings and distilling them into a harsh but honest reality. *The Street* is an imaginative and direct statement about how families respond to aging and death. It is also a virtuoso achievement in the development of a distinctive animation style.

BEAD GAME

1977. Canada.
National Film Board production. Directed by Ishu Patel. Produced by Derek Lamb. Music by J. P. Ghosh.
6 min. Color. Sound.

This extraordinary animation uses thousands of colorful beads, which are arranged and manipulated into the shapes of creatures both mythical and realistic. With evidence of the strong Eastern influences of his native India, Patel has created stunning images and explosions of color in this allegory of aggression and inevitability. Accompanied by the sound of an Indian tambour, the beads begin as simple organisms and progress through many layers of complexity, multiplying, absorbing, and devouring one another in an animated evolutionary chain. *Bead Game* ends with an analogy to the precarious state of the present world, visualized in the culmination of this process by an atom held in a cat's cradle.

BEAD GAME (1977)

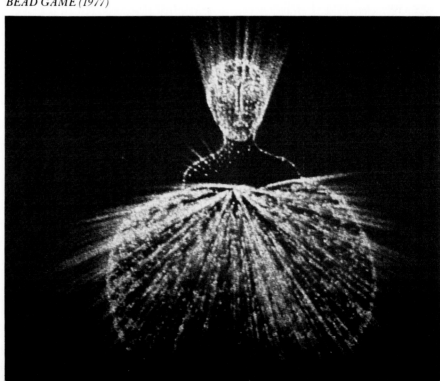

Co Hoedeman making THE SAND CASTLE (1977)

THE SAND CASTLE

1977. Canada.
National Film Board production. Directed by Co Hoedeman. Produced by Gaston Sarault. Music by Normand Roger. Edited by Jacques Drouin.
14 min. Color. Sound.

The Sand Castle is an animated fable of great humor and technical brilliance that becomes a bittersweet comment on the nature of experience. It begins with a sand storm that whistles through mini-ature dunes and changes their patterns. Suddenly, a sandman appears. This smiling character sculpts out of sand creatures with delightful shapes who then construct a sand castle. Enthusiastic about their adventure, they mold the sand and build their fortress under the spell of a common purpose. Shaped out of foam rubber, wire, and sand, and built in a tabletop sandbox, these figures are a tour de force of sand animation, winning Hoedeman an Academy Award in 1978. In the end, after celebrating the creation of their new home, the sand creatures are sadly interrupted by a predator they had not expected—the wind.

JOHN LAW AND THE MISSISSIPPI BUBBLE

1978. Canada.
National Film Board production. Directed by Richard Condie. Produced by Jerry Krepakevich. Animated by Richard Condie, Sharon Condie. Script and narration by Stanley Jackson. Music by Patrick Godfrey.
10 min. Color. Sound.

This humorous animated film tells the true story about the escapades of John Law's sensational get-rich-quick scheme. Armed with a plan to open a bank and exchange bank notes for gold at wildly inflated prices, Law goes from rags to riches and then back to rags when everyone decides to cash in on the notes. This monetary fable ends with John Law broke and brokenhearted.

LA PLAGE

1978. Canada.
National Film Board production. Directed by Suzanne Gervais. Produced by Francine Desbiens. Based on a story by Roch Carrier. Music by Maurice Blackburn. French titles only.
4 min. Color. Sound.

This elusive animation sets the stage for an unexpected accident by beginning with a calm beach scene. As the sun burns down, two people play dice and a man drinks a glass of water at a nearby table. While they sit with their backs to the surf, a woman drowns, unnoticed and alone. The viewer is the sole witness to a sadly unnecessary death in this film meditation on the themes of solitude and collective indifference.

PRETEND YOU'RE WEARING A BARREL

1978. Canada.
National Film Board production. Produced by Shelah Reljic. Directed by Jan-Marie Martell. Executive producer: John Taylor. Photographed by Doug McKay. Edited by Christl Harvey. Music by Ralph Dyck.
10 min. Color. Sound.

Pretend You're Wearing a Barrel is a vivid portrait of a toughminded woman who took control of her life. At age 35, Lynn Ryan decided, as a mother with five children and no husband, that she would learn a trade so that she could support her family and maintain a sense of personal dignity. After help from employ-

THE SKIFF OF RENALD AND THOMAS (1980)

ment counselors and a course in welding, she became an apprentice engineer in a Vancouver shipyard. This short is an effective document of one woman's courageous and positive encounter with life.

GOING THE DISTANCE

1979. Canada.
National Film Board production for the Minister of State for Fitness and Amateur Sport and the Commonwealth Games Foundation. Produced by Robert Verrall and Jacques Bobet. Written by Paul Cowan. Directed by Paul Cowan, Georges Dufaux, Reevan Dolgoy, Beverly Schaffer, Tony Westman.
90 min. Color. Sound.

Going the Distance is the official film of the XI Commonwealth Games, held in Edmonton, Canada in 1978. Like the Olympics, the Commonwealth Games is an international sports event held every four years. Unlike the Olympics, competitors are not required to meet special athletic standards in the ten official sports. Many small countries that cannot qualify for the Olympics can send one or more athletes to these "Friendly Games." In the Commonwealth Games, the idea of personal human contact is still a reality and the fostering of an understanding through competition is still a possibility. In order to explore the depths of human effort more fully, eight athletes were chosen by the filmmakers to be filmed in their home countries before the games and during competition. The film describes how they "go the distance in physical, emotional, and psychological miles."

SEA DREAM

1979. Canada.
National Film Board production. Produced by Margaret Pettigrew. Executive Producer: Kathleen Shannon. Directed and designed by Ellen Besen. Animated by Besen and Bill Speers. Photographed by Simon Le Blance. Music by Beverly Glenn-Copeland and Sharon Smith. Narrated by Trana Kroitor. Poem by Debra Bojman.
6 min. Color. Sound.

This animated children's tale tells the story of a little girl who, after suffering through a bad day, escapes into an underwater fantasy. She dives through her frustration into a sea world where she befriends a lady octopus who can execute as many dance steps as she has limbs and even plays baseball. The little girl returns to reality feeling fine and refreshed. The idea behind making this

THE SWEATER (1980)

film originated at a performance of the poem "Sea Dream" before an audience of children between the ages of six and ten. Impressed by the children's enthusiasm, the filmmaker resolved to bring the story to the screen. The result is a lively short film with exceptionally vibrant color.

THE SKIFF OF RENALD AND THOMAS (LE CANOT À RÉNALD À THOMAS)

1980. Canada.
National Film Board production. Directed and edited by Bernard Gosselin. Photographed by Jean-Pierre Lachapelle. Music by Alain Lamontagne. Executive producer: Michel Brault. In French with English subtitles.
57 min. Color. Sound.

Sixteen years after he assisted Michel Brault in filming *Pour la suite du monde* (1964), Bernard Gosselin returned to Île aux Coudres in the St. Lawrence River to make *The Skiff of Renald and Thomas*. The skiff of the title is a small boat built in three weeks by five men from this island, which was once reachable only by small boats like this one. The craft is built by "eye," with the care and tradition of these crusty, experienced builders. Gosselin, who proved his respect for craftsmanship in *Jean Carignan, Violineux* (1975), sensitively captures the camaraderie and skilled workmanship of these men.

A SUFI TALE

1980. Canada.
National Film Board production. Directed by Gayle Thomas. Produced by Derek Lamb. Music by Normand Roger.
9 min. Color. Sound.

This animated film is based on an old Persian parable. Using traditional images reminiscent of German woodcuts, the filmmaker tells the story of the habitants of a village who learn to overcome their fear of the unknown. This simple yet wise tale shows the intricacies of change and the benefit of the villagers' new-found knowledge.

THE SWEATER

1980. Canada.
National Film Board production. Directed and animated by Sheldon Cohen. Produced by David Verrall, Marrin Canell, Derek Lamb. Based on the story by Roch Carrier. Narrated by Carrier.
11 min. Color. Sound.

This animated interpretation of a short story by Quebec author Roch Carrier is set in the rural Quebec of his boyhood. Carrier recalls the passion for playing hockey which he shared with the other boys of his community and reminisces about the time of Rocket Richard, Canada's greatest hockey player. *The Sweater* is a funny, deeply felt story effectively animated in a style that evokes the period of the late 1940s.

Edward Weston in THE PHOTOGRAPHER *(1948)*

Films on the Arts

ANNOTATIONS
Marita Sturken

MARY WIGMAN DANCES (MARY WIGMAN DANSER)

1929. Denmark.
Anonymous production. Danish titles only.
10 min. B&W. Sound.

This anonymous footage of the famed dancer-choreographer Mary Wigman's most well-known dances was found among belongings which she left in Denmark. She performs four dances on a starkly lit background that isolates her movement: Seraphic Song, Pastoral, Summer Dance, and Witch Dance. According to the film's titles, the footage dates from 1929 because a sound camera was used and the dances are characteristic of that particular time. Mary Wigman began performing in 1919 after studying dance with von Laban in Switzerland. In 1920 she opened a school of her own in Dresden, where she taught her unique style of movement, which she termed "New German Dance." In 1931 a branch of her school was established in New York City, and it is through that institution that Wigman's dance theories became a major influence on modern dance within the United States.

L'ARCHITECTURE D'AUJOURD'HUI

1931. France.
Directed by Pierre Chenal. French titles only.
10 min. B&W. Silent. 24 fps.

L'Architecture d'aujourd'hui is a documentary about three villas designed by prominent French architect Le Corbusier with the assistance of Pierre Jeanneret. The film explores Le Corbusier's theory of form and function, comparing his buildings' functional aesthetic to that of an automobile, discussing their relation to nature and their surroundings and the fundamental importance of light to the architect. The colossal plan by Le Corbusier to demolish and rebuild a large, central slum area of Paris is presented at the end of the film as his next project. Never realized, this plan is one of the first designs for urban renewal.

IMMORTAL SWAN (LE CYGNE IMMORTEL)

1935. Great Britain.
Directed by Edward Nakhimoff. Photographed by Phil Greenrod and Guy Green. Edited by Julia Wolf. Commentary by Albert Grehan. With Anna Pavlova, Pierre Vladimoroff. French language version with some English dialogue.
33 min. B&W. Sound.

This footage of dancer Anna Pavlova, which was long presumed lost or destroyed, was found in 1935 by her husband and manager, Victor d'André, four years after her death on January 23, 1931. She performs several dances to the accompaniment of Weber's *Invitation to the Dance*, Anton Rubenstein's *The Night*, and Richard Strauss's *Don Quixote*. Interspersed with these dances are scenes of her daily life—at her home, strolling in the garden, feeding her pet swans, and socializing with guests. A brief sequence also includes the only known recording of Pavlova's voice.

THE STONE WONDER OF NAUMBURG (DIE STEINERNEN WUNDER VON NAUMBURG)

1935. Germany.
By Curt Oertel and R. Bamberger. Music by J. S. Bach. Organ played by Fritz Heitman. German titles.
20 min. B&W. Sound.

This cinematic essay on the stone sculpture of the Saxon cathedral in Naumburg, Germany, is also a study of camera movement through space. The dramatic statues, which are identified by titles, are isolated and shown in great detail, accompanied by the organ music of Bach. The gracefulness of the figures is accentuated by the fluid camera work, an early attempt to recreate the actual feeling of moving through an architectural space. The final shot from the cathedral tower gives a geographical perspective on the cathedral and the prewar city of Naumburg.

LA LETTRE

1938. France.
By Jean Mallon with Charles Peignot. Music by Jean Wiener. English narration; French titles.
8 min. B&W. Sound.

This early introduction to calligraphy and typography traces the evolution of lettering structures through the ages. Concentrating on the development of lower case lettering, animated drawings are used to trace letters as Roman scribes would have written them, analyzing the separate strokes. From Roman capitals to Renaissance script to modern lettering, changes in style are demonstrated, emphasizing the effect the invention of the printing machine had in freezing the evolution of a lettering style that was sparked by "the vitalizing influence of the human hand."

EVOLUTION OF THE SKYSCRAPER

1939. U.S.A.
Produced by the Department of Architecture and Design of The Museum of Modern Art. Photographed by Francis Thompson.
40 min. B&W. Silent. 24 fps.

This document of the history of the skyscraper up until 1940 is divided into three sections: the origins, the construction, and the design. Thorough explanations of the precursors of skyscrapers in American architecture are given and the economic and social factors that contributed to the skyscraper's birth are examined. The various structural factors in construction are detailed, with comparisons to skeletal design. Footage of significant structures in Chicago and New York includes the Tacoma, Monadnock, Guaranty, Daily News World, Empire State, Woolworth, Chrysler, and McGraw-Hill buildings as well as the construction of Rockefeller Center. Various plans of utopian urban centers by Le Corbusier and others are also included.

ALEXANDER CALDER: SCULPTURE AND CONSTRUCTIONS

1944. U.S.A.
Produced by The Museum of Modern Art. Filmed and recorded by Hartley Productions. Commentary by Agnes Rindge. Music by Arthur Kleiner.
10 min. Color. Sound.

This portrait of Alexander Calder concentrates on his use of motion in design through a documentation of his sculpture in exhibition at The Museum of Modern Art. He is shown at work and playing with his famous circus, and an analysis of his different working materials, such as wire and wood, is also presented. The basis of Calder's mobiles is described, and individual sculptures, such as *The Spider, Cage in a Cage, The Hourglass*, and *Dancers in Sphere* are analyzed.

THE PHOTOGRAPHER

1948. U.S.A.
Directed and photographed by Willard Van Dyke. Written by Ben Maddow. Commentary by Irving Jacoby. Edited by Alexander Hammid.

Alexander Calder in WORKS OF CALDER (1950)

27 min. B&W. Sound.

The Photographer is a portrait of Edward Weston as the quintessential example of the pioneer artistic photographer. Van Dyke uses a thorough study of Weston's subject matter, especially the California landscape and his friends, to explore the photographer as a distinct personality and father of a new and expanding medium. This film is an excellent example of the beginnings of an acceptance of photography as a medium of artistic expression that remains "a language that all can understand." The commentary discusses aspects of point of view, depth of field, and, most importantly, the process of selection involved in taking a picture. Weston emerges as a rustic, earthy Californian who is set in his ways, elusive, and intriguing.

GUERNICA

1949. U.S.A.
By Robert Flaherty. Edited by David Flaherty.
8 min. B&W. Silent.

This unfinished film by documentary pioneer Robert Flaherty is a study of Pablo Picasso's famous painting *Guernica*. Using a script by William S. Lieberman, Flaherty completed this preliminary shooting, which was later edited by his brother David. His camera begins with the entire painting and then explores the surface of the work. Through his isolation of the expressions of terror and violence in these figures, we can see how he approaches the mural through its detail. The painting, which hung for forty-two years at The Museum of Modern Art, is now housed at the Prado in Madrid.

IMAGES MÉDIÉVALES

1949. France.
Produced by La Cooperative Générale du Cinéma Français. Directed by William Novik. Photographed by Guy Delecluse. Commentary by James Johnson Sweeney. Narrated by William Chapman. Music by Guy Bernard Delapierre. English narration; French titles.
18 min. Color. Sound.

Using medieval manuscripts of the 14th and 15th centuries from the Bibliothèque Nationale in Paris, this film traces the daily life and dreams of people in the Middle Ages. Striking imagery includes scenes of the harvest, life in a manor, the hunt, jousting matches, war, the arts, love, marriage, religion, and death. With an understated, graceful quality these images combine realistic and metaphoric imagery to portray the medieval culture looking at itself.

WORKS OF CALDER

1950. U.S.A.
Produced and narrated by Burgess Meredith. Photographed and directed by Herbert Matter. Narration by John Latouche. Music by John Cage.
20 min. Color. Sound.

This poetic interpretation of the work of Alexander Calder relates his kinetic sculptures to images of nature. Through the scenario of a young boy's discovery of nature and his subsequent discovery of Calder at work in his studio, the film explores the wonder of this artist's work through a child's vision. Calder is seen at work, cutting metal shapes and forming wire sculptures. The grace and beauty of his mobiles and other sculptures are effectively combined with images of the surrounding environment to suggest the elegant movements of Calder's mobiles and the natural imagery that inspired them.

JOHN MARIN

1951. U.S.A.
Directed by James Davis. Produced by Robert S. Lindsay. Music by Bach.
24 min. Color. Sound.

Davis explores the work of painter John Marin (1895–1953) by filming the environments in which the artist worked. Starting out at Alfred Steiglitz's gallery, An American Place, Marin was rooted in Weehawken, New Jersey, overlooking Manhattan, and on the Maine coastline. His watercolors reflect and give life to these landscapes. Davis integrates Marin's eye and a camera's view by juxtaposing vistas with Marin's interpretations, all set to the music of Bach, Marin's favorite composer. "The paint must move," he quotes Marin as saying, "the line must move; it must have a life of its own." This film collage adds still more movement to the lines of Marin's work.

A JAPANESE HOUSE

1955. U.S.A.
Produced, photographed, and edited by Sidney Peterson for the Department of Architecture and Design of The Museum of Modern Art. Narrated by John B. Hughes. Music by Norman Lloyd.
18 min. B&W. Sound.

This is a pictorial survey of the 1954 installation and exhibition of a 16th-century Japanese house in the garden of The Museum of Modern Art. The purpose of the exhibition was to illustrate those aspects of Japanese architecture and design that have influenced modern theories of design. Peterson uses a Japanese aesthetic in documenting the details and graceful structure of the house and the complex reassembly of the structure in New York. The film describes the aesthetic concept of the Japanese house, which is based on the design of the roof, as well as the purpose of individual rooms. Decorative rafters, designs drawn into the sand of the surrounding garden, and the cultural implications of certain design aspects are explored in detail.

TEXTILES AND ORNAMENTAL ARTS OF INDIA

1955. U.S.A.
By Charles and Ray Eames. Music by Ustad Ali Akbar Khan and Panoit Chatur Lal. Narration by Mrs. Pupul Ja-

yakar.
11 min. Color. Sound.

Textiles and Ornamental Arts of India is a film record of an exhibition held at The Museum of Modern Art. With fast visual pacing set to Indian music, the Eameses use many still images of the expansive, diverse exhibit to create a cinematic portrait. The narration describes the rich cultural basis of the objects, rugs, and jewelry and the importance of color in Indian craftsmanship.

THEATER (TEATTERI)

1957. Finland.
By Sol Worth and Jack Witikka. Photographed by Ossi Harkimo. Music by Benjamin Lees. In Finnish and English.
20 min. B&W. Sound.

Theater is an impressionistic documentary of a Finnish production of Samuel Beckett's *Waiting for Godot* at the Finnish National Theater in Helsinki. Rather than a document of the play, the film is an experiment in interpreting theater. The camera captures with precision the nuances of the first readings of the script and the actors' transformation into these characters. Set design, lighting, costume design, scene blocking, and numerous rehearsals are woven together to present the various elements involved in the production. The director also describes the workings of the Finnish National Theater. With striking photography that not only captures the intricacies of these activities but also extends the play with a sensibility true to Beckett's style, ***Theater*** is a film that provides an extensive look beneath the surface of a play's production.

GLENN GOULD: OFF THE RECORD and GLENN GOULD: ON THE RECORD (1959). *See* National Film Board of Canada

HOMMAGE TO JEAN TINGUELY'S "HOMMAGE TO NEW YORK"

1960. U.S.A.
By Robert Breer.
10 min. B&W. Sound.

This tribute is an expressionist documentary of Swiss motion sculptor Jean Tinguely's auto-destructive sculpture as it is assembled and then self-destructs at The Museum of Modern Art. Tinguely's sculpture is an eclectic, massive conglomeration of wheels, bathtubs, piano strings, pulleys, and airplane parts that are constantly in motion. Breer overlays segments of the *Hommage* being set on fire with scenes of the original drawing

plan and welding, and extends his portrait by manipulating his imagery in kinetic collages which reflect the energy of Tinguely's work.

ANTONIO GAUDI

1965. U.S.A.
Produced by Ira Latour. Written by George Collins.
27 min. Color. Sound.

This film documents the work of one of architecture's foremost innovators, who built flamboyant and bizarre structures in Spain before his death in 1926. His architecture was derived from nature, using parabolic arches and tree, animal, and sea forms. This documentary centers on Gaudí's principle that "originality is a return to the origin," and clarifies the philosophical basis of his work through his writings. It presents him as the forgotten "prolific inventor of new forms," who was rediscovered in the 1950s and 1960s in reaction to the steel-and-glass cage trend of architecture. An extensive body of work is presented and discussed, including Casa Vicens, Palacio Güell, Finca Güell, Parque Güell, Casa Batlló, Casa Milá, Santa Coloma de Cervelló, and the famous unfinished temple, La Sagrada Familia.

DOROTHEA LANGE

1965. U.S.A.
Produced by Phillip Greene and Robert Katz for KQED. Directed by Richard Moore and Greene. Photographed by Greene.

PART ONE: *UNDER THE TREES*

30 min. B&W. Sound.

This portrait of photographer Dorothea Lange (1895–1965) shows her at work on a retrospective exhibit for The Museum of Modern Art, while fighting cancer in the last year of her life. Well-known for her work in the Farm Security Administration (FSA) project, Lange is credited with having photographed the most famous and important image of that collection, *Migrant Mother*. As one of the earliest women photographers, her straightforward and sensitive approach made her one of the foremost documentary photographers of our time. In this film, as she reviews her work for exhibition, she is self-critical and revealing. During a critique with the Museum's curator of photography John Szarkowski, and in discussions with her family, she goes through a vast number of images that she took all over the world, explaining how she felt when taking certain pictures. This is not only

a portrait, but a documentary of the difficult selection process involved in creating a retrospective exhibit.

PART TWO: *THE CLOSER FOR ME*

30 min. B&W. Sound.

The second part of this portrait of Dorothea Lange concentrates on her renowned work with the Farm Security Administration (FSA) project during the Depression. In describing what was one of the most important documentary projects ever initiated and produced in still photography, Lange tells of how she and the other FSA photographers were "turned loose in a region to find out what it looked like, what it felt like and what was the human condition." She reviews these images and her pictures of the war years, plus a project on "The New California," which occupied her during the last years of her life. Lange talks about photography as a universal language and her desire always to make thought-provoking photographs.

ALBERTO GIACOMETTI

1966. U.S.A.
Produced by Sumner J. Glimcher. Directed by Stuart Chasmar. Music by Arnold Gamson.
12 min. Color. Sound.

This documentary of Giacometti's last major retrospective, held at The Museum of Modern Art in 1965, surveys 50 years of the fascinating skeletal figures of Giacometti's painting and sculpture. The film soundtrack presents the artist's writings as the camera slowly scans his figures, silhouetted in bare museum space or standing in what he defined as the "common solitude" of crowds. Revealing and philosophical, Giacometti describes his desire to create "something alive and dead at the same time, transfixed in the void."

LE CORBUSIER DESIGNS FOR HARVARD

1966. U.S.A.
By Bruce S. Green. Narrated by Anthony Caputi.
15 min. B&W. Sound.

In reaction to the static and narrow style used in many architecture films, this documentary on the Carpenter Center for the Visual Arts at Harvard University uses cinema to document the movement of the eye through space. Le Corbusier's concept that "the path by which the spectator is led through the building should clarify the spatial conception of the structure" is systematically reiterated by Green's camera as it moves fluidly through the structure. In this concise articulation of the functional design of the Carpenter Center, Green also describes and analyzes the theories of one of the most important architects of our time.

THE CALDER MAN

1967. Great Britain.
Produced by International Nickel. Directed by D. G. Hannaford.
14 min. Color. Sound.

This film documents the conception, construction, and installation of *Man*, a 50-ton, 67-foot-high "stabile" created by Alexander Calder for Expo '67 in Montreal, Quebec. Calder calls the static sculptures that he made "stabiles," to distinguish them from his kinetic mobiles. He is seen at work in his studio in France and supervising the design and welding of this immense sculpture, as well as its assembly at its present site in Montreal.

NINE DAYS TO PICASSO

1967. U.S.A.
Produced by The Museum of Modern Art. Directed by Warren Forma. Edited by Phillip Messina.
25 min. Color. Sound.

Nine Days to Picasso is a documentation of the installation of a sculpture exhibition at The Museum of Modern Art in 1967. The late René D'Harnoncourt, who was then Director of the Museum, describes the criteria he used for designing the show. He begins by studying the catalogs of earlier shows by Picasso and redrawing all of the pieces to get an impression of scale. He decides to let the "affinities of form and content between the pieces" act as the organization of the show. The monumental installation of many of these "paintings on a curved surface," as D'Harnoncourt describes them, is presented, along with details such as lighting and sound. Many of the sculptures in the exhibition that are now well known had never been exhibited before.

SORT OF A COMMERCIAL FOR AN ICEBAG BY CLAES OLDENBURG

1969. U.S.A.
Directed by Michel Hugo. Photographed by Eric Saarinen. Edited by John Hoffman. Sound by Howard Chesley.
16 min. Color. Sound.

Image and sound operate as extensions of Claes Oldenburg's concepts as he considers the genesis and evolution of his *Giant Soft Icebag*, displayed at Osaka's Expo '70. This was the artist's first kinetic sculpture, and the film is straightforward and whimsical, educational and entertaining.

SONAMBIENTS: THE SOUND SCULPTURE OF HARRY BERTOIA

1971. U.S.A.
Produced and directed by Jeffrey Eger. Edited by Miriam Eger. Sound by Peter Hliddal.
16 min. Color. Sound.

This portrait of metal sculptor Harry Bertoia shows him at work on countless sound sculptures. These are composed of numerous tall metal rods which create eerie, haunting sounds when vibrated. Bertoia talks about the many tones and feelings evoked by the sounds as well as his progression as an artist. Taken outdoors, the sculptures are transformed in sunlight, and the imagery of these art works is related to natural images of the trees and sun.

THE ART OF THE POTTER

1972. U.S.A.
Directed by David Outerbridge. Photographed by Sid Reichman. Narrated by Edwin R. Newman.
50 min. Color. Sound.

The Art of the Potter has been praised by leading ceramists as one of the finest films on this subject. Featuring Shoji Hamada and Bernard Leach, both highly regarded functional potters, the film evokes a deft impression of this ancient art form. The scenes alternate from the seaside village of Cornwall, England, where Leach established a studio in the 1920s with Hamada's assistance, to Hamada's studio in the historic pottery village of Mashiko, Japan. The various processes of pottery are detailed faithfully, from the digging for clay and wedging it for use, to firing the finished pot. With Hamada at his primitive wheel, there is a quiet, sensual examination of throwing, shaping, and trimming the raw clay. Techniques in glazing and waxing are followed by a ceremonial loading of 2,000 pieces into a wood-burning kiln. The Mashiko potters then wait while the fire is stoked and the pottery cooled until they celebrate the unloading of the transformed, glistening pieces. Intercut with this process Leach examines the philosophy of the potter. He discusses the appeal of the handmade form and its relationship to the irregularities found in nature. The lush visual images in this film, beyond the natural beauty of the exotic locations, are the result of a painstaking and probing eye, complemented by a narration which is cogent and inobtrusive. Leach and Hamada died respectively in 1980 and 1981; this film is an informative documentary as well as a worthwhile tribute.

IAN HUGO: ENGRAVER AND FILM MAKER

1972. U.S.A.
By Ian Hugo. Music by David Horowitz.
8 min. Color. Sound.

This film is Ian Hugo's answer to the question of why he gave up engraving and went into filmmaking. In response he examines these two artistic processes and what makes them similar. Carrying a "sense of continuous motion" from the engraved plate to the cinematic image, Hugo shows the similarities of working in the different media. He is shown engraving a plate and explaining this process in depth. Then examples of his engravings and films are collaged together in an effective summary of his diverse work.

PICTURES TO SERVE THE PEOPLE: AMERICAN LITHOGRAPHY, 1830–1855

1975. U.S.A.
Produced and directed by Wheaton Galentine for the American Antiquarian Society.
24 min. Color. Sound.

A survey of American lithography between the years of 1830 and 1855, the film depicts the lithographic process and provides examples of traditional subjects. With the invention of the process in 1795, pictures became available in mass quantities and at reasonable prices for the first time in the history of the world. People began to rely on lithography for a documentary record of the world, and current events like the Mexican War were quickly translated into lithographic images. Other traditional subjects represented in the film are portraits of famous people, visions of the West, and scenes intended to teach morals.

AN AMERICAN POTTER

1976. U.S.A.
Directed by Charles Musser.
36 min. Color. Sound.

By creating a portrait of one potter, Musser succeeds in touching on issues of craftsmanship and the relationship of art and politics. New Hampshire potter Gerry Williams discusses the techniques of his craft, including his invention of wet-clay firing, as the camera deftly captures the beauty of his hands working with the clay. Williams describes how he uses his craft to present political issues with powerful clay sculptures, and how pottery is integral to his advocation of a specific, self-sufficient life-style.

CORNELL, 1965

1978. U.S.A.
By Larry Jordan.
7 min. Color. Sound.

This affectionate portrait of artist Joseph Cornell (1903–72) is composed of footage shot in 1965 by his assistant, Larry Jordan, at Cornell's home and studio in Flushing, New York. It includes some of the only known film footage of Cornell. In a personal homage, Jordan discusses Cornell's favorite artists and music and his influence on Jordan's own work (see **Duo Concertantes** [1964] and **Our Lady of the Sphere** [1969]). Close-ups of the work and the studio are presented in the collage aesthetic that made Cornell one of the most important artists of this century. Jordan describes the artist's intentions and feelings toward his collage boxes, saying, "his working concern was to bring certain threads of reminiscence together." Sensitively photographed, this tribute shows an elusive, complex artist whose influence is continuously growing.

MARCEL DUCHAMP IN HIS OWN WORDS

1978. U.S.A.
By Lewis Jacobs. Music by Henry Brandt.
34 min. Color. Sound.

This documentary on one of the most important artists of the 20th century opens with the familiar image of Duchamp studying a chess board. In recordings taken in 1968 in Cadaques, Spain, shortly before his death, Duchamp (1887–1968) discusses his work, jokes, and reminisces, saying, "I discarded brushes and explored the mind more than the hand." This informative and charming film is divided into segments: "The Art," which explores Duchamp's early drawing, painting, and Cubist period, including *Nude Descending the Staircase* and *The Bride Stripped Bare by Her Bachelors, Even* (the *Large Glass*); The "Object and the Gesture," which is concerned with his "ready-made" objects, "ready-made reciprocals," and Dada period, including humorous puns such as Mona Lisa's *L.H.O.O.Q.*; and the final section, which chronicles the last major work of his life, *Given: 1. The Waterfall 2. Illuminating Gas.* This mixed-media assemblage of different materials, techniques, and forms was erected at the Philadelphia Museum of Art in 1969. Built to be viewed by only one person at a time, it was produced in secret in the last years of his life. Jacobs approaches the artist through a visual style that reflects Duchamp's energy and humor. Using extensive collage, documentation of his work, photographs, and film footage of the artist, he creates a visual complement to Duchamp's fascinating dialogue.

JEAN DESPRES: THE DESIGNER (JEAN DESPRES: ARTISTE ET MAÎTRE ORFÈVRE)

1979. France.
Directed by Régis Prevost. In both French and English versions: please specify.
17 min. Color. Sound.

This portrait of Art Deco designer and craftsman Jean Despres combines extensive use of old photographs, footage of Despres at work, and an interview with the artist to recreate the atmosphere of the Art Deco movement and of Paris from the early 1900s to the 1950s. His prolific work in objects, jewelry, and figures is well documented in stills, as Despres discusses his life as a struggling artist living in the Bateau-Lavoir artists' community and his friendships with Jacques Dusset, Georges Braques, and Etienne Courault, among others. Describing how his fascination with machines began his Art Deco period, Despres defines the style as "an amalgamation of Greco-Roman curves fused with the explosive power of the engine form."

PISSARRO: AT THE HEART OF IMPRESSIONISM

1981. U.S.A.

Produced, directed, and written by Judith Wechsler for the Museum of Fine Arts, Boston, and La Réunion des Musées Nationaux, France. Photographed by Precision Film Group. Edited by Wechsler and Clark Dugger. Available in both English and French versions: please specify.
14 min. Color. Sound.

Pissarro: At the Heart of Impressionism traces the artistic development and the life of Camille Pissarro (1830–1903), who has been called the patriarch of the Impressionist movement. The evolution of Impressionism, its aesthetic aims, and Pissarro's role are presented through characteristic images, compositions, and techniques. The film relates Pissarro's work to that of Cézanne, Monet, Seurat, Sisley, van Gogh, and Gaugin and reveals how his receptivity to these artists, who were also his friends, influenced his paintings. We come to see and understand the evolution of his distinctive style. The camera focuses on the paintings and prints in close detail, suggesting a way of looking. The film draws attention to those qualities and elements that characterize Pissarro's work: quiet but lyrical imagery, the depiction of people in working interaction with nature. Drawing on the artist's twenty-year correspondence with his son Lucien, and using contemporary photographs, prints, and publications, Pissarro's personal, social, and political outlooks are sketched in order to reveal that these attitudes are reflected in his work. Cézanne called him "the humble and colossal Pissarro."

PISSARRO: AT THE HEART OF IMPRESSIONISM (1981)

POTEMKIN (ODESSA STEPS SEQUENCE) (1925)

Film Study

ANNOTATIONS
Eileen Bowser, Herbert Reynolds

THE BIRTH OF A NATION
(Battle sequence)

January 1, 1915. U.S.A.
Epoch Producing Corporation. Produced and directed by D. W. Griffith. Photographed by G. W. (Billy) Bitzer. With Henry B. Walthall.
14 min. B&W. Silent. 18 fps.

This excerpt from the famous battle sequences is a classic of camera placement and editing. The complete film, in both black-and-white and tinted versions, is also available. *See* Silent Fiction.

THE BIRTH OF A NATION
(Homecoming sequence)

January 1, 1915. U.S.A.
Epoch Producing Corporation. Produced and directed by D. W. Griffith. Photographed by G. W. (Billy) Bitzer. With Henry B. Walthall.
4 min. B&W. Silent. 18 fps.

This excerpt shows the moving episode in which Henry Walthall as the defeated Confederate soldier returns to his home, and his mother, unseen, puts her arm out the door to gently draw him inside. The complete film, in both black-and-white and tinted versions, is also available. *See* Silent Fiction.

CARMEN (GYPSY BLOOD)
(Escape from prison sequence)

1918. Germany.
Union-Ufa. Directed by Ernst Lubitsch. Script by Hans Kräly, from a novel by Prosper Merimée. Photographed by Theodor Sparkühl. With Pola Negri, Harry Liedtke. English titles.
17 min. B&W. Silent. 18 fps.

German cinema was not completely interrupted by World War I. Unable to obtain films elsewhere, the country subsidized film production then and after the war, laying the foundations of craftsmanship to support the great flowering of film in Germany during 1918–25. Ernst Lubitsch and Pola Negri were both products of the Max Reinhardt experimental theater. Lubitsch was already a popular film actor and director of farce comedies when he made this film to introduce the Polish star to German cinema. *Carmen* won great acclaim for both of them, although it was not to be seen in America until their later *Madame Du Barry* (1919) broke down the prejudices against German films. The Prosper Merimée story was filmed many times and in different countries. Pola Negri's version of the hot-blooded Spanish gypsy used all the vitality and magnetism that made her a star, and a much more convincing "vamp" than Theda Bara in *A Fool There Was* (1914). In this excerpt from the film, Carmen is seen charming her way out of prison, then scheming to help Don José escape, an aid that he refuses in order not to compromise his honor.

POTEMKIN (BRONENOSETS POTEMKIN) (Odessa Steps sequence)

1925. U.S.S.R.
Goskino. Directed by Sergei Eisenstein.
10 min. B&W. Silent. 18 fps.

The classic example of Eisenstein's montage style is this sequence showing the booted soldiers forcing the rebellious masses down the broad steps of the port, over the bodies of the dead and dying. The cinematic sense of time is expanded to extreme limits. The complete film is also available. *See* Silent Fiction.

THE LOVE OF JEANNE NEY (DIE LIEBE DER JEANNE NEY)
(Montage sequence)

1927. Germany.
Ufa. Directed by G. W. Pabst. With Fritz Rasp, Eugen Jensen.
4 min. B&W. Silent. 18 fps.

This example of creative editing contains more than forty cuts. The multiple camera positions, angles, cutting on action, and movements of the camera are carefully planned to reflect the psychology of the characters. This sequence is the one in which the repulsive Khalibiev (Fritz Rasp) comes to sell the list of Bolshevist spies to Alfred Ney. The complete film is also available. *See* Silent Fiction.

THE MAN I KILLED (BROKEN LULLABY) (Opening sequence)

January 19, 1932. U.S.A.
Paramount. Produced and directed by Ernst Lubitsch. Photographed by Victor Milner.
3 min. B&W. Sound.

Opening his dramatic film on the first anniversary of the armistice ending World War I, Lubitsch wished immediately to evoke the complex of memories and emotions held over from the war. Beginning with the title credits (which include the original head title, *The Man I Killed*), a montage of sound and image sweeps in a multitude of contrasting events: bells peal the victory celebration, cannon fire rouses fearful recollections, an ironic church service is held for officers in full military dress. A model of concise Hollywood style, concluding just before the introduction of the central character, the three-minute sequence expediently suggests the inheritance of war that will temper the mood of the entire story. The complete film is also available. See Sound Fiction.

TEST SHOTS FOR HAMLET

1933. U.S.A.
Pioneer Pictures. With John Barrymore, Irving Pichel, Reginald Denny, Donald Crisp.
5 min. Color. Sound.

These two tests for a planned, but never realized production are all that remain of John Barrymore's *Hamlet*, the most famous of his stage roles. Short scenes are filmed with the actors in full costume, before a curtain or rudimentary set. Notable is the use of early three-color Technicolor for these test shots: the process had been introduced commercially in the animated Disney short *Flowers and Trees* the year before but would not be seen by audiences of live-action until 1934's *La Cucaracha*.

ASSASSINATION OF KING ALEXANDER OF JUGOSLAVIA

1934. U.S.A.
The Museum of Modern Art. All footage taken for the Fox Movietone newsreel *Assassination of Alexander and Barthou* photographed by Georges and Raymond Mejat. Edited by Lawrence Stallings. Narrated by Lowell Thomas.
17 min. B&W. Sound (some portions silent).

Unanticipated climaxes are possible in the course of documentary filmmaking. In this case, two newsreel cameramen assigned to photograph the arrival of a foreign dignitary found their cameras witnesses to an actual assassination. On Tuesday, October 9, 1934, Yugoslavia's imperious King Alexander and French Foreign Minister Louis Barthou were both gunned down by a Croatian terrorist as they rode in a motorcade through the streets of Marseilles. Along with the footage of the explosion of the German Zeppelin *Hindenburg*, this assassination was one of the greatest scoops in newsreel history, and was unrivaled until the 1960s, when film and television records of assassinations became commonplace. This study film begins with the complete seven-minute Fox newsreel, edited by Lawrence Stallings with added music track and narration by Lowell Thomas, as released in theaters immediately after the assassinations. Then we are shown the complete and unedited footage of the events, including some sections with live sound recorded on the scene by a new Fox sound truck. It is interesting to note the way the raw footage is shaped and dramatized by the style of newsreel reporting and the remarkable economy of newsreel assemblage: nearly every scrap of camera original is used in the final release.

OUR DAILY BREAD (Concluding sequence)

1934. U.S.A.
United Artists. Produced and directed by King Vidor. Photographed by Robert Planck. Edited by Lloyd Nossler. Music by Alfred Newman.
8 min. B&W. Sound.

This final eight minutes of Vidor's Depression-era feature depicts a commune of farmers constructing an irrigation canal to divert the waters of a distant stream to their parched corn fields. This sequence is a paradigm of cinematic form, combining all major components of the sound film (camera placement and movement, lighting, editing, direction of actors, dialogue, music, and sound effects) to enjoin the audience's emotional participation and arouse us with its accelerating pace. Demonstrating the influence of Soviet and documentary films (particularly the styles and themes of Eisenstein and Flaherty) on some of the best of Hollywood fiction, Vidor's entertaining finale is similar to most of the great swiftly paced documentary sequences of the 1930s (compare, for example, the work of Pare Lorentz, Joris Ivens, and the British school). It is also a stirring symphony to man's industry and progress, an emblem of thirties optimistic faith in people's ability to shape their own economic and social futures through collective effort. The complete film is also available. *See* Sound Fiction.

YOU ONLY LIVE ONCE: PRODUCTION TAKES FROM A FILM IN THE MAKING

1937. U.S.A.
United Artists. Directed by Fritz Lang. Produced by Walter Wanger. Photo-

graphed by Leon Shamroy. Edited by Daniel Mandell. With Henry Fonda, Jerome Cowan.
10 min. B&W. Sound.

A valuable behind-the-scenes glimpse of actual Hollywood production, this short study reel first presents several uncut camera takes just as they were photographed by Leon Shamroy, and finally a complete sequence as edited by Daniel Mandell, from Fritz Lang's fine second American film. (At one point the director can be heard off screen, commanding in broken English, "I call you when you shall come: Come!") First we view four takes from different scenes, three featuring Henry Fonda. They show the anticipation before each shot and the relaxation afterward. Next we observe the laborious setting up and shooting of three takes for the famed bank robbery scene, then the extraordinary full 36-shot sequence as it appears in the finished film. As fascinating as they are instructive, these examples succinctly demonstrate how the slow, patient craftsmanship of big-studio filmmaking can yield such stunning results on screen.

OLYMPIA (Diving sequence)

1938. Germany.
Produced and directed by Leni Riefenstahl. Edited by Riefenstahl, assisted by Walter Ruttmann. Music by Herbert Windt.
6 min. B&W. Sound.

One of the most famous sections of Riefenstahl's monumental two-part documentary of the 1936 Berlin Summer Olympics, the men's diving sequence is perhaps the most justly celebrated aesthetically. For most of the events she covered in *Olympia*, Riefenstahl reconstructed her footage chronologically, to capture the mounting tension of competition; but with the divers she disregarded factual details altogether to create a visual poem with its own laws of time and space. The numerous contestants from across the globe were photographed, along with some spectators, by an ample camera crew over an extended period and from every imaginable point of view—below, above, even under water. Carefully chosen and arranged, the final order of shots begins somewhat conventionally but develops an increasing pace and variety of camera positions to match the growing complexity of the dives. By the time Riefenstahl introduces slow and reverse motion, the sequence has grown far out of the context of a competitive event and, with its music score as complement, into a free ballet of human form against a cloud-capped sky.

AN ANTHOLOGY OF THE ITALIAN CINEMA: THE SILENT FILM FROM 1896 TO 1926 (ANTOLOGIA DEL CINEMA ITALIANO: IL FILM MUTO DAL 1896 AL 1926)

1955. Italy.
Presented by Il Centro Sperimentale di Cinematografia. Produced in collaboration with the Cineteca Nazionale and the Cineteca Italiana. English narration.
152 min. B&W. Sound.

This valuable compilation film provides a historical survey of Italian cinema through the presentation of excerpts from its greatest cinematic works. The selections are often grouped by filmic genre or category and attest to the variety of styles that comprised the Italian cinema from 1896 to 1926. The visuals are accompanied by an English voice-over commentary, which, despite certain historical inaccuracies and generalizations, provides useful background information. The film's primary value, however, lies in its exhibition of film material not currently available in this country. This anthology explores the silent era, concentrating on the Italian spectacle film and including sequences from *Gli ultimi giorni di Pompei (The Last Days of Pompei)* (1913), directed by Mario Caserini; *Cabiria* (1913), directed by Giovanni Pastrone; and *Messalina* (1923), directed by Enrico Guazzoni. The excerpts afford the viewer an appreciation of the extraordinary sets constructed for such productions. Also represented are examples of films employing performers from the theater (for example, *Cenere* [1916] with Eleanora Duse), and female star vehicles, comedy films, and adventure serials such as *I topi grigi (The Gray Rats)* (1918) by Emilio Ghioni. Finally, attention is given to the origins of Italian realism, a movement that reached fruition in the 1940s. Thus we see footage from *Assunta Spina* (1914) and stills from *Sperduti nel buio (Lost in the Dark)* (1914). In general, what emerges from this overview is both a sense of what Italian silent film shared with cinematic development in other countries and an appreciation of what is distinctive about the Italian sensibility. (See also *An Anthology of the Italian Cinema: The Sound Film From 1929 to 1943* [ca. 1955].)

AN ANTHOLOGY OF THE ITALIAN CINEMA: THE SOUND FILM FROM 1929 TO 1943 (ANTOLOGIA DEL CINEMA ITALIANO: IL FILM SONORO DAL 1929 AL 1943)

EISENSTEIN'S MEXICAN FILM: EPISODES FOR STUDY (1955)

ca. 1955. Italy.
Presented by Il Centro Sperimentale di Cinematografia. Produced in collaboration with the Cineteca Nazionale and the Cineteca Italiana. English narration. Excerpts in Italian; no English subtitles.
189 min. B&W. Sound.

Following the monumental treatment of the silent period in *An Anthology of the Italian Cinema: The Silent Film From 1896 to 1926* (1955), many of the same associates produced this independent chronicle of the early sound era. It serves an important function in reintroducing the prewar Italian cinema so largely forgotten with the advent of Neo-Realism in the mid-1940s. The Italian early sound period produced most of the same genres of films as were conceived in other countries at that time, principally filmed theatrical productions and light operettas. This anthology focuses on the dramatic narrative film and provides excerpts from Italian dialect comedies and glamorous "white telephone" films. But what is most impressive in this survey of Italian sound cinema is the presentation of sequences from the films of several major directors whose work is virtually unknown in this country. Included are excerpts from Alessandro Blasetti's *Sole* (1929), *Nerone (Nero)* (1930), *La tavola dei poveri* (1932), *Palio* (1932), and *1860* (1933); Goffredo Alessandrini's *Cavelleria* (1936), *Seconda B* (1934), and *Luciano Serra, pilota* (1938); and several works by Mario Camerini.

EISENSTEIN'S MEXICAN FILM: EPISODES FOR STUDY

1955. U.S.A.
The Museum of Modern Art. Compiled and annotated by Jay Leyda, assisted by Manfred Kirchheimer, from footage shot for *Que Viva Mexico!*, directed by Sergei Eisenstein in collaboration with Grigori Alexandrov and photographed by Eduard Tisse. English intertitles. Available in two separate parts:
PART ONE: 120 min. B&W. Silent. 24 fps.
PART TWO: 108 min. B&W. Silent. 24 fps.

In 1953 Upton Sinclair donated to The Museum of Modern Art the remaining footage and negative that Eisenstein had shot during 1930–32 for *Que Viva Mexico!* Working with the material that had not already been excised for *Thunder Over Mexico* (1933), *Time in the Sun*

(1939), or various short subjects, Jay Leyda assembled this two-part study film to outline Eisenstein's original plan for the great epic and to illustrate his method of filming. Leyda had studied with Eisenstein in the years shortly after the aborted Mexican project and saw that the best way to appreciate Eisenstein's intentions for the film is to view sections of unedited camera rushes rather than rely on the versions put together by other parties, all of whom inevitably imposed their own designs on the footage. Thus, for **Eisenstein's Mexican Film**, Leyda chose more than a dozen sections of **Que Viva Mexico!**, and for each section includes all shots just as they were photographed by Tisse's camera. This footage not only demonstrates the director's technique, but the uniform brilliance of his exceptional cinematographer. Leyda's notes lend additional insight, and he has arranged these sequences according to their proposed order in the final work, which would have comprised six parts: a prologue, four independent novellas, and an epilogue, all linked by a central theme. **Part One** includes two introductory examples of Eisenstein's shooting method and covers the Prologue and first novella, "Fiesta," plus the bridging episode between them. Among the sections shown are the pre-Christian Indian burial ceremony; a religious procession after the Spanish conquest, which is an amalgam of Christianity and traditional Mexican rites; and both live and staged scenes from the bullfight episode. There is a glimpse of Eisenstein himself in one shot. **Part Two** covers the second novella through the Epilogue, with additional shots that caught Eisenstein or Alexandrov during the filming. We see scenes of the Tehuantepec matriarchal society, including a beautiful in-camera matched dissolve from a gold necklace to the husband in a hammock that it will buy ("Sandunga," second novella); several sections from the dramatic third novella, "Maguey," which became **Thunder Over Mexico**, including the Corpus Christi ceremony; a summary of the last novella, "Soldadera," never filmed; and three sections from the Epilogue, the carnival celebration of the Day of the Dead.

ORIGINS OF THE MOTION PICTURE

1955. U.S.A.
Naval Photographic Center. Drawn from Martin Quigley Jr.'s book *Magic Shadows—The Story of the Origin of Motion Pictures* and source material from the Library of Congress, the Smithsonian Institution, the National Archives, the Thomas Edison Foundation, and George Eastman House.
21 min. B&W. Sound.

A definitive history of the pre-cinema has yet to be written, but this instructive documentary contributes quite usefully to our understanding of the developments leading to the birth of motion pictures. It even takes some refreshingly different perspectives and cites some additional examples from those currently acknowledged by general film histories. Tracing most of the important optical devices and amusements, beginning with the 11th-century *camera obscura* and the 15th-century magic lantern, it illustrates each and explains its workings: the thaumatrope, Plateau's phenakistiscope, the zoetrope, Reynaud's praxinoscope, Muybridge's zoopraxiscope, Marey's photo-gun, Edison and Dickson's kinetograph and kinetoscope, Dickson's Mutoscope, and cameras and projectors by Armat, Jenkins, Lumière, and others. The film incorporates related contributions in still photography—Daguerre, Niépce, Fox-Talbot, the Langenheims, and Eastman—and illustrates several films from the turn of the century, chiefly from the Edison Company, including **Fred Ott's Sneeze (Edison Kinetoscopic Record of a Sneeze, January 7, 1894)**.

THE MAKING OF A MOVIE

1957. U.S.A.
Written and directed by Tom Ryan. Narrated by Patrick Barr. With Otto Preminger, Jean Seberg, Richard Widmark, John Gielgud.
21 min. B&W. Sound.

Short "documentaries" on the making of lavish commercial features have typically been used for advance publicity and are frequently included in the features' budgets. This look at the production of **Saint Joan** (1957) begins its story with producer-director Preminger's long-standing interest in Shaw's play and an ambition to film it. Initial public interest was aroused by a much-publicized talent search for the title role, ending in his personal choice of 17-year-old Jean Seberg from a reported 18,000 applicants. This chronicle of the year-and-a-half of work toward the film's completion comes to serve as a useful primer on large-scale moviemaking: we are shown every facet of production, including Graham Greene's script, Georges Perinal's photography with the 35mm Mitchell BNC camera, art design, set construction, costuming, make-up, lighting, blocking, rehearsals and actual takes, studio and location shooting, sound recording, and the post-production tasks of rerecording, editing, and musical scoring. Also shown is the frightening accident at the stake where Seberg was momentarily engulfed in flames.

SWEDISH CINEMA CLASSICS
(1959). See **Swedish Cinema Classics** (1913–22) in Silent Fiction

---

FROM DADA TO SURREALISM: 40 YEARS OF EXPERIMENT

1961. Switzerland.
Compiled by Hans Richter. All films by Richter except **Symphonie Diagonale** (1924) by Viking Eggeling.
Total program: 62 min. B&W and color. Sound (except **Symphonie Diagonale**).

SYMPHONIE DIAGONALE (excerpt)

1924. Germany.
By Viking Eggeling.
2 min. B&W. Silent.

RHYTHMUS 21

1921. Germany.
3 min. B&W. Sound (music track).

RHYTHMUS 23

1923. Germany.
2 min. B&W. Sound (music track).

FILM STUDY (FILMSTUDIE)

1926. Germany.
Photographed by Endrejat.
4 min. B&W. Sound (music track).

INFLATION (excerpt)

1928. Germany.
Ufa. Photographed by Charlie Metain.
3 min. B&W. Sound (music track).

RENNSYMPHONIE (RACE SYMPHONY)

1928. Germany.
Maxim Film. Photographed by Otto Tober.
5 min. B&W. Sound (music track).

TWOPENCE MAGIC (ZWEIGROSCHENZAUBER [ZWISCHENGROSCHENZAUBER(?)])

1929. Germany.
2 min. B&W. Sound (music track).

EVERYTHING TURNS, EVERYTHING REVOLVES! (ALLES DREHT SICH, ALLES BEWEGT SICH!) (excerpt)

1929. Germany.
Photographed by Reimar Kuntze. Music by Walter Gronostay.
4 min. B&W. Sound (music track).

GHOSTS BEFORE BREAKFAST (VORMITTAGSSPUK)

1928. Germany.
Photographed by Reimar Kuntze. Original music by Paul Hindemith. With Hans Richter, Darius Milhaud, Paul Hindemith.
6 min. B&W. Sound (music track).

DREAMS THAT MONEY CAN BUY ("Desire" episode)

1947. U.S.A.
Inspired by and with a monologue written by Max Ernst. Photographed by Arnold Eagle. Music by Paul Bowles. With Max Ernst.
10 min. Color. Sound.

8 X 8 (8 MAL 8) ("Black Schemes" episode)

1957. Switzerland.
Photographed by Arnold Eagle. Music by John Latouche and Robert Abramson. With Jacqueline Matisse, Yves Tanguy, Julien Levy, Marcel Duchamp, Richard Huelsenbeck.
13 min. Color. Sound.

DADASCOPE ("La Chanson Dada" episode)

1961. Switzerland.
Photographed by Arnold Eagle. Music by Georges Auric. With Tristan Tzara and Paul Falkenberg.
4 min. Color. Sound.

This comprehensive anthology by Hans Richter includes several short films and excerpts from his entire career. A thorough introduction to his extensive body of work, it follows Richter from the absolute animation of his early films to the complex narrative structures of his late Surrealist period. The filmmaker gives a brief history of the films and has added music tracks to all of his silent films. Of special interest in this anthology are five films which are rarely seen and not available individually. *Rhythmus 23*, the fullest version of a film which Richter never completed, develops Richter's planar work in *Rhythmus 21*. *Film Study* adds to abstract figures some representational images such as multiple eyeballs and faces, reflecting the influence of Léger's *Ballet mécanique* (1924). *Inflation* was produced as a prelude to the feature *Die Dame mit der Maske* (1928), and was cut from twenty minutes to eight by the Ufa studio. It is represented by an excerpt in which Richter's special effects reach their height, with pixillation, superimposition, and multiple imagery yielding a satiric comment on the runaway inflation in the Weimar Germany of the 1920s. (*Rennsymphonie* was also made to precede a feature, *Ariadne in Hoppegarten* [1928].) More tongue-in-cheek humor is evident in *Twopence Magic*, the most surreal of these films, using free association in its visual connections of illogical comparisons. *Everything Turns, Everything Revolves!* depicts a magician's sideshow at a country fair in which the audience sees cinematic tricks rather than conventional sleight-of-hand. The complete *Symphonie Diagonale*, *Rhythmus 21*, *Rennsymphonie*, *Ghosts Before Breakfast*, *Dreams that Money Can Buy*, *8 X 8*, and *Dadascope* are available individually; see separate annotations for descriptions of these films.

—

LOUISIANA STORY STUDY FILM

1962. U.S.A.
University of Minnesota. Prepared and assembled by N. H. Cominos. Study project directed by George Amberg. Narrated by Frances Flaherty and Richard Leacock. Opening sequence of *Louisiana Story* (1948) produced and directed by Robert Flaherty, story by Frances and Robert Flaherty, photographed by Richard Leacock, edited by Helen van Dongen, music by Virgil Thomson.
128 min. B&W. Sound.

This useful study begins and ends with the opening section of Robert Flaherty's masterful last documentary. Introducing the boy on his boat, traversing and observing the bayou, the sequence is composed of forty-one shots and runs five minutes. In between, unedited, are the hundreds of shots taken for the sequence—about two hours of them. Accompanying our viewing is a companionable dialogue between Richard Leacock, the photographer, and Frances Flaherty, coauthor of the script and lifelong advisor to her husband. They speak of Flaherty's dedication as an explorer and how it inspired his working method ("I was an explorer first and a filmmaker a long way after")—especially in this sequence, which was planned to project the magic and wonder of the swamp through the eyes of the young boy. As Flaherty, who grew up on the Canadian frontier, described the scene, "We are spellbound by the mystery of the wilderness." In addition to Flaherty's art, we gain an appreciation for Leacock's, and with the transition to the completed work, for van Dongen's editing and Thomson's score.

GERMANY, AWAKE! (DEUTSCHLAND, ERWACHE!)

1968. Federal Republic of Germany.
Norddeutscher Rundfunk. Produced, written, and directed by Erwin Leiser. English narration, and German dialogue with English subtitles.
89 min. B&W. Sound.

Shooting LOUISIANA STORY: see LOUISIANA STORY STUDY FILM (1962)

Documentary filmmaker Erwin Leiser, born in Berlin in 1923 and a refugee from the Nazi regime, has specialized in examining the rise of Hitler and the period of the Third Reich. Usually working in Sweden or Switzerland, he has directed a number of historical compilation films, including **The Bloody Years** (1960, released in the U.S. as **Mein Kampf**) and **Eichmann and the Third Reich** (1961, called **Murder by Signature** in Britain). In **Germany, Awake!** (the ironic title was a popular Nazi rallying cry) his subject is the cinema of the Third Reich, and specifically the dissemination of Nazi propaganda in the feature fiction films of that period. The films themselves, now rare, are of greatest value, and Leiser concentrates directly on dozens of excerpts which he carefully chose from virtually all the most significant examples, among them **Hitlerjunge Quex** (1933), **Flüchtlinge** (1933), **Bismarck** (1940), **Jud Süss** (1940), **Heimkehr** (1941), **Ohm Krüger** (1941), **Der Grosse König** (1942), and **Kolberg** (1945). Leiser's important book (entitled *Nazi Cinema* in its English translation), published in 1968, is a companion volume and supplement to this film. (**Hitlerjunge Quex** is available separately; see also **Nazi Propaganda Films** [1933–37], **German Newsreels** [1933–40], **Triumph of the Will** [1935], **Campaign in Poland** [1940], and **The Camera Goes Along!** [1936], **and Flieger, Funker, Kanoniere!** [*excerpt*] [1937]).

PIER PAOLO PASOLINI

1970. Italy.
Directed by Carlo Hayman-Chaffey.
With Alberto Moravia, Cesare Zavattini, Sergio and Franco Citti, Giancarlo Arnao, Ninetto Davoli, and Pasolini. English narration.
29 min. Color. Sound.

This iconoclastic Italian novelist, poet, and essayist entered the cinema as scriptwriter in the mid-1950s and, directing his own work from the 1961 **Accattone**, became one of the most controversial film artists of the next decade and a half. Brutally murdered at 53 in 1975 under circumstances as controversial as those that had embroiled his life, Pasolini remains an enigmatic and confounding figure, at once Marxist and mystic, Catholic and atheist. He had completed fifteen of his twenty-one films when this analytic profile was made. It serves to introduce his films and film theory, acknowledging the objections frequently brought against his work and seeking answers and explanations in the stress Pasolini placed on death as a theme and his growing need to restore an epic

and mythological dimension to life. Speaking in his behalf are Alberto Moravia, Cesare Zavattini, his collaborator Sergio Citti, and his actors Franco Citti, Giancarlo Arnao, and Ninetto Davoli. Special attention is given to Pasolini's **Medea** (1970), **Oedipus Rex** (1967), **The Hawks and the Sparrows** (1966), and **The Gospel According to Saint Matthew** (1964). The latter is available. *See* Sound Fiction.

GRIERSON (1973). *See* National Film Board of Canada

THE LANGUAGE OF THE SILENT CINEMA

1973. U.S.A.
Compiled by Vladimir Petric.
Available in two separate parts:
PART ONE: 100 min. B&W. Silent. 18 fps.
PART TWO: 90 min. B&W. Silent. 18 fps.

This is a teaching film in two parts, consisting primarily of excerpts from classic films of the silent era. Selections have been made to illustrate basic formal concepts central to an understanding of the art of silent cinema. **Part One**, covering the years 1895 to 1925, includes Louis Lumière's **Teasing the Gardener** (1895), to illustrate the recording of reality, and Méliès's **The Conjurer** (1899), to exemplify cinematic fantasy. Also included are sequences from Le Bargy and Calmettes's **The Assassination of the Duc de Guise** (1908), Serena's **Assunta Spina** (1915), Griffith's **The Birth of a Nation** (1915), Wegener's **The Golem** (1920), von Stroheim's **Foolish Wives** (1922), Clair's **Entr'acte** (1924), Stiller's **The Story of Gösta Berling** (1924), and Eisenstein's **Strike** (1925). **Part Two**, 1925 to 1929, is organized around such topics as the role of architecture in cinema and the use of lighting and camera movement. Included are excerpts from Kirsanov's **Ménilmontant** (1925), Lang's **Metropolis** (1927), Murnau's **Sunrise** (1927), Renoir's **The Little Match Girl** (1928), Epstein's **The Fall of the House of Usher** (1928), Dreyer's **The Passion of Joan of Arc** (1928), and Dovzhenko's **Arsenal** (1929). All of these films are also available individually (see Silent Fiction).

THE MEN WHO MADE THE MOVIES

1973. U.S.A.
Produced, written, and directed by Richard Schickel for the Educational Broadcast Corporation; except for **Alfred**

Hitchcock, produced for City Center of Music and Drama. Narrated by Cliff Robertson.

Broadcast on U.S. public television, this series is the work of the longtime critic for *Life* and *Time* and author of several books on film, Richard Schickel. It originally comprised eight films, each one spotlighting the work of a single prominent Hollywood director. All but one of these profiles (**William Wellman**) are currently available. For the most part, each profile traces its moviemaker's career chronologically, using excerpts from several major films. Alternating with these clips are segments showing the director himself, answering questions or speaking directly to the camera, reminiscing about his films or explaining details of his craft. Narration provides additional historical and critical observations. Because the excerpts are thoughtfully chosen from the strongest periods of these men's careers, all the profiles are helpful not only for introducing the best work of each filmmaker, but also for providing a broader sense of his style and range when viewed with a limited number of his feature films. Also valuable are the records of these men's personalities—presented as they would probably like to be remembered (six of the eight have died since the series was produced).

FRANK CAPRA

80 min. Color. Sound.

Along with **Raoul Walsh**, this is the longest and most detailed examination in the series. Sicilian-born in 1897 and California-bred, Capra made a big name for himself and for Harry Cohn's little Columbia Pictures during the 1930s. He combined the snappy comic style he had developed in his early career, working for Mack Sennett and directing Harry Langdon's best feature comedies, with subjects that exploited an idealist and sentimental brand of populism which he worked out in collaboration with screenwriter Robert Riskin. Like Hitchcock, Capra's success insured him a great deal of autonomy in his projects. Besides glimpses of Sennett and Langdon routines and of **Dirigible** (1931), substantial sequences are taken from **American Madness** (1932), **The Bitter Tea of General Yen** (1933), **It Happened One Night** (1934), **Mr. Deeds Goes to Town** (1936), **Mr. Smith Goes to Washington** (1939), **Meet John Doe** (1941), **Lost Horizon** (1937), **Arsenic and Old Lace** (1944, completed 1941), and **It's a Wonderful Life** (1946), as well as the **Why We Fight** documentary series (1942–45), which he supervised during World War II. Capra's last film was released in 1961. The complete **Why We Fight** series is available (see Documentary Film).

GEORGE CUKOR

58 min. Color. Sound.

Born in 1899, Cukor worked in the theater during his twenties, but moved to Hollywood when the new sound era created a market for directors who knew something about dialogue. Agreeable and urbane, he became a favorite of many performers, including Katharine Hepburn and Spencer Tracy, and mounted popular and honored productions for each of the major studios, moving from Paramount to RKO to MGM, free-lancing for Fox, Columbia, and Warner Bros. Featured are clips from twelve Cukor films through 1954: *The Royal Family of Broadway* (1930), *A Bill of Divorcement* (1932), *Dinner at Eight* (1933), *Little Women* (1933), *David Copperfield* (1935), *Camille* (1937), *Holiday* (1938), *The Philadelphia Story* (1940), *Adam's Rib* (1949), *Born Yesterday* (1950), *The Actress* (1953), and *A Star is Born* (1954). Cukor, who died in 1983 after beginning his sixth decade of moviemaking, speaks about his work with thoughtfulness and aplomb.

HOWARD HAWKS

58 min. Color. Sound.

A crackerjack craftsman in many genres, Hawks (1896–1977) benefited from his early experience as a film editor (around 1920) in putting together some of the best-paced comedies and melodramas of the 1930s and 1940s. These are the decades most closely examined in this celebration of many of his best works, chiefly for Warner Bros. and Columbia: *Dawn Patrol* (1930), *The Crowd Roars* (1932), *Twentieth Century* (1934), *Only Angels Have Wings* (1939), *His Girl Friday* (1940), *Air Force* (1943), *To Have and Have Not* (1944), *The Big Sleep* (1946), *Red River* (1948), *Rio Bravo* (1959), and *Hatari!* (1962). In addition to his lifelong obsessions with rugged professionalism, male camaraderie, and screwball repartee between sexual combatants, Hawks recollects his friendships with fellow writers William Faulkner and Ernest Hemingway.

ALFRED HITCHCOCK

58 min. Color. Sound.

The earliest of the film portraits in this series, *Alfred Hitchcock* varies its chronology to illustrate the personal obser-

Janet Leigh in PSYCHO from
THE MEN WHO MADE THE MOVIES: ALFRED HITCHCOCK (1973)

vations of the late director (1899–1980) rather than represent every phase of his career. After the British silent *The Lodger* (1926), film sequences are chosen liberally from seven of Hitchcock's American classics, concluding with his return to Britain for *Frenzy* (1972). The American excerpts include most of the classic moments from *Saboteur* (1942), *Shadow of a Doubt* (1943), *Notorious* (1946), *North by Northwest* (1959), *Psycho* (1960, four scenes in all), *The Birds* (1963), and *Torn Curtain* (1966). Forthright in his discussions while maintaining his characteristically wry posture, Hitchcock provides appropriate commentary on his deft blend of suspense and ironic humor. (Complete Hitchcock features available are *The Lodger* [1926], *Blackmail* [1929], and *Sabotage* [1936].)

VINCENTE MINNELLI

58 min. Color. Sound.

Born in 1913 to a Chicago family of entertainers, Minnelli is the youngest of this group of moviemakers and the last to begin work in Hollywood. Having started out as a theater director and set and costume designer, he was hired by producer Arthur Freed, who was organizing the excellent unit at MGM that would turn out the finest film musicals of the 1940s and 1950s. Minnelli directed most of the best, with a flair for color and exuberent staging: *Cabin in the Sky* (1943), *Meet Me in St. Louis* (1944), *Yolanda and the Thief* (1945), *Ziegfeld Follies* (1946), *The Pirate* (1948), *An American in Paris* (1951), *The Band Wagon* (1953), and *Gigi* (1958). Also illustrated are some of the most stylish segments of his nonmusical films: *The Clock* (1945), *Madame Bovary* (1949), *Father of the Bride* (1950), *Lust for Life* (1956), and *Some Came Running* (1958). Judy Garland (whom he married), Fred Astaire, and Gene Kelly bring added treasures to these excerpts.

KING VIDOR

58 min. Color. Sound.

Quite inclusive of his finest work, this record of Vidor wisely narrows its scope to his genuinely great period of the late 1920s and early 1930s, principally at MGM: *The Big Parade* (1925), *The Crowd* (1928), *Show People* (1928), *Hallelujah!* (1929), *The Champ* (1931), and *Our Daily Bread* (1934), films that guar-

Fred Astaire in THE BAND WAGON from THE MEN WHO MADE THE MOVIES: VINCENTE MINNELLI (1973) (p. 265)

antee his artistic reputation. Supplemental examples are drawn from **Northwest Passage** (1940), **Duel in the Sun** (1946), and **War and Peace** (1956). His directing career stretched from 1918 through the late 1950s (born in 1894, he died in 1982). It was his childhood fascination with moving pictures and his training during the silent era that brought him his exceptional sense for photographic composition and visually dramatic storytelling. As the film clips here demonstrate, Vidor's virtuosic camera positioning and mobility created many sequences that are unsurpassed in the history of the cinema. The complete **Our Daily Bread** and its **Concluding sequence** are also available. *See* Sound Fiction and Film Study.

RAOUL WALSH

88 min. Color. Sound.

In a career spanning half a century, Walsh (1899–1980) directed over a hundred features and a couple dozen two-reelers. Originally an actor, he is shown here as John Wilkes Booth in Griffith's **Birth of a Nation** (1915) and in his own **Sadie Thompson** (1928). After losing an eye, he stuck to directing and turned out one of the most varied lists of any Hollywood professional; most notable are his assignments for Warner

Bros. and Fox from the late 1920s through the early 1940s. At Warners, he was accomplished at gritty, contemporary action melodramas and charming romantic period comedies. He is very well represented by scenes from **What Price Glory** (1926), **The Cock-Eyed World** (1929), **The Big Trail** (1930), **The Bowery** (1933), **The Roaring Twenties** (1939), **High Sierra** (1941), **Strawberry Blonde** (1941), **They Died with Their Boots On** (1941), **Gentleman Jim** (1942), **Desperate Journey** (1942), **Northern Pursuit** (1943), and **White Heat** (1949). The complete **What Price Glory** is also available (see Sound Fiction).

—

THE MAKING OF SERPENT

1978. U.S.A.
Directed by Scott Bartlett.
34 min. Color. Sound.

Bartlett writes that his 1971 experimental film, **Serpent**, "embodies the primal chaotic life force in mythic symbology using natural and electronic imagery to particularize it." Seven years later, Bartlett analyzes the making of that work and its underlying philosophy. Among the issues discussed by the filmmaker are his sources for imagery— ranging from original live-action photography to "borrowed" footage from television,

spaghetti westerns, spectacle films, and newsreels. Bartlett also summarizes and explains the varied image-abstracting techniques he employed: cross-printing, scatter-printing, step-framing, matting, super-imposition and rephotography. All of these tools enable him to "transform the mundane into the sublime." **The Making of Serpent** is a valuable teaching film, offering audiences an unusual opportunity to understand the experimental filmmaking process, both on a technical and artistic level.

CORRECTION PLEASE, OR, HOW WE GOT INTO PICTURES (1979). *See* Contemporary British Independent Film

THOSE DARING YOUNG FILM MAKERS BY THE GOLDEN GATE

1979. U.S.A.
Produced and directed by Geoffrey Bell.
22 min. Color. Sound.

Numerous film stills and one surviving fragment illustrate the productions of the short-lived but pioneering California Motion Picture Corporation, which operated in the San Francisco Bay area from 1913 to 1917. The company's initial investment ($1 million), its studio near San Rafael in Marin County, and its goals for feature-length dramatic works were unusually advanced for its era, paralleling the grand contemporary designs of D. W. Griffith. In addition to the history of the company itself, this film gives an account of the first filmmaking in the Bay area in general and pays special attention to the advantages of the film medium over the early 20th-century theater from which it in part grew.

MAKING OFFON

1980. U.S.A.
By Scott Bartlett. Codirected and edited by Cindy Haagens.
11 min. Color. Sound.

Making OffOn is a video primer that documents the recreation of **OffOn** (1967), a film that combined film and video in a revolutionary fashion. This recreation took place in a class at UCLA taught by filmmaker Scott Bartlett. Explaining the history of **OffOn** and the progression of images through the 1950s and 1960s, Bartlett describes how he and his students reconstructed the film with film loops, a video studio system, and performers. Video special effects, such as wipes, fades, chroma sweeps, and debanning are demonstrated, and Bartlett touches on issues of low-budget production and the differences between film and video. *Making OffOn* is an exceptional teaching tool for students of both film and video.

BEFORE THE NICKELODEON: THE EARLY CINEMA OF EDWIN S. PORTER

1982. U.S.A.
Produced, directed, and edited by Charles Musser. Written by Warren D. Leight and Musser. Executive producer: Stephen Brier. Photographed by Rob Issen. Photo-colorist: Elizabeth Lennard. Narrated by Blanche Sweet, with the voices of Robert Altman, Peter Davis, Milos Forman, Jay Leyda, Louis Malle, D. A. Pennebaker, Robert Rosen, Robert Sklar, and others.
60 min. Color. Sound.

Investigation in recent years has added greatly to our appreciation of the early cinema, including the social and economic forces at work in its development. Filmmaker Charles Musser (see also *An American Potter* [1976]) is himself one of the leading scholars of the pre-Griffith period and a specialist on the work of Edwin S. Porter. Musser's *Before the Nickelodeon* lends a richly detailed view of the formative years of film production in the U.S., between 1896 and 1908. Centering on the turn of the century, the film sees Porter's early career as representative of the changing relations in the manufacture and presentation of moving pictures. Porter was a projectionist and exhibitor at the Eden Musée amusement center in New York before becoming America's first great film director working for the Edison Company (*The Great Train Robbery* [1903]). As film production evolved from one-shot views to more complex stories and as the public demand for films increased, editing and artistic control of film form shifted away from the exhibitor-showman and toward the producer-filmmaker. Correspondingly, the cinema became less a visual newspaper and more a storytelling medium just as the lure of current events (the Spanish-American War, President McKinley's assassination, Theodore Roosevelt's personal style) gave way to a popular taste for fairy tales and melodrama. *Before the Nickelodeon* introduces these significant trends with much fascination and joy, and includes many rediscovered photographs, hand-tinted in the style of turn-of-the-century lantern slides, period phonograph recordings, and a score of important films by Porter and others. Among the films shown here in their entirety (and, before now, mostly unavailable) are *Terrible Teddy*,

The Grizzly King (1901); *Kansas Saloon Smashers* (1901); *The Finish of Bridget McKeen* (1901); *Samson-Schley Controversy* (1901); *Taking President McKinley's Body from Train at Canton, Ohio* (1901); *The Execution of Czolgosz, With Panorama of Auburn Prison* (1901); *Capture of the Biddle Brothers* (1902); *Appointment by Telephone* (1902); *Jack and the Beanstalk* (1902); *How They Do Things on the Bowery* (1902); and *The Life of an American Fireman* (1903).

DIRECTORS AT WORK: THE DIRECTOR AND THE ACTOR

1982. U.S.A.
Produced by David Shepard for the Directors Guild of America. Written and directed by Carl Workman. Narrated by Lamont Johnson. Executive Producers: Robert Wise, Lamont Johnson.
28 min. Color. Sound.

Produced as a pair with *Directors at Work: The Director and the Image* (1982), this informative compilation combines interviews with actors and directors with an entertaining array of film clips. Exploring the relationship between directors and their actors, the film touches on issues of method acting, improvisation, the use of surprise tactics, the importance of casting, the actor's ego, and spontaneity. Directors King Vidor, Sydney Pollack, Paul Mazursky, Martin Ritt, George Cukor, Martin Scorsese, and Alan Pakula are featured, as well as actors Alan Alda and Charlton Heston. Acting performances by Marlon Brando in *On the Waterfront* (1954) and *Viva Zapata!* (1952), Jill Clayburgh in *An Unmarried Woman* (1978), John Voight and Dustin Hoffman in *Midnight Cowboy* (1969), Jane Fonda in *Klute* (1971), Robert DeNiro in *Taxi Driver* (1976), among others, are examined in detail.

DIRECTORS AT WORK: THE DIRECTOR AND THE IMAGE

1982. U.S.A.
Produced by David Shepard for the Directors Guild of America. Written and directed by Carl Workman. Narrated by Lamont Johnson. Music composed and performed by Gaylord Carter. Executive producers: Robert Wise, Lamont Johnson.
27 min. Color. Sound.

This companion film to *Directors at Work: The Director and the Actor* (1982) explores the importance of cinematic imagery to various directors. As the narration states, "A great director once said that there are a thousand ways to point a camera, but really only one," this film explores the different approaches directors use to construct imagery and illusion. Alfred Hitchcock, King Vidor, Alan Pakula, and others discuss their perception of a director's style and the importance of the visuals of their work, touching on issues of silent film, the iconography of key shots, camera movement, the use of color, and storyboards. Scenes from *The Crowd* (1928), *Way Down East* (1920), *Psycho* (1960), *Dirty Harry* (1971), *All the President's Men* (1976), *The Deer Hunter* (1978), and *Days of Heaven* (1978) are used to illustrate a variety of directorial techniques.

BEFORE THE NICKELODEON:
THE EARLY CINEMA OF EDWIN S. PORTER (1982)

TITLE INDEX

A

A . . . for English titles beginning with A, see the next word of the title.

À LA CONQUÊTE DU PÔLE: see CONQUEST OF THE POLE, THE (1912), 22

A LA MODE (1959), 184

ABANDONED CHILDREN, THE: see NIÑOS ABANDONADOS, LOS (1974), 139

ABOVE US THE EARTH (1977), 223

ABREUVOIR: see HORSES' WATERING TROUGH (1896–97), 20

ACCIDENT: see ÜBERFALL (1929), 75

8 MAL 8: see 8 × 8 (1957), 182

AFFAIR OF HONOR, AN (1897): see CLASSIC AMERICAN MUTOSCOPE, THE (1897–1907), 20

AI-YE (1950), 178

AIRSHIP DESTROYER, THE (1909): see BEGINNINGS OF BRITISH FILM, THE (1901–11), 22

ALADDIN (1953), 174

ALBERTO GIACOMETTI (1966), 255

ALCOFRISBAS, THE MASTER MAGICIAN (L'ENCHANTEUR ALCOFRISBAS) (1903): see MAGIC FILMS (1898–1905), 21

ALEXANDER CALDER: SCULPTURE AND CONSTRUCTIONS (1944), 253

ALEXANDER NEVSKY (1938), 88

ALL MY BABIES (1952), 133

ALL MY LIFE (1966), 190

ALLEGRETTO (1936): see OSKAR FISCHINGER PROGRAM II (1930–41), 171

ALLES DREHT SICH, ALLES BEWEGT SICH!: see EVERYTHING TURNS, EVERYTHING REVOLVES! (1929), 262

ALONE AND THE SEA (1971), 94

ALOUETTE (1944), 240

AMELIA AND THE ANGEL (1958), 91

AMERICA (1924), 61

AMERICA TODAY and THE WORLD IN REVIEW (1932–34): see FILM AND PHOTO LEAGUE PROGRAM II (1931–34), 114

AMERICAN MARCH, AN (1941): see OSKAR FISCHINGER PROGRAM II (1930–41), 171

AMERICAN MUSICALS: FAMOUS PRODUCTION NUMBERS (1929–35), 78

AMERICAN POTTER, AN (1976), 256

AMITIÉ NOIRE, L' (1944), 131

AMOR PEDESTRE (1914), 44

AMOURS DE LA REINE ÉLISABETH, LES: see QUEEN ELIZABETH (1912), 30

AMY! (1979), 227

AN . . . for English titles beginning with AN, see the next word of the title.

ANALOGIES #1 (1953), 179

ANALOGIES: STUDIES IN THE MOVEMENT OF TIME (1977), 203

AND SO THEY LIVE (1940), 126

ANEMIC CINEMA (1926), 167

ANGEL IN THE HOUSE (1979), 227

ANIMAL MOVIE, THE (1966), 246

ANIMATION FOR LIVE ACTION (1978), 224

ANIMATION FROM CAPE DORSET (1973), 247

ANIMATION PROGRAM (1908–33), 29

ANNA CHRISTIE (1923), 60

ANTHOLOGY OF THE ITALIAN CINEMA: THE SILENT FILM FROM 1896 TO 1926, AN (ANTOLOGIA DEL CINEMA ITALIANO: IL FILM MUTO DAL 1896 AL 1926) (1955), 260

ANTHOLOGY OF THE ITALIAN CINEMA: THE SOUND FILM FROM 1929 TO 1943, AN (ANTOLOGIA DEL CINEMA ITALIANO: IL FILM SONORO DAL 1929 AL 1943) (ca. 1955), 260

ANTICIPATION OF THE NIGHT (1958), 183

ANTOLOGIA DEL CINEMA ITALIANO: IL FILM MUTO DAL 1896 AL 1926; see ANTHOLOGY OF THE ITALIAN CINEMA: THE SILENT FILM FROM 1896 TO 1926, AN (1955), 260

ANTOLOGIA DEL CINEMA ITALIANO: IL FILM SONORO DAL 1929 AL 1943; see ANTHOLOGY OF THE ITALIAN CINEMA: THE SOUND FILM FROM 1929 TO 1943, AN (ca. 1955), 260

ANTONIO GAUDI (1965), 255

APALACHEE (1974), 199

APERTURA (1970), 194

APHRODISIAC (1971), 196

APHRODISIAC II (1972), 197

APPARITIONS FUGITIVES, LES: see FUGITIVE APPARITIONS, THE (1904), 21

APPLAUSE (1929), 79

APPOINTMENT BY TELEPHONE (1902): see BEFORE THE NICKELODEON: THE EARLY CINEMA OF EDWIN S. PORTER (1982), 267

ARABESQUE (1975), 201

ARCHITECTURE D'AUJOURD'HUI, L' (1931), 253

ARMS AND THE LEAGUE (THE LEAGUE OF NATIONS) (1938), 124

AROUND THE WORLD IN 80 MINUTES: see AROUND THE WORLD WITH DOUGLAS FAIRBANKS (1931), 80

AROUND THE WORLD WITH DOUGLAS FAIRBANKS (1931), 80

ARRIVAL OF EXPRESS AT LYONS (ARRIVÉE D'UN TRAIN) (1895): see LUMIÈRE PROGRAM I: FIRST PROGRAMS (1895–96), 1

ARRIVÉE D'UN TRAIN: see ARRIVAL OF EXPRESS AT LYONS (1895), 19

ARRIVÉE EN GONDOLE: see GONDOLA PARTY (1896), 19

ARROSEUR EST ARROSÉ, L': see TEASING THE GARDENER (1895), 20

ARSENAL (1929), 73

ARSENAL (excerpt) (1929): see LANGUAGE OF THE SILENT CINEMA, THE (1973), 264

ART OF LOTTE REINIGER, THE (1970), 174

ART OF THE POTTER, THE (1972), 256

ARTIST'S DILEMMA, THE (1901): see MAGIC FILMS (1898–1905), 21

ASSASSINAT DU DUC DE GUISE, L': see ASSASSINATION OF THE DUC DE GUISE, THE (1908), 30

ASSASSINATION OF ALEXANDER AND BARTHOU (1934): see ASSASSINATION OF KING ALEXANDER OF JUGOSLAVIA, 259

ASSASSINATION OF KING ALEXANDER OF JUGOSLAVIA (ASSASSINATION OF ALEXANDER AND BARTHOU) (1934), 259

ASSASSINATION OF THE DUC DE GUISE, THE (L'ASSASSINAT DU DUC DE GUISE) (1908): see FILM D'ART, THE (1908–12), 30

ASSASSINATION OF THE DUC DE GUISE, THE (L'ASSASSINAT DU DUC DE GUISE) (excerpt) (1908): see LANGUAGE OF THE SILENT CINEMA, THE (1973), 264

ASSUNTA SPINA (1915), 47

ASSUNTA SPINA (excerpt) (1915): see LANGUAGE OF THE SILENT CINEMA, THE (1973), 264

ASTRAY FROM THE STEERAGE (1920): see MACK SENNETT PROGRAM II (1916–20), 50

@ (AT) (1979), 207

AT THE CROSSROADS OF LIFE (1908), 29

ATMOSFEAR (1967), 191

AU BAGNE: see SCENES OF CONVICT LIFE (1905), 25

AUTOBIOGRAPHY OF A "JEEP," THE (1943), 130

AUTUMN FIRE (1931), 172

AVENGING CONSCIENCE, THE (1914), 45

B

BABY AND THE STORK, THE (1912), 38

↔ (BACK AND FORTH) (1969), 193

BACK-BREAKING LEAF, THE (1959), 243

BACKYARD (1976), 202

BAIGNADE DE NÉGRILLONS: see NEGROES BATHING (1898), 20

BAINS DE DIANE, MILAN: see BATHS AT MILAN, ITALY (1896), 19

BALLAD OF LOVE, A (CVOYE; TWO PEOPLE) (1965), 93

BALLET MASTER'S DREAM, THE (LE RÊVE DU MAÎTRE DE BALLET) (1903): see MAGIC FILMS (1898–1905), 21

BALLET MÉCANIQUE (1924), 167

BAMBINI IN CITTA (1946), 132

BANK, THE (1915): see CHAPLIN'S ESSANAY FILMS (1915–16), 47

BARK RIND (1977), 203

BARQUE SORTANT DU PORT: see BOAT LEAVING THE HARBOR (1896–97), 20

BASSIN DES TUILERIES: see BOYS SAILING BOATS, TUILERIES GARDEN, PARIS (1896), 19

BATHS AT MILAN, ITALY (BAINS DE DIANE, MILAN) (1896): see LUMIÈRE PROGRAM I: FIRST PROGRAMS (1895–96), 19

BATTLE AT ELDERBUSH GULCH, THE (1914), 45

BATTLE IS THEIR BIRTHRIGHT (1943), 239

BATTLE OF BRITAIN, THE (1943) [WHY WE FIGHT Series (1942–45)], 129

BATTLE OF CHINA, THE (1944) [WHY WE FIGHT Series (1942–45)], 130

BATTLE OF MIDWAY, THE (1942), 127

BATTLE OF RUSSIA, THE (1943) [WHY WE FIGHT Series (1942–45)], 130

BATTLE OF SAN PIETRO, THE (SAN PIETRO) (1945), 131

BATTLE OF WESTLANDS, THE (1980), 140

BATTLESHIP "MARYLAND" LAUNCHED (1920): see PATHÉ NEWSREEL, THE (1917–31), 109

BEAD GAME (1977), 249

BEAU GESTE (1926), 66

BED, THE (1968), 192

BED AND SOFA (TRETYA MESHCHANSKAYA) (1926), 66

BEFORE THE NICKELODEON: THE EARLY CINEMA OF EDWIN S. PORTER (1982), 267

BEGINNINGS OF BRITISH FILM, THE (1901–11), 22

BEGONE DULL CARE (1949), 241

BELLS OF ATLANTIS (1952), 178

BEN HUR (1907), 27

BERG-EJVIND OCH HANS HUSTRU: see OUTLAW AND HIS WIFE, THE (1918), 52

BERLIN, DIE SINFONIE DER GROSSTADT: see BERLIN: SYMPHONY OF A GREAT CITY (1927), 110

BERLIN: SYMPHONY OF A GREAT CITY (BERLIN, DIE SINFONIE DER GROSSTADT) (1927), 110

BETHUNE (1964), 245

BETWEEN NIGHT AND THE LIGHT OF DAY (1978), 205

BIG BANG AND OTHER CREATION MYTHS, THE (1981), 211

BIG BUSINESS (1929), 74

BILLABONG (1968), 192

BILLY SUNDAY BURNS UP THE BACKSLIDING WORLD (1931): see PATHÉ NEWSREEL, THE (1917–31), 109

BIRTH OF A NATION, THE (1915), 47

BIRTH OF A NATION, THE (Battle sequence) (1915), 259

BIRTH OF A NATION, THE (Final rescue sequence) (1915): see LANGUAGE OF THE SILENT CINEMA, THE (1973), 264

BIRTH OF A NATION, THE (Homecoming sequence) (1915), 259

BIRTH OF A NATION, THE [Wyborny]: see GEBURT DER NATION, DIE (1973), 199

BISMARCK (excerpt) (1940): see GERMANY, AWAKE! (1968), 263

BLACK AND TAN (BLACK AND TAN FANTASY) (1929), 79

BLACK DIAMOND EXPRESS, THE (1896): see FILMS OF THE 1890S (1894–99), 18

BLACK FIVE (1968), 220

BLACK SHEEP (1912), 38

BLACKMAIL (1929), 79

BLACKTOP (1952), 179

BLADE AF SATANS BOG: see LEAVES FROM SATAN'S BOOK (1921), 57

BLAUE ENGEL, DER: see BLUE ANGEL, THE (1930), 80

BLAZES (1961): see ROBERT BREER PROGRAM II (1954–68), 180

BLEEDING GERMANY: see BLUTENDES DEUTSCHLAND (Concluding sequence) (1933), 116

BLIND HUSBANDS (1919), 52

BLINKITY BLANK (1955), 242

BLONDE COBRA (1963), 187

BLONDE VENUS (1932), 82

BLOOD AND SAND (1922), 58

BLOT, THE (1921), 57

BLOT IN THE 'SCUTCHEON, A (1912), 38

BLUE ANGEL, THE (DER BLAUE ENGEL) (1930), 80

BLUE EXPRESS: see CHINA EXPRESS (1929), 74

BLUE MOSES (1962), 186

BLUEBOTTLES (1928), 71

BLUTENDES DEUTSCHLAND (BLEEDING GERMANY) (Concluding sequence) (1933): see NAZI PROPAGANDA FILMS (1933–37), 116

BOARDING SCHOOL GIRLS (1905), 25

BOAT LEAVING THE HARBOR (BARQUE SORTANT DU PORT) (1896–97): see LUMIÈRE PROGRAM II: EARLY LUMIÈRE FILMS (1895–98), 20

BOBBY, THE COWARD (1911), 34

BOILER LOADING (n.d.): see LUMIÈRE PROGRAM I: FIRST PROGRAMS (1895–96), 19

BONDI (1979), 208

BONUS MARCH 1932 (1932): see FILM AND PHOTO LEAGUE PROGRAM II (1931–34), 114

BORING AFTERNOON, A (FÁDNÍ ODPOLEDNE) (1965), 93

BOXER, THE (ca. 1925): see OSKAR FISCHINGER PROGRAM V (1923–27), 166

BOYS SAILING BOATS, TUILERIES GARDEN, PARIS (BASSIN DES TUILERIES) (1896): see LUMIÈRE PROGRAM I: FIRST PROGRAMS (1895–96), 19

BRAND NEW DAY, A (1974): see JANE AARON PROGRAM (1974–80), 200

BRANDING: see BREAKERS (1929), 170

BREAKERS (BRANDING) (1929), 170

BREAKFAST (TABLE-TOP DOLLY) (1976), 202

BREATHDEATH (1963), 188

BREATHING (1963), 188

BRICKWALL (1975), 201

BRIDE RETIRES, THE (LE COUCHER DE LA MARIÉE) (1904): see CORRECTION PLEASE, OR, HOW WE GOT INTO PICTURES (1979), 227

BRIDGE, THE (DE BRUG) (1928) [Joris Ivens], 111

BRIDGE, THE (1944) [Van Dyke and Maddow], 131

BRIDGES-GO-ROUND (1958), 184

BROKEN BLOSSOMS (1919), 53

BROKEN CROSS, THE (1911), 34

BROKEN DOLL, THE (1910), 32

BROKEN LULLABY: see MAN I KILLED, THE (1932), 82

BRONCHO BILLY WESTERNS (1913–18), 42

BRONCHO BILLY'S CAPTURE (1913): see BRONCHO BILLY WESTERNS (1913–18), 42

BRONENOSETS POTEMKIN: see POTEMKIN (1925), 65

BRONX MORNING, A (1931), 112

BROTHERS (BRÜDER) (1929), 74

BRUCE CONNER PROGRAM (1958–78), 184

BRÜDER: see BROTHERS (1929), 74

BRUG, DE: see BRIDGE, THE (1928), 111

BRUTALITY (1912), 39

BULLFIGHT (1955), 181

BURNING STABLE: see FILMS OF THE 1890S (1894–99), 18

BY MAN'S LAW (1913), 42

BY THE LAW (PO ZAKONU) (1926), 67

FILMMAKER INDEX

COUNTRY INDEX

SUBJECT INDEX

ABSTRACT FILMS: see ANIMATION, ABSTRACT

ACTUALITIES: see NEWSREELS AND ACTUALITIES

ADVENTURES AND SWASHBUCKLERS
HIS MAJESTY THE AMERICAN (1919), 53
THE MARK OF ZORRO (1920), 56
THE THREE MUSKETEERS (1921), 58
BLOOD AND SAND (1922), 58
ROBIN HOOD (1922), 59
MONSIEUR BEAUCAIRE (1924), 63
THE THIEF OF BAGDAD (1924), 64
DON Q, SON OF ZORRO (1925), 64
BEAU GESTE (1926), 66
WHAT PRICE GLORY (1926), 68
THE IRON MASK (1929), 75
MR. ROBINSON CRUSOE (1932), 83
THE LIVES OF A BENGAL LANCER (1935), 86

ADVERTISING FILMS: see COMMERCIALS AND ADVERTISING FILMS

AFRICA
NEGROES BATHING (BAIGNADE DE NÉGRILLONS) (1898), 20
DANCE CONTEST IN ESIRA (DANSTAVLINGEN I ESIRA) (1936), 120
L'AMITIÉ NOIRE (1944), 131
KENTU (1974), 138
MUKISSI (1974), 138
THE PRICE OF A UNION (LA RANÇON D'UNE ALLIANCE) (1974), 94

AGING
WHAT SHALL WE DO WITH OUR OLD (1911), 37
MAKE WAY FOR TOMORROW (1937), 88
INDIAN SUMMER (1960), 134
NELL AND FRED (1971), 247
CHESTER GRIMES (1972), 138
THE STREET (1976), 249
A PRIVATE LIFE (1980), 95

AGRICULTURE
A CORNER IN WHEAT (1909), 30
NEW EARTH (NIEUWE GRONDEN) (1934), 117
OUR DAILY BREAD (1934), 84
THE PLOW THAT BROKE THE PLAINS (1936), 121
THE RIVER (1937), 122
THE ISLANDERS (1939), 125
POWER AND THE LAND (1940), 127
THE LAND (1942), 127
THE BRIDGE (1944), 131
THE BACK-BREAKING LEAF (1959), 243
RICE (1964), 135
THE BATTLE OF WESTLANDS (1980), 140

AIRPLANES: see AVIATION

ANIMATION, ABSTRACT: see also ANIMATION, DIRECT
OPUS FILMS II, III, IV (1921–24), 166
RHYTHMUS 21 (1921), 166, 262
OSKAR FISCHINGER PROGRAMS I–V (1923–53), 166, 168, 171, 173
RHYTHMUS 23 (1923), 262
SYMPHONIE DIAGONALE (1924), 167
HANS AND OSKAR FISCHINGER PROGRAM (1931–32), 172
GLENS FALLS SEQUENCE (1946), 175
THE LONG BODIES (1947), 176
MOTION-PAINTING I (1947), 177
A MAN AND HIS DOG OUT FOR AIR (1957), 182
BLAZES (1961), 180
HORSE OVER TEAKETTLE (1962), 187
MOSAIC (1965), 246

66 (1966), 180
69 (1968), 182
70 (1970), 196
77 (1977), 205
TZ (1979), 209

ANIMATION, CARTOON AND CEL
ANIMATION PROGRAM (1908–33), 29
LES JOYEUX MICROBES (1909), 27
LE PEINTRE NÉO-IMPRESSIONNISTE (1910), 27
WINSOR MCCAY PROGRAM (1911–21), 38
THE SEX LIFE OF THE POLYP (1928), 77
JOIE DE VIVRE (1934), 173
TRANSFER OF POWER (1939), 126
A LITTLE PHANTASY ON A NINETEENTH CENTURY PAINTING (1946), 240
THE ROMANCE OF TRANSPORTATION (1953), 242
HUFF AND PUFF (1955), 242
CATS (1956), 180
OF STARS AND MEN (1961), 186
THE HAT (1964), 189
THE ANIMAL MOVIE (1966), 246
PBL 2 (1968), 181
WALKING (1968), 246
FABLE SAFE (1971), 137
HOT STUFF (1971), 247
ANIMATION FROM CAPE DORSET (1973), 247
COCKABOODY (1973), 199
HOWARD DANELOWITZ PROGRAM (1973–79), 199
CAT'S CRADLE (1974), 248
JANE AARON PROGRAM (1974–80), 200
VOYAGE TO NEXT (1974), 201
AN OLD BOX (1975), 249
THE STREET (1976), 249
DAVID EHRLICH PROGRAM I (1977–79), 204
GOING HOME (1978), 206
JOHN LAW AND THE MISSISSIPPI BUBBLE (1978), 250
LA PLAGE (1978), 250
DAVID EHRLICH PROGRAM II (1979–80), 208
SEA DREAM (1979), 251
STEP BY STEP (1979), 209
SKY DANCE (1980), 210
A SUFI TALE (1980), 251
THE SWEATER (1980), 251
THE BIG BANG AND OTHER CREATION MYTHS (1981), 211

ANIMATION, COLLAGE
UN MIRACLE (1954), 180
RECREATION (1956), 182
JAMESTOWN BALOOS (1957), 180
WHEEEELS, OR, AMERICA ON WHEELS, PART 2 (1958), 184
A LA MODE (1959), 184
SCIENCE FRICTION (1959), 185
BREATHDEATH (1963), 188
DUO CONCERTANTES (1964), 189
FIST FIGHT (1964), 189
OUR LADY OF THE SPHERE (1969), 194
LMNO (1978), 206
MARCEL DUCHAMP IN HIS OWN WORDS (1978), 257
RAPUNZEL LET DOWN YOUR HAIR (1978), 226

ANIMATION, COMPUTER
CATALOG (1961), 186
EXPERIMENTS IN MOTION GRAPHICS (1968), 192
PERMUTATIONS (1968), 192
MATRIX (1971), 196
MATRIX III (1972), 198
HUNGER (1973), 248
ARABESQUE (1975), 201
EUCLIDEAN ILLUSIONS (1979), 208

ANIMATION, CUTOUT AND SILHOUETTE
IRENE DANCES (IRENE TANZT) (ca. 1925), 166

ORDERING INFORMATION

The prices in this catalog are effective for 1983–85 but are subject to change.

Rentals

1. **Fees.** Rental charges are for one showing. Additional showings on consecutive days are 50% of the rental fee. There is a shipping-handling charge in addition to the rental fee for each film.

2. **Conditions.** Rental fees are for educational use with unpaid admissions. Any other use must be confirmed in writing by the Circulating Film Library. An asterisk (*) on the Price List indicates films for which no admission charge may be made at any time and for which no contributions can be collected. Two asterisks (**) indicate films that may be rented only for the sole purpose of classroom film study under the auspices of film study departments. *Films may not be duplicated or televised* without written permission from the Circulating Film Library.

3. **Returning films.** The renter is responsible for the return of the films, which must be shipped the day after the screening via UPS or U.S. Priority Mail. Features should be insured for $700 and shorts for $200.

4. **Reservations.** Films may be booked by telephone but this must be followed by a purchase order or a letter of confirmation before a film is shipped. A confirmation of the booking will be sent to the renter upon receipt of the written order. Cancellations must be received before a film is shipped, otherwise the full rental fee will be charged.

5. **Damage and loss.** The renter is responsible for the care of the films and will be charged for damage and loss. *To avoid damage always keep your projector gate clean and stay beside the projector during the screening.* Do not rewind the films, and make sure that the film leader is securely taped down for shipping.

Sales and Leases

1. Sales are in 16mm format and are for noncommercial, nontheatrical, and educational use for the life of the print. Sale prints may not be duplicated, copied, altered, or televised. Lease prints must be returned to the Museum at the end of the licensing period. Several of our recent films are also available on videocassette. "NA" in the sales column of the Price List indicates that a film is available only for rental.

2. A number of our titles are available for preview-for-possible-purchase by authorized persons in educational organizations. Features and silent films are not available for preview. Previewing privileges are not extended to renters.

3. For television and other rights, please apply.

Film stills may be ordered through the Museum's Film Stills Archive.

The resources of the Museum's Film Study Center are available by appointment to university students, researchers, and scholars.

A catalog of the Circulating Video Library consisting of work of independent video is available upon request.

PRICE LIST

TITLE		RENTAL	SALES
A			
A LA MODE		$20	$200
ABOVE US THE EARTH		$90	NA
AI-YE		$30	$350
ALBERTO GIACOMETTI		$20	NA
ALEXANDER CALDER: SCULPTURE AND CONSTRUCTIONS		$20	$110
ALEXANDER NEVSKY		$60	$575
ALL MY BABIES		$40	$550
ALL MY LIFE		$20	NA
ALLADIN		$35	$140
ALLEGRETTO (Rental: see OSKAR FISCHINGER PROGRAM II)		—	$115
ALONE AND THE SEA		$33	NA
ALOUETTE		$20	$100
AMELIA AND THE ANGEL		$35	$300
AMERICA		$60	NA
AMERICA TODAY and THE WORLD IN REVIEW: see FILM AND PHOTO LEAGUE PROGRAM II)		—	$225
AMERICAN MARCH, AN (Rental: see OSKAR FISCHINGER PROGRAM II)		—	$110
AMERICAN MUSICALS: FAMOUS PRODUCTION NUMBERS		$65	NA
AMERICAN POTTER, AN		$48	$475
AMITIÉ NOIRE, L'		$30	NA
AMOR PEDESTRE		$20	NA
AMY!		$40	APPLY
ANALOGIES #1		$25	$130
ANALOGIES: STUDIES IN THE MOVEMENT OF TIME		$30	$300
AND SO THEY LIVE		$35	NA
ANEMIC CINEMA		$20	$65
ANGEL IN THE HOUSE		$35	APPLY
ANIMAL MOVIE, THE		$40	$275
ANIMATION FOR LIVE ACTION		$35	$300
ANIMATION FROM CAPE DORSET		$25	$410
ANIMATION PROGRAM		$45	see individual titles
ANNA CHRISTIE		$45	$400
ANTHOLOGY OF THE ITALIAN CINEMA: THE SILENT FILM FROM 1896 TO 1926, AN		$55	NA
ANTHOLOGY OF THE ITALIAN CINEMA: THE SOUND FILM FROM 1929 TO 1943, AN		$55	NA
ANTICIPATION OF THE NIGHT		$55	NA
ANTONIO GAUDI		$40	NA
APALACHEE		$30	$300
APERTURA		$20	$165
APHRODISIAC		$20	$165
APHRODISIAC II		$20	$165
APPLAUSE	(high school)	$50*	NA
	(university)	$75*	
ARABESQUE		$20	$150
ARCHITECTURE D'AUJOURD'HUI, L'		$20	NA
ARMS AND THE LEAGUE		$20	NA
AROUND THE WORLD WITH DOUGLAS FAIRBANKS		$60	NA
ARSENAL		$60	NA
ART OF LOTTE REINGER, THE		$40	$360
ART OF THE POTTER, THE		$60	NA
ASSASSINATION OF KING ALEXANDER OF JUGOSLAVIA		$25	NA
ASSUNTA SPINA		$45	NA
ASTRAY FROM THE STEERAGE		$30	$130
@ (AT)		$20	NA
AT THE CROSSROADS OF LIFE		$20	$65
ATMOSFEAR		$20	NA
AUTOBIOGRAPHY OF A "JEEP," THE		$20	$65
AUTUMN FIRE		$30	NA
AVENGING CONSCIENCE, THE		$40	NA
B			
BABY AND THE STORK, THE		$20	$65
↔ (BACK AND FORTH)		$70	NA
BACK-BREAKING LEAF, THE		$30	$500
BACKYARD		$25	$225
BALLAD OF LOVE, A		$45	NA
BALLET MÉCANIQUE		$20	NA
BAMBINI IN CITTA		$25	NA
BANK, THE		$20	$80

TITLE		RENTAL	SALES
BARK RIND		$35	$450
BATTLE AT ELDERBUSH GULCH, THE		$25	$110
BATTLE IS THEIR BIRTHRIGHT		$30	$410
BATTLE OF BRITAIN, THE		$40	NA
BATTLE OF CHINA, THE		$40	$440
BATTLE OF MIDWAY, THE		$25	$250
BATTLE OF RUSSIA, THE		$40	NA
BATTLE OF SAN PIETRO, THE		$35	NA
BATTLE OF WESTLANDS, THE		$90	$750
BEAD GAME		$20**	NA
BEAU GESTE		$60	NA
BED, THE		$40	$375
BED AND SOFA		$50	NA
BEFORE THE NICKELODEON: THE EARLY CINEMA OF EDWIN S. PORTER		$100	$890
(Sept. 1 to Oct. 15)		$125	
BEGINNINGS OF BRITISH FILM, THE		$35	NA
BEGONE DULL CARE		$20**	NA
BELLS OF ATLANTIS		$22	$200
BEN HUR		$20	$65
BERLIN: SYMPHONY OF A GREAT CITY		$50	NA
BETHUNE		$40	$775
BETWEEN NIGHT AND THE LIGHT OF DAY		$25	$150
BIG BANG AND OTHER CREATION MYTHS, THE		$20	$225
BIG BUSINESS		$30	NA
BILLABONG		$22	NA
BIRTH OF A NATION, THE (black & white)		$75	NA
BIRTH OF A NATION, THE (color)		$75	$800
BIRTH OF A NATION, THE (Battle sequence)		$20	$65
BIRTH OF A NATION, THE (Homecoming sequence)		$20	$65
BLACK AND TAN		$30	$125
BLACK FIVE		$38	APPLY
BLACK SHEEP		$20	$65
BLACKMAIL		$55	NA
BLACKTOP		$20	$175
BLAZES (Rental: see ROBERT BREER PROGRAM II)		—	$170
BLIND HUSBANDS		$55	NA
BLINKITY BLANK		$20**	NA
BLONDE COBRA		$70	NA
BLONDE VENUS	(high school)	$50*	NA
	(university)	$75*	
BLOOD AND SAND		$50	NA
BLOT, THE		$50	NA
BLOT IN THE 'SCUTCHEON, A		$20	$95
BLUE ANGEL, THE		$60	NA
BLUE MOSES		$20	NA
BLUEBOTTLES		$30	NA
BOARDING SCHOOL GIRLS		$20	$50
BOBBY, THE COWARD		$20	$60
BONDI		$35	$275
BONUS MARCH 1932 (Rental: see FILM AND PHOTO LEAGUE PROGRAM II)		—	$225
BORING AFTERNOON, A		$28	NA
BOXER, THE: (Rental: see OSKAR FISCHINGER PROGRAM V)		—	see SPIRITUAL CONSTRUCTIONS
BRAND NEW DAY, A (Rental: see JANE AARON PROGRAM)		—	$100
BREAKERS		$25	NA
BREAKFAST		$30	NA
BREATHDEATH		$25	$300
BREATHING		$20	$225
BRICKWALL		$35	$330
BRIDGE, THE [Joris Ivens]		$20	NA
BRIDGE, THE [Van Dyke and Maddow]		$35	NA
BRIDGES-GO-ROUND		$25	$235
BROKEN BLOSSOMS (Color or B&W)		$50	$500
BROKEN CROSS, THE		$20	$65
BROKEN DOLL, THE		$20	$65
BRONCHO BILLY WESTERNS		$38	see individual titles
BRONCHO BILLY'S CAPTURE (Rental: see BRONCHO BILLY WESTERNS)		—	$65
BRONX MORNING, A		$20	$65
BROTHERS		$40	NA
BRUCE CONNER PROGRAM		$70	NA
BRUTALITY		$20	$50
BULLFIGHT		$25	$235
BY MAN'S LAW		$25	$110
BY THE LAW		$40	NA

TITLE	RENTAL	SALES
C		
CABINET OF DR. CALIGARI, THE	$45	NA
CABIRIA	$55	NA
CADET ROUSSELLE	$20**	NA
CAGE, THE	$45	$260
CALDER MAN, THE	$30	NA
CALIPH STORK	$25	$125
CAMERA GOES ALONG!, THE and FLIEGER, FUNKER, KANONIERE! (FLIEGER, FUNKER, KANONIERE! sells individually)	$30	—
CAMPAIGN IN POLAND	$40	NA
CAN CAN	$20	$125
CANON	$20**	NA
CARMEN (Escape from prison sequence)	$20	NA
CARS	$27	$250
CASTRO STREET	$20	NA
CAT AND THE CANARY, THE	$50	NA
CATALOG	$22	$110
CATCH OF THE SEASON, THE	$20	NA
CATS (Rental: see ROBERT BREER PROGRAM II)	—	$130
CAT'S CRADLE [Stan Brakhage]	$20	NA
CAT'S CRADLE [Driessen and Sarault]	$20**	NA
CENERE	$35	NA
CHAIRY TALE, A	$20**	NA
CHANTS	$25	$225
CHAPLIN'S ESSANAY FILMS	$45	see individual titles
CHAPLIN'S KEYSTONE FILMS	$40	see individual titles
CHARCOAL STUDY FOR SPIRITUAL CONSTRUCTIONS (Rental: see OSKAR FISCHINGER PROGRAM V)	—	see SPIRITUAL CONSTRUCTIONS
CHARMED PARTICLES	$125	NA
CHESS FEVER	$35	NA
CHESTER GRIMES	$30	$400
CHIEF'S DAUGHTER, THE	$20	$65
CHIEN ANDALOU, UN	$28	NA
CHILDREN	$45	NA
CHILDREN AT SCHOOL	$28	NA
CHINA EXPRESS	$40	NA
CHINESE FIREDRILL	$40	NA
CHRONICLE OF THE GRAY HOUSE, THE	$50	NA
CHURCHILL'S ISLAND	$30	$410
CINDERELLA	$25	$125
CIRCLES (Abstract version) (Rental: see OSKAR FISCHINGER PROGRAM II)	—	$110
CIRCLES (Advertising version) (Rental: see OSKAR FISCHINGER PROGRAM II)	—	$130
CITY, THE	$45	$300
CITY OF CONTRASTS	$20	$110
CITY OF GOLD	$30	$410
CIVILIZATION	$50	NA
CLASSIC AMERICAN MUTOSCOPE, THE	$22	NA
CLEVER DUMMY, A	$25	$110
CLINIC OF STUMBLE	$35	$250
CLOAK, THE	$50	NA
COCKABOODY	$25	NA
COHEN'S FIRE SALE	$20	$65
COHL, FEUILLADE AND DURAND PROGRAM	$25	NA
COLLEGE CHUMS	$20	$65
COLOR CRY	$22	$150
COLORATURA (Rental: see OSKAR FISCHINGER PROGRAM II)	—	$65
COLOUR BOX, A	$20	NA
COMING OF SOUND, THE	$35	NA
COMMUNICATIONS PRIMER, A	$30	NA
COMPOSITION IN BLUE (Rental: see OSKAR FISCHINGER PROGRAM II)	—	$160
COMRADES	$20	$65
CONSCIENCE	$20	$65
CORNELL, 1965	$25	$400
CORNER IN WHEAT, A	$20	$65
CORRAL	$20**	NA
CORRECTION PLEASE, OR, HOW WE GOT INTO PICTURES	$90	$750
CORRIDOR	$30	NA
CORTILE CASCINO	$50	$400
COTTAGE ON DARTMOOR, A	$50	NA
COUNTRY DOCTOR, THE	$20	$65
COVERED WAGON, THE	$60	NA
COWARD, THE	$45	$300

TITLE	RENTAL	SALES
CRADLE OF COURAGE, THE	$45	NA
CRAZY RAY, THE	$45	NA
D		
DADASCOPE	$125	$500
DANCE CONTEST IN ESIRA	$20	NA
DANCE IN THE SUN	$25	$185
DANIEL BOONE, OR, PIONEER DAYS IN AMERICA	$20	$65
DARK	$35	$250
DARLING, DO YOU LOVE ME?	$20	NA
DASH THROUGH THE CLOUDS, A	$20	$65
DAVID	$35	$300
DAVID EHRLICH PROGRAM I	$35	$325
DAVID EHRLICH PROGRAM II	$35	$300
DAY DREAMS	$30	NA
DAYBREAK and WHITEYE	$20	NA
DAYS BEFORE CHRISTMAS, THE	$30	$500
DEAD, THE	$25	NA
DEAD YOUTH	$25	NA
DEAR PHONE	$28	$250
DEATH MILLS	$35	$110
DEATH'S MARATHON	$20	$65
DESERT VICTORY	$45	NA
DESIRE (high school)	$50*	NA
(university)	$75*	
DESISTFILM	$20	NA
DESTINY	$50	NA
DETECTIVE'S TOUR OF THE WORLD, A	$20	NA
DETROIT WORKERS NEWS SPECIAL 1932: FORD MASSACRE (Rental: see FILM AND PHOTO LEAGUE PROGRAM I)	—	$150
DEUS EX	$50	NA
DEVIL IS A WOMAN, THE (high school)	$50*	NA
(university)	$75*	
DIRECTORS AT WORK: THE DIRECTOR AND THE ACTOR	$25	$150 (Lease)
DIRECTORS AT WORK: THE DIRECTOR AND THE IMAGE	$25	$150 (Lease)
DIVIDE AND CONQUER	$45	NA
DR. MABUSE, THE GAMBLER	$50	NA
DOCTOR'S DREAM, THE	$45	NA
DOG STAR MAN	$140	NA
DOLLAR DANCE	$20	$100
DON Q, SON OF ZORRO	$50	NA
DOROTHEA LANGE. PART ONE: UNDER THE TREES	$38	NA
DOROTHEA LANGE. PART TWO: THE CLOSER FOR ME	$38	NA
DOTS	$20	NA
DOWN THE CORNER	$75	NA
DREAM OF THE RACE-TRACK FIEND, THE	$20	$65
DREAM OF A RAREBIT FIEND, THE	$20	$65
DREAMS THAT MONEY CAN BUY	$125	$750
DUCK SOUP (high school)	$75*	NA
(university)	$95*	
DUO CONCERTANTES	$20	NA
E		
EARLY FILMS OF INTEREST	$25	NA
EARLY GERMAN FILMS	$38	NA
EARTH SINGS, THE	$40	NA
EASTER ISLAND	$30	NA
EASY LIVING (high school)	$40*	NA
(university)	$50*	
ECLIPSE	$50	NA
ÉCOLE BUISSONNIÈRE, L'	$45	NA
EDISON PROGRAM	$20	$50
EDWIN S. PORTER PROGRAM I	$40	see individual titles
EDWIN S. PORTER PROGRAM II: SOCIAL ISSUES	$40	see individual titles
8 × 8	$125	$750
1860	$50	NA
EISENSTEIN'S MEXICAN FILM: EPISODES FOR STUDY PART I	$50	$500
EISENSTEIN'S MEXICAN FILM: EPISODES FOR STUDY PART II	$50	$500
EMAK-BAKIA	$25	NA
EN PASSANT	$20	$100
END OF ST. PETERSBURG, THE	$60	NA
ENOCH ARDEN [D. W. Griffith]	$25	$100

TITLE	RENTAL	SALES	TITLE	RENTAL	SALES
ENOCH ARDEN (Extant reels: Conclusion) [William Christy Cabanne]	$25	NA	GEBURT DER NATION, DIE	$80	$1000
ENOUGH TO EAT?	$30	NA	GENERAL, THE	$40	$550
ENTHUSIASM, SYMPHONY OF THE DON BASIN	$50	NA	GEORGES MÉLIÈS PROGRAM	$48	NA
			GERMAN NEWSREELS	$28	NA
ENTR'ACTE	$30	NA	GERMANY, AWAKE!	$70	$750
ETERNAL MOTHER, THE	$20	$65	GETTING ACQUAINTED	$20	$55
ÉTOILE DE MER, L'	$20	NA	GETTING EVIDENCE	$20	$65
EUCLIDEAN ILLUSIONS	$25	$300	GHOSTS BEFORE BREAKFAST	$20	$80
EVENT ON THE BEACH, AN	$25	$125	GIRL AND HER TRUST, THE (Rental: see LONEDALE OPERATOR, THE and THE GIRL AND HER TRUST)	—	$65
EVERY DAY EXCEPT CHRISTMAS	$40	NA			
EVOLUTION	$20	$90			
EVOLUTION OF THE SKYSCRAPER	$40	NA	GLENN GOULD: OFF THE RECORD	$30	$500
EX-CONVICT, THE	$20	$65	GLENN GOULD: ON THE RECORD	$30	$500
EXCUSE MY DUST	$45	NA	GLENN GOULD: ON THE RECORD and OFF THE RECORD	$60	$1000
EXPERIMENTS IN MOTION GRAPHICS	$25	$200			
EXTRAORDINARY ADVENTURES OF MR. WEST IN THE LAND OF THE BOLSHEVIKS, THE	$40	NA	GLENS FALLS SEQUENCE	$20	NA
			GOING HOME	$20	$50
			GOING THE DISTANCE	$50	$925
F			GOLDEN POSITIONS, THE	$60	$500
			GOLEM, THE	$45	NA
FABLE SAFE	$25	$160	GONDOLA EYE, THE	$20	$375
FALL	$35	$350	GOSPEL ACCORDING TO ST. MATTHEW, THE	$85	NA
FALL OF THE HOUSE OF USHER, THE [Watson and Webber]	$25	NA	GOVERNOR, THE	$85	NA
			GRANTON TRAWLER	$20	NA
FALL OF THE HOUSE OF USHER, THE [Jean Epstein]	$48	NA	GRASS	$45	$375
			GRASSHOPPER AND THE ANT, THE	$25	$125
FALL OF THE ROMANOV DYNASTY, THE	$38	NA	GREAT ACTRESSES OF THE PAST	$45	NA
FALL OF TROY, THE	$20	NA	GREAT BLONDINO, THE	$75	$1000
FALLS, THE	$175	NA	GREAT TRAIN ROBBERY, THE (Color or B&W)	$20	$80
FANTÔMAS. Episode 2: JUVE VS. FANTÔMAS	$45	NA	GRIERSON	$40	$775
FAREWELL ETAOIN SHRDLU	$50	$400	GRIFFITH BIOGRAPH PROGRAM	$45	$325
FATHER SERGIUS	$50	NA	GRIFFITH'S WESTERNS	$45	see individual titles
FEELING OF REJECTION, THE	$30	$410			
FELIX GETS THE CAN	$20	$55	GUERNICA	$25	NA
FERDINAND ZECCA PROGRAM	$35	NA	GULLS AND BUOYS	$22	$325
FIDDLE-DE-DEE	$20**	NA			
FIÈVRE	$38	NA	**H**		
FIGHTING THE FLAMES, DREAMLAND and HIPPODROME RACES, DREAMLAND, CONEY ISLAND	$20	$65			
			H IS FOR HOUSE	$20	$200
			H_2O	$20	$80
FILM, A	$20	NA	HALLELUJAH THE HILLS	$80	NA
FILM AND PHOTO LEAGUE PROGRAM I	$70	see individual titles	HANDS UP!	$55	NA
			HANS AND OSKAR FISCHINGER PROGRAM	$28	see individual titles
FILM AND PHOTO LEAGUE PROGRAM II	$70	see individual titles			
			HAT, THE	$35	$275
FILM D'ART, THE	$45	NA	HEADSTREAM (Rental: see HOWARD DANELOWITZ PROGRAM)	—	$100
FILMS BY STAN BRAKHAGE: AN AVANT-GARDE HOME MOVIE	$15	NA			
			HEART OF SPAIN	$50	$400
FILMS OF THE 1890S	$22	$65	HEARTS OF THE WORLD	$60	$500
FIRESIDE REMINISCENCES	$20	$55	HEAVY METAL	$25	$250
FIST FIGHT	$20	$350	HER AWAKENING	$20	$65
FIVE EASY PIECES	$50	NA	HER CHOICE	$20	$55
FIVE FILOSOPHICAL FABLES	$35	NA	HER DEFIANCE	$28	NA
FIVE FOR FOUR	$20	$150	HIGH AND DIZZY	$33	NA
FLIEGER, FUNKER, KANONIERE! (Rental: see THE CAMERA GOES ALONG!)	—	$65	HIGH OVER THE BORDERS	$28	NA
			HIGH STEEL	$25	$350
FOOL THERE WAS, A	$45	NA	HIGHWAY LANDSCAPE	$20	$150
FOOLISH WIVES	$65	NA	HIPPODROME RACES, DREAMLAND, CONEY ISLAND: see FIGHTING THE FLAMES, DREAMLAND and HIPPODROME RACES, DREAMLAND, CONEY ISLAND	—	—
FORGOTTEN VILLAGE, THE	$50	NA			
FOUR JOURNEYS INTO MYSTIC TIME	$65	$750			
FRAGMENT OF AN EMPIRE	$60	NA			
FREE RADICALS (Rental: see RHYTHM and FREE RADICALS and LEN LYE'S AMERICAN FILMS)	—	$150	HIROSHIMA-NAGASAKI, AUGUST 1945	$35	$300
			HIS BITTER PILL	$33	NA
			HIS MAJESTY THE AMERICAN	$50	NA
FROG PRINCE	$25	$125	HIS MOTHER'S SCARF	$20	$65
FROM DADA TO SURREALISM: 40 YEARS OF EXPERIMENT	$125	$500	HISTOIRE DU SOLDAT INCONNU, L'	$25	NA
			HITLERJUNGE QUEX	$60	NA
FUJI (Rental: see ROBERT BREER PROGRAM I)	—	$325	HOMAGE TO MAGRITTE	$30	NA
			HOME, SWEET HOME	$35	NA
FUN AFTER THE WEDDING	$20	NA	HOMMAGE TO JEAN TINGUELY'S "HOMMAGE TO NEW YORK"	$25	$225
FUNNIEST I KNOW IS MUD PUDDLES, THE (Rental: see HOWARD DANELOWITZ PROGRAM)	—	$65			
			HORSE OVER TEAKETTLE	$20	$325
			HOT STUFF	$20	$275
G			HOTEL IMPERIAL	$55	NA
			HOUSE	$22	NA
GALA DAY	$30	NA	HOUSE DIVIDED, A	$20	NA
GALATHEA	$25	$125	HOUSING PROBLEMS	$25	NA
GALLANT LITTLE TAILOR	$25	$125	HOW TO BUILD AN IGLOO	$20**	NA
GAUCHO, THE	$50	NA	HOWARD DANELOWITZ PROGRAM	$48	see indivicual titles
GAY SHOE CLERK, THE (Rental: see EDWIN S. PORTER PROGRAM I)	—	$30			
			HUFF AND PUFF	$20	$200
			HUNGER	$20**	NA
			HUNGER: THE NATIONAL HUNGER MARCH TO WASHINGTON 1932 (Rental: see FILM		

TITLE	RENTAL	SALES	TITLE	RENTAL	SALES
AND PHOTO LEAGUE PROGRAM I)	—	$275	LAST OF THE LINE, THE	$25	NA
HYMN TO HER	$15	NA	LATE MATTHEW PASCAL, THE	$60	NA
			LAUGHING GAS	$20	$65
I			LE CORBUSIER DESIGNS FOR HARVARD	$20	$150
			LEAD SHOES, THE	$45	$300
IAN HUGO: ENGRAVER AND FILM MAKER	$20	$165	LEAVES FROM SATAN'S BOOK	$60	NA
ICE	$20	$150	LEN LYE'S AMERICAN FILMS	$40	see individual
IDÉE, L'	$44	NA			titles
IDYLLE SUR LE SABLE	$25	NA	LESSER EVIL, THE	$20	$65
IMAGES MÉDIÉVALES	$30	NA	LET THERE BE LIGHT	$40	NA
IMMORTAL SWAN	$48	NA	LETTRE, LA	$20	NA
IN PARIS PARKS	$30	$285	LEVITATION	$22	$165
IN PLAIN SIGHT (Rental: see JANE AARON			LIFE	$20	NA
PROGRAM)	—	$100	LIFE AND DEATH OF 9413—A HOLLYWOOD		
IN THE DAYS OF '49	$20	$65	EXTRA, THE	$25	NA
IN THE FOREST	$150	NA	LIFE OF AN AMERICAN FIREMAN, THE (Two		
IN THE STREET	$30	NA	versions)	$20	$55
INDIAN SUMMER	$38	$300	LIFE STORY OF BAAL, THE	$75	NA
INDUSTRIAL BRITAIN	$35	NA	LIGHT REFLECTIONS	$20	$100
INNOCENT FAIR, THE	$25	NA	LIGHTS OF NEW YORK	$35	NA
INSIDE OUT (Rental: see HOWARD DANE-			LINDBERGH'S FLIGHT FROM N.Y. TO PARIS	$20	NA
LOWITZ PROGRAM)	—	$250	LITTLE BOY	$90	$750
INTERIOR DESIGNS (Rental: see JANE AARON			LITTLE CHIMNEY SWEEP, THE	$25	$125
PROGRAM)	—	$150	LITTLE MATCH GIRL, THE	$45	NA
INTOLERANCE (black and white)	$75	NA	LITTLE PHANTASY ON A NINTEENTH CEN-		
INTOLERANCE (color)	$75	$750	TURY PAINTING, A	$20**	NA
INTREPID SHADOWS	$25	$160	LITTLE TRAIN ROBBERY, THE	$20	$65
INTRODUCTION TO JET ENGINES, AN	$25	$275	LIVES OF A BENGAL LANCER, THE		
IRELAND BEHIND THE WIRE	$90	NA	(high school)	$40*	NA
IRENE DANCES (Rental: see OSKAR FISCHIN-	—	see SPIRITUAL	(university)	$50*	
GER PROGRAM V)		CONSTRUCTIONS	LLANITO	$75	$700
IRON HORSE, THE	$60	NA	LMNO	$25	$325
IRON MASK, THE	$60	NA	LODGER, THE	$45	NA
ISLANDERS, THE	$25	NA	LONEDALE OPERATOR, THE and THE GIRL		
ISN'T LIFE WONDERFUL	$60	NA	AND HER TRUST (Sale price for THE LONE-		
IT AIN'T CITY MUSIC	$25	NA	DALE OPERATOR only; THE GIRL AND HER		
ITALIAN MELODRAMAS	$35	NA	TRUST sells individually)	$30	$65
ITALIAN STRAW HAT, THE	$50	NA	LONELY BOY	$30	$500
ITALIANAMERICAN	$30	NA	LONELY VILLA, THE	$20	$65
			LONG BODIES, THE	$20	NA
J			LOONY TOM THE HAPPY LOVER	$20	NA
			LOST IN THE ALPS	$20	$65
JACK THE KISSER	$20	$65	LOST SQUADRON, THE	$50	NA
JAMESTOWN BALOOS (Rental: see ROBERT			LOUISIANA STORY STUDY FILM	$65	NA
BREER PROGRAM II)	—	$225	LOVE EVERLASTING	$50	NA
JANE AARON PROGRAM	$35	see individual	LOVE GAMES (Rental: see OSKAR FISCHIN-		
		titles	GER PROGRAM IV)	—	$60
JAPANESE HOUSE, A	$25	$150	LOVE IN AN APARTMENT HOTEL	$20	$65
JAZZ OF LIGHTS	$25	$295	LOVE OF JEANNE NEY, THE	$60	NA
JEAN CARIGNAN, VIOLONEUX	$45	$925	LOVE OF JEANNE NEY, THE (Montage sequence)	$20	NA
JEAN DESPRES: THE DESIGNER	$35	$300	LOVE PARADE, THE	$60	NA
JOG'S TROT	$75	NA	LOVEMAKING	$28	$300
JOHN LAW AND THE MISSISSIPPI BUBBLE	$20**	NA	LOVING MEMORY	$45	NA
JOHN MARIN	$30	$140	LUMIÈRE PROGRAM I: FIRST PROGRAMS	$25	NA
JOIE DE VIVRE	$20	NA	LUMIÈRE PROGRAM II: EARLY LUMIÈRE		
JOURNEYS FROM BERLIN/1971	$200	$3000	FILMS	$25	NA
JOYLESS STREET, THE	$50	NA	LUMINESCENCE	$28	$200
JUDITH OF BETHULIA	$35	$185	LUTTE, LA	$30	$500
K			**M**		
KALEIDOFORM (Rental: see HOWARD			MACBETH	$50	NA
DANELOWITZ PROGRAM)	—	$65	MACHINE OF EDEN, THE	$25	NA
KEEP YOUR MOUTH SHUT	$20	$100	MACK SENNETT PROGRAM I	$40	NA
KENO BATES, LIAR	$25	$135	MACK SENNETT PROGRAM II	$40	NA
KENTU	$40	NA	MADAME DU BARRY	$48	NA
KINO PRAVDA (Selections)	$28	NA	MADE MANIFEST	$20	NA
KNIGHT OF THE ROAD, A	$20	$65	MAGIC CLOCK, THE	$48	NA
KNOCKOUT, THE	$25	$110	MAGIC FILMS	$50	NA
KRISTINA TALKING PICTURES	$150	$2000	MAIL EARLY	$20	$100
KYOTO	$40	NA	MAKE WAY FOR TOMORROW (high school)	$40*	NA
			(university)	$50*	
L			MAKING A LIVING	$20	$60
			MAKING OF A MOVIE, THE	$30	NA
LADY AND THE MOUSE, THE	$20	$65	MAKING OF SERPENT, THE	$45	$450
LADY WINDERMERE'S FAN	$40	$375	MAKING OFFON	$20	NA
LAND, THE	$40	$250	MALE AND FEMALE	$50	NA
LAND OF THE LONG DAY	$35	$575	MAN AND HIS DOG OUT FOR AIR, A (Rental:		
LAND WITHOUT BREAD	$30	NA	see ROBERT BREER PROGRAM I)	—	$130
LANGUAGE OF THE SILENT CINEMA, THE			MAN I KILLED, THE	$50	NA
PART I	$48	$400	MAN I KILLED, THE (Opening sequence)	$20	NA
LANGUAGE OF THE SILENT CINEMA, THE			MAN IN A BUBBLE	$45	$300
PART II	$48	$400	MAN WITH THE MOVIE CAMERA, THE	$50	NA
LAST COMMAND, THE	$55	NA			
LAST LAUGH, THE	$50	NA			

TITLE	RENTAL	SALES	TITLE	RENTAL	SALES
MANHATTA	$20	NA	MUSKETEERS OF PIG ALLEY, THE	$20	$65
MANHATTAN DOORWAY (Rental: see PERMANENT WAVE and MANHATTAN DOORWAY)	—	$60	MUTT AND JEFF IN THE BIG SWIM (Rental: see ANIMATION PROGRAM)	—	$65
MANIAC CHASE	$20	$65	MY AIN FOLK	$60	NA
MARCEL DUCHAMP IN HIS OWN WORDS	$35	$375	MY CHILDHOOD	$55	NA
MARCHE DES MACHINES, LA	$20	NA	MY NAME IS OONA	$20	NA
MARK OF ZORRO, THE	$50	NA	MY WAY HOME	$75	NA
MARRIAGE CIRCLE, THE	$50	NA	MYSTÈRES DU CHÂTEAU DU DÉ, LES	$35	NA
MARTYRS OF THE ALAMO, THE	$38	$350	MYSTERY OF THE LEAPING FISH, THE	$30	$175
MARY WIGMAN DANCES	$25	$175			
MASQUERADER, THE	$20	$65	**N**		
MASS FOR THE DAKOTA SIOUX	$33	NA			
MATCHLESS	$60	$500	NANOOK OF THE NORTH	$75	NA
MATERNELLE, LA	$50	NA	NATIONAL HUNGER MARCH 1931, THE (Rental: see FILM AND PHOTO LEAGUE PROGRAM II)	—	$150
MATRIX	$25	$100	NATIVE LAND	$150	$1000
MATRIX III	$25	$175	NAVAJO SILVERSMITH, THE	$25	$175
MAX LINDER PROGRAM	$35	NA	NAVAJO WEAVER, A	$25	$175
MECHANICAL PRINCIPLES	$20	NA	NAZI PROPAGANDA FILMS	$45	NA
MELODIC INVERSION	$25	$175	NAZIS STRIKE, THE	$40	NA
MEN IN DANGER	$40	NA	NECROLOGY	$20	NA
MEN WHO MADE THE MOVIES: ALFRED HITCHCOCK, THE	$40	$265 (Lease)	NEGRO SOLDIER, THE	$35	$225
MEN WHO MADE THE MOVIES: FRANK CAPRA, THE	$40	$365 (Lease)	NEIGHBOURS	$20**	NA
MEN WHO MADE THE MOVIES: GEORGE CUKOR, THE	$40	$265 (Lease)	NELL AND FRED	$30	$550
MEN WHO MADE THE MOVIES: HOWARD HAWKS, THE	$40	$265 (Lease)	NEUROSIS	$20	$130
MEN WHO MADE THE MOVIES: KING VIDOR, THE	$40	$265 (Lease)	NEW DRESS, THE	$20	$65
MEN WHO MADE THE MOVIES: RAOUL WALSH, THE	$40	$365 (Lease)	NEW EARTH	$35	NA
MEN WHO MADE THE MOVIES: VINCENTE MINNELLI, THE	$40	$265 (Lease)	NEW YORK HAT, THE	$20	$65
MENDED LUTE, THE	$20	$65	NIBELUNGEN, DIE. KRIEMHILD'S REVENGE	$60	NA
MÉNILMONTANT	$35	NA	NIBELUNGEN, DIE. SIEGFRIED	$60	NA
MESHES OF THE AFTERNOON	$40	NA	NIGHT MAIL	$30	NA
METANOMEN	$20	$100	NINE DAYS TO PICASSO	$30	$200
METROPOLIS	$50	NA	90° SOUTH	$50	NA
MEXICAN SWEETHEARTS	$20	$50	NIÑOS ABANDONADOS, LOS	$150	$800
MICKEY	$45	NA	NORTH SEA	$35	NA
MIDSUMMER NIGHT'S DREAM, A	$50	NA	NOSFERATU	$45	NA
MILLION, LE	$50	NA	NOTES FOR JEROME	$60	NA
MILLION DOLLAR LEGS (high school)	$40*	NA	NOTES ON THE PORT OF ST. FRANCIS	$30	NA
(university)	$50*		NUPTIAE	$30	$250
MINDSCAPE	$20**	NA	NUREMBERG	$45	$400
MIRROR PHASE	$50	NA	NUT, THE	$50	NA
MIRRORED REASON	$25	$300	N.Y., N.Y.	$30	NA
MR. FRENHOFER AND THE MINOTAUR	$45	$260			
MR. HAYASHI	$20	NA	**O**		
MR. ROBINSON CRUSOE	$50	NA			
MRS. JONES' LOVER, OR, "I WANT MY HAT"	$20	$50	OCTOBER	$60	$600
MOANA	$48	NA	OF STARS AND MEN	$90	$750
MODERN MUSKETEER, A (Extant reels: Opening)	$40	NA	OFFON	$24	$250
MOJADO, EL	$38	$400	OH DEM WATERMELONS	$28	$450
MOLLYCODDLE, THE	$48	NA	OKLAHOMA GAS (Rental: see OSKAR FISCHINGER PROGRAM III; For Sale with MUNTZ TV)	—	$75
MOMENT IN LOVE, A	$25	$225	OLD ANTELOPE LAKE	$20	$90
MONKEY BUSINESS (high school)	$75*	NA	OLD BOX, AN	$20	$275
(university)	$95*		OLYMPIA (Diving sequence)	$20	$65
MONSIEUR BEAUCAIRE	$50	$400	ON A PAVING STONE MOUNTED	$60	NA
MOODS OF THE SEA	$20	$125	100 TO 1 SHOT, OR, A RUN OF LUCK!, THE	$20	$65
MOON 1969	$30	$350	ONE SECOND IN MONTREAL	$30	NA
MOSAIC	$20**	NA	ONE STEP AWAY	$65	NA
MOTHER	$60	NA	OPUS FILMS II, III, IV	$20	NA
MOTHER AND THE LAW, THE	$48	NA	ORIGINS OF THE MOTION PICTURE	$22	NA
MOTHER'S DAY	$30	$300	ORPHANS OF THE STORM	$60	NA
MOTHERING HEART, THE	$25	$110	OSKAR FISCHINGER PROGRAM I	$38	see individual titles
MOTION-PAINTING I	$25	$275	OSKAR FISCHINGER PROGRAM II	$38	see individual titles
MOVIES MARCH ON!, THE	$30	NA	OSKAR FISCHINGER PROGRAM III	$38	see individual titles
MUKISSI	$40	$395	OSKAR FISCHINGER PROGRAM IV	$38	see individual titles
MUNICH-BERLIN WALKING TRIP (Rental: see OSKAR FISCHINGER PROGRAM V)	—	$75	OSKAR FISCHINGER PROGRAM V	$38	see individual titles
MUNTZ TV (Rental: see OSKAR FISCHINGER PROGRAM III)	—	see OKLAHOMA GAS	OTRO LADO, EL	$100	$800
MURATTI GETS IN THE ACT! (Rental: see OSKAR FISCHINGER PROGRAM III)	—	$140	OUR DAILY BREAD	$50	NA
MURATTI PRIVAT (Rental: see OSKAR FISCHINGER PROGRAM III)	—	$85	OUR DAILY BREAD (Concluding sequence)	$20	NA
			OUR LADY OF THE SPHERE	$20	NA
MUSEUM AND THE FURY, THE	$65	$650	OUTCAST AMONG OUTCASTS, AN	$20	$65
MUSICAL POSTER NO. 1	$20	NA	OUTLAW AND HIS WIFE, THE	$50	NA
			OUTTAKES—PAYSAGE DE GUERRE	$40	$435
			OVER SILENT PATHS	$20	$65
			OWL WHO MARRIED A GOOSE: AN ESKIMO LEGEND, THE	$20**	NA

TITLE	RENTAL	SALES
P		
PAINTED LADY, THE	$20	$65
PARADE	$20	$150
PART OF THE FAMILY	$60	$750
PARTICLES IN SPACE and TAL FARLOW (Sale price for PARTICLES IN SPACE only; TAL FARLOW sells individually)	$22	$150
PAS DE DEUX	$25**	NA
PASSAGES	$38	$300
PASSION OF JOAN OF ARC, THE	$55	NA
PATHÉ NEWSREEL, THE	$25	NA
PAT'S BIRTHDAY	$25	$260
PAUL TOMKOWICZ: STREET RAILWAY SWITCHMAN	$20	$275
PÊCHE À LA BALEINE, LA	$20	NA
PEOPLE OF THE CUMBERLAND	$35	NA
PERMANENT WAVE and MANHATTAN DOORWAY (Sale price for PERMANENT WAVE only; MANHATTAN DOORWAY sells individually)	$25	$50
PERMUTATIONS	$20	$120
PETRIFIED DOG, THE	$45	$250
PHANTOM CHARIOT, THE	$50	NA
PHILIPS-RADIO	$33	NA
PHOELIX	$75	$500
PHOTOGRAPHER, THE	$30	$150
PICTURES TO SERVE THE PEOPLE: AMERICAN LITHOGRAPHY, 1830–1855	$38	NA
PIE IN THE SKY	$20	NA
PIER PAOLO PASOLINI	$25	NA
PINT OF PLAIN, A	$40	$400
PISSARRO: AT THE HEART OF IMPRESSIONISM	$25	$250
PLAGE, LA	$20**	NA
PLOW THAT BROKE THE PLAINS, THE	$30	NA
PLUTO	$20	NA
POITÍN	$100	NA
POLICE	$24	$110
POLICEMAN'S VISION, THE	$20	NA
POLIDOR COMEDIES	$38	NA
PORCH GLIDER	$50	$600
PORTRAIT OF A YOUNG MAN	$35	$350
PORTRAIT OF AN AMERICAN ZEALOT	$85	$800
POTEMKIN	$55	NA
POTEMKIN (Odessa Steps sequence)	$20	NA
POTTED PSALM, THE	$45	$300
POUR LA SUITE DU MONDE	$50	$925
POWER AND THE LAND	$35	$200
POWERS OF TEN (First version)	$20	NA
POWERS OF TEN (Second version)	$20	NA
PRELUDE TO WAR	$40	NA
PREMIÈRE NUIT, LA	$33	NA
PRESIDENT VANISHES, THE	$40	NA
PRETEND YOU'RE WEARING A BARREL	$20**	NA
PRICE OF A UNION, THE	$75	NA
PRIMAL CALL, THE	$20	$65
PRINT GENERATION	$75	$800
PRISCILLA'S APRIL FOOL JOKE	$20	$65
PRISON TRAIN	$40	$375
PRIVATE LIFE, A	$50	$425
P'TITE LILIE, LA	$30	NA
PUMPKIN RACE, THE	$20	NA
PUSS IN BOOTS	$25	$125
Q		
QUIXOTE	$75	NA
QUO VADIS?	$55	NA
R		
R1 (Rental: see OSKAR FISCHINGER PROGRAM V)	—	$180
RABBIT'S MOON (First version)	$25	NA
RABBIT'S MOON (Second version)	$25	NA
RADIO DYNAMICS (Rental: see OSKAR FISCHINGER PROGRAM IV)	—	$180
RAIN	$20	NA
RAPUNZEL LET DOWN YOUR HAIR	$100	NA
RAQUETTEURS, LES	$25	$350
REACHING FOR THE MOON	$38	NA
REAL ITALIAN PIZZA	$22	NA
RE-BORN	$28	$200

TITLE	RENTAL	SALES
RECREATION (Rental: see ROBERT BREER PROGRAM I)	—	$130
RED CHURCH	$23	$225
RED PSALM	$50	NA
REDMAN'S VIEW, THE	$20	$65
RÉGION CENTRALE, LA	$190	NA
RENNSYMPHONIE	$20	$65
RESCUED FROM AN EAGLE'S NEST	$20	$65
RESISTANCE	$75	NA
RETOUR, LE	$35	$225
RETOUR À LA RAISON, LE	$20	NA
RETURN JOURNEY	$65	$690
REVENGE OF A KINEMATOGRAPH CAMERAMAN	$20	NA
REVOLT OF THE FISHERMEN	$38	NA
RHYTHM and FREE RADICALS (Sale price for RHYTHM only; FREE RADICALS sells individually)	$22	$50
RHYTHMUS 21	$20	$40
RICE	$30	NA
RIDDLES OF THE SPHINX	$100	NA
RIEN QUE LES HEURES	$38	NA
RISE OF LOUIS XIV, THE	$50	NA
RIVALS, THE	$20	$65
RIVER, THE	$35	$225
ROAD TO LIFE, THE	$60	NA
ROBERT BREER PROGRAM I	$45	see individual titles
ROBERT BREER PROGRAM II	$40	see individual titles
ROBIN HOOD	$55	NA
ROCKY ROAD, THE	$20	$65
ROMANCE OF HAPPY VALLEY, A	$45	$300
ROMANCE OF TRANSPORTATION, THE	$20**	NA
ROSE OF KENTUCKY, THE	$20	$65
ROSE O' SALEM-TOWN	$20	$65
ROSLYN ROMANCE	$38	NA
ROUNDERS, THE	$20	$65
RUBBER CEMENT	$25	$325
RUBE AND MANDY AT CONEY ISLAND	$20	$65
RUGGLES OF RED GAP (high school)	$40*	NA
(university)	$50*	
RUMPELSTILTSKIN	$35	$250
S		
SABOTAGE	$45	NA
ST. LOUIS BLUES	$25	$125
SALT FOR SVANETIA	$45	NA
SALT OF THE EARTH	$75	NA
SAND CASTLE, THE	$25	$350
SAUSALITO	$20	NA
SCARS	$25	$225
SCARY TIME, A	$35	$150
SCIENCE FICTION	$20	$150
SCIENCE FRICTION	$28	$300
SCORPIO RISING	$45	NA
SCRAP IN BLACK AND WHITE, A and THE WATERMELON PATCH	$17	$65
SCULLIONS' DREAMS	$20	NA
SEA DREAM	$20**	NA
SEA TRAVELS	$30	$200
SEASHELL AND THE CLERGYMAN, THE	$40	NA
SECOND WEAVER	$20	$100
SELF PORTRAIT WITH RED CAR	$30	$225
SELLING OF THE PENTAGON, THE	$38	NA
SERENE VELOCITY	$42	NA
SERPENT	$30	$350
"1776," OR, THE HESSIAN RENEGADES	$20	$65
SEVENTH HEAVEN	$70	NA
70	$15	$225
77	$20	$310
SEXUAL MEDITATIONS #1: MOTEL	$17	NA
SHADOWS ON THE SNOW	$20	NA
SHALLOW WELL PROJECT, THE	$25	$125
SHEPHERD OF THE NIGHT FLOCK, THE	$45	$495
SHEPHERDS OF BERNERAY, THE	$60	$725
SHORES OF PHOS: A FABLE, THE	$20	NA
SILENT VILLAGE, THE	$40	NA
SILK	$50	$600
SIN OF THE POET, THE	$25	$150
SIT DOWN SWEET SEPTEMBER	$40	$300
SIX LITTLE PIECES ON FILM	$55	$500

TITLE	RENTAL	SALES
69 (Rental: see ROBERT BREER PROGRAM I)	—	$225
66 (Rental: see ROBERT BREER PROGRAM II)	—	$225
SKEIN	$15	NA
SKIFF OF RENALD AND THOMAS, THE	$40	$775
SKY BLUE WATER LIGHT SIGN	$20	$150
SKY DANCE	$20	$225
SKY HIGH	$40	$350
SKYSCRAPER	$25	NA
SLEEPING BEAUTY	$25	$125
SLUICE	$15	NA
SMILING MADAME BEUDET, THE	$38	NA
SMOKE MENACE, THE	$25	NA
SNOW WHITE AND ROSE RED	$25	$125
SOC. SCI. 127	$40	$350
SONAMBIENTS: THE SOUND SCULPTURE OF HARRY BERTOIA	$30	NA
SONG OF CEYLON	$35	NA
SONG OF THE SHIRT, THE	$100	$1000
SORROWS OF SATAN, THE	$55	NA
SORT OF A COMMERCIAL FOR AN ICEBAG BY CLAES OLDENBURG	$30	NA
SPANISH EARTH, THE	$50	NA
SPANISH GYPSY, THE	$20	$60
SPARE TIME	$25	NA
SPIES	$55	NA
SPIRALS (Rental: see OSKAR FISCHINGER PROGRAM V)	—	$70
SPIRIT OF THE NAVAJOS, THE	$25	$175
SPIRITUAL CONSTRUCTIONS (Rental: see OSKAR FISCHINGER PROGRAM IV) (For Sale with THE BOXER, IRENE DANCES, and CHARCOAL STUDY FOR SPIRITUAL CONSTRUCTIONS)	—	$185
SPOOK MINSTRELS	$20	NA
SQUARES (Rental: see OSKAR FISCHINGER PROGRAM IV)	—	$120
SQUIBS WINS THE CALCUTTA SWEEP	$40	NA
STAGE STRUCK	$20	$60
STAR GARDEN	$40	NA
STARS ARE BEAUTIFUL, THE	$35	NA
STARS LOOK DOWN, THE	$60	NA
STATIONS OF THE ELEVATED	$65	NA
STEP BY STEP	$20	$125
STOLEN HEART, THE	$25	$125
STONE WONDER OF NAUMBURG, THE	$25	NA
STORM OVER ASIA	$60	NA
STRANGE VICTORY	$90	$900
STREET, THE [Karl Grune]	$60	NA
STREET, THE [Caroline Leaf]	$20	$275
STRENUOUS LIFE, OR, ANTI-RACE SUICIDE, THE and WAITING AT THE CHURCH	$20	$65
STRIKE	$55	NA
STRING OF PEARLS, A	$20	$65
STUDY IN DIACHRONIC MOTION	$20	$85
STUDY NO. 5 (Rental: see OSKAR FISCHINGER PROGRAM II)	—	$75
STUDY NO. 6 (Rental: see OSKAR FISCHINGER PROGRAM I)	—	$75
STUDY NO. 7 (Rental: see OSKAR FISCHINGER PROGRAM I)	—	$75
STUDY NO. 8 (Rental: see OSKAR FISCHINGER PROGRAM I)	—	$85
STUDY NO. 9 (Rental: see HANS AND OSKAR FISCHINGER PROGRAM)	—	$85
STUDY NO. 10 (Rental: see HANS AND OSKAR FISCHINGER PROGRAM)	—	$85
STUDY NO. 11 (Rental: see OSKAR FISCHINGER PROGRAM I)	—	$75
STUDY NO. 11A. A PLAY IN COLORS (Rental: see OSKAR FISCHINGER PROGRAM I)	—	$75
STUDY NO. 12 (Rental: see HANS AND OSKAR FISCHINGER PROGRAM)	—	$85
STYX	$20	$100
SUCH IS LIFE	$50	NA
SUFI TALE, A	$20	$200
SUMMER SAGA, A	$20	NA
SUNRISE	$60	NA
SURF AND SEAWEED	$20	$75
SURF GIRL, THE	$20	$100
SURFACING ON THE THAMES	$28	NA
SWEATER, THE	$25	$275
SWEDISH CINEMA CLASSICS	$45	NA
SWINGING THE LAMBETH WALK	$20	NA
SYDNEY=BUSH	$25	$275
SYDNEY HARBOUR BRIDGE	$22	$225
SYMPHONIE DIAGONALE	$20	NA

T

TITLE	RENTAL	SALES
T'AI CHI CH'UAN	$20	NA
TAKING OF LUKE MCVANE, THE	$25	NA
TAL FARLOW (Rental: see PARTICLES IN SPACE and TAL FARLOW; LEN LYE'S AMERICAN FILMS)	—	$50
TATTOOED TEARS	$150	NA
TAYLOR SQUARE	$30	$300
TEACHING DAD TO LIKE HER	$20	$65
TEDDY AT THE THROTTLE	$30	NA
"TEDDY" BEARS, THE	$20	$65
TELEVISION COMMERCIALS	$20	NA
TEST SHOTS FOR HAMLET	$20	NA
TESTAMENT	$40	$400
TEXTILES AND ORNAMENTAL ARTS OF INDIA	$25	NA
THAT CHINK AT GOLDEN GULCH	$20	$65
THEATER	$25	NA
THEY ALSO SERVE	$20	NA
THIEF OF BAGDAD, THE	$60	NA
THINGS I CANNOT CHANGE, THE	$40	$775
33 YO-YO TRICKS	$20	$195
THOSE AWFUL HATS	$15	$30
THOSE DARING YOUNG FILM MAKERS BY THE GOLDEN GATE	$38	$300
THREE MUSKETEERS, THE	$60	NA
THROUGH THE MAGISCOPE	$20	$190
THUMBELINA	$25	$125
THUNDER OVER MEXICO	$60	NA
THUNDERBOLT (high school)	$40*	NA
(university)	$50*	
THURSDAY'S CHILDREN	$28	NA
TIME AND DREAMS	$45	$400
TIME IN THE SUN	$40	NA
TIT FOR TAT	$20	NA
TO-DAY WE LIVE	$30	NA
TOL'ABLE DAVID	$48	$400
TOLL GATE, THE	$50	$350
TOM, TOM, THE PIPER'S SON	$170	NA
TONTOLINI AND POLIDOR COMEDIES	$45	NA
TOURISTS, THE	$20	$65
TOWN, THE	$25	NA
TRADE TATTOO	$20	NA
TRAIN WRECKERS, THE	$20	$65
TRAINER'S DAUGHTER, OR, A RACE FOR LOVE, THE	$20	$65
TRAMP, THE	$25	$110
TRANSCENDING	$33	$300
TRANSFER OF POWER	$30	NA
TRANSMIGRATION	$22	$190
TREADLE AND BOBBIN	$20	NA
TREASURE OF ARNE, THE	$50	NA
TRIP TO THE MOON, A	$20	NA
TRIUMPH OF THE WILL	$55	NA
TRIUMPH OF THE WILL (Abridged version)	$40	$375
TRUE HEART SUSIE	$55	NA
TRUT!	$30	NA
TWO	$25	NA
TWO FIGURES	$50	$600
TWO SIDES, THE	$20	NA
TWO TARS	$30	NA
TZ	$20	$325

U

TITLE	RENTAL	SALES
ÜBERFALL	$28	NA
UNCHANGING SEA, THE	$20	$65
UNDER CAPRICORN	$55	NA
UNDERWORLD	$55	NA
UNIVERSE	$30	$500
UNREACHABLE HOMELESS	$50	$1000
UNSEEN ENEMY, AN	$20	$65
UNTITLED FILM, AN	$20	$65
URBAN PEASANTS: AN ESSAY IN YIDDISH STRUCTURALISM	$60	NA
URBAN SPACES	$35	$375
USURER, THE	$20	$65

TITLE	RENTAL	SALES
V		
V FOR VICTORY	$20	$100
VALLEY TOWN	$30	$345
VARIETY	$55	NA
VERTICAL FEATURES REMAKE	$55	$600
VERY NICE, VERY NICE	$20**	NA
VITAGRAPH COMEDIES	$40	NA
VITAGRAPH ROMANCE, A	$20	$60
VOYAGE TO NEXT	$25	$180
W		
WAIT	$16	NA
WAITING AT THE CHURCH: see STRENUOUS LIFE, OR, ANTI-RACE SUICIDE, THE and WAITING AT THE CHURCH	—	—
WAITING FOR FIDEL	$40	$775
WALK THROUGH H, A	$50	NA
WALKING	$20**	NA
WAR COMES TO AMERICA	$40	NA
WARCLOUDS IN THE PACIFIC	$30	$500
WARGAMES	$22	NA
WARNING SHADOWS	$45	NA
WAS HE A COWARD?	$20	$65
WATER WRACKETS	$20	$225
WATERMELON PATCH, THE: see SCRAP IN BLACK AND WHITE, A and THE WATER-MELON PATCH	—	—
WATERSMITH	$48	$550
WAVE, THE	$48	NA
WAVELENGTH	$65	NA
WAX EXPERIMENTS (Rental: see OSKAR FIS-CHINGER PROGRAM V)	—	$110
WAY DOWN EAST	$65	NA
WAY OF THE WORLD, THE	$20	$65
WE ALL KNOW WHY WE'RE HERE	$35	$350
WEDDING IN WHITE	$50	NA

TITLE	RENTAL	SALES
WEDDING OF PALO, THE	$48	NA
WELCOME TO BRITAIN	$60	NA
WESTFRONT 1918	$48	NA
WHAT PRICE GLORY	$65	NA
WHAT SHALL WE DO WITH OUR OLD WHEEEELS, OR, AMERICA ON WHEELS, PART 2	$20	$200
WHEN ASIA SPEAKS	$30	$410
WHEN THE CLOUDS ROLL BY	$50	NA
WHITE CAPS, THE	$20	$65
WHITE HELL OF PITZ PALU, THE (high school)	$40*	NA
(university)	$50*	
WHITE MANE	$38	NA
WHITE ROSE, THE	$55	NA
WHO CARES	$25	$125
WILD AND WOOLLY	$40	NA
WINDOW	$20	$60
WINDOW CLEANER	$20	$65
WINDOW WATER BABY MOVING	$28	NA
WINDOWS	$20	$120
WINSOR MCCAY PROGRAM	$30	NA
WOLD-SHADOW, THE	$15	NA
WOMAN, A	$25	$100
WONDER RING, THE	$18	NA
WORKERS NEWSREEL UNEMPLOYMENT SPECIAL 1931 (Rental: see FILM AND PHOTO LEAGUE PROGRAM I)	—	$150
WORKS OF CALDER	$25	$225
WORLD OF GILBERT AND GEORGE, THE	$125	$1200
Y		
YOU ARE ON INDIAN LAND	$35	$575
YOU ONLY LIVE ONCE: PRODUCTION TAKES FROM A FILM IN THE MAKING	$20	NA

850298621

PHOTOGRAPH CREDITS

All photographs are from The Museum of Modern Art/Film Stills Archive except those (indicated by page number) in the following list of sources: Jane Aaron, 200; Arts Council of Great Britain, 227, 228; Robert Breer, 209; British Film Institute, 163, 212, 216, 220, 221, 222, 224, 225, 226 (bottom); David Ehrlich, 204; Fischinger Archive, 177; Hubley Studios, 198; Ken Jacobs, 187; The Len Lye Foundation, 6; Helen Levitt, 133; Danny Lyon, 138; Allen Moore, 107; Laura Mulvey/Peter Wollen, 226 (top); Charles Musser, 267; National Film Board of Canada, 230, 236, 241, 242, 243, 244, 245, 246, 248, 249, 250, 251; Lev Nisnevich, 95; Carl Schlesinger, 141; Stan VanDerBeek, 185; Judith Weschler, 257; Paul Winkler, 211.